DICKEBUSCH CHURCH—1917.

THE HISTORY OF THE 12th (Bermondsey) Battalion EAST SURREY REGIMENT

WRITTEN & COMPILED by

John Aston, M.A., and L. M. Duggan.

With LETTERS from

Lieut.-Gen. Sir Sydney T. B. Lawford, K.C.B., K.C.M.G.

and

Brig.-Gen. F. W. Towsey, C.M.G., C.B.E., D.S.O., J.P.

To the Undying Memory
of our Comrades
who fell in the Great War
mdccccxv——mdccccxviii

We of the
Twelfth (Bermondsey) Battalion
East Surrey Regiment
who remain
dedicate this book
mdccccxxxvii

Lieut.-General Sir SYDNEY T. B. LAWFORD,

K.C.B., K.C.M.G., G.O.C., 41st Division.

AT the invitation of the authors of the History of the 12th Battalion East Surrey Regt., I have much pleasure in writing these few lines of commendation of the splendid help which this battalion rendered to the 41st Division.

I feel sure that this history will record many of the great achievements attained, and many glorious deeds performed by its members; but the one point I should like to stress is the fact that the battalion was always ready to carry out any task which was presented, either in the front line or the training area.

The discipline always maintained was of a very high order, due to the devotion of all ranks from C.O. to the last joined private.

To the authors will be due the thanks of all those who were connected with the battalion for compiling a record which will bear witness to the memory of the many who readily came forward in the hour of need and gave their lives to uphold the honour of their Country and Regiment.

SYDNEY LAWFORD,
Lieut.-General.

Army and Navy Club.
June 14th, 1936.

Brig.-General F. W. TOWSEY,

C.M.G., C.B.E., D.S.O., J.P., Commanding 122nd Infantry Brigade.

IN its simple narrative form the history of the 12th East Surrey Regiment sets out the doings of those men of Bermondsey who answered their country's call not for any hope of personal gain or fame, but simply because they considered it to be their duty.

May England always have such men in her hour of need.

War has been defined as the expression of all that is worst in human nature, and yet, paradoxical as it may appear, it is only a great war that can call forth two of the greatest qualities of a nation, good-comradeship and self-sacrifice.

The history breathes the spirit and atmosphere of those stirring days and portrays more effectively than a more grandiloquent style would the quiet heroism of the man in the ranks.

All did their duty, and none make a better showing than the Quartermaster's department, the signallers, the runners, the stretcher-bearers and the regimental transport; the last two generally confused in the public mind with the R.A.M.C. and the R.A.S.C.

As their Brigadier for most of the period of their existence, I know that the 12th Battalion East Surrey Regiment never failed to respond to any call, however arduous, made on them, and, after reading this history, from which I have learnt much, I am prouder than ever to have served with them in the Great War.

Tollgate House, near Colchester. F. W. TOWSEY.

Brigadier-General.

March 15th, 1936. Late Commanding 122nd Infantry Brigade.

PREFACES

I.

THIS book appears as under joint authorship, but the labour has not been equally divided. The real credit is due to my friend Duggan, who, not content with founding the Association of the 12th Battalion and putting into that and its continuance the work of half-a-dozen men, conceived the idea of this volume and spent the best part of two years in copying records and writing the whole war history. All I have done is to add the "spit and polish." In his modesty he did not wish this so explicitly stated, but I have told him plainly that, unless he consents to the fact being known to all readers of the book, I will consent to no part in its publication.

Having got that confession off my chest, I must next explain that our aim has not been that of historians. While making every endeavour to be quite accurate (in which no doubt we have failed here and there), we have tried to provide a narrative, not so much for the general reader, as for the members of the Association and their friends to stimulate their recollection of those now distant events. It is for this reason that plenty of yarns are included in the actual words of the narrator himself, and we believe that these, whether grave or gay, will prove the best part of the volume. To those who have helped in this way we tender our heartiest thanks, and a full list will be found later, but we must especially praise Cpl. Southall, who wrote at the time a full account of his experiences with the Battalion, which has proved a mine of interest and information.

In 1934 Capt. R. O. Russell, M.C., produced his splendid history of the 11th Battalion, Royal West Kent Regt., our special pals in the 122nd Brigade. "Comparisons are odorous, palabras," as Dogberry remarked, and we do not venture to set our modest production in the same category. We would only suggest that Capt. Russell had, among other advantages, this especial one, that he served with his battalion almost through its whole existence. We had not that fortune, and our work inevitably suffers. Duggan was with the battalion from near the beginning till the very end, with the exception of two months after he was wounded at Tower Hamlets on September 20th, 1917, but his services in the combatant ranks with A Company were interrupted by the claims of the Battalion Orderly Room and B Company Office, where, though he had unique opportunities of knowing about every officer and man on the roster, he was not (except at Ploegsteert, Flers, Hollebeke and Tower Hamlets) in the firing line, and so has not first hand knowledge of much of which he writes. My own service with the 12th was a bare eleven months—September, 1916—July, 1917. The book inevitably suffers as a first-hand narrative, and is also something of a patchwork. The reader will quickly distinguish Duggan's sober style from my flamboyant and "purple passages."

We confess something of envy as we scan more than two pages of the names of those to whom Capt. Russell acknowledges indebtedness. To those who have sent in narratives we owe a very deep debt of gratitude for their truly valuable aid. If any members should criticize the accuracy or the presentation of our story, we can only say—

"Why did you not help us?" To all we would appeal in the words of a notice prominently displayed in a church out in the wild and woolly West—"Please do not shoot the organist; he's doing his best."

Lastly we feel that some explanation is necessary as to the use of such words as "Hun" and "Boche" in relation to our late enemies. These were words current at the time, and, as our object has been to use the vernacular in vogue during the war, we have done so with no intention of giving offence to the German soldiers whose fighting qualities eventually commanded our greatest respect. We feel that any evidence required as to our good relations with our former foes could be supplied by the people of the Rhineland.

Meadowside,
Uckfield, Sussex.

JOHN ASTON.

II.

It is because I feel that some further explanation is necessary with regard to the production of this book that I venture to add something to the preface written by Mr. Aston.

In the first place I never intended that I should be co-author with him, but that I should supply him with as much material as possible to enable him to produce an interesting and instructive story which I considered should be told before it was too late. Unfortunately Mr. Aston is a very busy man, much in demand by the heads of schools for lecturing to the younger generation on history, architecture, art and other subjects ranging from Coalmining to Hellenic Culture. As an Honours man in Modern History at Oxford, with the publication of several books to his credit, no one was better fitted to write our story in a manner which would appeal to the general public as well as to those who served with the Battalion. Since it was not possible for him to devote much of his time to writing for us, he was quite agreeable that, if I did the recording, he would attempt to put the matter into literary shape.

During vacations Mr. Aston has devoted a good deal of his time to doing what he promised, and has added many passages which go to prove that, had the whole work been done by himself, our production would have ranked with some of the best war books which have appeared.

With regard to myself, I have endeavoured to make the narrative interesting to read, but it must be remembered that my time too has been limited to a few hours in the evenings after a tiring day in an office. Most of the information I have had to gather myself, utilising a part of my annual holidays for that purpose. There was little time for me to attempt writing up the matter in a manner which would have given me entire satisfaction, and I simply recorded from the notes I had made at Audit House and left the rest to Mr. Aston. In addition I had to compile a complete list of everyone who served with the Battalion with the necessary information from Part II Orders to enable me write up the appendices. Although I have done my best to avoid error in the spelling of names, etc., I am afraid that I have failed in a few instances. The fault is not solely mine, for in the official records there is sometimes disagreement and inconsistency. I did attempt to get a complete list of the wounded, but owing to the fact that only those who were evacuated to England are recorded in Part II Orders I failed in this direction.

In parts of the narrative it will be observed that we have simply copied the entries in the War Diary. This has been done with the express purpose of ensuring accuracy and avoiding the tendency of some writers of history in bringing their imagination to bear on events of which they were not a witness. Some items recorded like this might not be of interest to the majority of our readers, but to others they might help to recall perhaps the biggest incident in their soldiering.

In conclusion I wish the book to be regarded not as a joint effort of two men only but as a concerted attempt by all those who have contributed to the story to place on record the doings of the 12th Battalion East Surreys for the use of their old comrades and the relatives of the fallen.

17, Aultone Way,
Carshalton, Surrey.

L. M. DUGGAN.

ACKNOWLEDGMENTS

IN order to produce this book the authors have had recourse to many sources of information, and thanks are due to all who have helped in supplying material, besides the authors of some excellent books on the war which have been mentioned in the narrative.

Without the help of the Official Historian, General Edmonds, and Mr. E. A. Dixon and his staff of the Historical Section of the Department of Imperial Defence at Audit House, we should never have been able to start the production. All the War Diaries of the Division, Brigade and Battalion were placed at our disposal together with Operation Orders and Part II Orders. As Duggan's time was limited in copying our own War Diary, extra facilities were granted to him to complete the task as soon as possible.

For the part dealing with the early days of the Battalion we have had to depend upon the files of the South London Press, which were placed at our disposal by the Librarian of the Southwark Public Library, Walworth Road, S.E.17. In addition, Mr. C. A. James has added his quota in touching on things not recorded in the Press or any other documents available.

Colonel H. W. Pearse, D.S.O., and Brig.-General H. S. Sloman, C.M.G., D.S.O., produced some years ago a very complete and excellent History of the East Surrey Regiment which has guided us throughout, while Sir J. A. Hammerton's Popular History of the Great War has come to our aid in many of the broader issues connected therewith.

Very few battalion histories contain a complete list of the cemeteries and memorials of the fallen; for this we have to tender our thanks to the Secretary and Mr. Farr, of the Imperial War Graves Commission.

We have had occasion to give extracts from or refer to the well-written publications of Sir Philip Gibbs, Sir Frank Fox, Siegfried Sassoon, R. H. Mottram, Roland Dorgeles, and Rudolf Binding, because we considered their experiences warranted us quoting them as authorities on the points at issue.

No statesmen have produced more interesting and instructive literature on the great upheaval than Mr. Lloyd George and Mr. Winston Churchill, who have written much which we have digested and introduced where we consider necessary. We are not concerned with the politics of these two statesmen, but the part they both played in the Great War has been acknowledged by our late enemies. We have also read Mr. Duff Cooper's disclosures in the "Life of Earl Haig."

The Histories of the 11th "Queen's" and the 11th Royal West Kents have been of immense service to us all through. In our task we have not only had the assistance of the authors' valuable record of their respective units, but their trusty henchmen, Burberry and Dawson, have, in addition to lending us blocks to save expense, been instrumental in putting Duggan in touch with the authorities to collect the necessary data and have, at all times, given him the benefit of their advice and experience. Perhaps it was Dawson who, more than anyone, decided Duggan on the step he took.

Of those who served with the Battalion, Mr. L. C. Southall set down his experiences *in extenso,* and his retentive memory and literary ability has served to refresh our memories of matters long since forgotten. In addition, his sketch of an incident at Tower Hamlets shows his versatility. Had others gone to the same trouble as he has, we are sure our personal side would have been much more interesting and amusing.

Mr. S. J. Nugent, in between his useful labours as Assistant Hon. Secretary, has found time to place on record many things connected with our trials and troubles overseas.

Despite the fact that Lieut. Norman Speller has had to shoulder great responsibilities for the last two years in the R.A.O.C., he has managed to produce a few stories and incidents in the usual "Speller" style.

We were fortunate in being able to call upon the two Walkers, Captains Hector and David, to read through our manuscript and supply further information, which we have used.

Colonel R. Pennell, Lieut. W. D. Mutch and Mr. J. Chamberlain, in addition to Messrs. Farrell and Keegan, have made our accounts of Hollebeke and Tower Hamlets more complete, while Mr. J. Radcliffe, besides writing of Tower Hamlets, has, with Lieut. R. C. Johns, given us an insight into the conditions prevailing behind the German lines after the great "Push" of 1918.

To the following who have contributed memories we are truly thankful:—Messrs. H. Budd, E. Connor, G. R. Daniels, T. Day, R. G. Fokes, C. F. Helliar, J. Jenkins, W. D. Mutch, H. T. Pike, H. J. Sherborne and H. Tice.

Our story has been read through by General Towsey, whose letter of appreciation sums up his impressions. In addition he has placed documents at our disposal which we have found useful.

Colonel Beatson very kindly read the chapters dealing with his command, and Colonel Brown went to great pains in checking our facts and supplying more information from March, 1918, till the end. Major Searle also helped to clarify some of the operations of 1918 by lending documents; a few anecdotes from him have been used in places.

Lieut. W. S. Hall placed in our hands a set of maps and certain papers which have ensured accuracy in dealing with events in 1918 which were rather involved.

To those who kept diaries we are very grateful for sending us extracts or the actual diaries for perusal. Particularly does this apply to Messrs. Cornish and Laws.

The task of typing the copy was not a light one, and in this respect our thanks are due to Capt. Gillett, Lieut. Pike, Messrs. Southall, Farrell and Press.

In the work of compiling and checking the appendices we have had the utmost assistance from Messrs. Crosby, Farrell and Lunn. The last named, with the ripe experience of one who followed our fortunes most carefully in the Brigade Office, has taken a very keen interest in reading through the matter and offering valuable suggestions.

Circumstances were such as to prevent Messrs. Lattimore, Crosby, and Herbert, of the Committee dealing with the publication, from meeting as frequently as they would have liked. It was, however, realised that the hub on which the publication turned was Mr. Herbert. To him the task of seeing the matter through was entrusted. No one understood the trials and pitfalls of publishing a limited edition of a book of this description as he did, yet he entered into the fray prepared to beg or borrow so that we should not be disappointed. With very little money to begin with he took the risk of sending the copy to the linotypers and accepted the responsibility of finding the paper and labour involved in the production afterwards. His idea was that talking would not get things done—action was essential. Taking on the production himself, he has been the means of saving pounds to the Association. Truly we can say that the real credit for the appearance of a history of the old 12th belongs to Herbert.

We must not be unmindful of those who have helped us financially, for without funds we could do nothing at all. To our generous donors we offer our heartfelt thanks.

Lastly, if there are any we have forgotten to mention who have in any way assisted us, we trust they will forgive our unintentional omission and accept our very best thanks.

CHAPTER I.

May to October, 1915.

Formation—Recruiting—Training and Equipment at Rotherhithe.

THE Infantry has been described as the "Queen of the Battlefield," but with equal justice nicknamed by Tommy the "P.B.I." At any rate through the greatest part of human history the main mass of manœuvre has consisted of this arm. For nearly a thousand years, from the fatal field of Adrianople in 378 A.D., when the Emperor Valens and his great army were overwhelmed by the mounted hosts of the Visigoths, through the Dark and Middle Ages the cavalryman in armour had his day. But in the 14th Century, at Halidon Hill, Crecy and Poitiers, and later at Agincourt, the English bowman redressed the balance, and since the introduction of gunpowder soon afterwards the infantryman, supported by artillery, has been the deciding factor in war. Whether the invention of the aeroplane may alter this fact in future wars, who knows? God forbid that there be any wars to come.

This book has but a modest aim—to record as simply and accurately as possible the history and exploits of a battalion of British Infantry in the Great War. It was but one of thousands in the mighty array of millions of armed men that bore arms for King and Country in that World-Earthquake. We do not here enter into the causes nor detail the general history of the conflict by land and sea. We can but trust that the story may help to dignify the memory of those brave men who gave their lives, may interest those who survived and help to recall incidents, localities, friendships and dangers to their minds, and may give to their families and friends a plain narrative of events calculated to fill their breasts with pride and to "be in their flowing cups freshly remembered."

Now, eighteen years after the Armistice of November 11th, 1918, there is no great nation in the world more pacific than our own. Certainly of those who served there are few who would willingly fight again. The hideous waste both of life and wealth, the cruelty of it, the futility of supposing that political dissensions can be really settled by the slaughter of millions, the injustice, the muddle, the inherent immorality and un-Christianity of War—these have burnt themselves into our minds and consciences in these unhappy eighteen years. But in 1914 there seemed no other way. The British Empire could not have stood aside and allowed Kaiserism triumphant to dominate Europe. Alas, there existed then no League of Nations. But to-day there does, and it behoves every man of goodwill to lend his aid and support our statesmen in their efforts to co-operate with those of other nations at Geneva in preserving world peace and eliminating causes of strife.

The 12th Battalion East Surrey Regiment came into being in the Spring of 1915. Already the War had lasted nine months. Those facile expectations of so many in the early days that it would be ended by an overwhelming victory before Christmas had been tragically falsified. Earl Kitchener, whom Mr. Asquith, the Premier, had called to be Secretary of State for War in the early days of August, 1914, had bidden the nation prepare for a war of at least three years in duration. Kipling in noble lines had lately warned us:—

"No easy hopes or lies
  Shall bring us to our goal,
But iron sacrifice
  Of body, will and soul.
There is but one task for all,
  For each one life to give.
Who stands if Freedom fall?
  Who dies if England live?"

In the first few weeks of the war the mobilisation of the Army consisting of Regulars, Reservists and Territorials had proceeded apace. The strength of the Regular Army in Great Britain and the Colonies was 156,110, all ranks, and 78,400 more were serving in India. The Regular and Special Reserves, all of whom were eligible for foreign service, came to another 200,000 odd, but a large number of these needed training to fit them again for the tasks they had to undertake. The Territorial Force, which was 63,000 short of its proper strength, numbered 250,000. Derisively known to some as "Saturday night soldiers," they were enlisted from men in industry and commerce for home service only, but soon after the outbreak of war most agreed to serve overseas.

Lord Haldane, Secretary of State for War, 1905-1912, had created a British Expeditionary Force for service abroad of 160,000 men, and the splendid work and amazing powers of organisation of this remarkable man should not be forgotten. Actually a force of 80,000 combatants, consisting of four divisions of Infantry and one of Cavalry, reached France in August, 1914, and effected at the end of the month the memorable Retreat from Mons, maintaining touch with the French in spite of all the efforts of Von Kluck's army to break that connexion, and so really saving the Allied cause from being overwhelmed in the first month by the German hosts. Two other Regular divisions followed in September. As A. E. Housman sang:—

"Their shoulders held the sky suspended:
  They stood, and Earth's foundations stay.
What God abandoned, these defended
  And saved the sum of things 'for pay'."

On taking office, Kitchener called for 100,000 volunteers, and ere long the call was repeated. From these were organised service battalions of existing regiments of the British Army. (In course of time Kitchener's divisions were numbered from 9 to 42, while 14 Territorial divisions carried the number to 56. Divisions with higher numbers were in existence before the War ended.) By the end of September, 1914, half a million of the flower of the British race had enlisted in the New Armies. Nothing can prove more convincingly to posterity the fact that England at any rate did not provoke the War than our utter unreadiness for a contest of such magnitude both in troops and equipment. It was not, in fact, till the War had lasted for nearly two years—years in which France and Russia had been bled white—that Great Britain was in a position on land to throw a weight into the struggle in the West commensurate with her position in the world. Our part till then was mainly naval and financial.

It was apparent from the heavy losses sustained by our "Contemptible little mercenary army," as the Kaiser called it, that recruiting under the voluntary system would have to be pushed to its limits. Despite its small numbers, it had shown to the enemy and to the world that for efficiency, skill in the use of arms, endurance and valour it had no equal anywhere. Its tenacity in holding up all attacks on the Channel ports until the Territorials and units of the new armies could arrive will ever live in the annals of the race from which it sprung. Whatever tribute we may pay to the "civilian" soldiers who fought for England, we must never be unmindful of the fine professional soldier who bore the brunt of those early days and possibly saved England from invasion and the ravages of war.

The time came when further efforts were needed to make good quickly the heavy losses which were being sustained on the Western Front. The idea was started in Lancashire that "Pals" battalions should be formed, in which groups of friends from one place should be enlisted in the same unit. Lord Kitchener issued an appeal to the mayors of boroughs. Mr. John Hart, Mayor of Bermondsey, received a request from the Secretary of State for War to raise a battalion of infantry, and this letter was discussed at a meeting of the Borough Council on May 4th, 1915. The terms of the letter were that men between the ages of 19 and 38 should be enlisted locally to serve together for three years or the duration of the War. Training would be carried out on the spot and the men fed and paid by the local authorities until the battalion was in a fit state for the War Office to take it over. The scheme involved an appeal to tradesmen and others for subsidies, but it was understood that the amount expended would be refunded in due course.

Some opposition was raised by certain members of the Council on the grounds that Bermondsey had done well as regards recruiting. It already had a Territorial unit in the 22nd ("Queen's") London Regiment which would need recruits to keep it up to strength. However, the scheme was approved, and the Borough Treasurer (Mr. J. Buckman) was appointed executive officer with Alderman Bulmer and Councillor Godden to represent the Council. For territorial associations it was decided to call the battalion the 12th (Bermondsey) Battalion, The East Surrey Regiment. A headquarters and training ground were necessary, and accordingly the Town Hall, Rotherhithe, and the Oval, Southwark Park, were acquired for these purposes.

Recruiting was started right away and the battalion officially formed on May 24th, 1915. Many of the first applicants to join were men well over military age who were keen as mustard but unfortunately had to be rejected.

On May 31st, 1915, Lieut.-Colonel L. F. Beatson, formerly of the Royal Warwickshire Regiment, was appointed to the command of the Battalion. With nothing to build upon except a few enthusiastic recruits, Colonel Beatson thus took on the colossal task of not only raising, but at the same time training, the new battalion.

The task of recruiting was not a light one. All sorts of schemes were adopted to try to get men to enlist. The main recruiting office was in the Rotherhithe Town Hall, whilst other offices (mainly unoccupied shops) were set up in different parts of the borough. Men had to take turns in these offices in an endeavour to secure recruits. Recruiting meetings were held throughout the district. On June 22nd, 1915, a meeting was held in the Bermondsey Town Hall, at Spa Road, which was addressed by Sir J. W. Benn, Mr. T. P. O'Connor and others. Special appeals were made at the Globe Picture Palace, in the Old Kent Road, where a patriotic picture was being exhibited, and at the South London Palace Music Hall in London Road, Elephant and Castle, where a war play depicting the agony of Belgium was being performed. At the Elephant and Castle Theatre some men appeared on the stage as "supers" in the grand finale of a play. As a result of these meetings many recruits were secured.

Battalion route marches also produced a crop of recruits. Mr. (now Sir) Harry Lauder's Pipers rendered assistance on one occasion, while the East Surrey Depôt band also helped. Lce.-Cpl. E. Dwyer, V.C., of the 1st Battalion, headed a march in which the Mayor and Mayoress of Bermondsey, in an open landau, took part on July 8th, and made his appeal as the youngest V.C. from the base of Colonel Bevington's statue in Tooley Street. The appeal of Dwyer, fresh from the awful fighting at Hill 60, met with a good response. Over 500 men of the Battalion took part in this march. The most memorable recruiting march took place on a Saturday in October, 1915. With the slogan "Wake up, South London," a vast parade was organised by Sir Francis Lloyd (G.O.C., London Command). The south-eastern section, which was led by Colonel Beatson, included the 12th Battalion East Surreys, the 11th (Lewisham) Battalion Royal West Kents and detachments of the Post Office Rifles and the 20th and 22nd London Regiments. The assembly point was Southwark Park, and the march was made through Deptford to Lewisham, tea being supplied to the troops at the Borough Hall, Greenwich.

The job of recruiting was much sought after, as it afforded freedom from parades and extra remuneration and privilege leave to the successful recruiters. Perhaps the worst job was when men were ordered to knock at the doors of the houses to find out whether there were any men of military age living in the house who were eligible and fit to join the army, for it often happened that some members of the households had already laid down their lives or were overseas fighting. To those of us who had not been overseas this was disconcerting. "My boy is already over there; when are you going?" was the rebuff we often got.

Before we leave the matter of recruiting in Rotherhithe, it would be as well to sum up the result of it all. Over 1,000 men joined, the bulk of the local recruits being dock and riverside workers with a good sprinkling of men from the tanneries. A great many "black-coated" workers living or working locally also helped to swell the ranks. There was a fairly big proportion of youths under and men over military age, and some not properly fit physically for the rigours of active service. This eventually had a great effect on the organisation of the Battalion. Recruits were posted to the companies, partially trained, and then either discharged or transferred to home service units. The wastage occasioned by this had to be made good before the Battalion was passed fit for overseas. To apportion the blame for this state of affairs would be difficult. Medical officers were badgered by unfit men who were anxious to serve their country. Time after time they would be rejected, until at last they would come across a doctor who in examining a great many recruits at one of our rallies was apt to overlook their defects. It must be remembered that medical officers were very much overworked during this period. With regard to those over and under age, some of the recruiting officers were not too scrupulous in dealing with these. They knew the great desire among most was to share the burden being borne by their friends and relations who were fighting in Flanders and other war zones, and suggested that "army ages" should be adopted for the purpose of enlistment. Despite the weeding out processes adopted afterwards many of the "overs" and the "unders" remained with the 12th practically to the end. There was another type of individual known in official parlance as the "absconded recruit." This fellow made a practice of attesting, receiving his first day's pay and clothing and not turning up again. Probably he would join several local units in this way until he was laid by the heels by the police. Unfortunately we had many of these wasters to contend with. Speaking of early desertions, R.Q.M.S. Speller states that the high incidence was traced to the machinations of a recruiting sergeant of all people! His *modus operandi* consisted of encouraging youngsters to enlist, get a free kit, and sell that same kit to the aforesaid sergeant in the evening, who in turn disposed of it to a notorious "old clothes man." A bit of detective work by R.S.M. Solomon resulted in the bemedalled hero getting three months' hard labour at Tower Bridge Police Court. All these things tended to retard the work of bringing the Battalion up to strength. In the light of this there is not much doubt that, had a system of compulsory military service (repulsive as it might seem to the free people of these islands), been introduced before the time it became inevitable, millions of pounds would have been saved, not to mention the thousands of lives of the early volunteers who grappled with the might of Germany before the new armies were able to take their place in the field.

Let us turn to the question of training and administration. Colonel Beatson surmounted this difficulty by the aid of some N.C.O.s from the 3rd Battalion and the Depôt of the East Surrey Regiment.

Foremost among these were Colour-Sergeant E. C. Solomon and Sergeant Norman Speller. Solomon's province was the parade-ground, Speller's the Quartermaster's Stores. There could not have been a more efficient or smarter R.S.M. in the British Army than "Ted" Solomon. Young officers and N.C.O.s were daily put through their paces on the Oval by him. As he had the eye of an eagle and a stentorian voice which could be heard a considerable distance from the parade ground, there was very little which escaped his attention and was not brought to the notice of the people concerned without delay. Solomon realised at the outset that he was not dealing with the ordinary type of soldier, and, although he maintained discipline, he managed to do it without incurring the displeasure of the N.C.O.s and men and in consequence was popular among all ranks. As to his efficiency, the fact that he finished his military career as a Captain speaks for itself. That he was unable, owing to his age, to accompany us overseas was a great blow not only to us but to Solomon himself. Having "reared" us he had to leave the fruits of his work to another. When the Association was formed in 1933, although a sick man, he attended our re-unions and was extremely happy to be among his "boys" again. Unfortunately, to the heartfelt regret of all who knew him, he died in October, 1934.

Speller, as R.Q.M.S., was just as successful in the stores as Solomon was on parade; in fact the name of Speller is intimately bound up with the history of the 12th Battalion. Quartermasters came and quartermasters went, but Speller went on for ever. Arriving after having been wounded on service with the 2nd Battalion, Speller set to work equipping, billeting, and generally catering for our multifarious needs. The public rooms in the Rotherhithe Town Hall made commodious office space, and the extensive hall and gallery were seized by Speller and made ideal "issue bays." "Fitting out" was an expeditious job, each recruit being presented with a kit bag and making a perambulation of the hall for the purpose of having the bag stuffed with the various items required. Then the customer ascended to the gallery, where boots, caps, and clothing were fitted. Soon after Speller arrived, Q.M.S. W. McEnuff, of the 7th Royal West Kents was appointed Hon. Lieut. and Quartermaster. Some of the men were billeted locally, others were living in their own homes. The acquisition of suitable billets in the district was therefore another matter which exercised the minds of the Quartermaster and his staff.

The Inns of Court O.T.C. supplied many of the first officers of the Battalion, and the 8th Battalion Gloucester Regiment parted with a very good officer in the person of Lieut. J. L. Buckman, the son of the Borough Treasurer, who later commanded B Company. Capt. H. de Courcy Blakeney was an early arrival and for a time acted as Adjutant before becoming commander of A Company, which was then in the course of formation. Capt. L. Tenbosch arrived later and assumed the Adjutancy of the Battalion. Other officers arriving about this time were: Capt. Spencer;

Lieuts. A. Fewings, R. A. McCulloch and C. York-Davis; 2nd Lieuts. R. A. V. Brearey, G. G. Briggs, J. R. Chesters, R. A. Elphicke, W. Hagen, J. W. Staddon and J. W. Tunwell

Sergt. L. C. Lunn has supplied some details of the officers who arrived in the early days:—

"Lieuts. Brearey and Chesters joined at the same time as J. W. Staddon and G. G. Briggs. I remember the first day these four arrived straight from the O.T.C. They were standing in Rotherhithe Town Hall, all looking very ill at ease, apparently waiting for the Colonel. We all thought, 'What babies!' (except for Briggs, who appeared older), and looked at them rather contemptuously, and wondered how we should have to knuckle under to them. How each of them proved to be 'men' is shown in later chapters of this history.

"Lieut. Fewings joined us at Rotherhithe and very soon became Captain and O.C., D Company. He was, I believe, the most popular officer there, and everybody was at a loss to understand why he was not allowed to go to Witley with us.

"2nd Lieut. J. W. Tunwell also joined B Company, and he used to go round with a N.C.O. to pay the landladies their allowance for billeting and rationing men who had joined the Battalion and did not live locally. On one occasion he went round with my brother to a certain lady who was very well known locally as a moneylender and to be very patriotic. After Lieut. Tunwell had paid her 17/6 (I believe) for billeting one of our men, she offered him 2/6 for himself. Of course he refused, but she was so insistent in stating that it was her patriotic duty to give it, that he was reluctantly forced to come out with the half-crown, which he immediately gave to my brother. When I met Capt. Tunwell in front of Ypres in 1918 (he was temporarily acting Staff Captain), he related this incident to me, and said that he would never forget his confusion at the time and had often laughed about it."

Parades consisting of squad drill and all the elementary training of the recruit were held in the Oval daily from 9.0 a.m. to 4.0 p.m., with a break of two hours from 12.0 o'clock to 2.0 for dinner. An hour of physical training under the able direction of Q.M.S. Instructor A. T. Carrell, of the Army Gymnastic Staff, produced its laughs as well as its pains. Carrell's funny remarks caused much amusement amongst the crowd of civilians who used to congregate by the railings of the Oval to watch the troops' antics on the parade. To the men of more mature years unused to strenuous exercise "jerks" were an agony, especially in the early stages of training; later, as one got used to them, they were not so bad. If the older men did not derive much benefit from them, the younger ones certainly did, for to those who had worked in offices and workshops it was like taking on a new lease of life.

As time went on, various formations began to take shape on the parade ground. Squad drill was succeeded by platoon drill, and, as officers and N.C.O.s were available, by company drill. Most of the N.C.O.s from the depôt had by now been promoted to sergeant-majors, quartermaster-sergeants and sergeants. To complete the complement, promotion was very swift for those who had previous service and those who had set themselves out thoroughly to digest the manuals of military training. At last came battalion and extended order drill. It was apparent now that it would not be long before the Battalion went into camp.

With the exception of exercises underneath the railway arches in Silwood Street, Bermondsey, carried out by a few squads with some old D.P. rifles (borrowed from the St. Katherine's Naval Brigade) arms drill was not done at Rotherhithe, for apparently there was a shortage of weapons. A class in Musketry for N.C.O.s was, however, held daily in the Rotherhithe Conservative Club, under Sergt. B. P. Horswell, the new rifle being used.

Orderly Room for defaulters and the Company offices were held in the Town Hall, but later A Company used a vacant house in Neptune Street. Prisoners awaiting trial, as well as those sentenced to detention, were at first placed in the cells of the Police Station in Paradise Street. In his account of the early days, R.Q.M.S. Speller states that our first "casualty" occurred in Rotherhithe Tunnel. An early 12th man was found guilty of highway robbery and thereafter served His Majesty in a different capacity to the rest of us. Later on the local Poor Law Guardians placed a portion of their Institution in Lower Road, Rotherhithe, at the disposal of the Battalion as a place of detention, where prisoners had a fairly good time. Food was supplied to them from a "coffee-shop" near by, while they were taken out for exercise daily by their guards, and it was even said that occasionally the prisoners, accompanied by their escorts, visited the local music hall! From all accounts heard at the time the prisoner's lot was not an unhappy one. Defaulters were put on tasks in the Quartermaster's Stores. The duties of Provost Sergeant devolved upon Sergt. T. E. Goss, whom Speller has described as "a rare combination of the London 'bobby' and fire-eater."

Concerts were organised by ladies for the entertainment of those billeted in the neighbourhood and two clubs were also available for their recreation. A Sports Day was held at Camberwell, in which troops from all the surrounding districts who were then in training participated, and this was followed in the evening by a torchlight tattoo in which the Battalion took a leading part. Cricket matches were played against local tradesmen and the 11th Royal West Kents and other units of the new armies. C.S.M. D. Saunders and Sergt. T. E. McDermott were the star players of the Battalion team. Both of them were selected to take part in a representative match at Kennington Oval on the 10th of September, 1915, where "Polly" Saunders had the best bowling average for the match—five wickets for 54 runs—while, in addition to taking two wickets, McDermott ran up a useful score.

During the sojourn at Rotherhithe, Church Parades were held at St. Mary Magdalen's, Bermondsey, and on the Oval at Southwark Park. The Roman Catholics attended their churches in Paradise Street and at Dockhead.

Men of the Battalion had a glimpse of the destruction wrought by Zeppelins when bombs were dropped near Peek Frean's factory in Keeton's Road. On another occasion some were commandeered by the police to guard the ruins caused by hostile aircraft in Wood Street, in the City of London.

The members of the Battalion were authorised by the War Office to wear collar badges supplied by the Mayor and Council of Bermondsey, the design being the Arms of the Borough. How this came about is explained by Colonel Beatson:—

"One day an official came to me and said the Mayor wished us to identify ourselves with the Borough, and suggested that we should change our cap badge for one incorporating the Arms of Bermondsey. I replied that I would not. I said that we were a battalion of a famous regiment, and if I were forced to change the badge, nothing would prevent me putting a proper badge in each man's pocket and ordering them to drop the other in the gutter as soon as we had crossed the borough boundary. I won the day, but, to appease them, I said that, if the Mayor could get permission for the men to wear the Borough Arms on their collars, we should be pleased to let them do so. That was done."

No account of the Rotherhithe days would be complete without reference to the "Jolly Sailor." No one is more competent to speak about it than Speller, who writes:—

"Next door to the Town Hall mine host of the 'Jolly Sailor' attended to our creature comforts. Officers in the drawing room, W.O.s in the lounge, sergeants in the private bars, and the troops in the public ditto; this suited everybody.

"At least one lasting romance resulted from this mutually satisfactory arrangement, and many existing friendships in the Battalion had their beginning within those hospitable walls. A small model of the 'Jolly Sailor' sign decorated the Battalion Sergeants' Mess wherever that happened to be during the restless 3½ years of war, and it is still in my possession."

All good things must come to an end. After six months' soldiering under "cushy" conditions orders were received from higher authorities for a move. Those who had the privilege of serving with the Battalion at Rotherhithe will retain many happy memories of those days. The more adventurous spirits may have resented having to spend such a long time in what they described as a "Fred Karno's" army at Rotherhithe, but doubtless this resentment was considerably qualified a few months later when training began in earnest, and later still when the heights of Passchendaele were reached.

On October 2nd, 1915, the last parade in the Oval took place. From a few raw recruits who assembled there six months before had emerged a partially trained battalion of Kitchener's Army. Led by Colonel Beatson, the column of fours wound its way through the main gates of the park, past its headquarters at the Town Hall, on its road to Waterloo Station. The Mayor and Civic Dignitaries of the Borough preceded the column, while the brass band from the Depôt played marches *en route*. Crowds of the inhabitants lined the streets and cheered as the troops passed, while wives, sweethearts and friends walked alongside the Battalion to the station. Within a few hours the 12th Battalion East Surreys were on their way to their next station—Witley.

Sergt. C. A. James, of A Company, provides an amusing and interesting account of the Rotherhithe days:—

"Unique! is the sensation of a man who, having leaped the fence of a double score of years makes his entry to the arena of a temporary military career. Suggestions that I might 'click' for being a soldier led to an experimental visit to Southwark Town Hall, in May, 1915, resulting with my being breeched with the sum of eighteen-pence, a three years' job and the singular privilege of soldiering in Rotherhithe and barracking in my own house at Kennington.

"The following morning, in fulfilment of directions given, I arrived about 9.0 a.m. at Rotherhithe. Outside the Town Hall a number of odd-looking men aimlessly shambled about, discoursing in knots or propping up the walls of the building. One particular individual engaged my notice; he wore carpet slippers and proficiently enlivened his mates with lyrics played on a whistle.

"I ascended the Town Hall steps and furtively looked inside for some regimental order to 'Fall in.' I ventured further; an A.S.C. sergeant was bureaued in an off-room, and I meekly told him who I was and was brusquely told to wait outside. As an outcast I descended the Town Hall steps, while all eyes of my future comrades in arms searched me up and down. Perhaps I flushed slightly, but my carpet-slippered friend struck up a lively ditty which relieved my embarrassment. Soon somebody essayed a conversation and then Bill Ireland (later sergeant of A Company), who seemed to be chummy with everybody, got us on terms of more intimacy. As the time wore on I wondered more and more what all this waiting might lead to. Finally a signal to file inside brought each in turn before an officer seated at a table who generously handed each man 3/6 and a warning to report next morning. These proceedings were repeated day after day, and some apprehensive doubts over this queer kind of soldiering began to oppress my soul.

"When our Colonel arrived, he took us under his wing, with an absence of any fussy scruples over our raw unsophistication and once or twice spoke in apologetic tones of the sad delay in getting us going as 'pukka' soldiers.

"At long last there was a stir, and the now swollen mass of raw materials assembled one morning on the cinder track of Southwark Park. We looked about for Generals, Captains, and other superior ranks in vain. For some time this rag-time crowd gazed about for some leaders. 'Look, here they come!' Yes, the figures of Colour-Sergt.

Barron with Cpls. Newing, Cook, Roberts and Toms were swiftly advancing to the rendezvous. The old Colour-Sergt. (he must have been about 70) raised his stick and gave the first command to the 12th Battalion, the East Surrey Regiment. 'Fall in, in two lines!' The corporals assisted us to get put. We were then divided into squads and left to the corporals to begin the process of licking us into shape. The corporals, experts at their job, were instantly enthused with the unusual types of recruit under their charge, so that progress was rapid and the impetus of training began, stimulated the course of recruiting, and the ranks expanded with great vigour, till it became expedient to select a few who had undergone previous military training for posts of sub-instructors. Amongst them was a sturdy South African War veteran and D.C.M., named Smith: a sterling man of duty later known as Sergt. Smith.

"We were, however, as yet un-uniformed, and, as training in the Park exposed us to the gibes of local onlookers—called forth by our frequent distortions of the drill book—our humiliation was increased by the consciousness of what guys we looked in our motley 'civvies' and how grotesquely unsoldier-like; and some perturbations arose about the long continuance of parading out of khaki, till one day, being deemed a sufficiently effective body for the purpose, we were marched to the Town Hall, where Colonel Beatson inspected us and in his pleasant tones intimated his eagerness to have us all in khaki and announced that stores of clothing were in the Town Hall awaiting the appointment of a Quartermaster to issue it. This latter was Mr. McEnuff, whose arrival with R.Q.M.S. Speller soon gratified our anxieties, and the 12th East Surreys at last went to the Park parading like the 'real goods' it turned out to be.

"Amongst those whose merits as sound soldiers and valorous men later fame attaches to the annals of the 12th, were a few whose former derelictions had become matters concerned with the Court at Tower Bridge, and the sudden appearance one day of R.S.M. Solomon at the Oval in Southwark Park had the psychological effect of 'scaring stiff' these poor lads with a panicky desire to scamper out of his reach. Whatever qualities may be ascribed to his court capacity, as our R.S.M. he was a great trump, and his martinet exterior was tempered with the keenest insight towards human qualities and a perfect estimate of how mercy should season justice.

"One day the R.S.M. on the parade ground said to me (I had attained Cpl. rank) 'I hear you can do a bit of spouting.' I assured him that I was never lost for a word or two. He thereupon detailed me on Thursday morning to march with thirty men preceded by the recruiting band from the Town Hall and halt at various points in the district. After the band playing had congregated a number of people, I should address the crowd, calling on all and sundry to join up and induce their menfolk to do the same, whilst my men were to pass among the crowd and tackle likely individuals. I might well have felt cocky leading my contingent at the head of a first-rate military band, as we proudly walked up Jamaica Road. The return to quarters was hardly so epic in character. The band of course did not escort me back, and I returned leaving, of my thirty men, twenty-five casualties on the field. My men had 'rumbled' that likely recruits were all concealed behind the breastworks of licensed houses and in raiding these lairs they had fallen.

"We had grown well seasoned to our slacks and puttees, all except one poor man named Pendry; somehow poor Ben could not be found a fit in stock clothing, yet like a Trojan he paraded each day a singular contrast in suit of dead black and bowler hat. He was a stocky little man whose breadth of shoulder should rightly have been attached to much longer legs; hence the crux of getting Ben into khaki. This misfortune however Pendry turned to some useful purpose. Many of us were being drawn out to distant evening recruiting drives, and when, after rousing speeches, lads willing to join up were invited to mount the motor waiting and get the job done on the spot, Pendry in 'civvies' would dramatically rush forward in a 'Come on, lads: follow my lead' manner! and like a leading sheep draw the shy ones into the fold. Pendry must have enlisted many times over.

"As stages of establishment advanced, a morale stealthily generated: officers won the esteem of men; the appointment of thoroughly efficient highly trained soldiers posted as sergeant-majors to the companies—'Polly' Saunders, 'Footy' Ward, Peterson and Jack Sheppard—brought the machine still higher towards a working standard, and the *esprit de corps* resulting was in no small measure engendered through the keen vigilance and discreet command of R.S.M. Solomon. Conspicuous in the ranks were to be found fathers and sons, brothers, uncles and nephews and sundry other ties of collateral relationship. Ardent local interest developed; kind friends promoted and maintained recreation and refreshment quarters in Jamaica Road; a concert and amusement hall opened in Rotherhithe; boxing contests of a high-grade revealed some remarkable pugilism; the Public Baths were set aside for our regimental scrub-down; the elegant cricket pitch in the Park became a cage within whose wide bounds there seethed daily the tense activities of a barrack square.

"To smartness in dress and equipment, fostered from the start, was added the amplification of 'Gym' exercises, undertaken primarily by our drill instructors and later raised to a peak by the advent of C.S.M. Carrell. Signals and ambulance sections came into being, and the all-important provision of a marching band was accomplished by "Drummy" Yates, whose selections out of the ranks effected the quick training of fife and drums and a band of buglers. A Medical Officer took sick reports at Bermondsey, consigning needful cases to Lewisham Hospital.* Sergt. Horswell was busily preparing a staff of musketry instructors. The sleepy Town Hall grew to a hive of hustle; the Public Library 'went west,' and one by one men, whose pens were mightier than the sword, left the drill ground to engage in formation of Orderly Room staffs.

"Frequent route marches in and around the district, to say nothing of Church Parades and Drumhead Services in the Park, attested the enthusiasm with which the Borough now regarded its very own battalion, and on the day when the Mayor—Mr. John Hart—in civic robes, and Colonel Beatson reviewed before the Bermondsey Town Hall the results of the task they had undertaken, our Colonel must have thrilled over the transformation effected from a rough nucleus into a disciplined corps, whose physique and bearing reflected high credit on the Borough whose Civic Arms were borne upon the collars of its citizen soldiers.

"The care expended in training us for good soldiers had not been extended to detailed instruction as to the procedure to be observed when we became 'men under arrest,' and those waiting in the vestibule to come before officers for their rep., admonishing or more serious awards, occasionally lapsed into some comic *faux pas* which marred the atmosphere of gravity. Furthermore, it became urgent to institute some detention quarter (hitherto the rather rare cases had been accommodated in the local police station). In a narrow *cul-de-sac* turning, nearly opposite H.Q., was a disused vagrancy ward with cottage adjoining. The vagrants department was a long passage of doors each opening to a cell where former clients had been given hospitality in requital for the performance of their delectable duties. Conversion of these premises into a guard room was opportune, gaining me the honour of being in charge of the Battalion's first guard-mounting. On a Sunday morning we paraded outside H.Q., six men and myself, and Sergt. Newing had undertaken to see the ceremony through. We bore arms no more lethal than swagger canes. As we were a pioneer guard, the ceremony of relieving did not occur. The house was commodious, and some mattresses had been thoughtfully laid on the floor. A sentry promenaded the *cul-de-sac* for two hours and was then relieved. The only occasion I recall the guard getting lively was one night when, as we were returning from one of our jovial concerts, the first Zeppelin raid happened, and the guard turned out to pacify the frantic 'wind up' of some of the gentler sex.

"On a morning in October we marched out of Southwark Park never to re-assemble there until an eventful parade in 1933 (Laying up of the Battalion Colour) gathered those of us who survived at the memorable old spot. At Waterloo a hitch over the Transport caused me to be left behind with a fatigue party to await the complete arrival and bestowal of stores. It was a tedious job. Leave had been granted to some dwelling near to re-visit their homes during an estimated time before the loads would arrive. Hours passed and darkness was advanced before the completion of our task allowed us to entrain for our destination. A few under arrest had to be collected from cages in the crypt of the station and placed under escort of Cpl. Sandell. From Milford Station it was a good march to Witley Camp. Night was well on us, and a bewildering maze of forest and hutments met me with my party on the Portsmouth road wondering how the dickens I could sort out my own lot from the numerous other lots quartered there. A light shone through a hut near by. I knocked; a kilted officer came; to my enquiry he could afford no assistance further than describe where he thought some unit had settled that day. We moved further down the road and the glare of the guard-room came in view. I walked across the bare ground and answered the sentry's challenge. Joy! it was our own quarters. Cook-Sergt. Turner ushered us into a messing hut and sumptuously regaled us with a solid meal, which I immediately amplified by reporting myself 'present' at the Sergeants' Mess."

* *The Rotherhithe Conservative Club was used for inoculation, Sergt. L. C. Lunn having the job of putting ether soap on a few hundred arms.*

CHAPTER II.

2nd October, 1915, to 2nd May, 1916.

Battalion moves to Witley Camp—Marches to Aldershot—Returns to Witley and then back to Aldershot—Proceeds to France.

THE Battalion detrained at Milford and marched to E.I. Lines at Witley Camp. Here it was posted to the 122nd Brigade of the 41st Division. The Brigade was eventually composed of the 12th East Surreys, the 15th Hampshires, the 18th King's Royal Rifle Corps and the 11th Royal West Kents. It is a matter of interest to know that the 13th East Surreys, which was formed in Wandsworth soon after the 12th, was originally posted to the 41st Division, but at the time the 12th arrived at Witley the 13th was transferred to the 39th Division. However, the 12th went out to France a month before the 13th, the latter being eventually posted to the 40th Division.

Witley had been a beauty spot in Surrey before the War. Surrounded as it was by pine trees, no healthier place could have been chosen as a camp even by the troops themselves, despite the muddy conditions in wet weather. By the time the Battalion arrived it had become a vast training centre, and wooden hutments were dotted about in groups all over the countryside. Canteens, recreation huts and other institutions used by the Army abounded. Established among the pine trees were Y.M.C.A. huts with reading, writing and concert rooms, which helped to supply the Tommies with the means of whiling away the hours after parades were done. For the officers and sergeants proper messes were established.

The huts, each accommodating a platoon, were raised from the ground with steps leading up to the interior. A stove was fitted in the centre and on either side were long wooden tables and forms. Three boards with trestles and "biscuits" (mattresses) constituted the bed of each man with the usual number of blankets (two or three, according to season). Opposite the Battalion Orderly Room was a large parade ground, and smaller ones for companies adjoined the huts.

Brigade Headquarters were situated near the Battalion lines, and very soon the 12th got to know their very amiable Commander, Brigadier-General F. W. Towsey, and his able assistant, the Brigade Major, Major Gwyn Thomas. General Towsey was an infantryman himself, having been an officer of the West Yorkshire Regiment, and a soldier of distinction and spirit, well versed in the training of men and ardent for his work. But what was of even greater value was his cheery outlook and wise humanity. He was always, both at home and on active service, indefatigible in seeking the well-being of the troops under his command. His bearing to junior officers or men in the ranks was never that of the aloof and precise "Brass Hat": there was always something paternal about him, and it was well-known that during some of the worst times suffered by the Brigade on the Somme and in the Salient his sympathy with the sufferings of his troops was so real and intense as to affect his own health. At home Mrs. Towsey always earnestly helped the Soldiers' Clubs and made every effort for the entertainment and relief of the Brigade. We were truly fortunate in being under such an essentially human and genial commander.

About this time there was much talk in the Press about waste. Witley had been singled out for one of these newspaper onslaughts, and cases had been quoted where food of the best quality had been thrown away in incinerators. Although the 12th may not have been guilty in this direction, there certainly was food in abundance. No doubt the cooking was not of the best until the cooks had gathered experience. However, in time there was little to complain of. Best Irish butter was supplied to the troops, and amongst extras canned fish and cake made their appearance on the tables, while tea was served in special pails which had to be scrupulously cleaned every day. Feeding under camp conditions was a novelty to most members of the Battalion. Feelings were mixed on the subject, but, like most things connected with soldiering, one got used to it in time and came to regard it as part of the usual routine.

Let Sergt. James give us his impressions of our entry into Witley Camp:—

"Witley Camp loomed up like a miner's settlement rattled together amid woods and heathlands, but within was a planned order of spacious huts, set as in company formation in extended order, with regulated alley ways and main thoroughfares, all liberally bestowed with sticky mud: there were spacious canteens dispensing refreshment: there was wide country for evening rambles and the convenient town of Godalming.

"Left behind were our home billets, feather bed kips and eiderdowns, now ruthlessly replaced by a harsh couch of three planks on two low trestles with a coarse blanket—perhaps two; these in roomy huts, boasting no furniture other than needful tables and forms, yielded what may in primitive ages have originated the term "Board and lodging." Another new feature was suddenly introduced: Reveillé at early morn with hurried ablutions, including shaving without the usual kettle on the fire to resort to.

"Our unit took over the guard-room shortly after arrival: rifles and side arms—except by the few N.C.O.s qualifying for musketry—had not yet been handled by the men, and our daily guard was limited to a sentry with a stick; until one week-end came a panic order, and some obsolete rifles arrived. Hastily endeavours were made to rush half-a-dozen men through the ceremonial, and again the honour of command was mine. The distant review of that zealous move to instil by cramming process rifle movements into men previously unacquainted with the drill is intensely humorous now, but at that period it was rather grave and serious, perhaps somewhat painful. It was a Sunday morning when the guard was inspected and despatched to duty: the close proximity of the Sergeants' Mess, lent occasion for a number of weatherbeaten old veterans to slip away from their beer to take a 'mike' out of us: and the keen interest they displayed over the event increased the nervous tremors of the poor lads undergoing the ordeal."

Training now began in earnest. Gradually the Battalion was equipped with rifles and bayonets: the short Magazine Lee-Enfield, Mark III was issued to each man. Lectures on the care of arms taught us that rifles were not merely weapons with which to fire at an enemy but they had to be continually cleaned, oiled, and prized above all worldly objects. To have a dirty rifle or use the gauze without the permission of an officer were heinous offences. A story was current of a sergeant instructing a squad of recruits. "Listen to me," he said. "You must take as much care of your rifle as you would of your wife. Mind you rub it all over with an oily rag every day."

Arms drill became part of the daily routine as well as bayonet fighting, when sacks were used to represent an enemy, and with wild yells men charged the sacks in accordance with their instructors' ideas of the spirit of the bayonet.

Specialists began to appear in different parts of the camp, Signallers, Lewis Gunners, Bombers and the like. The Transport began to be efficient, while the drum and fife band came very much into prominence, and buglers began to sound strange calls, which the troops were obliged to know.

The arrival of the 15th Hants and the 18th K.R.R.s was the signal for training on a more extensive scale. Brigade training was added to battalion training, and field days and night operations began to take their place in the programme. Trench digging was begun, and for this purpose we used the area around Hindhead. Here also various exercises were carried out in that well-known landmark, the "Devil's Punch Bowl." Open warfare was practised in the daytime, and relief and occupation of trenches during the night, while later on trenches were held for periods of about 48 hours. Officers, N.C.O.s and men attended various courses of instruction at the different schools set up for this purpose. Men going on courses had to take their rifles and equipment with them. A story is told of a private travelling with full kit and rifle in a compartment occupied also by an old woman. After glancing nervously at his equipment for some time, she leant across to him. "Young man," she said, "I'm very nervous of that 'ere gun o' yours. Would you please hold the spout out o' the window."

The privilege of week-end "Leaf" was extended to most members of the Battalion. At this time the pay of the private soldier was 1/- per diem; if he made an allowance to his dependants he would accordingly receive 3/6 on Friday. A week-end leave meant that he would receive nothing at all, as the cost of his ticket to London had to be defrayed from his pay; yet there was always a demand for passes.

The only incidents that broke the monotony of training at Witley were the passing of enemy aircraft over the camp soon after the Battalion's arrival, and the fire in the Power station. The first incident was remarkable for the fact that, on the alarm being given the Battalion was, apparently by mistake, ordered on parade, and, had bombs been dropped, there would have been a heavy casualty roll. Fortunately it was night time and the aircraft vented its spite on the neighbourhood of Guildford. In the second incident A Company was responsible for the fire picquet, which consisted of one platoon. When the alarm sounded, two platoons turned out and kept the flames in check until the local fire brigade arrived. That an additional platoon had rendered assistance was due to the fact that a certain platoon sergeant had forgotten that his platoon had been relieved from this duty the day before, and there was some muttering among his men when they were disturbed from their slumbers.

Two other incidents are called to mind by Cpl. Paddy Maguire and Sergt. James. Paddy states:—

"Some of the impecunious but adventurous spirits with the cry 'No money, no beer,' decided that it would be a splendid achievement to satisfy their thirst from the canteen which had 'bags' of it. Accordingly they decided on a plan which turned out successful. The attention of the N.C.O. on canteen duty being diverted by a riot staged at one end of the room, the double doors at the bar end were quietly opened and closed and a 36 gallon cask of beer was removed. The cask was not missed that evening and the N.C.O. on duty was given a rendezvous which was faithfully kept after staff parade. Going through the lines to a certain hut he saw an interesting sight; all the windows and doors were covered with blankets; propped up on two forms was the cask of beer, underneath which was a washing bath. Around the sacrificial table practically all the 'teetotallers' of the Battalion were offering up beer from the bath in any sort of utensil available. When the stock in the bath got low, the cask was rolled along until the bung-hole was over the bath, and the stock replenished. The cask was afterwards rolled away to the side of the canteen."

There was a sequel to this, as Paddy relates:—

"Shortly after this affair a barrel which appeared to be three parts full was noticed standing near the door of the bar. After a little manœuvring it was got out and rolled away to a small spinney adjacent. Guests were invited and several had a number of drinks before one of the party was invited to have a 'basin', tasted it, declared it was rotten, and at the same time pointed out the colour of the liquid. One enthusiastic toper then exclaimed, 'Garn, its stout!' When subsequently a notice appeared outside the canteen to the effect that a barrel of waste was missing, several members of the party walked down to where the barrel was standing, and investigating the remainder of the contents found such items as bits of swab, bottle corks, 'fag' ends and cigarette packets. They felt very squeamish, and, if the Battalion records were available for that particular occasion, the sick report would be found to be one of the biggest during the Battalion's existence."

Sergt. James's incident is concerned with the guard-room:—

"On one occasion the Brigadier and Brigade Major dropped into the guard-room unawares: a prisoner, Sergt, C—— had arrived in camp under close arrest, having exceeded the octave and violently resisted four strapping sergeant-majors. This N.C.O. was a sound trained old soldier, popular amongst us, and he had been brought from his cell to join us at the guard-room fire. For the moment I had visions of being consigned to join C—— in his cell, but the old sweat knew the road: instead of assuming a guilty look, he stood at attention with the rest, bold as brass, as though he was really of the company of the righteous. The officers detecting nothing retired to examine the premises whilst C—— slipped back to his cell. We had the unique spectacle later of seeing C—— being reduced before a parade of the whole Battalion."*

Route marches were frequent for it was said that Lord Kitchener considered marching the best means of making men fit and of trying their endurance. The real test came to the 12th Battalion when on November 8th, it was called upon to proceed from Witley to Aldershot. In addition to full marching order, each man had to carry an iron weight in each of his leather pouches in lieu of ammunition. These weights were nicknamed "Kitchener's Chocolate" owing to their resemblance to such bars. By the time the march was completed many pouches were empty, and the ditches on the road to Aldershot contained relics of the Battalion's great march. In recalling this march Sergt. James says that, although heavily laden, we accomplished the march without a casualty, thanks to the Colonel's watchful care to halt for rests whenever symptoms of exhaustion were manifested.

On arrival the Battalion was billeted in Oudenarde Barracks, situated in North Camp. Such an old garrison town was suitable in all respects for the intensive training which was to follow.

Some of the men were accommodated in brick-built barrack-rooms, others in wooden huts. Each barrack-room was equipped with iron bedsteads, tables, forms and cupboards for storing food and the enamelware used for meals.

The camp was well supplied with army institutes, including a garrison canteen where there was a large concert room, in which many of the leading lights of the music halls provided entertainment for the troops. A chairman in a little box adjoining the stage used to announce the turns by calling the audience to order with the aid of a hammer. From the look of the pint glasses of beer which surrounded the chairman's box it would appear that one had to have a big capacity to occupy the position. The audience was usually a very critical one; if the performers were good, the applause would be deafening, but, if the reverse was the case, demonstrations would be made in no uncertain manner. In many ways it resembled the old-time Music Hall. N.C.O.s had to take turns on canteen duty, which was not always a pleasant task. Their job was to see that the men behaved themselves and that army regulations, such as the prevention of gambling, were complied with. They had to report on staff parade just before "lights out," and if everything was in order they would answer the R.S.M.'s enquiry with, "Canteen closed and correct, Sir!" The Soldiers' Club was patronised by many, while the supper bar adjoining the barracks did a roaring trade in "Sausage and mash," especially on pay night.

* *This man afterwards got his three stripes back and was wounded at the battle of Messines.*

Training now approached the stage of advanced musketry instruction. Attached to the Battalion for this purpose were instructors from the School of Musketry; Staff Sergt. Instructor S. Shaw, after attachment for a month, was replaced by Staff Sergt. C. F. Helliar who remained to see the Battalion fire its course before it proceeded overseas. Daily men were to be seen taking aim at targets on parade, whilst others were clustered in groups around N.C.O.s, learning the parts and other essential points about rifles. An armourer-sergeant, Sergt. S. Tyrer of the Army Ordnance Corps also arrived, and his services were greatly in demand later on. He was to remain with us till the end.

C.S.M. W. H. E. Trewin of the Army Gymnastic Staff arrived on the scene to inculcate the troops with the spirit of the bayonet. With the aid of some of the officers and N.C.O.s of the Battalion who had been through a six weeks' course at the School of Gymnasia men became proficient in the art of sticking sacks, not to mention pointing, parrying and the rest.

Most of the officers had by now been through courses at the various schools to make them conversant with the part they had to play in preparing the men for the front. Lieut. E. V. Whiteway, who was connected with the famous cider firm, being appointed Transport Officer, was sent on a course to Pangbourne. With the aid of Sergt. George Nuttman and Sergt. Carpenter, who was attached from the Army Veterinary Corps, he brought the Battalion Transport up to a state of perfection which won for it a great name in the Division. The majority of the drivers came to the Battalion with a knowledge of horses, the others were horse masters before they left. Mules had come into their own by this time as the army beasts of burden. That they were difficult to manage was well known, but these civilian drivers not only curbed but mastered them. This is no idle boast, for it is on record that the Battalion interpreter in Italy who belonged to the much vaunted Italian Cavalry, handed over a month's pay for his failure to do more than grab the neck of one of Henley's mules which he had undertaken to ride.

Lieut. J. W. Tunwell took charge of the Lewis Gun Section, the advantages of which weapon were being slowly but surely realised. Its advocates had been fighting tooth and nail to get it more generally adopted throughout the British Army. Some Commanding Officers overseas were loath to adopt it, preferring to depend upon rifle fire, for which our Regular Army had made a name for itself. To those of us who watched the rise of the Lewis gun from 4 to 64 a Battalion this is hardly conceivable. The Vickers gun too was already a great force in the armament of the British Army, but its numbers were insufficient. Eventually each brigade had a company of Vickers gunners, and later on in 1918 each division had a battalion of them. Lieut. Tunwell became an expert instructor and for some time was attached to a school in France. Two of his able assistants were Sergts. A. Nash and Sam Lattimore. The former was a Regular soldier but the latter had been an accountant before joining up. "Lat" had acquired some knowledge of machine guns as a Territorial and, although he was first of all commandeered by C.S.M. Blatch as company clerk of C, he made it clear that so soon as the Lewis Gun Section started he wanted to join it. Lattimore had his wish, and became one of the most popular N.C.O.s of the 12th.

Bombers with the red grenade on the sleeves of their coats began to appear in charge of Lieut. Walter Hagen, a former Private of the Shanghai Volunteers, an organist and a wine merchant. Sergt. A. Bucknell of B Company became his right hand man and had such confidence in the "Mills" that often he scared the men in the pits by picking up bombs which failed to explode soon after they were thrown. To qualify as a bomber was to join the "Suicide Club." The Mills bomb was finding great favour with the authorities, and so everyone had to become familiar with it. Even with the greatest precautions accidents happened in the bombing pits, and the first casualties suffered by the Division happened in this way. Accidents could often be attributed to nervousness; not everyone was a Bucknell.

Guards and picquets were supplied in abundance. In addition to the usual guard on the Battalion guard-room, one was occasionally found for Government House, where the G.O.C. Aldershot Command resided. The guard for the latter had to be as smart and efficient as possible, and the greatest of care was taken in selecting it.

Sergt. James has an amusing story of one of our guards:—

"The main guard overlooked Queen's Parade, adjacent to G.H.Q., and there sentries required extra vigilance. One day an oddment—an awful little scrub—being on sentry and imagining two approaching Military Police were General officers, turned out the guard to present arms. Whether it was the guard or the poor Red Caps who felt 'silly' over the *faux pas* was never discovered."

It was said that it was impossible for anyone to escape from the guard-room at Aldershot. At Witley Camp this was not the case, for two or three prisoners had managed to get away owing to defects in the structure. However, an alarm was raised one night at North Camp when one of our prisoners (minus his boots) was missing, though how he had contrived to get out was not known. A S.O.S. was sent out to the different units in the Aldershot Command to try to catch the fugitive, who was eventually secured a day or two later in some woods near Twiseldon.

Perhaps the most interesting personality who was placed in the guard-room was the lad whose history is recorded by C.S.M. Helliar as follows:—

"At the outbreak of war his father—a reservist—took the boy with him to help him to carry his bag to the barracks. Father and son both stayed inside; both obtained uniforms; and, when the battalion went to France, somehow the boy accompanied it and acted as batman to his father and others. Apparently he managed to keep out of the way of officers and others who might challenge his identity. During the fighting in the autumn the boy was wounded, and, being admitted to hospital, gave the name and regimental number of his father. Complications arose when the wife was informed that her husband was wounded and in hospital at the time that she was receiving letters from him showing that he was still with his unit. The Padre at the hospital received particulars from the Depôt that the man was married and had several children, so he naturally came to the lad to clear up what seemed to him a glaring impossibility. The truth then came out. After explaining what had happened the boy was sent to another hospital, and in the summer of 1915 was discharged and sent to his home, the local clergy and police being instructed to keep an eye on him. The youths of Rotherhithe looked upon the boy either as a hero or something big in the way of liars, and he had a good time generally. When the 12th Battalion was formed, the lad enlisted and found himself in the army again, but under somewhat more arduous conditions. Squad drill, fatigues and discipline were new to him, and, as they became irksome, he disappeared and went home again. Having to keep out of the way of the police and being subject to the mocks and jeers of the local boys, the lad went away again, and, turning up at Birmingham, enlisted as a driver in the R.F.A., but he had by now learned to keep his mouth shut and get on with his job. The climax came when this particular battery was sent to Aldershot at about the same time as the 12th Battalion. It was not long before he discovered that the 12th was there, and, wanting to show off in his breeches and spurs to his footslogging mates in his old unit, he met some of them a number of times. One of them did the dirty on him and reported the facts to a N.C.O., with the result that he was arrested as a deserter and handed over to the 12th Battalion."

C.S.M. Helliar regrets that he does not know how the matter finished up. The lad, he states, was no myth, as he saw him himself in the guard-room at Oudenarde Barracks, and, although he forgets his name, he thinks the story is substantially true.

From Aldershot the Battalion marched back to Witley on January 7th, 1916.

In his amusing reminiscences Sergt. James recalls his second period at Witley:—

"During our next period in Witley, one night in the guard-room I had some men with musical bent. To beguile the peaceful hours, excerpts from our Church choir days were revived. We had melodiously harmonised 'Abide with me,' 'Swanee River' and suchlike; then for variation we had taken down the typed sentry rules to chant like psalms. We had nicely pointed 'He shall walk about in a soldier-like manner, and shall take charge of all Government property in view of his post,' etc., etc.; the solemn strain was rising, when the sentry's alarm, 'Guard, turn out! Visiting rounds!' scattered the choir for rifles, caps, etc., and hastily we fell in outside. I hurriedly saluted with 'Guard present and correct!' 'Yes,' responded the Brigade Major drawing near and touching my rifle at the slope, 'but your rifle is wrong way about' (toe of butt inward instead of outward). We entered the guard room, and they peered about.

'Were you holding a service?' Major Gwyn Thomas enquired.
'No, Sir,' I flushing replied.
'You were singing something sacred?'
'We were singing, Sir.'
'What were you singing?'
'Sentry rules, Sir.'
I flushed harder. Blandly they smiled.
'I think those words are sacred,' the Major playfully suggested."

Before becoming a soldier Sergt. James had had plenty of experience in the entertainment world. The men of his platoon used to refer to him as the "Actor." He was very well liked by all who came in contact with him and it was with regret that we had to leave him behind in hospital when the time came for us to go over the other side. He would have made a very useful member of the "Dickybirds." He was afterwards posted to the 1st Battalion in France, despite the fact that he was over age for the trenches. Thus A Company parted with one of its most cultured N.C.O.s.

The second period at Witley ended on the 14th of February, when the return journey by route march was made to our old barracks in North Camp, Aldershot.

The 41st Division now proceeded to carry out manœuvres preparatory to proceeding on active service. Field days were held near the Basingstoke Canal, which entailed long hours of waiting for a supposed enemy to arrive and a long trek back to camp in the evenings.

While we were at Witley and Aldershot, a weeding-out process was in operation. Old men and immature youths, together with those who were not considered fit enough for active service, were either sent to the Depôt Company at Rotherhithe to be finally merged into the 14th Battalion, or to the 3rd Battalion at Dover. The majority of these were subsequently sent overseas, being either posted to other battalions of the Regiment or transferred to other regiments. To replace these men drafts from the 3rd, 10th, 11th and 14th battalions. amounting in all to about 500, joined the 12th.

At the request of Lord Kitchener in October, 1915, Lord Derby was appointed Director of recruiting for the Army and soon afterwards propounded an idea later known as the "Derby Scheme," in which every recruiting organisation was to be employed on a canvass of unenlisted men of military age. Under a group system (46 groups—23 for single and a like number for married men, arranged according to age) men were asked to volunteer. Single men were to be called up first according to age; the married men not being called upon until the lists of the single had been exhausted. After simply attesting these men could return to their vocations until the time arrived for them to be called up for service. An armlet was issued to them, and those who wore it were dubbed by the troops "Civvy Sergeant-Majors," because at a distance the design on the armlet looked very much like the badge of rank worn by warrant officers. Not much time was lost in calling these volunteers up; a great proportion of the drafts joining at Aldershot being composed of them. The "Derby" men turned out to be some of the finest soldiers and fighting men posted to the Battalion. The courage and determination in action of these men, who had been prevented from enlisting earlier by family ties and responsibilities, proved that it was not fear that was the stumbling block to their being among the first volunteers. In this respect they put some of the old soldiers to shame.

The Battalion musketry course was due to start on March 1st, but, when the day arrived, snow had been falling for two days and was still coming down. As a wait of two or three days produced no improvement, instructions were received to start regardless of the weather. The course was fired on the range at Cæsar's Camp, which was one smooth mass of snow, and you could not tell firing points from ditches until you fell into the latter. The course went on seven days a week in hail, rain, snow, fog, thunder, lightning and gales. C.S.M. Helliar's returns, he states, were deplorable and never dry. However, towards the end of April when the machine-gun sections and details were finishing their courses, we had a burst of beautiful weather.

The final course produced some amusing incidents under such abominable conditions. Every man had to fire, no matter what his occupation was in the Battalion. The cooks from A Company were greeted on the range by their Sergeant-Major with the remark, "Here come the company snipers!"—a remark which produced some laughter from those assembled near the firing points. These men had not the same opportunity of learning as much as the other troops about musketry, and, if some of their shots did go over the butts, they were excusable.

At the end of March Lieut.-Colonel L. F. Beatson was relieved of the command of the Battalion by Major H. H. Lee, D.S.O., of the Cameronians. Fate decreed that, after raising the Battalion and organising it for service overseas, Colonel Beatson should not accompany it. His age and the fact that he had been out of harness for such a long time were the deciding factors. It was with real regret that all ranks heard the news and had to bid farewell to their genial commander, who had done the "donkey work" of the earliest days and had well earned his popularity. Colonel Beatson was afterwards posted to the Middlesex Regiment and later had charge of thousands of men in the Labour Corps; for his services he was awarded the Order of the British Empire. The Association is now fortunate in having him for its President.

Major Lee had already seen distinguished service with his regiment in France, and was a strict, though not harsh, disciplinarian. He was short, slight and wiry in physique, with a spruce moustache—every inch a soldier of the best "Regular" tradition.

The Battalion now being up to war strength, the final stages of training were carried out. Perhaps the most outstanding feature of the final training was the Divisional Route March, in which all units of the Division participated on a blazing hot day. It extended into the region of Farnham and was carried out with full marching order, including all the kit to be carried overseas. During the march the Divisional Commander, Major-General Sydney T. B. Lawford, took the salute at various points along the route. It was all right going out, but after two or three hours marching along the dusty roads packs began to weigh heavily on the shoulders, while perspiration through the heat made the men feel anything but comfortable. Some men of the unit in front of the 12th Battalion began to fall out, thoroughly exhausted, but no sympathy was extended to them by our fellows as they passed. "What time's reveillé, chum?" was how they were greeted. However, before the flying ground at Farnborough was reached, singing had practically ceased, and it was only with a great effort that men were able to rise after falling out for the usual ten minutes break in the hour. It was with great relief that the Battalion marched into the barracks at North Camp to the strains of our Regimental march. It says much for the stamina of the men that there were only two or three who failed to complete the course.

The time came when the King was to inspect the Division, and the Review was held on April 26th. His Majesty was accompanied by Lord French and Sir Archibald Hunter, and the Mayors of the various boroughs were also present with others who had worked in the raising of the battalions.

Final leave followed; only a couple of days could be spared for the men to settle their affairs at home. In consequence some took more time than was granted, and the Company Officers were kept busy in disposing of charges.

News arrived that the Battalion would proceed overseas on May 1st. Accordingly, relatives and friends began to stream into the barracks on the week-end preceding that date. Wives and children, fathers and mothers, brothers and sisters, sweethearts and friends came to spend the last few hours with those dear to them before they departed for a destination which at that time was unknown. As usual rumours were afloat. The Battalion was going to India, to Egypt, and even to Ireland; it was not up to the standard to take part in the fighting on the Western Front. But to those who were really in the know there was not much doubt about our destination, unless at the last moment it was changed. Had not Major Tenbosch and Capt. Blakeney already visited and been attached for a few days to units on the Western Front?

Pay books (A.B. 64) and identity discs had already been issued to the men, who received instructions to make their wills out on the proper page in the pay book. Particulars of vaccination and inoculation undergone before final leave was granted were also inserted in this book.

At 5.15 a.m. on May Day, 1916, the 12th Battalion paraded with a strength of 1,018 all ranks, and proceeded along the road to Farnborough to entrain for their unknown destination.

Even at such an early hour some of the relatives of the men were there to see them off, while the Details under 2nd Lieut. F. E. Elphicke also turned out. Amongst the latter was R.S.M. E. C. Solomon, who, being too old to accompany us, had reluctantly to give way to C.S.M. W. H. Nash of the 12th Essex Regiment who had only joined us two days before. The entrainment having been completed, the train left the siding and sped along the lovely English countryside towards Southampton.

What the thoughts of each man were during the first stage of the journey under sealed orders it is impossible to say, but soon after Farnborough was left behind the troops burst forth into song both sentimental and comic. "Homeland" and "We are Fred Karno's Army" both found a place in the repertoire of the Shiny Twelfth, and were sung with great gusto. While most of the soldiers of the belligerent nations marched off to the front with patriotic airs like the French "Marseillaise" and the German "Die Wacht am Rhein," the Tommy adopted such songs as "Tipperary" and "Who's your lady friend?" and "Whiter than the whitewash on the wall!" Not that he was less patriotic than the others, but he did not want to display his feelings to the world. The men of the 12th were no exception to the rest of the British Army, so that their marching songs were at times not only comic but of the type which would be unprintable,

When the sheds at Southampton were reached, a guard was placed on duty and men were not allowed to leave the docks. The troops had carried large tins of bully beef from Aldershot and consumed these while they were waiting to embark. In the docks were some large liners (including a German one) and these were objects of curiosity to many. Towards the afternoon we boarded the troopship Cæsarea and within a few hours the journey started.

There is no need to describe a troopship to those who experienced one during the war. Sufficient to state that there was very little room aboard to make one comfortable. As submarines were very active at this time, everyone had to don a lifebelt whether he liked it or not, and when the ship got a little way out, an escort of destroyers accompanied it. Nearly every unit of the 41st Division reported that it had either been delayed or chased by submarines. Rumours in the 12th had it that such was the case now. However, although it may have been so, there is nothing to confirm it, but members of the crew are said to have spread the rumour and smoking was prohibited on deck.

As the coast was perceived by the lights on the shore, men with great curiosity gathered on the upper deck. There was not much doubt now what our destination was. What kind of a reception should we get? Tales of the first expeditionary force were widespread among us owing to the presence of some who had served with the 1st Battalion. It was early in the morning when we disembarked and, apart from a few employees in the docks who took no particular notice of us, the place was deserted. We found that we had landed at Le Havre, and, after forming up on the quayside, we marched away to No. 5 Rest Camp, where we remained for a day.

The following list of officers, warrant officers and N.C.O.s who proceeded overseas with the Battalion will be of interest:—

Lieut.-Col. H. H. Lee, D.S.O., Commanding Officer.
Major H. J. Walmisley-Dresser, Second-in-Command.
Capt. and Adjutant R. A. McCulloch.
Lieut. R. A. V. Brearey, Signals.
Capt. J. W. Tunwell, M.G. Section.
Lieut. E. V. Whiteway, Transport.
Hon Lieut. and Quartermaster G. W. Lander.
Lieut. E. C. Lambert, R.A.M.C., Medical.

A COMPANY

Capt. H. de C. Blakeney, O.C.
Capt. F. D. Jessop.
Lieut. J. R. Chesters.
2nd Lieut. D. McCallum.
2nd Lieut. H. T. Pike.
2nd Lieut. H. S. Morgan.
R.S.M. W. H. Nash.
C.S.M. J. Wilkinson.
C.Q.M.S. B. P. Horswell.
Armourer Sergt. S. Tyrer, R.A.O.C.
Sergt. R. J. Calver.
Sergt. G. Claridge.
Sergt. W. L. Dorney.
Sergt. T. Dwan.
Sergt. T. Flanagan.
Sergt. W. L. Richards.
Sergt. E. G. Paisley.
Sergt. W. H. Sheppard.
Lce.-Sergt. W. Coughlan.

B COMPANY

Capt. J. L. Buckman, O.C.
Lieut. C. O. Slacke.
Lieut. H. S. Openshaw.
2nd Lieut. F. Beard.
2nd Lieut. A. T. Libby.
2nd Lieut. J. F. Tamblyn.
R.Q.M.S. N. Speller.
C.S.M. A. E. Peterson.
C.Q.M.S. F. Heydinger.
Sergt. A. Bucknell.
Sergt. J. Donnelly.
Sergt. E. H. Heywood.
Sergt. W. H. Ireland.
Sergt. C. Maguire (Signals).
Sergt. C. Norris.
Sergt. G. Nuttman (Transport).
Sergt. A. S. Taylor.
Sergt. C. A. G. Toms.
Lce.-Sergt H. R. Hawtin.

A COMPANY—*continued*

Lce.-Sergt. G. Simpson.
Cpl. E. Clark.
Cpl. V. B. Condon.
Cpl. W. Day.
Cpl. E. R. Durrell.
Cpl. C. W. Field.
Cpl. C. Jakens.
Cpl. R. Stringer.
Cpl. C. Tween.
Cpl. J. Williams.
Cpl. H. West.

B COMPANY—*continued*

Lce.-Sergt. C. Midson.
Lce.-Sergt. C. W. Turner.
Cpl. H. Clarke.
Cpl. G. C. Gosling.
Cpl. T. Maguire.
Cpl. P. R. Manning.
Cpl. F. W. Webb.

C COMPANY

Capt. C. York-Davis, O.C.
Lieut. G. G. Briggs.
Lieut. J. W. Staddon.
2nd Lieut. C. C. A. Lee.
2nd Lieut. S. Stimson.
2nd Lieut. E. M. Dove.
C.S.M. T. Blatch.
C.Q.M.S. A. Woods.
Sergt. N. Bowen.
Sergt. W. Cornish.
Sergt. W. Edlin.
Sergt. A. A. Joyce.
Sergt. F. Retford.
Sergt. B. Wilkinson.
Lce.-Sergt. W. Barnes.
Lce.-Sergt. S. Lattimore.
Lce.-Sergt. H. Richardson.
Cpl. G. A. Case.
Cpl. W. G. Clayton.
Cpl. H. Davidson.
Cpl. A. Garrard.
Cpl. G. Hatton.
Cpl. J. H. Hill.
Cpl. G. Morris.
Cpl. E. Taylor.
Cpl. J. T. Brewin.
Cpl. W. W. Taylor.

D COMPANY

Major L. Tenbosch, O.C.
Capt. R. A. Down.
Capt. W. Hagen (Bombing).
Lieut. C. C. Fox.
2nd Lieut. H. C. Reynard.
2nd Lieut. J. E. M. Crowther.
2nd Lieut. C. N. Pridham.
2nd Lieut. A. V. Reiner.
C.S.M. H. Jackson.
C.Q.M.S. E. M Warr.
Sergt. C. Aucourt (Provost-Sergt.).
Sergt. B. G. Burgess (Orderly Room).
Sergt. E. Critcher.
Sergt. C. Dibden.
Sergt. G. Freeman.
Sergt. A. Nash (L.G. Section).
Sergt. E. F. Sandell.
Sergt. E. C. Selby (Q.M. Stores).
Sergt. A. A. Smith.
Sergt. J. Sparks (Tailor).
Sergt. W. Turner (Cook).
Sergt. E. West (Pioneer).
Lce.-Sergt. P. W. Dove.
Lce.-Sergt. F. Fox.
Lce.-Sergt. L. C. Lunn.
Lce.-Sergt. P. W. Williams.
Cpl. R. Butterworth.
Cpl. R. Blencowe.
Cpl. J. Chifney.
Cpl. S. Easton.
Cpl. J. T. Hunt.
Cpl. R. Mitchell.
Cpl. H. Shulman.
Cpl. J. Sewell.

C.S.M. D. Saunders proceeded to Etaples as A/R.S.M. of the 41st Infantry Base Depôt together with Cpl. J. Cox as a pay clerk. Orderly Room Sergt. W. Parker proceeded to the Third Echelon, D.A.G. at Rouen.

CHAPTER III.

3rd May to 22nd August, 1916.

Battalion proceeds from Le Havre to Belgium—In the trenches at Ploegsteert—The raid on the Fort—Preparation for the Somme.

THE march to the Rest Camp outside Le Havre was not very pleasant. The men were weary with the journey and want of sleep, and the road was uphill, uneven and muddy. The camp was no home from home, deep in mud and with poor accommodation—only tents, into each of which as many as possible were crammed—so that all were glad next day to march back to Le Havre.

On May 3rd at 3.30 a.m. the Battalion entrained at the station, and for the first time experienced the French troop train with the inscription on the vans "Hommes 40-Chevaux 8." To the troops they were better known as cattle trucks, and a more apt description could not have been given to them. Men with all their accoutrements were herded together, forty and even fifty in number, in these draughty and generally uncomfortable trucks. It was impossible for them to lie down and rest even on long journeys. In order to get a breath of air the sliding doors were kept open, and some used to sit on the step and dangle their legs outside. The slow pace at which the trains travelled allowed the men to get down many times during a journey to stretch their legs. It was the usual practice to get hot water from the engine to make tea, and this was sometimes made on the footboards over a "Tommy's Cooker." At a stop crowds of men with their mess tins would gather round the driver and beg him to supply them with hot water.

The troop train the 12th had for its first journey in France was the forerunner of many more up and down the front. The saying that you could get out and pick flowers while making a journey in them was amply justified after the Battalion had been a few months overseas. Hardly any of us had been on the Continent before, and it was instructive and amusing to watch the passing scenery with its lack of hedgerows and lines of pollard elm or poplar, to see the old French Territorial soldiers with rifles and tremendously long bayonets and antiquated uniforms, and to greet the swarms of children screaming in chorus for "Beeskeet" and "Boulibif." There was one incident that brought home the realisation of what war meant. A hospital train drew up in a siding near the Battalion, and some of the wounded peered out and enquired who we were. At the time some of us were singing "Are we downhearted?" One of the wounded men shouted "No, but you'll soon be if you're going to the Refinery at Souchez!" We discovered that these were some of the wounded of the 47th (London) Division.

After a journey of over 25 hours the Battalion detrained at Godewaersvelde at 5.0 a.m. on May 4th, and from here made a gruelling march on a baking day to Outtersteen, where the Battalion stayed five days.

Situated some little distance behind the front, Outtersteene was a quiet little hamlet, where the men were billeted in barns. It was a new experience to clamber up a ladder and make one's bed in the straw of a loft, but, compared with later billets, these were a paradise. During the short stay parades were carried out as usual. Our first kit inspection overseas took place here; the number of men who had deficiencies, which were supposed to be paid for, was remarkable; Company Commanders were busy disposing of minor charges such as "Whilst on active service being deficient on kit inspection of one mess tin lid."

On the 9th the Battalion paraded and marched to the training area immediately west of Steenwerck, and was billeted here in various farms until the 28th. All old soldiers will remember such Flemish farms, a collection of houses and barns with a "rectangular smell," as Bairnsfather calls it, in the middle.

Training was carried out daily. Bombing pits were established, and every man had to throw a live bomb from a trench near the bombing pits. The first casualty suffered by the Battalion was the result of this; one man having thrown his bomb sat down with his back to the parapet at the extreme end of the trench; his elbow was projecting just beyond the sandbags and a piece of a "Mills" caught it and smashed it badly. Many of the men were handling their first live bomb and in consequence they were not too keen in holding on to it for long once the pin was extracted. Capt. Hagen and Sergt. Bucknell were at hand to help the nervous ones to extract the pins, and they must have had many anxious moments as some of the bombs just skimmed the parapet. The troops were also called upon to fire the Lewis gun on a range near Battalion Headquarters, and lectures on its use and mechanism were given by Sergt. Lattimore and other N.C.O.s of the section. Gas drill with the P.H. helmet and gas goggles was also carried out.

Fine weather prevailed while we were at Steenwerck, and, although we enjoyed the weather, we certainly did not enjoy the route marches carried out on two occasions. The cobbled highways were not to our liking, and some of the other roads were like cart tracks.

Our first pay day on active service saw us in possession of five-franc notes for the first time. At the time five francs were equivalent to about three shillings and eightpence, which amount was usually spent very quickly in the Y.M.C.A. close to our billets, or in the estaminets. The entry "Five francs" in the private soldier's pay book was to become an institution thereafter. About once every fortnight we would be given this princely sum to cut a dash on. Sport was not neglected, and boxing tournaments were arranged. We can recall a fine exhibition by our Adjutant, Capt. McCulloch, who pitted himself against a good exponent of the noble art in Major Sadd of the 18th K.R.R.s. Joe Mills and Sid Fowler also put up a good fight.

The task of breaking the Battalion in to trench warfare was begun on the 10th of May, when the Commanding Officer, Company Commanders, and 50 other ranks proceeded for attachment to units of the 9th (Scottish) Division, which was then holding the line. Other parties of 50 followed every 48 hours to relieve each other.

On May 13th the Germans made a raid on a battalion of the Royal Scots of the 27th Infantry Brigade in Ploegsteert Wood. At the time a party from the 12th was attached to the K.O.S.B.s, who were on the right of the Royal Scots. The enemy put down a heavy barrage on the sector occupied by our party, and in places the parapets were battered in. Fortunately we had no casualties, and the "Jocks" afterwards paid

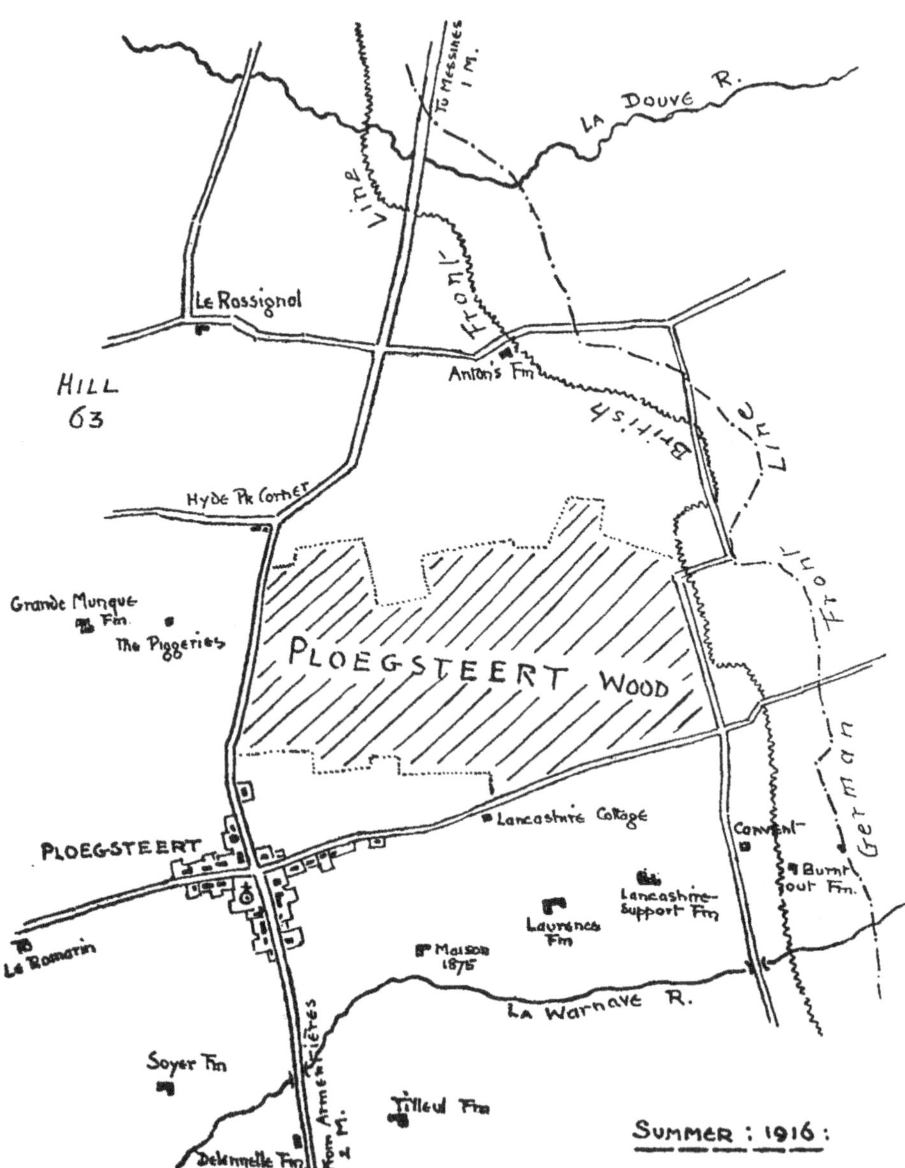

La Douve R.
To Messines 1 M.
British Front Line
German Front Line
Le Rossignol
Hill 63
Anton's Fm
Hyde Pk Corner
Grande Munque Fm.
The Piggeries
Ploegsteert Wood
Lancashire Cottage
Convent
Burnt out Fm.
Ploegsteert
Lancashire Support Fm
Laurence Fm
Le Romarin
Maison 1875
La Warnave R.
Soyer Fm
Tilleul Fm
From Armentières 2 M.
Delennelle Fm
Summer : 1916 :

a tribute to the steadiness of our men under very trying conditions. A party from the 15th Hants were not so fortunate, as they happened to be with the Royal Scots when they were attacked and suffered 10 casualties.

The time was now ripe for the 41st Division to take over from the 9th. Accordingly the Battalion moved into the Brigade Reserve area at Soyer Farm, in the early hours of the morning of May 28th. Next morning the Battalion paraded at 6.0 a.m. and proceeded to relieve the 7th Battalion Seaforth Highlanders in the Convent Position, Ploegsteert, always known in the British Army as "Plug Street."

The trenches were approached through the wood at "Plug Street," and at Lawrence Farm, where Battalion Headquarters were situated, a series of communication trenches led to the support line and Lancashire Farm. From this point a maze of trenches continued to the front line positions. Near Lancashire Support Farm there existed the remains of a Convent from which this particular sector had evidently acquired its name. The snipers and observers made full use of these ruins, and a pump still existed from which petrol tins were filled with water to be conveyed to the troops in front. Our front line was situated a short distance from the enemy's position, but on the extreme right there was an opening known as Gap E, with thick barbed wire separating us from the Boche, which had to be carefully watched during the day and actively patrolled at night. Built into the back of the parados were comfortable dugouts, accommodating four men each, with a blanket over the entrance to obscure the light of candles at night and to act as a gas stop. Behind the front line was a cook-house where, observing strict precautions against showing smoke during the day time, the cooks generally managed to prepare tea and bully beef and maconochie stew without the enemy being any the wiser.

Life consisted mainly in improving what appeared to be perfect trenches. Sandbags were filled each night from a recess at the back of the trench and carried to the different parts of the front line.

In common with all other troops along the front "Stand To" took place daily before daybreak and nightfall, this being, as we were told, the usual times when attacks by the enemy might be made and we had to be especially on the alert. (At this period of the war, and for some time after, daybreak attacks were persisted in by both sides until the value of surprise attacks in the middle of the day were fully realised.) The word "Stand Down" having been passed along, sentries would be posted for the day or night as required, and the rest would either try to snatch a few hours sleep in their dugouts or proceed on working parties or fatigues.

Which of the survivors of A Company, who with D occupied the front line for the first time at "Plug Street," will forget our first spell on the firestep? Sentries on the posts were instructed to fire an occasional shot to let the enemy know we were on the alert. Whether it was nervousness or the novelty of being able to put one's head and shoulders over the parapet and have a shot in the direction of "Fritz," it is hard to say; at all events men continued to fire incessantly throughout the night. When the German machine-guns started playing a tattoo on our parapet, the sentries would "duck their nappers" and then return to the alert and let off a round or two. To many it was great fun to stand boldly up and watch the Boche Verey lights drift towards our lines. Perhaps this first night's display was responsible for the board with the inscription "Welcome the 41st Division" exhibited by the enemy a day or two later. His Intelligence staff had had news of our movements, much as we acquired information of most of the German units facing our front.

Lieut H. T. Pike tells the following yarn of these early days:—

"When the Battalion proceeded overseas, it included quite a large number of very young soldiers whose patriotism had led them to overstate their age and who had by this means got themselves accepted for service. These boys, for they were little more, had plenty of courage, but, like everybody else, no experience of warfare and they were not aided by the more controlled nerves of older men. In point of fact, at a later date many of them were weeded out of the Battalion, I believe, and sent back for home service until they reached the required age.

"Some time during either the first or the second night during which the Battalion was in the trenches I was the officer on duty with A Company which was occupying the front line, when I received a message to the effect that the Germans were in the trench on the left. I proceeded to investigate and found one of our men with a bayonet wound in the leg and one of the boys referred to above in a very excited condition near by. What had happened was this. The boy in question had been on sentry duty on the fire step, and, it being his first turn at this duty, he had worked himself up into a great state of nervous tension. He thought he had seen someone moving inside our own wire (probably one of our patrols), and shortly afterwards, hearing a noise in the trench immediately behind him, had turned round, seen someone moving and promptly stuck his bayonet in. The unfortunate casualty was merely one of his comrades who was crawling from a dugout in order to go and relieve himself."

The morning after our first night on trench duty a German shouted over to our post in Gap E some scathing remarks about British swine, and for his trouble was rewarded with a rifle grenade, sent with the good wishes of the men on the post.

Owing to its close proximity to the enemy and the fact that we were able to converse with him there, Gap E afforded much amusement to the troops. Hardly a morning passed without an English-speaking "Fritz" shouting something to the sentries on the post. Here we heard about the *débacle* to the "Russian Steam Roller" and also of the death of Lord Kitchener before confirmation was received from the newspapers. This may have been a method employed by the German Intelligence staff to try to undermine our morale. If it was so, then it was a ghastly failure. Out usual manner of breaking off the conversation and thanking the enemy for the information was to send him a rifle grenade preceded by the remark, "Here's your breakfast coming over, Fritz."

Shelling by the Boche was mostly confined to Battalion Headquarters, where C Company were also in reserve. It was during one of these strafes that the first casualty caused by the enemy to a member of the Battalion occurred on the 31st of May. Work was in consequence started on trying to render Headquarters shell-proof. C Company aided by B who were in support, began this humanitarian task. Three men were wounded on the 1st of June and another on the 3rd; thus our first tour of duty had cost us five casualties. On the 4th the Battalion handed over the trenches to the care of the 10th (Battersea) Battalion, "The Queen's" Royal West Surrey Regiment.

Being now in reserve, the Battalion occupied billets as follows:—

A Company at Delennelle Farm, B Company at Roodee Farm, C Company at Maison 1875, and D Company, with Battalion Headquarters, at Soyer Farm. Although most of these billets were situated only a short distance from the line (Maison '75, as we called it, being less than a mile from Lawrence Farm), civilians were still in occupation and cultivated their fields despite the fact that the Germans used to shell the area. Enemy balloons were also able to observe, and roads were camouflaged to prevent too much being seen of our movements. Parades at Delennelle were sometimes interrupted by shelling, probably the result of being spotted by balloons. At Maison '75 very little movement was allowed, and built into the side of a bank was a dugout which accommodated a whole platoon.

The general Army method of holding the line of trenches was that a certain sector was assigned to two Brigades, one in the trenches for about six days at a time, and the other in so-called "Rest." This description was "rote sarkastick," for usually the men were as hard worked in Rest billets as when in the line, sometimes harder. Daily and often nightly they had to march up to the trenches to dig new communication trenches under R.E. supervision, construct bombproof shelters, or carry up heavy material, sometimes for miles. As every communication trench serpentined to prevent being enfiladed by the enemy's fire, to cover a mile often meant trudging nearly two.

Baths were situated in a brewery at Pont de Nieppe, where the men used to wash in huge vats of steaming water. Screened off from the vats by a canvas awning was a recess where Flemish girls washed the underwear of the troops, and all the time they kept up a running fire of comment in French and broken English. They also used to sing some of the songs which the men of the 12th as well as the British Army as a whole got to know. Amongst them were "Après la guerre finie," and "Mademoiselle from Armentières." Along the road from "Plug Street" to Pont de Nieppe were many cafés and estaminets, where it was a change to hear pianolas grinding out quick dance tunes instead of the roar of the guns. After a week or so in the trenches men became verminous, and after a visit to Pont de Nieppe there was a certain amount of freedom from the pests which all fighting troops, without exception, had to endure. Khaki was baked in ovens at the brewery, and the clean change of underclothing made one feel comfortable again—if only for a short while.

Towards the end of May the following officers were posted to and joined the Battalion:—2nd Lieuts. W. H. C. Binns, V. L. Clift, D. Walker, J. F. Walton, J. A. Rogers, A. Straker, N. G. W. Hancock, A. G. Howitt and W. M. Edwards.

Early in the morning of June 11th the Battalion relieved the 10th "Queens" in the Convent neighbourhood. During this tour of duty the enemy concentrated on shelling our guns in the rear rather than the trenches. Fulham, Hackney, Hampstead and Wimbledon had supplied the 41st Division with most of its brigades of artillery, and, as the batteries were now registering on their targets, no doubt they were causing some annoyance to the people on the other side of the line, and making them retaliate. In consequence much of our time was devoted to making "Plug Street" into a model set of trenches. Certainly along the whole front there could never have been a neater or cleaner system of earthworks. In the trenches sandbags were hung up at different points for the troops to deposit their rubbish in; even match ends had to be picked up and placed in the proper receptacle. "Peace-time" trenches was the Army sobriquet for such.

On the 14th our men in the front line were treated to their first bombardment by the enemy with trench mortars. They were of the variety known as minnenwerfers, or "Minnies" in Tommy's vocabulary. A "Minnie" could be described as a container for old iron with the addition of some explosive, and was fired with an almost perpendicular trajectory from an emplacement in the enemy trench. It was easily seen coming through the air, and when it exploded, it made a terrific noise and usually a tremendous hole in the ground where it burst. Speaking of his early days with the 1st Battalion at Kemmel in 1915, Pte. Joe Jenkins has described how a man of his company had his nose plastered with gramophone needles when "Minnies" were first used on them. However, as time went on precautions were taken to try to eliminate the danger from them, for, so long as men got due warning of where these horrors were going to land, there was always a sporting chance of casualties being averted. Accordingly sentries were instructed to keep a sharp look out and shout the direction of the missile to their comrades in the trench. At "Plug Street" a certain Lewis gunner renowned for his cheek and wit was instructed by a sergeant to call out "Minnie right" and "Minnie left" as the case might be, during one of these mortar bombardments. Quite religiously he carried out his instructions until a "Minnie" came in the direction of his post, when, without waiting to shout, he scampered to safety round one of the bays. It happened that the N.C.O. who had given him instructions came in the direction of the post just as the "Minnie" burst near it, with the result that, although not hurt, he got rather a bad shock. In an agitated condition he went in search of the sentry, who, at first he thought, might have been blown to atoms. Locating him in a dugout, he called for an explanation as to why he had not shouted out a warning. "Well," said the sentry, "you told me to shout 'Minnie right' and 'Minnie left,' but, as this one was neither, I just popped off before I lost my head!"

At about midnight on June 16th the gas alarm sounded along the 41st Divisional front. Strombos horns and empty shell-cases used for this purpose were sounded in the Battalion lines with the result that very soon everyone was standing to and adjusting P.H. helmets. Apart from a sergeant in A Company who put his helmet on the reverse way with the result that the dressing burnt his face a bit, no casualities resulted to the men of the 12th in the line, although it appears that other units in the Division were not let off so lightly. It was afterwards discovered that the gas attack had been initiated by the Boche further north of our positions and that before the attack two of his balloons had been released to test the direction of the wind, with the result that due warning was given to us to be on the alert. However, the gas reached as far back as the Brigade H.Q. and our Transport lines at Romarin, where some of the horses were affected.

The tour of duty ended on the 17th, when the 10th "Queen's" again took over. With the exception of the day when the gas attack took place the weather had been bad throughout. The casualties suffered were nine other ranks wounded. It was during this tour that, on the 15th of June, Summer Time was adopted for the first time and watches were accordingly put forward one hour. On relief the Battalion marched to billets at Soyer, Delennelle and Tilleul Farms and Maison '75.

During a bombardment by our artillery on a position in the enemy line known as the "Fort" it was discovered that gas cylinders were installed in their front line, and orders were issued that a raid should be carried out on this strong point by a party from the Battalion. The party selected included two officers, Capt. F. D. Jessop and Lieut. C. C. Fox, and Sergts. J. Donnelly and R. J. Calver. They proceeded on June 16th to Ste. Marie Capelle, near Cassel, where they were trained under Major Hall of the Dorset Regt., and here they remained until the time came for them to go over the top.

The first fatal casualties occurred on the 19th, presumably on a working party, when Cpl. A. Garrard and Pte. F. R. Russell of C Company were killed. Both of them were buried in Rifle Brigade Cemetery, not far from Soyer Farm. A draft of 62 N.C.O.s and men from the 3rd Battalion arrived on the 20th.

We have already mentioned what so called "rest" meant to us with regard to working parties, but there was another aspect which sorely troubled us at times, namely enemy shelling of the back areas with big guns. Being in reserve often was more trying than being in the front line. This, at any rate, was our experience at "Plug Street." The first realisation of this came on the 23rd when Soyer Farm was shelled between 8.0 and 9.0 p.m. and a H.E. shell exploded in the dining room of the H.Q. Officers' Mess, and was followed by others which burst close by. As a result Lieut. E. C. Lambert, R.A.M.C.

was severely wounded and Major L. Tenbosch suffered from shell shock, while R.S.M. W. Nash and a private were wounded at the same time. Lieut. Lambert, who was hit while dressing the wounds of a comrade, died of his wounds on the 30th of June, and Major Tenbosch and the R.S.M. were evacuated to England. The loss of the Doctor was a sad one. Cpl. L. C. Southall, his orderly, writes of Lieut. Lambert:—

"The doctor was one of the nicest men I have ever met. I still remember before our departure for France being introduced to his wife who had come down to Aldershot for a last visit and being asked by her to look after the doctor in France. Alas! no human agency could have protected him from the shell that wounded him so severely at Ploegsteert that he subsequently died from his injuries. He had 35 wounds of various sizes, and, although none was actually fatal, the shock must have made him succumb, and he died at the base hospital. I missed him terribly, as he proved a great friend to me during the early days of my life with the 12th."

The place of Dr. Lambert was taken by Lieut. L. W. Oliver, R.A.M.C.

R.S.M. Nash had a very short life with the Battalion, as he only joined us on the eve of our departure to France. The vacancy thus created was filled by C.S.M. J. Wilkinson of A Company; C.Q.M.S. B. P. Horswell being promoted C.S.M. of A in the place of Wilkinson.

Relieving the 10th "Queen's" in the trenches on the 24th, the Battalion occupied its old sector until the same unit took over again on July 1st. The time was spent in repair and upkeep of the trenches together with making final preparations for the proposed raid on the Boche lines.

The work of repairing trenches often brought to light evidence of the earlier fighting in the sector, for bodies of men who had been killed were found buried in the parapets. Owing to the heavy fighting which took place here in October, 1914, there was apparently little opportunity of collecting the dead and placing them in a spot where they were likely to be identified later, although at Lancashire Support Farm there were the graves of two Captains (Auchinleck and Roe) and a private of the Royal Inniskilling Fusiliers. Sir Frank Fox states in his history of the Inniskillings that these two officers were killed whilst rallying their men when the enemy stormed the village of Le Gheer on the 20th of October, 1914. At all events it conveyed to us then the common sacrifice which was being made to achieve victory.

Wiring parties were sent out during the night to repair and strengthen the barbed wire. During this tour of duty a large party under 2nd Lieut. J. A. Rogers, who had recently joined, was sent out together with a covering patrol consisting of Sergt. V. B. Condon, L/Cpl. H. Reffel and Pte. L. M. Duggan. At intervals in the front line were gaps in the parapet through which men could crawl to save them clambering over the top. In front of the parapet in No Man's Land were a lot of bully beef tins which had evidently been deposited there before the troops were instructed to place their refuse in the receptacles hung up in the trenches for that purpose. In consequence anyone moving about in this area would be bound to cause a noise which might be heard by the enemy, especially if their patrols were on the prowl. Condon's patrol made its way across to the Boche lines and for a time rested in a little sap, a few yards from their wire. Here they listened to some vile language from the men of the wiring party behind them. In driving the stakes in men would accidentally hit their comrades on the fingers with their mallets and bring forth heaps of abuse. To the patrol this was funny at first, but later, when in the darkness they observed an enemy patrol, the situation became more serious. Revolver in hand, Condon instructed the other two to keep their Mills bombs handy in case they were needed. The German patrol passed by, and still the noise from the working party behind continued. Condon then endeavoured to get back to give warning, but before he had got very far the German machine-guns started sweeping No Man's Land. The patrol lay low and listened to a scamper behind them. Soon all was quiet again: the wiring party had evidently gone back to the trench without warning the patrol. After a while Sergt. Condon decided to return also, but in the darkness he and his men missed their direction and found themselves inside the German wire close to their parapet. Just then a form was perceived creeping behind. Condon challenged. "Halt! who are you?" "A Battalion!" (the pass word at this time) replied the familiar voice of Capt. F. D. Jessop. With instructions to follow him quickly the patrol wormed its way through the wire to our lines. But for the timely intervention of Capt. Jessop and his concern for the men under him, the patrol would certainly have landed in the enemy line. A few days later his worth as a leader was to be proved.

The First Battle of the Somme opened on July 1st, 1916. Mainly in order to divert the enemy's attention from this main sector of the front, raids were carried out in other parts. To the 41st Division was given the task of raiding at Ploegsteert, and to the 12th in particular was assigned the position known as the "Fort" opposite the Battalion front.

A few days previous to the raid our artillery had bombarded the position, and the Germans, apparently fearing some big operation, had been keeping strict watch with their observation balloons over the sector. The day before the raid our men in the line were treated to a sight which made them raise a cheer. Several German balloons were up at the time, when out of the blue came a number of British planes, which, taking one balloon apiece, proceeded to destroy them with the aid of incendiary bullets. It was a magnificent and encouraging sight to see these "Sausages" go down in flames and to watch the vain efforts of the enemy anti-aircraft guns to bring our planes down. It was this sort of thing which gave us a moral ascendancy over our enemies when later we came to grips with them on the Somme.

For over a week working parties had been busily engaged installing 1,000 gas cylinders in emplacements in the parapets along the Divisional front, and, although the men groused and grumbled about carrying these loathsome burdens around the traverses, which gave them aching shoulders and tried their patience to the utmost, there was a certain amount of satisfaction in the thought that "Jerry" was going to get a good dose of his own medicine.

Early in the morning of the 30th of June, the artillery started the final bombardment of the selected points in the enemy trenches in preparation for the raid which was to take place in the evening. It concentrated on the wire in front of the "Fort" to ensure that the raiders would not have much difficulty in reaching the objective. The Boche retaliated fiercely, smashing our parapets in parts of the front line and causing many casualties. At one time the enemy fire was so accurate that the men had to crouch very low in the trench to avoid bullets from the man-killing shrapnel which burst overhead.

During the bombardment one man stood out in A Company—Lce.-Cpl. N. Beard, who had recently joined us from the 3rd Battalion. While everyone was crouching down, Beard, cool as a cucumber, started to shave himself, using a small periscope as a mirror. Shells burst overhead and on both sides of the trench, but still Beard continued until his task was accomplished. The coolness of this man amazed both officers and men alike, and it completely took their minds off what was happening around. To have to remain in a trench which was well registered by the enemy without any adequate protection from shell fire was no easy task. In the early days of 1915 the Germans began to build concrete shelters and emplacements for their troops, and this work continued up to the time of the battles of Ypres in 1917. These shelters were mainly built as a protection from our artillery and for the use of supporting and reserve troops. Often under intense fire the front lines were evacuated and protection sought farther back in these shell-proof structures. When we afterwards came across these wonderful dugouts and emplacements, it set us thinking why the British Higher Command had not adopted this means of minimising losses. The answer could only be that our General Staff were afraid that by employing these means of safety the troops would lose the offensive spirit; a feasible explanation, as, when one got used to living in the bowels of the earth, it was not an easy task to get oneself in the frame of mind to come to the top. Hence perhaps the expression "a Dugout" which was construed by Tommy as expressing one who was non-militant. When the ascendancy of our artillery made itself felt on the Western Front, German prisoners were fond of telling us that we did not know what a bombardment was. It shows how little they knew of the conditions under which the British Tommy lived. Whereas the Germans were usually out of sight when the British guns were playing on their lines, the Tommies had to remain in their trenches during a bombardment with no other cover than the parapet, or as Pte. Jenkins recalls in 1915 at Kemmel, just a privet hedge! It seems the fashion nowadays for some writers to praise the Germans and other combatants to the detriment of the British. Facts prove that there was not a better fighting man in the world than the Regular British soldier. Of the men of the New Armies it may be said that, if they were not so skilled in the use of arms and the art of warfare as their comrades in the Regular Army, or as well trained as the German conscript, they certainly were not lacking in courage, bravery and stamina. They did not suffer from an inferiority complex, nor did they fear the man on the other side of the line. The men who fought the Germans at Loos, who assaulted and carried the impregnable fortifications on the Somme, who advanced through the bogs to Passchendaele under conditions never before endured in warfare, who deprived the enemy of his ultimate objectives in March and April, 1918, and finally drove him across the Scheldt, were in the main peaceful citizens who detested war and who had never anticipated being called upon to serve their country as soldiers. They preferred to be known as "camouflaged" civilians and only donned khaki to save England and Europe from a military despotism which ultimately would have destroyed the freedom they cherished.

Throughout the day of the 30th our guns continued to pound the German lines in the region of the "Fort," while retaliation followed fast and furious. Everyone in the front line was anxious for the "Show" to start. The cry for stretcher-bearers seemed to grate on the nerves, and often some felt like going over the top to avenge the death or wounds of a comrade who had been taken away.

Dusk came at last and with it the order to stand to. The performance was about to commence. At 10.0 p.m. gas was emitted from the cylinders along the front after the artillery had intensely bombarded the enemy lines for three quarters of an hour. Three parties from the Brigade, from the 15th Hants, 11th R.W. Kents and the 12th Battalion now arrived on the scene of action.

At 10.28 p.m. the party from the 12th, consisting of Capt. Jessop, Lieut. Fox and 34 N.C.O.s and men, with blackened faces and armed with knob-kerries and bombs, left the front line trench and proceeded in the direction of the "Fort." They were met by a heavy machine-gun and rifle fire which caused two men to be wounded before they had left the parapet, but under the skilful and able leadership of Capt. Jessop they reached their objective. The "Fort" was found to consist of a parapet with firestep but no parados, together with three dugouts, two of them being concrete ones. A loophole plate was found in the parapet. The position had been blown in by our artillery and the occupants had evacuated it. To make sure, the dugouts were well bombed and then searched together with others in a trench further on, but without a prisoner being secured. After 10 minutes' stay the party returned leaving behind a board with a Black Hand painted on it. At 10.57 p.m. Brigade Headquarters were notified that the party had returned after carrying out the task allotted to them. Neither the West Kents nor the Hants reached the German trenches owing to the fact that the Hun had hastily repaired the wire cut by our shell-fire, and they could not get through anywhere.

"We were very busy at the Regimental Aid Post," writes Cpl. Southall, "during and following the raid, as Fritz retaliated pretty strongly, and we were dressing casualties till about 6.0 o'clock the following morning. It was my first real experience of what my duties were likely to be in France, and, while I was in a much more comfortable place than the lads who were having to put up with Fritz's retaliation, I must confess that this first trial was not a pleasant one."

This operation came to be known throughout the Battalion and also the Division as the raid of the "Black Hand Gang." Some of the raiders were said to be well known to the police in Bermondsey before joining up; at any rate these men proved to be some of the toughest fighters the Battalion ever had. One man in particular was singled out by General Towsey in a special Brigade Order, which ran as follows:—

"No. 12367 Private D. O'Sullivan, 12th East Surrey Regiment, was 46 years of age, and two of his sons are fighting. He refused all jobs that would keep him out of the trenches and volunteered for the raid. While getting through the parapet he was wounded, but refused assistance, saying, 'Go on, lads, carry on without me.' When the party returned he was dying. Truly we mourn the loss of a gallant comrade."

"Tuppenny," as he was known to us all, was a quaint character, full of fun. While we were in training he used to get up to all sorts of antics, but he was liked by all.

For conspicuous dash and gallantry and excellent leading, to which Colonel Lee attributed the light casualties (four) of the raiding party, Capt. F. D. Jessop was the first officer of the Battalion to be given the Military Cross. Sergt. J. Donnelly, an immigrant from Erin, was awarded the Distinguished Conduct Medal, and Sergt. R. J. Calver and Privates W. C. Camp and H. V. Rice (born in Cape Colony, South Africa) the Military Medal for services rendered in the raid. Of the recipients only Sergt. Calver and Pte. Camp survived the war. Major-General Lawford afterwards expressed his entire satisfaction with the manner in which the raid was carried out.

Although the raiding party only suffered four casualties, the remainder of the Battalion suffered badly throughout the day, the total casualties being 14 other ranks killed and 25 wounded. The trenches of A and D Companies were badly damaged and breached in parts. Welcome relief by the 10th "Queen's" came at 5.0 a.m. on the following morning, when the Battalion marched back to billets round about Soyer Farm. Before this was completed, the sign of the black hand left in the German trenches was plainly visible just above the parapet at the south end of the "Fort." Some time later the enemy shouted across to us and enquired when we were coming back to fetch our board. On another raid made before the Battle of Messines a similar board was left behind by our gang, so the Germans had cause to remember the 12th East Surreys.

In the afternoon following relief, burial parties in charge of the Brigade chaplains proceeded to Rifle Brigade Cemetery near by to give a decent burial to those killed during the operations. Foremost among the chaplains was that genial and popular R.C. Padre, Father Sheridan. A great many of the original members of the Battalion were of Irish extraction, and in consequence Father Sheridan's flock was a large one. There were few R.C.s in the Brigade that this ardent priest did not get to know personally; as soon as a new draft arrived he would be round to Orderly Room to get the names of those for whose spiritual welfare he was responsible, and, what was more, he clung to them until the end. In or out of the trenches he administered the sacraments and careless or lax Catholics derived great solace from the care and attention he exercised over them. Another very popular cleric was the Non-conformist, Padre Dobson. He was indefatigable in making constant excursions up the line and was a very familiar figure in the Brigade, unobtrusive, but ever helpful. We shall hear of him later in our story. The C. of E. chaplains were the Revs. Hilditch and Mayne.

The casualties suffered by the Battalion during June were as follows:—18 other ranks killed and 3 officers (one mortally) and 38 other ranks wounded. 2nd Lieut. J. F. Walton was the other officer wounded at this time.

The Battalion remained in rest from the 1st to the 5th of July finding working parties as usual. Considerable shelling of the back areas by the enemy took place during this period; Soyer Farm being again pasted with 5.9in. and 8.2in. high explosive shells.

On July 6th a move was made into billets at Grande Munque Farm, west of Ploegsteert, Battalion H.Q. and two companies being accommodated in the farm and the remainder in the Wood itself about 600 yards north-east of the farm. Here we remained until 10.0 p.m. on the 8th, when we proceeded to relieve the 11th R.W. Kents in the line north of Ploegsteert Wood, from 200 yards north of Anton's Farm to the little river Douve. B and C Companies occupied the front line, A Company a subsidiary line called "The Only Way," and D Company were with Battalion H.Q., 600 yards south of Le Rossignol. These positions were occupied until the 15th of July, during which time the weather remained fine and the enemy fairly quiet. The time was spent in supplying carrying parties and repairing or improving the trenches.

Carrying parties embraced the awkward task already referred to of manœuvring gas cylinders round the bays in preparation for a further gas attack on the enemy, in addition to bringing up bags of sand and rubble from the R.E. Dump at "Hyde Park Corner." The former task was perhaps the most detested one, as progress was very slow and the burdens very heavy. Rolls of barbed wire carried on a pole between two men and the carrying of "Toffee Apples" for the heavy trench-mortar batteries, were always a source of annoyance to the infantry, but even these jobs were sinecures compared with cylinder carrying. The ideal combination for wire and cylinder carrying was of course two men of similar height, but invariably it turned out that a tall and short man would be paired together. In consequence there was ample excuse for the "flowery" language which used to flow while these operations were in progress. The material carried from Hyde Park Corner was for the purpose of making some dugouts on the Messines road in preparation for a future offensive. Night after night men trudged along the road which was occasionally machine-gunned by the Boche. Often they had to drop their burdens and fall down flat to save themselves from being hit by bullets. Those not carrying had to take turns at excavating and hauling tons of Belgian mud by means of a pulley to the surface; not a light task in view of the fact that water was struck after you had dug down only a few feet.

A Company was employed on restoring what appeared to be a disused trench, which was in full view of the enemy on the ridge. Nothing startling happened until the work was well in hand, when "Jerry" took it into his head to disturb the tranquillity of things. Most of the men at the time were having an afternoon siesta little thinking of war, when suddenly "whizz-bangs" and 5.9's came pouring into the trench. It seemed as though the Hun artillery was having some target practice, as the shelling started at one end of the trench and finished up at the other. During the bombardment the company suffered some casualties, among them being Sergt R. J. Calver. The bombardment had its humorous side as well. Most of the men remained outside their dugouts while the "strafe" was in progress as a precaution against being buried in them, for in fact one of two were blown in. There were two N.C.O.s who fled down the trench after a shell had dropped near them. Seeing them in flight, some of the Lewis-gun team passed facetious remarks about them as they rounded their bay. One shout, "Next stop Rotherhithe!" sent us all into fits of laughter. Near the end of the bombardment a lance-corporal in charge of a post was heard to exclaim as a "whizz bang" landed in the trench where he was standing, "I've got it!" When we got to him, we found him holding the seat of his trousers and without further ado put him on a truck on the trench tramway close by, and pushed it down to the Battalion Aid Post. Imagine his surprise and that of those who had taken him down to find that he was not wounded at all; the splinters from the shell had simply torn away a portion of the seat of his trousers. Returning to the trench later on he was greeted with a great deal of chaff, although admittedly he had had a very narrow escape.

We have already mentioned how the Messines road was swept by enemy machine-gun fire. A calamity befell the Battalion at 12.30 a.m. on the 14th of July, when, on making his rounds near the Messines road, Colonel Lee was wounded in the foot. He was picked up by the stretcher-bearers and sent down the line to the 2nd Casualty Clearing Station, Bailleul, and evacuated to England on the 16th. The wounding of the Commanding Officer at such an early stage of the Battalion's career overseas was rather unfortunate, as there was no question that Colonel Lee was a most efficient and gallant officer, whose experience and sterling service with his own regiment, the Cameronians, at the front in the early days of the war, had well merited the command he had been given. In the place of Colonel Lee the Second-in-Command, Major H. J. Walmisley-Dresser of the Royal Warwickshire Regt., was appointed to command with the rank of acting Lieut.-Colonel. The duties of Second-in-Command then devolved upon Capt. H. de Courcy Blakeney, while A Company was taken over by Capt. F. D. Jessop.

During the night of the 15th/16th of July the 11th R.W. Kents took over, and the Battalion marched back to Grande Munque Farm and the billets in the wood.

Most of those who were serving with the 12th at this time will recall the Piggeries situated near our billets. A canteen had been installed here, and there was many a joyful re-union between some of our men and their friends in the 9th Battalion who were holding a part of the front at Wulverghem. It was strange that we should come in contact with the 9th Battalion before any other battalion of the Regiment on active service, for when hostilities had ceased the remnants of the 12th were merged into the 9th as part of the Army of Occupation in the Rhineland.

We remained in the neighbourhood of Grande Munque Farm until the 27th, and working parties were carried out usually at night while training took place in the day time. Another move took place on the 27th, when the 10th Battalion Royal Inniskilling Fusiliers, after its glorious but unavailing assault on Thiepval Ridge on the 1st of July, took over our billets and we marched to our original billets at Soyer, Tilleul and Delenelle

Farms and Maison '75, where we remained until the 2nd of August, finding working parties and enjoying very fine weather.

Our casualties for July were 1 man killed and 2 officers (Colonel Lee and 2nd Lieut. B. F. Dodd) and 36 other ranks wounded. 2nd Lieut. W. J. Palk arrived and joined A Company.

Trenches were again taken over at Ploegsteert on August 3rd, and on the 4th patrols under 2nd Lieuts. D. McCallum and D. Walker were sent out to inspect the wire in front of our lines; it was reported to be in good condition. During the nights of the 6th and 7th further officers' patrols went out from Burnt Out Farm to the enemy's saphead. Both the sap and the "Fort" were found to be manned, and the heads of about 10 Germans were reported to have been seen.

At 6.45 p.m. on the 8th, A Company opened fire on the Boche lines about 200 yards to the right of the "Fort," with 120 rifle grenades, which drew retaliation on our front. Our Stokes Mortars then brought their guns into action, causing the Hun further annoyance. By this time the 122nd Trench Mortar Battery was fairly well established at different parts of the Brigade front. One of our officers, 2nd Lieut. S. H. Morgan, had joined it on the 6th of August together with some men from the Battalion. While Stokes-guns were welcomed at times as offsetting the enemy's account of "Minnies," there were times, especially when things were quiet, when they were not so popular. The batteries had a nasty habit of "pooping off" behind a certain portion of the front line trench and then clearing away before the enemy had time to range on them. The result was that the troops in the part of the trench whence the guns were fired often got the retaliation which the Stokes Mortars had asked for. As the guns were portable, positions could be taken up and evacuated without much trouble.

The Stokes Mortars having done their work, the enemy again retaliated, but with our field artillery joining in the shoot, the enemy were silenced about 8.45 p.m. To see duckboards, planks, stakes, etc., being blown about 20 feet high in the air in the enemy lines was an unforgettable sight. Whether they suffered any casualties was of course unknown. At all events we did not have a single one during the operations.

This was to be the swan song of the 12th Battalion in the trenches at "Plug Street," as on the 9th of August the 10th "Queen's" took over and we marched out to rest billets.

From the 10th to the 14th the Battalion remained in reserve, finding working parties from those who were not in training as specialists. Signallers, Lewis-gunners and Snipers were among those who managed to dodge working parties. A new section was now formed for Battalion Runners. Men from each company were attached to the Snipers section, and Sergt. E. Durrell, a brilliant linguist, and a man of no mean distinctions in civilian life, was given the task of training them for the duties they would be called upon to perform at no distant date. Under the direction of Durrell these men were taught to read the map and compass, to tell their direction by the aid of the sun and stars and to make a reconnaissance of the countryside. Daily little parties were seen wandering in the direction of Le Romarin under the tender care of their very intelligent and interesting mentor.

The time had now arrived for the 41st Division to take its part in the great campaign which had been in progress on the Somme since the 1st of July. Units were accordingly withdrawn from the line and went into training in the back areas.

On August 15th the Battalion started its journey for the training area in preparation for its move to the Somme. A day was spent in La Crèche, another in the Meteren area, while on the 17th a further move was made to the neighbourhood of Flêtre, where billets were taken over in the small hamlet of Thieushouck. Here the Battalion stayed until the 23rd of August carrying out route marches, bayonet fighting, night operations, etc. The strength of the Battalion at this date was 40 officers and 934 other ranks.

The few days training and rest in this area was thoroughly enjoyed by all ranks, especially as Bailleul was not far away. Advantage was taken to spend a few pleasant hours in this rather lively town which was within range of the enemy guns. The inhabitants could tell some interesting stories of how in the early days of the war the Uhlans had advanced through the place only to be thrown back by the British cavalry. In 1918 the Germans came again and occupied Bailleul after it had been reduced to a shambles. As may be imagined, very few of us could speak French, and nobody a word of Flemish. A kind of "Lingua Franca" was evolved between the troops and the native population, a most amusing language too. Some words passed for a time into the English tongue, but by now have died out again. Everyone twenty years ago was familiar with "Napoo." It originated when our troops were constantly asking for commodities of which a supply had run out, receiving the reply—"Il n'y en a plus"—"There is no more." The word then developed into various shades of meaning, e.g., "This mess-tin's napoo" (worn-out, useless); " . . . . . is a regular napoo" (worthless); "The trench was napoo after that strafe" (destroyed after bombardment); "Poor Jones is napoo" (dead).

War slang was indeed a most interesting study. The present writer made a glossary of over 250 words in common use at the time, almost everyone of which to-day is as dead as Aramaic.

LIEUT.-GENERAL SIR SIDNEY LAWFORD, K.C.B., K.C.M.G.
(G.O.C. 41st Division)

BRIG.-GENERAL F. W. TOWSEY, C.M.G., C.B.E., D.S.O., J.P.
(G.O.C. 122nd Brigade)

GROUP OF OFFICERS TAKEN AT ALDERSHOT, MARCH 1916.

CHAPTER IV.

23rd August to 18th October, 1916.

Moves to the Somme—In action at Flers and near Le Sars.

ON the 23rd of August the Battalion, entraining at Bailleul Station, started about 11.30 p.m. on an all-night journey which ended at Longpré, between Abbeville and Amiens, at 10.0 a.m. on the following morning. The weather was hot, and the suffocating atmosphere of the cattle trucks made us yearn for the end.

After detraining, a halt of an hour and a half was made before proceeding by route march to the billets which had been allotted to the Battalion at Mouflers. The march, although not a very long one, was nevertheless most trying to men who had been cooped up in the trucks all night. Small wonder then that the Medical Officer and his staff were called upon to render first aid to those who simply could not finish the last stage of the journey, which was for some considerable distance uphill. The Adjutant, Capt. McCulloch, although he must have been dead-beat himself, urged those on who were inclined to fall out. Billets having been reached, everyone was glad to shed equipment and take a few hours well earned rest in the barns where they were accommodated.

During a spell of very fine weather the Battalion remained at Mouflers, carrying out training in attack and consolidation, wood fighting and the like. Ground had been chosen as nearly as possible similar to that over which the Division would soon have to operate.

On August 28th A Company under Capt. Jessop, with two detachments from the Machine-gun Section under Capt. Tunwell, proceeded to the Fourth Army Trench Warfare School at Flixecourt for demonstration purposes. In this party were 8 officers and 156 other ranks, and rumour had it that they were to be permanently attached to the school. Guards were supplied and complimented by the Commandant for their smartness and turnout. A demonstration on the use of liquid fire was given here by one of the instructors, who used a "Flammenwerfer" captured from the Boche in the Hooge sector where this form of warfare was used for the first time in 1915. A section of A Company had to man a trench while the instructor turned on the flame. Orders were given for the men to lie down in the trench while the huge conflagration swept across it, and to come to the top ready to receive the infantry attack when it was extinguished. It was an awful sensation to lie down in the trench while this ghastly weapon was being operated, and it made us shudder at the fate of the British Tommies who were caught unprepared when the contrivance was first used. Whilst all this was going on, officers were watching the performance as they did on other occasions when we were used to illustrate open warfare.

No better description of the school could be given than that supplied by Siegfried Sassoon in his excellent book, "Memoirs of an Infantry Officer."

"The Fourth Army School was at Fixecourt, a clean little town exactly half-way between Amiens and Abbeville. Between Flixecourt and the war (which for my locally experienced mind meant the Fricourt trenches) there were more than thirty English miles. Mentally, the distance became immeasurable during my first days at the School. Parades and lectures were all in the day's work, but they failed to convince me of their affinity with our long days and nights in the Front Line. For instance, although I was closely acquainted with the mine-craters in the Fricourt sector, I would have welcomed a few practical hints on how to patrol these God-forsaken cavities. But the Army School instructors were all in favour of Open Warfare, which was sure to come, they said. They had learned all about it in peace time; it was essential we should be taught to 'think in terms of mobility.' So we solved tactical schemes in which the enemy was reported to have occupied some village several miles away, and with pencil and paper made arrangements for unflurried defence or blank-cartridged skirmishing in a land of field-day make-believe.

"Sometimes a renowned big-game hunter gave us demonstrations of the art of sniping. He was genial and enthusiastic; but I was no good at rifle-shooting, and as far as I was concerned he would have been more profitably employed in reducing the numerical strength of the enemy. He was an expert on loop-holes and telescopic sights; but telescopic sights were a luxury seldom enjoyed by an infantry battalion in the trenches.

"The Commandant of the School was a tremendous worker and everyone liked him. His motto was 'Always do your best,' but I daresay that, if he had been asked his private opinion, he would have admitted that the School was in reality only a holiday for officers and N.C.O.s who needed a rest. It certainly seemed so to me when I woke on the first morning and became conscious of my clean little room with its tiled floor and shuttered windows. I knew the morning was fine; voices passed outside; sparrows chirped and starlings whistled; the bell in the church tolled and a clock struck the quarters. Flook entered with my Sam Browne belt and a jug of hot water. He remarked that we had come to the right place for once, and regretted that we were not there for the duration."

Mr. Sassoon goes on to describe the beauties of nature around and his various companions in the Mess from all units in the British Army. He mentions the gas expert from G.H.Q., who at lectures stated that "gas was still in its infancy," and the Artillery General who assured them that high explosive would be their best friend in future battles, unmindful for the moment that explosives often arrived from the wrong direction. "But," continues Sassoon, "the star turn in the school-room was a massive sandy-haired Highland Major whose subject was the 'Spirit of the Bayonet.' Though at the time undecorated, he was afterwards awarded the D.S.O. for lecturing."

The writer then gives a vivid description of this man's homicidal eloquence interspersed with genial and well-judged jokes, and of his assistant, a sergeant, who had been trained to such a pitch of frightfulness that at a moment's warning he could divest himself of all semblance of humanity. "When told 'to put on the killing face,' he did so, combining it with an ultra-vindictive attitude. 'To instil fear into the opponent' was one of the Major's main maxims. Man, it seemed, had been created to jab the life out of Germans. To hear the Major talk, one might have thought that he did it himself every day before breakfast. His final words were: 'Remember that every Boche you fellows kill is a point scored to our side; every Boche you kill brings victory one minute nearer and shortens the war by one minute. Kill them! Kill them! There's only one good Boche, and that's a dead one!' "

The description of the Bayonet Fighting instructor is of particular interest to the men of the 12th, as in 1918 a similar lecture was delivered to us, probably by the same man. Siegfried Sassoon also mentions the Jute Mill where one could get a really good hot bath in a dyeing vat, a fact which the survivors of A Company can substantiate.

Night after night our men watched the flashes and listened to the rumblings of the guns in action in the great battle which was taking place over 30 miles away from the peaceful town in which they were billeted. Most of them felt that they were going to take an inglorious part in the Battle of the Somme by staying in Flixecourt enjoying themselves while the other companies would be risking their lives in action with the enemy. In common with the rest of the Battalion A Company knew they were in France for more serious business than demonstration purposes and they were anxious to take their turn in attacking the enemy. It would be wrong to suggest that the men of the 12th had at this period the love for the enemy which some of the present-day writers are so fond of describing; they had an ugly job to perform and were anxious to get it over so that they could return to their homes again, nor did they consider themselves inferior to the Germans as soldiers. The morale of A Company was high. When parades and guards were finished, voices could daily be heard singing all the latest choruses from the shows in "Blighty." Sergt. Sid Fowler was the Company's greatest songster. With a repertoire ranging from the most sentimental to the utterly ridiculous songs which the troops delighted in singing, Fowler kept our spirits up to a very high pitch. One of Sid's songs went as follows:—

"Walking through the Churchyard,
I went my way,"
Thinking of my wife and child
So many miles away.
I could not find no work to do,
No matter how I tried,
And that's how I enlisted for a soldier."

In company with another man of his platoon named Hyams, Fowler would give a harmonious rendering of "When the swallows build their nest," in which was introduced a lady known as sweet Marie. Little did we dream that within a few days one of these voices would be stilled for ever. Fowler was a bit of a mystery to us all. He was nothing more than a big boy in his manner, with a laugh which was most infectious. He knew the manuals of military training from A to Z, even though, as Cpl. Southall recalls, he occasionally got a bit tongue-tied when he was rapidly detailing parts of a rifle. He was a most useful boxer, devoid of fear, and from what we gathered from him he had already (despite his youth) been wounded in the early fighting of the war. His body was recovered from the battlefields as recently as June, 1931, and is buried in Serre Road Cemetery, Beaumont Hamel. Fowler had his counterpart in the person of "Scotty" Williams of D Company, who afterwards became famous throughout the Division with his party of "Dickybirds." "Scotty" also laid down his life, and over his grave in Etaples Military Cemetery should be erected a monument to his greatness as an entertainer, who, besides doing his bit throughout in the line, devoted all his energies to making us forget the troublous times through which we were passing.

For the rest of the Battalion which was left at Mouflers training continued in accordance with the programme laid down by G.H.Q. for troops participating in the Somme offensive. A circular was issued by the High Command which reviewed the fighting that had already taken place and impressed upon the units preparing for the next attack the necessity of pushing forward with the utmost vigour, as the Germans were feeling the strain of the campaign in regard to their man power, whilst their morale was not very good. It was anticipated that victory would shortly come to us as the result of the battles which were then in progress. Whether the General Staff really meant what was said in this circular is open to doubt. That the enemy was able to continue for another two years can be partly explained by the Russian *débacle,* but perhaps one of the great factors was the heavy losses suffered by the British troops in comparison with the Germans. Mr. Winston Churchill in his "World Crisis" has put our losses down as three to two compared with the enemy's. When it is considered that the British had to break down the tremendous fortifications which the Germans had built, this is quite understandable, for the attackers usually suffer much more heavily than the defence.

The great series of actions lasting four and a half months known to history as the "Battle of the Somme" had begun on July 1st, 1916. By the middle of November, when the fighting died down in a sea of mud, no less than one million and a half had been killed or wounded, either German or British (the French took little part after the first few weeks). To the German troops it was known as the "Bloodbath." Only those who took part in this long Hell of horrors can realise what it was, but the truest description of the Inferno is best given in Sir Philip Gibbs' "Realities of War," a book which every young person of to-day might read with profit once every year.

The German Government had hoped to deal the knock-out blow to France before the English "New Armies" could come in force into the struggle, and in February, 1916, had begun the awful offensive at Verdun. How the French ever succeeded in repulsing these overwhelming onslaughts is a marvel, but they did. "On ne passera pas," was their grim watchword. The German casualties were 600,000, and the slaughter of the French was so appalling that they never properly recovered. We must never forget that France bore the main brunt of Germany's assault for the first two years of the war in the West. Some even question whether she will ever truly recover from that holocaust.

In the early part of 1916 Germany had no less than 130 divisions on the Western Front. But by the summer their hopes were dashed and their anxieties menacing. Their losses in front of Verdun had been frightful and the expenditure of ammunition enormous. The Crown Prince's armies had been badly shaken in morale by their failure to break down the French resistance. The Russians were conducting a formidable offensive in the East. And now the new armies of the British Empire, almost intact and supported by vast quantities of artillery and shells, were ready.

The German positions when the campaign began were of enormous strength. Huge concrete dugouts—some large enough to contain a battalion—had been constructed by the labour of prisoners and many of the inhabitants of the occupied territory, who were forced to toil in slave-gangs behind their lines. Barbed-wire defences, cement gun-pits, innumerable machine-gun positions rendered their front, as they trusted, impregnable. They knew of course where the attack must come, for our gigantic preparations were impossible to conceal.

At the end of June eight days intense "drumfire," in which 2,000,000 shells were fired, smashed most of these forward defences to smithereens, at any rate those on or near the surface, and many of them were captured at fearful loss both to the assault and defence. Our casualties on the first day alone were 60,000! To the north at Gommecourt, Thiepval and Beaumont Hamel, despite the most amazing valour, our attacks were mostly repelled. But further south the gallant British armies gradually pressed forward. The whole country was turned into a ghastly wilderness, where villages dissolved into a few mounds of brick, where scarcely a green thing showed on the tortured expanse of shell holes, and only a few torn tree-stumps here and there dotted the sky-line. It was impossible to recover all the dead and wounded. The grim fact that the Thiepval War Memorial commemorates 73,000 officers and men who were never found or identified is comment enough. About once every fortnight a fresh bombardment and a fresh "push" took place at some point or other. On these hideous fields fell by tens of thousands the flower of our race, from Great Britain and Ireland, from Canada, Australia, New Zealand and other dominions and colonies.

"They went with songs to the battle, they were young,
Straight of limb, true of eye, steady and aglow.
They were staunch to the end against odds uncounted;
They fell with their faces to the foe."

The pity of it: oh, the pity of it!

Our attacks in the Somme area relieved the pressure on the French just in time. By mid-September the German morale was cracking; their troops were frightened and almost mutinous if they found their destination was the "Bloodbath"; their reserves of ammunition were suffering a serious drain; our superiority in the air was manifest. Yet still they defended position after position with courage and tenacity. Our High Command was now trying to drive north-east so as to render the enemy salient at Thiepval untenable, and it was into this action that the 41st Division, till now unused to open warfare, were to be thrown.

The Battalion was inspected by Major-General S. T. B. Lawford, C.B., on the 2nd of September, and a special Order of the Day was issued from Brigade H.Q. as follows:—

"Major-General Lawford, C.B., commanding 41st Division, has expressed himself well pleased with all he saw at his inspection to-day and was good enough to add that he felt entire confidence that the 122nd Infantry Brigade when called upon would do its duty. The Brigadier-General Commanding trusts that all ranks will endeavour to show that this confidence is not misplaced."

(Sgd.) Gwyn Thomas, Major,
Brigade Office, 122nd Infantry Brigade.

At 6.0 a.m. on September 6th the Battalion entrained at Longpré, reaching Mericourt l'Abbé at 10.0, marching thence to Fricourt, where it was accommodated in bivouacs. On the 8th A Company and the Lewis-gun detachment boarded buses and bade farewell to Flixecourt. Singing at the top of their voices, the party passed through Amiens and joined the Battalion, whose strength now was 36 officers and 777 other ranks, near Fricourt.

The short stay in the region of Fricourt enabled the troops to get a little insight into the fighting which had already taken place. It was from here that the first advance had been made on the 1st of July, and the British and German positions were open for inspection. For the first time we were able to see the massive underground dugouts which the enemy had made during his occupation. It was said by some of the older soldiers of the Battalion who had occupied these positions with other battalions of the East Surreys that, before the British troops took over the sector, the French troops, who handed over to them, had spent most of their time here making souvenirs. Evidence was afterwards found by members of the 12th that the enemy certainly must have had a good time in this portion of the line.

It is a curious fact that before most of the big actions in which the Battalion took part there were a certain number of casualties caused by accidents. The first of these happened at Fricourt, when a party from D Company was on the march. One of them happened to kick a nosecap of a shell which exploded and wounded some of the party. After this orders were issued that all nosecaps which men had been collecting as souvenirs had to be thrown away; the Colonel, himself a collector, set the example by abandoning his.

12th (BERMONDSEY) BATTALION EAST SURREY REGIMENT—THE SOMME 1916

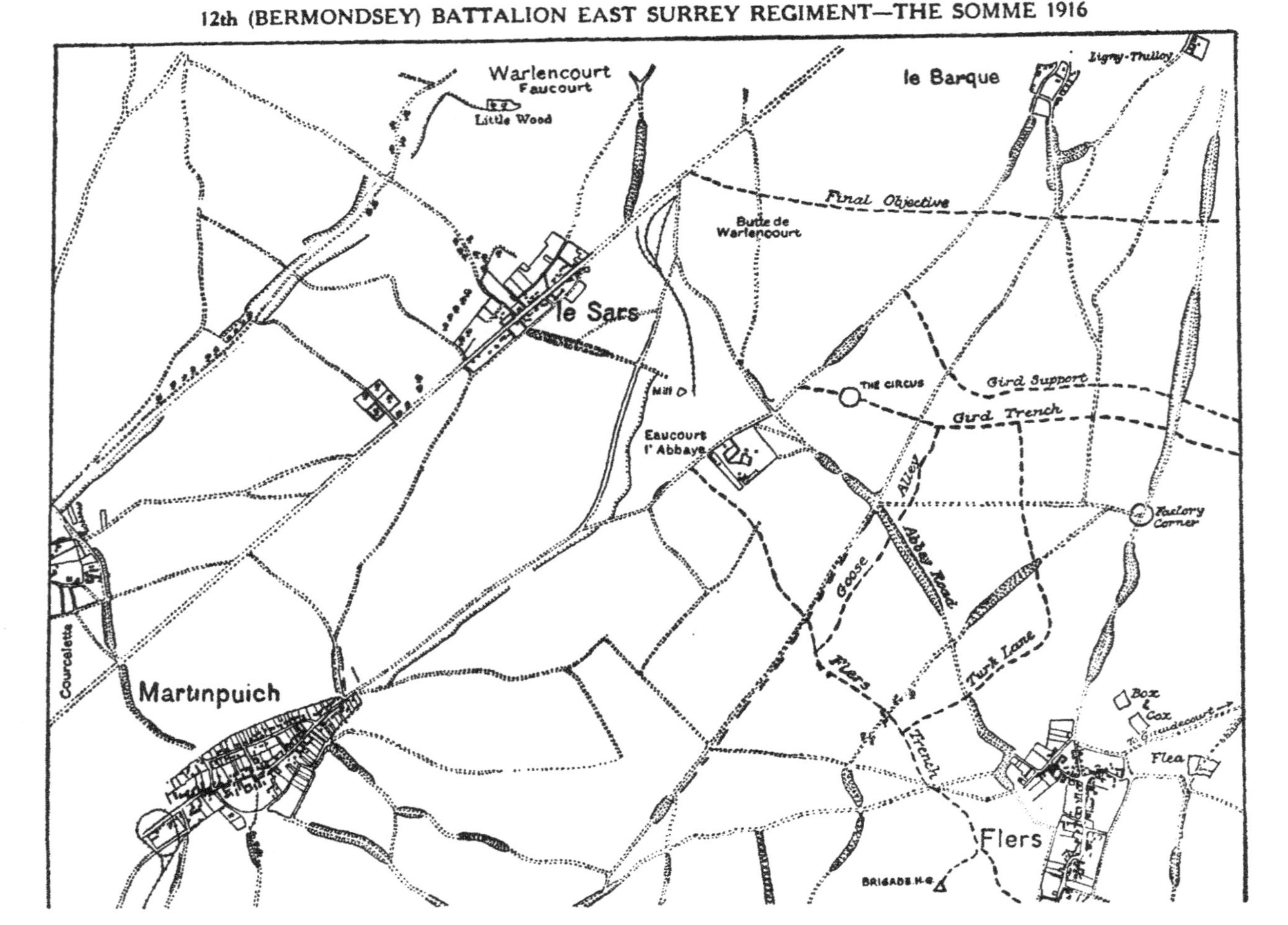

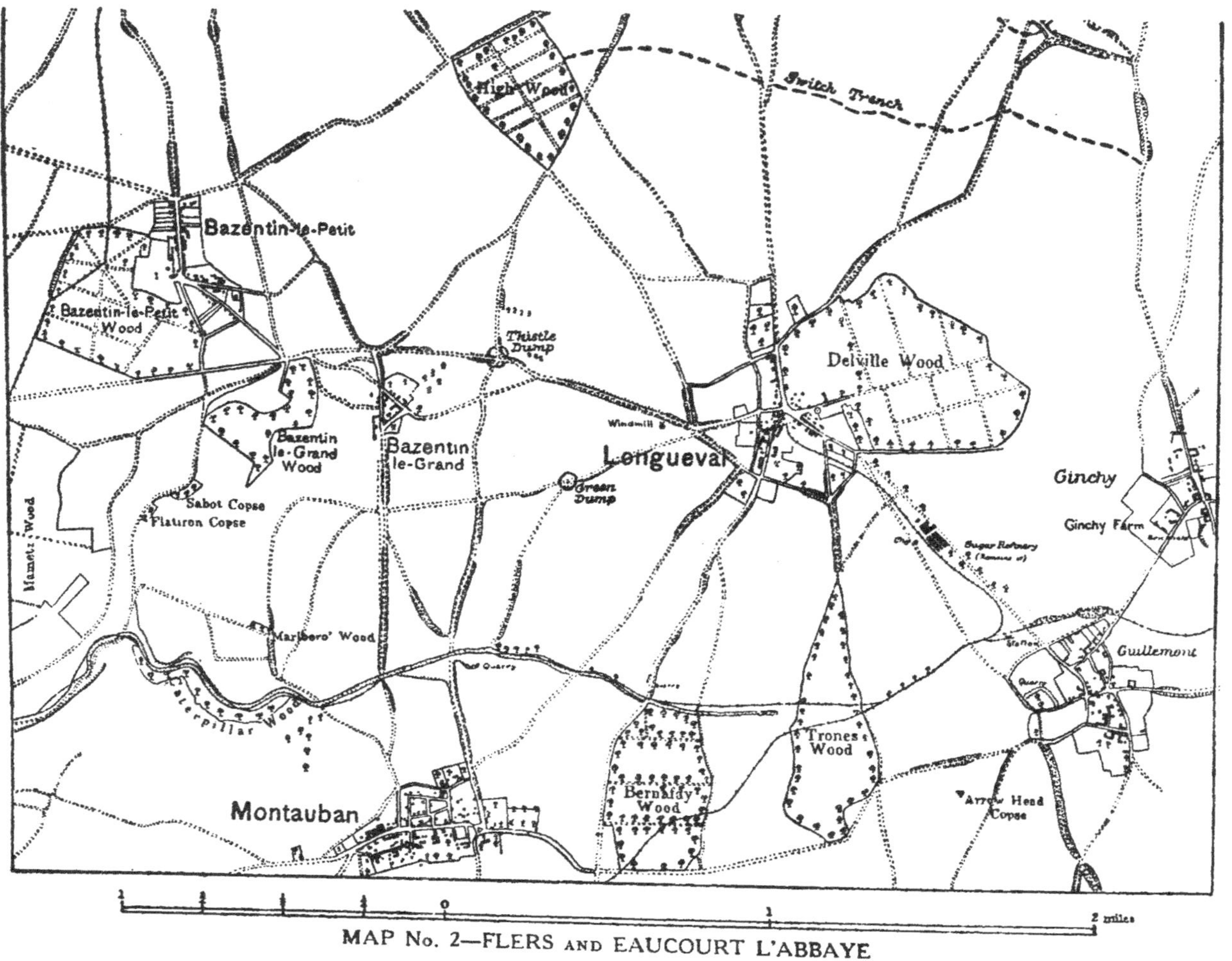

MAP No. 2—FLERS AND EAUCOURT L'ABBAYE

Day by day an enormous stream of transport and troops could be seen wending its way from and to the forward positions.

One of the first casualties of the Battalion, Pte. Dean of A Company, one day met us with a party of the "Queen's." He had exciting tales to tell of the fighting he had already been through on the Somme. After recuperating from a wound received at Ploegsteert, he had been posted to the "Queen's" and had been over the top three times with them. That was the last we were to see of Dean, as later on in the war he was posted as missing. A talk with him had convinced us that, once a man left his battalion through sickness or otherwise, there was no knowing to what unit he would be posted at the base to make good the severe casualties which were being suffered daily on the Somme. In fact there is evidence in the records that certain men who were posted to us never joined the Battalion. They were attached to other units such as the 2nd "Queen's" and the 1st R.W. Kents, and were either killed or wounded.

The time had now arrived for the 12th Battalion to take its part in the great offensive which had gone on almost unceasingly since the 1st of July. Battalion Orders issued by Lieut.-Col. H. J. Walmisley-Dresser on September 14th clearly explain the forthcoming operations and the part the Battalion had to take in them.

The situation was as follows:—

The Fourth Army, in co-operation with the Reserve Army and the French, was to attack and capture the enemy's system of defences up to and including the line Morval-Les Boeufs-Gueudecourt-High Wood. The attack was to be pushed home with the utmost vigour all along the line. The enemy's morale, it was stated, was known to be shaken; he had few, if any, fresh reserves; and it was considered that a combined and determined offensive would result in a decisive victory.

The 41st Division was to attack as the centre of the XV Corps (under Lieut.-General Horne), having on its right the 14th Division and on its left the New Zealand Division.

The 122nd Brigade was to be on the left of the 41st Division with the 124th Brigade on the right of it, a New Zealand Brigade on the left, and the 123rd in reserve. It was to attack in four stages, with the 15th Hants and the 18th K.R.R.s in the front line, and the 11th R.W. Kents and the 12th East Surreys in the second. The advance was to be in four waves on a four-company front, each phase of the operations being carefully timed. Orders in intricate detail were issued for the assaulting waves and their objectives by map reference, "mopping-up" parties, carrying parties, Stokes, Vickers and Lewis-guns, rockets, signalling both by ground and to aeroplanes, pigeons, dumps, ambulance positions, prisoners, etc., and all these had to be worked out by H.Q. and Company staffs. The appendix is of special interest, for this was the first time "Tanks," the very existence of which had been "wropt in mystery," were ever used in war.*

The Tanks, Heavy Section, Machine-Gun Corps, will co-operate in the attack, and will be in position in rear of our front line trenches by 4.0 a.m. on "Z" day.

These tanks will usually precede the Infantry. Their rôle is to destroy the hostile Machine-Guns and Strong Points, and clear the way for the Infantry. The Infantry will follow behind the tanks, and, should any strong point succeed in holding up the Infantry, they will call for a tank to assist them by using the signal "Enemy in sight" with the rifle. Should the tanks get in rear of the Infantry, an escort of one N.C.O. and 10 men will be detailed by the nearest unit to remove any wounded which happen to lie in the path of the tank. The escort will also protect the tank from close assault by the enemy Infantry or from attack from explosive charges. Should tanks become out

* *Appendix to Operation Orders*

of action, our Infantry are on no account to wait for them, but will advance at the hour arranged for the tanks, in order that they may derive the benefits of the artillery barrage.

Orders having been issued, the next thing that mattered was their execution. At 4.30 p.m. on the 14th of September the 12th Battalion, with a battle strength of 17 officers and 634 other ranks, set out in high spirits to participate in the seventh of the Battles of the Somme, known as Flers-Courcelette. The rest remained at Fricourt.

Passing the camp of the famous Guards Division, some of the men burst into song. The Guards, who at the time were preparing to take their part in the same action, respondered with cheers and wished the men the best of luck as they passed. Along the road to what had been the village of Mantauban, now a few heaps of rubble, batteries of artillery were keeping up a harassing fire on the enemy positions, while British planes soared overhead. In the distance some German observation (sausage) balloons were observed, and a great cheer went up from the troops when later they were brought down in flames by our airmen. It was a comfort for us to realise that at this period our planes were masters of the air.

As the evening advanced and transports made their way along the road, the rate of progress of the Battalion slackened. Night fell as the road near "the Quarries" was reached. In the darkness the weird monsters which we afterwards came to know as Tanks were encountered. At first we thought they were tractors used for conveying the heavy guns along the roads. Their secret had been so well kept that, apart from knowing that a new type of land cruiser was going to assist us in action, we had no real conception of what it looked like or of its capabilities. The tanks were kept in secret lairs and camouflaged in order to keep prying eyes off them.

Early in the morning of the 15th September the vicinity of Delville Wood was reached. The Germans were sending over tear-gas shells which had the peculiar smell of pineapple about them. Men's eyes began to water, and instructions were passed along for gas-goggles to be worn. The wreckage in this region was terrible, and here and there the bodies of dead Germans and "Jocks" were still to be seen, for the recent fighting had been of the severest kind; our tutors of the 9th Division had fought the enemy to a standstill and refused to yield any ground gained despite desperate counter-attacks.

As the positions behind the front line trenches were approached, some delay was occasioned by stretcher-bearers of the 18th K.R.R.s who were doing their best to evacuate their wounded before the dawn. A whimper from a badly wounded man on a stretcher brought forth the remark from one of the 12th, "Cheer up, mate; you'll soon be in Blighty!"

At 2.0 a.m. the Battalion had taken up its battle positions behind Tea Trench, N.W. of Delville Wood. The half-platoons were concealed in shell holes, and runners were utilised to keep touch with and report to Company Headquarters on any situation which needed attention. During the early hours of the morning a slight drizzle of rain was experienced, and the enemy, apprehensive of a possible attack at day-break, continued to shell with lachrymatory, while the British artillery kept up an intermittent shelling. Sheer exhaustion from wandering over the shell-pitted area to the battle positions caused most of the men to drop off to an uneasy sleep.

While men slept, the tanks gradually crept up on a line which had been taped out for them. The chugging of their engines could be heard by some of the runners who had been kept busy seeing that every order from the Commanding Officer and O.C.s companies had been complied with.

Zero hour was 6.20 a.m. Promptly to time our artillery opened a terrific bombardment, and automatically the troops in the front line began to advance behind the creeping barrage, the 12th Battalion followed behind the 18th K.R.R.s who could be seen moving to the assault on the first objective, Switch Trench (Green Line), which was taken by 6.30 a.m. The enemy machine-guns began to take toll as the troops advanced across No Man's Land. Reaching the old British front line, the 12th Battalion paused a few minutes and then went on in the direction of Switch Trench. Many casualties occurred at this stage of the proceedings through the men being too anxious to get forward to help the K.R.R.s, whose ranks were becoming sorely depleted through enemy machine-gun fire, which was very severe from the direction of the village of Flers.

The enemy, realising that his front line was gone, now began to bombard it. As the 12th Battalion was coming up to take up its positions before the final assault on the village, it suffered rather badly in consequence. Officers and men began to fall right and left.

Lieut. H. T. Pike who was wounded here, says:—

"One incident which shows the tremendously churned-up state of the ground in this area and the comparative uselessness of high explosive shells I well remember. The Battalion advanced in column of half-platoons, and in the middle of the barrage I looked to my left and saw what was apparently a large calibre H.E. shell explode in the midst of a half-platoon who of course were all knocked over, but within a few seconds they were mostly on their feet again and going forward as fast as they could over that terrible ground."

Reaching the second objective, Flers Trench (Brown Line), the Battalion now linked up with the K.R.R.s after an advance of about 1,000 yards. Very little opposition was experienced in taking the Brown Line, although a machine-gun team in front of A Company caused many casualties before it was rushed with the bayonet. The German survivors in the trench surrendered to C.S.M. B. Horswell, who had by now taken over some of the remnants of his company, Captain Jessop having been wounded soon after the first objective was reached.

So swift had been the advance that objectives were in advance of the creeping barrage, and very soon the men were caught between the British and German fire. Accordingly Sergt. C. Maguire of the Signal Section set about getting red flares lit and signalling to the planes overhead with panels. The planes, picking up the signals, soon got our artillery to lift on to the village. Some of the enemy retreated in this direction, while others made their way to our lines to surrender.

Meanwhile a tank slowly made its way towards our second objective. Up to now it had taken no really active part in the fighting, unless it was to frighten the enemy. It was a heartening sight to see this machine crossing trenches and deep shell-holes as if they had never existed. Nothing stopped its progress, slow as it was compared with the Infantry.

During the respite in Flers Trench an extraordinary incident took place. A stockily built German made his way towards a party of A Company to surrender and was greeted by a man who was renowned as a boxer in the Battalion. This man demanded of the German his watch as a souvenir, but "Fritz" refused to give it to him.

Thereupon this bruiser offered to fight the Boche for it. Judge the consternation of us all when we found the two adversaries going it hammer and tongs with their fists while shells dropped all round, till with a terrific punch to the jaw the German was sent sprawling into a shell hole. When he had recovered, the man from the 12th peremptorily ordered him to the rear and let him retain his watch. Asked afterwards why he did not take the watch, our man said he would not dream of taking anything from a man who had shown such pluck.

Six hundred yards still remained to be covered between the second objective and the village. As the barrage lifted, the 12th Battalion went forward, and, although held up for a little time by some wire in front, managed, with the assistance of one of the tanks,* to be the first troops to enter Flers.

Down the battered High Street the men of the 12th made their way, while the tank fired its machine and light guns into German posts which were still holding out in the village. It was now that one of our airmen wirelessed to H.Q. the famous words—"A Tank is walking up Flers High Street with the British Army cheering behind." Much confused fighting ensued, as the result of which we lost heavily in officers and N.C.O.s. Some of the Germans threw stick bombs at the tank, but these simply exploded on its sides without doing any damage to the machine or its occupants. The village was actually in our hands before 10.30 a.m. Dugouts and cellars were bombed, and prisoners taken and sent back to the rear. As the trees in the orchards were laden with apples, no time was lost by the men in stripping them.

Sergt. W. Barnes of C Company, after disabling a machine-gun in the village, secured about a dozen prisoners, some of whom were Red Cross men. Those of the enemy who were able to get away made off in the direction of Gueudecourt, and soon after they left the German artillery began to put down a terrific barrage, which caused our troops to evacuate the village. Flers was the third objective (Blue Line) and the final objective (Red Line), consisting of a double line of trenches on the other side of the village, had yet to be taken. With the shelling of the place a certain amount of disorganisation set in, especially as most of our officers had by now become casualties,

*With regard to the use of the tanks at Flers, the following which appeared in the "Times" on the 15th of September, 1935, is of special interest:—

"British tanks went into action on the Somme 19 years ago this week and overran a German line that had defied the attacks of infantry.

"A German artillery officer who was in an observation post in front of Flers said to a Press representative yesterday that when he saw the first tank on the ridge he thought it was a threshing machine. 'It did look something like a threshing machine,' he said, 'but why should it have arrived there in the middle of a war and on a most unhealthy sector at that? Should we turn our batteries on it or wait and see what might happen next? We waited and watched. Then it moved. It actually started to come towards us. But that was not all. Suddenly into view came another. It joined the first one and, side by side, they came on, ugly and ungainly, but terribly businesslike.

" 'Then, without warning, from both of them came streams of bullets. Next they were on top of us. . . . Those of us who survived will not forget that morning when your tanks first came into action. And to think that we thought they might be threshing machines!'

"Trained in secrecy in Suffolk, the crews had helped to smuggle their cumbersome landships across the Channel and up to near the front line without the secret being disclosed. Of the 49 tanks which set out, 17 broke down or became bogged. Nine of those which reached the front line got ahead of the infantry and another nine kept pace with them. One got astride the German line at Flers, raked it with heavy fire and then, ambling along behind it, helped to capture 300 prisoners."

but there is evidence that remnants of the Battalion went on, particularly from C Company under Lieut. J. W. Staddon, who was severely wounded in gruelling fighting beyond the village. At first Lieut. Staddon was reported missing, believed killed, but he was picked up two days after the action. Pte. E. Howell, who was also wounded near Lieut. Staddon, states that he too was not able to reach the dressing station for some considerable time after the Battalion was relieved. For the rest it is clear that positions were occupied on either side of the village by different parties from the Battalion. The final part taken by our men after the Germans had made the village untenable is difficult to piece together, as the account in the War Diary is so incomplete as to render it useless as a record of events. This is in the main explained by the fact that the Commanding Officer and all except one of the other officers (2nd Lieut. W. J. Palk) became casualties. The only reports officially made were by Mr. Palk and C.S.M. Horswell (the only warrant officer to come out of action) and these are too vague to be of much assistance. Consequently we have to turn to the official accounts by the Brigadier and his Brigade Major.

General Towsey states that, after the village was in our hands, practically all the officers of the Brigade had become casualties, units were all mixed up and there was considerable confusion. There was a tendency to remain in the village instead of all pressing on and consolidating. It was noticed that the Germans released pigeons before evacuating Flers and Switch Trench. The village was then heavily pasted with gas shells, and a barrage was placed between Flers and Switch Trench. Touch too had been lost with the Brigade on the right. About 11.0 a.m. groups of men began to go back on our left, and this movement spread along the line. Parties began to drift back towards the Brown Line (Flers Trench), but Lieut.-Col. A. F. Townshend, commanding the 11th Royal West Kents, endeavoured to stop this movement, till he was mortally wounded while consolidating a line south of the village to resist a possible counter-attack.

The situation as reported to the Brigadier at 11.0 a.m. appeared to be as follows:—

Elements of the Brigade were north of Flers in and beyond the Blue Line, together with some New Zealand troops. West and immediately south of the village in the Flers trenches portions of the Brigade were consolidating. Strong points were being built by the 228th Field Company R.E. attached to the Brigade under Lieut. Carter, and Switch Trench was also being consolidated by parties of the Brigade left there for that purpose. As a result of enemy shelling between 11.30 a.m. and 1.0 p.m. a period of inaction set in. On hearing that the troops were falling back from Flers and that the situation was obscure, General Towsey sent the Brigade Major at 1.0 p.m. to investigate personally.

Major Gwyn Thomas found on arrival that the advance, instead of pushing north of Flers, was stationary south of the village, and it was of importance to get the troops forward. As it was out of the question to advance through the village, which was being intensely bombarded by the enemy, Major Gwyn Thomas ordered Lieut. Carter to stop his work on the strong points and collect all the available troops of the Brigade west of the strong point and advance on the west side of the village. On the S.W. edge of the village the Brigade Major found a tank burning. He then moved west of Flers, taking with him what troops he could collect. These included the remnants of a New Zealand Battalion, believed to be the 2nd Battalion of the 3rd New Zealand Rifle Brigade under the command of Colonel A. E. Stewart, who moved his men forward in the most gallant manner N.W. of Flers. Elements of the Brigade followed the Brigade Major to the N.W. of the village and so averted any further withdrawal of troops who had previously advanced beyond the village and were retiring on the left of the Brigade.

The reinforcements advanced successfully to a point roughly 300 yards to the north-west and 100-150 yards north of the village, where flares were lit at 2.0 p.m. Here enemy rifle fire was encountered. Some New Zealanders with a machine-gun north of the village were also ordered to move forward and consolidate on the line about 100-150 yards nearer the enemy.

North-east of the village was a derelict tank, and here a party under Lieut. Carter and a Vickers gun under 2nd Lieut. Gilliat were directed by the Brigade Major to take up a position to cover the village close to the cross-roads, where there was considerable sniping. Passing back east of the village, Major Gwyn Thomas returned to Flers Trench and ordered forward further reinforcements, including a company of the 124th Brigade, to north of Flers. These dispositions rendered the village comparatively safe from counter attack, as, in addition to the infantry with Lewis-guns, 5 Vickers guns had been pushed forward by the Brigade Machine-gun Officer.

At about 4.15 p.m. the 123rd Infantry Brigade took over the line, and what was left of the 122nd Brigade was gradually withdrawn, being assembled and re-organised in York, Carlton and Savoy Trenches.

As the object of this book is to state the truth as verified from official documents, the foregoing accounts by General Towsey and Major Gwyn Thomas, two of the ablest men in the British Army, are given. Whilst those who survived might not be able to substantiate entirely the contents of these reports (for instance there were a few men of A Company in front of the village who, although they did not see the Brigade Major, can verify most of his facts) on the whole it is a true picture of the state of things at the time.

For the confusion that occurred no blame was attaching to the men who participated, for here let us quote the Brigadier in his report:—

"If, as is desired, everybody down to privates should know exactly what they have to do, orders must reach battalions in ample time and before they are in the trenches; otherwise it is impossible to explain them. In this case the orders were received too late, and officers and men went into action with a very confused idea of the long and complicated orders. I had only been able to impress on them the general instruction, 'Keep close to the barrage and take Flers,' and, when all the officers were down, it is probable that the men thought that, once in Flers, they had gained their objective. The time table must be simple, or it is not possible to follow it in the stress of action."

That the 12th Battalion had endeavoured to carry out all the instructions, where they were known, is proved by N.C.O.s and men who participated. In addition Sergt. L. C. Lunn of the Brigade Office has brought to light another factor which considerably increased our difficulties:—

"A copy of an entry from my notes may explain that the 12th not only had their own objective to take, but had first to help out the 18th K.R.R.C. owing to their unfortunate loss of the whole of their Battalion H.Q. About 9.0 a.m. we heard that Lieut. Notley, 18th K.R.R.C., was wounded and wanted to see the General before he was taken to the Dressing Station. The G.O.C. saw him, and he said. 'The Colonel, Major, Adjutant, two Captains and Signalling Officer have all been killed by one shell.' He was the only one who got out."

We have already mentioned how Lieut. Staddon and his party advanced beyond the village and fought until he and most of his men were put out of action. Although he was recommended for conspicuous gallantry, no award was made to him, although those with him considered that he had rightly earned one.

C.S.M. Bry Horswell took charge of A Company H.Q. staff after Captain Jessop was wounded. Later he was in command of a party which, after rushing the machine-gun post already mentioned at Flers Trench, he led to the final assault on the village. Horswell ordered his party to make full use of what cover there was in reaching their objectives, thus avoiding casualties from machine-gun fire. When the village was being heavily shelled, he brought the remnants of his party to the outer edge of the village, where a German dugout was discovered. Horswell's batman, Pocklington, proceeded to investigate with a Mills bomb in his hand. Before throwing the bomb he shouted down and two forlorn looking Bavarians came to the surface with their hands above their heads. One was wounded, while the other looked scared out of his wits. The prisoners were eventually handed over to the New Zealanders by a corporal who was with the party. Horswell then endeavoured to get in touch with the remainder of the Battalion by sending a runner through the village to find out what was happening. The runner hastily made his way through the village, which was being shelled very heavily, and, on reporting back stated that, apart from dead and wounded, the place appeared to have been evacuated by our troops. Joined by an officer of the Royal Fusiliers, the party (numbering now about 6) made its way to the north front of the village, where consolidation had to be carried out. The Germans then put down a heavy barrage which dispersed this small party. Men began to trickle back, as it was said the enemy was attacking. Two of Horswell's party (Cpl. W. Edwards and Pte. L. M. Duggan), remained in a shell hole in front of the village waiting for this supposed counter-attack, which apparently did not materialise. Both of them were tired out and dead beat: around them were many dead and badly wounded. Later a Staff Officer came along and ordered them to attach themselves to the Royal Fusiliers who had arrived at a position to the right of them, as he understood that the 12th East Surreys had been relieved. Accordingly they reported to the Fusiliers and stayed with them until they were relieved on the morning of the 16th. On the way out Cpl. Len Bishop of B Company was encountered carrying out of action his disabled Lewis-gun. The Fusiliers, having reached the road to Montauban, instructed the men of the 12th to try to find their unit. Fortunately for them Lieut. C. O. Slacke of B Company who was on water point duty, met them and, after saying that he had heard the Battalion was annihilated, took them along to his camp and instructed his servant to prepare breakfast for them, and never was a meal more enjoyed by the three. After breakfast Mr. Slacke's groom conducted the little party to the Details Camp at Fricourt, where after a short rest they had to fall in again and proceed with the remainder of the Details to join the survivors of the Battalion in reserve. The experience of these three men was typical of many more of our men, who never received the order that at about 4.45 p.m. on the 15th the 123rd Brigade was relieving the 122nd.

Of the many brave deeds in the action no evidence exists in the Battalion records now available, but men still speak of the great devotion to duty of a stretcher-bearer named W. Aitken. Hearing that the Colonel was severely wounded, Aitken scoured the countryside to find him and was mainly responsible for Colonel Walmisley-Dresser reaching the C.C.S. at Heilly, where, unfortunately, he died on the 17th. According to Sergt. Lattimore's recollection the Colonel was mortally wounded after the orders were received for relief when a shell landed in the shell hole occupied by Battalion H.Q. Although wounded, the Colonel continued to direct operations. His body was laid to rest in the cemetery adjoining the C.C.S., where it reposes to-day.

Cpl. Southall, who received the M.M. for the splendid work he did for the wounded, tells of the fine services rendered by Dr. Young and how he received his injury.

"We walked down the main street of the village and saw one of our tanks sitting in a large shell-hole apparently with engine trouble. Fritz was dropping shells in and behind the broken-down houses. We could not see any suitable place for an Aid Post, and accordingly the M.O. suggested we should look round outside for a good spot. We were walking back along a sunken road with a high bank on our right, the Doctor being on the left side with me on his right between him and the bank, when suddenly a shell burst on the bank and the Doctor spun round and fell. A piece of shell had hit him in the right side by the lung, and we found a small wound here which I dressed. Dr. Young then sat down and described the Germans in lurid terms for about ten minutes without repeating himself: he then collected a few things and asked me to help him down to the Dressing Station. It was a pretty tough job, as Jerry had now put down three barrages of 5.9's between us and our destination.

"In spite of his wound Dr. Young stopped to dress every wounded man he came across, and the day was well on before, with our slow progress, we got through the barrage, and the M.O. decided to rest for a bit. He was in a great deal of pain, as we made our way slowly to the Dressing Station, where I parted from him with much regret, for I had taken a great liking to him. He was very blunt, but a fine man and very brave."

The total casualties suffered by the Battalion during the battle were 16 out of 17 officers and 288 out of 634 other ranks.

The following officers, besides the Commanding Officer, became casualties:—

Killed: Captains F. D. Jessop, M.C. (after being wounded early on in the action), J. L. Buckman and C. York-Davis, and Lieuts. J. R. Chesters and C. C. Fox. With the exception of Capt. Jessop, whose body is buried at Bulls Road Cemetery, Flers, the names of the remainder are inscribed on the Thiepval Memorial.

Wounded: Capt. and Adjutant R. A. McCulloch, Capt. A. D. Crow, Lieut. J. W. Staddon, and 2nd Lieuts. F. Beard, J. E. M. Crowther, W. M. Edwards, A. G. Howitt, H. T. Pike and S. Stimson; and Lieut. E. W. G. Young, R.A.M.C.

Of the five officers who met their death one can still recall incidents which endeared them to the men they commanded. Colonel Walmisley-Dresser was a tall stately-looking man, quiet and unassuming and very far removed from our conception of the old time officers of the Regular Army. He had an utter disregard of danger. Capt. Jessop, although somewhat reserved, commanded our respect for courage and fearlessness. In Capt. Buckman we had a Company Commander whose men idolised him. He was a thoroughly efficient man in every way, and many feel that a brilliant Army career was cut short by his death at Flers. Capt. York-Davis who commanded C Company, besides being a very fine Rugby player, was well liked by the men because of the keen interest he took in all things pertaining to their welfare; little luxuries which the men enjoyed were the outcome of his generosity. "One of nature's gentlemen" is how one of our sergeants describes Lieut. C. C. Fox, and a truer description could not be given to him. He was one of the officers selected to lead the "Black Hand Gang" at Ploegsteert and one can imagine that he was an inspiration to some of the tough lads of D Company who volunteered to go with him. The memory of one of our best known sergeants goes further when he says that even in death Lieut. Fox looked beautiful. He found him lying in a shell-hole peacefully reposing with a smile upon his face. A tribute to the memory of Lieut. Chesters is given by Sergt. L. C. Lunn:—

"I have a very fond brief memory of Lieut. Chesters. I didn't really know him, although he was my platoon officer, until I went across to France with my platoon. Each night after dinner, he would come round to the barn in Outtersteene, where we were billeted, and talk to us individually and collectively, enjoy the jokes, and tell us, as far as he knew, the programme before us. After only one or two nights he had gained the confidence of the whole platoon, and we felt we had someone who was personally looking after our welfare. I had to report to Brigade H.Q. a few days after this, and I always was specially interested in any news concerning him that came through. When I heard he had been killed, I was especially grieved."

In addition to the officers we lost two very smart warrant officers, C.S.M. A. E. Peterson of B Company and C.S.M. H. Jackson of D Company, whose work in training the Battalion can never be over-estimated. The death of Jackson was a sad one inasmuch as a younger brother of his who was serving in another battalion of the East Surreys had only recently applied for a transfer to the 12th so that he could serve with him. Of C.S.M. T. B. Blatch of C Company who was wounded Q.M.S. Speller writes:—

"C.S.M. Tom Blatch possessed the physique and strength of an Apollo. At Steenwreck he lifted Tyrer (our cheery but diminutive Armourer) by the neck and ankles and literally hurled him at Sergt. Noad, who naturally went down like a ninepin! Tom and two brothers served many years as Regular soldiers in the East Surreys. Singularly, all three sustained serious neck wounds, all of which missed only by fractional margins, writing finis to three fine old soldiers. After Flers, where Tom lost an eye, we came across him with his Labour Company at Wieltje—a definitely warm place for old and C.3 warriors!"

Of the three brothers mentioned by Speller two of them actually served with the 12th—C.Q.M.S. W. Blatch joining us in 1918.

The names of the other ranks who were killed or died of wounds in this action are given in the appendix.

2nd Lieut. W. J. Palk was the only officer and C.S.M. B. P. Horswell the only warrant officer to come out of action. Both of them subsequently received the Military Cross. Other awards made for gallantry in these operations were:—
Military Cross: 2nd Lieut. J. F. Tamblyn (attached 122nd T.M.B.).
T.M.B.).

Distinguished Conduct Medal: Lce.-Cpl. W. Carter and Ptes. A. B. Giles and P. Huggett.

Military Medal: Sergt. C. Maguire, Lce.-Cpl. L. C. Southall, and Ptes. P. J. Budd, F. E. Butler, F. Coles, W. Hammond, G. Jones and J. Newton. Sergt. R. A. Langley also received the Military Medal for his part in the raid of the 30th of June at Ploegsteert and in action at Flers.

Many more recommendations were made, but the battles of the Somme were on so large a scale and the men who distinguished themselves so many, that rewards were given in a very meagre fashion particularly to Regimental officers. Of the deeds which won for the recipients their decorations information is lacking throughout this history; only where they are recorded in the diaries, related by old comrades of the Battalion, or where the authors had first-hand knowledge, have they been mentioned. In the case of Pte. A. B. Giles who received the D.C.M. Cpl. Southall recalls how after the action everyone was talking about Giles of the Signallers who had done great deeds with a German machine-gun, and had been blown up twice and buried by shells but not wounded, though he was a little shell-shocked. Giles became a familiar figure in the Battalion thereafter, being posted to the M.O.'s staff and serving to the end with the 12th.

At 7.30 p.m. on the 15th the order was received for the survivors of the Battalion to make their way to the Reserve trenches, where they remained until the 18th. Here a telegram from H.M. The King to the Commander-in-Chief was read to the troops:—

"I congratulate you and my brave troops on the brilliant success just achieved. I have never doubted that complete victory will ultimately crown our efforts, and the splendid results of the fighting yesterday confirm this belief."

(Sgd.) George R.I.

On the evening of the 16th, Major Blakeney brought a reinforcement of 6 officers and 60 other ranks from Fricourt and took over command of the Battalion.

LIEUT.-COLONEL I. F. BEATSON, O.B.E.

COLONEL H. H. LEE, D.S.O.

LIEUT.-COLONEL R. PENNELL, D.S.O., M.C.

LIEUT.-COLONEL G. L. BROWN, D.S.O.

I.W.M. Copyright

ROAD IN FLERS (LOOKING EAST FROM VILLAGE) September, 1916.

"DIDN'T SEE YOUR BADGES, SIR."

Back in the reserve trenches some attempt was made to reorganize the companies. After the battle comes the reckoning. In some cases platoons had ceased to exist through casualties. Information was sought from those who survived as to the fate of their comrades. Those who were wounded would be accounted for by the returns from the Casualty Clearing Stations, but the fate of the less fortunate would not be known for some time, unless they were picked up by burial parties and had means of identification upon them. Close on 50 other ranks of the Battalion were posted as "Missing." This number was gradually reduced as further information came to hand. Eventually, about nine months later, the deaths of 30 of these were accepted for official purposes as having occurred on the 15th of September, 1916. The names of these men are shown on the Thiepval Memorial together with others who were definitely known to be killed. It must be remembered that the tide of war turned in March, 1918, and in consequence cemeteries were churned up by the resulting bombardments. Crosses over graves were destroyed, and so, although a man might have had a grave which could be located in 1916, by the time the War Graves Commission undertook the task of putting headstones over the graves of the fallen, it was no longer possible to identify many thousands of bodies buried after the battles of the Somme in 1916. The result is that in most cemeteries will be seen the headstone commemorating the unknown soldier. In Bull's Road Cemetery, Flers, is the grave of an unknown Captain of the East Surrey Regiment, who, seeing that a good many of the 12th are buried there, is probably one of our officers.

For two or three days the remnants of the Battalion had more rations than they knew what to do with. In addition, parcels of perishable goods which had arrived from home for those who had become casualties were divided amongst the troops. Food was shared out, while articles not of a perishable nature were sent to the base with the effects of the men. The weather had now changed and was very wet and cold; a state of things which usually seemed to exist when the British Army took the offensive, who thus had to fight the elements as well as the enemy.

At 7.0 a.m. on the morning of the 18th of September the Battalion was relieved by the 4th King's Own Royal Lancaster Regiment. Proceeding viâ Savoy, Carlton and York Trenches, we took the road through Montauban to Mametz. From here we marched along the Fair Weather Track north of the Ribemont-Fricourt Road and arrived in a camp near Dernancourt, not far from Albert. The statue of the Blessed Virgin hanging from the top of the Basilica tower at Albert was seen on the way. It was a colossal bronze figure of St. Mary holding the divine Child high above her head. The following facts concerning the Church of Notre-Dame-de-Brebières are of interest.

Before the war as many as 80,000 people made pilgrimages to this basilica yearly, to see that ancient statue of the Virgin, discovered in the neighbourhood by a shepherd in the Middle Ages. The church was built at the end of the nineteenth century. The brick belfry, over 200 feet high, was surmounted by a dome on which stood a modern gilt statue of the Virgin, sixteen feet high, with the infant Jesus in her outstretched arms. The church was spared by the first bombardments in September, 1914, on account of two spies, who, hidden in the top of the tower, made signals to the Germans, but, as soon as they had been discovered and shot, the church became a target for the enemy artillery. A shell struck the top of the dome and burst against the socle of the statue. The base gave way, but did not entirely collapse, and the statue overturning remained suspended in mid-air. For several years it remained in this precarious position, and there was a saying that "the war would end when the Virgin Statue of Albert fell." It was said in some quarters that French engineers had riveted it to save it from falling. However, the ruin of the church was completed by the spring bombardments of 1918, and the belfry collapsing brought the statue of the Virgin to the ground.

The "leaning Virgin" of Albert was certainly the most prominent landmark on the Somme. To those who passed it, appeared as though she were looking pityingly down with her infant Son on the abomination of desolation which lay around.

Major C. H. Kitching of the 15th Hants was appointed to the temporary command on the 19th of September, and till the 30th, during wet and cold weather, the Battalion remained in camp re-organizing.

The heavy losses in officers were made good by the following being posted to and joining the Battalion on the dates stated:—

September 16th: 2nd Lieuts. J. Aston and W. L. Miller.

September 24th: Capt. J. A. C. McCalman, Lieut. L. S. Beaufoy and 2nd Lieuts. R. C. Baker, F. B. B. Dowling, P. J. Gibbons, A. G. Jennings, T. B. McWalter and S. A. Wheeler.

September 28th: 2nd Lieuts. A. M. Mackintosh and H. S. Todd.

September 30th: 2nd Lieuts. H. P. Bailey, F. J. Harding and F. R. Matthews.

Lieut. C. Cameron, R.A.M.C., temporarily took over the duties of Medical Officer.

The casualties among the warrant officers led to the appointment of the following as acting Company Sergeant-Majors: C.Q.M.S.s F. Heydinger and A. Woods, and Sergt. W. H. Sheppard.

Lieut. C. O. Slacke and 2nd Lieuts. H. C. Reynard and D. McCallum were appointed temporary Captains on the 16th, Capt. Reynard taking over the Adjutancy and Capts. McCallum and Slacke taking over A and B Companies respectively.

During the stay near Dernancourt bathing was carried out in the River Ancre. No clean clothing being procurable at the time, everybody in the Battalion was ordered by the C.O. to try to get rid of their "live stock" by the aid of creosote. Clothing was washed in the hopes that the vermin would be banished—hopes usually vain.

An amusing incident happened at one bathing parade. 2nd Lieut. J. Aston was in charge of a large party, and, seeing that there was a deep and a shallow place, he divided the men into swimmers and non-swimmers, and then took off his own clothes. He was just about to dive in, when he noticed a man still dressed. Thinking it was a skrimshanker, he said to him—"Are you an East Surrey?" "No," replied the man. "You must say 'Sir' in addressing an officer," said 2nd Lieut. Aston. The fellow grinned broadly. "Didn't see your badges, Sir," he said.

The men were accommodated in bivouacs, commonly called "bivvies," which were not at all comfortable, especially in wet weather, and a few bell tents existed for some of the officers and the Orderly Room staff. Troops in the vicinity of the camp were more fortunate in having Nissen and Armstrong huts. Casting a longing eye on these, one of the senior officers of the Battalion one day gathered together a small party of men and instructed them to move one of these huts to our camp. Some of the men were anxious to know how this could be accomplished without getting into trouble, but they were told there was such a thing as "winning" or "scrounging" in the British Army. The hut decided upon belonged to the Royal Engineers, and while they were away from the camp the hut disappeared. Whether they found out where it had gone to was not known; at all events it reached the East Surrey lines.

A few words on Scrounging might be inserted here for the information of the general reader. To be quite frank, it was stealing, but, as usually it was stealing

Government property from some other person or unit, it was naturally considered venial. It was all provided for the troops, so what harm if troops for whom it was not precisely intended got it? But some extended this to "winning" Government goods for which one would properly have to pay, such as food or drink from the canteen. From this it was easy to extend the principle by a little doping of the uneasy conscience to sneaking goods from the counters of French and Belgian shopkeepers. It was easy, with a dozen men all clamouring to be served at once in a tiny shop, where the vendor was some old woman or a girl of 14, to fill one's pockets with three packets of biscuits and only pay for one. And when troops were billeted on farms, fowls, eggs, fruit, disappeared like magic, fences or doors were chopped up for firewood, interpreters distracted by complaints from frenzied Flemish and French farmers, resulting in masses of correspondence, enquiries from the base, hunts for the offenders, and (occasionally) reparation made. The general argument was that the farmer or shopkeeper was making fat profits out of the presence of the British Army (which was frequently true), and therefore members of the British Army were justified in getting their own back in any way that seemed good to them. It was in the eyes of many a feather in one's cap to be a clever scrounger.

Here are a few random anecdotes. Their authors will probably prefer to be anonymous.

"I was in an estaminet with some of the boys who were drinking beer; I was drinking milk, as I had dysentery badly. Suddenly Fritz started shelling, and Monsieur rushed down to the cellar, leaving everything. At once chocolate, etc., disappeared. Private S—— jumped behind the counter and pumped beer into those long jugs they used, while I poured it into glasses for the boys, regretting my dysentery, you bet. Some were running out into the Square picking up the wounded and now and then running in again for the free beer. Every now and then Monsieur would pop up from the cellar, but no sooner did he appear than a shell would arrive, Bang! and bang went the cellar flap as he dived down again. This continued for three quarters of an hour, and we were very busy. All of a sudden swish went the beer pump. Monsieur had taken the pipe from the barrel. Napoo: Fini Beer."

"Whenever I got near the Q.M. Stores, Speller would chase me away. Young P—— and I cheated him once though, for going up to the Somme we 'knocked off' bread, strawberry jam, bacon, etc. We had to get over a high wall in a barn, and had our work cut out to do it, for the wall was impossible to climb, and we could not drive horse-nails into it. I found a big farm rope, and tried to throw it over a beam, but it was much too heavy. However, I got a ball of twine, threw this over the beam, then pulled the rope over, and P—— then took hold of the rope and I hauled him to the top of the wall. He then swung over, and I lowered him. After winning the stuff we were nearly caught, but, as we had our two horses next to the Q.M. Stores, we hid it in the manger and then dissembled. On coming back we found the horses had eaten all the precious bread!

Another old soldier writes:—

"On one occasion I lost my leather jerkin and was told by C.Q.M.S. Barnes of C Company to win one, which I proceeded to do. It turned out that the jerkin belonged to C.S.M. Love (afterwards R.S.M.). Shortly afterwards nearly all the cooks were killed, and M—— and I were detailed for the cookhouse. There C.S.M. Love, seeing his missing jerkin, promptly put me 'on the peg.' However, soon after I was slightly gassed in a trench near Bus House and was at the Advanced Dressing Station for ten days, and I heard no more of the incident."

But to return to our narrative.

While the Battalion was resting and re-organizing, the Campaign of the Somme continued. The Battle of Morval, fought between the 25th and 28th of September, resulted in the village of Gueudecourt being captured by British troops on the 26th.

The Battle of the Transloy Ridges began on the 1st of October, and Eaucourt L'Abbaye was captured on the 3rd. Now a fresh attempt to advance towards Ligny-Thilloy was to be made by the 41st Division, in which the 122nd Brigade was to be held in Divisional Reserve.

After spending the first two days of October in the camp near Albert and Dernancourt, the Battalion moved on the 3rd, and, passing through the famous "Happy Valley" towards Mametz Wood, rested for a while preparatory to going into action for the second time. The Transport, Q.M. Stores and Details were left behind in the south-east corner of Mametz Wood; then at 2.30 p.m. the Battalion, consisting of A, C, D, and 15 men from B Company, marched away to relieve the 3rd Battalion, New Zealand Rifle Brigade, holding the portion of Gird Support Trench, north of Factory Corner, about a mile due north of Flers. The weather at this time was appalling, and the troops experienced much misery in the chalky mud, which was several inches deep.

Guides were met at Thistle Dump, and companies proceeded to the line viâ Turk Lane and Fish Alley. Unfortunately the guides did not follow the recognized routes and led the Battalion across the open 600 yards south of Factory Corner. Heavy shelling was encountered, and in consequence companies lost touch and suffered unnecessary casualties. The relief was not completed until 10.45 p.m.

The battle strength was 15 officers and 311 other ranks. Besides the Transport and Details which we left south of Mametz Wood, another party of 50 other ranks from B Company had proceeded to Méaulte on fatigues.

During the night of the 3rd of October there was a continuous shelling along the whole front. It is of interest to note that on this date the reports speak of the use of burning oil by a special company of the Royal Engineers. During the attack on Flers gas was apparently used against the enemy, for a report had to be submitted by certain members of the Battalion as to whether any dead Germans were seen wearing gas-masks or bore evidence of gas poisoning. Some very yellow corpses at the southern exit of the village, which did not appear to have been hit by bullets or shells, were seen by some of our men, and this report was confirmed by an officer of the 18th K.R.R.s. The use of such diabolical inventions as burning oil and gas were simply the British retaliation for the "Flammenwerfers" and poison gas previously used by the enemy. Such is War, in which the opposite to every teaching of Christ and even to all ordinary morality is encouraged and belauded. However, it must be said in fairness to the British Army that the rules of war were only transgressed under great provocation from our opponents, and often Tommy himself grumbled at the delay by our Government in adopting measures of retaliation.

The enemy artillery continued to be active during the whole of the day of the 4th of October. Shell-fire was particularly severe in the neighbourhood of Factory Corner, and great difficulty was experienced in getting up rations and water. Salvage parties were organized, and, though greatly impeded in their work by the constant shelling, were able, to a certain extent, to cope with the situation.

On the following day the enemy fire slackened between noon and 6.0 p.m. Ration and carrying parties took full advantage of this respite, and in consequence all stores and supplies were able to reach the front line. The task was not an easy one as the ground was very much churned up and communication trenches were battered in.

We should here pay a special tribute to the work of the Transport section under Lieut. R. A. V. Brearey. Troops were helpless unless supplied with the necessities of food and water, the latter being specially needed for the wounded. We who saw the howling wilderness of shell-holes, foul mud, abandoned trenches full of dead, the stench of whom poisoned the air, and the labyrinths of rusty barbed wire, continually marvelled at the pluck and dogged resolution of these men who never failed to make their way through all obstacles and the dreadful shell-fire, which was concentrated on the ways by which alone they could proceed with carts or pack mules, in order that their comrades in the line might not lack the prime necessities of life.

The whole area was like a vast charnel-house. Putrefying corpses lay everywhere, in the trenches, built into parapets, in the open—a loathsome epilogue of horror to the fighting of the previous weeks.

Orders were received that at 9.0 p.m. the Battalion would be relieved by the 26th Battalion Royal Fusiliers, when a new line would be dug for the "jumping off" position for an attack which was to take place on the 7th of October. The digging operation was subsequently cancelled and fresh orders were given for the Battalion to take up positions in Flers Trench.

This was occupied until heavy shelling on the morning of the 7th had made it untenable, and orders were then received to vacate it at 12.30 p.m. Soon after an order was received from Brigade that the Battalion was to occupy Goose Alley at once and to hold itself in readiness to support an attack which was being launched by the 122nd Brigade. We moved by way of Abbey Road, and Goose Alley was occupied by 1.15 p.m.

Before we proceed any further, it is as well to review what had taken place in order to understand the position.

The French were attacking Sailly-Saillisel, three miles south-east of Gueudecourt, and in order to support them the Fourth British Army was preparing to attack along the whole front from the Albert-Bapaume Road to Lesboeufs. In this action the 122nd Brigade was to advance in the direction of the famous Butte de Warlencourt. This lofty mound, possibly the burial place of some prehistoric chieftain, had been made almost impregnable by the Germans, and indeed resisted every assault, till it fell to us months later, when the enemy secretly evacuated the whole area in February, 1917 and fell back to the notorious Hindenburg Line. It was honeycombed with underground passages, strengthened with concrete emplacements and dugouts, and from it a splendid view could be obtained of the whole British positions. No wonder it was held by the Boche with heroic tenacity. At the foot of the Warlencourt Ridge lay the village of Ligny-Thilloy, where 46 years before in the Franco-Prussian War a sanguinary battle had been fought, and this was now to be the ultimate objective of the 122nd Brigade. The order of battle was as follows:—

The 11th R.W. Kents and the 15th Hants in the front line; the 18th K.R.R.s in support, and the 12th East Surreys with a section of the 228th Field Company, R.E. in reserve. The battalions in front were to advance in two waves, each battalion on a two-company front. The supporting battalion had to conform to a similar formation, while special parties of bombers were detailed for "mopping up" and forming blocks in Gird Trench and Gird Support.

The Germans opposed to us were stout fighters, the 6th Bavarian Reserve Regt. under the command of Major-General J. Kiefhaber, and the 20th Bavarian Reserve Regt. under Major-General Scheler. They had not previously been in the "Blood-bath" and had come from the Laventie and Armentières sectors.

Punctually at Zero Hour, 1.45 p.m., the advance was made in accordance with the orders. Immediately the enemy put down a machine-gun barrage from both flanks, which was so accurate that the attack was at once held up all along the line at a distance of about 100 yards from our trenches, and the 11th R.W. Kents suffered terribly heavy casualties.

Soon after the attack had started, the 12th in Goose Alley was heavily shelled and was unable to move until 2.10 p.m. to occupy the newly dug trench whence the 18th K.R.R.s had advanced to the attack. At 4.30 p.m., in accordance with orders received from Brigade H.Q., the Battalion moved forward to reinforce the 11th R.W. Kents. As some difficulty was experienced in finding their positions, patrols were pushed forward to reconnoitre and lead the Battalion to its destination. These patrols did their work well, finding the trenches of the West Kents and leading the Battalion by the sunken road east of Eaucourt L'Abbaye through a heavy hostile barrage to the new front line without loss.

Reaching the West Kents, the Battalion consolidated and held the ground gained. A small party which had become detached from the rest of the Battalion reported at midnight and enabled communications to be dug. Throughout the night the enemy machine-guns and snipers were exceedingly active, but despite this fact working parties, scouts and covering patrols carried on as usual until dawn on the 8th of October, when they were called in. The whole of the 8th was devoted, as far as circumstances permitted, to improving the trenches dug the previous night. To prevent congestion and facilitate free movement in the new trench, 30 per cent. of the Battalion withdrew to the original front line in Gird Support. Relief by the 23rd Middlesex Regt. was supposed to have taken place at 8.0 p.m., but owing to an exceptionally heavy barrage which had been placed on the line in Gird Support and lasted over 4½ hours, this did not begin until 1.0 a.m. and was not completed until 3.30 a.m. New positions were now taken up in Switch Trench, where reinforcements from the details at Mametz Wood joined the Battalion later. Throughout the 9th and 10th things remained fairly normal, and on the 11th the Battalion left for Mametz Wood, where it was relieved by a unit of the 30th Division.

The Twelfth went into action on the 7th with a strength of 14 officers and 288 other ranks, and during the period 7th-10th sustained the following casualties:—8 other ranks killed. 47 other ranks wounded, and 8 other ranks missing. 2nd Lieut. A. V. Reiner was evacuated wounded on the 5th. Two officers of the Battalion, 2nd Lieuts. P. J. Gibbons and A. A. Wheeler, were attached to the 11th R.W. Kents for the operations. 2nd Lieut. Gibbons was killed in action on the 7th.

At 9.30 p.m. the Battalion left by Decauville train for the rest camp at Dernancourt. Here the conditions prevailing were so bad that a move had to be made farther away. The ground was deep in mud, and the men were crowded into small bivouacs with only a thin layer of straw between their ground sheets and the damp earth. The weather was cold, and a rum issue was ordered to try to put the troops into a better frame of mind. Some of the men who were known to be teetotallers took their ration of rum on this occasion in an endeavour to warm themselves internally. There was great delight when orders were received at 4.0 a.m. for us to strike camp and proceed to the rest area at Ribemont. Early in the morning of the 12th we left Dernancourt and, marching along the busy road to Ribemont, reached our billets at 10.30.

The 41st Division, after having taken a very prominent part in the operations of the Somme, was now to be withdrawn to enable it to be refitted and reorganized for future operations. Although among the youngest divisions in France, it had so established itself that thereafter it was given tasks which proved that the confidence the Higher Command had in it was not misplaced. The Commander of the Fourth Army paid his tribute to the Division in the following message which was subsequently received:—

4th Army No. 335 (G.S.)

41st Division.

"I desire to place on record my appreciation of the work done by the 41st Division during the Battle of the Somme, and to congratulate all ranks on the brilliant manner in which they captured the village of Flers on September 15th.

"To assault three lines of strongly defended trench system and to capture the village of Flers as well in one rush, was a feat of arms of which every officer, non-commissioned officer and man may feel proud.

"It was a fine performance, and I offer my best thanks for the gallantry and endurance displayed by all ranks.

"The work of the Divisional Artillery in supporting infantry attacks and in establishing the barrages deserves high praise, and I trust that in some future time it may be my good fortune to have this fine division again in the Fourth Army."

(Sgd.) H. Rawlinson,
General.
Comdg. 4th Army.

H.Q. 4th Army.
27th Oct., 1916.

The above was written soon after the events took place and in case it might be thought that the Fourth Army Commander was only sending out the usual communication to divisions under his command to spur them on to further effort, let us quote a passage from the "Life of Lord Rawlinson," published after the war:—

"Their assault and capture of Flers, surrounded as it was by numerous trenches and defended with great tenacity, the establishment beyond the Eastern lines of the village and their attempts to go on to Grandcourt constitute one of the finest feats performed during the War."

Despite the testimony of the Army Commander one can still pick up supposed histories of the war and read that the Guards or New Zealanders took Flers. The Guards, were some considerable distance away from us, and, although the New Zealanders and the 14th Division operated on the flanks of the 41st Division, the village itself was taken by the 122nd Brigade which had a total casualty roll of 1,200 out of 1,800 who went into action. Once a war journalist published anything, it seemed to be taken in some quarters as being official. Hence the spurious histories.

The story of the second phase of the Battalion's part in the Battle of the Somme has not yet been fully told, for the official records give very little insight into what took place, but it is the personal accounts which interest the reader.

The heroes of the second action were undoubtedly the stretcher bearers and runners. The former had a terribly slow and painful job in getting the badly wounded men back to the dressing stations. Communication trenches were narrow and in many places blown in, whilst the area over which they had to pass was usually under shell fire.

Most of them were tempted to leave the communication trenches and take the easier but more dangerous road over the open, but they invariably respected the wishes of their wounded comrades in keeping to the comparatively safer communication trench. With aching shoulders and extreme fatigue from their exertions these sterling men carried their burdens for miles and hours at a stretch. If the wounded man was suffering much from the jolts which were inevitable under the conditions in which stretchers had to be carried in trenches, they stopped to give him a respite and did their utmost to make his journey as comfortable as possible. How many alive to-day owe their lives to the patience and indomitable courage of the men who wore the red cross brassard! The 12th was well blessed with men of this description whose job was to preserve and not exterminate life.

Lce.-Cpl. W. Aitken will be remembered by many as one of the men who placed the lives of his comrades before his own. On the Somme Aitken set a high standard which was kept up by both him and his colleagues on the medical staff until the end. Like his successor (Cpl. Leonard C. Southall) as the Medical Officer's orderly, Aitken was in every action until wounds or sickness forced his evacuation from the Battalion. Southall was always to be seen working in conjunction with the Doctor at the Regimental Aid Post (a very unsavoury place during the course of a battle), while Aitken had a kind of roving commission between No Man's Land and the Aid Post. Southall richly deserved the Military Medal and bar he was awarded, although in both cases he was recommended for the Distinguished Conduct Medal. Aitken's reward for his courage and devotion to duty was two Courts-Martial and a belated Military Medal. Had Colonel Walmisley-Dresser survived the Somme, many are of the opinion that "Bill" Aitken would have received the most coveted decoration, instead of which he received a Court-Martial for insubordination and refusing to obey an order from a N.C.O. who was not very popular with a great many men of his company. Aitken had occupied a very good position in civilian life, and it was difficult for him to become amenable to Army discipline. He resented bullying in any form, which no doubt accounted for his being placed under arrest after the Somme. To the great joy of those who knew him the charge was dismissed, his ability in legal matters being, no doubt, partly responsible. In the second instance he also got away with it, when he proved to the court that, instead of being a man who had deserted his post to save his own skin, he was in reality performing feats of valour in the front line. His witnesses were officers of a unit of another division who testified to his bravery. This was the stuff of which the Battalion stretcher-bearers and medical staff were made.

The runners' duties were similar to those of the medical staff. Their task, an arduous one, was to keep up communication whatever happened. They wore a red brassard, but unlike the stretcher-bearers carried a rifle. Like the stretcher-bearers, there was very little rest for them in action, for their job took them all over the place until signals were established and even after, when lines were "dissed." While men took shelter in a trench, the runner would have to make his way through a barrage to find a spot, the position of which was very difficult to locate. It was the custom to employ officers' servants and certain picked men who were usually attached to the signal section both on the Battalion and Companies H.Q. staff. Men in the platoons often envied these men for certain privileges they enjoyed in and out of the line, but most will agree that in action their job was no sinecure. Cpl. Jim Rogers, "Scotty" Williams, Lce.-Cpl. G. Huxley and the twin brothers Daw symbolise the type of men who kept Battalion H.Q. apprised of what was happening in front. There are many more whose names are not mentioned, but who carried out their jobs splendidly. "Scotty" did great work at Le Sars during the operations in October and was rewarded later on.

Perhaps the oddest man who went into action was Cpl. W. G. Clayton of the Orderly Room staff. Clayton left Mametz Wood armed with a portable typewriter! The C.O. was an optimist if he thought that Clayton would be able to type out orders in the places which were afterwards occupied at Battalion H.Q. However it had the effect of causing a certain amount of amusement amongst the troops. Armed with his typewriter, Clayton slipped about all over the place in dodging from one position to another. Many times he cursed it and felt like slinging it away, but maybe the fear of the Colonel or the Orderly Room Sergeant made him hang on to it until bravely he brought it out of action without having used it!

Many recommendations for awards were made, and the following subsequently received the Military Medal:—Sergt. G. W. Simpson, Lce.-Sergt. J. Dawe, Lce.-Cpls. E. Morris and R. Collins, and Ptes. E. E. ("Scotty") Williams and F. C. Coomes.

The part taken by the 12th was not so prominent as that undertaken by other units of the Brigade, notably the 11th R.W. Kents, who lost 13 officers and 323 men out of a battle strength of 481 in a tragic advance of about 150 yards, but everything demanded of it was accomplished. Its assistance to the West Kents is acknowledged in their history.

Arriving at Ribemont with a strength of 530, the Battalion was comfortably billeted in barns and parts of farmhouses. It was found that facilities for football were available, and soon men began to forget the horrors of the last month. A few estaminets existed, which helped the men to forget the discomforts they had experienced and afforded them the opportunity of having "sing-songs" in which the average British soldier delighted.

During the next few days reorganization was carried out, and on October 14th a very fine draft of 259 men from the Middlesex Regt. and other battalions of the East Surrey Regt. arrived. On the 15th a draft of 191 men of the 2nd/1st (Q.M.R.) Surrey Yeomanry arrived in charge of 2nd Lieut. J. H. H. Pritchard. This draft, trudging up a hill from Mericourt Station, was of peculiar interest to the men of the 12th who saw them arrive. It was apparent to most that they were unused to "footslogging" and that an infantryman's pack was not the sort of thing they had enlisted for. R.S.M. Wilkinson, as the men paraded before the Orderly Room, soon realised that this was not an ordinary draft of infantrymen. However they were sorted out into four lots (in alphabetical order according to name) and posted to companies. Many of us have often wondered why Capt. Hector S. Walker did not personally conduct this draft to the Battalion. Let him explain in his own words:—

"I took out a draft of about 200 men of the 2nd/1st Surrey Yeomanry to France. On arrival at Oostrahove Camp, Boulogne, between 2.0 and 3.0 a.m. in the early hours. of the morning, I was told by the Commandant that I was a Draft Conducting Officer and would have to return to England by the 9.0 a.m. boat. I bluffed him so completely, although he was a full Colonel, that he sent me to the I.B.D. with the draft.

"After the usual busy time at the Bull Ring at Etaples, I was surprised when the authorities took away the Regimental numbers of the N.C.O.s and men and gave them new numbers and the badges of the East Surrey Regt. I was then sent off with a draft of men, not my own fellows, to Albert and after handing over returned to the 38th I.B.D. To my amazement my fellows had vanished. I went to the Adjutant for information and was told that he had purposely sent me off on a job as he felt sure I would raise the deuce of a row if my fellows were sent off without me. He was right. He then told me that he knew where the men had gone and was doing his best to get me posted to the same unit. Eventually I joined the 12th Battalion and my fellows at Huppy."

Most of the yeomen had been in the Army since the early days of the war, but trench warfare had rendered the cavalry impotent on the Western Front. The Battalion had already seen thousands of cavalrymen with their horses behind the positions at Flers awaiting the opportunity of getting into action, should a break-through occur as a result of the infantry operations. We passed them going into action and re-passed them coming out. It was patent after our experiences near the Butte de Warlencourt that the day was far distant when these splendid horses and men would be able to pit themselves against an enemy who was slowly but surely falling back on fortifications which had been specially prepared for a siege. While the infantryman sympathised to a great extent with the cavalryman that he could not be employed in the rôle for which he had enlisted, the infantryman saw no reason why the cavalryman should not share some of the burdens borne by the men in the trenches. Cavalrymen had already held the trenches in the early days of the war owing to the scarcity of infantry, and it was apparent now that the Higher Command had decreed that a wholesale transfer of cavalrymen into the infantry should take place. Thus it was that fate decided that the 12th Battalion should receive one of the best drafts that was posted to it since it was formed. Before becoming infantrymen the yeomen had been turned into cyclists. When, after a few months, they had settled down to the new conditions, two popular ditties were dedicated to them. They were as follows:—

"There's a rumour going round that the Surrey Yeomanry
Are to have their horses back and once again be cavalry,
You should hear the Yeomen shout, for it fills them with great glee,
For another little ride wouldn't do them any harm."

This was sung to the tune of "Another little drink." The other ran:—

"My horses are over the ocean;
My horses are over the sea;
My horses are over the ocean;
Oh bring back my horses to me."

This we used to refer to as the "Yeoman's Lament."

It was, by the way, one of these yeomen who went up to Q.M.S. Speller—a regular Warrant Officer—with the cheery enquiry—"Are you the Johnny who issues paraffin?" He afterwards obtained a commission, so perhaps his method of address was merely anticipatory.

On the day the Yeomanry draft arrived Lieut.-Col. H. H. Lee, D.S.O. returned and re-assumed command in place of Lieut.-Col. C. H. Kitching who returned to his unit. Before leaving us Colonel Kitching instructed the Adjutant to issue the following Special Order:—

"The 41st Division has now shown its value as a fighting unit and may well be proud of the part it has taken in the Battle of the Somme.

"We must uphold and increase this reputation and that already gained for work, smart turn out, and good behaviour. During the ensuing months every effort should be made to prepare for further active operations against the enemy, in order that all ranks may have full advantage over him when next met with."

(Sgd.) H. C. Reynard.
Lieut. and Adjutant.

On the 16th of October General Lawford distributed medal ribbons to the following:—

Military Cross: 2nd Lieut. W. J. Palk and C.S.M. B. P. Horswell.

D.C.M.: Lce.-Cpl. W. Carter and Pte. A. Giles.

Military Medal: Lce.-Cpl. L. C. Southall and Ptes. P. J. Budd, F. A. Butler, W. Hammond and J. Newton.

After the presentation General Towsey addressed the Battalion and commended it for its good work during the Brigade operations of the previous week.

The time had now arrived for the 12th to turn away from the Somme battlefields. Those who were in action there hoped it would be for ever, but fate decreed that such would not be the case. Eighteen months later it returned and passed over the fields which it had helped to conquer. On this occasion the positions were reversed, but that is another story.

The short but happy rest at Ribemont came to an end on the 17th of October, when we left for the station at Mericourt, where we entrained at noon. This was probably the slowest train journey we had, for it took 12 hours to cover the first 15 miles to Amiens. The old spirit of the Battalion seemed to have revived as the train made for the next detraining place—Oisemont. From here a march of six miles was made to Huppy, a few miles south of Abbeville. Oisemont and Huppy were old-fashioned villages which did not appear to have had a great many troops there before us. Billets were fairly comfortable, and the troops soon settled down to make the best of things. Capt. H. S. Walker and 2nd Lieuts. R. E. Edwards and O. E. Woollard of the Surrey Yeomanry joined the Battalion at Huppy, while Colonel Lee assumed command of the Brigade in the absence of General Towsey, Major Blakeney taking over temporary command of the Battalion.

Capt. Hector Walker recalls his first interview with Colonel Lee. Asked by the Colonel what active service he had had, he replied, "None, Sir." The Colonel then told him that he could not put him in command of a company. Capt. Walker assured the Colonel that he quite understood the position and that until he had been in action he had no desire to command even a section, as he had no idea which way he would go or what he would do. Since the day the war broke out he had been waiting, and, as he says, "At long last I had to face the plunge—I never did like cold water." How well Capt. Walker succeeded is recorded in subsequent chapters of this history.

CHAPTER V.

20th October to 31st December, 1916.

The Battalion returns from the Somme to Belgium—Takes over the trenches at St. Eloi—Life in the trenches and at Reninghelst.

ON October 20th the Battalion left Huppy for Pont Rémy Station, where it entrained. As the train pursued its leisurely way, everyone appeared to be in the best of spirits.

Although, as usual, our destination was secret, we felt that, after the gruelling times experienced during the previous month, and as so many new men had joined the Battalion, we were bound for a quiet sector. This proved to be correct. At 10.0 p.m. on the 21st, we reached Godewaersvelde; it had taken us a day and a half to cover the eighty or so miles. So here we were back again in the village where we detrained after our first journey on the Western Front! Much had happened even in the short space of those five months. Many thought we should return to "Plug Street," but that was not to be. Guides met the Battalion and led the way to the billeting area at Eecke, and by 2.0 a.m. it was reported that the companies were settled in. The billets were not too good, if the experiences of Battalion H.Q. staff is an index. Some of them were put into a cowshed where their sleep was disturbed by certain members of the bovine species who would persist in sticking their heads through a partition and showing some resentment to their next door neighbours.

Another move was made on the 24th, when we marched back to Godewaersvelde. Billets were scarce in this area and only two companies could be accommodated there: later on billets were found for C and D companies at Fontaines at the foot of the Mont des Cats. On the 25th the Battalion moved on to the village of Reninghelst and at mid-day was settled in Ontario Camp, the strength being forty-six officers and 1,014 other ranks.

The name Reninghelst will live long in the memory of those of us who had the good fortune to spend many happy days there while resting from the line for months during 1916 and 1917. Just above the huts rose a kind of Heath Robinson windmill, top-heavy and askew, with a few houses forming the hamlet of Zevecoten. This mill and a similar one on the top of the Scherpenberg near Kemmel were landmarks visible from afar. They were built of wooden storeys and looked as if they had been piled up carelessly by some freakish baby giant for amusement, and why they never fell over when the wind blew was a mystery. Alas! both were levelled to the earth in the furious fighting of the spring of 1918 in this area. We often referred to Reninghelst as a home from home, because everything was done by the staff of the 41st Division to make it a place where men could forget the worry and troubles of the trenches for at least two weeks in every month. The Battalion was accommodated in huts, which, although barely furnished, afforded fairly decent shelter from the elements. During wet weather the deep mud certainly caused no little inconvenience, but there were few places in Belgium where troops were billeted that mud did not prevail. When the Battalion arrived, the village boasted a Y.M.C.A. and an Expeditionary Force Canteen. Within a short space of time a Divisional Canteen, Supper Bar and Theatre had arisen next to the Divisional Headquarters. It was quite a treat to go into the supper bar and be served with a tasty dish by some of the neat Belgian girls who were employed there as waitresses. Prices were moderate, and the atmosphere was that of a restaurant in England. In the canteen English beer was sold, thereby taking away some of the custom from the few estaminets, including the "Swan," where the famous "Emma" dispensed hospitality. The theatre became the home of our well known Divisional concert party, the "Crumps," and some of the latest films from England were also shown there. The "Crumps" party was formed of members of the 41st Division and had some notable artists amongst them. How many laughs we got from Lce.-Cpl. O. Rae who presented Harry Tate's "Motoring" sketch. The "Drums of Oude," played by the party many times, gave an idea how versatile they could be. Pte. Purkiss of the R.A.M.C., better known to us as "Vera de Vierstraat," was so realistic in his rôle as the "lady" of the party that some Americans who saw him towards the end of the war would not believe that he was a man. Other members of the party were Captains A. H. Reid and Eric White, Cpl. Holden, Lieut. D'Arcy, Lce.-Cpl. Coffin, Gunner Burgess, Pte. McGruer, Lce.-Cpl. Edelston, Pte. Platt, Lce.-Cpl. Trethewey and Pte. Stone. The writer has before him a copy of the "Crumps" Play Pictorial, which is stated to be the pioneer "Play Pictorial" of just-behind-the-Front area. In it are given pictures of the members of the party and scenes from their shows. In the first picture Lce.-Cpl. O. Rae is seen "telling the tale" to Capt. Reid, and this is followed by "Glad Eyes," in which several members of the party are ogling "Vera de Vierstraat." Scenes from "A Seaside Burlesque," show Edleston, Purkiss, Stone and Lieut. D'Arcy in typical moods, while four pages are devoted to scenes from the dramatic Indian episode, "The Drums of Oude," in which the costumes and scenery would do credit to any West End theatre. Finally we see Holden, Rae (Major Harry Tate), Lieut. D'Arcy, Stone, and Capt. Reid (Pte. Bairnsfather) in scenes from the screamingly funny farce, "On the Staff," or "How Temporary-Major Harry Tate Won the D.S.O." The Bus House sector, occupied by the "Norty Worst Division," and the "Mud Patch," are given great prominence in a picture which shows a Hun spy captured by the Major to win him the D.S.O.

In addition to the "Crumps" another party was, at the instigation of Padre Hilditch, formed in the 122nd Brigade. The organiser was "Scotty" Williams, who before enlistment had been a music hall artist. "Scotty" could have demanded a place at any time in the "Crumps," but he preferred to stick to his comrades in the Battalion, for the Divisional party had a "cushy" job, never going into the line at all. His "Dickybirds" used to perform in the Y.M.C.A. Their opening chorus:

"The Dickybirds are we, ha! ha!
As you can plainly see, ha! ha!
We'll pass our time in fun and jollity,
Song and dance and gay frivolity," etc.

was a good introduction to some very fine performances. "Scotty" and his party actually produced a pantomime, "Cinderella," in December, 1916. Pte. W. R. Lallow assisted "Scotty" very considerably in the running of his party, as also did many men in other units of the Brigade. Len Young, Morice Hurling, Sergt. Hyland and Q.M.S. Germer, as members of the party from other battalions will be remembered by those who had the pleasure of being entertained by them. Other men from the Battalion such as Giles and MacKriell, gave their services to the "Dickybirds." "Scotty" did not confine his activities to the Brigade party, but organised concerts in the Battalion itself. Giles was one of his protégés, as also was Cpl. Harry Tarry, of the Signals. "Nelly from Abergelly" was Harry's favourite song, which he sang in his own peculiar cockney manner. It was a sad blow, not only to his comrades, but the Brigade as a whole, when "Scotty" Williams made the supreme sacrifice in March, 1918. General Towsey was grieved when he heard of the death of one whom he considered was of even greater value to the Brigade out of the line than in. Other talent was discovered later, and a full concert party from the Battalion was in existence near the end of the war, but without "Scotty's" influence and guidance it did not appear to reach the high standard he had set. One of our entertainers, Cpl. A. Brest, afterwards became a film star under the name of George K. Arthur, his best known film being "Kipps." Travelling concert parties used to give performances in the Y.M.C.A. hut; on one occasion Lena Ashwell's party entertained there. The band of the Royal Engineers also gave a concert there soon after the Battalion's arrival.

We should mention too that many friends in Blighty did their best to send comforts to the troops. For instance, Mr. Jimmy Moran, manager of the Palladium, sent over 100,000 cigarettes to the Battalion by consignments, having raised a fund for this purpose from patrons of that theatre.

Training began again on the day after we arrived in Ontario Camp. The new small box respirator was taking the place of the old P.H. helmet, and so one of the first things done was to practise the men in the use of it. Although at first it was not looked upon with favour by the troops, it was soon realised that it was a great improvement on the P.H.

It was the usual practice, when units joined an army, that the Army Commander should make a point of inspecting them as soon as he could after their arrival in his sector. Accordingly, on the 27th of October, the Battalion was paraded before General Sir Herbert C. O. Plumer, G.C.M.G., K.C.B., Commander of the Second Army, and in the afternoon the General inspected the camp. In recalling this parade, Capt. H. S. Walker writes:—

"One of my earliest impressions of General Plumer was the inspection by him at Reninghelst. The Battalion was paraded in the mud, which came up to one's putties in places. He rode up followed by his glittering staff. I thought to myself that he would remain mounted and that we would have to march or rather wallow past him. To my amazement he dismounted, as did his staff, and he walked up and down the lines of men, inspecting them by companies. He spoke to a number of the men and I noticed that the mud was well over his spurs. This made a great impression on me when I realised that he could no doubt have been quietly ensconced in his club at home, telling the members how to run the war. Instead, here he was, hard at it and letting the men down as lightly as he could. How I admired him!"

The history of the 12th Battalion is intimately associated with the Second British Army and its Commander, and the old gentleman with the monocle became a familiar figure to us all. Other army commanders under whom we served will be forgotten, but "Plum," as we knew him, will not. There is no doubt that he was a painstaking and very efficient man at his job, surrounded by an efficient staff, notable amongst whom was his Chief of Staff, General Harington. Schools of all sorts were organised throughout his command, and he saw to it that the men were well fed and that the catering was the best that could be provided on active service. He realised the capabilities of the troops under his command and believed in getting men away from the scenes of action as soon as it was possible to relieve them. Plumer was not the sort of general to waste his man power, if it could possibly be avoided. The successful Battle of Messines is proof of this. Lord Plumer (as he afterwards became) remained silent to the end regarding the Third Battle of Ypres. Whether we shall ever get his views on the continuance of the battle after the rain of July, 1917, made the conditions so abominable, is questionable. In some quarters it was stated that he was against it, but Mr. Duff Cooper, in writing from Earl Haig's diaries, asserts the contrary. Sir Philip Gibbs writes of him:—

"As there are exceptions to every rule, so harsh criticism of our High Command (he speaks elsewhere with much truth of some officers on the staffs 'who had the brains of canaries and the manners of Potsdam') must be modified in favour of the generalship and organization of the Second Army, which was of rare efficiency. . . . The staff work was as good in detail as any machinery of war may be, and the tactical direction of the Second Army battles was not slipshod or haphazard, as so many others."

He writes too of the

"Abominable mismanagement of other troops, the contrast being visible to every battalion officer and even to the private soldier."

Altogether the 12th East Surreys were very fortunate in being usually under the command of this fine, humane, efficient soldier, who was one of the very few army commanders not a cavalryman, and unquestionably far the most successful general on the Western Front. Was this a mere coincidence?

Three of us were able to be present at Whitsun, 1933, when in the English Church at Ypres the Bishop of London dedicated a banner and brass to his illustrious memory.

The 41st Division had by now taken over the line from the 4th Australian Division. Accordingly, orders were issued on the 28th of October for the Twelfth to relieve the 20th Battalion Durham Light Infantry in the trenches on the following day. Now was to begin a trek up to the line which was to be repeated very many times during the next six months. Men became so used to it that they could almost do the journey blind-fold. So for the first time let us make the journey.

Companies paraded outside the huts at Ontario Camp and moved off at intervals soon after 10.0 a.m. The route taken was through the village of Ouderdom, along the road to Hallebast Corner into Dickebusch, passing just before the entrance to the village a dummy house made of canvas, inside which was a huge howitzer. Up to this point hutments and transport lines were to be seen on either side of the road; there were also a few farmhouses where eggs and chips could be procured for a few francs. Dickebusch was at this time a fairly large village with a few houses still fit for habitation, and also boasted a Y.M.C.A. Brigade Headquarters were established near by at Burgomaster's Farm. Along the road on either side of the village camouflage netting was erected to obscure the enemy's vision, while here and there a few tall trees still remained intact.

The column then proceeded along the side of Dickebusch Church, which had been badly battered by the Germans. From the church the fields were in a swampy condition and to overcome this a duckboard track had been made leading towards Ridge Wood, where guides met the companies and led the way across the "banana-skins," as the troops nickname the duckboards from their slippery nature. Reaching Ridge Wood, platoons were broken up into small parties, as the short road to the Brasserie of Elzenwalle was under direct observation from the enemy on the Messines Ridge. A Y.M.C.A. was established in Ridge Wood, and not far away from this stood a farmhouse which was still occupied by civilians. From the Brasserie, which was the Regimental Aid Post, on the south side of Elzenwalle Château, another duckboard track led along by a hedge to Dead Dog Farm, where Battalion Headquarters were situated. The Headquarters consisted of about half a dozen fairly large sandbagged dugouts built above the ground and obscured from the view of the enemy by a few shattered trees. A short trench leading off from the main communication trench gave it the appearance of a place which was intended for cover, should the Boche be fortunate enough to discover that it was a centre of great activity. Dead Dog Farm may be said to have been the parting of the ways of many sections of the Battalion. Some little distance away on the left was an old farm in which the reserve company was accommodated, the track to which ran alongside a stream or "beek." Out of it on the right a sap led to the H.Q. Officers' Mess and cookhouse, and also a dugout which was used as a canteen and later on as a drying room. Further along was Battalion H.Q. cookhouse, and a short distance from here the Reserve Farm, already referred to. The front and support line companies would then proceed along a communication trench, known as "P and O," and reach "Suicide Bridge" where a few planks crossed the Diependaalbeek at its junction with the Bollardbeek. From here the last few hundred yards led through the smashed trees and fetid squalor of Bois Confluent, and you were in the front line. The portion occupied by the Battalion was rather less than half a mile, reaching from the top of "P and O" Trench to about 200 yards from the cross roads where the hamlet of St. Eloi used to stand. On the map Belgium 28 (1/20,000) S.W. it was from 0.7.b.5.9 to 0.2.c.6.8. The general reader must realise that, as we always saw the country from ground level, we had a most imperfect knowledge of the landscape, e.g. we should never have known that any roads existed, if our maps had not shown them. Imagine the field of vision of a terrier; that was ours. Just beyond our junction with the unit on our left at the top of "Queen Victoria Street" was the famous "Mound." Here in the spring, when the Canadians had held the sector, four mines had been blown. These four craters were held by the enemy and the lips of the craters formed his front line. Only forty yards at this point separated the combatants, and a good bomber could lob a Mills bomb into the craters. This sector was usually held by the 18th K.R.R.s, and several of our officers (among them the writer) who were lent for two months to that battalion, remember the spot well—distinctly "unhealthy."

On our extreme left, facing "Crater Lane," was a short sap connecting up with a fifth abandoned Mine Crater in the middle of No Man's Land, held by a few men with a Lewis-gun or two—in winter a foul midden with reeking slimy sides round a deep pool of yellow mud some 25 feet in diameter. From the support line by Queen Victoria Street a sap led to some tunnels about 60 feet from the surface, where, in the mephitic filth and gloom, Canadian Engineers were burrowing under the German lines in preparation for the great explosion of the following summer. The entrance was heavily camouflaged. This shaft was occasionally used as a refuge in very hot bursts of shelling.

The joke about "P and O" Trench was that it was in the winter usually under water, and this, as often as not, overflowed into the support trenches. Some of us thought that its name implied that it was intended for ships. This was owing to the fact that the Diependaalbeek traversed it, and this brook often overflowed in winter when the whole area was waterlogged. The greatest part of the country here was indeed a swamp. Four miles away to the north appeared the shattered tower of the Cathedral in the martyred city of Ypres.

The relief was reported complete by 4.30 p.m., sentry posts fixed, stores and equipment taken over from the "Bull Durhams," and weary men began to try to "kip down" as comfortably as circumstances would permit. But rest was not yet. Ration parties had to be found, water pumped out of the trenches, working parties detailed to carry out the hundred and one tasks that went on unceasingly. "Stand To" meant that everyone for about twenty minutes before dark had to be on the alert ready to repel an enemy attack in case one might materialise. Dusk fell, and "Stand Down" was passed along: then a little party stumbled along the tumbledown sap leading to the Crater. Separated from their comrades, these sterling fellows took their lives in

WHITE CHATEAU, 1917 (German Official Photograph)

VOORMEZEELE (MAIN STREET), 1916

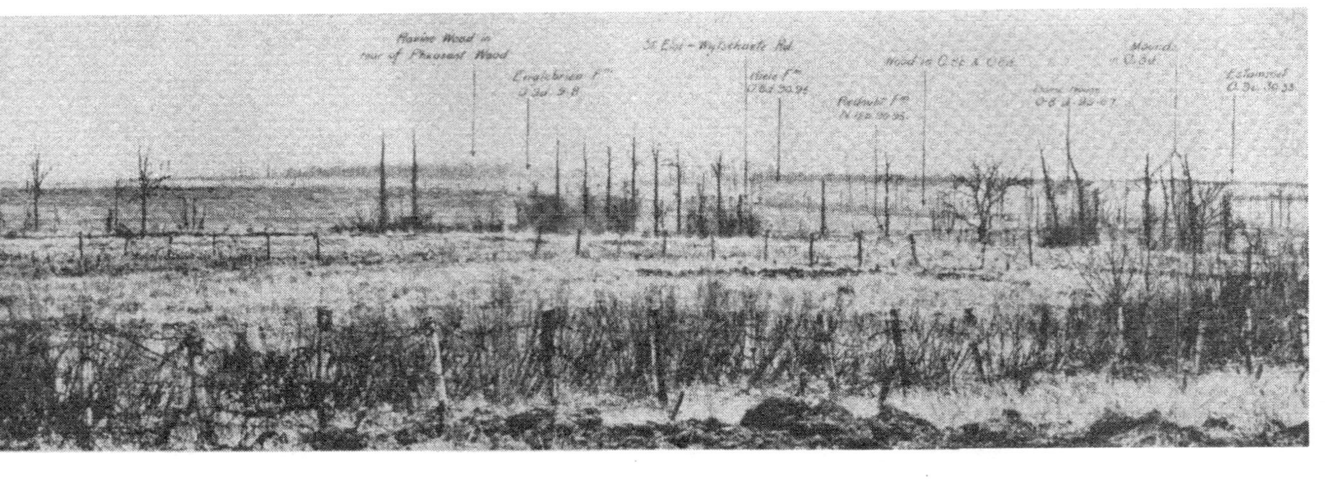

VIEW OF THE FRONT FROM ST. ELOI.

their hands every time they made this journey. The Crater, which was in a very bad condition when the Battalion arrived, had to be drained, built up, and terraced under R.E. supervision. It was only 50 yards from the enemy, and when the Germans baled their trenches out, the water used to run into the Crater to the intense discomfort of the occupants. Underground mining operations were being carried out by both sides, and there was no knowing when the earth would open and entomb the troops in the vicinity. In point of fact a few explosions occurred during the stay at St. Eloi. A small "camouflet" or mine was blown in the tunnels to give us an idea of what was likely to happen later on. Inside the mine-workings men toiled day and night excavating chambers which were afterwards filled with high explosive, and listening apparatus was used below by the engineers to enable them to locate where the enemy was sapping. In some parts the Germans actually broke into our chambers and fired on the sappers, and this necessitated the chamber being sealed up again with the aid of a bangalore torpedo. For about ten miles from Hill 60 to Messines, where nineteen large mines were later to be blown, this sort of warfare was waged during 1915 and 1916. With the thoughts of what might happen below them and the extreme discomfort of the effects of the elements on top, not to mention the danger from shell and rifle-fire, the men in the Crater and the front line stood on guard for a week at a stretch for very many periods before the Battle of Messines. The winter of 1916 was a hard one, and frost-bite, "trench feet" and trench fever took heavy toll of the strength of the Battalion. Whale oil had to be rubbed into the feet, and "gumboots thigh" were used with socks which had to be changed or dried two or three times a day. It was bad enough at Battalion H.Q., where charcoal and coke fires could be kept going in the dugouts, but to the men nearest the enemy, life was at times almost intolerable. One cannot speak too highly of those who braved all these hardships so that victory might be achieved. This is what holding the line at St. Eloi meant to the men of the 12th Battalion during a period which is described in the historical records as being a fairly quiet one.

Nightly, whilst the Battalion was in the line, the transports left Reninghelst and made their way along the Vierstraat Road to the Brasserie with rations and other supplies. The journey was not an easy one, for the road was "rocky" and the enemy active. The quartermaster-sergeants would often report to their company headquarters in a breathless state after having an uneasy and hectic journey on the way up. One N.C.O. and old warrior, who at times reported to Battalion H.Q., could tell hair-raising stories of shells exploding under the belly of his horse. While we laughed at his exaggeration we had cause to know that the missiles used to land in most uncomfortable fashion along the Road. The Brigade Transport was in charge of Capt. E. V. Whiteway, of the 12th, who had been responsible for organising the Battalion transport before taking over that of the Brigade. At the time of which we are speaking the duties of Battalion Transport Officer devolved upon Lieut. R. A. V. Brearey, who was still in his teens. It was usually arranged for the Transport Officer and Quartermaster to take turns in bringing rations up. In the absence of the Transport Officer Sergt. G. Nuttman used to take charge of the Transport, and R.Q.M.S. N. Speller deputised for the Quartermaster. Whatever happened, the rations always arrived. Even in the gruelling days of 1918, as we shall see later, the Transport was not known to fail. It would be interesting to know the total number of miles travelled by the quartermasters in bringing up rations and returning again to Reninghelst, some six miles away.

From the Brasserie of course all stores had to be humped by the working parties from the reserve and support companies, and this job would take many hours of the dark. Sleep had to be snatched at any odd hours of the day or night.

Pte. G. R. Daniels has an amusing story of one such party.

"A lot of us had the job of ration-carrying from the dump at the Brasserie, while Jerry was sending over a few shells causing some casualties. Near by we came across a smashed up waggon and some rations belonging to the artillery. We had the fags, dumped the tobacco and carried away what we thought was a jar of rum in a long box. We hid this and later went to fetch it, thinking what a good time we should have. Imagine our feelings when we opened the box and discovered a consignment of pickled walnuts!"

It should never be forgotten that both the severity and the continuousness of the strain in the European areas of the Great War were such as had never been experienced before. In the wars of previous centuries campaigning was almost limited to the summer: from October to April armies retired into winter quarters. For the combatant troops in the Great War there was no respite from one year's end to another. The only chance of getting away from the tension of active service was to fall sick or be wounded, which explains the envy of any man lucky enough to get a "Blighty," i.e. a wound not too severe but serious enough to send a man home to England for a time. Remember too the nervous strain caused by the diabolical inventions of modern science, poison-gas, enormous shells fired from twenty miles away that on explosion made holes large enough to bury a house in, liquid-flame and phosphorus, and, most dreadful of all, especially as the war drew to its close, the constant night-bombing by aeroplanes, when men exhausted by their spells in the trenches could get no sleep, even in rest-camp, because of the terror by night, or else were helplessly mangled and butchered as they lay.

At the time the Battalion first entered the trenches at St. Eloi, Colonel Lee was still acting Brigadier and Major Blakeney was in command of the Battalion. Capt. H. C. Reynard was Adjutant, Lieut. D. Walker, Signalling Officer, and Lieut. G. P. G. Reah, Intelligence Officer, though some months later he was appointed I.O. of Brigade.

On the 1st of November the enemy shelled Bois Confluent, killing Ptes. W. H. Norman and W. G. Ellis, besides wounding six other men. Norman was one of the Surrey Yeomanry draft which had recently joined.

In the morning of November 3rd, the 20th D.L.I. arrived to take over. The companies of the 12th gradually handed over positions and made their way from the trenches across the duckboard track to Dickebusch. Thence the route via Millekappelleken Farm—Ouderdom—Reninghelst, back to Ontario Camp was followed. No casualties were suffered on relief; there was, however, an accident which might have had serious consequences. On the way back, Major Blakeney was thrown from his horse and sustained injuries to his head. He was taken to hospital, and Capt. W. Hagen, who had just returned from leave to England, took over temporary command of the Battalion. Major Blakeney recovered from his injuries and returned to the Battalion some time later.

Kit and rifle inspections were carried out on the 4th and also training in the use of the small box respirator. On the following day most of the Battalion was on working parties, and on the 8th the same sort of activity prevailed. It would be idle to suggest that the men welcomed these working parties. In the line or out they were never free from them. If the Royal Engineers wanted some trenches dug, earthworks made or material carried, they sent for the infantry. If the T.M. artillery wanted "toffee apples" carried to their mortars in the line, again the infantry was pressed into service. Loading parties for the A.S.C. and jobs connected with other corps were always pushed on to the P.B.I. Next to the mule the infantryman was the beast of of burden on the Western Front. It was not an uncommon spectacle on the Somme and in the region of the Ypres Salient to see the mules loaded up with panniers of shells followed by parties of infantry carrying all sorts of material for the trenches. No wonder that the infantryman groused, for as the worst paid man in the army he undertook the most hazardous job and did all the dirty work that was going. His pet aversion was the Royal Engineers. If the sappers who used to lead parties to the different tasks could have heard half of what the infantrymen thought of them, they would have wished for the earth to open up and swallow them. Yet, poor chaps, they were only acting on orders from their superiors. One fatigue, however, was welcomed with joy. Now and then a large party was sent to the Cornwall R.E. workshops at Abeele, some ten miles off. It was a real holiday. The lucky men travelled to and fro by lorry, and at Abeele the work, usually some quite pleasant job, such as nailing duckboards together, was deliberately made as light as possible, while the officer in charge could sit by a blazing fire in the officers' mess or get a luxurious deep hot bath by himself instead of squatting in a brewery tub with twenty others round him. The men, too, were often supplied with small luxuries for their meals. But these glimpses into the sappers' paradise were rare.

Bathing was carried out at the Divisional Baths on the 6th of November, and in the afternoon of the same day men had to go through gas chambers with their small box respirators on to test them against phosgene and other gas. On many occasions a test of this description had to be carried out, the less deadly lachrymatory gas being used for the purpose.

During this period reference is made in the War Diary to Salvage. The economy wave was sweeping France about this time and the work of the Divisional Salvage Corps was beginning to make itself felt by the numerous dumps of all sorts of material which were springing up near the trenches. Such slogans as: "What have you salved to-day?" and "Salve shells and save shipping" began to appear on the walls of some of the houses in Dickebusch, while in the trenches sandbags were hung up at intervals, with the motto: "Pick it up, it may come in handy."

On the 9th, the Battalion paraded before Colonel Lee, who had returned to the command, and proceeded by the usual route to relieve the 20th D.L.I. with a trench strength of 756. The trenches were still in a very bad state, and Capt. F. C. Chatt, of the Durhams, was attached to the Battalion as Drainage Officer. The work of pumping the water out of the trenches and repairing them began without delay, the enemy remaining fairly quiet until the evening, when they shelled Bois Confluent without causing any casualties. It must be remembered that the enemy were in possession of the Messines Ridge, a low elevation some ten miles long, from which the ground sloped gradually westwards. Two results followed. First, water always flowed down in our direction, and our trenches assumed during the winter the function of dykes, for the underclay prevented proper drainage. Owing, too, to the sopped ground it was useless to dig deeply, and the so-called "trenches" were really, in the main, alleys between walls of sandbags. These were constantly collapsing of course, bulging in all directions; often it was impossible to pass along without exposing head and shoulders or more, and this was the Boche sniper's chance. Advantage was taken of the night to repair these and other weak spots, so that men got no rest by day or night. It was pitiful to see men who had dropped off by day into the sleep of exhaustion on the crazy duckboards, when in a few minutes a N.C.O. would come along and shake them, shouting, "Come on, my lad, you're wanted for a fatigue."

Secondly, the enemy had an uninterrupted view over our positions. When, in the following June, we had stormed the ridge, it was amazing to look over this expanse of country, where every trench could be plainly seen. The greatest marvel of all was that reliefs were always conducted by day and must have been plainly visible to the Hun, yet he never shelled the crowded communication trenches. The only explanation is the preponderance of our gun power, the Germans well knowing that any such shelling would incur a four-fold retaliation.

The situation remained quiet on the 10th until 2.0 p.m., when our own trench mortars in Bois Confluent bombarded the enemy's front line under cover of artillery fire. This caused some retaliation, but fortunately no casualties resulted. As the weather was fine, advantage was taken of it to continue drainage work.

The 11th of November, 1916, marks a tragedy in the history of the Battalion. The day had been quiet and everyone had prepared for a restful night, when suddenly the stillness was disturbed by bombing and machine-gun fire. No orders out of the ordinary appeared to have been issued from Battalion H.Q., and the Adjutant, who was in the H.Q. dugout at Dead Dog Farm at the time, was at a loss to understand what was taking place. Some little time later Sergt. C. Turner, of B Company, entered H.Q. dugout and gave a report of what had happened. Sergt. Turner stated that at 10.0 p.m. Acting Capt. C. O. Slacke, O.C., B Company, who had recently returned from leave, had taken out a patrol consisting of 2nd Lieut. J. F. Walton and four others to reconnoitre the enemy wire on the left of No. 1 Crater. On arriving at the wire the patrol was heavily bombed and fired on with machine-guns, as a result of which one man was wounded. Stretcher-bearers were sent for, and on their arrival the party was again fired on by machine-guns, sustaining more casualties and being dispersed. In consequence, Capt. Slacke was missing, believed wounded, 2nd Lieut. Walton was wounded and missing, and four other ranks, including Ptes. Budd and Brenton, stretcher-bearers, were missing. The matter was reported to the Colonel, who at once began to investigate. Patrols went out to try to locate the bodies without success. Pte. J. Kirk, who was in the front line at the time, states that he vividly remembers the figure of Capt. Slacke looming over his sentry post and calling out the pass-words, "Is Mrs. May in?" and then in the next breath, "For God's sake get the stretcher-bearers!" He then went back into No Man's Land and never returned. From the account of one of the survivors it appears that, when 2nd Lieut. Walton was wounded, Sergt. T. G. Mackenzie, who was with the patrol, got the assistance of Lce.-Cpl. A. Kitchen and Pte. T. J. Young in order to bring him in. It was then discovered that Capt. Slacke was also wounded. This little party endeavoured to get both the officers back, but it was found that 2nd Lieut. Walton was again wounded (this time mortally) and that Capt. Slacke had disappeared. Two of the men were known to have been killed. The firing became such that Mackenzie and his gallant assistants had to get back to the trench. The next day instructions were issued to the observation posts in the sector to scan No Man's Land thoroughly for any vestige of the bodies. No trace was ever found of them. It sometimes happened that, when men were missing on patrols and captured by the enemy, he exhibited a board in his front line trench giving us details. It did not happen on this occasion, neither were any of the missing reported as prisoners of war. In Capt. Slacke's case it was presumed that he fell into a large shell hole and was drowned. Any doubt that may have existed as to the fate of the missing on this occasion can soon be satisfied if one looks on the panels of the Menin Gate. For their services, Sergt. Mackenzie, Lce.-Cpl. Kitchen and Pte. Young were subsequently awarded the Military Medal. The loss of both the officers was serious to B Company, as they were the senior company officers and generally popular. The command of the company temporarily passed to 2nd Lieut. J. Baker.

The enemy showed more activity on the 12th, his snipers getting busy about No. 1 Crater and enfilading a portion of the front line trench from the left. In consequence A Company suffered the loss of a good N.C.O., Lce.-Sergt. W. J. Hemmings, who was killed. The Boche also turned his attention to the Reserve Farm, where C Company was stationed, and for a time he made things very uncomfortable there. Pte. A. J. Mark, another of the recently joined Surrey Yeomanry draft, was killed during the bombardment.

By this time the 41st Divisional Artillery had taken over positions, and it is recorded that on the 13th the artillery registered on the enemy lines in front of No. 1 Crater and that several shells were falling short close to our front line. This was a common complaint of the Battalion at St. Eloi. There was a Belgian Battery too which used to fire over us; it was known to fire short on a few occasions, and whenever anything went wrong with the shooting of the artillery, it was always put down to this unfortunate battery and even ascribed to treachery. Experience taught us later that with the daring shoots and the close barrages carried out by the artillery it did not matter whether it was the British, French or Belgian batteries firing; "shorts" were inevitable. It is impossible to compute the number of our men who were killed by their own artillery, but there is not much doubt that there were many. The artillery worked to a schedule, as also did the infantry. Whereas the former usually remained in their gun pits until the close of an action, the latter had often to follow up a fleeing enemy before he was able to gain the shelter of new positions. In the heat of action there was not the time to consult schedules and watches, and consequently times out of number we went through our own barrages. In action we came to expect this state of affairs, but in trench warfare we considered that artillery fire should have been so organised and controlled as to eliminate danger of casualties occurring from it.

The Ypres Salient was a very definite one. Standing in the trenches at night, one could watch the Verey lights going up at intervals in almost a complete circle, while the trenches themselves serpentined in a most irregular manner. Thus British batteries were at times actually in rear of the enemy, and theirs in rear of ours, so that what we took to be "shorts" from our guns might well be from the Germans'.

On the 13th the order "Gas Alert" was given. At Headquarters and other parts of the sector weather-vanes were erected in order to determine the direction of the wind. To be successful, a gas attack had to be launched while the wind was in a favourable quarter towards the objective. In the line and even out a strict watch was kept on the direction of the wind, and precautions taken accordingly. A situation report had to be rendered to Battalion Orderly Room at certain intervals daily, in which the direction of the wind had to be stated, and, if it was in an unfavourable position, the words "Wind dangerous, Gas Alert on" were usually added. The "Gas Alert" order often remained on for days at a stretch; on this occasion it lasted for two days, extending to the 14th.

The Battalion was employed on fatigues most of the next rest period, with bathing and a little company work thrown in. The baths were situated in a brewery in Reninghelst and were gladly welcomed after a tour of the trenches. The men shed their underclothing and all went naked into a large shed full of open brewing-tubs, where each man could get a hot bath; some got just a hot shower under pipes pierced with holes. The steam was thick on these occasions. Then out at a door opposite the entrance into another shed, where fresh underclothing was supplied, and it may be imagined that large men often got very shrunken garments. The clothing they had abandoned was all put into huge boilers where it was subjected to very high steam pressure, by which all lice and other live stock were supposed to be killed, though many a louse seemed to enjoy the experience and come up to scratch again with a healthier appetite than ever. The army term for this universal pest of war was a "chat": thus, if you saw a row of men in a hut "chatting," that did not mean light conversation, but that they had got their shirts off and were hunting for lice. The clothing which had been "deloused" was then washed and dried and served out to another batch of men. Officers got their laundry done at the various Belgian farms.

Lieut.-Genl. Sir T. L. N. Morland, K.C.B., D.S.O., commanding the X Corps, presented medal ribbons to the following on the 20th:—

Military Cross: Lieut. H. S. Openshaw.

Military Medal: Sergt. G. W. Simpson, Lce.-Sergt. J. Dawe, Lce.-Cpl. E. Morris and Ptes. F. C. Coomes and E. E. ("Scotty") Williams.

Lieut. Openshaw had just returned from leave and assumed command of B Company: his work in the Battalion was for some time associated with the Lewis-gun Section. After the war he went to the Far East and was met at Shanghai in 1929 by Q.M.S. Speller. Sergt. George Simpson received his decoration for helping to dig out men who had been buried by shell-fire on the Somme; eventually he became C.S.M. of A Company. Lce.-Sergt. Dawe was a most dependable man in the Lewis-gunners. Coomes was one of the hard-worked stretcher-bearers who carried on this work from the time the Battalion went out until he was demobilised. "Scotty" Williams well merited his decoration for his work as a runner. Lce.-Cpl. E. Morris, or "Ted," as he was known amongst his friends in the Signal Section, was an expert linesman, often much to his regret. Ted's job was to find breaks in the line whenever they occurred, and it took him all over the trench system at all times of the day and night. At St. Eloi he was out in all sorts of weather for hours at a time, testing and trying to find where the line had gone "dis." Often he would do the necessary repair and think his day's work was done, only to find on his return to the Signal H.Q. that another break had taken place somewhere else, and cursing the whole German army he would go out again to mend the other break when he found it. In the middle of the night he was often roused to do a job of this kind. Ted thought that, because he was so much in demand, he must have been the only linesman in the British army. Other linesmen, such as R. Scott, may have become famous later, when Ted found there was such a corps as the Royal Engineers willing to avail itself of his services, but, while he remained, Morris was unrivalled at his job.

Owing to the conditions in the trenches at St. Eloi the idea of more frequent reliefs was devised, and accordingly the next tour in the line lasted only from the 23rd to the 28th, when the trenches were handed over to the care of the Durhams. It was a nasty day for marching, but an ideal day for relieving, as a fog descended and covered any movement. It was not a happy experience groping across the duckboard track to Dickebusch, but to know that the slight comforts of Ontario Camp awaited us at the end of the journey spurred us on.

During the month the casualties had been 1 officer and 7 other ranks killed; 13 wounded; and 1 officer and 4 other ranks missing. 2nd Lieuts. A. Jennings and C. J. F. Beauchamp had been evacuated sick. In addition to those already mentioned Cpl. W. Day and Pte. H. Scott died of wounds on the 15th and 26th respectively. The strength of the Battalion at the end of the month was 38 officers and 997 other ranks. We should remember that the "Trench or Ration strength" was always from

100 to 200 less, as men were on leave, in hospital, on Command, at Army and Divisional Training Schools, and the like.

December opened with the Shiny Twelfth training at Reninghelst. Boxing was always fostered as a sport in the Battalion, and some of the men were adepts at the art. The recent arrival of Pte. Johnny Creamer from the 1st Battalion had caused a stir amongst the boxing fraternity. Some of the old 1st Battalion men now serving with the 12th considered that Johnny ought to be fixed up with somebody, as he had a good reputation in India. But who was there capable of giving him a good fight? The original members of the 12th seized upon Joe Mills of the Transport, who they knew was bound to put up a good show. The opportunity came when on the 2nd of December a tournament was organised in the afternoon. The principal bout, Creamer v. Mills, drew a large growd of all ranks on the parade ground in front of the Orderly Room at Ontario Camp, where the ring was arranged. Speculation on the fight raged furiously. The Transport men were with Joe Mills to a man, while Creamer was well supported by his friends of the 1st Battalion. The fight went the full number of rounds scheduled, much to the annoyance of Creamer's supporters, who reckoned on his knocking Mills out. There was not much doubt that Creamer was the better boxer, but Joe Mills was as hard as nails. He drew some laughter from the crowd as he put his chin forward for Creamer to hit; Creamer struck, and struck hard, but Mills simply shook his head.

Most of us can still recall many incidents of a humorous nature which occurred during our occupation of Reninghelst. Here is one sent in by Q.M.S. Speller, dealing with our famous Sergeant Shoemaker:—

"Sergt. Ernie Noad was perhaps our 'queerest awk.' He confessed to having tried everything once and had travelled the world in the trying. A genius with a pack of cards, an erstwhile diamond dealer (for a limited but hectic period), he left a modestly flourishing boot and shoe business when he died in Lambeth in 1930. He was an accomplished 'leg puller' but met a veritable Waterloo, together with his assistant 'Snobs,' at Reninghelst. Their shop consisted of a den built of odds and ends of sacking, boards, and what not—a comparatively cosy hovel anyway. One particularly disgusting Flanders night some wag emptied half a kilo of pepper down the stove pipe, plugging the latter with wet sandbags, and nearly accounted for all the shoemakers at one fell swoop!"

During our next tour, on the 4th the enemy was unusually active with field-gun fire distributed over the whole Battalion front, reserve, and communication trenches. In the night time fixed rifle and machine-gun fire was experienced in P and O Trench. As a result of this activity 2nd Lieut. J. W. Barrow and two other ranks were wounded. 2nd Lieut. Barrow, who was usually given charge of draining and repair work in the trenches because of previous experience, remained on duty, and the work of improving the front line was carried on without delay.

A pleasant interlude, and one that showed the chivalry which existed between rival airmen, occurred on the 4th. Pte. H. Budd, who kept a diary, relates the incident:—

"News had filtered through that something unusual might happen during the afternoon. What happened was that from behind our lines a small balloon appeared, from which was suspended a small parcel. Blown by a breeze gently towards our lines it was escorted by one of our planes which circled round until it reached the enemy lines. There was an absolute lull in both rifle and shell-fire during its progress, and one can imagine the rapt attention of all the men who watched this novelty. The balloon and the plane crossed over the German lines at a low altitude, and later a German plane appeared and took on the task of escort while our own plane returned to our lines. When well over the German lines the balloon was brought down.

We afterwards heard that on the body of a German airman who had been brought down behind our lines was some personal property, which for some particular reason we were willing to return to the relatives, and that as soon as a favourable wind occurred we had adopted this means of returning it—our intention undoubtedly having first been communicated to the enemy."

On the 5th the enemy carried out a systematic bombardment with "Fishtails" of the front line, damaging C Company's trenches and causing five casualties. In the afternoon the British field-guns and howitzers retaliated and soon silenced the Boche. Despite this the work of repairing the front line trenches was carried on. The enemy brought his "Fishtails" again into action on the following day, and although he damaged Crater Lane, no casualties were reported, in spite of the bombardment lasting on and off from midnight to dawn.

The 7th being a misty day, advantage was taken of this to send wiring parties out during the morning. In connection with this Capt. Hector Walker relates how, when Colonel Lee came along to inspect the wire he pointed out to him the large number of rolls of barbed wire in the frozen shell holes. The wire was still on the reels and this made it abundantly clear how our opposite number was able to put out such quantities of wire each tour, though the wiring never seemed to get any thicker. Capt. Walker had specially trained wiring parties, but they could never get out anything like the Durhams, try as they would. In the afternoon the mist rose, and the enemy artillery became very active again, using heavier shells on the reserve line and field-guns on the front: as was so often the case, no casualties were caused, but the strain on the men was great. However, later on in the day Pte. F. Collins was killed by a sniper in No. 1 Crater.

A shoot was carried out by our guns on the enemy's back area on the 8th, which brought forth retaliation on our front and reserve lines without very much damage being done.

The preceding paragraphs shows the constant strain on troops in trenches during the winter months, when the newspapers informed the public—"All quiet" or "Nothing to report." Another fact of which mention might be made is this. Folk at home were under the impression that everything a man in khaki said was gospel, and the most absurd reports gained credence. As a matter of fact the men at the front knew less than anyone, even of events in their own sector. For instance, one night, when we were in Rest Camp, a fearful bombardment lasting for hours was heard from the Salient: it was not till newspapers arrived from England three days later that we knew what had occurred. The truth in fact was curious. A gas sentry had had an attack of giddiness and caught hold of the gas alarm. This went off: the alarm was taken up for miles along the line by our own and the enemy's alarms. Thousands of troops stood to, hundreds of guns started protective barrages, casualties were considerable, and perhaps £100,000 expended in ammunition. All for nothing.

It may be to this that Q.M.S. Speller refers when he writes:—

"I remember a joker who let off a smoke candle in the Sergeants' Mess Hut. A semi-somnolent sentry started the gas gong, and within ten mintues the whole front was a solid clot of S.O.S.'s, Klaxon horns, frightfulness and retaliation. The next issue of "Comic Cuts" duly reported, "A determined attack by the enemy, accompanied by gas, was everywhere repulsed with great loss to the attackers'."

After a period of rest, during which some snow fell, trenches were taken over again on the 15th. The 17th was foggy, and this gave another chance of parties being sent out to put up more wire in No Man's Land in the day-time. The night, of course, was always a time of activity in the trenches, as work could be done unseen by the enemy. Sentry groups of two men were posted at intervals, one man up on the firestep, and his fellow seated below, each relieving the other now and then. The groups were relieved at stated periods. To be asleep on Sentry duty was the most heinous crime: it was an offence for Court-martial, and the extreme punishment was death, though in actual fact it was seldom inflicted. The difficulty was to prove that the man was asleep: in practice the best proof was that the man's rifle had been taken from him without his knowledge. This sometimes happened: if the officer or N.C.O. were kind-hearted, the man would be only severely reproved and warned of the terrible consequences of the second offence. It was pitiful to see the poor fellows—often mere boys—weighed down with fatigue and drowsiness, but not allowed to walk about in order to keep awake, fighting with the natural tendency to fall asleep. The sentry on duty had to keep head and shoulders above the parapet, though he might duck his "napper" when a machine-gun was traversing. Meanwhile working parties were active, some putting up wire in No Man's Land, some putting up fresh sandbags of earth where parapets were collapsing, some draining off mud and water with pumps, some bringing up rations, "A" frames, duckboards, etc. All this too often in drenching rain or bitter cold, and of course in complete darkness.

We must not forget the rats. They were ubiquitous, and were as bad in Rest Camp as in the trenches. It is scarcely an exaggeration to say that the ground was alive with them. They ran over us while we slept, gnawed the men's haversacks and attacked every store of food not sealed in tins.

The romance of it all! "Pride, pomp and circumstance of glorious war!!" Perhaps they did exist in Othello's day. We never discovered them on the Western Front.

With regard to the rats which infested St. Eloi trenches Pte. H. Budd recounts the following amusing incident:—

"One wintry night when the parapets were covered with snow, a comrade and I were in a reserve trench, and during our spell of guard we repeatedly saw a large rat come along the top of the parapet in front of us. Having been unsuccessful in hitting it with any missile which lay handy, at last my chum said, 'The next time it comes along I'll fire at it with the corporal's revolver.' (We were machine-gunners and No. 1 carried a revolver). Strangely enough a suitable opportunity did not occur when he was thus equipped, much to his regret. Then an idea came to my mind. We were wearing the regulation gloves: a wash leather, thickly padded two partitioned affair, one for the thumb and the other for all the fingers. Each glove was joined to its partner by a tape, four or five feet long. At an opportune moment when my chum was not looking, I threw one glove over the parapet and by gently pulling the tape brought it within a few inches of the top. Then, when my chum turned round, I warned him with a quiet, Hist! and pointed meaningly to the top of the parapet. He quickly grasped my meaning, and, with revolver ready, stood waiting the rat's next appearance. I allowed several moments to elapse, and then gently pulled the tape, taking care not to let him see me do it. Soon the glove came up and bang went the revolver. My chum was glad at having achieved his object of frightening the beast and speculated as to the likelihood of having hit it. 'Well," I said, 'we can quickly find out,' and once more pulling the tape brought the glove back and then congratulated him on having placed a bullet neatly through the centre. Unfortunately my chum did not appreciate the joke quite as much as I did."

On the 18th the enemy was quite active in the afternoon with shells and rifle grenades on the left front, while later on machine-guns swept the road past Battalion H.Q. This road was frequently machine-gunned during the night, and ration and working parties were warned of the danger. A certain sergeant in B Company was proceeding along this road one night when a bullet caught him in the leg. It was apparently a ricochet, and, while not doing any severe damage to him, was sufficient to get him evacuated to the clearing station. As he had his leave warrant in his pocket, he did not report the matter until he arrived in England, with the result that he not only got his leave but an extension for his slight wound.

The Reserve Farm came in for some "strafing" by the enemy on the 20th, and as the result of a direct hit by a 5.9 Pte. G. Johnson was killed, and 2nd Lieut. H. E. Winder and four other ranks wounded. The weather was fine and in consequence there was much aerial activity on both sides. There was a certain airman whom we called the "Mad Major." All the time the Battalion was at St. Eloi this pilot performed remarkable feats in the air. He was apparently attached to the artillery, for usually after he had flown just above the enemy trenches our guns would open out. Day after day he used practically to skim the parapet, and the report from his machine-gun could be heard as he headed for the German lines. The Germans below would kick up a terrific din with machine-guns and rifles, and later their anti-aircraft guns would join in the racket. Despite this he managed to get back to our lines, so low on occasions that we could see him wave to us. This was undoubtedly the man who first realised that an airman could be very useful in keeping the infantry on tenterhooks without bombs. With a man like this above you there was little chance of defending yourself against his machine-gun, for he was able to get away before you had time to take aim at him. Later the German airmen employed this method on us, especially when we began to advance across the swamps towards Passchendaele. Many a dog-fight in the air was witnessed at St. Eloi; often on a clear day we would watch British and German planes circling round trying to get at grips with each other. The rat-a-tat of machine-guns would be the prelude to seeing a plane come down in flames or a headlong dive to earth. On one occasion we saw two of our own machines collide with each other in mid-air. On another a British plane was attacked by a German and made a dive towards earth, but just before reaching the ground it seemed to right itself. We afterwards heard that the pilot had been killed whilst in the air and that the observer had managed to get hold of the controls in time to right the machine. The observation balloons at Hallebast Corner would also come in for attention from the Boche. Many times the occupants were forced to take to their parachutes and make landings wherever they could. It was a thrilling sight to see these men being carried through the air attached to their parachutes. Most of them would not attempt to leave the balloon until the enemy had commenced to fire into it. It was said that the German airmen deliberately fired at them while they were coming down in their parachutes, and there is evidence to support this in the case of one German plane before the Battle of Messines, but it is more than likely that this was done while the men were preparing to leave. It was usual for the enemy plane to give warning by circling round the balloon before firing incendiary bullets into it. Those who delayed getting away were sometimes enveloped in the flames from the gasbag.

The Battalion returned to Ontario Camp on the 22nd, and the entry in the Diary for this day ends on the note, "A rum issue was ordered," which seems to suggest that the weather was very cold. The Medical Officer had much to do with the ordering of rum to the troops. It was issued in the trenches in winter, if hot soup was not available. Of course the troops always complained that they never got their full ration; others were supposed to have "dipped" well into it before the turn of the privates came for their tot. Hence the song that was often heard.

"If the sergeants pinch your rum, never mind.
If the sergeants pinch your rum, never mind,
They're entitled to their tot, but if they drink the blessed lot,
If the sergeants drink your rum, never mind."

There may have been some truth in this in certain cases, for it was noticeable that there was always a reserve of rum at Headquarters when we took over from other units. There was no direct evidence that the same sort of thing obtained in the 12th, for where R.Q.M.S. Speller had a say in the matter, which he usually did, he always saw to it that the men in the front line got as much as those farther back and more, if he could manage it. This applied to all rations. On a certain occasion Speller returned some of his staff to duty with their companies, because he found a loaf of bread concealed behind a pack.

The mention of hot soup reminds us of the blessed invention of the Vacuum Portable Canteens. These huge containers, full of boiling hot soup or stew prepared at the cookhouses in the reserve line, were strapped to the backs of men who toiled with their weighty loads up the communication trenches. What joy when they arrived! Dixies might get upset, and their contents anyhow were usually tepid, but here was steaming hot fare, "bonn for the troops!" as the saying went. During this winter the C.O. instituted a vote in the Battalion on the men's preference for Rum or Hot Soup, and the latter easily won the day. It should be mentioned that the rum issue had to be supervised by an officer, so that men only had a moderate amount each, and teetotallers were not allowed to pass on their share to a comrade.

Speaking of the issue of rum, Capt. Hector Walker recalls an incident which happened at St. Eloi:—

"One of my early recollections of life in the front line at the top of P and O was when, as Commander of C Company, I detailed a junior officer, whose name I forget, to issue the rum. Later on I heard a spluttering and much cursing near my dugout. On investigating I found that the officer had gone to the far end of the Company complete with rum jar and had dished out tots on his way back of Unsweetened Lime Juice! I always felt that the 12th generally called a spade a blank shovel and they did so on this occasion, excellently. It was a cold, frosty morning."

By the way, it was commonly believed at home that our troops in a push had to be doped with big tots of rum before going "over the bags," to put Dutch courage into them. We cannot positively state that this never occurred, but it certainly did not in the 41st Division, and we doubt if it was the practice in any other either.

It was notified that the Divisional Commander would present medal ribbons to Sergt. Mackenzie and Lce.-Cpl. Kitchen at Chippewa Camp on the 24th, and so the 23rd was spent in cleaning up and getting ready for the parade. As it turned out, only two companies paraded at 8.0 a.m. for the march to Chippewa, the remainder of the Battalion having to go on working parties.

Christmas Day—the day of peace and goodwill—broke upon the Battalion in the hutments at Ontario Camp. It is a time-honoured custom in the Army that on this one day of the year officers and senior N.C.O.s are allowed to fraternise with the men even to the extent of waiting on them at table. In the circumstances it was not possible for things to be carried out in the same way as they would be in the more palmy days of peace. However everything possible had been done to ensure that the men should have a good dinner and as much enjoyment as it was possible to give them. A visit of Major Blakeney to Bailleul had resulted in some Christmas cheer reaching the troops. Plum puddings from "Blighty," plenty of cigarettes, and barrels of beer made their appearance on Christmas Day. The Regimental Depôt and the people of Bermondsey through Mr. Hart did their best towards helping the men to enjoy their first Christmas on active service, and individual officers with the aid of their relations and friends at home contributed much to make the day more enjoyable. The Christmas dinner took place at 2.0 p.m. and was thoroughly enjoyed by all. Afterwards impromptu concerts were held throughout the camp, and later in the evening the Brigade and Divisional concert parties helped men to forget the war and revive the spirit of Christmas.

On Boxing Day the G.O.C. held an inspection of the Regimental Transport. On the 29th we were back again in our usual sector, the trenches being in a fearfully waterlogged state.

Snipers, firing obliquely from the left, were active on the 31st, and two men were wounded in the crater. C.Q.M.S. H. Tice of D Company gives us an experience of this period:—

"About Christmas time 1916 I was in charge of 'Crater Party,' not a very pleasant job, as all will remember who came in contact with it. The Crater consisted of a big hole in the mud in the middle of No Man's Land and could only be relieved after dark, and it was in full view of the enemy's lines and quite close. Why it was ever occupied by us I could never understand: one would have had no chance of doing anything, had a raid or attack taken place at any time. We could (on a moonlight night especially) see small German patrols and wiring parties moving about, but could not be certain who they were, as often our own people were prowling about too. This particular Christmas time Jerry was very "pally": they had a cornet going nearly all night long playing well known carols and hymn tunes, and occasionally shouted to us, 'How would you like to be in Leicester Square tonight?' 'We know you, East Surreys,' and so on.

"On one occasion I had a very unpleasant time after being relieved. It was a horrible place to get in and out of: from our front line trench duckboards were put down to walk on, but there was no proper trench or much cover till one actually got into the crater. By some means or other I got off the beaten track and slipped into a real bog, and quickly sank in over my knees. I was bringing up the rear of the party, and only one man heard me call (it did not do to shout very much, or something would have come over pretty quickly). He could do nothing; however, he went to the front line and got half a dozen men who after a terrible struggle got me out minus my trench boots. It was a much more difficult job than one would imagine, as they dared not get too near me or they would have been bogged themselves. I was only stuck an hour, but it seemed a good deal longer to me. I suppose I looked a bit shaky when reporting at Company H.Q., but the spot of Scotch given me by Capt. Pridham soon cheered me up again, and I strolled off to the old farm house in reserves and slept the sleep of the righteous."

As Tice was one of the biggest men in the Battalion one can imagine the difficulties his rescuers encountered.

Another of the same N.C.O.'s experiences comes in well here. He is assuredly a lucky man to be alive to tell the story to-day:—

"We were holding the line in 1916 in front of Voormezeele, and while I was waiting for Mr. Puttock to come out from the officers' dugout to go on front line patrol, a trench-mortar bomb burst between my legs. It landed me clean inside among the officers, and, although it "holed' my trousers and tunic, cut my belt clean through and busted my bayonet scabbard, I had not a piece of skin knocked off me, and, except for a couple of bruises sustained when falling, felt no ill effect at all. I was a walking wonder for a couple of days till another suit came along for me. The Brigadier somehow heard of it, and I had to parade before him. Everyone still considers it a miracle, as I do, that not a particle of the numerous pieces which went through my tunic and trousers touched my flesh in any part whatever."

The casualties during the month were 4 other ranks killed; 2 officers and 23 other ranks wounded. 2nd Lieuts. R. C. Baker and W. R. Miller left us to join the Machine Gun Corps (Heavy Section).

So ended 1916. The stupendous efforts made by this country had brought a measure of success in the Somme area, though at frightful cost. The losses and gains for the Allies and Germany through the year seemed to have brought on a position of stalemate. Rumours however were current that the U.S.A. might be joining in on our side, and the fact was becoming obvious in our sector at any rate that we were easily "top dog" in artillery and in the air. Any Boche strafe now brought retaliation of three shells to his one. Thus there was a general feeling of optimism and almost more than a hope that victory would be ours before the end of 1917.

Though war-weariness was not yet much in evidence, still the men, as they dragged one foot with difficulty after another towards the end of a march from the trenches to Rest Camp, would put real feeling into the well-worn words:—

"I want to go home.
I don't want to go to the trenches no more,
Where bullets do whistle and cannon do roar.
I want to go over the sea;
Where the Allyman can't get at me.
Oh my! I don't want to die.
I want to go home."

But often they were too "done to the wide" to sing at all, poor beggars.

LITTLE TICH.

(Killed in action)

'E was a rummy sort of bloke;
It wasn't often that 'e spoke,
A reg'lar dugout, as they say,
An' fifty, if 'e was a day.
'E wasn't one to swing the lead
Or tell the tale—an' now 'e's dead.
A washout, so they called 'im. Yus,
'E always looked ridiculous,
A standing wiv 'is patient face
An' belt a little out o' place,
Grey 'air like wire a stickin' out
Beneaf 'is cap, feet all about
Like Little Tich. We called 'im so:
It come to us in 'arf a mo'.

Our Capting Barker—rare good chap,
In spite of 'is Gorblimey cap—
'E did 'is level best, an' tried
To give ol' Tich a proper pride,
But 'tweren't no use: 'e'd never be
A soldier, same as you an' me.
At last one fine day on parade
The Capting lorst 'is wool an' said,
"Major, that blighter is no good—
No more sense than a block o' wood.
You take an' make 'im what you choose:
I'll 'ave no more of these Napoos."

So Little Tich they turfed 'im out
An' made 'im carry cans about.
In billets, trenches or in camp
You'd see 'im on the blinkin' tramp,
A petrol tin in either 'and.
I never couldn't understand
What 'is perfession was before
'E joined up for the bloomin' war.
I arst 'im once. "Say, chum," says I,
"Excuse my curiosity:
What was your stunt in civvy life,
Before you left your kids an' wife?"
'E looks at me wivout surprise
In 'is ol' patient weary eyes:
"Ye know the cawfee-stalls," says 'e,
"Open all night wiv cups o' tea
For cabbies an' such likes at 'ome
In Blighty streets: well, round I come
An' takes 'em water every night.
They gives me tuppence an' a bite,
An' sometimes too a cup o' tea.
An' that's the way I lives," says 'e.
Then off he toddles wiv a grin
To fetch anuvver petrol tin
O' water for 'is ol' platoon.
"It's 'ot," he says, "this afternoon."

'Is job it was no cushy one,
But no man's job was better done.
If Fritz was on 'is evenin' strafe,
An' whizzbangs flying by—not 'arf.
Minnie or coalbox, 'twas the same,
Our Little Tich was always game.
'E'd turn up wiv' a friendly grin
An' 'is ol' petrol water tin.
But it was only yesterday,
A fishtail burst close where 'e lay.
We found 'im later, pore 'ol' dear;
I couldn't 'elp but drop a tear.
Properly 'urt 'e was, but bright.
"They got the water-tins all right,
Eh, chum?" 'e smiled an' gently said,
Then sighed a bit an' lay back dead.

Pore Little Tich, 'e's now gone west,
No soldier, but 'e did 'is best.
A dud? Yus, but 'e played the game
Pray God we all may do the same.

1917. Voormezeele.

John Aston.

CHAPTER VI.

1st January to 31st May, 1917.

In the trenches at St. Eloi—Severe winter—Training at Nordausques for coming Battle of Messines.

FEW people ever realise the extraordinary difficulties placed in the way of efficiency by the constant changes of officers, N.C.O.s and men. They were sent off on courses in the various training camps of the Second Army, were evacuated sick or fell out as casualties, were transferred to other posts, went (very occasionally) on leave. Thus almost daily there were changes. Let two examples suffice. In the nine months between September, 1916, and the Battle of Messines in June, 1917, eight different C.O.s commanded the Battalion, which involved no less than 22 changes of command during the period. In two months there were 15 changes of O.C. B Company. It was very rare for any officer to be as long as a month continuously at one job. Imagine a school being run efficiently, where the Headmaster was changed 22 times in 9 months, and the assistant masters no less! Could any business prosper properly where the manager was changed once a fortnight? Yet that was our fate, and the same could be said of most battalions at the front. It was sometimes a marvel, considering such conditions and the stupendous difficulties of transport, rationing, equipment and life in a foreign country, that the Army ever functioned at all.

Four more months were to be spent in and out of the trenches at St. Eloi. The preparations for an offensive in the summer were beginning: more and more time was spent during so-called "Rest" on working parties. New corduroy roads were constructed leading up to the front, for the existing ones would not suffice for the vast amount of transport that was to be involved. Further back Decauville railways were constructed, new camps formed; more and more till June the back areas assumed the appearance of a great mining settlement.

On the 1st of January, 1917, a fierce bombardment took place. It had been a quiet day in the line, and at dusk "Stand To" took place as usual, then "Stand Down" and placing of sentry posts. Shortly afterwards heavy firing was heard some miles to the north in the Ypres direction, then to the south, then whizz-bangs exploded in our front line, followed by "Minnies." "Stand To" was shouted all along, officers and men tumbled out of dugouts, S.O.S. rockets went soaring into the darkness, and in ten minutes the trenches on either side of No Man's Land were crowded with troops on the alert to repel an attack, and the guns belching shells into the enemy. It was "Wind up"—the prairie-fire of the trenches—and no bad picture of Europe to-day, with every country terrified of attack by the others. What was the original cause was never discovered. Our trenches were badly breached in places, and our casualties one man, Pte. A. E. Ridley, killed, while Pte. W. H. Charman died next day of his wounds; 2nd Lieut. J. W. Barrow was again slightly wounded. On the 3rd it was announced that Sergt. Durran had been awarded the M.M.

After the next rest period we were in the line again on the 8th. In the evening six dummy figures were placed in No Man's Land and attached by wires to the front line trench in preparation for a dummy raid which was to take place on the 9th to distract attention from a real raid to the north. Our trench mortars cut the enemy wire without much retaliation. At 6.55 p.m. on the 9th the figures were pulled up by the wires from the front line trench and at 7.0 p.m. our batteries opened fire on the enemy trenches. Smoke was to have been sent over by us, but the direction of the wind prevented this. An intensive bombardment lasting 30 minutes drew no retaliation from the enemy, and after the bombardment a quiet night was passed. It was evident that the Boche was not to be fooled, as he was probably aware somehow of what was going to take place.

The same sort of trick was tried on the following day, when a dummy was placed in No Man's Land and a party of bombers under 2nd Lieut. Harding lay in wait for any of the enemy who came out to investigate. None came. Dummy figures were "napoo" thereafter.

Bois Confluent and Queen Victoria Street were shelled on the 10th and 11th, and again shelled and trench-mortared on the 13th, and the trenches were flooded.

One unhappy incident marred the next rest from the trenches. During practice in a bombing pit a Mills prematurely exploded and 2 officers (2nd Lieuts. Woollard and Pritchard of the Surrey Yeomanry) and 5 other ranks were wounded. 2nd Lieut. Woollard was Capt. H. S. Walker's chief patrol officer while he was with us. It was a snowy period. The 11th "Queen's" on the 20th sent a party of raiders into the enemy lines, dressed in white shirts and trousers and whitewashed helmets and their faces covered with flour.

The Battalion proceeded to the trenches again on the 21st and relieved the Durhams. Thick snow was on the ground, and the going was so difficult that it was not until 9.30 p.m. that the relief was reported complete. Two of our planes were brought down in flames by the German anti-aircraft guns on the 24th, one sinking in flames in the enemy support line opposite Bois Confluent.

Hard frost and low temperatures were experienced throughout this tour, although the weather was favourable for artillery fire. On the 25th Reserve Farm was shelled with 77 m.m.s during the morning and sustained 13 direct hits, as a result of which Pte. W. J. Backhouse was killed. Counter battery work did not keep down the enemy's fire, and later they put the Belgian battery of light field guns near Dickebusch Lake out of action. Queen Victoria Street was blown in and Bois Confluent shelled on the 26th and 27th. During relief on the 28th two machine-gunners were hit in Dickebusch.

In many tours of the trenches during this period scares were frequent. Perhaps it was, as Capt H. S. Walker suggests, the boredom and brain stagnation inseparable from trench life that made people imagine all sorts of things. Here is an incident related by him:—

"The Company Commander from the unit on our right came to me one night, saying that there were noises of mining under his trench. I went along to his dugout and heard distinct tappings as of steel on steel. It was a dark night, but I could find nothing to explain this tapping. I went along again in the morning and found after a time, that a bottle floating in the stream that passed through the trench was tapping intermittently against one of the iron stakes which held the wire across the opening."

The following officers joined during January:—

Capt. C. T. Williams, Lieut. A. V. Baker and 2nd Lieuts. S. Lasenby, A. V. Hutchinson, A. R. Puttock, R. N. Haine, B. C. Stenning, A. T. Duncan, S. E. Bennett, W. A. Vanner, and G. P. Cooper. Lieut. M. C. Morris was evacuated sick to England.

The M.O. for many months till the middle of February was Capt. F. W. Wilson, an unconventional son of Erin, relieved on occasions by Capt. W. L. A. Harrison. Cpl. Southall writes:—

"Dr. Wilson was extremely popular with the rank and file, and with most, if not all, of the officers, but there did not appear to be a great amount of co-operation between him and the C.O. He transferred his quarters from H.Q. to the Transport, then to D Company and finally to C. He was always full of fun, like all Irishmen, and ever had a twinkle in his eye: his manner, soft brogue and kindness endeared him to all the men in the Battalion. . . . . I have known instances when sick men had come down to the Regimental Aid Post at the Brasserie and had been detained there for rest, and owing to our being short of rations we were unable to feed our patients as we should have liked to. The doctor would send to the canteen and pay for biscuits and milk for the men out of his own pocket. I was very sad indeed at his going."

The casualties during the month were 2 other ranks killed and 3 officers and 12 other ranks wounded.

During the 4th of February on our next tour P and O Trench was shelled with heavy trench mortars. Visibility was poor and frost continued.

On the 8th Sergt. F. J. Howlett was killed by a sniper in the sap leading to the Crater. Howlett was a very popular N.C.O. of B Company, a quiet and unassuming character. He was one of those to whom war was abhorrent, yet he did his duty well and unobtrusively because it was the obvious thing. There were many such. Another man, Pte. G. A. Read, was killed on the following day by a sniper. Accordingly, the 18-pounders were directed on the spot where the sniper was suspected, but failed to hit him. Another shoot on the sniper's lair was made on the 9th, but owing to the state of the ground the shells did not burst well and the sniper was not put out of action, as, after we were relieved by the Durhams on the 10th, one of their men was sniped. At least one officer and another man of the Battalion met a similar fate while entering the Crater in the early days of March. If the same snipers were responsible, it is evident that they were cleverly concealed or that the artillery had failed to carry out the work allotted for their destruction. Pte. E. Herbert states that he located this lair by the aid of a small periscope fixed on a bayonet which he exhibited from the front line trench. The periscope was smashed by a bullet coming from the direction of the wood near the White Château. By carefully watching a suspected tree Herbert observed a slight movement of leaves when future shots were fired. Later on after the Battle of Messines, when he was passing through the wood, out of curiosity he searched for the tree from which he thought the snipers fired. At last he found a tree with an iron ladder leading up to the branches with a platform on top. As he says, the marvel to him was that our artillery did not destroy it considering the amount of shelling this wood had been subjected to. This is probably the one shown in the photograph

In the afternoon of the 6th, Bus House, about 400 yards behind the front line, was shelled with light shrapnel. Bus House derived its name from the fact that in the early days of the war it was the rendezvous of the buses used to convey the troops to rest billets after the stirring and arduous times in the Salient. On the same day our 18-pounders silenced a trench mortar which had been active on our right.

A barrage of minnenwerfers was put down on Crater Lane at 10.30 p.m. on the 8th, resulting in the portion between the front and support lines being blown in. With great energy a working party managed to make it passable again within a few hours. This was probably connected with the successful raid of the 11th West Kents in the Spoil Bank sector, a mile to the east.

During the period February 11th to 16th the usual training was carried out in the Rest Camp interspersed with working parties—the whole Battalion being employed on the latter for two days. H.Q. and B and C Companies were inspected by Colonel Lee while we were at rest. The C.O. did not usually inspect H.Q. Company as much as the others, and one can imagine the stir among the specialists when the news of the inspection was announced. No doubt there were a few borrowed rifles on the parade, as the H.Q. men were often too busily employed in other directions to take the same care of their arms as their comrades in the companies. A voluntary Church Parade was held on a day when the majority of the Battalion were on working parties, while the usual baths were allotted to the Battalion on the only real day of rest. In the afternoon of the 14th there was a route march via Westoutre-Mont Rouge-Kastel Molen. Westoutre, as has already been stated, was well known as a landmark because of its windmill of which strange tales of espionage were told. Mont Rouge, or the Red Hill, was a fairly high one for Flanders and at this period was a very quiet and restful place, but later on it became a target for the enemy when he made his terrific onslaught in 1918.

Intensely cold weather prevailed almost the whole of February, and the men had a cruel time. Once or twice the frost broke, and then P and O Trench would be flooded to the waist with thawed dirty water, and the fire trenches sometimes to the knee. Those who were sent to the various training camps were better off, but even here in tents the cold was rigorous and frostbite not unknown. Luckiest of all were those few sent to the Army Schools far back near St. Omer, where they were billeted in houses, and had fires to sit round when off duty. 2nd Lieut. Aston was on one such course at Norbecourt in March, when a comic incident occurred.

His batman, Pte. J. Rogers, had borrowed a rubber bath and brought it in triumph to his "bloke." In the evening Rogers brought up two tall cans from the cookhouse full of boiling water and emptied them into the bath, departing with a "satisfying feeling that his duty had been done." Mr. Aston had to wait a good half hour till the water was cool enough to enter. He thought it looked even muddier than usual—a deep brown hue—but sat down, filled a good spongeful and poured it over himself. Horror! Beetles? No, tea-leaves. The mystery was solved. Rogers had gone in the dark to the cookhouse and filled up the cans in which the men's tea had been made, but at the bottom of which the leaves were still lying. Next morning Rogers appeared, eager to receive praise for his thoughtfulness. "Good morning, Rogers." "Morning, Sir. Had a good bath last night?" "'M, not bad, but you forgot something." "Very sorry, Sir, what was that?" "The milk and sugar, Rogers. Look at the bath!"

Here is another anecdote from Capt. Hector Walker concerning a course he was sent on:—

"I was sent on a course at the Lewis-Gun School at Paris Plage with a party. We arrived late at Etaples, and, after seeing that the men were all right for the night, I went back to the 38th Infantry Base Depôt to see some friends there, including the old Major I had met on my arrival overseas. The Major at once asked me what I was doing there. I explained to him that I did not like the way the war was being carried on up at the front. I had always been under the impression that one went into action waving a sword and cheering, but that I found that we had to more or less crawl up a dirty muddy trench for hours and had to make as little noise as possible. You were then expected to stay in the front line trench, which was both wet and muddy, for a week or ten days, and then crawl out again. As I did not like that sort of thing,

I had come down to see if they could give me a job more to my liking; if not, I thought I would go back to England and see what could be done there. I had no idea how well I had pulled their legs until the dear old Major insisted that I should share his quarters for the night. He then spoke to me very seriously and begged me to return to the line at once. When I told him that I was on my way to the L.G. School, he was so pleased that he turned out my old friends and we had a good time of it."

The conditions prevailing at the Army Schools during the hard winter of 1916 and 1917 were certainly very much better than those the Battalion had to contend with even back at Reninghelst, which we considered a Paradise compared with the trenches at St. Eloi. Let us here quote Q.M.S. Speller.—

"I remember," he writes, "dear old 'Billy' Warr, whose naturally refined speech became so absolutely 'refaned' after a bottle or two that he was dubbed the 'Marquis.' Scrupulously particular in his person, during the bitter weather early in '17 it was his nightly habit to divest himself of all his undergarments, which he hung over the company notice-board, and then, with a roar of 'Freeze, you asterisks, freeze!' to the small inhabitants, he draped himself in a blanket and slept. In the mornings it was an education to see Billy slipping into garments stiff as a board with hoar frost with no more fuss than if they had come straight from an airing cupboard. He was the complete 'soldier and a man.' "

Though casualties from shell and rifle fire had not so far been very heavy in the St. Eloi sector, much sickness was occasioned by the conditions, resulting in wastage of man power: so far there had been three fatalities from sickness, Ptes. T. Thorogood, G. Thorogood, and W. Hoadley having succumbed to trench fever, nephritis and pneumonia respectively.

At the end of December a draft of 50 men joined from the 5th (Territorial) Battalion, while towards the end of January, 1917, a draft of 100 other ranks came from the 3rd Battalion, and about 50 from the 1st arrived early in February. Drafts from every battalion of the East Surrey Regiment joined the 12th while it was in England and also on active service: in addition they arrived from many other regiments and corps. The wisdom of the authorities at the base at Etaples of sending men to units other than their own is questionable. Perhaps the exigencies of the service demanded that such a practice had to be adopted, but the troops concerned never regarded the practice as one that was likely to lead to harmonious working. Men had been taught in Blighty the value of *esprit de corps* only to find when they got overseas that they might be sent to any unit without having a word to say in the matter. It was well known among those who were unfortunate enough to spend any time in the "Bull Ring" at Etaples that the instructors or "Canaries" (so called because of the yellow armlets they used to wear) were only too glad to send them up the line with the greatest possible speed. It was not uncommon to find a real Cockney posted to a Highland regiment in which he had to wear a kilt, or a broad Yorkshireman posted to a London regiment. In fact before the end of the war had been reached, some units could have boasted of having received men from every regiment in the British Army (excluding colonials) besides the Engineers, R.A.M.C., Army Service Corps and others. Up to this period the 12th had received in addition to men from all battalions of the East Surrey Regt., drafts from the Surrey Yeomanry and Middlesex Regt., together with some men who had voluntarily transferred from other units, including the Royal Artillery. To weld these into a homogeneous whole was a task that beset the officers and N.C.O.s. How well it was accomplished is reflected in the work afterwards done by the Battalion. Later drafts came from the Royal Fusiliers, Royal Sussex, Royal West Surreys, Manchesters, Northamptons and also Territorial units such as the 2nd/5th and 2nd/6th Battalions of the East Surreys, the Hertfordshires and the 22nd ("Queen's") London Regt. When the man-power of the Army was under review, fit men from the R.A.M.C., A.S.C., and

R.E.s were also posted to the Battalion. It is also of interest to note that the Battalion was never commanded by a senior officer of the East Surrey Regt.

On the 24th Capt. R. A. McCulloch returned to the Battalion and resumed the duties of Adjutant. Unfortunately he only remained in this position for a few days, as owing to his wounds causing him trouble he had to relinquish the appointment on the 1st of March, when he took over acting Quartermaster in place of Lieut. A. T. Libby, who had been admitted to hospital on the 28th of February as the result of a fall from his horse. Capt. McCulloch was eventually transferred back to England on the 8th of April, and Capt. H. C. Reynard acted as Adjutant.

On the 13th Lce.-Cpl. A. E. King died of wounds. On the 26th Pte. F. C. Look died of double pneumonia, and on the same day Pte. J. Spink was killed. During the month 4 other ranks had been killed and 11 wounded. 2nd Lieut. R. L. Oates had been sent sick to England.

It was about this period that an order came from Army H.Q. stating that the Army Commander had noticed with displeasure that men were often found to be ignorant of the very names of their officers. Nothing else was possible, when officers and men were shifted almost daily. Never mind that. Every man was to be instructed in the name of the Army Commander, the G.O.C. Division, his Brigadier-General, C.O., Adjutant, O.C. of his company, etc. And thereby hangs a tale. One fine day General (now Sir) Sydney Lawford was making a tour of our trenches. He was a fine soldier, constantly inspecting every detail in his area, and even in foul weather usually contrived with riding crop, gaiters and gloves to look as if he were taking a constitutional down Bond Street. He fetched up in front of a Bermondsey lad. "Now, my man," he said, "tell me the name of your Brigadier-General." The fellow scratched his head dubiously, then—"B'lieve 'e's a bloke called Lawford, Sir."

During our first tour in March there were several casualties. One of the recently posted officers, 2nd Lieut. A. T. Duncan, was killed by a sniper while going out to the crater. Pte. A. Hewitt died the same day. On the next day Pte. R. Armstrong was sniped at the fatal crater. Pte. A. Fewtrell was killed on the 4th.

Pte. H. J. Sherborne relates a story in connection with the enemy snipers at St. Eloi:—

"The Battalion's turn for duty in the line had come round once again, and so through Reninghelst, past Ouderdom, where some bright wit had stuck up the notice 'This way to the War,' and on to the Dickebusch road we wended our way. During the customary ten minutes halt our platoon officer was joined by two other officers (one a new man). They sat down and one of them handed round his cigarette case, struck a match and then all three lit up. The sergeant sitting near noticed this and mentioned that he would not do such a thing, and a chorus of 'Nor me' came from the men. The new officer laughed and said he had heard about the old superstition and in his opinion it was all 'tommy rot.' One of the other officers however said, 'One of us will get it this time up.' The whole affair was passed over with a laugh, and we proceeded on our way.

We had been in the line our allotted time and were expecting the relief up within an hour. The young officer came round on trench patrol for the last time and stopped in our bay for a while chatting with the men, and, after informing us that the Durhams were on their way up, turned into the next bay out of sight. We then heard the crack of a rifle, but, as this was quite a common occurrence no notice was taken of it. Then the Corporal went round the corner to see if our relief was in sight. He came back looking very white and told us to pass the word along for the stretcher-bearers as Mr. —— had got it right through the back of the head. A message was sent through to Headquarters reporting what had happened, and shortly afterwards officers came up, a consultation was held and we were then informed that there would be a Corps artillery strafe to wipe out the sniper's post. Meantime the relief of the front line would be postponed and the Durhams put in the support line.

About an hour afterwards the strafe started and the din was appalling. The whole of the artillery concentrated on this one spot in front for some time with the result that the post was literally blown from the face of the earth.

"Coincidence, you say. Well, may be, but the other two officers got theirs during the month, both Blighty ones."

We were delighted to hear on the 4th that the C.M.G. had been bestowed on our popular Brigadier. On the 7th Lieut. G. P. G. Reah took over the duty of Brigade Intelligence Officer and was succeeded by 2nd Lieut. J. Aston as Intelligence Officer of the Battalion and assistant adjutant.

A few words here as to his duties. He was in charge of about 25 N.C.O.s and men, observers and snipers, besides having to keep the War Diary daily and act as general liaison between the Battalion and Brigade. The observers were picked as the most intelligent men, and their job, when in the trenches, was to watch the enemy's lines from dawn to dusk through telescopes and field glasses and report anything of special interest. There were two chief Observation Posts ('O Pip's in Army language); one, where a tunnel had been driven into a Windmill Mound, and a small gap made where it could not be detected by the enemy observers, for it was concealed by the wreckage of the old mill. This being some 15 feet above the level afforded a view over a fair space af country. The mound was shelled now and then, but only a direct hit could knock out the O. Pip. The other was more precarious. In a ruined farm known as the Moated Grange a room had been concreted and sandbagged inside, and a few bricks taken out of the wall, while close by a ladder had been rigged up inside a shaky chimney, where an observer could peer through a tiny gap. It was not a pleasant post. In a high wind the old chimney swayed to and fro, and if the place was shelled it rocked alarmingly and was untenable*. The observers became very clever, watching as they did the same enemy lines day after day. They could report on weak spots in their trenches, where men's heads could be seen passing, they noticed where fresh sandbags had been placed during the night, they spotted new machine-gun posts and Hun O.P.s. Every evening the Intelligence Officer had to make up a report for Brigade H.Q. from their information, and this would be all sifted at Divisional H.Q. and compared with aeroplane photographs, and the information published in "Comic Cuts," as the daily Divisional Intelligence Report was called. Map-making too was done by the observers. They were a most attractive and intelligent set of men.

The snipers, the crack shots of the Battalion, had rifles with special telescopic sights and became deadly in their accuracy. They would construct sniper's posts in the trenches—tiny chambers of sandbags with a large steel armour plate pierced with a hole about 1½ inches in diameter. This hole had a steel flap on a hinge, and the plate was sandbagged on the outside and camouflaged to look innocuous. Snipers and observers became so super-cute on both sides that they had to take excessive precautions. A canvas sheet hung at the doorway, and anyone wishing to enter had to give warning first, so that the sniper might close his flap. Otherwise a watching enemy might see a sudden blink of daylight through the tiny hole and have his suspicions confirmed. In these holes a man might crouch for hours—even days—watching some point in the sandbags opposite, from which a flash might at last prove that an enemy sniper was lurking there, or with his rifle pointed at some gap where Jerry might incautiously show a head in passing along. A dummy tree was used for a short time, but the flash soon gave it away, and the enemy shelled it "to glory."

*Note.—We are fortunate in being able to give a panorama photo actually taken from an O.P.—probably Moated Grange.

On the ridge were two Hun contraptions we knew well. One was a sniper's post in a tall tree (the one mentioned previously by Pte. Herbert), which was ere long knocked out by our guns; the other a cart on the skyline, used, we knew, as an O.P. Each side knew most of the other's O.P.s, but refrained from knocking them out. The Intelligence Officer one day got the battery behind us to range on the cart, then a few days before the action at Messines it was blown sky high and the enemy observers deprived of their look-out at an awkward time.

The snipers used dummy heads on a short pole to raise behind the parapet and try to draw enemy fire. These were most realistic, produced by an atelier under Solomon J. Solomon, R.A., and it was always a joke to conceal them in a dugout with the head looking out from behind a packing case or pile of clothing. They would give rather a turn to anyone entering the dim light from outside.

The 8th of March produced a scare in the Rest Camp. During the day the men had been in training, while a special party, under Lieut. V. L. Clift, had been giving a demonstration before Colonel Lee of a proposed raid which was to be made on the German lines. Tea over, most of the men had repaired to their usual resorts like the Y.M.C.A., the Divisional Theatre and the few estaminets, when soon after 6.0 p.m. a wire was received for the Battalion to stand by in case of need to support the 16th (Irish) Division, whose lines had been raided by the enemy. The order was subsequently cancelled at 7.0 p.m. as the Irish Division managed to restore the situation. The amusing part about the affair was that during the scare "Scotty" Williams and his "Dickybirds" were giving a show in the Y.M.C.A. Runners from the West Kents, Hants and K.R.R.s. arrived during the performance, telling their men to return to the camp at once. No runner arrived from the Twelfth, so that those of us who were in the Y.M.C.A. heard nothing about the scare until we returned to our camp after the show was over. Had the remainder of the Battalion moved off to support the Irish, there would have been many absentees. As it turned out, we enjoyed the concert, quite oblivious of the fact that the bombardment we could hear in the distance was something more than one of the usual nightly "strafes."

We do not detail the events of every day during the winter and early spring, only the chief features. Visits of inspection were often made by the Divisional and Brigade Generals. General Towsey was always indefatigable in doing all he could, while keeping up efficiency in every way, to alleviate the discomforts and often the suffering of his troops. We can never be thankful enough that we were under his command. Colonel Lee, too, would often be seen in the company of that fine soldier, Colonel Corfe of the 11th West Kents, with whom he was on intimate terms. This month, too, we had the pleasure of welcoming as Second in Command Major L. A. Hickson, of the Royal West Kent Regiment, a man of extraordinary charm and fine character, and a *beau ideal* of the Regular officer, efficient, modest, kindly, and a true gentleman. Those who came to know him well were deeply grieved when later he had to go to take command of a battalion of his own regiment elsewhere.

Patrols were now constantly out under junior subalterns in No Man's Land, examining the enemy's wire and defences by night in view of the coming raid. These dangerous feats were taken as a matter of course, but the patrols took their lives in their hands every time, creeping from shell hole to shell hole in the mirk, covered with slime, compelled to remain absolutely motionless on their bellies for minutes at a time, when the Verey lights shot skyward shedding their unearthly blue glare over the hideous waste and then fading out to leave a blacker darkness than ever. Occasionally similar Boche patrols could be detected by our own. Each would give the other a wide berth; if firing started, both parties would have small chance of getting back alive.

No Man's Land serpentined in and out between the often ruinous parapets, and it was very easy in the dark to lose all sense of direction, even with luminous compasses. On one occasion a small party of a neighbouring battalion were going along a front line trench near the "Mud Patch" of evil memory, well-known to Lieut. Aston, when he was attached to the 18th K.R.R.s in November and December. This was a section of trench some fifty yards long, collapsed in most places and knee-deep in mire, and entirely "in the air," for the front line on either side had disappeared, leaving two seventy yard gaps, and no communication trench led to it, so that reliefs, rations, etc., had to go by night over the open, and in day time the little garrison was completely isolated. The three men in question, believing they were crossing the gap to the Mud Patch, at last found themselves in a trench and proceeded a short way, when they fell into a German working party. They had actually crossed No Man's Land and the wire entanglements and were in the enemy front line! But they kept their heads. Shouting "Hands up!" before the Boches could get to their rifles, they drove them out and shepherded them across No Man's Land, thus capturing nearly a dozen. For this smart piece of work they received decorations.

It was decided that the proposed raid should take place on the 14th. The day opened with considerable shelling by the enemy of the Reserve Farm and Headquarters area with 77 mm.s. It was obvious by now that the enemy was beginning to find the range of Dead Dog Farm and to realise that it was some sort of headquarters. Although on this day he did not do any damage there, it was a pointer as to what was to happen later. The front line was bombarded with minnenwerfers in the morning and also in the afternoon, much damage being caused; there was considerable hostile machine-gun and rifle fire between 6.0 and 8.0 p.m. It was plain from this that the Boche was aware that something out of the ordinary was going to take place.

At 8.30 p.m. one of our planes flew over and dropped a coloured light over the enemy lines. Simultaneously the British guns behind us opened up a terrific bombardment. 2nd Lieut. A. R. Puttock with an advance party had left our trench in order to lay the tapes for the raiders to line up on, when they were perceived by the enemy, who had installed a searchlight, and fired on, with the result that two men were wounded. It was discovered that the enemy had manned No Man's Land with machine-gunners. Meanwhile the raiders with blackened faces and knobkerries were anxiously waiting in the front line to go over and get the job finished. With sound judgement Lieut. Clift, who was in charge of the raid, decided that in the face of things it was impossible to carry it out. 2nd Lieut. H. S. Todd was in command of the actual raiders, and it must have been with great reluctance that he accepted Lieut. Clift's decision, which was afterwards confirmed by General Lawford as being a very wise and praiseworthy one. Some of the raiders themselves were rather annoyed that after training for the "stunt" they were unable to carry it out. In fact it was said that a corporal had to be restrained from going over the parapet even after the order to abandon the raid had been issued. 2nd Lieut. Todd and his raiders would certainly have gone over, had the chance been given to them, but to do so would have meant sure suicide, for it is evident from the enemy's attitude during the day that either his espionage had worked well or that he had gauged that the smashing of his wire was the prelude to a raid. Soon after the raid was cancelled the enemy began to bombard our front line, wounding two other ranks. His bombardment in the afternoon had wounded six men in the Crater. The enemy barrage was so heavy and maintained for such a long time that the party who went out to lay the tape could not get back till after midnight—a frightful four hours for them. Thus ended a day which was to prove the quality of which the vast majority of the men of the 12th were made. The raiders with heavy hearts came to Headquarters later, where many of them were given refreshment. 2nd Lieut. Puttock, who was a very brave and well respected officer who was always volunteering for patrols, did his bit as far as possible. Those who knew 2nd Lieut. Todd would have followed him anywhere; his carefree manner made him very popular amongst the men of his platoon. Like very many of the young officers who joined us, he realised that in order to get the best out of his men he had to gain their confidence and respect, and to this end he devoted himself to their welfare in and out of the line, and, while strict, maintained discipline without incurring wrath. Lieut. Clift, whose foresight undoubtedly saved many lives, was a very sound officer who carried out the duties of Machine-gun officer and also Adjutant for a time.

During the morning of the 17th the British guns in Scottish Wood carried out a bombardment during which Duggan and Sloots, of the Orderly Room staff, proceeded to the cookhouse near the Reserve Farm to draw breakfast. Having filled their dixies with tea and their lids with bacon for the whole Orderly Room staff of five, they took the duckboard track back to Dead Dog Farm dugouts. Suddenly a noise like an express train coming through the air came to their ears. Without hesitation they fell on the duckboards and a few seconds later were greeted with a terrific explosion and a shower of dirt. In a few more seconds they were on their feet again and making their way as fast as possible through a cloud of smoke to their dugouts, minus their tea and bacon. On their arrival it was discovered that one of our own shells had burst prematurely and that the artillery had rung up to know what damage had been done. It then dawned on the scared ones that a certain Charlie Heasman had been washing out his dixies at the time the explosion had taken place. They thereupon retraced their footsteps only to find Charlie a bit shaken up but still carrying on the job of preparing for the move out to rest. It was then discovered that the shell had made a big hole less than 20 yards from the cookhouse.

Here is another amusing story from C.Q.M.S. Tice:—

"When I was C.Q.M.S. of D Company, there was always a standing joke about 'paying out.' One evening when taking rations into the line, we were having a very rough time between Ridge Wood and the Brasserie. Shells were falling thick and heavy, and everyone was more or less 'windy'; in fact everyone was hot and bothered. I was running from the Wood to the Brasserie, which was pretty open country, when a real Bermondsey voice came from a small dugout: 'When yer payin' out, Quarter?' I and the other Q.M.S.s with me could hardly get along for laughing after that little remark, for, as you can imagine, our thoughts were a long way from the pay-table at that moment. It certainly did us all good, and by the time we reached the communication trench we were quite normal again."

"On March 22nd, at 6.0 p.m.," notes the War Diary, "a special performance of the Brigade Pantomime 'Aladdin' was given to the Battalion at the Y.M.C.A." This struck the right note. All the ingenuity of the "Dickybirds" was used to make this show a success, and right well they did it. Aided by the Padres, they turned out costumes and props. excellent for a show on active service, while the scenery did great credit to the artists who laboured on it. A duet sung by "Scotty" and one of the "ladies" of the show went something like this:

"My child, my child, I'm in an awful mess,
Poor papa! Poor papa!
I'm stony broke, and that I must confess.
Poor papa! Poor papa!
I kept on pawning till I couldn't stop,
I've pawned everything that I can pop,
And if you don't marry, I shall go down flop.
Poor papa."

Here we found "Scotty" right bang in form with all the latest jokes, surrounded by a galaxy of talent, all of whom contributed to a wonderful evening's entertainment.

With the assistance of Lce.-Cpl. A. B. Giles we are able to reproduce the programme.

By kind permission of Brigadier-General F. W. Towsey, C.M.G.,
the "Dickybirds" will produce

A GRAND PANTOMIME

ALADDIN.

Produced and arranged
by SCOTTY WILLIAMS.

Scenery painted by
Bandsman ELLIS,
11th R.W. Kents.

CHARACTERS.

THE EMPEROR—A monarch in difficulties. ... Sergt. H. Hyland, 18th K.R.R.C.

THE VIZIER—Is supposed to have cleared out the Exchequer,
Rfn. L. YOUNG, 18th K.R.R.C., or Pte. W. H. COLBECK, M.G. Coy.

PEKOE—The VIZIER'S hope and his own pride. Bandsman ELLIS, 11th R.W. Kent. Regt.

ALADDIN—A lively youth, though universally looked upon as a sad boy.
L/Cpl. A. W. KINGSTON, 15th Hampshire Regt.

ABANAZAR—A magician who is after the lamp.
SCOTTY WILLIAMS, 12th East Surrey Regt.

SLAVE OF THE LAMP
GENIUS OF THE RING } ... ... Sergt. H. L. WILLIE, 15th Hampshire Regt.

WIDOW TWANKAY—Aladdin's mother, rather old and not beautiful.
Pte. W. R. LALLOW, 12th East Surrey Regt.

PRINCESS BADROULBOUDOUR—Possessed of great beauty.
Cpl. MORFORD, 11th R.W. Kent Regt.

FULL ORCHESTRA and CHORUS under Pte. HURLING, 11th R.W. Kent Regt.

Music written by Ptes. M. HURLING, W. R. LALLOW, W. K. HURLING.

On the 24th heavy firing was heard in the distance to the south-east between 4.0 and 5.15 a.m. About this time the Germans were retreating further east in the Somme area after a systematic destruction of the countryside, to shorten their line and install themselves in the strongly prepared and fortified "Hindenburg Line." The British and French were following up and were now experiencing great resistance from the enemy, who had reached what they considered the limit of their retirement. On the 24th the British occupied Roisel, seven miles west of Péronne, while the French had reached the western bank of the Oise between St. Quentin and La Fère. The bombardment we heard was probably the outcome of these operations.

At 9.15 a.m. on the 24th an enemy aeroplane was brought down in No Man's Land by our anti-aircraft guns and fell beyond the four enemy craters which were about 100 yards east of the limit of our posts. The K.R.R.s usually held this sector, which included the "Mud Patch" further on; the sector thence to the Canal was usually occupied by the 11th R.W. Kents. For the remainder of the day trench mortar and artillery bombardments predominated on both sides. P and O Trench and the line in Bois Confluent were damaged, and the telephone wire to Headquarters and the batteries was cut. During the bombardment 2nd Lieut. Bennett was sent to the Brasserie suffering from shell-shock.

An enemy patrol was driven off by the fire of our Lewis-guns at 12.30 a.m. on the 25th; one of our wiring parties was fired on by the enemy soon after, with the result that a sergeant and another man were wounded.

General Lawford made a visit to the line in the morning and again in the afternoon of the 28th. The day was a noisy one, for planes were active up above, while Stokes, Minnies, "Fishtails" and other trench mortars pounded the trenches on both sides. A little damage was done to our positions, and one other rank was sent down with severe shell-shock.

Capt. H. C. Reynard at this time was sent as Anti-gas Instructor to the 16th (Irish) Division. It is strange how rumours got about in the Battalion. The disappearance of Capt. Reynard gave rise to the tale that he had been specially selected for a mission on the other side of the lines dressed as a German officer! It was said that he was to try to glean information as to the enemy's defences, and that as a German linguist he was most suitable for the hazardous task.

During March the following officers joined:—2nd Lieuts. W. G. Robinson, L. V. W. Clark, W. R. Gurrin, R. D. Brown, L. W. B. Russell, A. Hemsley; and Capt. C. N. Binney, R.A.M.C. was appointed M.O. He was almost a direct opposite to Dr. Wilson —rather reserved, interested in Art and Literature, quietly efficient and genial.

"I recollect one incident," writes Cpl. Southall, "which shows his coolness under fire. He had gone round the line one day, when Fritz started to shell the support line very heavily. One or two casualties came down, and, while I was preparing to dress their wounds, I enquired if anyone had seen the Doc. 'Oh, yes,' said one, 'I saw him sitting beside the stream in the support line washing the mud off his gumboots'."

The casualties during the month of March were:—

Killed: 1 officer and 4 other ranks. Wounded: 1 officer and 17 other ranks.

The beginning of April found us resting at Reninghelst. Church Parade was held on the 1st, and bathing parade on the 2nd. Training with reference to the attack was carried out during the remainder of the period of rest. The weather was severe on the 2nd and 3rd, when a heavy blizzard swept the countryside.

Major L. H. Hickson, Second in Command, was sent to hospital on the 4th with measles; this was the second case of an officer being affected with this malady, 2nd Lieut. C. C. A. Lee having been evacuated on the 22nd of March.

The Battalion relieved the Durhams on the 5th in the old sector, when Capt. C. T. Williams took over the duties of Second in Command and handed over A Company to Lieut. J. A. Rogers. In the evening, after relief had taken place, heavy firing and a raid took place to the south of our line at 8.45 p.m. The enemy shelled our reserve line and P and O Trench heavily late at night, killing four of our cooks and wounding another with one shell which landed direct on their cookhouse. The dead were Ptes. J. Seagrief, J. Hammond, A. Latter and A. E. Lewington.

The next day was Good Friday, and heavy artillery fire took place all day, during which Pte. B. Burbidge of C Company was killed, while another man was wounded. The Germans responsible for the great activity of the last two days were the 204th Division which was now holding the sector opposite to us.

On the 7th of April, 1917, one of the most successful raids on the Western Front was carried out by the 7th Londons of the 47th Division in the Bluff sector on our left just across the Canal. In order to deceive the Germans, it was decided that the 12th East Surreys should make a demonstration in the St. Eloi sector in co-operation with the Artillery with the idea of making them believe that a raid was going to take place in that neighbourhood. In the meantime the sector where the raid was to take place was to remain fairly quiet. It was slowly being realised that these surprise raids and attacks were fruitful, besides being the means of saving man-power. It was generally understood hitherto that, if a certain part of the line was bombarded consistently, a raid or an attack would follow. In the Divisional War Diary it is recorded that on the 26th of January, 1917, it was considered by G.H.Q. that an attack on the Salient was imminent. The reason for this may have been the activity shown by the enemy guns along different parts of the front just about this period.

To return to the rôle of the 12th Battalion in the operations. Throughout the day our artillery bombarded the enemy lines opposite, and in consequence we received retaliation. At 7.50 p.m. one of our planes flying over our lines dropped "golden rain," and immediately afterwards all guns opened up an intense bombardment. Simultaneously, smoke bombs were discharged from our front line. The guns covering the Bluff sector also opened up, and the Salient became a ring of fire. The enemy, fearful of what was going to take place, sent up his S.O.S., and soon whizz-bangs and 5.9's began to crash our trenches in, Reserve lines, Queen Victoria Street and Crater Lane being breached in many places. Meanwhile the raiders on the left were over in the German lines, making a big bag of prisoners and machine-guns from a surprised enemy. Despite the awful barrage on our front line our men carried out their task of lighting smoke candles and bombs in order to delude the enemy. At 10.45 p.m. the Boche blew a camouflet in Queen Victoria Street sap, and at 11.0 p.m. all was quiet again. All this did not happen without the usual toll, which considering the conditions was fairly light. Pte. R. Peachey of B Company was killed, and 5 other ranks were wounded.

Lieut. J. Aston has a rather amusing story of this evening. A few days previously sitting in a tub at the Reninghelst baths he perceived through the steam some well-known features—those of a fellow-cadet with whom he had been friendly during the previous summer in training at Oxford. Mutual salaams followed, and he found that C—— occupied a dugout only a mile or so from our H.Q. at Dead Dog Farm. "Come along and have some dinner about 7.45 on Saturday," was Mr. Aston's invitation, which was gratefully accepted. Alas! The invitation was soon forgotten by the host, and Saturday evening came. Punctually at 7.45 arrived C——, just five minutes before zero hour for our Raid! Imagine Mr. Aston's shame, horror and apologies. Rogers the batman seized some plates of tepid food (dinner had been at 7.0 because of the raid) and some drink, and C—— sat down in a dugout to snatch this unsavoury meal just as our guns opened. In ten minutes the Boche was retaliating heavily on Dead Dog Farm dugouts. There were several direct hits, impedimenta were sent flying, the drink upset, and a shindy arose in which conversation was futile. Soon an orderly "blew in"—"Colonel's orders, Sir. Evacuate the dugouts." C—— seized his plate, and Mr. Aston a mug of tea, and with others they did the 100 yards in record time to a ditch near by, where the next two hours or so were spent till things were quieter. C—— finally departed, followed by profuse apologies, and it was heard later that on his way home he had had a flesh wound in the leg from a rifle bullet. C—— never accepted another invitation!

Easter Sunday was a fairly quiet day, on which there was a good deal of aerial activity on both sides.

Since his return from ten days leave to Paris on the 31st of March, Colonel Lee had been busily engaged on a scheme for the defence of the sector and particularly the mine shaft in our lines. This no doubt accounted for the many visits paid by Generals and staff officers. Major-General Lawford, and Brigadier-Generals Towsey and Clemson, and Colonel B. L. Anley arrived on a tour of inspection on the 9th. Colonel Clark, commanding the 32nd Royal Fusiliers, and other officers of that battalion also came along preparatory to taking over the sector later.

On Easter Monday at about 10.30 a.m. the enemy bombarded the top of P and O Trench with rifle grenades and fishtails, and later at about 3.30 p.m. blew in the front line in the right sector with minnenwerfers with the result that Ptes. W. C. Brown and S. Hooker of A Company were killed instantly, while Pte. W. Parsons of C Company died of wounds soon after. Another man was wounded.

As was the usual practice during this tour, the enemy started the day quietly but livened up during the evening. At 7.0 p.m. on the 10th the front line at Voormezeele Extension was badly smashed with 5.9.s, and one bay completely blown in. C Company had three men killed or mortally wounded—one while wiring—during the night and early morning. Ptes. A. Godfrey, H. Barnard, and R. Tinsley were the men who died: two other ranks were wounded. The whole night was a disturbed one, and during the morning of the 11th the enemy remained active with his artillery, blowing in Queen Victoria Street and Crater Lane. Fortunately the afternoon was quiet.

During this period of trench duty Dead Dog Farm was subjected to a great deal of shell fire. No doubt the enemy was aware by now that this was our Battalion H.Q. and singled it out for special attention. Promptly at 5.0 a.m. on the mornings of the 11th and 12th an intense bombardment was opened on the dugouts, and these had to be evacuated temporarily until the shelling had subsided. On the 12th the C.O.'s dugout was hit while he was in there with Major Williams, but fortunately no harm came to these officers, although they must have been badly shaken up. Under Lieut. David Walker, Signalling Officer, the remainder of the H.Q. staff took to the ditch behind the sandbagged wall close to H.Q., where shells dropped all round them without causing any casualties. During the "strafe" Sergt. J. Hawkins and Pte. Wheatley remained on duty in the Signal Office, which only a week before had been penetrated by a shell while the Durhams were in it. Both of them were afterwards complimented by the Brigadier.

Relief from a very trying time came on the 12th, when the 32nd Royal Fusiliers took over.

The period from the 13th to the 17th of April was spent in Ontario Camp, where the programme was the usual training, baths and Church Parade. Special attention was paid to bayonet-fighting. At various times the powers above thought the men were not aggressive enough. Brass hats living in comfort at Cassel or Montreuil amused their leisure in devising schemes to keep them up to the mark. One such was bayonet-fighting, to which we have already referred in extracts from Siegfried Sassoon's "Memoirs." The instructors, large beefy men who could make horrifying grimaces and had a flow of the filthiest language, urged quiet chaps from the office stool to plunge their bayonet with horrid yells and blood-thirsty growls into sacks, which were marked to show vital points. "Stick him in the belly, man," was the cry. "Call that a —— jab?" would howl the instructor. "That wouldn't take the —— skin off a —— rice-pudden!" The argument was that war was Hell and it was useless to wage it with kid gloves. Then go the whole hog, and be as devilish as you can make yourself. A very sound proposition for a supposedly Christian nation! However, most of those who were in action can testify that there was usually no need to use the devilish or fancy tricks of bayonet-fighting taught by these instructors. There were few soldiers among the belligerents who stopped to face a bayonet charge. It was nearly always a question of who was taking the offensive. If we were rushing a German trench the defenders scuttled away before we had time to plunge our bayonets in them. At times some of their machine-gunners stayed on, but, with their hands up in surrender, it was only the most callous that could bring themselves to give them a few inches of cold steel. The same might be said of our own fellows when they were in a similar predicament. It must be remembered that in the last war the destruction by artillery was so great that the defenders were often so badly shaken up as to render them absolutely incapable of resisting the attackers when they reached their objectives.

The weather was severe throughout this period of rest, gales, blizzards and stormy nights being commonplace occurrences. These conditions were very serious for the health of the troops. The conditions in the line were, of course, very much worse, as despite strict instructions about putting whale oil on the feet and the constant changing of socks and wearing of gum boots up to the thigh, men were being evacuated daily with frost bite and trench feet. The malady known as "Trench fever" began to assert itself, while pneumonia attacked others. One had to be very hardy to escape any sickness, but it was usually only the very bad cases that were evacuated. When a man left the Divisional area with sickness, it was usually a case for Blighty or the grave. Two men, Cpl. H. Mitchell and Pte. V. Eason died from pneumonia. Mitchell, who had also been wounded, expired on April 25th and Eason on the 26th of May. Some were sent to England in a crippled condition, especially the older men, though some of them "stuck it out" valiantly. Quite a number it must be remembered were over 40, and a few over 50. Ned McCarthy, the R.Q.M.S.'s batman, enlisted at the age of 57! He was the patriarch of the Battalion, and saw some service overseas until Speller thought it was time he sent him home. Of him Speller has written:—

"Old Ned McCarthy was my unofficial batman throughout his time with the Battalion. At the age of 57 he enlisted as 42 and maintained a solemn cheeriness under all sorts of circumstances. As compensation for his personal attentions Ned relieved me, by mutual arrangement, of 1 franc each day. With this he hurried off every morning to "Emma's" at Reninghelst, and there quaffed five glasses of very French *bière* at about 8.0 a.m.! He deserves a niche in the records of the Battalion if only for his gifts as a 'finder' of charcoal and an extraordinary facility for producing hot water for a tub whenever I hinted at one."

Besides the older ones there were some of the youngsters who put up with the extreme rigours of active service right to the end. In some cases these boys were claimed by their parents in 1917, and were sent to England until they were old enough to be sent overseas again. There was the case of Lce.-Cpl. W. Edwards, a Lewis-gunner of A Company. Having enlisted in June, 1915, he served with the Battalion at "Plug Street," Flers, and throughout the winter of 1916 and early '17, before being sent home at the age of 16! This was one of the boys who used to man the Crater and was responsible for a Lewis-gun team.

About this time a craze for taking commissions was rampant in the Battalion. The first man to be given a commission overseas was Cpl. R. Butterworth, who on the 6th of November, 1916, was posted as a Subaltern to the 11th Yorkshire Regt. Ptes. T. J. Young, M.M., T. C. Greves and R. Tyrrell proceeded to England as candidates soon after Butterworth was gazetted. Then came the Surrey Yeomanry: Cpl. W. G. Saunders, Pte. A. W. Floyd, Cpl. E. Noakes, Pte. S. Everett, Sergt. H. G. Herring and Pte. R. Collier followed at intervals up to the end of March, 1917, while C.S.M. F. Heydinger left for England for the same purpose on the 28th of February. The procedure adopted was for the candidate to make application to his Commanding Officer, fill in the necessary form, and then appear before the Brigadier and Divisional Commander before proceeding home. When the demand for officers became more urgent the Brigadier utilised the power of recommending candidates after interview without having recourse to the G.O.C. Division, but it was also made a condition that candidates had to be N.C.O.s and that they should continue to serve in the line till their movement orders were received. To qualify as N.C.O.s selected privates were given two stripes for which they drew no pay. The system of men applying for themselves was considered by many to lead to abuses and discontent among the others, who, although sometimes possessing better qualifications as soldiers and leaders, and also socially and educationally, did not like the idea of putting themselves forward in a manner that might suggest a temporary escape from the fighting. Realising this, Company Officers often approached suitable candidates with the object of getting them to make application. Without any disparagement to those who went home as candidates, it is acknowledged by officers and men that quite as good men remained in the ranks right up to the time that the Battalion was disbanded. The life of a subaltern on the Western Front was a short one, and it often struck us as peculiar that private soldiers who had shown no aptitude for leading men or even the ordinary qualifications of a Tommy should suddenly conceive the idea of becoming officers. To see such fine soldiers as C.S.M. R. Mayston, C.S.M. W. Hall and Sergt. S. Lattimore, to mention a few, remain in the ranks till the end would seem to indicate that the system was wrong. Of those who went home no records exist to tell us how they fared, although from what one hears from others they were, with one or two exceptions, all gazetted in due course. Sergt. ("Kip") Herring, who was a most popular N.C.O. in A Company, eventually became a Captain in the Cavalry, while Cpl. Saunders was given a commission in the Artillery.

To some extent the difficulty of finding suitable N.C.O.s among the men also existed. Many good soldiers refused to take promotion because, although they could be depended upon to lead men in action, they had an abhorrence of the parade ground and the often irksome job of ordering men about. It was not every N.C.O. that could maintain discipline and keep the friendship and respect of his comrades, especially in the companies. With the specialists, such as signallers, snipers and to a great extent the Lewis-gunners, things were slightly different. The Battalion Orderly Room staff, which was usually under the supervision of the Adjutant, who invariably looked after their welfare and saved them from many disagreeable parades and distasteful jobs, consisted of a sergeant, corporal, and three lance-corporals. In their capacity they got to know most of the officers and non-commissioned officers. They could be helpful to all ranks in many ways, and, as far as lay in their power, they tried to accommodate where it was possible. It was not such a bombproof job as some were led to believe, for it will be recollected that in trench warfare the whole staff went into the line at H.Q. and that in action one clerk at least always accompanied the C.O. and Adjutant. Where they differed from the rest of the Battalion was that their work was never finished. Day and night the "Paper war" was waged furiously during the Battalion's existence. All sorts of returns and reports, frivolous and otherwise, had to be drawn up for the Higher Authorities. One has only to visit the offices of the Official Historian to realise the enormous amount of paper used by the Army during the war. All orders were issued by Higher Authorities and thus it was a constant repetition of being "passed to you for necessary action." Masses of correspondence, instructions, operation orders and the like were thus passed on from G.H.Q. to Army, Army to Corps, Corps to Division, Division to Brigade and thence to Battalion.

Part II orders had to be compiled, principally by Cpl. W. G. Clayton, for forwarding to Orderly Room Sergt. Parker at the Base. Sergt. B. G. Burgess, who had been specially enlisted by Colonel Beatson applying to the War Office for authority to accept him despite the fact that he was under the minimum height, was in charge of the staff with the Battalion and got so used to King's Regulations that he could almost recite them backwards. A complete record of every movement of the officers and men of the Battalion was kept by the other clerks, and much of the material for this history is the result of their painstaking labours. A mutual respect and friendly feeling for one another was the keynote of the success of our Orderly Room staff, and so it was rarely that Sergt. Burgess had to "stand on his dignity."

Most of the Battalion were on working parties on April 18th, which was a snowy day. In the afternoon a Battalion team played the 18th K.R.R.s at football, the score being 2 all. Lce.-Cpl. A. Bowry, formerly of the Old Kingstonians, played in goal for us on this occasion.

The activity shown by the Boche on our last tour of the trenches at St. Eloi was evidently the preparation for an incident which took place at 9.0 p.m. on the 20th. The 11th West Kents this time took over the sector that had always been our charge. After heavy shelling a party of the enemy, estimated at 50, raided the line in the vicinity of the mine shaft. With the assistance of the Canadian Tunnellers and the Hants the West Kents drove the party back to the German lines, but not before the men in the Crater had been overwhelmed and either killed or taken prisoners. In his report of the raid General Towsey paid a tribute to the satisfactory working of the mine shaft defence scheme which was instituted by Colonel Lee. It was hard luck on the Kents that they should have got what in the normal run of things would have been the lot of the 12th Battalion. However, the 12th had had its share of the defence of the mine shaft, and if, as the historian of the West Kents records, the trenches were better and deeper and the area less boggy than at Spoil Bank, he is really paying a tribute to the work accomplished by the 12th East Surreys and the 20th D.L.I., who had found it a veritable swamp and a badly constructed line of defences a few months before.

On the 21st of April the C.O. proceeded to Recques, 10 miles N.W. of St. Omer, to reconnoitre the future training ground and returned in the evening. The 22nd was spent as a rest day and baths were indulged in. A football match with the 26th (Bankers) Battn. Royal Fusiliers resulted in a draw 2—2.

The quietness of the day at Ontario Camp was disturbed at 11.0 a.m., when two enemy planes flew low over the place. At the time training was going on in an adjoining camp, and whistles were blown to take cover. Outside the Battalion Orderly Room was a Lewis-gun post, to which Sergt. Lattimore rushed in order to have a "pot" at the planes. Lattimore states that owing to the low altitude at which the planes were flying it was not possible for him to range on them in time and also that there was the danger from bullets to our own troops to be considered. Thus the enemy was able to get away in the direction of the Mont des Cats before Lattimore could do what he intended. Meanwhile the anti-aircraft guns were firing so low that shrapnel fell on the camp. As the enemy made a similar appearance on the following day, it was obvious he was getting a bit concerned about what was happening behind our lines, but again he escaped. The Battalion played another football match on the 23rd against the Queen's Royal West Surreys which we lost by the only goal scored. Major L. H. Hickson relinquished the duties of Second in Command on the 23rd on being appointed to command the 7th Royal West Kents, and there was very great regret when he had to leave us.

The 24th of April was spent in gathering together all the different sections of the Battalion, including the men on command, in preparation for departure to the Brigade Training Area. Everyone knew that the period of winter warfare was nearly over, and the time for great offensives was approaching. The prospect was horrifying, but in war men perforce develop a devil-may-care insensitiveness to the future. "Let us eat and drink, for tomorrow we die." We were going to be out of the stink and the slime. away from minnies, whizzbangs, gas and rats, for a few weeks. What was beyond?—well, best not think of that.

At 10.0 a.m. on the 25th the Battalion with the First Line Transport, to the number of 29 officers and 935 other ranks, marched out of Reninghelst towards Steenvoorde en route for the training area. The weather was fine, and the troops in good fettle as they marched along the cobbled roads flanked on either side with hop poles. Rest was at hand, and the men gave vent to their feelings by singing as they marched along to the billets, which were reached at 2.0 p.m. The Divisional and Brigade Commanders watched the Battalion on the march and both expressed their high admiration of the general turnout and bearing of all. The Battalion could always be depended upon to present a good appearance when away from the fighting line, and the nickname "Shiny Twelfth" was in every way warranted.

A day's rest was enjoyed at Steenvoorde, a nice little town which boasted of a good deal of civilisation, including shops, which were well patronised by the men.

The march was continued on the 27th to Lederzeele and Wulverdinghe—a distance of 17½ miles. In case it might be thought that after such a lapse of time imagination has been brought to bear on the narrative, let us quote the entry in the War Diary for the date. "Falling out on the march was conspicuous by its absence. The Battalion finished the march in splendid condition and spirit. En route passed the Corps Commander, who expressed great satisfaction." Who could have helped being other than in the best of spirits passing through the countryside on a lovely spring day, with cows lowing in the fields as we passed and little children with their mothers turning out to make us realise that there were still better places on earth than the muddy and unhealthy area around St. Eloi! To hear the distant mutter of the guns instead of the deafening roar of the explosions was a change we much appreciated. Into fairly comfortable billets in the farmsteads men gladly threw down their packs, and then went in search of fresh milk, eggs and chips and other delicacies not so easily procured in the regions they had come from. Headquarters were situated in a farmhouse where a good many were able to make themselves comfortable in a fairly large kitchen.

On the 28th the road was taken to Nordausques, Le Panne (not to be confused with La Panne on the coast), and Quemberghe, which were the final destinations of different sections of the Battalion in the training area. The day after arrival was a Sunday, and after Church Parade there was a kit inspection. The remainder of the day was free for the men to do what they liked without getting into trouble.

The end of April found the Battalion parading at 5.15 in the morning and marching to the training ground. Night operations were carried out from 9.0 p.m. until 2.0 a.m., the general idea being to march and form up on taped positions in waves, ready to attack at dawn.

The casualties during the month were 2nd Lieut. S. H. Morgan (attached 122nd T.M.B.) killed on the 4th, and 12 other ranks also killed; 11 other ranks were wounded.

For the next fortnight the Battalion continued training in the area around Nordausques during a spell of very fine weather. The billets were comfortable, and with plenty of rations, well cooked joints and puddings made in the field ovens which had been installed, the troops began to think that soldiering on active service was not so bad after all. After parades men were free to spend their evenings in the few estaminets in the villages. Funny what an attraction these estaminets had for Tommy. Some of them were very bare and offered no other attraction than a warm stove over which coffee was brewing and some cheap indifferent beer or white or red wine, commonly referred to as "Vin Blong" or "Vin Rouge." Yet at all times these places were well patronised by the men. Wherever a crowd of Tommies gathered together, there was sure to be an impromptu concert. Even in the darkest days of the war the strains of some old Music Hall song could be heard coming from estaminets and billets where British troops were congregated, and it would have been an instruction to present-day crooners to listen to some real harmony. Nordausques was no exception. These men who had faced death and knew that ere long they would have to face it again could still afford to sing. It was this spirit that distinguished the British Army from most of the other belligerents, although it must be stated in fairness to the others that, whenever we had the opportunity of serving alongside them, they tried to emulate us in this direction. Two ditties sung in harmony stood out as great favourites with the men: "Love's Old Sweet Song" and "Nelly Dean." How many happy memories these two songs will recall despite the sentiment expressed in them!

Football matches were arranged between the companies, and during the course of one of these Sergt. G. Nuttman—one of the best full backs the Battalion ever had—accidently dislocated the collar-bone of Pte. C. A. Sly of the observers. Sly got to Blighty, and rumour had it that he wrote to Nuttman thanking him for what he had done and enclosed some cigarettes as a thank-offering. Sly, who to-day is an active member of the "Toc H" movement, cannot confirm the rumour, although many may think he was somewhat remiss in not suitably rewarding Nuttman for his trouble. H.Q. Company got into some trouble over football. Requiring a field, they searched round and came across a bit of a mud heap on which they started to punt the ball about. Unfortunately, they forgot to get permission of the farmer, and very soon the game was disturbed by a Frenchman who, with fury in his eyes, demanded that the ground should be cleared right away. After a heated discussion and a great deal of gesticulation it was decided to abandon the game and make representations elsewhere in order to get a ground for the purpose. With the aid of one of the French-speaking men of the company the same field was eventually secured, which showed the advantage of being able to speak the language.

Passes to St. Omer were granted to us, and for the first time we were permitted to spend a whole day in the town which had served for a time as British Headquarters. Lorries conveyed us there, and the town was found to be a very lively place, probably the liveliest part of the Second Army area. Cafés and canteens abounded, in which music was played throughout the whole day. English nurses and W.A.A.C.s used to visit there, and it was because of the possibility of seeing or speaking to womenfolk of their own race that the troops always tried to get into the town whenever they were near it. A large number of Australians were always there, and it was noticeable that many of the English girls sought these Colonials out for their attentions. It may have been just simple curiosity that drew them to the Australians, but the average English Tommy was convinced that it was because the "Aussies" had more money to spend. The private soldier used to draw five francs a week while out at rest, which did not leave him a lot to go gay on, whereas his Colonial brother-in-arms was more adequately paid for his services. The English infantryman was very conscious of the disparity between the pay of the Imperials and Colonials. However, what little cheer there was in St. Omer was a tonic to men who had spent months in the trenches.

Battalion sports were held on the 9th, and some good performances were put up for prizes offered for the different events.

All good things must come to an end, and so it was with great reluctance that the men of the Twelfth took the road back to Wulverdinghe and Lederzeele on May 15th after a fortnight of forgetfulness of the war and its horrors. After a night's rest there the march to Steenvoorde was continued. Another night's rest, and the Battalion paraded on the 17th and marched viâ Poperinghe and Reninghelst to Mic Mac Camp near Dickebusch. The other battalions of the Brigade returned to their old camps at Chippewa and Alberta. Mic Mac was situated closer to the line than our old Camp Ontario, and at this time was the centre of a hive of activity. A new railway had been

GROUP OF OFFICERS TAKEN AT NORDAUSQUES, 1917.

constructed along the road from Reninghelst through Ouderdom to Dickebusch, along which came two big naval guns—"Bertha" and "Bella." Their particular job was to fire a few shells into the German lines and then retire to a more secure place behind. In addition artillery dumps were being erected all along the road, with horse lines, drinking or watering points and prisoners' cages. It was clear that the great day was approaching. At Mic Mac the "practice" bombardments of our artillery soon became a daily and nightly occurrence. The star shells and bursting shrapnel gave the Salient the appearace of a Brock's benefit on a tremendous scale. In these circumstances the short stay of two days at Mic Mac cannot be said to have been the sort of rest which was usually associated with this encampment. Heavy German guns had already started to take toll of the roads, for, as we afterwards discovered, the enemy could see from the ridge as far back as Reninghelst.

The Battalion set out to relieve the 20th D.L.I. in the old trenches at St. Eloi on the 19th. They were found to be in a badly damaged condition owing to the enemy retaliation for two raids made by the Durhams on the preceding nights, but as the weather was sunny, the conditions were not so bad as when we had last been there.

Apart from a great deal of aerial activity which fine days usually brought, there was little to report in the sector on the morning of the 20th. In the air six of our planes fought six of the enemy, one of our machines being brought down in the German lines. Bus House was heavily bombarded for about an hour and a half in the evening, when a rain of 5.9.s was responsible for one man being wounded. On the 21st an artillery duel took place, in which the enemy must have got the worst of the deal, as our guns were still firing long after his had ceased. Just before 10.0 p.m. the sectors on our right and left were heavily bombarded by the Boche, a few shells dropping in our lines.

To the great regret of all ranks it was learned on the 22nd that Colonel Lee was leaving us and handing over the command of the Battalion to Major E. Knapp, an officer of the South African Defence Force, at present serving with the 23rd Middlesex Regt. Colonel Lee, feeling that his health, which had been poor for many months past, was not such as to enable him to undertake the strain of the coming offensive, with reluctance gave up his command and proceeded to Reninghelst. Lieut.-Col. H. H. Lee, D.S.O., was a very efficient commanding officer and was highly thought of by the Brigade and Divisional Commanders. There is not much doubt that, had he remained, he would have later received a Brigade in the same way as Major Gwyn Thomas, our first Brigade Major. Out with the Cameronians in the early days of the war he had experienced a trying time before taking the 12th overseas. Wounded at Ploegsteert, he came back at a time when most of his old command had been put out of action on the Somme. The bad conditions at St. Eloi must have had their effect on him, for he never missed his daily tour of the trenches, whatever the weather. Though he was a strict disciplinarian outwardly, those who were intimately associated with him saw the other side of his nature. Off the parade ground he was kindly and genial, concerned mainly with the men's welfare.* In Major Knapp a good successor was found. With reference to the new C.O., Capt. H. S. Walker writes:—

"He had been on Kitchener's staff in the South African War. I forget where he served in the early part of the Great War, but he got to London and went to the War Office to ask for a job on the Western Front. He was politely 'turned down,' but, having in the meantime discovered which was K. of K's room in the War Office, somehow got

*Note: Colonel Lee's after-career was as follows: C.O. Depôt Battn. Tank Corps—November, 1917—March 1918; C.O. 26th R. Welsh Fusiliers and 1st Cameronians, 1918; served in Kurdistan, 1923; retired, 1930. He was three times wounded in the Great War and four times mentioned in despatches.

near there, met an officer in the corridor and explained his difficulty. The officer told him that nothing could be done. Major Knapp then kicked up such a row that K. of K. looked out of his room to see what was wrong. He recognised Knapp, called him inside and sent him to France.

"When he took over command of the 12th he summoned all Company Commanders to Battalion H.Q. at Dead Dog Farm, and when we were all assembled he came into the dugout and said in his short clipped way of talking, 'Good day, gentlemen, I have taken command of this battalion. Our opposite numbers have told me that there are no Boche opposite us. They are wrong. To prove it, the Battalion will do a raid.' Short and to the point, as I always found him to be, there was no doubt that he was a Hun Strafer."

Doc. Harrison, who got to know him very well, says that during his command the 12th were dubbed by some "Knapp's Nippers," for his smart soldierly figure was on the short side.

An incident happened on the 22nd which will be well remembered by those present at the time. At 8.0 a.m. a man was seen—by one of our sentries—in No Man's Land followed by a German. The matter was reported to 2nd Lieut. Puttock, who shot the German, whilst the other continued to crawl towards our parapet. Meanwhile C.S.M. W. G. Hill, who had taken over B Company in place of C.S.M. Heydinger, climbed over the parapet and pulled the man into our trench. It turned out to be Lce.-Cpl. Faulkner of the 7th Battn. South Lancashire Regt., who had been captured four days before in an enemy raid in the sector on our right and had lived three days without food in shell-holes behind the enemy front line after breaking away from his escort. During the night he had managed to cross the enemy front line, and, though in a thoroughly exhausted condition and wounded, managed to make for our lines in the morning. In rescuing the man, "Pompey" Hill, as we called him, was shot at by the pursuing German before the latter was shot by 2nd Lieut. Puttock. So bad was the plight of Lce.-Cpl. Faulkner that he had to be conveyed to our Aid Post on a stretcher. It is not recorded in our Diary whether he received a decoration for his pluck, but certainly he deserved one. "Pompey" Hill was afterwards awarded the Military Medal, which was well earned.

The 23rd of May was a sunny day with the usual war in the air. Several fights took place over our lines, and five of our machines were brought down to only one of the enemy. Von Richthofen's "Circus" was very active about the front at this time. His red plane was occasionally seen very high up, while the remainder of his crack airmen were in close proximity. Our airmen were brave and daring, but it was often evident that they unnecessarily courted trouble by fighting at odds of about one to six. When the Germans found that they were outnumbered, they usually broke off the fight as soon as possible and made for their lines with the greatest speed. It was rarely an Englishman turned tail, whatever the odds.

From now until the 26th when we were relieved, our artillery continued to pound away at the enemy lines by day and night. Of course, we got some retaliation in which two men were wounded in the front line on the 24th. Many times we cursed our own artillery for keeping us awake at night and causing Fritz to sling over every variety of trench-mortar shell into our front line. Observers reported that the enemy front line was in a very bad condition and that the wire was almost gone. In these circumstances many of us thought that it was impossible for the Boche to hold it, but when 2nd Lieut. Puttock tried to enter it with a patrol on the night of the 25th it was found to be well manned, possibly in view of the fact that the 18th K.R.R.s on our right had made a raid earlier on. Fights in the air continued daily, our young airmen striving to gain the ascendancy before the great battle opened. In the evening of the

24th it is recorded that four of our planes fought 35 of the enemy! The result of the fight is not stated, but it is apparent with such odds it would have been wisest for our machines to make off for reinforcements.

On the 26th the Battalion was relieved by the 23rd Middlesex Regt. and marched back to Reninghelst, but this time to Alberta instead of Ontario Camp. Alberta Camp was situated some little distance away from Ontario, on the road to Westoutre. It was surrounded by various brigades of Artillery which had just moved into the area for the coming offensive. These were known as "flying columns," as they moved from one part of the front to another to take part in big "stunts." Higher up than Ontario Camp, Alberta enabled us to get a better view of what was happening up the line. It was a wonderful sight to watch the flashes from the two thousand and odd guns of all calibres firing on the Messines Ridge. It was a veritable ring of flame accompanied by a continuous thudding from the guns. Verey lights and rockets of all hues shot into the sky, accompanied by metal from our lines. As we stood there, we wondered how it was possible for men to live in such an inferno. And yet they did. As we afterwards discovered, the Germans were living like rats in a hole; their deep dugouts came to their assistance. In the words of the troops, Fritz was getting it "thick and heavy."

For the next four days the Battalion was employed on working parties in the line. So congested were things at the time that often it was impossible to get in or out of the trenches. The roads leading up to them were as bad, and it was wonderful how the traffic police managed to control the tremendous number of lorries laden with ammunition which were making their way to the advanced dumps. At this period 18-pounders had been installed in the reserve line at Dead Dog Farm awaiting "Zero" day. Shells had to be carried to these batteries, and of course the task of bringing them up fell as usual to the infantry. It was not a pleasant sensation to be seated on top of a cargo of shells in a lorry while the enemy was sending over his "heavies" on the road which was congested with traffic. Such was the predicament in which most of the Battalion found themselves on these working parties. It became so hot at times that drivers and carriers had to scatter to what cover they could secure in the vicinity. Even after this had been accomplished, there was the extremely delicate task of bringing the shells to the guns through the crowded trenches on which the enemy was venting his fury. Can it be wondered at that the men were only too glad when the haven of Alberta Camp was reached each evening, despite the fact that the enemy airmen chose to make nocturnal visits in order to disturb their slumbers?

On the 30th our Transport was shelled out of Mic Mac Camp during the night and had to move to Chippewa Camp. This was not surprising considering that the German balloons had been keeping watch during the day and that planes had been overhead many times.

On the 31st we relieved the 11th (Lambeth) Battn. The Queen's Royal West Surreys in the G.H.Q. line in front of Scottish Wood. The day was again sunny, and the heavy bombardment of the enemy lines still continued; the enemy retaliating on the back areas with H.E. and gas shells during the night.

The casualties during the month of May were 12 other ranks wounded, and the strength at the end of the month was 43 officers and 1,020 other ranks.

THE LARK AND THE INTELLIGENCE OFFICER.

The Lark. Upon my flickering wings I rise
And spurn the dewy ground,
To pour my matin ecstasies
In wave on wave of sound.

The I.O. You foolish bird, to throw your hours
So fruitlessly away!
Had I your wings, I'd put my powers
To better use today.

The Lark. Yes, brother. Would you had! We two
Could mount together straight,
And, soaring upward to the blue,
Sing praise at Heaven's gate.

The I.O. Dull thing, I do not long to fly
On a fool's errand. No.
But I could unsuspected spy
On German lines below.

The Lark. 'Tis true, their trenches everywhere
Are spread, as I can see:
But what the men are doing there
Is nothing, sure, to me.

The I.O. But much to me, for, could I know
Their every nook and gun,
'T would be an easier task, I trow,
To extirpate the Hun.

The Lark. And do you seek to kill him then?
If that's your aim, my friend,
Rather than stay on earth with men,
My life in air I'd spend.

The I.O. Your wits are slow. You cannot tell
The wrongs he does to us.
So we must answer shell for shell,
And teach him better thus.

The Lark. And, if you kill him, tell me true,
Nay, should you millions slay,
And should he millions slay of you,
Is this the only way?

The I.O. I cannot stay and argue more
With one whose brain is blind
To all our high superior lore,
The wisdom of mankind.

The Lark. Goodbye, my master. One last word
Your mind's beyond my span.
Thank God who made me but a bird
And not superior man.

1917. St. Eloi. John Aston.

CHAPTER VII.

1st June to 5th July, 1917.

The raid before the Battle of Messines—The explosion of the mines and assault on the Dammstrasse—In action near the White Château—Working parties near Dickebusch Lake and Vierstraat—Visit of His Majesty.

ALL was now in readiness for the stupendous Battle of the Messines Ridge. This was a brilliant military success, standing out in high relief against all the other so-called victories of 1916-1917, which were in truth sanguinary failures, said to have been persisted in against all reason by our High Command. On May 7th, Haig asked Plumer when he would be ready to deliver the attack, and he replied—"A month to-day." This calm confidence, fulfilled exactly, was based on deliberate, exact and business-like preparation and on will-power tempered by commonsense and unbiassed judgment. Trust and receptiveness to ideas and criticisms were the keynotes of the Second Army. Harington, the most brilliant strategic brain in the British Army and the finest organiser, was yet never pontifically aloof from those holding subordinate commands, but built up his plans on the advice or warning he received.

We felt at the time, and we still hold, that, if only Plumer and Harington had been the pair in supreme command, the history of 1916 and 1917 would have been far different, hundreds of thousands of lives might never have been thrown away, and far better strategic results gained. But on the Western Front, where the whole conflict was a siege-war, almost every high command, including the command-in-chief, was held by a Cavalry general, and the result was ruinous—with the exception of Messines.*

Before we proceed, it would be profitable to compare this, just one of the actions of the Great War, with the famous battle of Waterloo, fought 102 years earlier, and also fought within one day. In that fearful struggle 170,000 men in all were engaged, French, British, Prussians, Hanoverians, Belgians, Dutch. The artillery under Wellington's command comprised 156 guns, whose extreme range was a few hundred yards—half a mile at most. The battle front was about 3 miles in breadth. Thus the carnage was fearfully concentrated—dead and wounded in places piled in heaps upon each other. The French suffered 25,000 casualties, the victorious Allies 16,000.

*Since the above was written, Mr. Lloyd George's War Memoirs for 1918 have been published, and in them there is a letter from Lord Milner to Lloyd George in which the suggestion is made that "the Army would be quite happy with Plumer and Harington" at the head of affairs. It is also revealed that Plumer was offered the post of C.I.G.S. in place of Sir William Robertson, but declined it. We suspect that his refusal was based on loyalty to his chiefs and the fact that he had no axe to grind with politicians of any shade.

Now for a few facts about Messines. The attack had been devised and preparations begun many months before. The battle front was 9 miles from Mont Sorrel just North of the Ypres-Comines Canal to La Douve Brook. Those who have never seen the country should realise that there was nothing in the nature of true hills: the highest point of the enemy position was less than 250 feet above the sea. Most of it was merely gently rising ground. Just South-West of Mont Sorrel was a wide open area torn and wasted by shell fire, bisected by the Canal, now almost dry, its banks crumbling into ruin, with here and there huge chunks of cement or masonry, where a lock had once existed. As the canal had ceased to operate and all the beeks and ditches in the country, which usually carried the water off from the sodden soil, had been choked and breached, it was not strange that it had become a huge swamp during the winter. But now, after two months of fine weather, it was dry. Going South-West from the Canal, you follow a line of low heights in the shape of an unstretched bow, forming an obtuse salient. It was Plumer's object to storm this crescent and establish himself on a line formed by the chord of the bow, of which the village of Oostaverne would be about the middle point. About 300 yards South-West of the Canal on the gradually rising ground stood the "White Château." This handsome mansion, though in Belgium, belonged to two French brothers Mathieu—both of whom were killed in the war—and, being a prominent spot, had of course, suffered badly. By kind permission of the Director of the Imperial War Museum we reproduce an excellent German photo of the ruin about the beginning of 1917. In June, 1917, it was merely a heap of rubble so deep that no projectile could penetrate it, while the huge cellars formed a great nest of machine-guns. To the South of the ruins were the shattered stables and a stinking morass, once a charming little lake, with about 50 acres of woodland, now merely grisly stumps. The drive from the mansion to the main road ran almost due East and West along the high ground and was known to us as the Dammstrasse; this had been strongly fortified. Three miles South-West on the highest point of the little ridge, were the gutted remains of the houses, hospice and church of Wytschaete (known to us as Whitesheet), and beyond that, out of view of our sector, the village of Messines.

Why was this battle fought?

The situation, as we pointed out earlier, was by the end of 1916 a stalemate. But important events had occurred since. The Russian revolution and collapse had seriously shaken the fabric of the Allied cause. The U.S.A. joined in and declared war in February; but her weight could tell but little for at least a year. Rumania had joined the Allies too, but had been dealt a knockout blow in a few months. A great French offensive under Nivelle had began early in April and had been repulsed so bloodily that the French Army for nearly a year was shaken and unable to do more than hold on, so that the British had continually to make vast and expensive attacks in order to keep the enemy pressure off them. The Hun submarines were taking a fearful toll of our merchant shipping every week, using Ostend and Zeebrugge as their chief bases. It was of immense importance for the Allies in the West to retain the initiative gained in 1916 and to keep up the pressure in order to prevent Russia from being overwhelmed, to relieve the French, and, if possible, to clear the hostile forces from the neighbourhood of Ypres and disengage the coast.

The first thrust had been the successful capture of the Vimy Ridge in April and the subsequent series of battles east of Arras, which had ended, like the Somme offensive, in a stalemate; the clearing of the enemy salient of the Messines Ridge was to be the second great operation and this was to be followed later by tremendous assaults on the Passchendaele heights. Since October, 1914, manœuvre had been impossible, and the only feasible method of attack for either side was a direct frontal assault, seeing that the trenches stretched for a distance of 650 miles from the sea to the Swiss frontier. Frontal attack was fearful enough in the days of Malplaquet or Borodino, but in modern war the invention of the machine-gun and magazine rifle behind *chevaux-de-frise* of barbed wire makes the defence almost impregnable. The only possible method of breaking it down was then held to be by absolutely overwhelming artillery fire. This should, if in sufficient weight, completely pulverise the defences, and to the infantry was left the task of walking over, occupying the shattered ground and constructing new defences. That at least was the idea. It almost never worked according to plan. Only once did the fact even approximate to the intention, at the battle of the Messines Ridge. Later of course the tank, when its capacities were at last realised and fully used, solved the problem.

The preparations were on the most formidable scale ever yet devised in war. The Somme had shown what tragic muddles and waste of life resulted from offensives improperly planned, where the troops went "over the plonk," unaware of what they were intended to do, inadequately equipped and directed. General Plumer, General Harington and their competent staffs were determined not to repeat that débacle. They had thought out to the smallest detail every item of the operations, they were adequately supplied by the Home Government with every engine that modern science could devise for complete success, but, most important of all, they had ensured that every officer and man should know precisely what he was expected to do on the day of battle. The troops had practised assaults in waves over open country selected as resembling the actual terrain they would have to cover, and just behind Mont Kemmel a large scale model about an acre in extent was constructed, to which parties of officers and men were taken for study—a remarkable instance of the meticulous care given to the preliminaries.

The whole countryside for many miles behind our trenches was a vast encampment, light railways, dumps, workshops, cantonments; and everywhere guns, guns, guns, from the huge 15 inch howitzer (a representation of which horror stands as the R.A. memorial at Hyde Park Corner) and the long-barrelled "Silent Susan" that had a range of 25 miles, down to the 18-pounder field gun. There were no less than 2,374 of them (over 800 of them being heavies), the greatest concentration of cannon ever till then assembled in such an area in the history of the world, one gun to every seven yards of front. The gunner personnel numbered 120,000, and 321 trainloads of ammunition were brought to the guns, whilst in the course of the preliminary bombardment, which lasted 19 days, 18,000,000 shells weighing 300,000 tons were hurled at the enemy lines. The British troops taking part in the battle numbered 155,000. The cost has never been estimated—£100,000,000 would certainly be far below the truth.

And the combatants were the most civilized peoples of the world!

But two further prepartions were devised "to make assurance double sure." In the air for many weeks we had almost complete preponderance. Our machines, fighters, bombers, observers, were in hundreds; and rarely did an enemy plane succeed in getting across. Several miles back from the front line there hung in the sky at least 50 "Sausage" balloons anchored by wire cables to the ground, each containing two observers. Thus our furious gunfire was accurately directed, and the whole enemy area plastered and riven, while the gunners were rendered almost blind, and his retaliation was feeble compared to our barrage. Lastly, the device by which the battle will always be remembered, the key factor to its success. For two years miners had sweated in the foul clayey depths, driving 8,000 yards of galleries eastward and southward, till now 19 huge mines, charged with 1,000 tons of ammonal, were only waiting the spark to explode and hurl thousands of the foe into eternity in one awful cataclysm. In fact, the whole "Show" as it was blithely called, was a Titanic example of how man can pervert his God-given powers of mind and body to the service of the Devil.

A glorious 1st of June found the Battalion occupying trenches in the G.H.Q. line between Voormezeele and Scottish Wood. It was a treat to see a few blades of grass again and to rest in dugouts which were fairly comfortable and well concealed. Our artillery in a constant crescendo continued to play havoc with the enemy lines. Not an inch of the German front seemed to be free from explosions, as we gazed across the ridge while these rehearsals for the big day were being conducted. "Poor old Fritz," we would say, "he must be getting it in the neck." Observers reported seeing him scuttle out of his deep dugouts and get to earth as soon as possible. Volcanoes of fire and smoke spouted from the Boche trenches, hurling up clods, fascines, limbs of men, branches, 200 feet in the tormented air. In the words of Scripture that describes the destruction of Sodom and Gomorrah—"The smoke of the country went up like the smoke of a furnace." Letters found later in German dugouts and statements made by prisoners showed the ghastly ruin effected and the state of nerve-wreckage to which they were reduced. Our guns were never quiet, day or night, for a fortnight before Zero day, and on the day of the battle itself they fired no less than 3,550,000 shells!

At 9.45 p.m. that evening our artillery opened up a furious bombardment on the enemy front line near No. 1 Crater. This was the signal for a party, commanded by Capt. W. Hagen, to get ready for a raid on the German front and support lines known as "Obey" Trenches. 68 other ranks accompanied 2nd Lieuts. A. G. Howitt and H. S. Todd across No Man's Land and entered the Boche front line at 10.0 p.m. The trenches were found to be demolished, but the raiders pushed on to the support lines, bombing dugouts and picking up prisoners here and there. Altogether they spent close on half an hour in the German lines and returned with 2 Unteroffiziers and 5 other ranks of the 44th Infantry Regiment, 2nd (East Prussian) Division, one machine-gun, a telephone, several rifles and some equipment, but not before leaving their visiting card—a board with the "Black Hand" painted on it. A dugout with a dozen Germans in would not surrender and accordingly it was bombed, with the result that the inmates were in all probability killed. Our casualties were 5 other ranks slightly wounded. The prisoners were brought before Major Knapp, our new C.O., who, being a fluent speaker of German, interrogated them, but without getting much information. They were fine strapping men, but looked very dazed owing to the terrible bombardments they had been experiencing. So the Major was right after all. There were some Boches opposite us, and the "Black Hand Gang" had once again demonstrated what could be done with a minimum of casualties. The raid was admirably planned by Major Knapp, who received much credit for the way the action was carried out. The machine-gun was sent as a trophy to Bermondsey.

For their services in the raid the following decorations were awarded—Military Cross: 2nd Lieut. A. G. Howitt; Military Medal: Sergeants D. S. Maddison and R. W. Mayston, Cpl. H. C. Richardson.

After the raid our artillery continued to bombard all night; following this up the next day, they brought all guns in the sector to bear upon the ridge in a practice shoot between 3.0 and 3.30 p.m. As the Diary pithily records, "It was a warm day; very hot for the enemy."

Capt. David Walker has an anecdote about this raid.

"Part of the plan was to establish in No Man's Land and close to the Boche lines a forward signal station, where telephone communication could be kept up. The night before I was given the job as signalling officer with a N.C.O. and two men of laying a line out and connecting up with a telephone which would be left ready for the raiding party the following night. Our front line trenches were held by the 123rd Brigade: the raiding party was to come up from the G.H.Q. Line and then rejoin the Battalion there. All was arranged for us, and the company holding the front line was advised that we were out in No Man's Land.

"We had just completed our job and the telephone line was in operation, all without a hitch. We may have imagined a lot but actually saw no Boche patrols, and wasting no time in such an unhealthy spot, we began the return to the trenches. Immediately there was a clap of rifle shots and a cry of pain at my side. Down into the bottom of a shell hole! Had we been spotted? Were we cut off from our lines? Certainly we were being shot at from the direction of our trenches. Another shot! This time I was certain that the men holding our front line trenches were firing at us and for some reason did not know we were in No Man's Land. This was a very awkward situation and my signaller by my side was in great pain, having been shot through the muscle of the right biceps. Hastily a tourniquet was put on his arm, and he was able to get up. Frantically waving a white handkerchief, I dashed for our trenches, the others coming on as best they could. Through the barbed wire we lost our way, in making such great haste, our uniforms and our hands and legs being torn to bits on the barbs. The awful moment was not over until, one by one, we leapt down into the front line trench to find an officer, full of apologies and 'telling off' a very young and conscience-stricken sentry."

The Battalion during this tour of duty had been employed on working parties, chiefly at night. The conditions were not too favourable for this sort of work, as the enemy gave us severe bursts of shelling with the object of hampering the preparations which were going on. The back areas in particular were subjected to very heavy shelling, and a large dump not far from our positions was exploded. The work of the Transport was very praiseworthy, for nightly it was "strafed" very badly. Gas shells too were constantly dropped day and night, and the new devil's invention of "Mustard" gas that blinded the sufferer was making its appearance. We can recall still the fluttering noises of these shells, followed by soft plops, almost more dreaded than the usual explosions. Despite these difficulties rations arrived as usual. The Transport Officer—2nd Lieut. F. W. Matthews—had a bad experience one night, when his charger bolted and ended up in Dickebusch Lake. Some of the mules also got adrift and were lost to the Battalion. How these were replaced is best left to the imagination. If a stray horse or mule was found, it was usually "adopted" by the unit finding it.

At 8.0 a.m. on the 5th of June the Battalion was relieved by one company of the 26th (Bankers) Battn. Royal Fusiliers, and marched to Chippewa Camp. As he was coming down the duckboards by Elzenwalle, the Medical Officer, Capt. C. N. Binney, R.A.M.C., was badly wounded in the jaw by a shell. 2nd Lieut. J. Aston, who was with him, bound him up, and he was able to walk to Dickebusch. When the Provost Sergeant (Charlie Field), conveyed the news to Battalion H.Q., it was received with great regret. Dr. Binney had endeared himself to all ranks by his charm of manner and his outstanding abilities as a Medical Officer. It was a greater blow to his orderly, Cpl. Southall, who had only left him a short while before, after the Doctor had told him that he was going to try to get a lift in an ambulance. How prophetic his words seemed to be! Dr. Binney was succeeded by Capt. H. H. Prentiss, R.A.M.C., who joined the Battalion on the following day—a "tremendous figure of a man," as Cpl. Southall well describes him.

It was notified on the 5th that Major E. Knapp had been promoted to Lieut.-Colonel as from the 22nd of May.

The eve of the great day in the history of the British Second Army on the Western Front had at last arrived. Feverish activity was displayed everywhere. Sign boards pointing to the location of dumps, routes and prisoners' cages had sprung up behind the lines. In the woods at Chippewa Camp men began to detonate bombs ready for the morrow. As usual one or two accidents happened through detonators being carelessly handled—one man having two or three fingers blown off. Inserting detonators in bombs was a job which needed very great care, but there were some men who considered they were so adept that they did not take the same care as the less experienced, with the result already stated. In addition, there were also faulty detonators over which no one had any control. Conferences between the Commanding Officer and Company Commanders were held, and final instructions issued to the troops. N.C.O.s were given small maps which could also be used as message forms for notifying H.Q. of the progress of the troops under their command. The maps gave a very clear outline of the objectives to be attained, whilst the message forms provided for almost every eventuality. Here is a copy:—

MESSAGE.

..........................DIVISION.
Map reference or
Mark on Map at back.

1. My (Company.
2. My (Platoon has reached..
3. My (Company
(Platoon is at..and is consolidating.
(Company
(Platoon is at..and has consolidated.
4. Am held up by M.G. at..
5. I need:—Ammunition.
Bombs.
Rifle Grenades.
Water.
Verey lights.
Stokes shells.
6. Counter attack forming up at..
Right
7. I am in touch with..on Left at..................
Right
8. I am not in touch with..on Left
9. I am being shelled from ....
10. I estimate my present strength at..rifles.
11. Hostile Battery
Machine Gun } active at..
Trench Mortar

Time..m.
Date..

Name..
Platoon..
Battalion..

This form of message was also used in subsequent operations of the Second Army and proved to be very useful on more than one occasion.

Both the Divisional and Brigade Commanders inspected the Battalion and gave a few words of encouragement. 2nd Lieut. Aston was sent to the Headquarters of the 140th Infantry Brigade at Lock House, Spoil Bank, to act as Liaison Officer for the following day.

The following was the list of officers for the attack:—

Headquarters: C.O. Lieut.-Col. E. Knapp.
Understudy: Capt. Hector S. Walker.
Acting Adjutant: Lieut. V. L. Clift.

A Company O.C. 2nd Lieut. W. G. Robinson: 2nd Lieuts. W. J. Palk, M.C., R. N. Haine and A. W. England.

B Company. O.C. Capt. H. S. Openshaw, M.C.: 2nd Lieuts. B. F. Dodd, A. G. Howitt and W. A. Vanner.

C Company. O.C. Lieut. J. A. Rogers: 2nd Lieuts. L. W. B. Russell, A. Hemsley and L. A. Rossiter.

D Company. O.C. Capt. A. V. Baker: 2nd Lieuts. A. R. Puttock and F. A. Samuels.

At 9.0 p.m. the Battalion, with the men carrying their full battle kit with Lewis-guns, rifle grenades, bombs, flares, entrenching tools and the rest, set out in fairly good spirits to take up its positions for the attack. To illustrate the intricate details thought out, every man was provided with chewing gum to prevent thirst when water bottles were emptied. The fact that the mines were to be blown had acted as a tonic to the men. As one of the companies marched out of the camp, the band, which had turned out, played the familiar strains of "Good Byee." The men took up the air as they marched along, and those who were left behind with the Details were choked with emotion at the wonderful spirit displayed by their comrades—some of whom they knew only too well would never return, while others would probably be maimed for life. With a faint cheer the Details withdrew from the scene, as the last section of fours passed the camp. It may have been that some of them were jubilant at staying behind, but most had no such feeling. They felt like sneaks because they knew they were to be spared—temporarily at any rate—the trials and troubles of their comrades. They had no delusions about being brave, but they were conscious of the feeling that, if it was good enough for their own particular pals to risk their lives, it was good enough for them. It was with heavy hearts that many of them lay down to rest that night at Chippewa Camp.

The Battalion followed the route by Mic Mac Camp and rear of Dickebusch and thence between English and Scottish Woods to the concentration area in front of Old French Trench.

A desultory bombardment was in progress as the troops moved up, and unfortunately the enemy was dropping shells at intervals, as he had done daily of late, close to the point where the Regimental Aid Post and Battalion Dump had been sited. About eight 4.2's fell and caused some casualties in D Company, for the route was much congested with the troops of the 123rd Brigade and those of our own. By 1.30 a.m. June 7th, the Brigade was in position and waiting for Zero hour.

The scheme of operations was as follows:—The Second Army was to capture the Messines Ridge and the enormously strong positions along it, which had been held by the Germans for nearly 2½ years, along a front of 9 miles from Mont Sorrel on the North to La Douve Brook on the South. On the South was the II (Anzac) Corps, in the centre the IX Corps, largely Irish and Ulstermen, and on the left the X Corps under General Morland, of which our Division formed the right. The objective of the 41st Division was the Dammstrasse and the woods and positions beyond it up to the "Black Line" known as Oblong Reserve. The first objective ("Blue Line") just over the Dammstrasse, was to be taken by the 123rd Brigade, the 124th Brigade acting on the Right; the second ("Black Line") by the 122nd Brigade, the 124th Brigade at the same time continuing forward with them. On the left of the 41st Division was the 140th Brigade (47th Division), consisting of the 6th, 7th, 8th and 15th Battalions London Regt., whose objective was the ground immediately south of the Canal. On our right was the 19th Division. After the capture and consolidation of the "Black Line" a period of 8 hours was to elapse, and then the 24th Division was to advance through us on to the extreme objective, the village of Oostaverne, known as the "Green Line."

At Zero hour the 19 mines were to be sprung along the entire Army front and the intense bombardment was to begin. No troops within half a mile of any of the mines were allowed to be in any dugout or narrow trench, lest the explosions should cause these to collapse and bury the occupants. The tense moments passed. A few shells were dropping here and there. Our guns were almost silent. Officers kept looking at their watches. No one who was there will ever forget those fateful minutes.

Suddenly at 3.10 a.m. the great mine at St. Eloi, which had been driven by the Canadian tunnellers (charged with over 50 tons of ammonal), was blown beneath No. 2, 3, and 4 Craters, causing a terrific explosion, killing many of the enemy and demoralising the occupants of their lines. Simultaneously the other 18 mines flared to heaven. At the same instant every single gun and howitzer opened intense fire on the enemy trenches and batteries. It was Hell broken loose. Under this fearful barrage the first assaulting waves went over, accompanied by tanks; by 5.0 a.m. every position on the Dammstrasse had been gained by the 123rd Brigade, and a good number of prisoners were coming back. There was hardly any resistance, except on our left by the machine-gunners at the White Château, which caused some delay to the 140th Brigade.

How the German troops lived at all in the Inferno is a mystery: still more wonderful is it that groups of brave men here and there actually stood to their machine-guns. Most however of their troops in the front line and support trenches who survived the explosions and drumfire surrendered. Groups of prisoners, pale and shaking, some hysterical, came down through out lines, shepherded by our Tommies. Many were wounded—some carrying others on stretchers—some who were unhurt supporting wounded Englishmen. One hefty R.S.M.—a typical "Hun"—attracted attention as he passed Spoil Bank dugouts, scowling to right and left and grinding his teeth with hate. But most of the prisoners seemed only too thankful to be captured and out of the infernal regions they had inhabited.

The sun was now well over the horizon, and, as the day went on, the heat and glare became intense. Still the Devil's Tattoo, the orchestra of the guns, continued, now diminishing, now swelling to thunder, as our fire was directed on the different targets.

At 5.10 a.m. under some shell-fire the 122nd Brigade moved forward through the shattered trenches just taken by the 123rd Brigade and the corpses of the dead, and by 6.0 a.m. were in position in front of the Dammstrasse formed in waves for the assault. At 6.30 our waves moved up over the shell-torn wrack close behind our barrage. At 6.50 this began to move forward by 50 yard leaps, and our men pressed on close behind it, clearing the enemy dugouts and "Obscure" trenches in Pheasant Wood and Denys Wood and taking many prisoners who were too demoralised to offer more than a very slight resistance. The Commanding Officer established Battle Headquarters in a shell hole in Pheasant Wood, using as a battle sign a piece of paper stuck on a twig, on which he sketched a Dagger, the code sign of the Battalion. The "Black Line" was occupied according to time table by 7.15 a.m. Unfortunately, as the troops went forward in front of the enemy's lines in Obscure Support to dig themselves in, the barrage appeared to drop back, and a good many casualties were thus caused by our own fire. The line was soon consolidated, and four advanced posts and one Observation Post established by 8.30 a.m., when our contact aeroplanes came over. The enemy continued to shell the area intermittently with H.E., causing some casualties. Our bombardment now slackened, though our guns still kept up a considerable shelling of the positions ahead in the "Green Line" area. Indeed, but for our barrage, our troops might have gone a good way further and captured some of the hostile guns. In front of our positions on the left, a battery was seen abandoned, but the gunners returned and got their pieces away, moving at some 500 yards distance across our front. B Company opened on them with Lewis-guns and rifles, but without effect. The position of these guns, as shown on a map lent by Cpl. Fokes of the Observers, was midway between Denys Farm and Bug Wood. 2nd Lieuts. D. Walker and L. H. Jennings—who were in charge of the Brigade advanced signal party—came up behind the troops and established a post on the Dammstrasse, doing excellent work in keeping up communications with Brigade Headquarters in Voormezeele Switch. Later 2nd Lieut. R. W. Gurrin brought up a party with material for consolidation.

At 3.10 p.m. an intense bombardment opened on the "Green Line"; the 24th Division came up and "leap-frogged" through the positions we had won, passing on to the final objectives. By 5.0 p.m. these had all been gained. The enemy shelled our positions at intervals during the evening, but did little damage. A thunderstorm broke about 6.0 p.m. with a heavy shower of rain.

The 12th Battalion took 268 prisoners (44th I.R. 2nd Division and 139th I.R. 24th Division, German IV Army), 6 machine-guns and 2 trench-mortars, besides much smaller material. Six officers, Capt. A. V. Baker and 2nd Lieuts. W. G. Robinson, W. J. Palk, A. R. Puttock, W. A. Vanner and A. W. England, were wounded. Of the other ranks, 30 (7 of whom were reported missing but afterwards accepted for official purposes as dead) were killed, 8 died of wounds and 152 were wounded. The full list of dead will be found in the appendix. C.S.M. E. M. ("Billy") Warr, whom R.Q.M.S. Speller regarded as the "complete" soldier, was one of those who laid down their lives. He had only recently taken over as C.S.M. of D Company. Lce.-Cpl. Bowry, the Battalion goalkeeper, was also killed.

Messages of congratulation were later received from the Corps, Divisional and Brigade Commanders.

"Thus on this glorious day" (we quote the War Diary) "the Second Army drove the enemy out of positions immensely strong by nature and every resource of military art, which he had occupied for 2½ years and from which he commanded observation of all our movements and preparations. At least 30,000 of his troops must have been put out of action, over 7,200 prisoners were taken, with 51 guns, 242 machine guns and a vast amount of other military stores and equipment. Our casualties did not total 10,000, and every objective was taken in 14 hours. At very few points was there serious resistance, and the counter-attacks the enemy attempted were dispersed with heavy loss by our artillery fire almost before they left their trenches.

"The wonderfully successful result of these operations was chiefly due to the explosion of the mines and the vast preponderance of our artillery, the concentration of which was 30 per cent. greater than any previously known. By this means the hostile trenches were pulverised for a fortnight with H.E., the wire destroyed, the guns silenced or shattered, the dugouts smashed in and the troops demoralised. All this was made possible by the magnificent work of the Royal Flying Corps. The Staff work too was admirable. In short it was the co-operation of all arms of the Service in harmonious working that effected this splendid victory, the most striking yet gained over the armed might of Germany."

The above abstract is from the official account of Messines as recorded at the time in the War Diary. With very few exceptions—mostly in regard to captures of guns—

this differs very little from the accounts now current in histories of the war. The official figures now give 67 guns, 94 trench-mortars and 294 machine-guns; and our casualties as 16,000. The British Artillery are reported to have made a hole in every nine square yards of ground during the course of the battle and, as all the enemy gun positions were known beforehand, over them fell a standing barrage. Altogether 45 square miles were taken from the enemy.

At Hill 60, where one of the mines was blown, it was known that the enemy had tunnelled above our chambers which were full of ammonal when part of the roof fell in. Here some of the Australian miners waited to see the culmination of the task they had undertaken and after the explosion went into the attack and captured some of the Wurtembergers who had survived.

The fact that the mines had been blown two or three days before the enemy expected saved the British troops from a similar fate to that of the enemy at the Mound, as it was found that the Germans had driven a shaft some distance into the British lines on the plain south of Ypres.

The Dammstrasse, on which German engineers had laboured since October, 1914, was considered by them to be impregnable, and it is some consolation for us to know that, although our troops were observed assembling for the battle in shell holes, the German officer in command of the sector thought that only a raid was intended and shelled only a small portion of the unprotected troops, as he did not like unnecessarily to expose all his battery sites.

Although the Prime Minister, Mr. Lloyd George, is said to have heard the explosion of the mines in England, there were some of our men at Chippewa Camp, two miles off, who did not, possibly because they were in the dead slumber of exhaustion.

As the day advanced, activity behind the lines became very great. Transport lines began to shift forward and the railway lines were being extended. The arrangements for water were the most amazing. All had been prepared beforehand, so that water drawn from Dickebusch Lake, chlorinated and filtered, was being carried through pipes rapidly laid down and delivered that evening from taps in the front lines, which were now four miles beyond what had been No Man's Land two days earlier. At our own Quartermaster's Stores enemy machine-guns and mortars were exhibited for the first time since the Battalion had been overseas. These were captured by men of the Battalion, and they were sent home to Bermondsey or the Depôt as souvenirs. Perhaps one of the most humorous sights was that of Pte. C. Redding of D Company (one of the smallest men in the Battalion) leading to the prisoners' cages a party of about 50 of the enemy with a couple of their officers.

Kindly night at length dropped her veil over the sickening scene. Headless trunks, disembowelled bodies, detached limbs were strewn about, and it was days before all could be disposed of by burial parties; while back at the Field Ambulances and Casualty Clearing Stations, surgeons, orderlies and nurses were worked to a standstill.

The authors of this book with Cpl. Rogers visited in 1933 the scene of the St. Eloi mine-crater. It is now a lake in private grounds, and a country house has been built on its bank by a Frenchman from Lille. His daughters were bathing in this "pleasure pool" and fishing there, while ducks paddled over its waters! He told us that he often came across corpses, when planting his shrubs.

"Little they think on those strong limbs
That moulder deep below."

Although Messines has been considered the perfect example of the limited offensive conducted on the "Leap-frog" principle, it will be debated for many a day by those who took part in it whether a golden opportunity was not lost in not pushing on while the enemy was in a state of demoralisation. We have already recorded how our men could see guns being hauled away and were powerless to do anything but fire their rifles and machine-guns at the brave gunners and drivers. With more tanks and more reserve divisions there seems little doubt that there might have been a repetition of what the Germans did in March, 1918. The weather was perfect, as was the whole organisation, while the enemy was in a very bad state owing to the terrible time he had experienced at the hands of our artillery. Within a month the Germans were able to bring up fresh reserves and strengthen their positions, while, when the time came to strike the next blow at the start of the Third Battle of Ypres, the weather broke and continued bad right up to November.

The following decorations were granted to the Battalion for the Battle of Messines:—

Distinguished Service Order: Lieut.-Col. E. Knapp.
Military Cross: 2nd Lieuts. A. F. Samuels and H. P. Bailey (attached 122nd T.M.B.).
Distinguished Conduct Medal: C.S.M. W. G. Hill, M.M.

Military Medal: Cpl. W. R. G. Mallett; Lce.-Cpls. J. Dove and R. Collins; Ptes. A. Floyd, A. Pegg, W. A. Southwood, W. J. Thompson, W. J. Varrow and H. Wells.

Cards of Commendation from the G.O.C. 41st Division: Capts. H. S. Walker and A. G. Howitt, M.C.; Lieut. V. L. Clift; 2nd Lieut. A. W. England; Sergt. E. Hambleton; Lce.-Sergt. J. Ferney; Lce.Cpls. E. G. Bartlett and A. J. Linford.

Personal accounts are perhaps of greater interest to readers than the official ones, so here is one from Capt. David Walker, M.C., which gives a vivid description of the battle:—

"For the attack on Messines Ridge of June 7th, 1917, I was detached from the Battalion along with selected signallers to organise a forward Brigade Signal Station. This forward Signal Station was the only line of communication available to battalions forming the attack, and messages delivered to the signal post were transmitted by telephone if possible, or by pigeon, runner, or visual signals. The company of signallers under my command went forward with the attacking troops, and when the objective of the attack was reached, a spot was chosen and an effort made immediately to maintain telephonic communication. This was no easy matter. Shelling went on all the time, of course, and linesmen out repairing the wires had no pleasant job. We often, however, secured a satisfactory means of communication, and our signallers were complimented on the way they stuck to their usually most heartbreaking job.

"On this occasion, awaiting the 3.10 Zero hour, we signallers formed up immediately behind the St. Eloi craters with the second wave of attacking troops. It was an interesting viewpoint, for we knew that at that time half the hill top was going 'sky high,' and that the four craters, that we had all learned to dislike intensely, were to be blown up as the result of tunnelling and mining operations. We would be about 100 yards—not more—away and we hoped that we would not go 'sky high' too.

"It was a wonderfully fine dawn. Half an hour before the sun rose our eyes were on the second hands of our watches. Then our moment—Zero hour. The ground shook, then came a marvellous sight; we forgot for the moment the noise and the guns. A fierce tongue of flame shot up, then slowly and almost majestically it climbed to almost 300 feet, shaping eventually like a huge mushroom, topped with dense black cloud. Earth and pill-boxes the size of houses went up too. I wondered why they shouldn't fall on us! No, they all came straight down and helped to fill the awful hill top that was now one huge crater.

"For previous attacks the Zero hour was fixed by hundreds of independent, though synchronised, watches. This meant a somewhat ragged commencement of artillery barrage—some gunners fired three, others possibly two or four rounds, before the general clap of the barrage. This tongue of flame from the St. Eloi mine, fired by electricity from Kemmel Hill, and seen, if not actually felt, for hundreds of miles, was the most marvellous Zero hour. Every gunner and machine-gunner with his hand to the lanyard or trigger, gave it a jerk. Tens of thousands of shells and bullets were in the air on the second. In this one second, the comparative peace that had held the night for the assembling troops was broken and a tremendous battle was begun. Two minutes after Zero hour we attacking troops moved off past and round that crater.

"To return to the signallers, they had reached the Dammstrasse with the attacking troops, and as a signal station I chose an old enemy dugout at a corner of a trench by the sunken road. The first signaller to enter saw, sitting huddled together in the dark against the wall, three terror-stricken German schoolboys. These lads, not more than 14 or 15, were beyond crying, though later they wept real tears. They were cadets, sent to the line on a course of instruction, and, when the enemy retired fighting from their position, they were told to stay there, as being the safest place, and hope for the best. This was not the only time that the signallers under my command actually encountered the enemy, but they did not often have the further worry of prisoners to add to their job of work!

"During the attack one of our corporals was slightly wounded in the arm early on. In spite of encouragement from his men around him he would not consider it a 'Blighty,' and he had only one answer: 'I have a job of work to do to-day.' So he manfully carried on. A few hours later I happened to see the same corporal, this time on a stretcher and very seriously wounded in the leg. He was pale, and, if not unconscious, he said nothing, but held, in almost a death-grip, a sandbag. To see what it contained this was taken from his grasp. Inside were five gold watches—and our corporal was, I believe, a peace time jeweller!"

On the other side of the Dammstrasse was a cemetery, and it must be to this that Capt. Hector Walker refers when he writes:—

"The enemy trench in which we massed for the attack was packed—we stood more or less shoulder to shoulder—and things were not improved when the Boche started shelling the trench. The shells fell short and smothered us with the remains of their dead who had been buried there. We had to wear gas masks."

On the 8th the Brigade was moved out of the positions it had won, and the Battalion, being relieved by the 7th Northants, went back to Old French Trench, where it remained till the night of the 12th. On relief we were visited by Generals Lawford and Towsey who paid tribute to the work accomplished, and Capts. C. T. Williams, J. A. C. McCalman and W. Hagen came up from the Divisional Reinforcement Camp. The men were employed in salvage and the clearance of the battlefields; most were in bivouacs, which were shelled about 7.0 p.m. without any casualties being sustained. At 10.0 p.m. heavy gunfire heralded a counter-attack by the enemy; this was broken by our artillery which was now moved forward. One 18-pounder and two 60-pounder batteries were established close to us, and the roar of their explosions made sleep difficult.

Pte. E. Connor, M.M., has a reminiscence of Old French Trench at this time:—

"My pals and I," he writes, "had built a dugout, as, at 'Stand to' time we all had to go down a sap where there was not enough room for us all to lie down. Accordingly I decided on the second night there to spend the night in the dugout we had built, as I thought it would be more comfortable, although not so secure as the sap. That evening there was a race by the boys for the sap at 'Stand down,' so I proceeded to make myself comfortable in the newly built dugout and soon went off to sleep. All of a sudden I woke with a start to find that 'Jerry' had put an awful barrage down on the trench. One shell fell at the back of the dugout, part of which fell in on me without doing me injury, then another burst in front, the gas and smoke from it coming in, with the result that I had to get out, crawling on my hands and knees alongside of the trench. I do not know how many 'Our Fathers' I said; I think I was praying for about two hours until the shelling stopped. When it was quiet, I crawled back to the dugout (it was still there) and lay down again and went to sleep. In the morning my pals came up from the sap and asked me how I had enjoyed the 'strafe.' I told them I did not hear it, but, believe me, I was the first down the sap that night."

DEAD DOG FARM.

I.W.M. Copyright

OLD FRENCH TRENCH, JUNE 1917.

Newspaper Illustrations Copyright

KEMMEL, 1918.

While the Battalion was in Old French Trench, an official photographer visited the scene and took the picture which is reproduced. Several members of the Association will, no doubt, recognise themselves in the group.

There is also an excellent photograph of L/Cpl. A. B. Giles, which must have been taken at this time, in a book recently published, entitled "The War of the Guns," written by Aubrey Wade.

The construction of fresh roads up to the Dammstrasse was pushed on with the utmost vigour despite the enemy shelling. The excessive heat through all this period made life more trying.

At 11.0 p.m. on the 12th the Battalion moved forward to occupy new positions in Oak Support and Oak Trench, North of the White Château, relieving the 7th London Regt., and Battalion H.Q. was established in a sap in the Canal Bank. We were in support to the 18th K.R.R.s and the 11th R.W. Kents.

In the evening of the 14th the two front line battalions, under a heavy barrage, carried out a minor operation to straighten out the line, driving the enemy out of Olive and Optic Trenches and Oblique Row,* inflicting considerable loss and suffering a good many casualties. A spirited account of this hot engagement will be found in Capt. Russell's History of the 11th R.W. Kents. (Pte. F. Brunt was killed and 7 other ranks wounded this day.)

Things were fairly quiet on the 15th apart from occasional shelling. In the evening however, the enemy counter-attacked the 11th West Kents in the new front line positions, apparently on a large scale. Our artillery frustrated this to a large extent, and only a small bombing attack materialised, which was easily repulsed. A 5.9 fell at the entrance to Headquarters sap and a dump near by was blown up. During the day 5 other ranks were wounded, one of whom, Pte. P. Chipping of D Company, died soon after.

The area round about the Transport Lines at Hallebast had been a hive of activity during the offensive, so it is not surprising that the enemy decided to shell it on the 16th, and so persistent was the shelling that new quarters had to be acquired at Chippewa Camp. At 10.0 p.m. the Battalion moved up and relieved the 11th R.W. Kents in the front and support lines, Headquarters being established in a strong point in the cellars of the White Château. The 47th Division, in attacking this position on the 7th of June, had entered the ruins at the first rush, but were afterwards held up by about 300 Germans who, with bombs and machine-guns, emerged from their underground cellars and momentarily drove them back, but with smoke bombs and incendiary missiles the Londoners eventually gained possession. It was in truth at this time a most "unhealthy" spot. The enemy gunners had it "taped," and during most of the day and a good deal of the night H.E. shells were falling on it. To get

*Note.—Some readers may be puzzled by the curious names of enemy trenches. By means of air-photos accurate maps of all the enemy positions had been printed and issued. These maps were divided into large squares marked by a capital letter of the alphabet; each square was subdivided and numbered and each smaller square again subdivided into four marked by small letters. Every enemy trench and position in each large square was given some name beginning with the capital letter of that square. The area we had captured was all in the square O: hence the names Obey, Oblique, Obscure, Oblong, Olive, Oasis, Obtuse, Octagon, Oat, Oak, Owl, etc. The map reference for e.g., a post in Optic Trench was 0.5.d.4.6.

either in or out without hurt was the problem. The shells usually burst about one a minute. Thus, to get out, you waited near the entrance to the cellars till the explosion took place overhead and bits of metal and brick had stopped falling, then legged it over the shell holes like blazes before the next shell burst. To get in, you approached from one shell hole to another, lying doggo till an explosion was over, and then made a dash for the entrance which was not too easy to spot.

Inside the scene was a macabre one, worthy of Rembrandt's brush. The Headquarters of two battalions, and some other units too, occupied the cellars. About a hundred men were sitting or lying about in the dim light of a few candles, mostly asleep, a few cooking or "chatting," cleaning equipment or shaving. At two points a little daylight filtered in, but these were dangerous places, for, if a shell pitched just outside, the blast must be deadly, and it was thus that the casualties happened on the 17th. The place was swarming with vermin, and on the walls were sketches and mottoes drawn by the German soldiers, many very uncomplimentary to the British. The place was fetid in hot weather, though the roof was 15 feet high, supported by huge baulks of timber. It was not pleasant to sit in this mantrap, hearing the thud of the explosions overhead, expecting the next shell to come through and finish us all, and shaking off the bits of brick and dirt that fell continually.

The companies were now in Oblique Row, Optic and Oblique Trench (in the middle of which was a bombing post and block, for the enemy held the rest of it) and Opal Reserve. These trenches were still much damaged but were gradually strengthened, and a communication trench was dug up to them. We were now over the low ridge and commanded an extensive view across miles and miles of country never seen till now. Our observers had established an O.P. out in front of our lines in an old German dugout. It was a risky situation, with its open door towards and in full view of the enemy, and to get into it you had to get along a trench full of Boche dead, who in the hot weather were decomposing rapidly. Between our lines and our H.Q. were the smashed trees of the White Château copses and grounds.

On the 17th the enemy kept up considerable shelling of our area, particularly about the ruins of the White Château. Typical of the conditions prevailing is the entry in the Diary for this date: "The White Château was heavily shelled from 9.45 a.m. to 12.45 p.m. making egress and ingress difficult." Pte. Sam Harber, the H.Q. officers' cook, was severely wounded when a shell entered the ruins at 11.0 a.m. Lce.-Cpl. F. Goble was also hit together with another member of the Mess staff, while Lce.-Cpl. A. B. Giles of the M.O.'s staff was slightly wounded, but not evacuated. Harber died of his wounds two days later in the C.C.S. at Lijssenthoek, where he was buried.

The enemy continued to hold Oblique Trench and Optic Support and various shell holes to our front with small parties which were strengthened at night. Enemy planes constantly hovered above us: they came in droves and made themselves most objectionable. To fire a machine-gun at them was only to invite further trouble, for they had become most daring and flew very low, firing their machine-guns for all they were worth. Meanwhile our artillery was not quiet, but kept up a harassing fire on all points of the enemy front. The Brigadier visited the line in the morning and the Commanding Officer in the afternoon. In order to straighten things out a bit it was decided to make a bombing attack on Oblique Trench at dusk. 2nd Lieut. R. D. Brown led a party over, but unfortunately it was at once observed and came under severe machine-gun and rifle fire, 2nd Lieut. Brown and one other rank being wounded.

Pte. T. Clarke, M.M., late of B Company, tells an anecdote of this raid:—

"Sergeants Turner and Davey, two courageous young men, found a bombing post which was apparently not occupied during the day: they resorted to taking the detonators out of the enemy's bombs and planned to surprise him by night. However the raid did not meet with much success, as Jerry, apparently getting wind of what was to happen, met the party with a good supply of egg bombs which were similar to our own 'Mills,' but, being smaller, could be thrown further.

"Being a runner, I had no easy job, carrying messages to H.Q. in the White Château. It was shelled by big guns every few minutes, and it was some job trying to get in, and worse still to get out."

Tommy Clarke has probably the unique distinction of serving with the 12th throughout its existence, and never leaving it for wounds or sickness the whole time! He was under age when he joined and received his decoration for good work as a runner.

Here too is a yarn from Q.M.S. Speller of "a better (but smaller) 'ole'."

"Having successively and successfully sprinted from the White Château, the four C.Q.M.S.s and I met near Spoil Bank. We had gone only a few yards, when an outsize shell with a roar like an underground train intruded upon our conversation. Without wasting a word or a moment we made a simultaneous head-first dive into a small abandoned trench. The "woofer" fell near enough to partially close the trench on us. The spectacle of 10 legs frantically waving in the air as we tried to extricate ourselves 'in reverse' so convulsed a passing runner that he was incapable of rendering immediate aid. His joy was short-lived, and he visibly wilted under 'Bill' Barnes's completely shattering flow of high-pitched invective."

Besides the casualties mentioned, Pte. W. Weller of A Company was killed and four other men were wounded on the 17th. Weller was one of those quiet unassuming men who had been in every action so far. He was slightly deaf, and owing to his utter disregard of shell-fire it was suggested by some that he could not hear a shell even if it burst a couple of yards away from him. At all events Weller was the perfect example of the undecorated hero of the war who carried on steadily in and out of action without doing anything spectacular to bring him to the notice of the Authorities.

The 18th of June, which, as the Diary records, was the anniversary of the Battle of Waterloo, was again unsettled. The White Château continued to get its usual "dose," the support lines were strafed considerably, while hostile planes again swept our area with machine-gun bullets in the early morning and late evening. This was getting too much for our own air fighters, and it was some satisfaction for us to see a fighting squadron come over and engage the enemy, with the result that two of them were brought down. It was a bad day for the Signal Section, for two of their number, Ptes. Tom Easter and A. F. Tondeur were killed, the latter outside the White Château. During the shelling of D Company's lines Capt. Walter Hagen was wounded in the ankle. At 4.0 p.m. a violent thunderstorm broke over the lines, and soon the mud of Flanders began to assert itself.

On the night of the 19th our old "opposite number," the 20th D.L.I., came to relieve us. It was a very dark cloudy night, and it was most difficult to steer a course over the muddy waste of shell holes.

The Battalion now moved back to Voormezeele Switch and Middlesex Lane, Headquarters being situated in our old trench in Queen Victoria Street, close to Voormezeele. To the regret of those who knew him it was learned that the Brigade C. of E. Chaplain, the Rev. C. F. Schooling, C.F., had been mortally wounded by a large shell in Dickebusch. He had been with the Brigade about six weeks, since Padre Hilditch went home, and was a man greatly beloved, very retiring and unobtrusive but always doing his utmost to minister to the men both spiritually and in more material ways. He had been conversing with 2nd Lieut. Aston only half an hour before he met his death. This occurred owing to his unselfishness. He was in a place of safety when he saw a party come along the street; he ran out to warn them that shells were falling a little further on, when a "Crump" burst. When the smoke cleared, they saw him go up to a lorry and climb on board, and never suspected that he was hit. A piece of metal had actually punctured the abdomen. He got out of the lorry at the Field Ambulance and walked in. Within an hour he had passed away.

The weather now broke. Rain constantly fell, and we were cooler after the intense heat which had lasted since the end of April.

The enemy now began a war on our observation balloons. At 5.0 p.m. on the 20th one of his planes brought down two; on the 23rd four more were brought down; on the 24th another one, and on the 27th two more were fired and sent to destruction. It seemed to us that the ascendancy our airmen had established over the Boche before and during the Battle of Messines was gradually being lost. Day after day the puffs of white smoke high up in the sky heralded the approach of German planes. In vain would our "Archies" create a fearful din, while the planes would approach our balloons, circle round and then dive with the rat-a-tat-tat of their machine-guns with incendiary bullets ringing in our ears. The occupants of the balloon would then jump with their parachutes, while the riggers below would do their utmost to try to bring the gas bag to earth with the aid of the windlass. These were trying times for observers, for, as soon as one balloon was destroyed, up would go another one. The watch on the enemy front had to be maintained, and many lives must have been sacrificed in doing so.

The activity of the enemy planes had also resulted in our back areas being disturbed. Shells began to find their way to Reninghelst, and Divisional Headquarters, hitherto immune, now began to realise what it was like to have heavy shells bursting around them. The news was hardly received with regret by the troops in the line. "Why shouldn't these posh merchants in cushy jobs have a dose of the medicine as well as the fighting troops?" was what one heard on every side.

A Brigade Church Parade was held on the 24th near the Brigade Headquarters at Elzenwalle Château. It was an impressive sight—some 3,000 troops in hollow square, but some of us felt it rather a risk, if so large a gathering had been observed by some Boche plane.

The Battalion took over some dugouts in the banks of Dickebusch Lake from the 22nd (Bermondsey) "Queen's" on the 26th and remained there finding working parties until the 1st of July. During all this period the enemy continued to shell a great deal in the neighbourhood. There was however one spot which seemed to be free from shell-fire, an old farmhouse occupied by an aged couple who supplied the troops with coffee and eggs and chips. Every place around had been practically razed to the ground, but this farm did not appear to have been hit, and of course everyone suspected that spies occupied the place. Whether such was the case was not disclosed whilst the 12th was near Dickebusch. At Café Belge and Belgian Battery Corner working parties had to congregate; there was a very large amount of traffic at these places and in consequence they became especially "unhealthy."

The 122nd Brigade, minus the 12th East Surreys and the 15th Hants, who were remaining in reserve for working parties, moved to the Berthen area on the 28th of June.

During the month Hon. Lieut. and Quartermaster W. W. Easter, late R.S.M. of the 23rd Middlesex Regt., joined the Battalion as Quartermaster, and 6 other ranks arrived as drafts, while the casualties had amounted to 38 other ranks killed; 8 officers and 203 other ranks wounded; and 2 other ranks missing.

The Battalion left the dugouts at Dickebusch Lake on the 3rd of July and proceeded to billets near Vierstraat. Major C. C. Clifton now joined the Battalion and took over the duties of Second-in-Command, and, as he had come from the East Surrey Regiment, many thought there was at last the possibility of our having a Commanding Officer from our own regiment, instead of, as hitherto, from other units of the Division. This was not to be however, as Major Clifton was evacuated to England sick on the 21st of July.

At 8.30 a.m. on the morning of the 4th the troops were surprised to see a number of cars coming along the Vierstraat Road. It was discovered that it was none other than His Majesty the King, accompanied by the Prince of Wales and some General Officers. As the procession passed there was shelling in the vicinity of Dickebusch. We afterwards found out that His Majesty had been up to see the craters caused by the mines and forward into the Wytschaete area. This was the first occasion on which we had seen any Royalties overseas, though later we were to see a great deal of the Heir to the throne.

CHAPTER VIII.

6th July to 15th August, 1917.

Resting, training and refitting at La Roukloshille—In action at the start of the Battle of Pilckem Ridge and at Hollebeke—Appalling conditions and heavy casualty list.

AFTER five weeks of practically continuous sojourn in the line, we all felt very eager for some relief. For the first three weeks it had not once been possible to remove even one's boots, and for the whole time no clothes could be removed, despite the hot weather. A bath was what most of us chiefly longed for.

But the time had now come for the 12th Battalion to be relieved from the fighting zone and to proceed to the training and rest area. Accordingly, on the 6th of July the road via Hallebast, La Clytte, Locre and Bailleul was taken to La Roukloshille. Battalion Headquarters were established in a farm, and the troops were housed in barns and tents. Although not many miles from the line, the hamlet was a nice quiet spot, disturbed only by occasional nocturnal visits of planes to Bailleul and Hazebrouck and the long distance shelling to which both these towns were subject about this time. Meteren and Flêtre were within easy reach, and, when funds permitted, the men paid visits to both these places. A couple of miles away was the Mont des Cats with its monastery on the sky line. Most of the time at La Roukloshille was spent in re-organization, refitting and sport. Flanders, even in June, cannot be compared for beauty to most places in rural England: there are comparatively few trees, and those almost all pollard elms in rows, and not many hedges. But here and there were coppices, and anyhow it was almost heaven to be out of the bestiality of the line with its dust and noise, its muck and grime and constant toil and danger. Yet curiously enough it was this very quiet which these boys from Bermondsey did not appreciate. 2nd Lieut. Aston, chatting one day with one of his snipers, remarked on the pleasure of being in the blissful peace of the country. "Lord, sir," said the lad with emphasis: "what I want is to get back to the streets and gas lamps."

The weather throughout remained fine, except for one severe thunderstorm in the night followed by heavy rain during a Church Parade. Many of the men resorted to the fashion of wearing shorts (service trousers cut down) for two good reasons; coolness and the fact that they were not so likely to harbour vermin. Even to-day photographs exist of some of the younger members of the Battalion, in which they look more like boy scouts than youths who had seen over twelve months of very active service on the Western Front. The photographer at Flêtre did a roaring trade in the rough studio at the back of his house. Some of the officers and N.C.O.s turned a blind eye to the wearing of shorts, but others, especially quartermaster-sergeants, frowned on them. It was rather an awkward predicament to be in when one was told not to appear on parade without the regulation service trousers after they had already been cut down. All sorts of dodges were resorted to in order to obtain a new pair of slacks before the next parade. Fortunately some of the rank and file had so well tailored their shorts that it was possible to give them the appearance of slacks until the opportune moment arrived to exchange them.

The 7th and 8th of July were spent in baths (very welcome) and resting, but regular training began on the 9th, on which day General Towsey visited the Battalion and cheered us up, as he always did.

The Diary records an air raid being made on Bailleul on the night of the 6th. Occasionally the enemy planes dropped bombs very close to us as most of the training area adjoined towns which the Germans knew only too well were full of essential services connected with the thorough organization of the Second Army. The same sort of conditions prevailed when about six weeks later we were billeted in this same area. To be precise it was the 19th of August when a plane flew over us and dropped two bombs in an adjoining field without causing any damage except putting the wind up everybody. The 10th (Battersea) "Queen's," however, who were cantoned in the village of Thieushouck (where the 12th were billeted before proceeding to the Somme) were not so fortunate. A bomb dropped on their camp, killing 40 and wounding 70. Those of us who saw the plane which possibly did the damage are convinced that the bombs were really intended for Hazebrouck, and that, owing to the work of our anti-aircraft sections in keeping the plane in the rays of the searchlights and shelling it ferociously, the airman was glad to unload anywhere in order to make for home again.

Pte. G. R. Daniels has a scrounging yarn of La Roukloshille:—

"A few of us came across a field of peas, and, getting a sack, soon filled it up. While we were shelling them, an officer came along and wanted to know where we got them. We told him we had 'won' them, whereupon he handed us a five-franc note and told us to go and win some more for the officers' mess. Some days later the old farmer came along with the interpreter, picked us out of the whole company on parade and, in addition to the charge of taking his peas, accused us of breaking his fence down to get some wood. The result was that we were all stopped a franc from our pay to make good the damage done."

It was on the 12th that the contest for the barrel of stout began. The fight consisted of an inter-company football tournament, in which all the teams entered with the greatest of zest. Officers and men vied with each other to be in the winning team. The question arose whether Transport and Battalion H.Q. men should play for their companies or whether they should enter a team of their own. Eventually a Headquarters team appeared which included acting R.S.M. Bry Horswell, Sergt. George Nuttman and Lce.-Cpl. Len Southall, to mention a few of the men who had represented the Battalion in big games. Headquarters became favourites after the first round, but in the Final, played on the 14th, C Company won the honours and the barrel of stout. During the period of rest the Battalion team did quite well in winning the inter-Battalion competition in the Brigade, beating the 18th K.R.R.s by 3—2 on the 14th and the 11th R.W. Kents by 2—1 on the 16th. The team went on towards the Divisional Championship, but some hefty fellows from the Artillery gave them a rough house with their ammunition boots, and though Sergt. Nuttman and Cpl. J. W. Lingwood put up a gallant defence in rear, we had to retire beaten by the closest of margins and nursing some lacerated shins.

On the 13th there was an inspection by Major-General Lawford accompanied by the Brigadier at 9.30 a.m., after which and some exercises, the following were presented to the Divisional General to receive medal ribbons and cards in recognition of services rendered:—

Military Cross: 2nd Lieut. (A/Capt. from 27.3.17) A. G. Howitt.
D.C.M. and M.M.: C.S.M. W. G. Hill.
Military Medal: C.S.M. D. Maddison; Sergt. R. Mayston; Cpl. M. Coghlan; Ptes. H. Richardson, W. Thompson and A. Varrow.

Mentioned in Despatches: Sergts. B. G. Burgess and S. Lattimore.

A route march at 2.0 p.m. was followed by an entertainment by the "Crumps" in the evening. A special platform had been erected for the party, who gave us a thoroughly good show with topical jokes directed at members of the audience. On the 14th the Divisional General gave a garden party at Headquarters, a château at Berthen, to all officers of the 41st Division.

B Company proceeded to Ridgewood on the 18th for working parties, being attached to the 228th Field Co. R.E. till the 23rd: during the five days 6 men were wounded.

In the course of the next two days the direction of the Battalion was to pass to two officers of other units of the Brigade: Capt. A. W. Puttick, M.C., of the 11th R.W. Kents took over the duties of Second-in-Command on the 18th, and in place of Major H. de C. Blakeney (acting C.O. instead of Colonel Knapp on leave) who proceeded on leave on the 19th, Major R. Pennell, M.C., of the 18th K.R.R.s took over command. The history of the 12th Battalion must be unique in having so many senior officers of the Division sent to command it at one time or another. The standard of a battalion could usually be gauged from its commander. Just as the Colonels of the 12th began to get to know their officers and men, they were either rendered *hors de combat* or transferred to other units. When one reads of Colonel Corfe of the West Kents being with his unit from its inception to its demise, one can appreciate the task confronted by the different commanders of the 12th. Yet it can be said with truth that these officers left the Battalion with many regrets.

There was not a finer soldier or disciplinarian in the Division than Major Pennell, and it was with the 12th Battalion a few weeks later that he won his D.S.O. This order was given to Commanding Officers mainly in consideration of the successful work accomplished by the troops under their command; three different C.O.s gained this decoration whilst serving with the Battalion. The men of the 12th never claimed to be any better than other troops in the Division, but their records show that ever since the first raid by the "Black Hand Gang" they had never failed to do what was required of them. The original members from Bermondsey were as hard as nails and set an example of courage and endurance which all drafts emulated.

The following movements of officers took place during our stay at La Roukloshille. Evacuated sick—Major Clifton, Lieut. R. A. V. Brearey, Hon. Lieut. and Q.M. Easter (he went to England and was pronounced unfit for further active service), 2nd Lieuts. T. B. McWalter and F. Beard. Capt. H. H. Prentiss, R.A.M.C., too sprained his ankle in the Battalion sports and had to go: his place was taken by Capt. R. Herdman, R.A.M.C., a very quiet elderly doctor who wore a beard (a most unusual sight on active service) and performed his duties in the line courageously and coolly, but the rigours of Hollebeke were too severe for his age, and to our regret he was not long with us. Cpl. Southall describes him as "extremely cool in all trying circumstances." Lieut. Pridham took command of B Company, while Capt. Openshaw went on leave, and Temporary Capt. A. G. Howitt took over D Company. 2nd Lieut. Palk returned from hospital, though clearly by no means fit. 2nd Lieuts. C. R. Haynes and E. Aucutt joined.

It was at this time too that the Rev. F. E. A. Williams joined the Brigade as C. of E. Chaplain. He quickly became a general favourite with his cheeriness and sympathetic goodfellowship; indefatigable in ministering to the troops at all times, he brought to mind Chaucer's lines:—

"But Criste's lore and his apostles twelve
He preched, but first he folwed it himselve."

Padre Williams was a member of our Association and preached the sermon at Rotherhithe Parish Church at the Laying-up of our Battalion Colour in October, 1933. His services with our Battalion gained him a well-deserved M.C. After the war he became Vicar of Temple Ewell and River-with-Guston, near Dover, where he was greatly beloved. In November, 1935, he died after a very short illness in Dover Hospital, aged 65.

During this period, too, some N.C.O.s and men went home for commissions—Cpl. T. W. Sabine, Ptes. C. S. Jones, F. Smith, W. R. Lallow, C. Hughes and H. Tuppen.

The period of rest now came to a close, and the Battalion was about to take part in the most criticised campaign of the war in the West, "Third Ypres," or "Passchendaele." It was the last of the great artillery engagements. The spade now definitely defeated the gun, and the defence the attack.

The vast systems of entrenchment used in 1916 and 1917, where trench was dug behind trench to a depth of, in some places, several miles, offered unmistakable targets to guns aided by spotting planes. An enemy provided with enormous gun power could pulverise such defences. The British Army being in this situation from July, 1916, to July, 1917, did indeed on the Somme and at Vimy Ridge by incredible expenditure of shells partially succeed. But the method was prodigally wasteful and expensive to the attacker, and, if any rain fell, the whole area became a vast morass, over which no sane person would dream of risking his life by walking in peace time, but which (unbelievable as it must nowadays seem) men, weighted with all kinds of equipment, were expected to negotiate, under a hail of bullets, stunned and lacerated by a tornado of huge shells exploding on all sides without cessation, drenched with poison gas, so plastered with mud that their weapons could not work and they themselves bore no resemblance to human beings, haggard, sleepless, filthy, like creatures of the primeval slime.

For the Germans wisely altered their defensive strategy. When assault was imminent, they disposed their men by small groups with machine-guns in shell-holes or in "Pill-boxes." These were square or round emplacements of reinforced concrete of immense thickness, impervious to anything but a series of direct hits by the largest shells, having a wide field of fire through narrow slits. In these a few stout men with machine-guns were impregnable, unless and until the pill-box was blown to bits by H.E. or by a field gun fired at close range from a tank.

Tanks! Ah, they were to do the trick. Since Flers much improved ones were available in greater numbers. The High Command apparently believed that they could do anything. So they could, or almost anything, on ordinary ground. But over the huge quagmire that stretched round Ypres they could not move at all. They sank helplessly and became bogged, death-traps for their crews and completely useless in the attack. It was not till the end of November that tanks were used in conditions favourable to their tactical use at Cambrai, where 4,000 tank soldiers put out of action nearly 10,000 of the enemy and captured 8,000 prisoners and 100 guns at very small loss. But that, and its grievous sequel, is another story.

On the 23rd of July, at 8.0 a.m., the Battalion moved from La Roukloshille and proceeded via Piebrouck, Berthen and Westoutre to Wood Camp. On reaching the camp, 2nd Lieut. J. Aston went up to Lock House to reconnoitre the positions to be occupied by the Battalion on the following day.

The contrast between the preparations for this "Show" and that of the Messines Ridge was very marked. The historian of the 11th Royal West Kents states that the Battalion had detailed orders for their operations: it was certainly not so with the 12th. Day after day our I.O. went to Brigade H.Q. to try to discover exactly what we were expected to do on Zero day, but Brigade could not tell him: they were waiting on Division, and they presumably on Corps. And when battle was joined, the weather conditions were utterly different. On June 7th no rain had fallen for many weeks, and the ground, though torn by shell fire, was quite dry. At the end of July the weather broke; rain fell in torrents, week after week, till the entire battle area became an immense swamp, practically impassable, in which the wretched troops, continually urged on by orders from the High Command in comfort 50 miles away at Montreuil, floundered, drowned and died. But we anticipate.

After a Company Commanders' conference had been held on the 24th, the Battalion proceeded to relieve the 8th Battalion London Regt. in the line. A Company moved off at 2.10 p.m. and was followed at intervals of thirty minutes in the following order:—C Company, Headquarters and D Company. A distance of 500 yards between platoons had to be maintained. The route taken was Wood Camp—Cross Roads—Overland Track to Mic Mac Camp—Hallebast Corner and Ridge Wood to just S.W. of the Canal behind the old White Château. B Company marched from Ridge Wood and arrived at the positions soon after 4.30. The disposition of the companies was as follows:—Battalion H.Q. at Lock House, in Spoil Bank; A Company, Ecluse Trench; B Company, Old British Front Line, from Oak Dump to Norfolk Bank: C Company, Dugouts in Lock House Bank; D Company, Bois Confluent and Old French Trench. During the relief there was much shelling from our batteries with the consequent retaliation in which one other rank was wounded.

Lce.-Cpl. S. J. Nugent recalls some details about Spoil Bank. It was a long, wide bank, some 40 feet high and a quarter of a mile long, formed by the earth thrown out when the Canal had been dug, and was covered with scrub and small trees. The saps were very deep, and, apart from the evil smell which came from the water under the duckboards, the accommodation was fairly comfortable. The tunnels were lit with electric light, and were used as a means of egress and ingress, but leading off from these were roomy dugouts and also recesses, in which were beds built in three tier style, made of wood with wire netting stretched across, similar to a spring mattress. Besides being the 12th Battalion Headquarters, it was also used as Brigade Headquarters. Along the side of the Bank ran the Canal, which through constant shelling had lost all semblance of what it had been before the war. It consisted of a series of pools of filthy water, mantled with green scum; most of the locks had been smashed in, and the surrounding country was practically a bog. In the bank itself gun emplacements also had been built, and near by was a warm spot known as the Brickstack, where some dead mules were seen as the Battalion made its way to the Bank. The whole place was a regular target for 5.9.s.

For the next five days the Battalion was mainly on working parties; one particularly nasty job being that of salvaging around the White Château, which Pte. F. G. Laws records in a diary he kept. Officers were also becoming acquainted with the positions the Battalion was to occupy during the coming offensive. Capt. H. S. Walker and 2nd Lieut. J. Aston reconnoitred the forward positions on the afternoon of the 25th, and on the following day the C.O. with the M.O. and Capt. Walker also examined the area. 2nd Lieuts. H. S. Todd, C. R. Haynes, E. Aucutt and F. A. Samuels, with runners, also went forward on the 26th to find out the positions their companies were to occupy on Y-Z night.

2nd Lieut. J. Aston was seriously wounded near Optic Trench on the 27th. Going across the open in full view of the enemy at a point where no other way was possible, he was potted at by an enemy field battery. A shell burst a few feet from him, and a fragment passed through the abdomen into the spine. Lieut. G. P. G. Reah, Intelligence Officer at Brigade H.Q., a great friend of his, received the news at Spoil Bank and was given permission by the Brigadier to make enquiries. He hurried to the Advanced Dressing Station at Voormezeele, but Mr. Aston had just been passed through. The M.O., however, who had attended him, told Lieut. Reah, "There's no chance for him: he must have died by now." 2nd Lieut. Aston's faithful servant, Cpl. J. Rogers, accompanied him to the Dressing Station and stayed with him at the C.C.S. until he was evacuated. For three days he was not expected to live, but made a wonderful recovery, and after nine months was discharged for wounds in 1918. The piece of shell was not removed from the abdomen till 1926. The duties of Intelligence Officer were taken over by 2nd Lieut. L. A. Rossiter. On the same day, 2nd Lieut. B. C. Stenning was severely wounded and died of his injuries soon after, and two other ranks were also wounded.

The enemy was very active on the Canal area on the 28th and 29th, when the tunnels at Spoil Bank were heavily bombarded with gas shells and H.E. 2nd Lieut. W. J. Palk was sent to the Transport lines sick. The weather continued very bad.

Operation orders were now issued in connection with the battle. The Battalion was to assemble on Y-Z night in the positions allocated to it for the attack. Battalion Headquarters were to be established by 12.0 noon on Y day in a dugout by the "Iron Bridge," on the banks of the Canal, and were to be marked with a Dagger (code sign) painted on a canvas screen. The final positions to be taken up before Zero on the day of the battle were to be:—"A" in Opal Reserve; "B" in Old German Front Line; "C" in New Support Trench in front of Opal Reserve, and "D" in Oblique Row. The orders for the action were sent out by Lieut. Clift, who had taken over the duties of Adjutant.

According to orders the Battalion moved on the 30th, Headquarters leaving Lock House during the morning, and proceeding to the "Iron Bridge." The remainder of the Battalion moved up to the assembly positions at 11.0 p.m. There had been only one casualty during the day, which had been a noisy one on both sides.

The stage was now set for the Third Battle of Ypres, which lasted from the 31st of July until the 6th of November, 1917.

Mr. Lloyd George, in his "War Memoirs," has described this campaign as one of the costliest military blunders of history in which the valour, patience and resolution of the soldiers who took part was unsurpassed in all time. The finest army ever commanded by a British General was sacrificed hopelessly and uselessly after Petain, Foch, the British Army Commanders who participated in the actual operations, the Tank Corps, not to mention the statesmen, Lloyd George, Bonar Law and Lord Milner, are said to have raised their voices in protest against the continuance of it after the heavy rains had made the conditions so appalling. In the course of a battle in which it was estimated that the British guns had helped to churn up the already swampy ground with 25,000,000 shells, our casualties had reached close on 400,000, many of whom, we know only too well, sank into the mud and were lost for ever. We read of how the cavalry were supposed to thunder across the impassable bog to complete the rout of a fleeing enemy! Although many may not entirely agree with what Lloyd George has written about the battle, those of us who took part in it will bear witness that what he has written of the conditions prevailing is in no way exaggerated. Who was to blame for this frightful waste of human life? Lloyd George puts it down to the deceit of the High Command. There was always resentment among the generals that statesmen should intervene where military operations were concerned, but after all the statesmen were responsible to the people of this country that the soldiers should not indulge in operations which incurred losses far out of proportion to the ultimate gains. The object of the writers is not to place the responsibility on any particular person; that will be left to the historians after they have weighed up all the facts. But to the simple soldier who had to obey orders there seemed to be no military genius required to send men in frontal attacks over swampy ground against an enemy who had prepared fortifications which even our own heavy shells were unable to reduce. The 41st Division had its full share in the operations, and if, as Mr. Lloyd George also records, it was considered to be one of the best divisions on the Western Front, then that reputation was gained by the Regimental officers and men, many of whom sacrificed their lives in gaining it. To our General Officers one must extend a meed of praise. Being on the spot, they realised the agony and sufferings of the troops under them and, no doubt, did all they could to let the High Command know their views. In General Lawford we had an officer who personally did not shrink from constantly visiting the scene of operations, while Brigadier-General Towsey, with a first hand knowledge, did, we know, everything possible to alleviate our sufferings.

According to the initial plan the Fifth (British) Army, under General Gough, was to attack on a front extending from Boesinghe, three miles north of Ypres, round to the Zillebeke-Zandvoorde road. It was to be supported on its left by the First French Army under General Anthoine, attacking north of Boesinghe, and on its right by an advance astride the Canal of the Second (British) Army, to which the 41st Division belonged.

At 3.50 a.m. on the 31st of July another terrific bombardment opened on the enemy lines, and in a drizzle of rain the 122nd Brigade went forward to the attack. The 12th Battalion, being in support, remained in the trenches, but continually sent forward carrying parties to the 11th R.W. Kents and the 18th K.R.R.s who were the assaulting battalions. The 10th Bavarians, whom General Towsey describes as stout foes and not the rabbits which some correspondents seemed chiefly to hear of, put up a great resistance in and around Hollebeke (which was the ultimate objective), and the West Kents and K.R.R.s found great difficulty in progressing, the K.R.R.s being mown down by frightful machine-gun fire from the flank. Hollebeke held out for a long time, being defended by a courageous German officer and about 20 men, who had previously put up a splendid defence in some battered houses before withdrawing to the village. According to the history of the 11th R.W. Kents the village of Hollebeke was eventually cleared of the enemy by a party of that battalion, but this does not agree with the official records of the 12th Battalion or personal accounts. Lieut.-Col. R. Pennell, our C.O. at the time, states that at about 4.30 p.m. on the 31st of July the Brigade Major (Capt. A. Y. Graham Thomson) came into Headquarters and reported a very unsatisfactory state of affairs. The two battalions in attack had reported earlier that Hollebeke had been taken, but it was now found that this was not so, and he brought orders for the 12th Battalion East Surreys to go forward, take Hollebeke, and establish the line. On completion of this operation a coloured light was to be fired to acquaint Brigade H.Q. that the operation had been successful. Company Commanders were then sent for and the situation explained, and at about 6.15 p.m. Capt. Howitt moved with a composite company to the attack. The operation was entirely successful, and the coloured signal was fired at 7.59 p.m., showing that Hollebeke was in our hands. Owing to the skilful leadership of Capt. Howitt we suffered very few casualties. The Brigade Diary reports that the K.R.R.s were in a most disorganised state, every reinforcement having failed to get through the barrage, and then a company of the East Surreys under Capt. A. G. Howitt, M.C., moved forward to attack an enemy strong point which was still holding out in Hollebeke and was successful in gaining its objective and establishing a line beyond the village. The Brigade Major reported that at 7.0 p.m. Capt. Howitt moved up from the Red Line with his company behind the West Kents on the left, took some houses on the road S.W. of Hollebeke from the flank, captured and took eight more prisoners—a very neat little manœuvre—and extended the line to about 250 yards from Forret Farm. Those who were at Battalion H.Q. at the time can remember Lieut.-Col. C. H. Kitching, who was in temporary command of the K.R.R.s, rushing into our sap and informing Major Pennell of what had happened to his men, who had been severely mauled in front of the village. It was after this that instructions were issued to Capt. Howitt. Whatever happened, there is no disputing the fact that D Company and other men of the Battalion were in Hollebeke on the first day of the battle, as we shall see as the narrative continues.

Four German officers and 60 other ranks passed through the collecting station during the day, while so far our casualties had been light, only seven (one gassed) being recorded in the Diary. This figure is surprisingly small considering that the Battalion had been actively engaged carrying material and supplies to the assaulting troops and in view of the successful operation, but it may be that some of our casualties did not pass through our Aid Post and are included in the figures which are given later on for the whole operations. Indeed it was difficult at any time during the course of a battle to give even approximate numbers of casualties, and more especially in the Salient, where men were scattered in small groups owing to the difficult terrain. However, it also serves to prove what has already been said about Capt. Howitt's skilful leadership. Two officers of the Battalion who were attached to the 122nd T.M.B. became casualties during the day, 2nd Lieut. H. P. Bailey being killed and 2nd Lieut. A. M. Mackintosh being wounded.

The casualties during the month were:—Killed or mortally wounded: 2 officers and 4 other ranks. Wounded: 2 officers and 45 other ranks. Ptes. H. Dale and C. A. Watts proceeded to England as candidates for commissions. Both of them left us at Spoil Bank, and it was amusing to see them both running from the sap during a bombardment, when they were in possession of their movement orders. The strength on the 31st of July was 37 officers and 950 other ranks.

Early on August 1st the remainder of the Battalion moved up to forward areas as follows:—A and C Companies in Optic Support, while B Company proceeded to join D Company in front of Hollebeke extending along to Forret Farm. Battalion H.Q. moved to "Bow" Headquarters in the Canal Bank. The rain of the last few days had reduced the trenches to an appalling condition. Before B Company moved to join D, 2nd Lieut. F. A. Samuels with a patrol reconnoitred Forret Farm and reported it unoccupied by the enemy. Here Capt. Howitt eventually established his Headquarters. An indiscriminate shelling of our forward and back areas was carried out by the enemy throughout the day.

On this day Major Blakeney, who had returned from leave, left the Transport lines to take up employment on the Lines of Communication.

With Capt. H. S. Walker, who was acting as Second-in-Command for the operations, the C.O. inspected the positions now held and found the support trenches (occupied by A and C Companies) in a very wet and damaged condition. In consequence of this many were forced to go sick with trench feet, trench fever and exhaustion. Some were up to their waists in mud and water, and the conditions were so galling that ration parties had the greatest difficulty in getting up supplies. Men struggled grimly with bags of rations to reach their comrades, but the task was one that would have beaten the stoutest of hearts. It took hours to move a mile or two over the reeking morass to which the constant shelling and rain had reduced the ground, which was also in places soaked with gas. In addition, the enemy kept a barrage on the back areas to prevent supplies or guns coming forward. One ration party was lost for 48 hours and turned up in a totally different part of the sector. Even when rations arrived, they were unpalatable, as bread would be covered with mud through men falling in shell holes. It was pitiable to see miserable objects, hardly able to drag one foot behind the other, wearily make their way to the Regimental Aid Post, where they usually collapsed. Battalion H.Q., situated on the edge of Battle Wood which was constantly shelled, was bad enough, despite the fact that it was a dugout which would resist shell fire on top. Its entrance had been flooded by the rains; some damaged steps led down to its interior, and there were few dry spots inside.

B Company reported on the 2nd being in contact with the left of the Loyal North Lancs. Regt. in the region of Forret Farm. On the 3rd the enemy artillery continued active at intervals throughout the day on our forward positions in the neighbourhood of Hollebeke and Optic Trench. An enemy document showing the key to his Verey light signals was found in Hollebeke and forwarded to Brigade H.Q. The strong point at Forret Farm was completed, and our new forward line consolidated.

The 4th was a quieter day, although the wood near the White Château received a good deal of attention. A and C Companies were by now badly depleted in numbers owing to sickness caused by the incessant rain and the abominable conditions of the trenches. 2nd Lieut. Aucutt reported sick and was evacuated.

Having regard to the conditions under which the Battalion had been called upon to hold the line since the 31st of July, we cannot wonder at what happened on the 5th of August. The morning was a misty one, visibility being confined to not more than twenty yards, and very early in the morning the enemy put down a heavy barrage lasting two hours. At 4.45 a.m. a corporal of the Machine-gun Corps arrived at Headquarters and reported that a strong force of the enemy had not only retaken Hollebeke but was almost at hand. On hearing this the C.O. ordered the Adjutant to collect all maps and secret papers and burn them. All lines to Headquarters were "dis," as also was the line to Brigade and the Batteries. S.O.S. rockets were fired without success and then runners were despatched to the 15th Hants and Brigade H.Q. Without hesitation Major Pennell then ordered all the Battalion H.Q. staff, with the exception of one signaller, to follow him and proceed to counter-attack. At the time the order was given, acting R.S.M. B. Horswell, had to awaken some of the men who had been trying to snatch a few hours' sleep in the very uncomfortable surroundings. Some of them had taken off their boots for the first time for a week owing to the fact that their feet were hurting them badly. Some had only time to slip them on and tie them round without lacing them up, while others, as Colonel Pennell recalls, fought without them through not being able to get them on or losing them in the mud on the way. All sorts of news were prevalent, after the first report had stated that the enemy had taken the village and was in the vicinity of Battle Wood, practically outside Headquarters. At all events the last reserves of the 12th made their way out and began to move forward in the thick mist towards the village through a barrage of enemy shell-fire.

This motley collection of observers, signallers, batmen, orderly room clerk, cooks and even stretcher-bearers, wallowed through the mud to within a couple of hundred yards of the village. Trussler, a stretcher-bearer, joined in with a rifle and Lewis-gun, but they were quickly choked with mud and useless. (He received the M.M. later.) On the way we met Capt. C. N. Pridham, who informed the C.O. that the enemy was in the village and bombing for all he was worth. Very soon it was apparent that we were in touch with the Boche although the mist obscured our vision. The guttural German voices could be heard distinctly, while a machine-gun swept the front over which we were advancing. One of the first to fall was Lce.-Cpl. W. Richens, of the observers, who was struck in the heart by a bullet—a very fine man, both in intellect and physique. In continuing the advance, Lce.-Cpl. L. M. Duggan, the orderly room clerk, fell into a deep shell-hole and with the assistance of a comrade was extricated from the mud minus a boot. In vain did he try to retrieve his boot, but without success, and he had to move on without it. German riflemen and machine-gunners became busy as the last hopes of the Battalion were joined by the remnants of a company of the 15th Hants just in front of the village. Suddenly out of the mist three or four of the enemy ran towards us with their hands up. They were seized upon at once by Major Pennell, who tried to get some information out of them. They could not speak French or English, and in consequence it was not possible to ascertain from them the numbers or location of the enemy. Major Pennell then instructed the orderly room clerk to conduct them to Brigade H.Q. They were well-built fellows who, it was clear, had been specially brought up for the attack. Their clothes bore no signs of belonging to men who had been holding the line in front of Hollebeke. According to the numbers on their shoulder straps they belonged to the 209th and 213th German Regiments.

It must have been amusing to see Duggan conducting the prisoners across the awful waste towards Brigade. With only one boot on, over a week's growth of beard on his face, and a rifle choked up with mud, he must have looked the very picture of misery. Hopping about on one foot (the other was sore through being cut by wire), whilst his charges, a little scared, walked on in front, he was glad when he had got rid of them and had his foot attended to at an aid post.

Meanwhile Colonel Cary Barnard, commanding the 15th Hants, on our right, had received Major Pennell's message. He sent on Major Amery and 2nd Lieut S. Lasenby (12th East Surrey Regt., then attached to the 15th Hants) for further information, organised two platoons in Opal Reserve, which with some Twelfth East Surrey men made a counter-attack under Capt. Oxborrow, and sent another of his platoons forward towards Forret Farm. By 8.15 Colonel Cary Barnard had gone right forward and had found Major Pennell successfully holding Hollebeke village with a strong fighting patrol, having taken 17 prisoners. About the same time some East Surreys had got back into Forret Farm, and on the arrival of a platoon of the 15th Hants a little later, a Staffordshire officer was found re-organising these men, whom he handed over to 2nd Lieut. Shields of the Hampshires. This combined force then retook the whole of Forret Farm, while a half-company of the Staffords of the 19th Division, who were on our right, were brought to a point 200 yards in rear as supports. At Hollebeke the whole line was then pushed forward, and positions were established slightly forward of the line we held before the attack on the village. By noon the situation was completely restored, and Lieut. (acting Capt.) C. N. Pridham then took over command of the survivors. With a party estimated at 25 other ranks, and a protective barrage in front of his new positions, Capt. Pridham had to hold on till relief came later.

Gradually the story of the attack was unfolded. It appeared that in the mist the posts of B and D Companies were surrounded before they could give any alarm. When it was realised what had happened, the officers and men made a stubborn resistance before being overcome. For the first time since the Battalion arrived overseas some of its officers and men became prisoners.

2nd Lieuts. F. A. Samuels, M.C., and L. H. Jennings were reported missing, together with the following other ranks:—Cpl. F. Francis; Lce.-Cpls. E. G. Bartlett, H. G. Farrell, N. Goold and R. Smith; Ptes. A. Bacon, C. Berwick, G. P. Bourne, V. Brown, P. Carrod, A. W. Childs, W. J. Clark, H. Cloak, F. Cornish, G. Day, P. Diplock, F. Ford, W. A. Forster, G. A. Gull, W. Hammond, W. Harmer, A. Harris, F. Head, A. T. Jelly, C. Joyce, T. W. Keegan, W. King, F. H. Knight, W. Lidbury, S. F. Lowers, J. McAllister, A. McKay, L. B. Marsh, J. Mason, F. Miles, G. A. Norman, W. H. Page, C. Roberts, A. C. Robins, E. R. Roffey, H. G. Rose, F. Shaw, H. B. R. Smith. S. W. Smith, A. Spicer, W. Tarling, A. Thompson, W. G. True, R. L. Wanstall, W. Watts, T. Wells, D. A. White and T. Wright.

All were eventually reported prisoners and transported into Germany to such places as Hamburg, Limburg, Gustrow and Parchim, with the exception of the following:—Ptes. Bacon, Cloak, Diplock, King, Knight, Robins, Rose, Shaw, True, Wells and White. These latter were afterwards reported as killed, and their names are inscribed on the Menin Gate. Pte. Spicer must have been wounded when captured; he died later on the 19th of August and is buried at Harlebeke.

Capt. A. G. ("Jock") Howitt, M.C., will remain the legendary hero of the 12th Battalion. If there was anything to be done needing courage and a cool head, "Jock" was the man for the job. Badly wounded at Flers, he was back again with the Battalion in time for Messines and for the raid in which he earned the Military Cross. Then came his attack on the strong point at Hollebeke. On that misty morning of the 5th of August, when the Boche came over it would appear that Capt. Howitt was caught unawares in his Headquarters at Forret Farm. A message received at Brigade H.Q. from the 24th Division during the action stated that he had been killed by a sniper, but the real facts were not forthcoming until a runner from D Company reported that he had found the captain dead at Forret Farm with several of the enemy dead around him. Beside him was a man of his company severely wounded. Dead men tell no tales, but, knowing the man as we did, we could only assume that he and the man beside him made a gallant fight against odds which were too great for them. "Jock," the name by which the men under him knew him, received no posthumous award for his gallantry and skilful leading at Hollebeke, but his memory is enshrined in the hearts of the men whom he led as a gallant and lovable personality. To-day his name appears on the Menin Gate. Who his severely wounded comrade was it is not possible to say with certainty. Lce.-Cpl. Nugent thinks it was his servant, but Lce.-Cpl. Farrell is under the impression that his servant was taken prisoner.

So much for the account of the operations taken from official documents and other reliable sources. Let us now have recourse to personal accounts from some of those who participated.

Capt. Hector S. Walker, who went through the whole operations, gives his impressions of them:—

"A great deal of the sickness suffered by us in this action was due to orders from Higher Authority for our troops to occupy certain definite positions. These were no doubt picked out on the map. In my opinion the man on the spot must, or ought to be the one to decide. We were told to occupy a certain trench and I had to report to the C.O. that "C" were in what probably had once been a trench, but was now a trough of yellow slimy mud. A rifle placed on the so-called parapet sank into the mud about a foot, and the men were sinking when standing in it. Definite orders from Higher Authority through Division and Brigade—in spite of all difficulties—had to be obeyed. Had some of those responsible for planning details such as these visited the spot, things would have been very differently planned. Once the orders had gone out, apparently nothing could be done to have them changed. By the time we had finished arguing, or should I say requesting, it was too late—the irreparable damage had been done, and nearly the whole of C Company was evacuated sick.

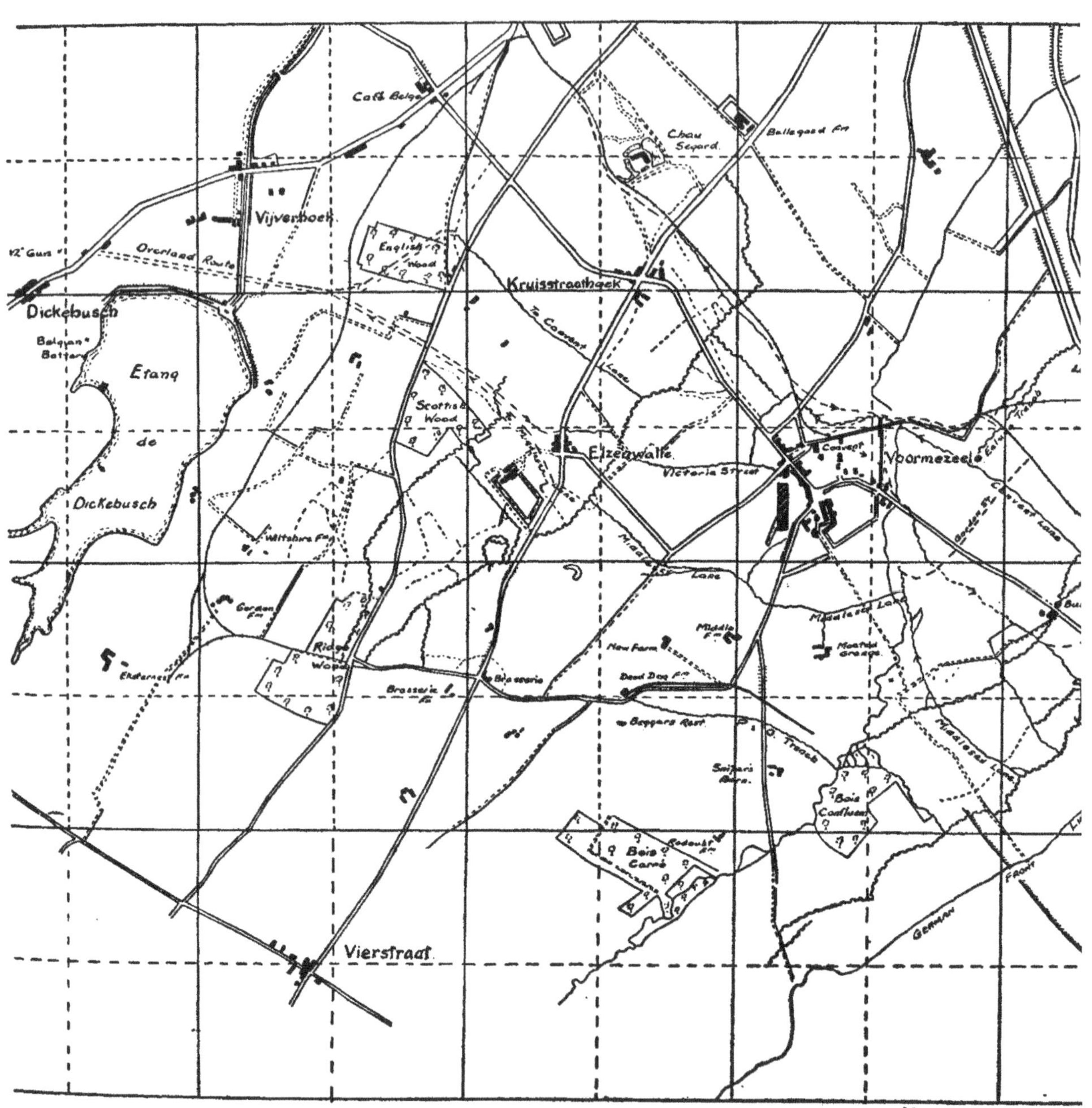

Café Belge
Chau Segard
Bellegoed Fm
Vijverhoek
12" Guns
Overland Route
English Wood
Kruisstraathoek
Dickebusch
Belgian Battery
Etang de Dickebusch
To Convent Lane
Scottish Wood
Elzenwalle
Convent
Voormezeele
Victoria Street
Wiltshire Fm
Middlesex Lane
Gordon Fm
Middle Fm
New Farm
Moated Grange
Ridge Wood
Brasserie
Brasserie Fm
Dead Dog Fm
Beggars Rest
P. & O. Trench
Snipers Barn
Bois Confluent
Redoubt Fm
Bois Carré
Vierstraat
German Front

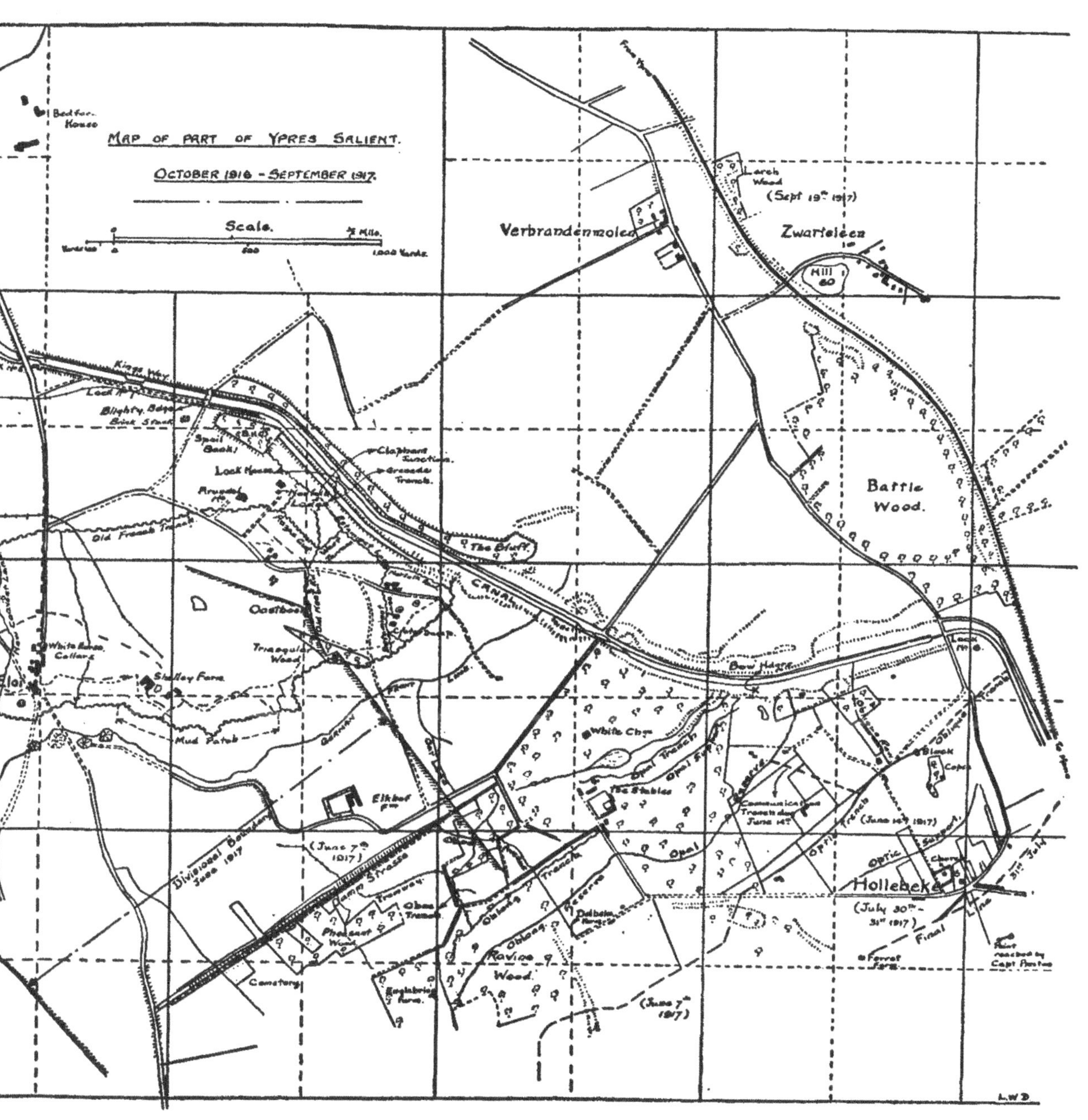
MAP OF PART OF YPRES SALIENT.
OCTOBER 1916 - SEPTEMBER 1917.
Scale.
Verbrandenmolen
Zwarteleen
Hill 60
Larch Wood
(Sept 19th 1917)
Battle Wood.
The Bluff.
CANAL
Bow Hague
Lock No 6.
Oostbook
Triangular Wood
Lock House
Spoil Bank
Kings Way
Old French Trench
Mud Patch
White Chau
The Stables
Opal
Opal Trench
Elkhof Farm
Divisional Boundary June 1917
(June 7th 1917)
Damm Strasse
Tramway
Oblong Trench
Oblong Reserve
Ravine Wood.
Pheasant Wood
Cemetery
Optic
Optic Trench
Hollebeke
(July 30th - 31st 1917)
(June 14th 1917)
Communication Trench dug June 14th
Black Copse
Final
Ferret Farm
(June 7th 1917)
L.W.D.

"It was my job to detail Capt. "Jock" Howitt to take his company and clear up the situation at Hollebeke. I saw him there afterwards in a Boche dugout and he was quite merry and bright. He had done his job well and had his company out in posts in front of the village or rather what was left of it, just a heap of rubble.

"During the early morning of the 5th there was a thick white mist and I was told afterwards that the officer then on duty, failed to order "Stand to." The mist allowed the enemy to get between and behind the various posts and also to the Company H.Q. dugout. There was hand to hand fighting there, but the enemy knew every inch of the ground, and against superior numbers and bombs, in addition to the surprise, Capt. Howitt had no chance. He made a gallant last stand and left many dead as proof that he went down fighting to the end.

"I was with Major Pennell in the retaking of the village. The thick mist and the heavy bombardment made the going very difficult. All men in the H.Q. dugout were turned out; one man I remember was without boots. As we approached the village we saw men of another battalion (?K.R.R.s) lying in line along a ditch. They were all dead, probably caught by M.G. enfilade. Richens was lying next to me. He was shot dead. I believe he was an expert camera man and should have been with the Photographic Dept. of the R.F.C. where his special training would have been so useful. Like many others, he stuck to the men in the line rather than try for a more cushy job.

"The mist suddenly lifted and we saw some of our men about to be marched off as prisoners. We shot the escort and released the prisoners. The mist kept lifting and falling again and completely obscured everything. Hollebeke was once more in our hands."

Capt. David Walker writes:—

"July 31st will ever remain a date to be remember by those who took part in the assault on Hollebeke. It had rained in torrents and without ceasing for some days, and, once the battle had begun and the heavy rains continued, the weather took control of the situation.

"It is difficult for a reader to imagine the awful expanse of slimy mud just south of the Ypres—Comines canal, which was our Divisional Sector. Our attacking troops plodded on through this until all but beaten by physical exhaustion. Many never rose from the mire; evacuations through nothing else but just these weather conditions reached a high proportion of those of us who consolidated the ground gained in the successful advance on the ruined village.

"I was again in command of the group forming the Brigade Forward Signal Station and had established telephone communication with Brigade at the H.Q. of the West Kents, who occupied a newly captured enemy dugout in the Canal bank, half-way up the slope rising before Hollebeke. It was a tremendous effort to maintain this important link in communications as Division was still uncertain of our positions after the attack. Man after man was sent out repairing the line, and to do this meant tracing it through mud indescribable. When the linesmen returned, covered with mud up to the neck, as likely as not, the wire was again broken by artillery fire, and cheerily they would face their task again out in the open. They were heroes.

"Runners had a task, if possible, more difficult still. We kept up a supply of carrier-pigeons, and these runners not only carried important messages but also maintained our supply of pigeons by transporting the empty baskets to Brigade H.Q. a mile away, there to be furnished with fresh birds to bring back to us. In these hectic days, as conditions got nearer to the impossible, the pigeons served us best of all: anyhow, by one means or another our communications were maintained.

"Our very good friend, Col. Corfe, of the West Kents, waged war on the telephone with the Staff Captain at Brigade H.Q. During one of these brief periods of telephonic communications he was asked by the Staff Captain to give the pin-point map references where the dead were being buried. The story of his volcanic repartee is excellently told in the West Kents war history, and I can only add my testimony as to what a good friend Col. Corfe was to have near you when in trouble.

"Later that morning the East Surreys took over from the West Kents. Major Pennell, in temporary command of our Battalion, was having a scratch lunch during one of these waits to get the telephone to function again, our linesmen being all out in the quagmire repairing the line. At last there was a Buzz Buzz in the dugout. I was called to the phone: we were through once again to Brigade, and the Staff Captain wanted to speak to me. I recognised the voice, and with some pique I called: 'What, Captain A——! The general has told you to complain that the Brigade Signal Sergeant reports the empty pigeon baskets as being sent back from the line in a dirty and filthy condition!

"I intentionally raised my voice, as I knew that Major Pennell was within earshot. Hearing the subject of conversation, he jumped up from his lunch and was in a trice at my elbow. All ears were open in astonishment. To think that our heroic runners could carry pigeon-baskets a mile through several feet deep of mud, not to mention shell-fire from the enemy, back to Brigade H.Q. without getting them into the same mess as they themselves were in—mud from head to foot!

"Major Pennell took up the phone. His cool, collected voice must have sounded ominous to the Staff Captain at the other end of the wire: I am sure at that moment he must have wished it could receive the attention of a 5.9. To use the C.O.'s own words —'he cursed A—— well and truly and told him to fetch the —— baskets himself.'

"He further dictated a personal letter to the General as follows:—'I regret the Staff Captain having to complain of the pigeon baskets being received back from the line in a dirty and filthy condition. I cannot understand how they could possibly get dirty, as we are under such clean and ideal conditions here. I suggest that the Staff Captain might keep his sense of proportion and have a better idea of the real conditions, if he would pay *a personal visit* to the troops in the line.

"Sure enough General Towsey did send Capt. A—— up. He arrived about two hours later full of apologies. The C.O., after saying a little more about his thoughtless complaint, took him to the front line. The Staff Captain must have enjoyed that trip! It was a bad day for him."

The consolidation of the line in front of Hollebeke and the capture of the village itself, which had given so much trouble, was the job of the East Surreys. This was accomplished with comparatively few casualties, and Capt. Jock Howitt with D Company occupied a line just in front of the village. Four days later (5th August) all Headquarters were disturbed by the noise of an enemy barrage in the early hours of dawn. Quite obviously the enemy were making a serious counter-attack to regain the Hollebeke position. Outside our dugout it was easy to see the helplessness of the position, for there was a heavy mist and it was hardly possible to see 10 yards. Our telephone lines were cut, and the only pigeon we had left was being kept so that we might be able to send later some definite information on the situation. The enemy were shelling very heavily, and we were very anxious to get some artillery support and counter-battery fire, but as yet no sound came from our guns. Whether S.O.S. rockets could be seen in the mist was very doubtful, but this was a chance. We fired one, and then another, and another, but only to find that like everything else they had been steeping in mud for a fortnight. Only one out of eight rockets gave any encouragement, and this was really futile.

We had no real information from the front line, but our C.O. did not for a moment doubt what was happening. The enemy might be at strength, and with the aid of the early morning mist any organised attack must succeed against our weak defences. The enemy shelling continued, and then, with a hasty note to Brigade which was despatched by our remaining pigeon, our Commanding Officer ordered every available man who could be found to follow him and advance towards the enemy. The C.O. also despatched messages by runners to Brigade and the Hants. He soon had a following of perhaps 40 men—H.Q. staff runners, signallers, sick and slightly wounded. The C.O. with only a heavy walking stick trudged on, never looking back even to see the strength of his supporters. In the mist only those who were close up could see him, so determined and so quick a pace did he set towards the enemy. By good fortune this little band, following its leader, fell in with Capt. H. S. Walker with part of his company. Originally on the right of our front position, they had fallen back and came over to the left and were in touch with the enemy. Immediately Major Pennell himself set out on a reconnaissance round Hollebeke. He found the enemy Storm Troopers who had carried out the attack retiring, and the enemy battalion in the line coming forward to consolidate their advance. With the morning mist now in our favour for attack, the C.O. ordered us to advance and occupy the village. This was carried out just in time and surprised the enemy. Our advanced line in front of Hollebeke was regained and the surprised enemy left many prisoners in our hands.

It was however a sad sight that told its tale in Hollebeke. In the organised attack on D Company during the early morning the company had been completely wiped out. Some were taken prisoner, but the Commander with many of his men lay there, having been obviously surprised in the mist by the attack on their position. I lost a fellow-countryman and friend in Jock Howitt, but Major Pennell's prompt action and extremely brave leadership saved Hollebeke for the 12th East Surreys.

An interesting account of the action has been supplied by one of the prisoners, Lce.-Cpl. H. G. Farrell, which runs as follows:—

"On the 31st of July D Company took up their positions on the edge of a trench from which the K.R.R.s were jumping off to the attack. I don't know how long the K.R.R.s had been there, but they seemed very 'fed up,' which was not to be wondered at considering the weather. At Zero hour our guns opened up and the K.R.R.s went over the top and we took what shelter we could in their trench. Within a few minutes the wounded started coming back. The first man I saw came running back minus his trousers and with a nice 'Blighty' one. Within a short time the trench we were in, which was used as a first dressing station, was packed with wounded. Whether they ran forward too fast into our barrage (which was a jumping one), or whether 'Jerry' had got the range, I do not know, but it was evident in a very short time that the attack on this sector had failed. Somehow some Germans got through the barrage and gave themselves up. They were used as stretcher-bearers after a time, but everything seemed useless, for as soon as they started back the whole lot were usually blown up, as 'Jerry' by this time had put a barrage behind us to stop supports arriving. During the period I saw many V.C.s earned. The stretcher-bearers worked like heroes, but I am afraid that very few returned to get their rewards.

"However, to return to the East Surreys. As the day advanced, things slowed down a bit, and then Capt. Howitt came along and told us to get ready to go over, as there was a break on our part of the line and we had to advance to Hollebeke village. It was peculiar to go over without a barrage of any sort, and all seemed quiet. I was crawling along with my Lewis-gun when the man just in front was caught by a sniper in the centre of the forehead, so after that we lay doggo a bit and then went forward again led by Capt. Jock. We bombed a few dugouts and soon arrived at some heaps of bricks, which after a bit of map reading etc., Capt. Jock decided was the village, the red bricks being the church. Our orders now were to dig in and make a strong point, which we did as well as possible, although the water did not allow us to get very deep. However, we found a 'Jerry' trench later on and tumbled in. We soon went off to sleep, dead beat, but woke to find the water over our necks and my Lewis-gun gone. I dug into the mud and found it.

"During the next day the sun came out a little, and we managed to clean our guns and walk about a bit in between 'Jerry's' attentions. During this day a sniper got busy and picked off several of our men, so Capt. Jock and a sergeant decided to find him. Off they went with revolvers, and a couple of hours later came back saying that the sniper would not trouble us again. A brave action this to find a sniper in broad daylight. The next night found us in the same position with no food and our numbers getting smaller. During this time we saw one 'Jerry' only, and he was wandering about lost, so we took him in tow, and he was a very surprised man when Capt. Jock gave him a drop of whiskey from his waterbottle instead of shooting him. We scrounged around and found a dugout that had been 'Jerry's' telephone headquarters with a fine switchboard and (glory be) some flasks of rum and hundreds of cigars floating about. However, we found a few dry ones and managed a smoke, but we were hungry by this time. We had one or two casualties, as 'Jerry' strafed us twice during the day, but otherwise it was quiet.

"On the night of the 4th a ration party got through and left us a fine supply, including some rabbits, which we were going to have in the morning. Unfortunately, we did not have them, because 'Jerry' came and took us early.

"There was a heavy mist during the night and 'Jerry' must have crawled right up to our strong point, for suddenly a barrage opened up which lasted about ten minutes, and then he was in the midst of us with the bayonet.

"Lce.-Cpl. E. G. Bartlett and I were in an old German dugout. I could hear cries of 'Oh mother!' as the Germans plunged their bayonets into some of our fellows. Hearing the hubbub we ran out and were greeted by the enemy who were slinging bombs behind their backs, and Bartlett was badly wounded with one of these. At the same time a German ran at me with a sword bayonet. I can't quite make out how, but I evaded it and ran forward. Soon afterwards the enemy cooled down a bit and brought me back to assist Bartlett. We stood no chance, as rifles were useless, and it was horrible while it lasted; very few of us were eventually gathered together in 'Jerry's' dugout where wounds were dressed. We were then marched back a few kilos, being followed this time by our own barrage. Only 25 of us marched along that weary road to Courtrai. The troops that carried out this very smart raid were Bavarian Storm Troopers, and the first thing one asked me was how the Strand was looking these days. He had been a waiter for many years in some of our big hotels.

"I was particularly struck with the smartness of their officers. They were well dressed, and one wore a monocle. He spoke to me and others in perfect English: 'You take a hundred yards of mud to-day,' he said, 'we take it back to-morrow.' These chaps treated us very well, and eventually we arrived at Courtrai—25 hungry and dirty 'Englanders'."

Cpl. T. Day, of B Company, supplies some details of the part taken by his company in the operations.

"On July 31st I was one of a party detailed to carry wire and stakes over behind the West Kents. Later the same day the same men had to take rations up to D Company. When we arrived, we were told that they were going over at 6.0 p.m. and that we must follow with the rations. This done we got back about 9.0 p.m. only to be told that our Company was going up to strengthen 'D.'

"We were given two hours to have some rest and food before reporting to H.Q. near Spoil Bank, where we were detained from 3.0 a.m. until 2.0 p.m. on the 1st of August when we rejoined B Company. When we reached the trench, we found the men stuck in a place with water up to their thighs. We remained there until about 6.0 p.m. and then moved off to some dugouts where we remained until it was dark. We then moved forward and dug in alongside D Company and there we remained for close on a week, sitting in water. The Lewis-gunners stayed in the trench all the time, the others took turns in the dugouts.

"On the 4th of August the rain ceased and late that night the officer in charge of 'B,' who, I believe, was Mr. Gurrin, came along and told us that the 19th Division were going over on our right and no doubt we should have something slung at us. True, we did. Then a thick mist came up in the early morning and behind it came Jerry. He apparently attacked D Company first and then came along to us. I remember Sergt. Myers calling out, 'Lewis-gunners, they are here!' We quickly mounted the gun, which failed to respond owing to so much wet and mud. Then we retired back to a pill-box and dugouts to arouse the boys who were asleep. It was then that I saw Mr. Gurrin walk as if towards Jerry, when he and his servant, George Willows, were shot down, both dying of wounds. We fell back upon a strong point held by the Staffords, in charge of an officer and a sergeant-major. They asked us who we were and what the trouble was. When told, they formed us up in line and led us back to recapture our lost ground, pill-box and dugouts.

"Here Pte. Harry Collins (better known to us as 'Billy') distinguished himself. Our rifles were useless, being completely coated with mud, but Collins got hold of the branch of a tree and led us. We formed one line and then split into two, so as to attack the pill-box from both flanks. Collins was on the right. We made a rush, and out came two officers and eighteen men* to surrender to a practically unarmed party! Not a bad counter-attack. Jerry then posted snipers all round, and several of the boys were killed or wounded, and Collins attended to them under hot fire. We all afterwards said he should have had a decoration, and tried to get his name sent up, but for some reason it never was. Poor Collins later was mortally wounded at Gheluwe and died on October 1st, 1918.

"The roll call next morning after we had been relieved by the Hants was answered by 30 men."

Lce.-Cpl. S. J. Nugent relates an incident which took place before the "Show" which might have had serious consequences.

"An incident happened at Spoil Bank on the 29th of July, which, had it been a day later, might have had far reaching effects. B Company was in a position a little forward of Headquarters, and the telephone line linking the Company with Battalion H.Q. failed on two or three occasions, usually during the night, necessitating turning out a signaller to find the cause and remedy the defect. At about 1.0 a.m. on the 29th of July this line was found by the signaller on duty to be broken, and the linesman was detailed to turn out and put the matter right. He took a D III (portable telephone) with a lighted candle and set out along the duckboard track running parallel with Spoil Bank. Within a few minutes, however, there was a terrific explosion which rocked the whole sap and extinguished all lights. Candles were lit, and a few moments later the linesman returned, white as a sheet through the mud which plastered his face and still carrying the D. III. He almost collapsed and managed to gasp out, 'The ——s must have seen my candle.' It was then discovered that all lines, both Battalion and Brigade, had been cut, and when daylight arrived, it was found that a large ration dump built into the side of the bank had collapsed through the explosion of a huge shell, which not only cut but buried the mass of wires which provided communication in all directions. It took practically all the day before the attack to clear the débris and repair the damage."

* The capture of these prisoners is confirmed in the Brigade report of the operations.

Speaking of the German attack on the 5th of August, Nugent writes:—

"When the attack opened, all means of communication having failed, two signallers were detailed to repair the line to Brigade in an effort to restore communcation. By this time Battle Wood had come under a very heavy bombardment, and these two men were continuously repairing the breaks as they occurred, although it proved of little avail. Both of them afterwards received the Military Medal. The only other methods to get messages through were by pigeon and runner. Both methods were tried, and a signaller who was detailed to make for Brigade H.Q. took an hour instead of the normal twenty minutes to reach there owing to the state of the ground. Some of Major Pennell's party had no puttees or socks, as they had to dispense with them through the thickness of mud with which they were coated. Others had cut the legs of their trousers off up to the knees in order that movement should not be restricted."

Cpl. Southall also tells something of the difficulties of this time. He and his men wandered for long trying to find a spot for an Advanced Dressing Station. At last they were installed in a small concrete German pill-box close to the stretch of mud that had been the lake of the White Château. They pumped two feet of muddy water out and even then the pill-box was too low to stand upright in it, but there were wire beds in wooden frames in tiers.

"When I woke in the morning," he says, "the water was in again and gently lapping against the bottom of the bed. We waded in and pumped it out and during the day kept it out by baling. It wasn't exactly a home from home, but it was a palace compared to the trenches our men were occupying.

"The conditions were appalling; numbers of the fellows came down with trench feet, and we kept a constant supply of hot drinks going, chiefly Oxo and Glaxo mixed. In the attack in the early morning of August 5th when the C.O. took the whole H.Q. staff with him, Trussler, of the stretcher bearers, was filled with war-like ardour and joined the attack with a rifle and Lewis-gun. He told me they weren't of much use as they soon got choked with mud. However, he behaved very gallantly and received the M.M. for his activities."

From the questioning of the prisoners at Brigade H.Q. it transpired that Hollebeke was attacked by 200 Storm Troopers specially brought up for the attack. They were ordered to capture and stay in the village. Further light is thrown on the affair by the report in the Divisional War Diary. This states that the enemy, consisting of detachments from the 207th Division (fresh) and a large detachment of Assault Troops, 4th Army, which had been brought up on the previous day from Menin, attacked Hollebeke and Forret Farm and after a very heavy barrage managed to establish themselves in the aforesaid places. The report continues:—

"The supporting troops of the East Surreys and Hants who were holding the line, although very tired, and in numbers far less than the enemy's, counter-attacked with splendid vigour and determination and succeeded in driving the enemy out and re-establishing themselves in front of their original front line."

What the Divisional and Corps Commanders thought of the operations in which we had taken so prominent a part can be gauged from the following wires which were received at Brigade H.Q. on the 5th of August:—

To G.O.C. 122nd. Inf. Bde.
5/8.

Please congratulate troops of the 122nd Inf. Bde. on the splendid way in which they counter-attacked and regained their positions this morning.
From:—Lawford. 1.0 p.m.
To Bell (122nd Bde.). August 5th.

Wire from X Corps. Army Commander wishes to congratulate 41st Division on the stubborn defence and recapture of Hollebeke and Forret Farm. The defeat of fresh enemy troops, put in for the purpose, by your troops who have been holding the line since its capture is most creditable to all concerned.

Addressed to all concerned 41st Division. 4.25 p.m.

In the evening of the 5th the Battalion, about 90 strong, moved to Bois Confluent, but the Details at the Transport lines, under Capt. H. S. Openshaw, moved up the line as a platoon of a composite company formed from each battalion of the Brigade. Lieut.-Col. E. Knapp, who had returned from leave to the Transport lines on the 2nd, then reassumed command of the Battalion.

On the 6th a few other ranks who had attached themselves to the Staffordshire Regt. during the attack on Forret Farm reported back. The enemy continued to plaster the back areas, and a shell falling into our lines killed Ptes. W. Daston and W. Parsons. These men were staunch friends of Richens who had been killed near Hollebeke, so that the snipers and observers had lost three very fine men within a few hours. They were all of exceptionally high character and intelligence, and the I.O. had repeatedly tried to induce them to take commissions, but they steadily refused not only this but any other advancement. Fate had indeed dealt a very severe blow to that happy family of the H.Q. staff—the Snipers and Observers—with the wounding of Mr. Aston and the death of these three close pals.

After General Lawford had visited Battalion H.Q. on the 6th, orders were received for a move to De Zon Camp, near the Scherpenberg, on the morrow. It rained at intervals and in between there was much aerial activity. Next day we moved from Bois Confluent, motor buses meeting the men at the Brasserie and conveying them to De Zon Camp. General Towsey was known to be greatly distressed at the fearful hardships his men were suffering and the heavy casualties, and he did everything in his power to relieve them.

The casualties suffered by the Battalion in the operations from the 24th of July to the 7th of August were as follows:—Killed: 23. Died of Wounds: 7. Wounded: 115. Missing: 54. Sick: 125. Total: 324. It will thus be seen that sickness took the greatest toll, owing to the terrible conditions under which men had to fight. The full list of those who lost their lives will be found in the appendix. Some of the wounded died of their injuries later, while the number of missing was also decreased by reports from burial parties. Among the officers 2nd Lieut. Palk was wounded and sent to England on the 2nd of August. 2nd Lieuts. R. W. Gurrin and C. R. Haynes were also wounded, the former, mortally.

In reviewing the operations Colonel Pennell has expressed his surprise that our casualties were not heavier, but it must be remembered that during the Third Battle of Ypres battalions went into action very much below normal strength. We have already stated that only 90 survived the operations, so that the casualties suffered were high for the number which participated.

The gallant acts performed were not only many but also done in places where there was no possibility of them being suitably recognised. However, as a result of recommendations the following awards were afterwards made:—

Distinguished Service Order: Lieut. (Temp. Major) R. Pennell.

Military Cross: Capt. H. S. Walker; Lieut. D. Walker and 2nd Lieut. A. M. Mackintosh (attached to 122nd T.M.B.).

Distinguished Conduct Medal: Sergt. G. D. Prosser.

Military Medal: Sergt. H. Dickson; Cpl. S. G. Sarvant; Lce.-Cpls. J. A. Baker and E. E. Bolton; Ptes. A. Broderick, C. Daw, J. T. George, A. Hoare, D. Lynch, H. Manley, H. Scott, A. Trussler, C. Turner, C. T. Tustin and G. Wilkins.

In regard to the decoration so well merited by our acting Commanding Officer the following Commendation from General Lawford speaks for itself:—

"I wish to place on record my appreciation of your gallantry and devotion to duty.

"In the action near Hollebeke July 31st, 1917, you commanded the 12th Battn. East Surrey Regt. with skill and judgment. On August 5th, 1917, hearing that the enemy had recaptured Hollebeke, you organised and led a counter-attack under heavy machine-gun and rifle fire. The attack was completely successful and the village re-occupied by our troops."

Major Pennell had started the war as a sergeant, and was severely wounded at the Battle of the Aisne in 1914, then sent to England for a long sojourn in hospital and placed on light duty. Many a man would have felt his duty well done for the duration, for he was practically patched together with a silver plate supporting his anatomy. But he worked until he was appointed R.S.M. to the 18th Battn. K.R.R.C., then 2nd Lieut., then Lieut. and Adjutant, and in April, 1916, Temporary Captain. He proceeded in May, 1916, to France with his battalion, was soon appointed Temporary Major and was Commanding Officer before the end of that year. Soldiering was his meat and drink, and he did not know what fear was. Somewhat dour and taciturn, he was not popular with everyone, for he was rightly impatient with slackness or inefficiency, but those who came to know him well admired him intensely and realised that there was no stouter soldier or leader of men in the British Army.*

After recounting Major Pennell's early zeal for soldiering, Capt. Hector Walker writes:—

"He was a fine C.O. When he took over the 12th he inspected my company and ticked me off for allowing some of the men to have boots that showed a little wear on the heels. 'Whose job is it to see to the outfitting of the men under your command?' I informed him that the Q.M. assisted by the R.Q.M.S. and the C.Q.M.S. as a rule attended to this. 'It is not their job,' he barked, 'it is the duty of the company commander—remember that.' I did. I became friends with him, liked and respected him in every way, and discovered that his uncle was the hero of the school I was at—a V.C.—which was rather rare in my young days."

Capt. Hector S. Walker had acted as understudy to Major Pennell throughout the operations and on the morning of the 5th had rallied the remnants of C Company when things looked blackest. Lieut. David Walker, being responsible for maintaining forward signal stations for Brigade, found himself pitch-forked into a battle on the 5th and was of the greatest assistance to Major Pennell during its progress.

Of the other recipients records are not available which would be of assistance in assessing the value of the acts they performed, and they too would not desire that their deeds should be considered any greater than those of their comrades who laid down their lives and whose only reward was a wooden cross.

Throughout this history mention has been made of individuals only where the writer had first hand knowledge himself or where others have since written and paid tribute to the acts or the men concerned have sent details.

The majority of the awards went to men like Dickson and Sarvant who had been with the Battalion since its early days. They were known to us as the "Old Twelfth." Their consistent good work was bound to be recognised some time or another, if they were fortunate enough to survive. Three of these were transport drivers, and, as all the transport men had taken an equal share in the awful task of getting rations up, it was decided to ballot for them. Clem Daw was one of two brothers who joined us from the Middlesex Regt. He was a runner who never failed to get his messages through in all sorts of weather and conditions. His brother who, like himself, was very well liked amongst the H.Q. staff, was wounded towards the end of the war.

Of Scott and Manley here let us quote an episode of the Great War by Pte. H. J. Sherborne, D.C.M.:—

"The Battalion H.Q. Signal dugout was a fairly comfortable spot. It was deep and a welcome place to return to after a day out in the open in the cold inclement weather at this time. The dugout was situated in the reserve line with some hundred yards to go for the support line through a wood. The lines to Company H.Q. ran through this wood and had been badly knocked about during the last few days and nights until they were practically a mass of joints. The wood was in an exposed condition and movement through it was at considerable risk even if use was made of the communication trench; out on the top was of course considerably worse.

"In the signal dugout were two linesmen, one called 'Scotty.' They were close pals and always operated together if possible. They were tired out after a hard day and were lying down to sleep. The signaller on duty called out that he believed that the line to the front line had gone. Amid much cursing and swearing the two linesmen were roused from their slumbers and told of the trouble. 'Scotty' said it was hopeless trying to repair that line again and the only thing to do was to run out a fresh one. Accordingly they grabbed a drum of cable, which, by the way, is no light weight, and started out on their trip. One or two of us who were standing by in the trench climbed up on the parapet to have a look at them. They had got as far as the wood in front when suddenly Jerry opened fire and commenced to search the wood with shells. We

*Note.—A few words as to his later remarkable career would be appropriate.

Only a month or so after winning the D.S.O. for his fine action with the 12th at Hollebeke he was awarded a bar to this decoration for his gallant actions at Tower Hamlets and was promoted Temporary Lieut.-Colonel. In November he was temporarily commanding the 122nd Brigade. After the return from Italy he was again severely wounded in March, 1918. During the war he was four times mentioned in despatches and was also awarded the M.C.

After the war his rank was reduced to Lieut. and he did hard service in Ireland in the dark days of 1921. He finally retired in 1927 with the rank of Lieut.-Colonel, and is now one of the Military Knights of Windsor, residing at the Castle. Truly a romantic and honourable career.

could see these two men out there caught in the bursting shells and fully expected them to go to ground and take what cover they could. To our amazement however we saw 'Scotty' bend down and then stand up with the drum of cable above his head on a stick and start running forward with his mate tailing him up behind to see the line dropped in position all right. Shells were bursting everywhere around them and in the mist their figures showed up like demons in the flash and glare of the bursts: now disappearing entirely from view in front of the clouds of smoke and earth, then their figures being lit up again by other shells. Stumbling forward, falling, picking themselves up again, they carried on until they finally vanished from view altogether. Meantime the firing had increased considerably, a terrific barrage being put down by the enemy. We became anxious as to what was happening up there when the buzzer sounded. To our astonishment the signaller on duty informed us that he had heard 'Scotty' say that the line was all right now and that, as Jerry was attacking, would he put them through to the Colonel."

Throughout the day on the 8th the Battalion was employed on reorganisation of Companies, issues of clothing, baths, etc. Lieut.-General Sir T. L. N. Morland, K.C.B., Army Corps Commander, inspected us at 11.0 a.m.

Despite what the Battalion had been through, relief was not yet at hand. After a temporary reorganisation orders were received on the 9th for it to move to the forward area on the following day with a fighting strength of 5 officers and 253 other ranks. Accordingly on the 10th De Zon Camp was left behind and buses taken as far as the Brasserie: thence on foot again to the foul and hated area south of the Canal: Battalion H.Q. were fixed at the Iron Bridge. Capt. Openshaw with another officer and 64 other ranks who had rejoined from the Brigade Composite Company occupied Oblique Row; one officer and 64 other ranks occupied Optic Trench, and 50 other ranks the White Château. Two officers and 75 other ranks reported to the O.C. 11th West Kents at Wood Camp and later relieved D Company of the 15th Hants in the line in front of Forret Farm. The troops in Optic Trench, Oblique Row, and the White Château now came under the C.O. of the 11th West Kents for tactical purposes. The Details marched to the Transport lines at Murrimbidgee Camp, La Clytte, where 2nd Lieut. F. B. B. Dowling had reported back from the Base Training Depôt at Etaples. Pte. C. Thrussell was killed on the 10th.

At dawn on the 12th and 13th the enemy, evidently in anticipation of further attacks, shelled the lines, but owing to the activity of our planes and artillery remained fairly quiet for the remainder of the time. Battalion H.Q. received attention from the enemy's heavies on the 13th, on which day 5 other ranks were wounded.

Referring to this period Capt. H. S. Walker writes:—

"I was O.C. Details attached to the Royal West Kents and we were sent to hold Forret Farm. The party consisted of Lieut. Dowling (?), Sergt. Mayston and a smattering of all companies. Ration parties had great difficulty in finding us, and in consequence we were short of food and water most of the time. We could not move at all by day as our position was at the foot of a slope facing the enemy. Enemy planes flew low over us and our only protection was to lie still under ground sheets. Although we were only about two platoons strong the position we held was most important—the junction of the line between two divisions. I had a battered old dugout as Headquarters, which filled with water until we drained it at night.

"Orders from Colonel Corfe to do a raid on the enemy dugouts in front of us were cancelled."

On the evening of the 13th the Battalion was relieved by two companies of the 12th Sussex Regt. and two companies of the 15th Hants. The relief was going well and three platoons were out, when the enemy commenced a gas shell bombardment on Spoil Bank and the Ration Track. On the way down Lce.-Cpl. E. E. Bolton (who received the M.M. for his part in the earlier operations) was killed at Oak Dump. A rest was taken at Wiltshire Camp in the neighbourhood of Elzenwalle Château during the night, and on the 14th the Battalion, about 250 strong, marched viâ Dickebusch Lake to Hallebast Corner, where lorries conveyed the gallant remnants to La Roukloshille, which was reached at 1.15 p.m. The Details and the Transport had in the meantime paraded on the Reninghelst-La-Clytte Road and proceeded through Westoutre and Berthen to the old billets at La Roukloshille which had been occupied before the operations at Hollebeke.

Continuing his account of the period Capt. H. S. Walker says:—

"The incoming troops who took over from us in the line amounted to a battalion, and as they had to occupy a line which we held with two platoons I have often wondered where they were all put.

"I took a compass bearing from my H.Q. to the Battalion H.Q. for the use of our relief. On 'Relief Complete' I had ordered each section to move off as soon as relieved. Our little H.Q. party consisting of Dowling, Mayston, Pilcher (my servant) and Dowling's servant, and myself then moved off. We were led by a really good runner whose name I cannot remember, but he is a member of the 12th Association. As he proceeded I checked him by my compass. He was sure he was right and I was equally sure that he was wrong. The night was pitch black; no moon, no stars, not even a Verey light, and all very quiet. Eventually we reached some dugouts, but not the ones we were looking for. It was a row of enemy dugouts. Very quietly we retraced our steps for a bit, and I then led out by corrected compass bearing, the runner all the time being sure that we were going towards the enemy. At last we felt we were near a trench, so we carefully lay down to hear voices. A working party moving along the trench kicked a resting man and we heard a wonderful flow of language. I called out 'Is that Dagger?' and someone recognised my voice and addressed me by name. After reporting to Colonel Corfe we went on out and arrived at a camp, very tired and very very dirty and unwashed."

After these terrible three weeks rest was an absolute necessity. But the gaps in the Battalion were shocking: many a fine comrade had "gone west," and their loss cast a gloom over the camp. This was perhaps the most tragic side of the war, the close friendships formed only to be soon severed by Death, and this not once but many times. Ah, the stupid cruelty of it!

NOTE 1.

Most of us must have wondered at times what became of our comrades when they were unfortunate enough to fall into the hands of the enemy. Lce.-Cpl. Farrell therefor continues his reminiscences with an account of events after his arrival at Courtrai on the 5th of August, 1917:—

"We were kept at Courtrai two days, fed very well and made quite a fuss of. We found the reason for it later, as this was a 'Pumping station' and they did their best to pump us. All the orderlies could speak English, though we did not know it until later, so they were able to listen to our conversation. I don't think they learned much, as from this time until December at least our one talk was Food! Food! Food!

"At any rate from Courtrai we were taken to Dendermonde. This was a typical occupied town as Germans understood it, and apart from our own suffering it was terrible to see the way the Belgians were treated. We were taken to a kind of prison, where there were hundreds of other English prisoners, and packed in cells so tight that there was not room for all of us to lie on the floor at night. We had straw to lie on and an iron bath to use as a latrine. The latter was not big enough and before morning it used to overflow on to the straw, which in a few days was a moving mass of lice. We had been used to lice in the trenches, but here it was unspeakable. No shaving tackle was allowed, and food consisted of a ladle of vile soup per day and one tiny piece of black bread. We were here nearly four weeks, during which time the straw was unchanged and the food ration the same. At this time there must have been 800 men—scarecrows I should say—in the place, and almost too weak to take the little exercise we were allowed. The wonderful thing was the spirit of the men. They even got permission to hold a concert in the yard one evening, and one man sang 'I'm Burlington Bertie from Bow' (without food so long, I've forgot where my face is, etc.). Then the leader, a little Welsh fellow, said 'Let's all sing, "God save the King".' We did, and had got nearly through it before the Commandant realised what it was, and then we were packed helter skelter to our cells.

"It would need the pen of a Dickens to describe the condition of the men at this time; dirty, starved and ill-clothed (they even took our shirts if they could get at them). Some of us got together and made plans for a mutiny, but the Commandant was informed, so on the 2nd of September a large number of us were marched to the railway station and put in cattle trucks. We were in the train three days, during which time we had two meals only, and on the 5th of September reached Dulmen in Westphalia. Here was a properly organised camp, and we received a bath and a haircut (proper No. 1, whiskers and all).

"We left Dulmen on the 17th of September and arrived at Bayreuth Camp on the 19th, and from here were sent to work. I then lost sight of my East Surrey comrades and did not see them again until I returned to Bayreuth Camp after the Armistice.

"I do not think any account would be complete without reference to the marvellous work and organisation of the Red Cross Society. But for them many thousands of our prisoners would have starved to death."

NOTE 2.

Pte. T. W. Keegan, of D Company, who was taken prisoner of war on August 5th, kept a valuable diary during his captivity which lasted till December, 1918.

The fearful hardships of our prisoners, of which this account and that of Lce.-Cpl. Farrell are typical examples, should not be forgotten. We admit that Germany, owing to our blockade, was experiencing great shortage of food and other necessaries during the latter part of the war even for her own civilian population, and we know that in some camps, as Pte. Keegan testifies, prisoners were treated with decent consideration, yet many suffered inexcusable inhumanity and neglect and often deliberate cruelty, especially at the hands of the Prussians.

It is often the fashion in post-war days to speak as if all combatants were tarred with the same brush, and to maintain that, if it be true that Germans were too often treacherous, brutal, callously cruel bullies, we were the same. The authors emphatically hold that this is entirely contrary to the known and proved facts.

In case it might be thought that the authors are being unfair to our late enemies, let us here quote from the book by Ernst Junger (a Prussian Storm-Troop Officer), "The Storm of Steel," which was published in 1929. Referring to the German retreat to the Siegfried line in March, 1917, he writes:—

"The villages we passed through as we marched to the front line had the appearance of lunatic asylums let loose. Whole companies were pushing walls down or sitting on the roofs of houses throwing down the slates. Trees were felled, window-frames broken, and smoke and clouds of dust rose from heap after heap of rubbish. In short, an orgy of destruction was going on. The men were chasing round with incredible zeal, arrayed in the abandoned wardrobes of the population, in women's dresses and with top hats on their heads. With positive genius they singled out the main beams of the houses and, tying ropes round them, tugged with all their might, shouting out in time with their pulls, till the whole house collapsed. Others swung hammers and smashed whatever came in their way, from flower-pots on the window ledges to the glass-work of conservatories.

"Every village up to the Siegfried line was a rubbish heap. Every tree felled, every road mined, every well fouled, every water-course damned, every cellar blown up or made into a death-trap with concealed bombs, all supplies of metal sent back, all rails ripped up, all telephone wire rolled up, everything burnable burned. In short, the country over which the enemy were to advance had been turned into an utter desolation.

"The moral justification of this has been much discussed. However, it seems to me that the gratified approval of armchair warriors and journalists is incomprehensible. When thousands of peaceful persons are robbed of their homes, the self-satisfaction of power may at least keep silence.

"As for the necessity, I have, of course, as a Prussian officer, no doubt whatever. War means the destruction of the enemy without scruple and by any means. War is the harshest of all trades, and the masters of it can only entertain humane feelings so long as they do no harm. It makes no difference that these operations which the situation demanded were not very pretty."

Perhaps the above sums up the whole attitude of the German system in waging war. We do not condemn all the Germans as individuals, but the ruthless means advocated which the soldiers, sometimes reluctantly, had to carry out.

Here are some extracts from Pte. Keegan's diary:—

1917. August 5th. Taken prisoner by Hamburg marines. Treated well and given cold coffee from their flasks—my first drink, except shell-hole water, for five days. . . . Badly wounded go to hospital, remainder taken to Menin in lorry for dinner: a good meal and plenty.

2.0 p.m.—Photographed—then lorry to Courtrai for tea—bread, soup, sausage. Send home cards, then bed (paper mattress and pillow): what a glorious sleep after five days and nights at Hollebeke.

August 8th. Dendermonde. Old Barrack. Fifty men in our room (30 x 18 feet). Stone floor; one blanket. Exercise one hour walking round yard daily: rest of time locked in. Rations for day—nettle tea without sugar and milk, two small slices of bread: small quantity of jam or sausage every other day: at dinner and tea very weak soup.

August 21st—24th. Sick. Very weak. See doctor and ordered to sick room. Temp. up to 104. Food as in barrack, but cannot eat.

August 25th. Back in barrack. About 2,000 men in Lager, mostly K.R.R.s and Northants taken at Ostend, July 10th. All in very poor state through lack of exercise and insufficient food. Many collapse.

August 26th. First shave since July 31st.

August 29th. Belgians in town send in baked fruit. Delicious.

September 2nd. 6.0 a.m. breakfast—thin veg. soup and two slices. Entrain 7.30 a.m. Twenty-one hours without food.

September 3rd. Next meal Aix-la-Chapelle, 3.0 a.m. Thick macaroni soup. Next meal 12 midnight. Thin soup only. Bed.

September 4th. Bath and fumigation. Food better than Dendermonde. Roll call five times a day. Allowed out in compound all day. Sleeping accommodation good.

During September moves to Dulmen, Haltern, Opladin, Hammelburg. Food fairly good. On several days five Woodbines supplied by other East Surreys on Lager Staff and N.C.O.s.

September 21st. First wash with soap for seven weeks. Fifty prisoners volunteered for work, but with many others I refused.

October 6th. At Lichtenfels. Start work 6.0 a.m. Heavy work unloading coal from trucks. Six men working. Finish 6.0 p.m. Meat or fish once daily, otherwise greenstuffs, carrots or potatoes. Food insufficient for long hours.

October 8th. One day off per fortnight spent in room, windows barred, not allowed out except for meals. We are discontented, having no pay, no smokes and poor food.

November 5th. Pay day at rate 60 pfennige per day. Several lots of potatoes given us by German workers.

November 12th. We have several good friends. Food not enough. Getting weaker. Hands very sore from catching and stacking coal bricks.

November 14th. Written home weekly since September 8th. No news yet from Blighty. Weight just 8 st.

November 21st. Two letters arrive. We are not forgotten.

November 30th. Weather very cold. Parcels arrive for several chums.

December 21st. Parcel of bread arrives. My first. Delighted.

December 25th. Christmas. Share conserve with chum "Jock."

December 26th. Boxing Day. We get day off, and have best meal since taken prisoner. Under-boss is good.

December 27. Five parcels bread for me, but four loaves bad through delay. Forget hard work having so much food.

1918. Clothes and boots arrive as well as parcels of food, so that Krieg bread issue could be given away to German civilians. By end of April weight over 10 stone. But things often stolen from parcels. By August food getting scarce and very poor. Boils on neck and rupture from lifting heavy weights. On good terms with French prisoners. Tobacco very scarce.

November 10th. Great excitement. News of Republics everywhere. Kings resign, including our own. All say we shall be home by Christmas.

November 13th. Vorstand and Postern tell us we are no longer considered prisoners. Pay to be five marks a day, from which 3½ deducted for food and lodging. Allowed to walk in town. Returning troop transports all fly the Red Flag.

1918. At the end of November moved to Lichtenfels Lager. Austrian, Russian and French troops everywhere. Bad conditions at beginning of December. Many sick and deaths in Lager Lazarette (Hospital). On December 21st start to entrain. Journey up the Rhine via Karlsruhe. Over Swiss frontier. Arrival at Basle. Red Cross ladies provide good dinner: "Tipperary" sung by request. Across French frontier at Delle. Band on station play us in. Journey via Lyons to Calais, arriving home late on December 31st.

NOTE 3.

CARRIER PIGEONS.

Cpl. S. J. Nugent has some interesting remarks on the Carrier Pigeons used by the Signal Section under Lieut. David Walker. These birds, he says, were used in war as far back as 1174, and were widely used by the French during the Siege of Paris in 1871.

"In the Great War many men observed white wooden structures behind the lines, where large numbers of pigeons were looked after by a special staff. They were taken out in rotation and sent from Corps to Battalion H.Q. in wicker baskets which held five or six birds. This was only of course when a battalion was in the line waiting to take the offensive or expecting an attack.

"Messages were written on special thin paper to reduce the weight to a minimum, and after being rolled, were placed inside a small metal cylinder fixed to the bird's leg. The bird was then released, and, after circling round a few times, followed the homing instinct and made for Corps Headquarters, where the message was retrieved. Even in adverse weather and bad conditions these birds performed some good work, and the only things which daunted them were heavy barrages and thick mists or fog.

"Owing to the many occasions when the enemy put over gas, it was found necessary to provide some protection for the birds, and this took the form of a canvas cover, which could easily and quickly be adjusted to envelop the whole of the basket when the need arose.

"Birds brought up overnight were seldom kept in their baskets for a longer period than one day, and any remaining in the baskets after a certain time were released one by one after a fresh lot had been brought into the line.

"When all other means of communication failed, provided the weather conditions were not too unfavourable, the pigeon was the medium through which a message could speedily be sent back, although many were killed in flight, as may be expected.

"It was the usual practice in the 12th Battalion to place the pigeons in charge of a runner who was held responsible for them, and this recalls a humorous incident which occurred whilst Battalion H.Q. was in Spoil Bank awaiting the Hollebeke stunt of July 31st, 1917.

"A number of signallers and runners were sitting on their wire netting beds in the sap enjoying a quiet game of cards, when the sentry sounded the gas gong and dropped the gas curtain. No notice was taken of this quite common occurrence and the game proceeded for about ten minutes, when a faint smell of gas reached the players, one of whom was Patsey Higgins, the runner in charge of the pigeons, which had been placed in a safe position outside at the head of the sap.

"Somebody casually asked Patsey if his pigeons were all right. 'Begorrah, me poor pigeons!' exclaimed Patsey, jumping up, and without waiting to put on his cap or gas mask, he rushed to the steps and through the gas curtain into the open.

"In a few minutes he came back, choking, his eyes running through the effects of the gas, with the basket of pigeons around which he had fixed the canvas cover. He would not play cards after this, and every few minutes would peer into the basket to see how the birds were. Fortunately neither Patsey nor the pigeons came to harm over the affair, and the birds were duly released the next day after a fresh lot arrived."

CHAPTER IX.

16th August to 23rd September, 1917.

The Battalion in training at La Roukloshille and Zudausques—Inspection by Sir Douglas Haig—In the line once more—Action at Tower Hamlets in the Battle of the Menin Road Ridge—Heavy losses.

FROM the 16th to the 19th the Battalion remained at La Roukloshille, and during the period there were some ceremonial parades. After the Commanding Officer had inspected the Battalion on the morning of the 16th, General Towsey carried out an inspection in the afternoon and congratulated all ranks on the recent operations at Hollebeke. There was a catch in his voice as he related the sufferings the men had to endure and how he had tried to get them relieved as soon as possible. General Towsey was a very human commander. As a soldier he knew where the path of duty lay, but it was apparent to us that he did not relish the idea of sacrificing his men. It appeared to many of us that the General was not altogether satisfied with the way in which the 122nd Brigade had been called upon to bear the brunt of the last operations. There was a suspicion, rightly or wrongly, amongst the men that other brigades in the Division were not sharing as much of the burden as we were. On the 17th we marched to the neighbourhood of Meteren where the X Corps Commander, General Morland, inspected and congratulated the 122nd Brigade on the recent operations. He spoke of the difficult work that had been allotted to the Division, and particularly the 122nd Brigade, at Hollebeke. On the next day an inspection was carried out in the same place by General Sir H. Plumer in command of the Second Army.

On the 20th the Battalion paraded and marched via Caestre, Hondeghem and Staple to Zuypteene, where billets were taken for the night. As Pte. P. Cornish recalls in his diary, we were marching for about six hours, and everyone was glad to rest in fairly comfortable barns owned by farmers who were very nice people.

Mention by Pte. Cornish of the type of people we met at Zuypteene is a pleasant change from what was the popular conception of the French and Belgian civilians we met behind the lines. It was often thought that the British troops were singled out for special treatment by greedy, grasping and ungrateful peasants who seemed to forget that we were fighting for their country and did not at all give us the reception we considered we were entitled to. But, if such was our experience, so too, on the authority of French writers, was it the experience of our French comrades-in-arms. Henri Barbusse in his "Under Fire" relates incidents similar to what we went through, while Roland Dorgeles, in "The Cabaret up the Line," very aptly expresses our sentiments when he writes:—

"It was true that we were the means of saving their land, that thanks to us they could still milk their cows and till their fields; but as one of them said grumblingly to a beribboned soldier who was trying to bargain for a couple of pints of milk, 'Medals are all very fine—but just look at the cost of living!'

"Complainingly they would get out a few odds and ends of food, mumbling the while that they couldn't get much from the town nowadays 'with all these cursed gendarmes about,' and as they pocketed our money, they would murmur tearfully of 'their own poor boy who was in the army too.'

"In spite of all, we were grateful to them—an hour of comfort was so precious in that precarious life which might be cut short so soon—but as we got our money out we prayed to God that 'their own poor boy' was being rooked as unmercifully as we were. Occasionally, of course, we came across wonderfully fine people who would willingly have given us all they had. People who loved the 'poilus,' they spoiled every passing soldier—all of them different, but, none the less, all of them brothers; they used to look after us with the most touching care, and even cried when the time came for us to go."

The march was continued in columns of three, on the 21st to Le Nieppe, approximately a distance of five miles. The village was a very rural one in which there were a few brooks where the men were able to wash their feet.* Later buses picked us up, and we were conveyed through the lovely countryside, far from the maddening guns and swamps of the Salient, to the peaceful pastures and homely farmsteads of the little village of Zudausques, near St. Omer. The troops were in high glee as the buses sped along the dusty roads, and the singing of the old choruses brought the inhabitant of the villages to their doors as we passed.

Zudausques was reached by noon, and soon all the companies were settled down in billets. Battalion H.Q. were established at the Château Noir Carme; the Officers' Mess was situated in the Château itself, while the signallers, runners, observers, Orderly Room staff, etc., were billeted in various barns and outhouses around it with the usual midden in the centre of the farm. A few of the H.Q. staff made their temporary home in a farm cart, and Battalion Orderly Room was situated next to a cowshed. The companies were housed in barns and sheds scattered about the village, which boasted of two of three shops and a similar number of estaminets. As far as rest areas went, Zudausques was as good as any we had met up to now. It was only a few miles from St. Omer and in consequence passes were issued to that town, the allotment, as recorded in Pte. Cornish's diary, being five N.C.O.s and men per company each evening. It was usually reached by "lorry-jumping"; an A.S.C. park being established in the town, there were always plenty of lorries from our own division and others on the road, and the drivers were invariably only too pleased to give the men a lift. At this period of the war St. Omer was visited nightly by the enemy planes, and it was not safe to be in the streets when they were overhead. The inhabitants would retire to their cellars when the hum of the German planes was heard in the distance, though many of them sought refuge in the village of St. Martin, situated a short distance out of the town. It was a distressing sight to see old men and women and little children making their way down the road to St. Martin, carrying blankets, just before dusk. Some of them must have slept in the hedges during these nocturnal bombardments by the "Gothas." Much damage was done as a result of these raids. On one occasion a Chinese labour camp was bombed, and it was said that the infuriated "Chinks" went round next day to a German prisoners' cage and started throwing Mill's bombs at the Boches without extracting the pins! We were to see a great many of these curious little Orientals who delighted in clothing themselves in the most grotesque costumes, including some battered straw hats.

Here is a most amusing yarn of this spell from Cpl. Southall.

"The farmer here was very surly and refused to sell us either eggs or milk. At last we found some of the hens were getting up to the top of the machine for stacking hay, and hearing them clucking we investigated and found they were laying freely. Our supply, however, did not last long, for the farmer also found the spot and used to get up before us.

* A party of Uhlans had reached this village in the early days of the war and were killed and buried there after a brush with the British Cavalry.

"The only thing then to do was to entice the hens to come into our barn and lay eggs for us there. We therefore sloped two stretchers from the manger to the floor, one on each side, and then draped blankets on the stretchers so that they could be dropped to the floor at the right moment. A climb to the loft supplied some maize with which to tempt the chickens in. A trail of maize was then laid outside our billet and into the barn where it led under the stretchers. We then sat down to await events and hens.

"Sure enough the bait was too much for the fowls, and after eating up the maize outside they came in for the rest: under the stretchers they went, and down came the blankets. Finding themselves in darkness, the good hens became resigned to the position and settled down to lay eggs by numbers. Our Heath Robinson egg-producing machine worked long and smoothly."

Training began in earnest on the 22nd, on which day Colonel Knapp (most thorough in everything he undertook) formed a class consisting of all officers, N.C.O.s and a few selected privates. The C.O. took the class himself; the remainder of the Battalion was under the Adjutant.

During the recent operations in the Salient drafts had joined the Battalion from the 6th and 7th Bedfords, the 1st Herts, the 5th Northants and the 5th East Surreys. These men from Territorial units in England had been transferred to the 12th Battalion on arrival at Etaples. Most of them had been classified as specialists in one way or another, such as Lewis-gunners, bombers, signallers, etc., a slip in A.B. 64 (Pay Book) stating the qualification. They were probably more up to date in the latest methods of training than the older members of the Battalion. This system of specialisation made for efficiency in re-organisation of units after heavy casualties. Men had only to be placed in the section they specialised in and then be taught to act in concert with the other men of the section. Each platoon had three main sections, Lewis-gun, Bombing and Riflemen. The bombers were also divided into ordinary bombers and rifle-grenadiers. In the forthcoming operations it was considered that rifle grenades would play an important part owing to the number of pill-boxes. It was to the task of making the Battalion an efficient fighting force under the new organisation that Colonel Knapp set himself by taking parades personally and giving lectures.

The 23rd of August will be remembered by all those present at the time as the day on which Sir Douglas Haig inspected the 41st Division at Leulinghem, near Wisques. The parade had to be as spick and span as possible; accordingly a deal of preparation had to be made beforehand. The Battalion marched to the parade ground of the Division and formed up on the extreme right of the line. The weather was showery and we were in no mood to be kept hanging about, but we had to wait for the other units to take their place. At last the stage was set for the arrival of the Commander-in-Chief. A lancer in front of the parade dipped a pennon as the band struck up, and on to the parade ground rode an officer followed by many others. He rode towards the 12th as the order to "open ranks" was given and simply rode round and away to the next unit. The order was then given to us to re-form ranks, march off on to the road and then double a few hundred yards to enable the other units to get away as soon as possible. It was a most disappointing "show" for us all, for we had expected something different to this. Never before had we had such a cursory inspection by a Commander. Perhaps it was the rain which prevented a more complete review; nevertheless we felt that all our efforts to impress had been wasted. We did not even have time to see what the Commander-in-Chief looked like, but we did notice our own Divisional Commander, General Lawford, spruce as ever, perhaps the most striking figure on the parade.

In the latter half of August the following officers joined the Battalion:—2nd Lieuts. T. B. Jolly, G. L. and R. E. White (brothers), W. S. Hall, H. N. Dunkley, C. F. W.

Faith, T. H. Lloyd, and 2nd Lieut. J. McL. Hutcheson rejoined from the R.F.C. Lieut. V. L. Clift became adjutant, replacing Lieut. T. B. McWalter (appointed vice Capt. Reynard at St. Eloi) who resumed regimental duties at his own request. Capt. Herdman, Medical Officer for the trying month July to mid-August, rejoined the Field Ambulance, and our old friend Capt. Harrison took his place and remained with us for many months.

The casualties during the month of August were:—Killed or mortally wounded: 2 officers and 48 other ranks. Wounded: 1 officer and 97 other ranks. Missing: 2 officers and 42 other ranks.

In the morning of the 1st of September the Battalion was inspected by General Towsey in the new attack formation over the battalion shell-hole training area. This was carried out again on two or three occasions during the next few days, and on the 9th and 11th the companies were marched to the Divisional training area to view a model of the ground over which the next attack would be made and carry out a practice of it. As at Messines, it was the intention of the Authorities to give the troops participating a very good idea of what was expected of them. We were afterwards to learn that models could not convey the true conditions of the ground over which we had to advance or of the resistance we were to encounter.

Inter-Company football matches were played when circumstances permitted, but perhaps the most noteworthy part of the recreational training during this period was the cricket matches arranged by Lieut. Libby and others. Where the gear came from we did not know, but the fact remains that we enjoyed a few games, despite the fact that the pitches available were like ploughed fields. Sergt. Jack Hill of the observers was a very useful man with bat and ball, and according to all accounts some of the matches were rather one-sided. Pte. Cornish of A Company recalls a match in the afternoon of the 4th of September when the Privates beat the N.C.O.s by 20 runs. It was rarely that the opportunity of playing the summer game came to the fighting men of the infantry because of the difficulty of getting suitable grounds and kit. It is recorded in the history of the 11th Battalion The "Queen's" that in May, 1916, a match was played at Strazeele between a company of the "Queen's" and the Brigade Bombing Company, with only four stumps and two bats, one of which was broken! W. J. (Bill) Abel, who was a bomber in the "Queen's," played in the match and only scored 21 in two innings. As Capt. Neave says, "Surrey's cricketer, W. J. Abel, could never have played on a worse pitch." At some of the base camps opportunities were afforded, but on matting wickets. Battalion sports were also held on September 8th, following the usual practice of having at least one day during a rest period devoted to a sports meeting.

During this time, Lieut. (A/Capt.) R. A. V. Brearey left to join the R.F.C., in which he had been accepted as an observer on probation. The recent casualties to officers were made good by the arrival of the following: Capt. D. McCallum, who rejoined on the 7th and was posted to his old Company, A, Capt. Z. N. Brook, and 2nd Lieuts. R. C. Johns, W. D. Mutch, C. H. Fisher, M. T. Johnson and H. C. Ward. Drafts of close on 100 other ranks from the 8th and 9th Battalions joined between the 12th and 14th, to bring the Battalion up to strength again.

A few notes from the diary of Pte. Cornish of A Company might help to recall certain incidents of the period.

August 25th. "Cpl. taking us to a gas lecture at a school. Walked about 5 kilos; no school to be found, so we all came back again."

August 27th. "After dinner marched about 7 kilos to Divisional Baths. Some baths; open air! Poured with rain on parade ground, most of us wet through and then marched back to billets."

September 4th. "Battalion practised the attack in front of General and 11th R.W. Kents. Bread ration rather short these last few days; three loaves between thirty-three men to-day and no biscuits. Chaps talk about tossing for it."

September 9th. "At Church Parade the Chaplain gave a broad hint that we should be in action before another Sunday."

Preparations were now well advanced for the next part the Battalion was to play in the Third Battle of Ypres. On the 5th, Major A. W. Puttick, Capt. H. S. Walker, and 2nd Lieuts. T. B. Jolly and R. E. White reconnoitred the line occupied by the battalions in the neighbourhood of Shrewsbury Forest, near the hamlet of Zwarteleen, and on the 7th a further reconnaissance was carried out in the same area by Colonel Knapp, Capt. Openshaw, Lieut. Clift and 2nd Lieuts. L. W. B. Russell and W. S. Hall.

The return to their companies, because of a very strict combing out, of men who had been on Headquarters staff for some time but who were extra to the number allowed on the establishment of the sections, made it apparent that the question of man-power was being felt in certain quarters.

The officers had a final dinner in the Mess: how many of the laughing, happy-go-lucky members of that party were soon to be amongst those who made the great sacrifice! The men, too, had their sing-songs, for nothing stopped Tommy from making the best of things while it lasted. "Scotty" Williams had not let the grass grow under his feet while we were at Zudausques, for he had arranged concerts amongst the men in the billets and as usual discovered some talent for future occasions.

The trek back to the desolate region of the Salient commenced on the 14th of September, exactly a year to the day since the original members of the Battalion had gone forward into the Battle of the Somme in the highest of spirits. What changes had been wrought since then! The last officer survivor of that action, Lieut. W. J. Palk, M.C., had recently been wounded, while only a handful of the other ranks who were lucky enough to get away from Flers unhurt were now with the companies. New drafts had since joined, but many of these had been wounded once, twice, and even three times with other battalions of the regiment, besides other units. It was generally admitted that those who had already been in action were liable to be more "windy" than those who were new to the game, and the arrival of fresh men who had never been over the top often acted as a stimulus to the veterans in action. Most of the men with the 12th at this time had already received their baptism of fire, and many of them at such a deplorable place as Hollebeke. There were, of course, some who had such a wonderful control over their nerves that they never displayed any signs of fear, but to the vast majority shell-fire, especially at this period of the war, was a nerve racking ordeal. Even the strongest of men were known to collapse under the strain of it. Yet few could have imagined the ghastly hell we were to go through.

A story is related by Mr. Lloyd George, for the truth of which he vouches. When the campaign of Passchendaele had been in progress for a long while, a staff officer was sent up from his comfortable home at Montreuil near the coast, where G.H.Q. was established, to make a special report. As the car proceeded further and further into the zone already fought over, that interminable area of infernal swamps and desolation, he became more and more shaken. At last he gasped out—"Good God! Did we send men into this?" His conductor tersely replied—"This? This is nothing to what is further on." The Staff officer sunk his head in his hands and burst into tears.

Forming up on the road near the Brasserie at Zudausques the Battalion marched away in the direction of St. Martin, through Arques and Le Nieppe to Staple, where billets were taken for the night. The march was continued the next day, the Battalion parading in mass behind Crêve-Coeur Farm soon after 10.0 a.m. and taking the route Hondeghem Station—Caestre—Flêtre to La Roukloshille, where another halt was made. Thus in two days about twenty-four miles had been covered with the prospect of a further nine miles on the morrow. Before leaving Staple, 2nd Lieut. W. D. Mutch, now our Intelligence Officer, had been sent forward to the battle area to reconnoitre the positions the Battalion would have to take up for the impending battle.

Continuing the march soon after midday on the 16th the Battalion and Transport moved to the Murrumbidgee area, La Clytte. In columns of threes on the La Roukloshille—Noote Boom Road we moved off and marched through Piebrouck, Berthen and Westoutre. After a short halt we were on the road again, through our beloved village of Reninghelst (now a vast concentration area for all sorts of units), thence by the Overland Track to Chippewa Camp which was reached at about 5.0 p.m. Here the men were only too glad to "kip down" in the huts.

On the 17th the slow approach to the scene of operations brought us to Ridge Wood, where supplies of bombs, flares, etc., were issued. The usual pick or shovel had to be carried by the men who had come to regard these tools not only as unnecessary adjuncts to fighting order but also as implements of torture. Only those who had the misfortune to have to carry a pick or shovel underneath the haversack of a man's fighting order can realise the agony this involved. It was really impossible to run or make any progress with these things sticking in one's back. Needless to say they were "dumped" as soon as the men found it convenient to do so. Most of the men were accommodated in dugouts for the night.

The old cheery spirit evident on other occasions when we were preparing to go into action was now absent. Rather was there an ominous silence. Hollebeke was too near to make one forget the awful times spent there. From what we were able to gather, some rather confused fighting had taken place since we were last in the region. We had heard, and from our own experience had no reason to doubt, how the pill-boxes were giving so much trouble, and we knew full well that the rain of recent weeks would make the going very uncomfortable. We were not slow to learn that the concentration of artillery on both sides was greater than it had ever been. It was generally felt that we were up against something even worse than we had before experienced, and we were more concerned with what would be our ultimate fate than driving the enemy from the ridge with the homely name of Tower Hamlets. The officers realised as much as anybody what the feelings of the men were. Who can forget the anxiety for the welfare of his men of that sterling commander of A Company, Capt. Duncan McCallum? Right up to the time when the barrage opened he was making enquiries as to the comfort of his men in the circumstances in which they were placed. He was one of the original officers of his Company who had only recently rejoined us, but was to lead them for the last time. Well! it had to be done. There was no going back. Death lurked in either direction, and it was better to die in the face of the enemy. Besides, if we did not advance, the enemy eventually would. Then all the hopes we cherished of a final victory to our arms would be in vain. Perhaps it would not be as bad as we thought; the enemy must surely be feeling the strain of this fighting in bogs as much as we; may be our artillery would silence his as the advance progressed and destroy his pill-boxes before we reached them. Whatever happened, the job had to be done; so we resigned ourselves to our fate.

On the 18th we moved forward to Lankhof Farm, near Lock No. 8 on the Canal, and one and a half miles south of Ypres. Here we remained until 11.0 p.m. on the 19th, having a very uncomfortable time owing to the fact that we had to lie in funk holes in front of our batteries; owing to the retaliation for their fire we had to move further up in the morning of the 19th. Waking up rather cold in the morning, we cooked our own breakfast as best we could and then listened all day to the deafening noise of the artillery putting down barrages on the enemy front.

On the 19th, Colonel Knapp held a conference of Company Commanders to explain the final directions.

The series of operations known as the Battle of Ypres, 1917, had already lasted over seven weeks and was yet far from its end. Right up to the 10th of November, 1917, these actions continued in rapid succession and constituted one of the greatest struggles in the history of the War. Owing to the terrible weather conditions experienced they probably entailed a higher degree of endurance on the attacking troops than any other group of battles, possibly than any others in recorded history. The third great action, known as the Battle of the Menin Road Ridge, which opened on September 20th, was fought on a front of about eight miles, and save that it did not extend beyond Langemarck on the north, it covered nearly the same ground as did the operations of July 31st. General Sir Hubert Gough's Fifth Army again attacked on the left, and Sir Herbert Plumer's Second Army on the right. The X Corps, in which was the 41st Division, was near the extreme right of the Second Army's assault. In this area the British front line was now after a month and a half of continuous struggle about a quarter of a mile east of where it had been before the battle of Pilkem Ridge!

The order of battle for the 41st Division was the 124th Brigade on the right, the 122nd Brigade on the left, with the 123rd Brigade in reserve.

In the 122nd Brigade the order was—Right: 18th K.R.R.s in the front line, and 12th East Surreys in the second line. Left: 15th Hants in the front line and 11th R.W. Kents in the second. These dispositions were similar to those at Flers a year before.

The objectives were divided up into three phases—Red, Blue and Green Lines, and the attack was to be carried out on the leap-frog principle. The Red and Blue Lines had to be occupied by the 18th K.R.R.s and the 15th Hants, each of which had to attack on a two company front; the leading two companies having to reach and consolidate the Red Line, while the other two would pass through them, cross the Bassevillebeek and take and consolidate the Blue Line. The 12th East Surreys and the 11th R.W. Kents were then to assemble on a two company front in rear of the Blue Line after its capture by the K.R.R.s and Hants and then attack and consolidate the final objective (Green Line) some 700 yards further, known as Tower Hamlets Ridge.

The dispositions and formation of the 12th Battalion for the attack were as follows:—A Company on right front, B Company on left front, C Company behind A and D behind B, each company occupying a two platoon front.

The assembly of the battalion was to be with its front resting on a tape at right angles to the line of advance. The flanks of the battalion were to be marked by notice boards and the dividing line between right and left companies by a tape. It was anticipated that the marsh by Bodmin Copse would prevent the right and left from maintaining contact on assembly, but instructions were issued for the waves to obtain contact on clearing the marshy ground. Each company on a two platoon front was to advance in column of sections until the Blue Line was reached. Here platoons of A and B Companies were to extend to battle formation, while C and D were to continue to advance in sections until 200-300 yards in rear of the Green Line, where they were to extend and, after occupying the final objective, consolidate.

At Zero hour the barrage was to be put down 150 yards in front of the assembly area. Our battalion had to conform to the movements of the 18th K.R.R.s, 50 yards behind that unit, until they attacked the Blue Line. After the Blue Line had been captured, A and B Companies were to pass through and form up closely under the barrage. When the barrage lifted, they were to follow it forward and attack and consolidate the Green Line.

Each assaulting company was responsible for "mopping up" in its area. Supporting and reserve platoons were to examine all shell-holes and dugouts to ensure that none of the enemy was left in rear of our creeping barrage. Headquarters were to be established in the south corner of Clonmel Copse. Bombers were to carry 100 rounds of S.A.A. and five bombs; Riflemen 150 rounds and two grenades each. The necessity of being thoroughly acquainted with the plan was impressed upon all ranks, and strict orders were issued to preserve the utmost secrecy concerning it. All papers had to be returned in sealed packets to H.Q. before the troops went into the line to the assembly point behind Bodmin Copse.

Such were the admirable intentions of the Army Commander and Staff; the reality, as will soon be seen, was quite otherwise. It all appears so simple on paper and on the map. Whether any battles in history have ever been fought according to the intentions of the attacking Commander is most questionable: in most battles of the Great War what actually occurred was hardly even approximate to the design.

Consider the circumstances.

The plan is explained in every detail to the officers, who pass on the general idea to the N.C.O.s and these then give a bare outline to the men, these last, of course, never seeing a map. Before Zero hour the force is lying in the dark in shell holes in a spot where not one of them has ever been before, except possibly half a dozen of the officers—once. At Zero hour the barrage starts, i.e., huge shells from our guns miles behind begin bursting a hundred yards or so ahead. Every man has to go forward and lie down 25 yards or so from this horrible inferno, and, as soon as it "lifts," i.e., when the guns are elevated and the shells burst further on, the officers and men have to stagger on through a waste of thick mud and shell-holes, dead and wounded, enemy shell-bursts and a stream of machine-gun bullets to attempt to capture some pill-box and trench occupied by desperate men. By this time a quarter of an hour has elapsed, probably half the officers are casualties and half the N.C.O.s and men. No one has the faintest idea in the smoke and racket and spouting earth and mud where they are or where are the objectives they are supposed to be making for. Everything around looks the same. One's natural instinct the whole time is to get into any cover from the rain of missiles. Yet on you must go. And when a trench has been occupied and rendered defensible, as far as possible, the officer, if there be one, in charge of the remnant, may decide that he is at a certain point on the map, when he is really half a mile awav. How can he or anyone tell what is Blue Line or Green Line, if those fragments of wall are the village of X, or Y Farm, or Z Church, if yonder tree trunks are A or B or C Wood? And then ere long some brave runner manages to reach you alive through this hell with a filthy piece of paper—"Captain ——'s compliments, and what the . . . are you doing? Where the . . . are you? Give map reference."

This certainly, if an imaginary picture, will be recognised as truly depicted. Most of the battles of the autumn of 1917 were of this kind. Thousands of men, of course, even when no action was in progress, fell in the dark into shell-holes and sank, weighed down by their heavy equipment, till the slime closed over their agony.

Yet still the High Command, many miles away in comfortable châteaux in the rear, moved their little flags about on their big wall maps and issued orders for fresh holocausts or complained of objectives not reached, some of the Brass-hats even grousing that the spirit of our troops was poor! Small wonder that Tommy was always wishing that the men who directed or organised war in all countries—the politicians, the brass-hats, the profiteers, the hundreds of thousands in cushy billets in Blighty or at the base, the workers at home dissatisfied with £4 a week and striking to get more—could have just had 48 hours in a "Show." Peace wouldn't be long in arriving, Tommy thought. And he was probably not far from the truth.

It was difficult not to weep then: it is hard to keep the tears back or restrain the pangs of sorrow and indignation in recalling it all now. But what is still more difficult to understand is why is not the united conscience of mankind mightily stirred till War—the stupidest, cruellest of all man's follies—is outlawed for ever?

But we must return tó our narrative.

It was a dark night and rain had set in to make the conditions anything but favourable. The enemy, apprehensive of what was coming, kept up a nervous bombardment of the area through which we had to pass. Slow progress due to guides having lost their way put most of us in a very bad mood. The troops passed along "Towsey's Track," but the assembly point near Bodmin Copse, about one and a half miles east of Zillebeke, was not reached until 3.0 a.m. in the morning of the 20th. Capt. R. O. Russell, M.C., of the 11th R.W. Kents, explains the delay of the 12th Battalion in assembling as being due to the fact that the officer, presumably from Brigade, detailed to lay the tapes for the East Surreys had become a casualty, and the Brigade Major, Capt. Graham-Thomson, assisted by Capt. Russell, had to complete the job. The Kents were in position by 1.0 a.m., and, on reporting to Brigade soon after, Capt. Russell learned that Colonel Knapp and his battallion were missing. The Brigade Major and Capt. Russell were sent to discover them. To quote Capt. Russell's own words:—

"It was assumed that they would have missed their way at certain branches of the system of duck-board tracks. Luckily we hit on the right one, eventually discovering a long, swearing, jostling, rattling snake on a track in the left Divison's area. It was no easy task to guide them safely across the maze of water-logged shell holes until Tor Top was reached. Thence all was plain sailing, a short distance along Towsey's Track, up round Clonmel Copse and so on to their tapes. The Surreys, in no happy frame of mind after this long wandering in the dark, eventually settled down to take their place in the attack. They did not have a quiet time forming up, for by this time the Boche was beginning to open up for his usual 'early morning hate.' Fortunately a number of their casualties were walking cases, so that it was possible for us to get them safely down, when we went back to Tor Top for a much needed rest."

Capt. Russell has very aptly described the circumstances attending the assembly of the 12th for the battle, but further light is thrown on the affair by Capt. Hector Walker in his account of the action:—

"While out of the line at rest," he writes, "we had visited and reconnoitred the positions we were to take up, Brigade H.Q. etc., and all was set and ready for the 'Show,' but one fatal mistake was made on the day we started up Towsey's Track or thereabouts. So far as my memory serves me, the Battalion was to report at Brigade H.Q., but owing to enemy action with artillery, Brigade H.Q. had to move and guides from our Signal Section were taken up to learn the new directions. I believe that

Capt. David Walker or Lieut. Harding was called to Brigade for some particular job. The main point I wish to bring out is that the officer in charge of our Battalion Signals received an order from the Brigade Intelligence Officer to send two of his men who were NAMED. He obeyed the order, but failed to advise me that he had received this order and that the two men called for by name were the two guides—the only two men who knew where we were to go. I repeat that neither Colonel Knapp nor I knew that these two guides had been called to Brigade. When the Battalion was on the move, A Company was late in moving off, so I went to the head of the column and made enquiries. I asked the Company Commander where his guides were. I was then informed that no guides had been seen. Going back to the officer in charge of Signals I then discovered our plight. Probably the officer in question had not realised that the two men already referred to were the only men who knew the new positions we had to make for. This explains why the Battalion was wandering about in the pitch dark, running into other troops, none of whom knew anything to assist us to find Brigade H.Q. How we picked up the Brigade Major, I do not know. We got into position, led by him, with all too little time to spare. Colonel Knapp then stuck a stick into the parapet of a trench we were in and set it by compass so that it pointed towards our objective."

On the way up two other ranks were wounded, but before the "Show" started this number had been greatly increased.

Arriving at the tapes at 3.0 a.m., B Company took up position on the left flank of the Battalion front, A Company on the right, with C and D Companies behind on the second tape. The 11th R.W. Kents were already in position on our left, as also were the 26th (Bankers) Battalion Royal Fusiliers of the 124th Brigade on our right. Heavy rain, as usual, fell during the night, and in the early hours of the morning of the 20th our artillery continued to batter the enemy strong points, to which he replied, causing some more casualties. Promptly at 5.40 a.m. (Zero hour), our barrage opened and remained for three minutes 150 yards in front of our front line to allow the 18th K.R.R.s to form up close to it. The barrage then moved towards the Red Line at the rate of 200 yards in eight minutes and then at 100 yards in six minutes, until it reached a point 200 yards beyond the Red Line. The 12th then proceeded close behind the K.R.R.s and reinforced them, when they were held up at a strong point about 150 yards east of Bodmin Copse. After being held up for an hour at this point, we eventually dispersed the enemy with rifle grenades and went on over the shell-torn ground to the Blue Line, where we had to form a defensive flank on our right owing to the 124th Brigade being unable to gain its objective, thus leaving our flank open to machine-gun fire and snipers. It was now about 7.30 a.m., and we proceeded to consolidate the position we had attained, throwing out strong points in front with machine-guns under the command of 2nd Lieut. H. C. Ward. After this, re-organisation was made for the final advance on the Green Line. There were still no troops on our right, so that the 12th, whose business it was now according to the plan to follow up the barrage, could not advance, being engaged with the enemy on the right who were still unshaken and pouring in a hot fire from machine-guns, enfilading our positions and mowing down any who attempted an advance. This delay, of course, in its turn, hampered the 11th West Kents on our left, who were obliged to throw back a defensive flank, which was annihilated before it could dig in.

It was then decided by the West Kents to consolidate a line in their rear and so link up with our men, who were now about 100 yards in front of the Blue Line. By 10.0 a.m. this was effected.

At 11.30 a.m. the following wire was sent to Brigade H.Q. by Colonel Knapp:—

To Bell.

Ref. my situation message, I have fought a flanking fight right from the beginning, the Battalion of the 124th Brigade retiring almost as soon as the attack opened. I have also assisted the 18th K.R.R.s in taking Red and Blue Lines. I attach situation report from the only officer left. There are still no troops on my right. Have consulted with the R.W. Kents and come to the conclusion that ridge cannot be held in case of counter-attack with present forces. Am protecting my flank as best I can. M.G. at J.26.b.80.25. most annoying. Ammunition and bombs much required. Also protective barrage (strong).

11.30 a.m.
20.9.17.

(Sgd.) E. Knapp.

Report from A/Capt. H. S. Todd.

J.20.c.85.30.

With 2nd Lieut. Ward, C.S.M. Maddison and 40 other ranks am holding a line from approx. left battalion right flank on GREEN Line and running into Wood down Bassevillebeek on right of our battalion boundary. No troops on right. One officer and 12 men from another division also with us. The 124th Brigade retired.

10.55 a.m.

(Sgd.) H. S. Todd.

From the report of Capt. Todd it is clear that, as is claimed by Lieut. Mutch, Pte. Cornish and others, some of our men had reached their objective, the Green Line, long before the remainder of the Brigade. Unfortunately, for reasons which will be related later by Capt. Hector Walker, messages from us to Brigade were not received by the Brigadier. For the whole of the operations only two from Colonel Knapp and one from Capt. Walker were received under the code name of "Dagger," the majority of messages with the Divisional records being signed by "Hamlet" (The Hants).

The first sign of counter-attack came at 2.0 p.m. when the enemy were seen massing on the high ground on our right front, but Lewis-gun and rifle-fire checked this assault, which was a little later also caught and smashed by our quickening barrage. Meanwhile machine-gun and rifle-fire continued heavy from the right flank and seriously harassed our men, so much so that to strengthen our protective flank the C.O. had to bring up Battalion H.Q. into action. An attack to complete the capture of the Green Line was then out of the question.

Another message was despatched at 4.0 p.m. by the Colonel, as follows:—
To Bell.

Situation unchanged. Enemy has re-occupied positions from J.26.b.80 to J.27.a.0.5. From here he is most annoying with M.G.s and shelling. I have one officer and 40 men under my command, and am fed up generally.

4.0 p.m.
20.9.17.

(Sgd.) E. Knapp.

There was one thing the Colonel forgot to mention and that was that he had already been wounded himself in trying to dispose of enemy snipers.

At 6.30 p.m., however, the 123rd Brigade had forced their way forward on our right, reinforcing the disorganised 124th Brigade, so that our right flank was clear. Lieut.-Col. Cary Barnard brought up 130 men of the 15th Hants from the Blue Line, and Hampshires and Surreys together moved forward to the assault of the final objectives on the ridge. These were stormed before nightfall, and 28 prisoners were captured, but 50 per cent. of the attacking force were put out of action. Except for bombing encounters with the enemy on our right who had not yet been dislodged, the night passed fairly quietly, several posts holding these forward positions.

Let us take the experiences of some of the men of A Company who formed one of the first waves of the Battalion.

"Weary and cold we lie down in our shell holes which are almost full of water. Behind us, badly wounded in the leg, lies one of our sergeants, who, despite the pain he must be in, stoically stifles his cries for the assistance which we badly want to give him but cannot in the circumstances. Capt. Duncan McCallum, dog-tired and well nigh exhausted, goes round to see that his men are in position. With a cheery word here and there he gives us some final instructions, advising us to steer clear of the Bassevillebeek, make our way round the sides and avoid bunching together, if possible. Fagged out by our exertions to reach the jumping off point, many of us try to snatch a little sleep in the two hours which remain before Zero, oblivious of the shelling and the galling conditions in which we are placed.

"With the faint streaks of dawn we wake to hear the mighty crash of the guns, limber to limber, behind us. Rat-a-tat-tat comes a tremendous chorus of Maxims almost shoulder to shoulder in our rear, and firing indirectly to cover the advanced troops. In the semi-darkness we see in the distance the forms of men looming before us. Like automatic machines we follow in the direction of those in front. The air reeks with fumes of bursting shells, as we scramble a hundred yards or so through a maze of old earthworks and shell-holes before confusion ensues. That the enemy is replying with his 'Crumps' is evident from the upheaval of the earth in front and the black and blue haze in the air. With gunfire on every side of us and a mist which makes it difficult to locate our bearings, we feel that we are descending into the inferno as described by Dante. We stop. No one seems to know what to do next. The bursting shells have caused us to scatter into shell holes or take cover behind what earthworks remain within reach. We are dazed by the shell fire: it is impossible now to tell which are the enemy bursts and which are ours. Then our Captain crawls forward in front of us, and shouts out something which in the tremendous din we are unable to discern. He then signals us to follow. Scrambling up, we follow the Captain who is making his way over the difficult and treacherous ground towards a group of men in front. In a cloud of smoke and mud the leading men disappear; a big shell having made a nasty gap in their ranks. Disregarding their cries we press on. Towards the Bassevillebeek we wend our agonising way. Crump! Crump! Crump! and more men fall over. Appealing eyes of our pals ask for assistance which we have reluctantly to refuse. We are too obsessed with the thoughts of what awaits us to trouble over others. We are not callous and indifferent to their ultimate fate, for we realise that our heroic stretcher-bearers who have never failed us are not far behind. The sulphuric fumes almost suffocate us, while the effort to get through the mud over the churned up ground is tearing the inside out of us. Again we stop to try to find our bearings. No one seems to know much except that the remnant of a stream is the Bassevillebeek on which the enemy is concentrating his fury and which, for obvious reasons, we were ordered to steer clear of. An order, presumably from the Captain, to make our way a little over to the left arrives. We do so while the enemy artillery, or perhaps—who knows?—our own, reaps a harvest of death in our depleted ranks. We reach a pill-box, uprooted by the force of our time-delayed fuse shells. Machine-guns on both sides are now coming into their own. Turn where you may, there does not seem any place which will afford us cover from the weapons of destruction. Moving forward in the open we are getting machine-gun fire in front, on either flank, and even, it appears, behind. In the shell holes we are shaken up by the explosions all around. We are no longer an organised unit. Casualties have removed most of our own comrades from us and instead we become a mixed collection of different units. Instinctively we move on, crawling from shell hole to shell hole with machine-guns raking across our path. As we advance we come across a body of men crouching low in shell holes, while a short distance away to our front we perceive the dim outline of a concrete emplacement. We are now informed that the enemy is still firing through the aperture. Like a flash we dive into the sea of mud. 'Digger' Stanley, mad with fury, wants to rush the pill-box on his own! He is pulled back and then brings some rifle grenades to bear on the offensive emplacement. A short silence from the German pill-box makes us think it is safe to proceed. Advancing cautiously, while Lewis-guns fire into the stronghold, we are within a few yards of our goal when suddenly the enemy opens up a murderous fire with a machine-gun through the opening. The line breaks, and for many of us it is the last part we shall take in the advance to Tower Hamlets. Wounded we crawl into shell holes, and after the first shock has worn off find out the extent of our wounds and, if possible, try to staunch the flow of blood with the aid of our field dressings. Meanwhile we can still hear the machine-guns of both sides playing the Devil's tattoo. A stretcher-bearer then comes along and tells the 'walking cases' where to find the Aid Post. From shell hole to shell hole we make our way backwards, passing a good many of our comrades, some stark and still, others crying to us for stretcher-bearers as we pass. Reaching an Aid Post at last, we find it crowded out. The doctor and his staff are working like Trojans to get the wounded ready for the next stage of their journey down the line, but their difficulties are increased by the enemy shelling round about. Without waiting, those of us who are able to make our way along the wooded track to Voormezeele, do so. C.S.M. E. Fenner, badly wounded in the side, is helped along by some of us. We pass the British guns, which are still bellowing for all they are worth. A kindly sergeant of Artillery shouts to us to keep clear of the blast of his battery firing and puts us on the right road to the Dressing Station. Voormezeele is reached at last, and down into the cellars we descend, where particulars are taken and the badly wounded cases put on stretchers. Walking cases are then put into lorries and transported to La Clytte, where we are given an anti-tetanus injection by an orderly, our wounds are properly dressed and we are treated to a good feed of Maconochie stew. Cigarettes are distributed by a Padre, and very soon we begin to feel that we are back again in a civilised land. Any hatred we may have had for the enemy disappears as we gaze at a stretcher on which a young German lad, obviously in agony, looks appealingly towards us. One of our men offers him a cigarette which he gratefully accepts. In the afternoon we are conveyed to the Casualty Clearing Station at Godewaersvelde, where there is a re-union of some of the men of A Company, including the sergeant who was wounded before the action started. Here we are in the tender care of Red Cross nurses. A hospital train draws into the siding in the evening, and, while the enemy is bombing overhead, we leave for the port of Boulogne, which is reached in the morning. Some then go over 'Blighty' on the boat, while others are taken to the various base hospitals along the coast."

This is the story of Passchendaele as it affected some of A Company and many more members of the Battalion who were put out of action in the morning of the 20th.

Another man of A Company, Pte. P. Cornish, who survived the operations, writes:—

"The action was a nightmare to most of us. After having a tot of rum about 3.0 a.m. I went to sleep for a bit, but woke pretty quick when the barrage opened. Away we went, and all went well till we ran up against a pill-box which was bombed out, and on we went again. It was hell; we were mixed up, and a lot had fallen before we got to the foot of the Ridge. It was better going up as it was a bit sheltered. We took a bit of trench right on top of the Ridge where we could see back the way we had come. Time must have been getting on, but I couldn't judge now, as it seemed a lifetime. There were some Hants in our trench and one of our officers (of D Company, I believe). Soon afterwards this officer came to me and sent me back to find Battalion H.Q.: he said that they were supposed to be at the bottom of the Ridge, but he did not know where. He gave me a map of the position we were in and a request for ammunition and help, as there was no one on our right and he expected a counter-attack. He explained this to me, and off I went. The 124th Brigade had not taken their objective then. It was a rough journey, as the enemy were sniping from the hill. I could not find Battalion H.Q. or anything else till some stretcher-bearers directed me to the duckboard track, so I went to Hedge Street Tunnels and found Brigade H.Q. I took my message and map right down and gave them to General Towsey himself. He gave me some rum and told me to stay there till the ration party went up. This I did, but didn't find the spot I had left earlier. It was further on the left, I think."

Lieut. W. D. Mutch, the Battalion Intelligence Officer, who had previously reconnoitred the positions, states that the officer who was responsible for laying the tapes came from Brigade H.Q. He thinks it was the Brigade Intelligence Officer. On other occasions he had carried out this task himself.

With regard to the attack he has written:—

"As regards the actual advance, directly our Battalion came out of the wood, we came under machine-gun fire from a concrete pill-box direct to our front. Cross fire also came from the remains of a farm building on our right flank, which was the cause of holding up the 26th Royal Fusiliers of the 124th Brigade. There was also a concrete dugout about 12 to 15 yards to our front, which, owing to a dip in the ground, was obscured from view excepting the roof which could just be seen. This was manned by two Boches, whom I wounded with rifle grenades after they had killed dozens of our men. I however despatched these two fellows to the Almighty as they were escaping.

"I afterwards gathered together as many men as I could muster and went on to our objective, taking as much cover as possible. Now I can definitely say that the East

Surreys were the first to reach their objective on the Divisional front. The men who came with me I did not know, as I was quite a stranger to the Battalion. On reaching our objective, we worked our way to the rear of a concrete machine-gun post and with Mill's bombs dispersed the men who were inside. There were about six of them, whom I sent back as prisoners. With me was a very brave fellow who was a machine-gunner. I was afterwards very sorry that I did not get his particulars, but things were happening very quickly at the time.

"By this time we were also to the left rear of the remains of the farm which I mentioned was holding up the Royal Fusiliers. Our machine-gunner cleared this, and I can assure you that he did mow them down."

For his services in the attack Lieut. Mutch was afterwards awarded the Military Cross. The commendation card given to him by General Lawford reads:—

"I wish to place on record my appreciation of your gallantry and devotion to duty on 20th September. When Battalion Intelligence Office, on seeing a party without any officers held up by a strong point, you took command, firing rifle grenades into the strong point until captured, then led them on and gained their objective. Your prompt action undoubtedly saved the advance from being held up. Your personal disregard for danger was a fine example to all.

(Sgd.) Sydney Lawford,
Major-General. Comdg. 41st Division.

We shall give some other personal accounts later on in this chapter, but as the foregoing deal almost exclusively with the operations on the 20th of September, we have seen fit to insert them here so that the reader might be able to follow the narrative more easily.

One would have thought that a day under these terrible conditions should have been enough for the attacking troops, but there was no such luck for the survivors. Other attacks were due to take place later on, and any fresh troops who were behind us had to be conserved for that purpose. So it was that our men had to hold on to their gains until the early morning of the 23rd. Those who remained lost all count of time, and even to-day are surprised to learn that they were there for three whole days.

The Battalion continued to hold the line on the 21st, although heavily shelled by the enemy. Several posts were still forward on the ridge, but the situation on the right flank was still unsatisfactory, as enemy snipers in a strong point caused many casualties throughout the day. Machine-gunners were also active, and in consequence our stretcher-bearers and ration parties suffered casualties. During the afternoon the enemy shelling increased to great intensity and was responsible for Battalion H.Q. being broken up and the C.O. being badly wounded. Colonel Knapp, who had been wounded in the hand earlier on by an enemy sniper, now received a severe shell wound which eventually cost him the use of his right arm. Capt. Hector Walker, who had been buried by a shell and dug out by his servant, then took over command of the Battalion, or what remained of it.

The following wire, which was despatched to Brigade by Capt. Walker, gives the position as he saw it at the time:—

21st. 5.10 p.m.
With Bow H.Q. alone.

H.Q. shelled out and scattered. Bombs believed buried. These are urgently needed in the line. No news from my front. Two platoons at most is all I have of Battalion. Can relief be hurried forward, please?

Dagger.
(Sgd.) H. S. Walker.

At about 8.30 p.m. the enemy gun-fire died down.

The Battalion remained in position on the 22nd and was relieved at about 1.0 a.m. on the morning of the 23rd by the 13th Battn. Royal Sussex Regt. and moved viâ Towsey's Track to Ridge Wood. Here let us quote the entry in Pte. Cornish's diary for this date: "Arrived back at Ridge Wood somehow, dead beat, about 9.0 a.m. Thank God, to be out of that." This must surely express the sentiments of the majority of the survivors. Throughout the action the right flank of the Battalion was exposed owing to the 124th Brigade not being able to move forward. No blame would seem to attach to this Brigade, who were up against a determined and desperate enemy with a nest of machine-guns which even our masses of artillery had failed to destroy. Even to-day the pill-boxes on the road to Passchendaele stand as a grim reminder of the tremendous task which the 12th Battalion and other units of the 41st and many more divisions had to accomplish over the bogs. That they withstood the fearful volume of our gun-fire is a tribute to their designers. While making every allowance for their comparative security from shells and immunity of their garrisons from our bullets, we cannot but have a great admiration for the men who manned them. Ernst Junger in "The Storm of Steel" has given a graphic description of how the German storm troopers fought in the Third Battle of Ypres. They had instructions to fight to a finish, and well they did it. Stunned by the concussion of the explosions they manned their machine-guns till the end. "The timid ones, artillerymen, signallers and others were at times thrown into the line by means of entreaties, commands and even blows with the butt-end, to stop the advance of the English," writes Junger. But with all his bragging, this courageous Prussian Officer finds time to pay a tribute to the men who fought against him at Passchendaele and other sectors on the Western Front. "Of all the troops who were opposed to the Germans on the great battlefields," he says, "the English were not only the most formidable, but the manliest and most chivalrous." And we too can say with honesty that after Tower Hamlets we had a greater respect for the fighting qualities of our opponents.

Leaving Ridge Wood the Battalion marched to Ouderdom where it entrained for Caestre. The command of the Battalion now passed to Major A. W. Puttick, M.C., of the West Kents.

During the fighting from the 20th to the 23rd the Battalion had suffered very heavily. Out of the 18 officers and 447 other ranks who went into action, 14 of the former and 287 of the latter, a total of 301, were *hors de combat*. Of the other units of the Brigade the Hants had 331 casualties, the West Kents 260 and the K.R.R.s 245. When it is remembered that none of the battalions was 500 strong, the high proportion of the losses can be gauged. Our officer casualties, as at Flers, were higher than any other unit in the Brigade, 9 of them being killed or mortally wounded. The dead were: Capt. D. McCallum; Lieut. A. T. Libby; 2nd Lieuts. H. N. Dunkley, L. W. B. Russell, J. McL. Hutcheson, S. Lasenby (attached as Signalling Officer to the 15th Hants), F. J. Harding, T. B. Jolly and R. E. White (died of wounds 28.9.17). Those wounded were: Lieut.-Col. E. Knapp, D.S.O.; Capt. H. S. Openshaw, M.C.; Lieuts D. Walker, M.C., and C. N. Pridham, and 2nd Lieut. F. R. Matthews.

Of the other ranks 33 were reported as killed and 57 missing. A full list of these appears in the appendix, and most are commemorated on the Tyne Cot Memorial.

According to accounts Capt. McCallum was sniped when attacking a pill-box, and his servant Pte. C. Holmes, sacrificed his life in attempting to get at the sniper afterwards. Capt. McCallum had served with A Company as a platoon commander and his loss was a personal one to those of us who had served with him since the early days of the Battalion. His quiet manner and unfailing concern for our welfare, both as a platoon and company commander, won our love and obedience.

Lieut. A. T. Libby, a veteran of the Boer War, was another one of our original officers who enjoyed great popularity amongst all ranks. At his own request he had returned to his company after holding the post of Transport Officer.

2nd Lieut. R. E. White who died of wounds, was the brother of 2nd Lieut. G. L. ("Jumbo") White, and according to the particulars shown in the records the stretcher-bearers, E. H. and F. Piggott, who were both killed, appear to have been related.

Cpl. A. Miles, the very well respected Company Clerk of A Company, who had been wounded on at least two occasions during previous service in France, also met his death.

Amongst others who laid down their lives were Lce.-Cpl. ("Golly") Linford of C Company, an ex-yeoman, who had established himself in his company as an expert on patrols, and C.S.M. Dan Maddison of D Company who, as already stated, was with Capt. Todd in the Green Line, and took over C.S.M. after the demise of C.S.M. Billy Warr. Billy Warr.

The wounding and consequent loss of the future services of Colonel Knapp was a sad blow to the Battalion. Although his command had not been a long one, it was realised by all that with his kindly consideration coupled with his efficiency as a soldier he was likely to get the best out of those under his command. The Colonel encouraged others to think for themselves and make suggestions for his consideration. The story is told by a lance-corporal of A Company how before the Battle of Messines his Company Commander approached him with reference to the disposition and other matters in connection with his Lewis-gun team. Having made certain suggestions he was surprised later at having to appear before the Commanding Officer. "Are you Corporal ——?" "Yes, Sir!" replied the man. "I understand that you have made certain suggestions in connection with your Lewis-gun section in the coming offensive." The flabbergasted corporal spluttered out, "Yes, Sir, but I never intended my Company Commander to convey them to you." Colonel Knapp then went on to say how pleased he was to know that some of his men were showing such a keen interest in their job. He ended by saying, "I have considered your suggestion which is a good one, but think mine is better. As I am the Commanding Officer, I suppose what I suggest will have to stand." The corporal retired with a great admiration for his colonel, for he had expected to get a good "wigging" for having the audacity to differ from his arrangements.

Another man tells how, when the H.Q. Officers' Mess staff returned to Reninghelst after a gruelling time in the trenches, the Colonel told them to supply the officers with the same fare as the men, bully and biscuits, instead of preparing a course dinner. He said the batmen were tired out and badly needed a rest that night.

With the wounding of Lieut. David Walker (Signal Officer), and the return to England through sickness on the 22nd of September of Lieut. V. L. Clift (Adjutant) and 2nd Lieut. L. A. Rossiter (Intelligence Officer), the whole H.Q. staff had to be re-organised. The position of Adjutant was temporarily taken over by Lieut. B. F. Dodd, but later Capt. H. S. Walker took on the duties. Lieut. Mutch had taken over the duties of I.O. soon after 2nd Lieut. Rossiter was sent to hospital.

Owing to the loss of the Colonel and most of the officers there were no doubt many brave actions which were never brought to the notice of the Higher Authorities. However, after investigation the following honours were awarded for the Battle of the Menin Road Ridge:—

Military Cross: Capt. W. L. A. Harrison, R.A.M.C., and Capt. E. V. Whiteway (122nd Brigade Transport officer); Lieut. J. A. Rogers, and 2nd Lieuts. W. D. Mutch (now Intelligence Officer) H. C. Ward and 2nd Lieut. (A/Captain) H. S. Todd.

Distinguished Conduct Medal: C.S.M.s C. J. Love and R. W. Mayston and Pte. A. W. Trussler.

Bar to Military Medal: Lce.-Cpl. L. C. Southall.

Military Medal: C.Q.M.S. W. Barnes; Sergts. G. Hammond and J. F. Radcliffe; Cpl. S. Woodcock; Lce.-Cpl. W. Aitken, and Ptes. E. Connor, T. Cunningham, F. Davey, G. F. Greaves, G. L. Huxley and H. Kenyon.

Belgian Croix de Guerre: 2nd Lieut. (A/Capt.) H. S. Todd; C.S.M. R. W. Mayston and Pte. G. Reeves.

The most pleasing feature of these awards was that at last Lce.-Cpl W. A. ("Bill") Aitken had been recognised. Never was a decoration more richly deserved. The courage of Aitken was unsurpassed throughout the Battalion.

Capt. Harrison, known throughout the Battalion as "Mad Jack," was always up to some funny prank or other and was unorthodox in most things he did. For all that he was a most courageous man, who personally superintended the removal of the wounded as soon as his duties at the Aid Post permitted. How many men owe their lives to the doctor's determination at Tower Hamlets will never be known, but the fact remains that he called upon all and sundry to carry stretchers and get the wounded away. In this work of mercy he was ably assisted by Pte. A. Trussler and Lce.-Cpl. Len Southall who for the second time was recommended for the D.C.M. only to receive a bar to his well-deserved M.M. Southall was like a second Medical Officer to the Battalion. Quiet, unobtrusive and polite to all, Southall could not have had an enemy in the whole unit. Two decorations in actions following one another was Trussler's record. No better men could have been found anywhere to see to the evacuation of the wounded than Trussler and Aitken. In the biggest bombardments these two men were an example of courage and coolness. Further on will be found some exciting reminiscences of the Medical Staff at Tower Hamlets.

Capt. E. V. Whiteway, the Brigade Transport Officer, and one of the first officers of the Battalion, so organised the transport arrangements during battles that the men in the line received their rations even under the most trying conditions. To our great regret he was mortally wounded some months later.

Lieut. J. A. Rogers, one of the most modest and unassuming officers ever posted to the 12th, came from America to join up. Before he left the Battalion on account of wounds he had the distinction of adding two bars to the M.C. awarded for Tower Hamlets.

2nd Lieuts. Mutch and Ward, who have already been mentioned in the narrative, had the distinction of winning a decoration in their first action with the 12th Battalion although both had seen previous service.

A/Capt. H. S. Todd, as we have already seen, took a prominent part in the operations. He was one of the most likeable officers we ever had. Members of A, C and D Companies will remember him with his boyish exuberance, his well tilted Service cap or tin helmet (Beatty style) and his never-failing care for the men of his platoon and company. Captain Todd, as he was later, managed to supply his men with cigarettes and other comforts when all other means of supply had failed. He left us on account of sickness in March, 1918, and was afterwards posted to the 8th Battalion, where on September 1st, 1918, he again distinguished himself in the capture of Le Priez Farm (halfway between Combles and Rancourt) for which he was awarded a bar to his M.C.* Unfortunately he was killed while advancing towards Ronnsoy with the 8th Battalion on September 18th, 1918, and was buried in Péronne Military Cemetery.

C.S.M. C. J. ("Wag") Love afterwards became R.S.M.

C.S.M. "Bob" Mayston of C Company was one of the finest soldiers produced by the Surrey Yeomanry. Nothing seemed to ruffle him, and his smiling and rosy countenance was a pleasure to behold.

In C.Q.M.S. W. H. ("Billy") Barnes we had a "Quarter-bloke" who, as a platoon sergeant of C Company, had done good work at Flers. Never was a task too hard for "Bill" if it meant delivering rations to his comrades in the line. Barnes had a reputation among the men in all the companies as being so devoted to his job that failure to deliver the goods was looked upon as an impossibility as far as he was concerned. Like many good fellows we knew he is said to have died of his wounds received later on in the war, after the cessation of hostilities.

A very refreshing account is given in Capt. E. W. J. Neave's history of the 11th "Queen's" of a genuine conscientious objector, Cpl. Roland Lee-Warner, who joined that battalion as a stretcher-bearer, and, after being taken prisoner in March, 1918, succeeded in escaping from his captors on three occasions and finally reached our lines when the Grenadier Guards reached Solesmes on the 8th of November, 1918. It is recorded that, although his principles did not allow him to fight, he was not satisfied to remain in comfort and safety while his countrymen were giving their life's blood to preserve that security. Of a similar type was Pte. G. L. Huxley, one of the most famous men in the section of runners. A godly man, Huxley would often be seen reading his Bible in and out of the line. He had a conscientious objection to killing, and even in the tightest of corners never did he resort to the use of the weapon which as a soldier he was forced to carry. But there was not a braver or cooler man amongst the runners than he. With Huxley men seemed to bear a charmed life. He would go anywhere through the thickest bombardment and could be depended upon to deliver his messages when others failed. Subsequently he received a bar to his M.M., and those who knew him testify to this day that they have never known a better practising Christian.

Radcliffe, Greaves and Kenyon (we shall hear more of these later), Connor, Cunningham, Davey and Reeves, were men who came out with the Battalion and had been doing consistently good work right through. Sergt. Hammond, who succeeded C.S.M. Maddison as C.S.M. of D Company, and Cpl. S. Woodcock were old 1st Battalion men.

*It is interesting to note that in this action another old member of the 12th, Sergt. C. Jenkerson, was awarded the D.C.M. He shared the same fate as Capt. Todd on October 23rd, 1918.

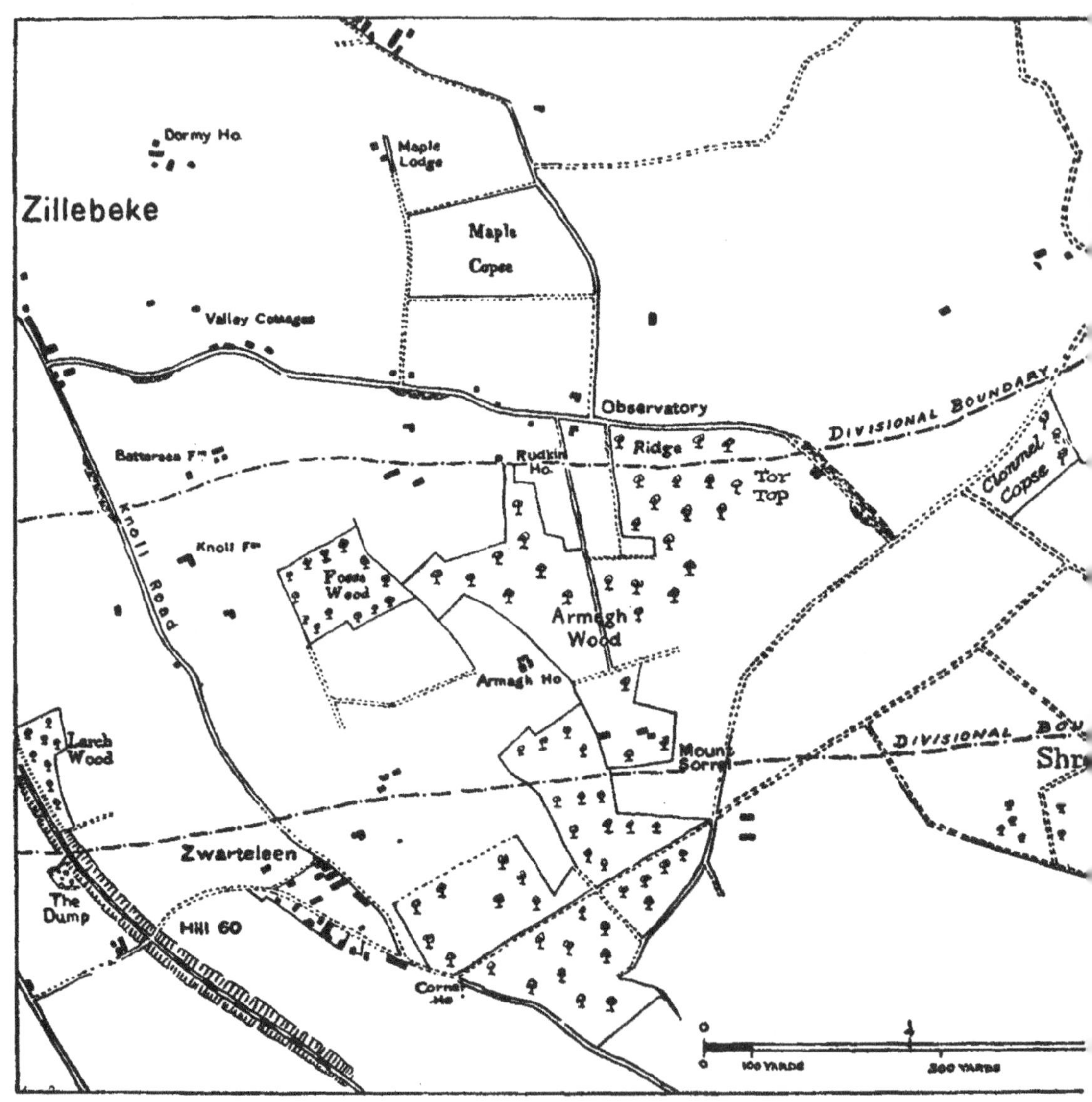
Dormy Ho.
Maple Lodge
Zillebeke
Maple Copse
Valley Cottages
Observatory
DIVISIONAL BOUNDARY
Clonmel Copse
Battersea Fm
Rudkin Ho.
Ridge
Tor Top
Knoll Road
Knoll Fm
Armagh Wood
Armagh Ho
Mount Sorrel
DIVISIONAL BOU
Larch Wood
Zwarteleen
The Dump
Hill 60
Cornet Ho
100 YARDS
200 YARDS

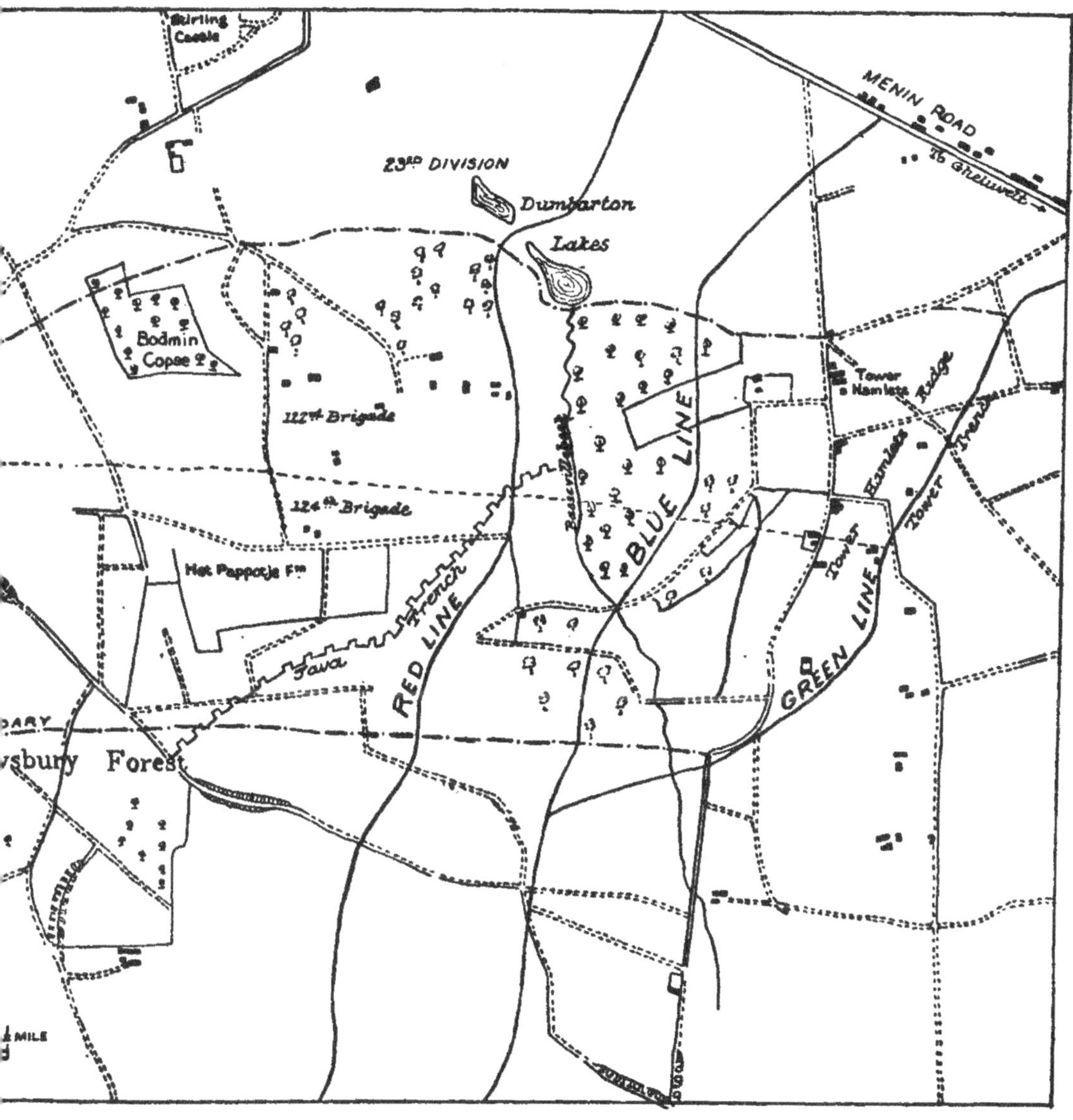
Stirling Castle
MENIN ROAD
To Gheluvelt
23RD DIVISION
Dumbarton
Lakes
Bodmin Copse
Tower Hamlets
Tower Hamlets Ridge
Tower Trench
122nd Brigade
124th Brigade
BLUE LINE
Basseville beek
Het Pappotje Fm
French
Java
RED LINE
Tower Hamlets
GREEN LINE
ARY
sbury Forest
½ MILE

Let us now return to some personal accounts which serve to prove many things which have been recorded in the Diary and official records.

Capt. H. S. Walker, in his capacity as the senior officer who came out of action, has supplied some notes:—

"As soon as we moved off, I noticed the troops on our right were doing a "left incline" which we had to correct. Then Lieut. Russell's servant ran up to me to say that Lieut. Russell had been killed by a sniper from a pill-box in a shell hole which had not been destroyed by our barrage. This temporary hold-up was cleared by the use of rifle grenades.

"We moved steadily forward and at the bottom of the slope a shell hole was selected as Battalion H.Q. Colonel Knapp saw some enemy snipers to our right front up the hill, and taking a rifle he dropped two or three of them. He was just closing the bolt of the rifle with it still at his shoulder, when an enemy rifle bullet struck the shank of the bolt. The bullet broke and part of it went through the Colonel's right hand while another piece whizzed over me and wounded Lieut. David Walker who was lying by my side. After having his wound dressed, Lieut. Walker went up the hill for the Aid Post, under fire all the way.

"The Brigade on our right had been held up very early, which left us with an exposed right flank. I went up to the front line. Our Left was on its objectives,* and I ordered the Right to fall back and face their right to form a defensive flank. This was duly reported by me to Colonel Knapp.

"Our H.Q. had been shelled heavily throughout the 20th, and on the 21st this shelling increased considerably. Although we had improved our shell hole by digging a narrow trench, things got so hot that the C.O. said we must move and ordered me to go forward, while he went back to get his hand dressed and to see the Brigadier. Just then a shell burst just short of our little trench, and I was buried, but Pilcher, my servant, got me out by cutting my equipment, which he salved later in the day. We had no sooner got out of our H.Q. and were starting on our different ways, when a shell dropped in the middle of us and we were all thrown to the ground. My little party then moved forward and over the stream and crept up the slope towards the front line. We were all pretty well dazed, and during a pause I looked back and saw the C.O. tying up his right arm. There was someone with him, probably his servant. I cannot describe my feelings at the moment. I had no idea that any of us had been hit, and when I saw that the Colonel had been wounded for the second time I felt awful. We watched him move off and we went in the opposite direction, where we found a pill-box occupied by Capt. Henderson of the West Kents. I see in the history of the 11th West Kents that I placed myself under his command. This is news to me, but I was very shaken at the time, and I feel sure there was some misunderstanding.

"Capt. Henderson's servant scrounged a bag of rations from a shell hole. The bread was sodden, and the bacon was covered with green slime. But I never tasted better. It was cooked over a fire of splinters of wood no thicker than a match stick. As the entrance to the pill-box was facing the enemy, a ground sheet had to be held over the door to prevent them seeing the light.

"The enemy were massing for a counter-attack, and I got off messages by pigeons we had salved from our blown-in shell-hole H.Q. The result was that our artillery dispersed the enemy with many casualties.

"Having sent a good number of messages back, I was surprised to hear later, at a C.O.'s Conference, that none had been received from Dagger. I was ticked off by the Brigadier. I took it quietly, the only thing to do, but I saw the Brigadier and Brigade Major afterwards and produced my copies of messages. All had been received, but not over my signature. They had been opened and re-written at a relay post.*

"The re-bombardment for the Brigade on our right caused many casualties to our men forming the defensive flank.

*This confirms Capt. Todd's report and Lieut. Mutch's assertion that some of our men had reached their objective.

*Most of the messages received at Brigade H.Q. were signed by Hamlet.

"After the relief I had much writing to do *re* casualties, etc., and no one to help me in this difficult task."

Lce.-Cpl. Joe Chamberlain, who was practically in charge of our signal arrangements, has given an interesting account of the operations, which he has in no sense exaggerated:—

"Having spent the best part of the night marching in silence, most of the time in single file, getting mixed up with other troops all on the same journey, sorting ourselves out and getting mixed up again; taking orders in whispers, not knowing where we were or hardly who we were, we eventually found ourselves in position just behind the front line in the early hours of the morning of the 20th of September.

"There were just five of us signallers: Lce.-Cpl. Dan Crawley, Reg. Hall, Jack Sharpe, "Ross" Chatfield and myself. Our Signal Officer, whom I had seen for the first time the day previously, and whose name I never knew*, was with the Colonel just to our front. (Lieut. 'Hookey' Walker, our regular Signal Officer, was with the Brigade Forward Party for this advance). Being senior lance-corporal (our two signal sergeants had, for some reason or other, been left down the line) I was in charge.

"We had an hour or two to go before Zero, so began to make a couple of shell holes as comfortable as possible. We were well loaded with signal equipment, reels of wire, lamps and stands, telephone, etc., as well as our rifles, ammo, and other things, so we could not make ourselves too comfortable. The guns were quiet, and one could hardly imagine that shortly Hell was to be let loose. We had strict orders not to smoke, but, 'boys will be boys' (we were all in the 19's or early 20's) and we smoked continually without, of course, anyone being the wiser. We were none of us too happy, but kept most of our thoughts to ourselves. Our Signal Officer crawled over and gave me final instructions, also telling me that he would be over with a spot of rum before the 'kick off.' Well, I never saw that officer again, nor the rum. Whether he was killed or wounded I cannot say.

"It was getting near Zero hour, and I had that sinking feeling which can only be felt and not described.

"Jerry had apparently sensed something and was getting busy with his Verey lights and a shell or two, but our guns were silent. Then our barrage opened; one moment silence, the next Bedlam. What a barrage! It seemed to me as if the whole of the guns on the Western Front had concentrated on this one spot. Then came Jerry's effort at retaliation, and a very good effort it was. We were quite content to dig our heads into the earth while the shells dropped all around. Dan Crawley was lying on his side facing me. I could see him shouting but could not hear a word, until he moved over and shouted in my ear, 'He'll drop one right in here in a minute.' Well, Dan was a good prophet. Within the space of a few seconds Fritz sent over two for our especial benefit; one landed on the edge of our shell hole, and before we could shake the dirt off another landed slap bang inside. I felt a clout in the back and, whereas a moment before I had been pressing my face into the earth, I now found myself half out of the shell-hole with Jack Sharpe lying ocross me; Dan and the others had been blown the other way. On pulling ourselves together we found that we had got off lightly. Dan Crawley was hit in the leg, and Reg. Hall had his chin and lips badly knocked about. The long tripod which I had strapped across my back was smashed in two, which must have been a near thing for me. Jack Sharpe and "Ross" Chatfield were spitting out dirt, but were not hurt. Without more ado, except shaking of hands and good luck, Dan and Reg promptly started off for the dressing station and within a few minutes we were over the top in the other direction. Being now short-handed, I dumped some of the signal equipment, keeping only the wire and telephone, and we started to go forward. We had just jumped what had been Jerry's front line trenches, when a machine-gun opened fire on us from directly in front. Sharpe and myself promptly dived into the nearest shell-out. Hearing our signal pal shouting out that he was hit, we clambered into the next hole and found that he had got one clean through the foot. We left him and moved forward and in one of our dives to earth came across Lce.-Cpl. Mathias (Sniping Section). Both his legs were badly smashed about, and the poor chap was in a very bad way; he was only semi-conscious and did not know us. He was calling for water, which we gave him. There were several more of our chaps lying close to him, all dead. We covered Mathias's legs with his ground sheet and then left him.* The advance came to a stop, and our

*He died later.

H.Q. was made in a couple of shell-holes about half way up the ridge. Here we were joined by Lieut. Walker and some of the Brigade Forward Signal Party, and I was pleased to see that Cpl. Harry Tarry and Harry Harding, who were with that party, had come safely through, although I heard that Jack Lovell had been hit. After fixing us up with a Power Buzzer the Brigade Forward Party left us, with the exception of 'Hookey' Walker and Harry Harding who remained with H.Q. I was surprised to find that it was still early in the day, as it seemed like a lifetime to me.

"Jerry shelled a bit during the day, and Harding and I had the job of trying to comfort a young machine-gun sergeant (Machine-Gun Corps, I think) who had been hit in the chest and was dying. He died holding Harry's hand and mumbling about his wife and curly-headed boy. It was very pitiful and completely put me off my rations. Harry Harding still has the lanyard of the poor chap's revolver.

"During the operations we were amazed to see a signal flag waving from the front line and read the S.O.S. message* sent out by Signaller W. Taylor, for which gallant action he received a 'Soup Ticket' (a card from the Divisional General). We had a few scares at dusk and during the night and had to ask for retaliation on the Power Buzzer. Then I lost the last signaller who had started off with me, Sharpe being badly wounded by a shell which burst as we dived into a shell-hole for our rifles during a scare. We had to use a little 'gentle' persuasion to make some Jerry prisoners carry Sharpe and some other wounded down.

"The next morning we were troubled by a Jerry sniper who seemed to have us bang in line and eventually he got Lieut. Walker. Things went quietly until later in the day, when Jerry started shelling us. At first we thought they were just a few strays, but it was soon evident that he was on to us, and the shells started to drop thick and furious right amongst us. The Colonel was wounded and gave the order to shift. As we clambered out of the shell-hole my tin hat was blown off. I made a grab for it only to find that some other chap wanted it as well. Whilst we were tugging away, we were both blown straight up by a shell which must have exploded directly underneath us. When I landed I felt as if my head was bursting and then discovered that I had been hit in the arm and shoulder. I then started running, not caring much which way I went so long as I got out of that Hell. I must have run into instead of out of it, for I was blown over quite a number of times before getting clear of the shelled area. I eventually reached what must have been part of Jerry's front line trench and sat down to try to pull myself together. I felt in a bad way, not from my wounds, but from my head and ears (I suffered a lot from my ears for weeks afterwards). The trench I landed in was not exactly a comforting sight, as parts of dead Germans were scattered about, and I found I was resting my arm on a gum boot with a leg still in it. Four legs were protruding from a smashed-in dugout which told its own tale. Jerry must have had a bad time here. I had been sitting there a few minutes and was wondering how to find my way down to the dressing station, when who should come along but Q.M.S. Speller with one of his men. His first words were: "Hello, Sonny, where's Headquarters?" I pointed to where the shells were still bursting and told him they were somewhere round about there, if they weren't all blown to pieces. He decided to wait a bit until it had eased up and asked me where I was hit. I told him I had got it in the arm and that it was beginning to feel stiff. He gave me a drink of rum and pointed out the way to the dressing station, wished me good luck, and away I went feeling a bit better for that drink. I passed through the C.C.S. and eventually found myself in the 2nd Australian Hospital at Boulogne. I was there six weeks and rejoined the Battalion at Nieuport."

From the point of view of C Company, Sergt. Joe Radcliffe writes:—

"We had been under cover of a hedge in reserve for a day or two previous to the attack, and things were very quiet.

"The night before we went over we moved into position. Although we were supplied with a guide, as usual he managed to lose us, and it must have been early morning before we arrived at our final destination. Considering the amount of walking

*According to the Divisional War Diary, at 11.0 a.m. on the 20th September, a message was received from the 23rd Division stating that they had intercepted a visual message from the 12th East Surreys timed 10.25 a.m. which ran as follows:— "Right flank open. Reinforcements required for Green objective."

backwards and forwards the men were in fairly good spirits before settling down at the 'jumping off' point.

"Before leaving the reserve line N.C.O.s had been given a time table of the programme of attack, and final instructions were given some little time before Zero hour. I personally was concerned only with my own platoon, and, if I remember rightly, C Company had some new officers for this 'stunt.' Just before the bombardment opened, we all had a tot of rum which was most welcome.

"At last it was time to go, and go we did under a terrific bombardment from our field and heavy artillery. We had not gone far when we met very strong resistance. The German shells were dropping right into us, causing a great many casualties. We attacked as best we could under this storm of fire but progress was rather slow. No. 9 Platoon had lost about twelve men either killed or wounded up to this time. In our advance we were temporarily held up on our right by an enemy strong point which we attacked with rifle grenades and bombs. Eventually the Germans inside surrendered, but not before they had caused us several casualties, including Cpl. Vic Cooper of No. 10 Platoon. After we had taken them prisoners we searched the stronghold and found it consisted of several concrete dugouts and pill-boxes. We also found six more Jerries who had secreted themselves in the ruins, evidently with the intention of waiting until we had gone forward so that they could attack us with their machine-gun from the rear. These were also sent back as prisoners.

"Soon after leaving this fortified position I had a touch of 'wind up,' or perhaps it was a bit of luck. In my tunic pockets I was carrying two ground flares for signalling to aeroplanes (a green one to let them know where we were and a red in case we were counter-attacked) and two Mill's bombs. The incident I am recalling caused some excitement amongst my Lewis-gun team. We were advancing all together when somebody saw smoke coming from one of my pockets. I tried to undo my equipment to seek the cause, but in the meantime Kenyon and Greaves (two of the gunners) managed to undo the pocket concerned and extract two smouldering flares. On examination of my tunic it was found that a bullet had cut a slit about three inches along the side, entered the pocket and then set light to the flares. However, I was all right and that was all that mattered.

"We delayed our attack here for a while waiting for the barrage to lift. About this time I ran into some of the Battalion H.Q. staff and well remember Lieut. 'Hookey' Walker urging us on. As we advanced I saw Lewis-guns and ammunition lying about, so we picked up two extra guns which the gun team carried while I carried some ammunition. Not many of C Company appeared to have been left by this time, and my platoon consisted of a Lewis-gun team with four guns, a couple of others and myself. Before we started the attack I had a waterbottle full of rum which I had completely forgotten. However, we all had a drop out of the bottle and felt much better for it.

"We carried on further, not knowing exactly where our objective lay. At this period we were meeting with little resistance and I well remember two British planes circling over our heads. I don't know whether this was a signal to us that we had reached our objective, but at all events I took it as such, seeing that there did not appear to be a great many troops on either side of us. Here we got into shell-holes to consolidate our position.

"The German artillery had quietened down a bit, and everything was peaceful. This caused us to keep a sharp look out, as we had a suspicion that this was just the lull before the storm.

"We had no idea of the time of day, but presumed that it must have been afternoon by now. We continued to consolidate in readiness for a counter-attack which I fully expected would come at dusk. I went along for some distance to the right and left to find what troops there were on either side of us, but only found a few scattered here and there. Some time afterwards it was with great relief that I saw an officer coming towards our position. Luckily for us it was Capt. H. S. Walker who enquired how we were feeling and gave us a 'nip' out of his flask. He told us that we were in front of the remainder of C Company and stayed with us a while, probably to cheer us up. He certainly bucked us up considerably when he told us that we were being relieved as soon as it was dark. Capt. Walker then left us and we waited in expectation of relief, as we considered that we had had enough for one day. Relief did not come that night, for to our great surprise C.Q.M.S. Barnes brought rations up, as usual.

"When relief did come, we were more than pleased to march away out of it to a camp behind the lines, where we found out how many of our pals were either killed or wounded."

Cpl. Southall writes of the Tower Hamlets action:—

"Dr. Harrison certainly added to the gaiety of nations, always cheery and always doing something unexpected but humorous. . . . Tommy Walker, the M.O.'s servant, and I went up from Bedford House past Zillebeke Lake, a dreary mass of mud and shell-holes, where transport continually passed, then to Larch Wood Tunnels in an old railway cutting. These were lit with electric light, and the number of corridors and rooms which had been constructed by the Canadian tunnellers was a revelation to us. It seemed safe as houses, but was obviously no use as a First Aid Post.

"As we moved on, Fritz started a heavy strafe. We took refuge in a decayed trench about three feet deep and crouched there waiting for the worst. Mud and dirt rained round us and bits of spent shrapnel, but we were not hit.

"After about half an hour the strafe ceased suddenly, and after searching for the M.O. we found him smiling as usual. . . . .

"On the 21st of September we finally arrived at Battalion H.Q., where we learnt that the C.O. had been wounded and Capt. H. S. Walker had taken charge. We moved on up the slope, picking up a couple of shovels en route. We had been given a present of a small flag with a red cross on it, left behind by the Germans during our advance.

"We wandered on up the Tower Hamlets Ridge, the Doctor's idea being to find a suitable hole which could be turned with the shovels into an Aid Post. Suddenly the M.O. slipped into a shell-hole full of liquid mud; he was rapidly getting deeper, so we pushed out a rifle for him to hold on to and hauled him out in a horrible state.

"Towards evening we tramped back after first marking our shell-hole with the flag so that we could locate it next morning, and dug a little sap some distance back and slept there 'two deep.' The Doctor stretched himself on a ground sheet, and I slept with my head just above his chest and my legs projecting beyond the end of the sap. Half way through the night the Doctor asked me if I felt cold: I said I wasn't too warm, whereupon he said it was time we changed over, so I got underneath and he on top.

"Just as dawn broke, Jerry started a counter-attack, and bits of shrapnel and shells came flying around. One shell hit the ground a few yards away, and we felt the ground beneath us heave and waited for our last hour. We went on waiting until we came to the conclusion that it wasn't going to burst at all, and heaved two sighs of relief. We then went up again to our shell hole.

"Towards evening Padre Dobson arrived with two cans of water, of which we were rather short. Then he and the Doctor urged me and finally ordered me back to Larch Wood Tunnels for a good night's rest.

"Early in the morning the Doctor sent a message by Trussler telling me to collect some R.A.M.C. bearers and all the stretchers and dressings we could carry and go up to him. We reached the foot of the ridge to find Fritz had put down a barrage between us and where we could see the Red Cross flag flying halfway up the slope. When we arrived we found the Doctor sound asleep!

"He awoke soon after and gazed around drowsily. Then he noticed clods of earth, etc., on his ground sheet. 'Fritz has altered the landscape a bit,' he said. 'What's been happening, Southall?'

" 'They've been shelling, Sir,' said I.
" 'Was it bad?'
" 'Yes; it has been simply raining 5.9.s.'
" 'Why on earth didn't you wake me up?'
" 'Well, Sir, to tell the truth, you were sound asleep, and I thought, if you were going, it would be better that the 5.9 with your name on it should find you in that blissful state, so I didn't wake you.'

"But how he had slept through that pandemonium was really astonishing.

"I learnt from Trussler what had happened the previous night. When it became dark, the Doctor and he retired a little way to a small concrete pill-box occupied by the Hampshire's M.O. and Staff. There was no room to accommodate them in the pill-box, so they settled down in a shell hole behind it. They had many casualties in, and while they were dressing one case a shell passed between them and landed the other side of the hole without harming them. They had a pretty rough night, but, not satisfied with his good work all through the night, the Doctor, hearing that some wounded were lying out before the front line, went up with Trussler in the early morning mist and cleared them all down, even collecting R.E.s to work as stretcher-bearers.

"We at last were told to leave, as the Battalion was going out of the line. We had a terrible time coming down dodging the enemy's shells, Once we dropped into a shell-hole as one shell burst close, and Dr. Harrison, who had run a piece of barbed wire into his heel and was dog-tired, couldn't crawl out, and we had to hoist him up. But at last we reached the Tunnels."

Here to end our chapter, is a vivid description by Q.M.S. Speller of the work of the Transport:—

"Rations were taken up to the troops in the line in sandbags hung on pack ponies, for the last part of the route was quite impassable for limbers.

"Taking our usual route, our 'circus' passed a 60-pounder battery which had moved up during the night and was in action on a sunken road just in front of Moated Grange Farm. In crossing a small ridge (which brought us temporarily into enemy vision), we unavoidably masked the battery's fire for a minute or two. Lieut. F. R. Matthews and myself brought up the rear of the column, and just as our ponies were pulling clear, out popped a very irate figure whom I recognised as the Divisional C.R.A. Almost purple with choler he asked, 'What the asterisked asterisk are you asterisks doing here?' to which Matthews, with a cheery nonchalance which added to the Brigadier's discomforture, replied: 'We're winning the asterisked War. What are you doing?' Before the C.R.A. could annihilate us verbally, we were out of earshot!

"Organised ration parties were, of course, impossible, and we merely distributed bags, containing five complete rations, to whatever troops we found in holes and ditches. Matthews made for Battalion H.Q. and I carried a bottle of mess whisky and a couple of personal letters.

"What a journey!

"Shell holes full of muddy and bloody occupants, the turgid countryside churned up all around by an unceasing smother of shells of all sizes and descriptions.

"Suddenly Matthews trod on a partially submerged duckboard which see-sawed and shot me over. He also missed his footing and as we reached 'terra wetta' I sat on his chest!

"After what seemed miles we reached the hole occupied by Colonel Knapp, Capt. H. S. Walker and a couple of runners. (I cannot recollect definitely but fancy David Walker and R.S.M. Love were in the adjoining hole.)

"The bottle survived miraculously and was gratefully disposed of without further ado. The C.O. cheerily called us a pair of blank fools, and told us to get back, an order which in the circumstances I had no hesitation in trying to obey. I say 'trying,' because at that moment the scattered attacking troops recommenced to push on, and the movement was the signal to the watching 'Jerry' to open up with every weapon he could get to bear on our people.

"Whilst we waited for a lull, Colonel Knapp and Capt. H. S. Walker went forward and after a few yards were blotted from our vision by an enormous explosion, and then, like magic, reappeared beyond the smoke.

"The immediate area was literally a shambles. Bodies lying everywhere, and some no longer even bodies! I remember vividly a personal sickening fear, a fear of mutilation which accompanied me throughout the thirty-five months I spent in France, and which transcended a curiously remote fear of sudden death.

"I confusedly remember how on that day my fear gave place to a raging fury at my impotence, a helplessness to render help to the poor stricken devils on every side.

"Then Matthews crumpled up suddenly, and I scrambled over to find him dazed and speechless, blood streaming from both ears, and lying in a still smoking shell-hole. Near by was a youngster, shouting incoherently in the appalling din, with a piece of shrapnel sticking out of his upper arm. I took his field dressing and plugged Matthews' ears, and decided to leave the youngster's 'souvenir' where it was, as the limb did not appear to be fractured.

"Between us we got Matthews to his feet (he was about 6 feet 4 inches) and after pulling and pushing and half dragging each other for what seemed an eternity, I was relieved at handing them both over at a dressing station at Zwarteleen.

"Matthews turned up after a few days, and cheerily counted his temporary deafness as a blessing. He couldn't hear shells coming and he couldn't hear 'asterisked Generals,' and so he 'didn't care an asterisk for either or both.'

"Gay and gallant Matthews met his death at Achiet-Le-Grand in March, 1918, in very similar circumstances to Lieut. A. Libby, a South African veteran. Both acted as Transport Officers, and both asked if they could rejoin their companies in the line, and having got there died fighting."

CHAPTER X.

25th September to 17th November, 1917.

Battalion moves to La Panne and takes over a part of the Coast Defences—Bad times at Oost Dunkirk—Start for the Italian Front.

ON September 28th the Battalion was transported by lorry to the Belgian coast, billeting one day at Uxam, and on the next arriving in Furnes Camp in the area of La Panne, which was the temporary home of the King and Queen of the Belgians for a long period during the war. Here in the little slice of their country left to them the small remnant of the Belgian Army stood with their gallant monarch looking across the area which they had deliberately flooded in 1914 to their martyred country, where their parents, their wives and families must, they knew, be still living under German thraldom. Only a few miles off, yet for four years there was no chance of communication. Think of the agony of it. It was the custom of many English to sneer at the "braves Belges!" Some of us never ceased to protest against this unlovely attitude. There were indeed some Englishmen whose staple conversation was the incompetence or cowardice or inferiority of every other unit in the British Army but their own and of every one of our allies. They were usually those whose ill-manners were only equalled by their gross ignorance, but they were a vastly irritating crowd.

The story of one Belgian might be of interest here. At the beginning of the War Mr. Aston was headmaster of a preparatory school near Deal, and in September, 1914, a convoy of wounded arrived at the local hospital. Several residents took in walking cases. Among the four he received was Fernand Corbisier, a young baker of Braine l'Alleud near Waterloo, a broad-shouldered upstanding fellow with fair hair and a charming smile. He was full of gratitude for our hospitality and always trying to find some job in which he could lend a helping hand. After a couple of months he was sent to Le Havre, where the Belgian Army was reorganising. In the summer he came back to the school for a week's leave, for, as he pathetically said, "I know nothing of my family: you are my father now." For the next three years he regularly corresponded, signing himself "Ton fils," full of gratitude for parcels sent and now and then returning some little souvenir, but after September, 1918, no news came. At the beginning of 1919 a touching letter was received by Mr. Aston from the father. "My dear son Fernand," he said, "was killed in the last advance. We had no news of him since 1914. All his belongings have been sent to us, and among them a packet of all your letters, showing us who had befriended him all those years." The letter was an outpouring of thanks for what Mr. Aston had been able to do for him.

The martyrdom of little Belgium is often forgotten now, or even unknown to the younger generation. As Robert Bridges says in "The Testament of Beauty":—

"Memory is so complacent that we well may fear lest our children forget,"

and it is tragically true.

After the frightful experiences of the last three and a half months La Panne was a home of rest for our troops. There were still signs of civilisation here, though the town was within easy reach of the enemy guns and hostile planes were fond of unloading missiles over it.

Two big drafts from the 2/5th and 2/6th Territorial Battalions of the East Surrey Regiment joined the Battalion soon after arrival in this area.

We have already made reference to the "combing out" which took place in the Battalion, especially on Headquarters staff, before Tower Hamlets. On a larger scale this was taking place throughout the British Army. Recent drafts to the 12th had included men who had enlisted in Corps such as the Royal Engineers, R.A.O.C., etc. The posting of Territorials to ordinary service battalions was another step in the direction of filling up the ranks from trained soldiers. Many of the new drafts had seen previous service in France. Amongst them too were qualified musicians who had been in the bands of their old units, and with the arrival of brass instruments a Battalion brass band was formed under the conductorship of Sergt. Crabtree with Cpl. Rogers as his second in command. For the 12th this was an innovation which, although not appreciated at first when the earlier practices were taking place, was the means of affording us much enjoyment later on. With the arrival of these new drafts there was also a loss to the Battalion of some of our men who had been found unfit for the rigours of the trenches and were transferred to the Labour Corps. Posted to Area Employment Companies and the like, these men did not have a "cushy" time, for they worked just behind the lines, on dumps and in some of the most "unhealthy" places one could imagine. Many of them had already been wounded several times in the infantry, while others were well over Army age.

The casualties during the month of September were—Killed or Died of Wounds: 9 officers and 68 other ranks. Wounded: 5 officers and 226 other ranks.

During the next fortnight the Battalion remained in the neighbourhood of La Panne, carrying out training, mostly under company arrangements, principally in trench warfare and routine. N.C.O.s were under instruction by the R.S.M. in a class which was formed for that purpose. Baths at St. Idesbalde were allotted during the period, and Church Parades were held in the Y.M.C.A. at La Panne on two occasions. Route marches, bombing and grenade practices, miniature range work and protective sandbagging were also carried out.

General Towsey during his command kept in touch with the Mayor and Council of Bermondsey, and, having written to them with reference to our recent operations, received the following reply from the Mayor, which he circulated for our information:—

Mayor's Parlour,
Town Hall,
Bermondsey, S.E.
2nd October, 1917.

Dear Sir,

I have just received your favour dated the 26th Sept., and am so glad to hear of the great success that has attended the fighting of the 12th East Surrey Battalion.

We in Bermondsey feel proud of the Boys; we were sure in the early days of the recruiting (when I personally did some work in this way) that the men of Bermondsey could be relied upon for their sterling fighting qualities, and they would do anything for those who led them well. The Battalion has been fortunate in its officers, and it has been a real pleasure to me to read from time to time of the many wonderful achievements performed by the whole of the men in your Brigade.

I thank you for your letter and note that you will be sending shortly a roll of the honours and awards which we shall read with much interest.

Lieut.-Col. E. Knapp has promised us some guns which the 12th East Surrey Boys captured some time since.

Your letter fills us all with pride.

I am,
Dear General,
Yours faithfully,
(Sgd.) Henry J. Vezey, J.P.
Mayor.

The presence of the Battalion on this part of the front was not solely for a rest cure, for the 41st Division had now relieved the 66th Division and certain units were now holding the line along the sand dunes which are a prominent feature of this part of Belgium. On the 4th of October Major Puttick, our C.O., reconnoitred the trenches in the Nieuport sector, and a further reconnaissance was carried out by Capt. Hector Walker; he had taken over the Adjutancy after handing over the duties of Second-in-Command of the Battalion to Major C. T. Williams, who had rejoined on October 1st. When Capt. Walker made his tour of the sector he was agreeably surprised to find it exceptionally quiet, not hearing a shell burst all day and only seeing one so far away that he could not hear it.

Cpl. Southall recalls some incidents at La Panne in connection with two well known men in the Battalion, Sergt. "Jock" Turner and Cpl. A. W. Trussler:—

"Our hut was a commodious one. We had three rooms along one side, and a high partition separated us from the Band and the Canteen which occupied the other. Of our three rooms one was used as a medical room, one to sleep in, and one for stores. The Doctor decided that it would be possible for us to accommodate men who were not fit to carry on with duty but not quite bad enough to be evacuated. We had a stretcher fitted up as a bed in the medical room, and, as it was draughty, we hung it with blankets to make it cosy. Sergt. Turner (who acted as Q.M.S. to H.Q. Company, besides being Sergeant Cook) used our hut as his sleeping and living quarters. He was most interesting to talk to and was a man of many parts—a master cook, a master tailor, and many other things besides. He had seen much army service: in his capacity as a R.E. he helped to lay the charges which blew up the stockade at Atbara in the Sudan campaign before Omdurman.

"There was a hole in the floor through which, one day, we saw a small rat poke his head. We therefore laid a little bit of cheese by the hole, and, when the next rat put his head through we heaved at it anything which came handy. 'Don't throw anything at the poor little chaps,' said Jock Turner: 'they're my mascots.'

"A few nights after the Boche came over on one of his numerous bombing raids. The plane was caught in the searchlights and dropped a whole load of bombs in the next field to our hut, causing many casualties to men and mules, so that we were kept very busy, and it was a long time before we settled off to sleep again. I was just getting off to sleep when I felt a rat crawling up my blanket. I waited till it got near enough and then hoisted it in the air with a hefty punch. The rat fell into Jock's eye: he had just dropped off to sleep and let out a tremendous yell. 'What was that?' he shouted. 'It's all right, Jock,' I replied. 'It's only one of your mascots.'

"Not long after an unfortunate incident occurred which robbed us of our home. Sick parade had just finished one morning, and Trussler was heating up some water over a shell case containing wool soaked in methylated spirit. The flame appeared to die out, and Trussler picked up the large drum of meth. in which two holes were punched, and poured on some more spirit. But the wool must have been smouldering underneath, for it caught alight, flared up and exploded the drum. In a second the blazing meth. was all over the room.

"Our patient in bed in the medical room leaped out of bed in his pants and hared across the camp as hard as he could run. The flames ran up the blankets hanging round the walls: a large drum of paraffin exploded also and shot over the partition into the canteen. The man in charge grabbed the cash and bolted for safety. I dashed to the communicating door and was met by a sheet of flame that singed my eyebrows off. Trussler ran out of the medical room with his clothes alight, and we rolled him in the sand to extinguish the flames, but he was badly burnt on the face and hands and had to go to hospital. All our equipment and personal belongings were destroyed, and the only thing I saved was my volume of Shelley with burnt edges."

Orders were now issued to proceed to the Divisional Reserve area in the Nieuport Bains Sector, at St. Idesbalde. On the 15th we proceeded by the Coast tracks in relief of the 10th "Queen's" of the 124th Brigade, who were holding the line in the Right Battalion Sector, Eolian Road, which was reached by the route Coxyde, Coxyde Bains to Oost Dunkerke Bains. We were now on the extreme left of the whole Anglo-French line of 650 odd miles, the extreme right ending at the Swiss frontier.

During the night the beach everywhere was under military control. During darkness the whole of the area between the wire entanglements and the sea was to be considered No Man's Land and those entering liable to be fired on. The sole exception was the La Panne section, where every person was to be challenged twice and if possible apprehended. If such persons evaded apprehension, they were to be fired on as in other sections. No firing at night was permitted except for hostile landing or reasons stated above. Sentries were to use their discretion at all times and were particularly warned not to fire on British or Allied planes forced to land.

We held the line from the 15th to the 29th of October, during which time the daily reports were usually "Situation normal," with occasional shelling by the enemy of Oost Dunkerke Bains and Nieuport Bains and activity by his planes. There were two other ranks wounded, Pte. A. H. Willis on the 19th and Pte. C. D. Cooper on the 23rd. As Capt. Hector Walker has recorded: "Things did not long remain so quiet, as our Artillery soon started and things got more lively. But it was peace and quiet after our recent operations."

Another change in the command took place on the 16th, when Temporary Lieut.-Col. A. W. Puttick, M.C., relinquished the command on being transferred to the 15th Hants, and handed over to another officer of the 11th R.W. Kents, Acting Lieut.-Col. C. F. Stallard, M.C. This was the third officer of the West Kents who had commanded the Battalion for a period. The fact that there were no senior officers of our own regiment to take over command of us will give rise to a great deal of discussion. There were many brilliant officers in other battalions of the East Surrey Regt. who could have been safely entrusted with the command, but most promotions were made inside the Division. Regular and Special Reserve officers naturally were selected where possible, but there were some cases where officers who had only been commissioned during the war were given commands. The casualties among senior officers of the Battalion at Flers and other battles made the selection a very limited one. One officer in particular, Capt. J. L. Buckman of B Company, was considered by many to be a promising candidate for a higher rank. Then there was another officer, Capt. A. G. Howitt, who was not only a good soldier but a born leader. Lieut. J. F. Tamblyn, M.C., who was staff Captain of the 122nd Brigade for a time and was afterwards Brigade Major of the 71st and 120th Infantry Brigades was another young officer who could have been depended upon to do justice to any position given to him; his work at Flers had proved this. When it is considered that Lieut.-Col. E. Bowden of the 11th "Queen's" was only 21 years of age when he was killed in 1918, there is much to be said for some of the younger and capable officers of the 12th taking over command, failing efficient Regular and Special Reserve officers being found for the job.

On October 29th the 1st South African Brigade of the 9th Division relieved the 122nd Brigade, and the Battalion was moved by bus viâ La Panne and Dunkerque to Coudekerque Branche over the French frontier.

During the month the following officers—some of whom had been serving with Territorial battalions of the East Surrey Regt. since the beginning of the war—joined: Capt. A. R. K. Edsell; Lieuts. A. C. Edgar (appointed Musketry Officer), G. C. Davenport (appointed Lewis-Gun Officer), A. A. Wright, E. St. J. Ryan, A. F. Copp, E. B. Gillett, E. H. Barry, L. Dawson; 2nd Lieuts. R. N. Haine, A. K. Watts, and L. L. Linford. Several of these were before long commanding companies.

Casualties had been few during the month, only 5 other ranks being wounded. Various drafts had now brought our strength up to 40 officers and 864 other ranks.

The period from November 1st to the 11th was spent mainly on constant route marches, tactical exercises and outpost schemes. Even Sunday was not free from marching, for after Divine Service in the morning on November 4th, there was a march from 1.45 to 4.0 p.m.

On the 5th of November the Battalion proceeded by route march to St. Pol-sur-Mer, where, after an inspection by the Divisional Commander, the ribbon of the Military Cross was presented to Capt. W. L. A. Harrison, R.A.M.C., and 2nd Lieuts. W. D. Mutch and C. H. Ward. This was followed by a practice rearguard action in which the 12th Battalion was to cover the retirement of the 15th Hants.

From all the outpost schemes, route marching, etc., it was apparent that something was in the air. In the deadlock on the Western Front there was really no need to practise open warfare, for there was little likelihood of the break through which we had been seeking since the Battle of the Somme.

Through the downfall of Russia, owing to the machinations of the Bolsheviks sent there by the Germans, there had been a change in conditions which were likely to have serious consequences for the Allies. Rumania after a short life in the war on the Allied side had practically ceased to exist, thanks to the masterly tactics of Von Mackensen. In Von Below the High Command of Germany had placed its trust to dispose of Italy. With the release of troops from the Eastern Front there were great possibilities of this in addition to stiffening resistance at Passchendaele. Had Russia been able to survive for a few months longer than she did, the whole history of the war from 1916 onwards would have to be rewritten. There might have been a break through at Passchendaele instead of the war of attrition which went on there for five months. The Rumanians and the Italians would not have suffered the débacles which happened on their territories, nor would the German offensive of 1918 on the Western Front have been possible.

At the end of October German planes flew over the Italian lines on the Isonzo front and far over their back areas dropping millions of leaflets, which brought about a widespread "defeatist" spirit among the Italians. The Austrian Army, stiffened by several crack German corps, then suddenly made a terrific assault. The whole Italian front gave way. Within a fortnight 650,000 men were lost—300,000 killed, wounded and prisoner, and 350,000 scattered far and wide as fugitives and stragglers. Back across the Tagliamento their line sagged, and at last the remnants reached and managed to hold the line of the River Piave, 125 miles back but still covering Venice. Diaz, called to the supreme command in this emergency, proved a real rock, rallied his country and army, and so just saved the situation.

But the Caporetto disaster was a resounding blow at the whole Allied cause. The chief English and French statesmen hurried to Italy for a conference, at which it was decided to send a strong force of picked English and French troops to stiffen the Italian army, and this resolve was at once carried out. The Germans, having effected their purpose of forcing a large withdrawal of Allied troops from France and Flanders, soon withdrew their corps and handed over the new front to the Austrians.

We wish here to correct a widespread impression regarding Italy's effort in the War. Our own troops who went to that front too often base their low opinion of the "Macaronis" or "Ice-cream merchants," as we nicknamed them, on those they came across just when Italian morale was at its lowest. We must remember that the country in which the Italians operated was about the most difficult of any theatre of the World War—the Alps and the stony Carso plateau. To overlook the prelude to the tragic episode of Caporetto is even more ungenerous than to forget the victorious sequel at Vittorio Veneto in October, 1918. We do well to remind ourselves that the Italians had before Caporetto fought eleven Battles of the Isonzo, most of them offensives in which they showed the utmost heroism. It is no small tribute to the Italian fighting spirit that they should have rallied so quickly from such a crushing disaster, for we must emphasise the undoubted fact that they brought the enemy's advance to a standstill themselves before any Allied reinforcements entered the battle line.

It was decided that five divisions from the British Army on the Western Front should be sent with General Plumer to operate on the Italian front. Mr. Lloyd George says in his memoirs that five of the best divisions were selected for that purpose, the 5th, 7th, 23rd, 41st and 48th. The first two were Regular divisions who had distinguished themselves at Mons and Ypres, the 23rd was another Regular division with a great reputation, while the 48th was a division of Territorials with a great deal of service overseas. Thus it will be seen that on the 41st Division was conferred the honour of upholding the traditions of Kitchener's Army.

To return to the Battalion in billets at Coudekerque-Branche. The short period spent here was not a happy one; we were on the outskirts of Dunkirk, which the Germans were constantly shelling with "Long Max," a 15-inch naval gun at Leugenboom, 23 miles away, and also bombing by planes, so that things were even more unsettled than in the trenches.* Four more officers joined, 2nd Lieuts. R. McKechnie (from the 15th Hants), A. Bell, F. L. Warland and F. R. Barry. Lieut. McKechnie, who took over the position of Transport Officer from Lieut. Matthews, was a well-seasoned veteran. As Q.M.S. Speller has written: "He reeked of horses and horse lore all the time, and his Cape Dutch stood him in good stead with the few 'Belgiques' we met."

Lce.-Cpl. S. J. Nugent gives an account of the district we were in, and of the events leading up to the move to Italy:—

"For some time we had been stationed at Coudekerque, a suburb to the South of Dunkirk, where the companies were accommodated in several large buildings. Two were in a building with a stone floor which was exceedingly uncomfortable and cold. The M.O.s staff were billeted in what had been a wine store judging from the layout of the interior and the number of empty bottles which were in evidence.

*Besides being shelled by long-range guns, Dunkirk was bombed once by Zeppelins, seventy-seven times by planes and bombarded four times by warships.

"The district was not a pleasant one. During the day the enemy occasionally sent over a heavy shell from his line near Ostend, and during the night air raids were frequent, being in two or three relays on occasions. Warning of a raid was given by means of a raucous factory hooter near by. Sometimes the 'Take cover' would be sounded, and after the raid the 'All clear' signal would be given, only to be followed a few minutes later by the 'Take cover' again. This happened sometimes four or more times during the night.

"Route marches, which gradually increased in the distance covered, were frequent and gave rise to much speculation. What was the meaning of it? Some said we were off to Egypt, others Italy, but nobody in the ranks knew.

"One day after a great deal of cleaning equipment, etc., we were ordered to parade before the Divisional Commander, and then we guessed that something out of the ordinary was about to be disclosed. After the inspection the Divisional Commander gave a short address to all on parade and announced that the Battalion was shortly being sent to Italy. This was welcome news and explained the reason for all the route marching, as we were given to understand that on arrival in Italy a long march had to be undertaken."

The orders to proceed to the Italian Front were carried out on the 12th of November, when the Battalion entrained at Loon Plage. Two trains were allotted; the first occupied by A and C Companies, the Transport and part of H.Q. was under the Commanding Officer, assisted by R.S.M. Love, and the second, consisting of B and D Companies and the remainder of H.Q. under Major Williams, assisted by C.S.M. Horswell. The first train left at 1.0 p.m. and proceeded viâ Calais, Boulogne and Longeau; the second left at 5.0 p.m.

Capt. Hector Walker says that, when we entrained, neither he, as Adjutant, nor the Commanding Officer, had any idea of our final destination. He was in possession of various papers, warrants, etc., and had to see numerous officials *en route*

The first train arrived at Mesgrigney at 9.0 a.m. on the 13th and left at 10.0 a.m. On the 14th two halts were made during the day for meals; on the 15th the Riviera was passed, and on the 16th the train halted at Campomorone in Italy, where a cordial reception was given to the Battalion, sandwiches and cigarettes being given to the troops whilst the C.O. was presented with a bouquet!

So far the journey to Italy had been accomplished by the first train without mishap, but unfortunately this could not be said of the second train which followed some hours later, as 2nd Lieut. M. T. Johnson was accidentally killed, being electrocuted while the train was passing through a tunnel. It will be remembered that there were overhead wires on the railways, and it may have been that the members of the second train did not receive the same warning of the danger as those on the first. Capt. Walker recalls how going along the Riviera he had a compartment more or less to himself during the day, as the C.O. was seated on the driving seat of a G.S. waggon. On arrival at a certain station a British officer came rushing into his compartment in a terrible rage. It took some time for him to cool down, and he then went through Capt. Walker's papers again and again. He next asked for a certain paper which Capt. Walker informed him he had never received. It transpired that this referred to a definite instruction that nobody was allowed to put his head out of the train while in motion owing to the danger of electrocution in tunnels. Needless to say the Adjutant referred the excitable officer to the C.O. still enthroned on the G.S. waggon.

Let us have the experiences of two of the members of the Battalion.

Cpl. Southall says that he had just returned from leave when the news of the move was spread about. Even Ireland was suggested as a possible place for the next operations, but owing to the disaster at Caporetto, Italy was the most favoured. The medical staff laid in large stocks of bread, chocolate and cigarettes for the long journey, but these were all exhausted before it ended.

"It was a bleak morning in November with snow about and sleet in the air when the Battalion entrained," Southall continues. "The Doctor went on one train, and I was put in charge of the medical arrangements on the other. The medical staff had a real compartment to itself—not the usual horse-box—and on the pretext of his having a septic hand which would need constant fomentation I wangled Sergt. Perce Manning into our compartment.

"The first day or two of the trip was very cold and the carriage draughty, but we were nevertheless fairly comfortable. We skirted Paris but did not see much of the town, and gradually as we got further south the weather began to get warmer. We ambled along and stopped often. Sometimes a long stop would be announced, and everybody would jump off the train and run up to the engine driver for hot water from the boiler to make tea. Some would light fires at the side of the track for the same purpose and often would be interrupted at their tea-making when it was suddenly decided that the train would proceed instead of stopping. It was funny to see the fellows running for the train and climbing in as it was going. Not that there was any need to rush, as the speed of the train was so slow most of the time that it was quite easy to catch it. In fact I walked along the footboard of several compartments on one occasion when the train was in motion in order to attend to an officer who required some small attention in the way of dressing or medicine.

"As we approached the South of France the scenery became very delightful. At one spot the hills rose on our left hand in a series of terraces all under cultivation, whilst villas painted in pastel shades of cream, pale blue, pink and so on, nestled in amongst the trees. On our right was the sea—a beautiful deep blue—and above a cloudless sky from which the sun shone warmly. At San Remo, I believe it was, where we stopped a short time, oranges were picked and handed to us.

"We made a short stay at Marseilles and were entertained by four soldiers, who we understood were Serbians, and who stood on a waggon in the railway siding singing quartets. They all had fine voices, and I, at any rate, enjoyed the impromptu concert.

"We then passed through Genoa and began to get our first glimpses of Italy. The train passed through numerous vineyards, and the Italian girls who were picking the grapes gave us several bunches. Sergt. Manning held out one of the canvas horse-buckets which the Transport men used for carrying water to the horses and invited the girls to throw the grapes into it. One girl threw an enormous bunch with such good aim that it caught Manning in the neck, and as most of the grapes broke he got large quantities of juice running down inside his collar. We were amused, but I hardly think he was."

Nugent states that two blankets were issued to each man on entraining and that some managed to obtain by devious means various utensils such as buckets and also a supply of coal or coke to provide the wherewithal for a fire.

"It was not unusual," he goes on, "when looking to the front or rear of the train to see several braziers being swung round to produce a clear glow, as the smoke in the trucks was very trying.

"For the first few nights sleep was not deep owing to the movement of the train over the rail joints, which not only produced much noise but caused soreness at the hip through the continuous jolting. We soon got used to this, and instead of lying awake when the train was moving found ourselves waking up when the train stopped, the noise acting as a lullaby. As we progressed further south, stops were numerous owing to the fact that we had to be shunted off the main line now and then, and at some wayside places waits were experienced of anything from 30 minutes to an hour. This led to some amusing experiences when certain of the troops would alight to stretch their legs and have a look round. Without warning the train would start, and then followed a frantic rush to get on board. A story was told of two men who on one occasion strayed so far from the train during a halt that the train was away before they could reach it, but plodding along the permanent way they managed to get on board a few miles further on where the train came to rest.

"In the beautiful Rhone valley the scenery was finer than ever before experienced; vineyards arranged in tiers on both sides of the river and luxurious vegetation abounded all around. It was noticeably warmer here, and this, combined with the winter clothing we were wearing, tempted many to discard outer garments. Travelling through the night we missed many of the larger towns like Lyons and Avignon, but one morning we arrived and stopped in the station at Cannes. This was the signal for a general exodus. Some turned out in shirt sleeves, the weather being really hot. Some of the men conversed with a number of English people who were apparently staying there on holiday. After a short halt here we proceeded along the edge of the coast to Nice.

"We viewed the Principality of Monaco, with Monte Carlo; the sea was a beautiful tint matching the cloudless sky. The frontier was passed at Vintimiglia. A short stop was made at a place where Italian ladies distributed ripe figs and other fruit from baskets. Sufficient to say that these were very welcome, and although only one man, Pte. Jonescu (a Rumanian) of C Company, was able to speak Italian, I am sure the donors appreciated our thanks given in English. At another station, San Pier d'Arena, picture postcards depicting panoramic views of Italian scenery were distributed by Italian ladies on behalf of the 'Società di M.S. Opera, Addetti alla Società Anonima Fonderia di Cogoleto.' These were gratefully received and after being hastily completed by the troops were handed back and, as events subsequently transpired, were posted on the 17th of November and duly delivered to the addressees. The reverse side of these postcards bore the inscription 'To the valiant English brothers our welcome—Ansaldo's Direction and Staff—San Pier d'Arena, Novembre, 1917.' The train stopped at Turin and Milan for a few minutes. Later the Alps were observed in the distance, the air being wonderfully clear.

"At last Mantova, or Mantua, where the mantle originated, was reached, and here we detrained, thankful to be on *terra firma* again. Here the troops strolled about, interested in the unfamiliar surroundings. Much comment was made on the dress of the Italian men, who mostly wore large sombrero hats with wide brims and had large capes or mantles flung about their shoulders. The womenfolk wore brightly coloured attire, some with gaily coloured handkerchiefs on their heads.

"At last the 'Fall in' sounded, and we marched off through what must have been the main street. Tram-cars displayed the Italian flag and the Union Jack side by side, whilst large posters were exhibited bearing the words 'Viva l'Inghilterra' and 'Welcome to the British.' "

The accounts of the first part of the journey by Southall and Nugent can be taken as an accurate description of the reception given to us by the Italians. However they appear to omit the war cry of the troops, "Oh! oh! Antonio," and the story of his ice-cream cart which used to be a popular music-hall song in England before the war. Many of the men apparently expected to find ice-cream carts and baked potato and chestnut vendors as seen in England. In this they were disappointed. The Italian Bersagliere with the lovely plumes in his hat at the frontier station at Vintimiglia was also an object of curiosity. There was some crowing aboard the trains when these soldiers were referred to as the "roosters." Trust the 12th to have their little joke, but the Italian took it smilingly.

As we were going into another foreign country in which a knowledge of the language would be of the utmost assistance to him, one of our men took it into his head to do some swotting on the train. With what result let him tell us in his own way.

"The method in which a man of the 12th achieved a 'bubble reputation' is worth recording. On the long rail journey from Loon Plage to Genoa, I busied myself with an Italian—English Dictionary and managed to master the equivalents for water, food, etc. At Genoa, the Colonel alighted and exchanged salutes and felicitations with numerous and gorgeously attired uniformed station staff whilst I approached a lesser light and made this phonetic noise: 'Quala la via per Verona, Signor?' To my gratification the apparent Admiral-cum-General replied with a sweeping bow and a 'Là, Signor,' as he pointed to a road running north-east. Colonel Stallard called me over and asked if I spoke Italian. I modestly and truthfully replied, 'A little, Sir!' but I did not tell him that I had just exercised the whole of my vocabulary!"

CHAPTER XI.

18th November, 1917, to 5th March, 1918.

The Battalion in Italy—Arduous march from Mantova to the Montello—Three months there holding the line—Return to France.

THE region in which the "Shiny Twelfth" arrived, and across which the Division was to make its notable march was historic ground, though probably few were aware of this at the time. At Goito the Piedmontese beat the Austrians in 1848 in the short campaign that ended in their fatal defeat at Custozza a few miles to the North. The whole of this part of the Lombard plain is a "cockpit of war." Mantua, Peschiera, Verona, Castiglione, Solferino are all within a 25-mile radius.

The first train reached Mantua at 1.0 p.m. on the 17th of November, and the second at 2.0. A and C Companies proceeded by train to Guidizzolo where billets were allotted, whilst B and D Companies marched to Goito, where they were billeted for the night. The strength of the Battalion was 42 officers and 876 other ranks.

A and C Companies rested during the 18th at Guidizzolo and were joined later by the other two companies who had left Goito at 10.0 a.m. to march there. From Guidizzolo on the 19th a march was made viâ Marengo* to Malavicina, where billets were taken for the night.

Continuing on the 20th in very cold weather through Trevenzuolo, we reached Isola Della Scala. A day's rest was spent here on the following day, and rifle and kit inspections were carried out. Billeting parties, including Pte. Jonescu, met 2nd Lieut. W. S. Hall (now our Signalling Officer) with cycles on the morning of the 21st, and the Battalion paraded at 7.30 and marched through Oppeano to Albaredo on the swiftly flowing River Adige. The march was continued on the 22nd to Presina, passing through Bagnolo (close to Bonaparte's battlefield of Arcola) and Lonigo. Hitherto the country had been dull and flat. Now it became more hilly, and to the North mountains loomed up.

On the 23rd the Division was instructed to march in two columns, the 124th Brigade being the right or East column, the 122nd the left or West column, followed by the 123rd. An advance guard for the left column consisting of the 18th K.R.R.s, one section of the 122nd M.G.C., one battery from the 187th Brigade R.F.A. and the 228th Field Co. R.E. under the command of Lieut.-Col. R. Pennell, D.S.O., preceded the main body which consisted of the 12th East Surreys, the 11th R.W. Kents, the 15th Hants, the 122nd M.G.C. (less one section), the 122nd T.M.B., 199th M.G.C., No. 2 Company of the 41st Divisional Train and the 187th Brigade R.F.A. (less one battery). During the night of the 23rd/24th outposts were established on the line San

*Not the Marengo where Bonaparte's great battle was fought in 1800.

Gottardo to Valla (just N.W. of Brendola). The 12th had to find the outposts on the line stated above, an approximate distance of four kilometres. The remainder of the Battalion had to march to Vo, where Battalion H.Q. were to be established.

The route was now across the range of hills South of Vicenza, rising to about 1,000 feet, called the Monti Berici, lovely in spring or summer, as all travellers on the main railway line to Venice know well, but at this period of the year bleak and forbidding in the early mornings or evenings. It was intensely cold, and a drizzling mist hung over everything except during the midday hours, when the sun was very hot. The going was bad, and the troops suffered considerably. On the following day we marched to Longara, just South of Vicenza, where another rest was taken.

The 25th saw the Battalion again on the road, this time for Pieve, a distance of about 28 kilometres being covered.

A good rest came at last, for on the 26th and 27th of November the Battalion remained at Pieve, and (better still) baths were allotted on both days. On the 28th a further move was made to Casacorba; on the 29th viâ Trevignano to San Luca and on the 30th viâ Selva to Giavera, where this historic march of nearly 150 miles in a fortnight ended.

There had been only one casualty during the month, but on the 25th we lost the services of Dr. Harrison who was forced to go to hospital with a septic finger. He eventually reached England, and thus we lost one who besides being brave and fearless had a very lively sense of humour. A good successor was found in the person of Capt. G. W. Christie, R.A.M.C.

Lieut. E. H. Barry, who had recently joined us, left to take up a Commission in the Indian Army.

Speaking of the march from Mantua, Cpl. Southall writes:—

"We finally detrained at Mantua, and I saw my first snow-capped mountain looming up in the distance. From here we marched to the line, the journey taking us about a fortnight. Most of the country was flat and uninteresting for the first few days, and the marches were made longer by the fact that a lot of the Italian roads were made in a series of right angles skirting the edges of square fields. Our food was not very varied, consisting mainly of bully, biscuits, jam and occasionally cheese. We tried to buy bread at various villages, but, as the bakers' shops were only too pleased to make a quick sale to the British troops, the result was a shortage of bread for the inhabitants, and an order was issued forbidding us to buy it.

"Dr. Harrison, who had rejoined us with the rest of the Battalion, was suffering from a bad septic finger. It was extremely painful and needing constant fomenting, which unfortunately could not be done, as our days were occupied with marching. He had picked up a little dog which he had named 'Rags' coming down on the train. He saw the dog running along the track, got out of the train whilst it was in motion, picked up the dog and climbed in again. 'Rags' either rode on top of the Maltese Cart or on the doctor's horse in front of him; he was a friendly little fellow. The doctor's finger got worse, and I remember one night on our arrival in billets endeavouring to obtain some boiling water from the lady of the house where the M.O. was billeted. The lady had no English, and we didn't know the Italian for boiling water. The local priest who was in the house was called in to assist but without success. I thought he certainly must have a knowledge of French, so I tried my poor efforts at French on him, but without success. Finally, by means of signs we managed to get what we wanted.

"The next night the doctor could bear the pain of his finger no longer, and he asked Lce.-Cpl. Aitken (who was in charge of the stretcher-bearers) to make an incision. Aitken was afraid of hurting the doctor, I think, so I was asked to do it instead. The finger got no better, and finally the doctor left us and was sent home sick. He wrote and told me that the finger had remained stiff after it had healed up, and I have often wondered whether I cut a tendon or did some other damage when I lanced it.

"I remember particularly one day of our march. We started very early after having been up most of the night before caring for the feet of the Battalion. We had an enormous sick parade, practically all sore feet cases, and we were dealing with them until nearly midnight. It was a misty morning and bitterly cold when we started off. We had to pass through the hills, and it was a tremendous job getting the transport up the slippery road. Our cart was almost the last in the transport line, and I waited with it for some time. Finally Dr. Harrison suggested that we should walk on alone, which we did. Some way up the hill we came to a farmhouse from which came the delicious smell of newly-baked bread. We could not resist the temptation and went in and bought several loaves. A little further on we came across some of the Battalion resting by the roadside, and most of our loaves were distributed amongst them; unfortunately the loaves didn't go far among so many.

"We reached the highest point of the road, and a magnificent view met our gaze. On our left the hills towered up above, and down below, where the base of the hills formed a kind of bowl, the mist, which had dispersed from around us, still floated up and down, while the sun shining on it caused it to reflect the most lovely colours. Far away on our right stretched a wide plain crossed by various rivers and dotted with little villages, each with its church and campanile painted in blue, pink or cream, and the smaller houses in a variety of colours, while directly in front of us was the road winding away into the plain like a snake. We sat on a wall by the side of the road and had a meal and enjoyed the view. It was here that I first heard the news of General Byng's attack on the Boche at Cambrai.

"Some time after our arrival in the village where we were to stay for the night Read came in with the Maltese cart and told us of a very narrow escape he had had coming down the hill. Apparently a collision had occurred between the Maltese cart and the cooker in front. Read had been thrown off the cart under the horse, and the cart had toppled over the edge of the road and would have gone hurtling down the hillside but for the fact that a tree a short way below the road managed to stop the fall. Read had rather a bad cut over the eye, which however soon healed.

"One other impression which remains with me is the crossing of a river by a bridge built on pontoons and arriving in a little village at the other side. After settling down and getting cleaned up a bit we went for a short stroll, and turning to go down one street saw a glorious sight. It looked as though a tremendous hill which was outside the village actually blocked the end of the road. The sun had just sunk behind the ridge of the hill leaving the side nearest us in almost complete darkness while the ridge was silhouetted against a background of fiery redness. It was most impressive.

"At one place in the early stages of our march—I think it was just before entering Isola della Scala—I was marching along by myself some distance behind the Battalion, having stopped to dress the feet of some of the fellows who had fallen by the wayside, when I passed the Prince of Wales with another Staff Officer. I heard that he had given some sandwiches to some of our boys.*

"I believe it was at this place where we had a day's rest* that a concert was given in the evening, at which our band played the Italian National Anthem amidst great enthusiasm, some of the Italian soldiers and civilians who were present getting wildly excited and standing on chairs waving their handkerchiefs and cheering wildly.

*At least one member of the Battalion vouches for this. He had fallen out, and was approached by a Staff Officer who enquired of him the reason he had done so. The man told the officer that he had started off on the march with a little bit of 'bourgoo' (porridge) and had no stomach to march on. The officer promptly took some sandwiches from his haversack, handed them to the man and then departed. After he had left, another Staff Officer approached and asked our man if he knew to whom he had been talking. The man replied that he did not. When he was informed that it was none other than the heir to the British Throne, he exclaimed, 'If I had known that sir, I would have kept the sandwiches as a souvenir!'

*It was the day after the incident of the sandwiches that the Battalion rested, and it was generally assumed that the Prince of Wales had interceded with the Higher Authorities, although Sergt. L. C. Lunn thinks it was according to plan.

"I was very sad at heart when Dr. Harrison left us. He was always such a cheery companion, and, while he looked on me as a 'weird chap,' he was extremely kind to me and did a lot towards making life bearable in those days. About midday on the day after he left our new M.O. Dr. Christie joined us.

"I recollect one amusing incident in connection with Dr. Christie. We were on the march one day and stopped for a short time at a little village where the doctor hoped to get some bread. There were some Italian soldiers about, and the doctor addressed to one of them the Italian word for bread, which I believe is 'pane.' His pronunciation must have been a little incorrect, because the Italian soldier appeared to be a little nonplussed at first. However, he subsequently understood what the doctor meant, and after repeating the word with a slightly different accent said to the doctor, 'Oh, you mean bread. If you turn to the left at the corner you will find a baker's shop on the right-hand side where you can get some bread.' 'How do you come to speak English?' asked the M.O. 'I was in America for several years,' replied the Italian.

"The end of the long march came at a little village named Giavera. The last day was a painful one for me as I had a very sore toe, which I found on reaching billets had turned septic."

In recalling the march Capt. Hector Walker says that our mail and rations went astray. The Authorities, not knowing what was in our mail van, detained it at the frontier, while the ration difficulty was overcome by the issue of Italian rations consisting of a small flask of wine, some salad oil, a cupful of flour and other things which called for some caustic remarks from the troops. Our Canteen also disappeared, and Capt. Walker had to get permission of the C.O. to go shopping in Padua, where, finding a brewery with good beer he bought £30 worth, only to find that he had to pay another £30 on the casks. The trouble did not end here, as, the sellers not liking the look of a cheque on Cox's, he gave them one on the Westminster Bank, which they trustingly accepted, despite the fact that they did not know him. The beer was sold at a price which refunded Capt. Walker all his outlay, and the casks supplied funds for further purchases. A large crate containing ten gross of eggs was also purchased, and the eggs and the beer arrived safely at our billets on a G.S. Waggon.

At last we were within range of the guns, for, as Cpl. Nugent has written, "situated less than 200 yards from our billets in Giavera, they fired at intervals during the night."

On the 1st of December the Battalion marched to the Montello Range area and took over reserve lines from an Italian regiment. The approach to the positions was up steep roads which were numbered to ensure that we took the right one. It took three hours from the time we arrived to complete the relief, and we then found that we were in reserve to the 11th R.W. Kents, who were holding the right front line sector of the left brigade.

The positions now taken over by the 41st Division were on the River Piave, to which the Italian armies had retreated after the Twelfth Battle of the Isonzo. From the 2nd to the 8th the Battalion was employed in making dugouts and erecting bivouacs. Contrary to what we had been used to in reserve, there was no real necessity to have the same kind of fortifications and shelters as on the Western Front. In fact whole houses still existed, and there were many dips in the ground where "bivvies" could be erected to afford comfortable shelter. A river separated us from the enemy and behind him were snow-clad mountains.

The Montello is a hilly mass rising in parts to an extreme height of about 1,000 feet, some eight miles long and three wide. Its Northern and Eastern faces front the Piave, which at this time was a shallow ice-cold stream of many channels, some half a mile wide, though, when the snows of the Carnic Alps melt in spring and early summer, it can become a wide mass of foaming water, like all the rivers of Northern Italy. The escarpment facing the river is extremely steep, in places sheer cliff. From the top an amazing view is obtained over the Venetian plain to the right. To the front are hills, among which at some 15 miles distance is the little town of Vittorio Veneto, which gives its name to the final great victory of the Italian Armies in the autumn of 1918. To the left are the masses of the Carnic Alps, rising range upon range, many peaks exceeding 3,000 feet.

Few trenches could be dug owing to the rocky nature of the ground, and positions had to be held by isolated posts of a few men. Movement by daylight in the front posts was impossible, for the slightest motion could be seen by the enemy in that clear air, and his artillery was active and accurate.

Only a few miles east of the Montello is the little town of Asolo, which gives its name to the last volume of Robert Browning's poems, Asolando. It is worth mentioning, for almost the last lines he wrote are the famous ones on himself, which might well have been a motto for every Englishman in those dark days:—

"One who never turned his back but marched breast forward,
Never doubted clouds would break,
Never dreamt, though right were worsted, wrong would triumph,
Held we fall to rise, are baffled to fight better,
Sleep to wake."

Did any of the Twelfth recall those inspiring words, we wonder?

Let us have recourse to Cpl. Southall's notes of our arrival in the sector:—

"In the evening we marched up the hills and landed finally in a small house. It was very cold, and I remember having a slice of cold Christmas pudding issued to us. We finally moved to another small house with a wood behind sloping down the hill. We were well under observation from the enemy lines, and it wasn't wise to walk about too much in daylight nor to make fires which would give away our position by the smoke. During the daytime therefore we had a job to keep warm, and we got a little exercise by going out into the wood and chopping the logs for the fire we intended to have at night. A short distance away was a dugout where the doctor slept at night.

"We explored a bit and in an outhouse found a large butt of wine* and upstairs in the house a large bed in which we decided to sleep at night. The first night of our stay in the house we lit an enormous fire on the big brick fireplace, heated up some wine* and water into which we put sugar and settled down to a comfortable evening. We then went upstairs to bed, but had only just got in when the enemy put about ten whizzbangs round the house. We were down the stairs, and down the hill to the doctor's dugout like lightning, myself with only one boot on; a sore toe making it difficult for me to wear the other boot. We crept into the dugout, where the doctor was sleeping peacefully, and stayed there a few minutes. Then, as the evening hate appeared to be over, we went back to our house and slept the rest of the night and every subsequent evening on the floor in front of the fire. In the morning the doctor came over and asked us where we slept. We told him. He said: 'I shouldn't sleep there if I were you. I've just been to the house over there (pointing towards the line) and a shell was put through the wall last night and landed just about where you

*Capt. H. S. Walker states that many of the houses we lived in on the Montello had large butts of wine in them, the butts being built into the house so that they could not be removed without taking down a wall at least.

*The Italian soldiers were issued with "Vino" much the same as the British were issued with rum, except that the Italians always had large stocks in the line, and apparently consumed a good deal of it. The wine was of a very cheap variety and had a devastating effect on the Englishman, even if taken in small quantities. To the troops it was known as "Dragon's blood," and after its purgative effect became known, the drinking of it was strongly discouraged by the Higher Authorities, whilst the men themselves soon took a strong dislike to it.

fellows would have been sleeping.' We thanked him for his cheering news and continued to sleep in the same spot. We might just as well have used the bed as we were never disturbed again."

A bit of excitement was caused on December 8th when an Italian airman brought down an enemy machine in our vicinity. The Medical staff was startled to hear the roar of an aeroplane flying very low over their house, and rushing out Cpl. Southall saw an enemy plane about to come down. It crashed a short way off, and soon afterwards the pilot was brought to our Aid Post on a stretcher. The airman, who gave the name of Lieut. Berthes Meyer of Hanover, had been shot in the eye by a bullet, and was attended to by our M.O. He was of German nationality and was very surprised to find English troops holding the line. By papers found on him it was presumed that he had lately been on the Russian Front. His machine, a single-seater Albatross with two machine-guns, was numbered D.5384/17. Lieut. Mutch still retains a piece of fabric of the plane which shows the trade mark of the designers, while Cpl. Southall recently tried to trace the airman in Hanover to hand him back his cigarette-case which is still in the possession of one of our stretcher-bearers. Unfortunately the Authorities cannot trace him.

It was now our turn to occupy the front line, and so in the evening of the 8th we proceeded to relieve the 11th R.W. Kents in the right sector of the Divisional front, the relief not being completed until 12.30 a.m. The front was held by A, B and C Companies; D Company being in support and supplying road patrols and guards. The enemy artillery was active on the 9th, several 15-inch shells being distributed over our front, Battalion H.Q. receiving special attention. The enemy planes were also active.

On the 10th Battalion H.Q. again came in for some strafing. It was a frosty day with good visibility. Our artillery registered on several houses at Falze di Piave and also carried out several shoots on Collato, a village in the enemy lines to the right of our front. Civilian movement had been very marked in villages well to the front of the Austrian lines.

The enemy artillery and aircraft were active throughout the morning and afternoon of the 11th, some planes flying low, only about 300 feet above our positions.

The 12th was more lively, for during the morning there was a heavy bombardment of our lines, in which the enemy sent over about 1,500 shells, including shrapnel, H.E. and several 15-inch. A Company suffered the loss of Ptes. J. W. Chaplin and L. Menzie (Manszi), who were killed, and 7 other ranks who were wounded. B Company had 2 men wounded. Pte. Lorinco Manszi, although a Londoner by birth, appears to have come of Italian stock, and it was the fortune of war that he should be our first fatal casualty in defence of the land of his forefathers. Unfortunately details are lacking of some brave acts which were performed by some of our men during this bombardment, but later on the award of the Military Medal to Lce.-Cpls. T. Long and G. Ponman and Pte. G. Harbridge was announced.

Great difficulty was experienced by the ration carriers owing to the steep incline of the cliffs, for the majority of our posts were situated on the face of the escarpment which ran along the entire front. This state of affairs was gradually overcome by the ingenuity of the men themselves. They made toboggans from sheets of corrugated iron, and sticks out of branches of trees were used as alpen-stocks. It was only by these means that men were really able to get up and down the steep slope.

It was now notified that Pte. A. Spicer, who had previously been reported missing, had died on August 19th, 1917, as a prisoner of war at Feldlaz, Wervelghem. The following were also reported as having been mentioned in despatches:—2nd Lieuts. R. N. Haine, W. S. Hall and F. R. Matthews; R.Q.M.S. N. Speller, C.S.M. C. J. Love, Sergt. L. C. Lunn (Brigade Office), Lce.-Sergt. F. I. Osborn and Cpl. A. Durrant.

Although the enemy artillery was quiet throughout the 13th, aircraft activity was above the normal. It was observed on this day that civilians in several of the villages behind the enemy front appeared to be moving away, as many waggons full of furniture had been noticed on the roads travelling north. This was probably due to the increased activity of our own guns during the last few days.

During the night of the 15th the enemy guns were active. We were also troubled with two searchlights, which for several nights previously had played on our roads during the night. The snow having melted, the ground became muddy and more difficult to negotiate. Thanks to a sharp frost things were a little better on the following day.

In the evening of the 16th the 11th R.W. Kents again took over, and, relief being completed by 1.30 a.m., we marched back to Giavera South in a slight snow-storm.

The usual billets were allotted at Giavera, such as barns, etc., and conditions at rest were similar to those prevailing on the Western Front (baths—occasional—and working parties—frequent).

It would not be out of place here to mention what these working parties entailed. First of all there was the march to the place where the work had to be done. The roads to the line, 16 in number, were numbered from one upwards; they were in the main very steep and winding and not very wide. The transport used these roads or "stradas" as well as the troops, and so progress was usually slow. (The Italians had an overhead cable system or wireway for conveying rations and supplies along these roads and across valleys.) After the weary tramp, often in the snow, the positions would be reached, and with pick and shovel men would endeavour to excavate through rock and chalk. There would be very little to show for a night's work; the only way to make progress was to use some blasting powder. There would then follow the trek back to billets which more often than not occupied hours; pea soup was never so much enjoyed by the men as after one of these nocturnal visits to the line.

By a Brigade Order the 21st was granted as a general holiday to the Battalion, and a special dinner was provided for the men by Colonel Stallard.

On the night of the 24th/25th December, the Battalion moved off viâ "Pall Mall" to the cross roads on Road No. 3, and with a distance of 200 yards between platoons proceeded to relieve the 18th K.R.R.s on the left front sector of the right Brigade on the Montello Range.

The men in the front line posts were employed in repairing the wire which stretched in front of them. There was an island too which had to be held. This consisted of a series of rifle and Lewis-gun posts, fifteen in all, but the occupation of it was soon given up as useless. Above the cliffs which stretched behind the island was a line of resistance which was only to be garrisoned in case of invasion.

So here we were, spending our second Christmas on active service in front of the Austrians and Germans on the opposite side of the River Piave. During the night music floated over from the enemy positions. Some say that a band was heard, but most agree that the enemy sang carols and other songs. Singing on the Italian front was not an unheard of thing, for had we not often listened to the Italians serenading us while things were quiet? However, the official Christmas of the Battalion was to come later on.

Boxing Day saw between 30 and 40 planes of the enemy fly over and bomb our back areas. It was a wonderful sight to see these planes flying low, and those of us who witnessed their antics were of the opinion that the airman had been dining well but not too wisely. But it was fatal for 14 of them, when they were sent hurtling to the earth by the sober methods of our gunners and airmen.

During the rest of the month the Battalion was engaged in draining and strengthening the defences. There is a note in the Diary on the 30th that the R.E.s superintending the work praised the Battalion on its efforts in this direction.

There were two casualties as the result of shell-fire on the 30th, which made the total casualties for the month 2 other ranks killed and 15 wounded. Two new officers, Lieut. W. P. Selbie and 2nd Lieut. A. J. Rodd, joined on the 26th and a draft of 87 other ranks reached us on the 14th.

At the end of December we were relieved by the 15th Hants and went into support to the two front line battalions. So ended another year of the war, and we seemed further from final victory than a year before.

From the 1st to the 5th of January, 1918, the Battalion was employed on making and improving dugouts to replace bivouacs which were being found inadequate shelter against the enemy guns. The dugouts were excavated into the slopes of dells which abounded here. Battalion H.Q. was heavily shelled on the 5th together with villages two or three kilos behind our positions. In retaliation for shelling Nervesa our artillery shelled Susegana.

Capt. J. A. C. McCalman was sent to England sick on the 6th. He was a good deal older than most, and was never fit for the most active duties. On the 8th Lieut. E. B. Gillett assumed command of B Company in place of Capt. A. R. K. Edsell, and 2nd Lieut. A. J. Rodd assumed the duties of Acting Quartermaster. Pte. H. Green died as the result of an illness on this date.

Three or four inches of snow fell during the night of the 9th and greatly delayed the Transport, which had a steep incline to negotiate before reaching the Battalion. This sort of thing prevailed for most of the time while we were in Italy. When a frost set in, it was most difficult for marching and also for the horses.

The 20th D.L.I., our old opposite number of the St. Eloi days, came to relieve us on the 10th. After relief we marched a considerable distance to Volpago, where we took over houses which had recently been evacuated by the civilian population. The houses were found to be exceedingly good as rest billets and appeared to have been subjected to very little shelling. Part of the village was occupied by Italian soldiers, and a few civilians still remained.

Divine Service was held on the 13th, and later General Towsey inspected the billets and afterwards presented medal ribbons to Capt. J. A. Rogers (Military Cross), and Lce.-Cpls. G. Ponman and T. Long, and Pte. E. Harbridge (Military Medal).

We enjoyed our postponed Christmas dinner on the 15th of January, when, with the assistance of the Mayor and the kind people of Bermondsey, an excellent repast was provided.

The Battalion was now about to be relieved from the sector, so we will deal with some of the incidents, not of course recorded in the official Diary, which happened during the period.

Cpl. Southall again comes to our assistance, and his experiences are typical of many.

"After a short time in the line we returned to billets in a small village. It was bitterly cold and there was a shortage of fuel, many schemes being considered to overcome the difficulty of obtaining it. When we arrived in the village, we noticed lying alongside the road opposite the medical hut, a huge pile of saplings which had been stacked there by the Italians for their on use. The following morning it had disappeared, and there is no doubt that various sections of the Battalion were well set up for wood for burning for a few days. The Italians lodged a complaint, but it did not result in their getting their wood back. We of the medical staff weren't fast enough workers to share in the spoils and were cold, so Giles said he would go out and scrounge some wood. After being away some time he returned, and we were surprised and amused to see him stagger in carrying a huge window shutter, almost as big as himself. 'Where did you get that?' we asked when we had stopped laughing. 'Well,' said Giles, 'I walked all through the village without seeing any wood and at last I passed a house with two window shutters hanging at the side of the window, so I just unhooked one and brought it home. It was a bit of a job getting it off without being spotted because there was one of our guards walking up and down past the house.' Nobody would have recognised the shutter as a shutter a few minutes afterwards.

"A great event here was the opening of the canteen. As we had been very short of cigarettes, etc., since we came to Italy the canteen was sold out in about 15 minutes. The shortage of cigarettes was one of the drawbacks of our Italian experiences. I remember while we were in the line the M.O. having a few sent to him. He shared them out amongst the various officers, keeping very few for himself, and came down to our little hut with two which he broke in half and handed us a half each. We really appreciated his kind thought, and we gave more value to this little gift than in more prosperous times we should have done to a box of 100 'gaspers.'*

"To make some sort of Christmas celebration the officers of A Company considered that an effort should be made to give the company a slight change of diet. So one of them set off with a N.C.O. on Christmas Eve to see what could be obtained. They bought a calf, thinking no doubt that a little tender veal would be delicious. The calf was killed, transported back to billets and duly cooked the next day. It was as tough as old boots owing to its being cooked too soon after being killed!

"We were soon back in the line again, and this time we had a dugout at the bottom of one of the deep cone-shaped depressions which abounded in this part. It was a very snug spot practically immune from shell-fire except from high trajectory missiles from a howitzer or some similar weapon. We got very lazy here and used to sleep till 11 or 12 o'clock. Casualties were very rare, and we had little to do.

"We found some maize flour* while we were here, and the doctor made a huge cake of polenta, a kind of heavy bread of a pudding-like consistency, of which we offered slices to the sick when they came down. As the majority of them were suffering from disorders of the stomach, there weren't many takers.†

*This shortage was felt throughout the Battalion. Some of the men are said to have followed one of our officers who was smoking a cigarette to try to get the end when he had finished with it. Unfortunately the officer used a pin to enable him to smoke it to the bitter end. Padre Williams also found some cigarettes which were greatly appreciated by those to whom he gave them. Many of the men used brown paper and dried leaves as a substitute for their favourite weed.

"It used to be great fun going out to obtain water. The springs were usually at the bottom of a steep incline and these slopes were often frozen and tremendously slippery, so that it was always a toss up whether one arrived at the top with the water or without it.

"After a time we moved further over to the left of the line, and our new Aid Post was in a stone-built shed on the side of a hill in full view of the enemy. Behind the shed to the top of the hill was a wood, and in daylight it was considered inadvisable to move from the post unless one went out of the door into the wood and used the trees as shelter. Snow had fallen and the air was wonderfully clear, so that in the open the slightest movement was visible to the enemy. Headquarters and the companies were in trenches and dugouts some distance to our left, and, as we were drawing our rations from H.Q., it meant a long trek every morning before we obtained our breakfast. Owing to the cold weather we usually woke half frozen and to get our blood circulating we used to run the whole way to H.Q. It was an exhilarating atmosphere, and one felt very fit.

"One day somebody found a spare bit of corrugated iron, turned up one end of it and was soon using it as a toboggan. If we managed to strike the path over the ditch at the bottom of the hill, everything was plain sailing, but otherwise we went into the ditch among the acacia thorns and not seldom with the corrugated iron on top of us. It was a damp journey too, as owing to the snowballs thrown at us by the spectators on the journey down the hill we were soon sitting in a pool of water. The fun was finally stopped just about lunch time by a salvo of whizzbangs from the enemy. Fortunately nobody was hurt, but all were a bit mad at having their innocent fun ruined.

"One afternoon the doctor came to tell us that there would be a raid across the Piave‡ that night and that as things were likely to be pretty hot, it would be as well if we went down to the trench when the time came for the show to start. After the doctor had gone, we decided that, as we were more comfortable where we were, we would stay in our little hut, unless we got shelled out. Zero hour arrived and with it a deathly silence. No guns roared and still we waited. We kept on waiting, and long after the time of the start of the raid the doctor came in and asked us how long we had been back. We explained that we hadn't gone and asked him when the raid was to start or had it been postponed? He said that at the last moment it was decided to make it a silent raid and that it was all over. We heard various stories about this raid subsequently; how the troops were taken across in pontoons and how silent they were, dropping shovels and rifles in the bottom of the boat, while somebody would shout out, 'I'll go pontoon!' We were told that very little opposition was encountered and that Major Lauder and Capt. Fergusson of the R.A.M.C. went for a long walk in the enemy country. It was also mentioned that one prisoner met with an untimely end by drowning on the way back, although whether by accident or design was not stated.

"We left for Volpago shortly afterwards. Here we found some welcome parcels, in which were hundreds of cigarettes, whilst we had a great feast in the schoolroom. Many comforts were sent out by the good people of Bermondsey to enable us to celebrate Christmas."

The Battalion was relieved by the 2nd "Queen's" Royal West Surreys on the 16th of January, and, concentrating on the Selva-Volpago Road, marched to Altivole where billets were taken for the night. The march was continued on the following day to Loria where a course of training was to be undergone, and the new billets were found to be very comfortable and clean.

*This was usually made into a pudding by the local inhabitants and sold to the troops as "Polenta," and was invariably well covered with marmalade or jam by the men before they consumed it. A more indigestible dish we never tasted, but it served the purpose of alleviating the pangs of hunger.

†There were many cases of dysentery and kindred ailments owing to dry vegetables and certain Italian rations, not to mention "Dragon's blood," which did not agree with the men.

‡The 23rd Middlesex made a raid across the Piave on January 1st, 1918. They took four prisoners of the 25th Schutzen Regt., one of whom was drowned during the passage of the river, which, at the point they crossed, was 2½ to 3 feet deep with a very strong current. Seven of the Middlesex were wounded.

For the remainder of the month we carried out training in the mornings and indulged in football, boxing, running and other sports in the afternoons. Training consisted of squad and platoon drill, bayonet fighting, gas drill, musketry, demonstrations of telling off a platoon (not to be confused with scolding), instruction on bugle calls, extended order drill, outpost drill, battalion drill, bombing and advance and rear guard drill. In addition an officers' riding class was held each morning at 8.0 a.m. In other words it was "Blighty" soldiering all over again. Well might the note in the Diary for this period be, "A marked improvement has been noticed in the drill and general turnout of the Battalion." On the 29th the Brigadier came to inspect us and afterwards sent the following letter:—

"The turnout of the 12th East Surrey Regt. at my inspection this morning was excellent, and, under the conditions we live in, I know that a great deal of trouble must have been taken to obtain such a good result. I have seldom seen better packed valises and the boots were in good order. The Battalion moved and handled its arms well. The transport was most satisfactory."

On the 31st the following letter was also received from the Brigade Office:—

"The G.O.C. wishes me to say how pleased he was with Cpl. Greenslade and his six men who have been on guard over Brigade Headquarters during the past week. They performed their duties in a way which was a credit both to their Battalion and Brigade."

The above testimonials from the Brigade give a good insight into the conditions prevailing at the time. It must be remembered that the Twelfth had always a good sprinkling of Regular instructors in its ranks, and, when "peace time" soldiering came about—as it did in Italy—the Battalion could be depended upon to hold its own. We could now boast of two good bands, the brass, in charge of Sergt. Crabtree, and the drum and fife, under Sergt. Levett. The brass band was composed of many good musicians from other battalions of the East Surreys, besides other units; the drum and fife contained many of the old members of the Battalion. It had a varied life and after many vicissitudes had been resuscitated. The brass band was welcomed by us all, because it was able to provide concerts with all the latest tunes from "Blighty," besides classical music and excerpts from operas. With its stirring march tunes the journeys along the road were made lighter. "Marching through Georgia" and the French "Sambre et Meuse," which the band played accompanied by "Skin" Levett's buglers, were great favourites. "Sambre et Meuse" was known to most of us as "San Farian" because that distorted French phrase (Ca ne fait rien) fitted in with a part of the tune which was repeated many times. "Colonel Bogey," "Old Comrades," "The Great Little Army," and the Regimental March, "The Lass o' Gowrie," when played now by Military bands must conjure up many memories in the minds of those who served with the Twelfth during the last year of the war. The Regimental march was changed a few times during the time the Battalion was in existence. It started off with "A Southerly Wind and a Cloudy Sky" to which we used to sing, "One more River to Jordan," went on to "The Farmer's Boy," then to a tune to which we used to sing:—

"The Kaiser said, 'Before I die,
There's one more mob I want to try.'
The Crown Prince said, 'What shall it be,
The Shiny Twelfth or the A.S.C?' "

Finally we got the "Lass o' Gowrie" which remained to the end. The last tune we liked immensely and often felt like doing a jig to it.

Sergt. "Skin" Levett was not to be outdone by the brass band. His Drum and Fife Band was noted not only for their gallant efforts in the musical direction, but also for their smart appearance. "Skin" with his mace swinging would lead his men with their pipeclayed cords and trappings and shining bugles and brass. Beating tattoo nightly, the "Drums" would cause crowds to gather who stared open mouthed at the march and counter march which "Skin" would superintend. Bert Cole, the big drummer, also became a familiar figure. It was not an easy job to select a man capable of taking on the big drum with any success. Men were usually selected because of their height and strength. Bert had both, but, unlike some of his predecessors, he mastered his instrument. The way he used to flourish his sticks provoked admiration from the crowds who used to watch Levett's performances. The side drummers were equally successful with the sticks and altogether "Skin" was immensely proud of his men and they in turn got on well with him. The Brass Band, although not so "showy" as the "Drums," was very versatile. One favourite piece they used to play was "Sizlietta," in which the solo cornet player used to give a rendering some distance away from the band, preferably behind a cluster of trees if we happened to be in a wood. The effect was that of an echo, in which the whole band would join after the soloist had done his bit. In addition to Sergt. Crabtree the band had two good N.C.O.s in Cpls. T. Rogers and G. Maloy. What Rogers did not know about music was not worth knowing; he was also, by the way, an excellent football referee.

Speaking of bands and turnout brings to mind that it was at Loria that we came in contact with some of the French troops which had been sent to Italy. We were greatly surprised one day to see an exceptionally fine body of "Poilus" in their horizon blue marching through the village, preceded by a smart band playing "Sambre et Meuse." Never before had we seen such a fine and orderly unit of a French regiment. There was not much doubt that they had been specially selected to make an impression on the Italians. We gave them a cheer when they passed, and right well they deserved it.

Turning to the other side of training, Sport, we had our full share of it. Hardly a day passed without a football match. Inter-company and platoon matches were played as well as a match between the officers and sergeants. The latter provoked a great deal of fun. C.S.M. Bry Horswell was a good footballer when he cared to be. On this occasion he kept goal and kept it quite well until R.Q.M.S. Norman Speller came on the scene. The officers had a fairly good team, as also did the sergeants, but unfortunately for the sergeants Speller kept on enticing Horswell away from his goal just at the moment the officers were in a position to shoot. It was amusing to those of us who watched to see Speller giving the goalkeeper some refreshment just as an officer would shoot into an empty goal! On another occasion a stir was caused by our very fine referee, Cpl. T. Rogers, ordering one of his own company off the field for an infringement of the rules.

Major C. T. Williams, besides being a good footballer who had on occasions played for the Battalion, was also a boxing enthusiast. Accordingly competitions were arranged. There was no lack of talent in the 12th in this direction, "Smudger" Smith, Joe Mills, Bourne, Sergts. Mackenzie and Lewis and that great sportsman, Jack Greenslade, were all adepts at the noble art. But it was to novices that Major Williams specially turned his attention at Loria. Who will forget the splendid performance put up by that courageous and heroic stretcher-bearer, Pat O'Malley? Pitted against one of the best boxers in the Battalion, Pat held his own until superior ringcraft and a terrific punch put Paddy out of the running. A Company cheered O'Malley to the echo during and after the bout. Towards the end of the war Pat was the hero of another episode when he sacrificed his life in bringing in a wounded German cadet.

About this period officers and men were granted leave to Rome. Of course the numbers were few, but those who went all spoke of having a good time.

Leave to England was also granted, Capt. Hector Walker being O.C. Train of the first Divisional leave train which left. It usually took six days to reach Le Havre, where the lucky ones embarked. Fourteen days and the return journey meant an absence of a month from the Battalion. The trains from Le Havre only ran once a week, so that a day overdue would entail reaching the Battalion a week after one's leave warrant expired. There were a few who spent a week among the "Yanks" and the Non-combatant Corps at Le Havre, owing to having missed their train at Waterloo and the boat at Southampton. They were of course punished for their carelessness or otherwise when they eventually reached the Battalion.

Le Havre was also used as a concentration place for the Italian details, who proceeded from there to the Italian Expeditionary Force base at Arquata, where there were also some of our officers, including Lieuts. Linford, Lloyd and Ryan, who, being surplus to establishment on our arrival in Italy, were sent there until such times as they were required by the Battalion in the line.

Towards the end of 1917 the pay of the fighting soldier was raised by varying rates, from threepence a day upwards. This came to be known as "War Pay." In consequence there was a demand for bigger amounts on pay days. The lira was of less value than the French franc, and therefore it was felt that the usual method of paying out five francs or the equivalent in lire was a bit out of date. Company officers, being aware of this, made arrangements accordingly, but for a time there was a certain amount of difficulty over the new money. Tommy always liked to talk in terms of sterling, so that a lira became a sixpence and 10 centesimi a penny. But even this was not a satisfactory method of assessing the value of things, for, as Capt. Hector Walker says, "Turkeys cost 4/- when we arrived in Italy, but they were 16/- or more before we left, a good deal of the rise in the price being due to the altered rate of exchange." Fruit could be purchased cheaply, but apart from that there was very little which could be bought in the villages where the 12th were billeted. Those who visited Padua, some 30 miles away, could make other purchases. When our own canteens were established, there was very little need to go outside the organisation of the British Army to purchase cigarettes, canned fruit, chocolate and other luxuries in which the troops indulged when funds permitted. The "Crumps" had provided themselves with a theatre near the Divisional H.Q. at Selva. Nightly performances were given by the party for which a small charge was made for admission. Many of the troops patronised them, and H.R.H. The Prince of Wales attended one day and got a great reception from the audience. The Prince was very much amongst us in Italy; many times he had been seen in dangerous spots in or near the line, and the Headquarters at Montebelluna where he lived was bombed on more than one occasion.

Whilst the Battalion was training at Loria, baths were allotted at Riese, the people of which were particularly proud of their village, as it was the birthplace of Pope Pius X. He had an intense horror of war, and it was the shock of the outbreak of the Great War that is said to have caused his death on August 20th, 1914.

At Loria part of A Company occupied the top rooms of a private house. Opposite was a café where Italian soldiers used to congregate and sing, as only Italians can sing. One evening some of them had a bit of a fracas, and to quell the disturbance a sergeant of A Company turned out the billet guard with fixed bayonets to restore order. The Italians soon dispersed, much to the relief of the café proprietor. There is not much doubt that about this time there were many subversive forces trying to undermine the morale of the Italian troops. Through the machinations of the Germans in Russia and elsewhere a spirit which we afterwards came to know as "Bolshevism" was abroad. Some of the Italians realised that our arrival on their front meant the continuance of the war. There were no outward signs of hostility towards us and many of the Italian troops were very friendly, but others, who wanted peace at any price, were cold and indifferent. If there was any doubt at the time, the manifestation of the true conditions prevailing in Italy was shown after the war, when a period of several years anarchy ensued.

With few exceptions the civil population of Loria and other places were very kind and considerate to the British troops. We were comfortably billeted with them, and in many cases they practically regarded us as members of their own households. The peasantry had little to offer us, but what they had they gave ungrudgingly. Their stone floors on which we had to sleep were poor substitutes for beds, but they were a great deal better than some of the old cowsheds and other unsavoury places where we were forced to sleep on the Western Front.

Corporal Southall writes thus:—

"We moved to Loria, where we were billeted in a room on the ground floor of an *albergo*, or small inn. When the lady of the house found that she was not having officers billeted on her, she was at first very indignant, but later, having discovered that we were unlikely to wreck the place, she became very friendly. We had some very jolly evenings at our billet. After the place had closed for business we used to get out the cards, order a large basin of macaroni and wait till we heard a tap on the shutter outside. We would then open the shutters, and Sam Lattimore would step over the window-sill into the room, and we would play cards until he felt it was time to go home, when we let him out the same way as he came in.

"We had one delightful day in Padua. Our party amongst others included the Band Sergeant, Sergt. Lattimore and myself. In addition to sight-seeing we had to call in at Ricordi's, the music people, to obtain some music stands and other necessaries for the band. It was a glorious frosty morning when we set off and we passed through Castelfranco* on our way, thinking it a quaint old town. We were very early, but even at that early hour the Italians had got their Austrian prisoners out on the way to work, and a very unhappy lot they looked.

"On arrival at Padua we found the town enveloped by a thick mist which completely spoilt our desire to have a good look round. We made a short tour and then went to lunch, which we enjoyed thoroughly. Our bill resulted in our having as change one lira which we generously gave to the waiter. As there were at least four of us, imagine the look on his face at the smallness of the tip, especially as we gave it to him in a manner which made it look as though we were giving him something worth having. We then walked out of the restaurant highly pleased with our leg pull, having left the waiter's real tip under a plate on the table.

"We then visited the music shop, and, while the Band Sergeant was obtaining his requirements, we asked if we might listen to a Melba record which we saw lying around. We were given permission, and while we were listening to that lovely voice, the proprietor, an interpreter with the British Army, came in. He gave us the freedom of the shop and told us we could have all the records on which we wished to hear. We had three gramophones going, and, as soon as a record on one was completed, we would start the next one without a pause. The proprietor stood around with us listening, just as much enraptured as we were and growing wildly enthusiastic at intervals over some fine note in an operatic aria or a lovely orchestral passage.

"One thing that used to amuse the inhabitants of Loria was our drum and fife band. Not to be outdone by the brass band, Sergt. Levett got his men all pipeclayed and polished and used to make a brave show marching up and down the main street of the village in the evenings. The villagers used to stand and gape at them, being especially amused at the wonderful arm work of the big drummer and the drum-major (Levett). Sergt. Levett had achieved fame in the Battalion before this however. It was, I believe, at La Panne that an English paper sent out to one of the fellows contained an advertisement for Phospherine with inset a photograph of "Skin" Levett and an unsolicited testimonial from him telling the world what a lot of good he had experienced from taking this famous medicine. Naturally "Skin" had his leg well pulled as a result of this effort.

*Birthplace of Giorgione, one of the world's greatest painters.

"The time arrived at last for us to leave Loria. The lady of our billet and her daughter wept when we left, and we too, were sad at leaving. They had been extremely kind to us."

During the period the Battalion was at Loria news was received of the death in hospital at Bordighera of Pte. F. W. Underwood. The only other casualty during January had been one other rank wounded.

From the 1st to the 15th of February we continued to train at Loria, carrying out the most up to date methods of infantry training besides listening to lectures on sanitation by the M.O., firing on the range and taking part in tactical schemes. A new Quartermaster, Hon. Lieut. H. Amoore, formerly a R.Q.M.S. of the R.H.A., was appointed to the Battalion on the 3rd.

At last the very enjoyable stay at Loria came to an end. Orders were received for us to proceed to the Altivole area on the 16th. Accordingly, we proceeded in columns of threes, with 100 yards between companies, to Altivole, where we rested for the night. On the following day the march was continued to Veneazzu, where we relieved the 10th Northumberland Fusiliers, 23rd Division. We were now in support of the right brigade of the Montello left divisional sector.

From our positions, which were some miles from Monte Grappa, Venice could be seen in the distance. Visions of gondolas, carnival and Venetian nights that we had heard and read about, came before our eyes. But that was not to be in these times. For the time being, the Venice of romance and gaiety was, through the fortune of war, dead. Nevertheless to us veterans of the Western Front nothing but beauty abounded in the view from those high hills of the Montello compared with the flat devastated plains of Flanders and the hideously scarred uplands of the Somme. The glorious sunrise over the mountains behind the Austrian positions each morning was a sight that many of us had never dreamt of witnessing. What a difference from those dull and heavy mornings at Passchendaele!

Strange as it may seem to those who fought in other theatres of war, being in support of this part of the line meant carrying out training in company and even battalion drill. Yet such was the case. Bombing practice was also carried out, including the discharging of rifle grenades. B Company Office was situated in an old farmhouse with windows still intact. Near by an 18-pounder battery dug itself in, and all went well until the battery fired its first salvo. Then, while the Company Clerk was busy at his table preparing returns, a window frame fell on him, and the impact caused a pane of glass to break over his head without doing him any hurt.

Cpl. Southall again gives his impressions:—

"We went into the line again to the right of Monte Grappa. The weather was much warmer, and, as we had a very quiet time our stay was rather enjoyable. The Italians used an overhead cable system for carrying equipment, rations, etc., up to the line from the valley below and I was told that some of our blankets were sent up in this way. The N.C.O. who had charge of transporting them saw them safely packed into the car at the start of the journey. Yet when the car reached its journey's end, it was discovered that some of the blankets had been 'knocked off,' presumably by the Italians. A smart bit of work, but how it was done we didn't know.

"The observation advantages were all in our favour on this portion of the front, for on the enemy's side of the river was a plain about nine miles wide on which nothing could move without being seen on our side. Consequently we were only disturbed by 'heavies' from the other side, and that was rarely. They were really heavies though. The holes the shells made were so big that, as one of the fellows said, you could put a G.S. waggon and horses in them.

"Life was so peaceful here that it was possible to walk round the front line in broad daylight quite safely without even the necessity of wearing tin hats. Giles used to spend most of his spare time at the bottom of one of the deep conical holes which abounded on this front, where he could stretch himself out in the sunshine minus his tunic and read away to his heart's content. To our shame it must be admitted that we didn't let him thoroughly enjoy his rest. We used to lie hidden in the bushes at the top of the slope and bombard him with clods of earth and grass.

"Very soon however our peace began to be disturbed by rumours of another move. Egypt, Salonica, India and various other places were mentioned; the one everyone disliked mentioning but knew to be our certain goal was France. It would be difficult to describe our feelings of hopelessness when we knew that without doubt we were once more to exchange the sunny skies and 'cushy' times of Italy for the mud and frightfulness of the Western Front."

On February 20th the following appointments were notified:—Temp. Capt. C. F. Stallard, M.C., to be acting Lieut.-Colonel whilst commanding the Battalion from October 16th, 1917; Lieut. E. B. Gillett (5th Battn.) to be acting Captain whilst commanding a company from January 19th, 1918. On this date Pte. G. Gould was admitted to hospital and died the same day.

By this time it was patent that all was quiet on the Italian Front. The Germans who had been putting a stiffening into the Austrian troops, were being recalled to the Western Front to prepare for the next great gamble of the Boche. Storm troopers of the German Army were not the sort of people to let matters remain at rest in the sectors where they were called upon to operate. They were men with the offensive spirit fully developed. Bereft of German support, the Austrians were inclined to adopt a pacific attitude. Their policy was live and let live. Although we were not aware of it at the time, as events turned out, they were beginning to feel the strain. In the autumn when the Italian Army with a few British units attacked across the Piave, they fled like sheep.

It was to the Western Front that attention was now to be turned. Since the 12th Battalion had left there, the fight for the Passchendaele heights had ended with the capture of the village of that name by the Canadians on November 6th, 1917. Thus ended a battle of 3½ months' duration, during which time the British Army had defeated 78 German divisions, but at a cost which had greatly exhausted its strength. Following upon this on the 20th of November, 1917, the British Third Army under Sir Julian Byng had made a successful surprise attack with tanks and infantry on the Hindenburg Line in front of Cambrai. Ten days later the enemy counter-attacked and retook most of the ground captured. In addition to this it had been decided that the British Fifth Army should relieve the French of another 28 miles of front in the west up to the village of Barisis, south of the River Oise. Thus a depleted British Army was called upon to hold a line of 125 miles against an enemy, who, having disposed of Russia, was now sending train-loads of troops from the Eastern front to participate in an impending German offensive which one of the ablest generals of the World War, Von Ludendorff, had already published his intention of launching for a decisive victory on the Western Front. The U.S.A. had long thrown in her lot with the Allies, but many miles separated the continent of America from France, in addition to which there was the difficulty of transport and training which the British Army had already experienced. Comparatively few of their troops were yet on the Western Front. All available men would be needed to meet the new German menace, and so it was that the 41st Division was again selected to take its place on the Western Front. Later the 5th Division, in which our own 1st Battalion had made a great name, followed suit.

In accordance with orders received the 12th was relieved by a battalion of the West Yorkshire Regt., on the 25th of February. After relief a march was made to Pederiva (Mercato Vecchio), where we stayed the night.

At 8.30 a.m. on the following morning we marched to and took over billets for the night in Ca Amata. On the 27th a further eight miles was traversed through Castelfranco, Soranca and S. Martino to Lovari. On arrival it was found that there was a shortage of billets; in consequence H.Q. afterwards moved to Tombolo, and B Company to Cra Spetto.

There were no casualties in action during the month, but two other ranks had died, Pte. Green and Sergt. V. B. Condon, the latter at the Base at Arquata on the 7th. "Con," as we knew him in A Company, was one of the most popular N.C.O.s who enlisted at Rotherhithe. Vincent Byron Condon, who was born in Belleville, Ontario, Canada, was a much travelled, intellectual and interesting personality. His greying hair seemed to indicate that he was past military age, but there was not a gamer man in the company. His quaint accent and funny sayings marked him out amongst his contemporaries. How he met his death we shall never know, for some unknown assailant had foully struck him down on the road to his camp.

On the 1st of March the Battalion proceeded to Carmignana, where entraining was carried out, the Battalion occupying two trains, the first of which left at noon, and the other some time later.

After passing through Vicenza, Verona and Brescia we reached Milan soon after midnight. The train passed through Turin and reached Modane on the French side of the Mt. Cenis tunnel, 7 miles long, on the 2nd. At Modane there was a scramble to change lire into francs, the exchange being 64 lire=50 francs. The 3rd found us passing through France viâ Amberieu, Bourg, Gray and Langres. We did not seem to get the same lovely journey we had on the way out by the coast route. Some of the places we were passing we had never heard of before.

Passing as we did through Châlons-sur-Marne, Epernay and Estrées, we perceived that we were cutting in on a part of the front which was held by the French. By 10.0 p.m. on the 4th Amiens was reached, and at 3.30 a.m. on the morning of the 5th of March the first train stopped in a siding at Doullens, where detrainment took place. The first half of the Battalion then marched to billets at Halloy, and the second half, after detraining some time later, followed. So here we were back again in the last place in the world we wanted to return to after the experience of four months in the sunny land of Italy. Even some of the horses seemed to resent their return, for one can still remember a couple of them bolting in the station at Doullens.

Here is Cpl. Southall's account of the return journey:—

"The weather changed for the worst the moment we began to move. It rained and became very cold, and the journey back was comfortless. We travelled in the usual cattle trucks.

"We passed round Milan, and I was delighted to get a view of its fine Cathedral. Up the Rhone Valley we were given some very beautiful views, and the snow on the islands and over the countryside rather added to the beauty. It was bitterly cold however, and we didn't keep our truck doors open too long to admire the scenery. One incident happened on the journey which caused us a certain amount of amusement. One of the R.A.M.C. men attached to us had a small primus stove on which he was boiling a canteen of water for making tea. The train was proceeding at its usual leisurely gait, when suddenly there was a terrific jerk and our friend with the stove knocked over the canteen of hot water, falling on the hot stove as he did so. He got up with the hot stove adhering to the seat of his pants. It certainly wasn't there long, but the sight of him dancing around with his stove sticking out behind was too much for the rest of us, and we just collapsed with laughter. It transpired that the couplings of the train had broken, causing the jerk. One man was thrown head first on to the end of a truck and received a nasty gash on the top of the head which had to be stitched up by the doctor.

"We finally detrained in France at Doullens. It was of course a miserable day, and everything was muddy and dirty. We marched to the little village of Halloy and there went into billets."

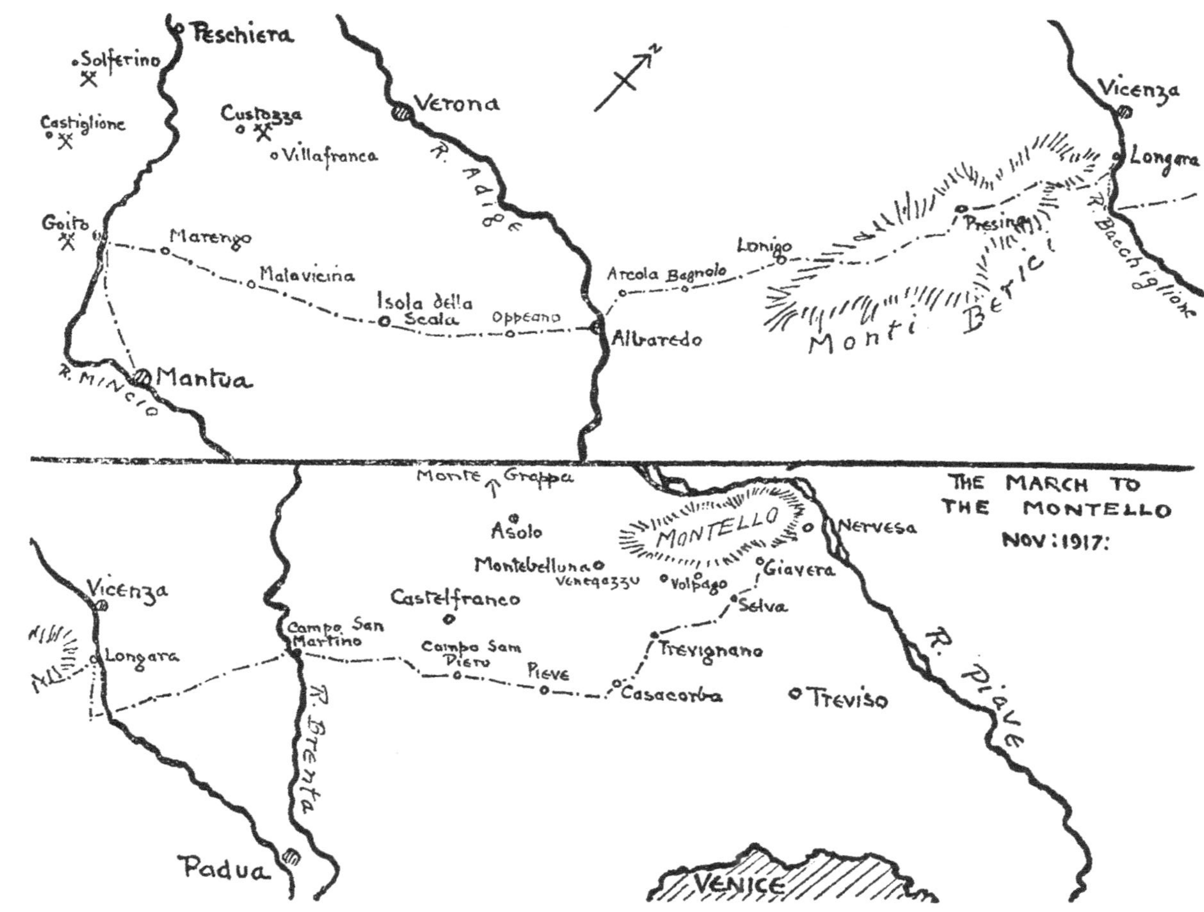

THE MARCH TO THE MONTELLO NOV: 1917:

CHAPTER XII.

6th March to 3rd April, 1918.

The Battalion in the Great German Offensive of March, 1918.

ON arrival at Halloy it was found that billets were insufficient to meet the needs of the 12th Battalion and the 11th Royal West Kents, who were also cantoned there, and so B Company was moved to the outskirts. Halloy was another of those little villages behind the line which the average Tommy enjoyed immensely as being a complete change from the fighting area. As usual there were a few shops and estaminets, and many farms where the men were billeted. B Company, more or less isolated from the remainder of the Battalion, were in fairly comfortable quarters in barns, and the other companies were also well situated. One of the curious features of the place was what we termed the "Village Crier." This individual used to beat a drum and, when the local inhabitants gathered round him, he would recite the latest news. Of course the majority of us did not understand what he was saying, but his excitability amused us greatly. We met him soon after our arrival, and he was still distributing the news when we left.

From the 6th to the 20th of March, the Battalion remained in Army Reserve at Halloy. It was generally understood that we should not be called upon, unless something very serious happened in the line. Most of us had the confidence that such an emergency would not take place, for we had become used to thinking that our superiority on the Western Front, especially in gunfire, since 1916 was so great that the enemy would simply knock his head against a brick wall. No doubt we had lulled ourselves into a false sense of security, but it was better to be thus than to dread what was in store for us.

Training was carried out as usual, route marching perhaps occupying too much of our time. Were the Higher Command expecting a retreat in which march discipline would be an important factor?

Tactical schemes were carried out and also range practice. Church parades were held on two occasions: the first in conjunction with the 11th Royal West Kents on the 10th, the last parade the Kents were to attend as a unit of the 122nd Brigade. As it was becoming increasingly difficult to keep battalions up to strength on the Western Front, the powers that be had decided to reduce the number of battalions in a brigade to three. The effect of this on the 41st Division was that the 11th Royal West Kents, the 32nd Royal Fusiliers and the 21st K.R.R.s were to be disbanded, and the officers and men to be sent to reinforce other units of the British Army. Our sympathy went out to our neighbours the West Kents, for we had a great deal in common with them. In the first place they were raised in Lewisham, an adjoining district to that in which the 12th was formed. Their first Commanding Officer, Lieut.-Col. H. L. Searle, was a Major in the 8th Battn. East Surreys, and during our sojourn in England we were usually stationed in adjacent billets; again at Reninghelst our camps adjoined. Lieut.-Col. H. H. Lee, D.S.O., was a brother officer in the Cameronians of Lieut.-Col. A. F. Townshend who took the 11th Kents overseas and was killed at Flers. Three officers of the Lewisham Battalion—Major L. H. Hickson, and acting Lieut.-Colonels A. W. Puttick, M.C., and C. F. Stallard, M.C.—commanded our Battalion for varying periods. We were the keenest rivals in the field of sport, while in action we usually advanced alongside each other and at the final objectives were usually to be found together. For their C.O., Lieut.-Col. Corfe, who was acting Brigadier at the time of their demise, we had a great admiration. We had often come in contact with his immense figure at St. Eloi. He looked a typical soldier and fighter, and was renowned for showing the greatest consideration for the troops he commanded.

Capt. R. O. Russell, the official Historian of the 11th West Kents, says:—

"Here may we express a word of thanks and appreciation to those good friends, the East Surreys. Their sympathy with us in our sad fate was almost as if they were sharing it. They entertained us both at table and on the sports ground. They did all in their power to soften the blow—and they succeeded in no small measure.

"The football matches, officers versus officers and sergeants versus sergeants, were great occasions. One forgets the results—they do not matter—but one will never forget the remark of that immortal wag who cheered us on with the words, 'Go it, the Spare Parts!' "

And so it was that we bade farewell to the 11th (Lewisham) Battalion Royal West Kent Regiment.

At the time the West Kents were disbanded, the 7th East Surreys were likewise dealt with in the 12th Division. Many of them were afterwards posted to and joined the 12th. For record purposes Colour-Sergt. Samuda, the 7th Orderly Room Sergeant, and others were attached to the 12th Battalion at the base. Drafts of 64 other ranks joined on the 18th and 19th.

Orders were now received to be ready to move at a moment's notice. One day everyone packed up and proceeded to Mondicourt Station, where, after dumping our packs and waiting to entrain, we were given a lecture on the spirit of the bayonet by a senior officer, presumably from one of the schools. This over, we marched back to billets. It was evidently a test to see how quickly we could move to the entrainment point.

Cpl. Southall writes.—

"A big Boche attack was expected not far from our front. That it was going to be a desperate one was evident by the practice we put in for packing up and making a quick move. Several times we established record times in getting on the march, and, after careering round the country, not knowing whether this was the big day, finally found ourselves back in billets again."

As had happened on other occasions before a big stunt, the command of the Battalion passed to another unfamiliar officer, Lieut.-Col. G. L. Brown of the Middlesex Regt., who came to us from the 21st K.R.R.s on March 17th. The change, however, was one that augured for the best. In a short while our new C.O. had endeared himself to all ranks by his charming manner and kindly consideration. He was to stay with us until the end.

Of our new Colonel's thoroughness and consideration Capt. H. S. Walker, the Adjutant, writes:—

"One of his first instructions to me was to see that all chits to Company Commanders were to be written out in quintuplicate and put on small spikes for 'A,' 'B,' 'C,' 'D,' and 'H.Q.' These chits were to be sent out at 6.0 p.m. unless of course, there was an urgent one which would be sent out at once. He would not allow a chit to be sent out to be read and initialled and returned to Orderly Room. He insisted on orders being out early, so that Company Commanders could arrange for their day's work before they went to bed. Another thing he impressed upon me was that he wished Company Commanders to deal with minor crimes, saying that, if anyone was brought before him, he would either get off scot free or would be for it properly."

The story of the 12th Battalion's part in the great German Offensive of March, 1918, really starts on the 20th, when "A" Echelon of the Transport moved at 11.0 a.m. to Achiet-le-Grand, some three miles north-west of Bapaume, and six miles north of Flers, where the Battalion first went into action on the Somme 18 months before.

Early on the following morning, the 21st of March, the rest of the Battalion at Halloy awoke to hear a furious bombardment some distance away. There was not much doubt what this meant, but we hoped that the noise we could hear was that of our own artillery driving the enemy back. It was a fine day and not the sort to which we had been used at this time of the year. While the drum-fire continued in the distance, the men stood about in little groups discussing the situation. Should we be called upon to take an active part in the operations was the thought uppermost in our minds. However, no time was lost in Battalion H.Q. notifying the companies to be ready to move off at any moment.

The orders to move came at last when at 4.0 p.m. we paraded and marched to Mondicourt Pas Station, where entrainment was carried out. Instead of the usual cattle trucks we had ordinary coaches with broken window panes. The Brigade War Diary reports that entrainment was made at Mondicourt for Remy where concentration into the IV Corps area was to be effected, but that the train was diverted to Achiet-le-Grand.

With us were some who had their movement orders to go on leave but at the last moment were prevented owing to all leave being cancelled, and amongst them was Capt. R. O. Russell of the 11th West Kents, who, after the disbandment of his battalion, was temporarily posted to the Twelfth. It was ironical that some of these were either taken prisoner or made casualties within the next few days. The train made its way through country over which we had been before in 1916, but as it was dusk we were unable to make out where we were. At last we came to a halt in a station, and one of the first people to greet us there was the Sergeant Shoemaker, Ernie Noad. When we espied Noad (his familiar expression: "Wot cher, me old mate," drew our attention to him) he was taking cover behind some packs. We then enquired where we were and found out that we were in Achiet-le-Grand, halfway between Arras and Albert, and at that very moment the station was being shelled. It was now 2.0 a.m. and the order was passed along to get out of the station as quickly as possible and parade on the road outside. Very little time was lost in executing this order, as it was "unhealthy" to remain in the station. Soon the Battalion was making its way along the road at a cracking pace to Savoy Camp near Bihucourt, where accommodation was found in huts.

Before we proceed any further, it would be as well to review certain aspects of the situation which had arisen.

The great day for which the Germans were waiting arrived on March 21st, 1918. It was known to them as "Michael" day, Michael being a Teutonic national figure. The Germans used heroes of mythology and the like as symbols: Hindenburg, Wotan and Siegfried being names connected with fortifications; even to-day we have another name which holds Germany—Hitler. The German armies participating had the operations explained to them about three days before zero day. The idea was that three immense armies were to make a general advance in a westerly direction to the estuary of the Somme at Abbeville, where it was anticipated that lack of bridges over the widening stretch of water would leave the British Army separated from the French. France, it was thought, would then quickly come to terms when left to bear the whole weight of the German arms; thus it would be necessary to make the first attack on the British Forces. The plans had been so carefully prepared that failure was regarded as impossible. So secret had the date of "Michael" been kept that some of the armies moving up on the 14th of March were of opinion that the British line had been broken already and that they were moving forward to exploit success. By March 18th the secret was a fairly open one, and even the British Staff had learnt something which made them alter certain dispositions. It is thought that some prisoners captured just before the day disclosed the actual date. The Germans estimated that their attacking gun power was four times stronger than our defending artillery, or one piece of ordnance to every ten men of their shock regiments.

March 21st, a misty morning in the front positions, saw the vast German machine of 64 divisions set in motion. A hurricane bombardment of every kind of shell, including gas, preceded the attack before dawn had broken. The British Third and Fifth Armies were assailed between the rivers Oise and Scarpe. Thus on less than half of the front occupied in the West by the British a force considerably greater than the total strength of the British Armies in France and Belgium advanced to the attack. Before the men in the front posts knew where they were, the enemy was upon them. Below St. Quentin, where Sir Hubert Gough's Fifth Army, consisting of 14 infantry divisions and three cavalry divisions, was attacked by 40 German divisions, the enemy gained a great measure of success, but in the North, where 24 German divisions fell on the 15 divisions of the Third Army under General Byng, things did not turn out as he had anticipated. It was to the area where the stiffest opposition had been met that the 41st Division was now hurried.

At 6.0 a.m. on the 22nd of March orders were received from the IV Corps for the Division to move into the Favreuil neighbourhood, the Corps Reserve area. One Brigade was to be prepared to hold the Rear Zone ("Green Line") between the Beugnâtre-Vaulx Road and the Corps Left Boundary, and one company of the 41st Battalion, M.G.C. (formed as recently as the 17th of March) was to move into the line at once. The 124th Brigade concentrating at Favreuil was ordered to reconnoitre and hold the line forthwith.

The G.O.C. 41st Division was placed in command of the Rear Zone with the 7th Infantry Brigade (25th Division, attached 6th Division) also under his command. At this time the 122nd Brigade had not arrived, and only two battalions of the 123rd Brigade were in the Favreuil area. These two battalions were ordered up from Achiet-le-Grand to a position west of Favreuil at 10.0 a.m. to be in Divisional Reserve.

Soon orders were received from Corps that two battalions, in addition to the 124th Brigade, were to be held in readiness to occupy the Rear Zone. Two battalions of the 122nd Brigade were detailed for this purpose. By noon the Brigade had arrived and were concentrated just east of Sapignies. This is the position as recorded in the narrative of operations carried out by the 41st Division.

Let us now return to the 12th Battalion, whom we left in the hutments at Savoy Camp on the morning of the 22nd.

It was with some difficulty that men, tired after the tedious journey of the night before were awakened from deep slumbers. Breakfast was taken and instructions issued to move off again. Certain specialists were left behind as Details, and then, with the sun shining on the buckles of their equipment (the result of the "poshing up" in Italy and at Halloy), the Battalion marched off and proceeded to take up a line north-east of Sapignies and facing Mory.

At 6.0 p.m. fresh orders were received for the Battalion, in conjunction with the other two battalions of the Brigade, to move about a mile to the eastward and take up a line astride the Bapaume-Vaulx-Vraucourt Road, but we were moved back to the line in front of Sapignies again, where A and B Companies took up a line on a ridge overlooking Mory and forming a defensive flank on the right flank of the VI Corps and left of the IV Corps. This position was reached at 5.0 a.m. on the morning of the 23rd.

Information explaining these instructions was now issued. Mory was the point of junction of the 41st Division (IV Corps) with the 40th Division (VI Corps) to the north of it. The VI Corps was being heavily attacked, and, in view of the possibility of its being forced back and of the village being captured by the Germans, the 12th Battalion was to form a defensive flank for the 41st Division. To carry out these instructions A and B Companies moved forward early over the crest and dug themselves in on a line covering Mory, which lay in the valley below. The remainder of the Battalion was in support in rear, where the ground afforded cover from view. There was considerable aerial activity during the day, and small parties of the enemy began to enter Mory, only to be thrown out in the afternoon by the 13th East Surreys of the 40th Division, whom we met for the first time in France in such gruelling circumstances. The 13th, after retaking Mory, remained there until nightfall, when they withdrew to a position west of the village. A gap existed between the 12th and 13th Battalions, and to close this D Company was moved up in line with A and B Companies.

Several patrols were sent out to get in touch with the troops to the north, who had not apparently been identified as the 13th East Surreys. One of these patrols was in charge of Lieut. F. R. Matthews, who was afterwards reported missing. It subsequently transpired that Lieut. Matthews was killed while chasing an enemy scout. Matthews dashed after the German as he was escaping and ran into a party of the enemy and was shot down. In consequence of this the proximity of the 13th Battalion does not appear to have been reported to our Headquarters.

The 23rd had been a fateful day for the 41st Division, for at Beugny and opposite Vaulx Vraucourt the 123rd and 124th Brigades were heavily attacked soon after 4.30 p.m. The 123rd Brigade was surrounded by the enemy, and that fine soldier, Colonel Corfe, now in command of the 10th Royal West Kents, found himself a prisoner together with his staff, and the Colonel of the 11th "Queen's" and his H.Q. staff met a similar fate. The 124th Brigade, on the other hand, strongly supported by the 20th D.L.I. beat back no less than six separate attacks, in two of which the enemy brought up cavalry and guns.

The 12th Battalion remained in its positions until the evening of the 24th, when orders were received to concentrate west of Sapignies. During the day there was considerable artillery and aerial activity on the part of the enemy, and, as the Diary records, "very little was seen of our planes throughout the day."

The order to withdraw and take up positions west of Sapignies was subsequently cancelled, and instead the Battalion took up a position east of the village* with orders to hold out as long as possible, in order to give the remainder of the Brigade sufficient time to organise a new defensive line near Bihucourt, about two miles to the westward.

Colonel Brown has written an account of the circumstances attending the issue of these orders.

"At about 7.30 p.m. on the 24th of March, whilst the Battalion was on the move from the line west of Mory to a point west of Sapignies where it had been ordered to concentrate, Capt. Snell, the Brigade Major, met me and ordered me to halt the Battalion in the low ground to the east of Sapignies, and to proceed myself to the village for a conference.

"I halted the Battalion and about half an hour later went with Capt. H. S. Walker to a house (or rather part of a house) in the village where I met Brig.-Gen. Towsey, Brig.-Gen. Clemson and Capt. Snell (there were others present whom I cannot remember). I was told that a gap existed between the Fifth Army which had been forced back and the right of the Third Army which had more or less held its ground, and that the Third Army would have to withdraw to close this gap.

"The result of the conference was that the 12th East Surreys were to prepare and hold a line east of Sapignies and to deny that village to the enemy whilst the remainder of the Brigade prepared a new defensive position east of Bihucourt. I asked the General how much time he thought the rest of the Brigade would require and he said that by 9.0 or 10.0 a.m. next morning the work should be completed.

"I was told that other battalions would prolong my line on both flanks, and this I found to be correct.

"It was then about 10.0 p.m. and Capt. Snell accompanied me back to the east of Sapignies and showed me the approximate line which was to be held."

In recalling the conference referred to by the C.O., Capt. Walker says he remembers the three Brigadiers looking very tired and worn, and Capt. Snell, who had a large map on the table with a guttering candle as the only light, pointing out the positions of our troops and also those of the enemy.

The withdrawal took place immediately after dark, and the Battalion dug in on a line behind Favreuil. A, B, and C Companies were in the front line, while D Company took up a line on the Arras-Bapaume Road. The right flank was the dangerous one and it was for this reason that Colonel Brown moved D Company into the area of the battalion on our right. During the day a letter of appreciation of the work accomplished on the 23rd was received from General Lawford.

On either side of the new positions taken up was a Composite Battalion. At intervals during the night small parties of British troops who had been in continual contact with the enemy for the last two days withdrew through our line, and before daylight on the 25th it was discovered that the units on our flanks had been withdrawn together with D Company, which, according to orders, had conformed to their movement. Six tanks were sent up by General Towsey which materially assisted in covering the infantry retirement by vigorously operating about Favreuil. A party of Wilts under two officers had been observed at 3.30 a.m. retiring through our positions, and it was an hour later that the discovery was made that our flanks were in the air. Colonel Brown now realised that A, B, and C Companies with both flanks bare and

*It might be of interest to remember that all this ground was the scene of the Battle of Bapaume, one of the few French successes in the Franco-German War of 1870-71. A monument just south of Sapignies commemorated this action in January, 1871.

with an open slope of some 600 yards in rear of them would stand very little chance of getting out of this awkward predicament, should the enemy attack. It must be remembered that the C.O.'s orders were to hold the line to enable other units of the Brigade to withdraw and consolidate further back; consequently no blame would have attached to him, had he decided to remain in his positions and let the enemy gradually surround the three companies. However the decision he made in order to carry out his orders was to sacrifice only one company. That company was C, under Capt. A. F. Copp. Colonel Brown also decided that he himself with some machine-gunners should remain with C Company. Sending the Adjutant, Capt. H. S. Walker, with A and B Companies back to a ridge west of Sapignies, the Colonel then disposed C Company in a series of posts occupying about 300 yards of the newly dug trench.

Now followed an heroic incident in the annals of the 12th Battalion. It was 5.30 a.m. when the Colonel sent the rest of his forces back, and soon after sunrise the enemy attacked. He was immediately met with a withering fire from C Company's rifles and Lewis-guns, and repulsed. At about 6.30 Capt. Copp was severely wounded in the thigh. It was impossible to convey him back on a stretcher, so, with the assistance of Pte. H. J. Sherborne, a signaller, he crawled back some 600 yards to the troops in rear. With a broken thigh this was no mean feat of endurance. Although communication between all the various posts was impossible owing to the enemy's continuous fire, C Company held its ground until 10.30 a.m. At that time the Germans were firing into the Company from behind, and it was obvious that both flanks had been turned. Colonel Brown therefore, observing the position, gave the post with which he was able to communicate, numbering some 40 men, permission to attempt a retirement. Out of these, 16 men with the Colonel tried to get back. Of these only Colonel Brown and Lce.-Cpl. Fry were successful, the others being either killed or taken prisoner, as were the rest of C Company. The plight of C Company was very bad, and there was no option but to surrender when once the enemy had got round the flanks and in rear. From the distance some of our men could see the gallant remnants being sent back under escort. Right well they had performed the rôle allotted to them. They did not know what they had accomplished, but the gallant defence put up by them was something of which they could all be proud. Through their stand they saved 60 guns at Achiet-le-Grand from capture, besides affording to a number of British troops of more advanced units who were in danger of being cut off an opportunity of regaining the British lines. Amongst the latter were the Hampshires, who were digging a line in front of Bihucourt.

In the meantime the companies under Capt. H. S. Walker had been holding a line between Sapignies and Bihucourt, where they were joined by D Company. About noon they were withdrawn to the new line dug in front of Bihucourt by the 15th Hants, where Colonel Brown rejoined. Here a stand was made, the Battalion also supporting an attack by the Hants on Bihucourt Wood.

Continuing his account of the operations of the 25th of March, Colonel Brown says:—

"There was an open slope of some 600 yards behind the position and daylight showed that it would be almost impossible to extricate any force in safety if they were engaged by the enemy. The situation arose from the fact of siting the line during darkness, and, had A and B Companies been kept in the line, they would undoubtedly have shared the same fate as befell C. I had some 16 men in the post that I was in when I ordered the withdrawal at about 10.30 a.m., and so far as I could see the only other posts still holding out at that time were the ones on my immediate right and left. Communication with outside posts was impossible, and, although efforts were made to signal to them to withdraw, I have always been doubtful as to whether the signal was ever understood.

"At the time I could not understand how the enemy got round my right flank without my seeing them until they appeared almost behind me, and to clear up this point I visited the scene of the action in 1922, some four years afterwards. I found that there was a sunken lane just north of the main road which gave a covered line of advance and which must have been left open and unguarded after the troops on our right had withdrawn.

"The left flank was turned by parties of the enemy advancing from the direction of Mory and gaining possession of the high ground which had been occupied the previous night by the Composite Battalion on our left."

Further light is thrown on the movements of the Battalion by Capt. H. S. Walker. After relating how the Battalion had been digging in at different places for a day and a night and then found themselves back where they started, he comes to the night of the 24th.

"We remained in these trenches for a bit and then moved out and were told to dig in on the west side of the Arras-Bapaume Road by Sapignies.

"As we were moving by companies independently to the new position we were to take up, we were met by the Brigade Major and told that plans had been altered and that we had to dig in at the foot of the slope below Sapignies. One Company had already gone on to the other position and I had to go and fetch them back. Our line was made up of various details on our right and left. Lieut. Dowling was on the right of this composite line actually on the Arras-Bapaume Road. He had one platoon with him.

"I went along the line to the left and found that the troops on C Company's left had been withdrawn without Capt. Copp being advised. I informed the C.O. who gave me a time limit to go to the right and find out how we were placed there. At the end of our line I found a gap of about 400 yards where the troops had also been withdrawn between our right flank and Lieut. Dowling on the road. I told Dowling that he was 'in the air' and ordered him to act independently of us in case we were driven in, pointing out his best line in case of having to withdraw. By this time the day was beginning to break, and the enemy machine-guns were peppering us pretty heavily.

"As soon as I reported to the C.O. the state of our line, he ordered me to lead out 'A' and 'B' up the hill to the place we had been told to occupy on the night before. With H.Q. and the two companies I proceeded up the hill which was being well sprayed with rifle and machine-gun fire and later was bombarded with light shells.

"I had been trained as a machine-gunner, and when the enemy attacked I saw C Company with a target which machine-gunners dream about; enemy troops in mass formation moving obliquely across their front! The rifles of 'C' and the Lewis-gunners, assisted by a section of the M.G.C. who were a little higher up on the hill, were simply mowing down the enemy. But numbers will tell in the end.

"When Colonel Brown, who had remained with C Company, rejoined us, he was fagged out and we put him into the entrance of an enemy dugout, where he went to sleep reclining on the steps. Lieut. Hall brought some sandwiches from our cooks (wonderful fellows they were), and I suppose we made rather a noise munching and disturbed the C.O., who muttered: 'Is there anything for me?' Hall quickly replied, 'Something's just coming for you, Sir,' and the next second a 5.9 arrived, struck the roots of a tree and burst. A large clod of mud fell on to Lieut. Mutch. He was very quiet for a moment and then said, 'I'm blinded.' Then I saw that the mud had completely covered his face; but, on our peeling it off, he was none the worse. His tin hat saved him.

"C Company had been sacrificed, but they did their job and did it well. The fact that they checked the enemy attack allowed positions to be consolidated further back which enabled us still further to hold up his advance.

"Then followed that dreadful experience: going back, then digging in, troops retiring through us, and then we again retiring through them. This seemed to go on for hours and more or less without a shot being fired. A hopeless feeling."

Of the actual attack on C Company Sergt. Joe Radcliffe supplies some details.

"On the night of the 24th of March, C Company came out of one part of the front line. I do not remember being relieved by any other company or battalion, although we were given to understand that we were being relieved.

"We were on our way back when we were suddenly halted and told to dig ourselves in as quickly as possible. There was absolutely no protection whatever, so it was a case of dig for your life. Luckily things were very quiet; not a shot could be heard anywhere. We had no idea how serious things were, but of course we soon found out at daybreak. Lieut. Dawson told me to detail a N.C.O. and three men to go out on patrol to locate the enemy front line. This I did. I forget the names of the men who went, but do not remember seeing them return.

"Just before daybreak on March 25th there was a great deal of shelling and shouting on our right in a wood. This had hardly died down when our turn came. We were shelled for a while, and then 'Jerry' advanced in mass formation from a wood in front of C Company. The order was given to open rapid fire, and I know No. 9 Platoon did their share with the rest of the company.

"The three officers, Capt. Copp, Lieut. Dawson and 2nd Lieut. Johns, were with the platoon on my left. We were certainly holding up the enemy, for, try as he did, he could not get us. Two guns of the M.G.C. were firing for all they were worth. We were in a trench on the enemy side of a ridge, which was bad for anybody who tried to get back, for under cover of a smoke screen the Germans were able to get round and so enfilade us.

"Just about this time Colonel Brown, who was in a trench on a ridge in the rear of us, was urging the men to make a dash for his trench. We opened rapid fire to cover up several who tried to reach him, but they fell before reaching the trench which was only about 50 feet away.

"Some time after the order was passed to me from my left not to fire if attacked again. We were attacked again very soon and had to give in. We left our arms in the trench and were soon collected together by some Germans, who took us behind the lines to an officer. If my memory serves me right, Lieut. Dawson was wounded when I saw him here. After having told us all to fall in, the German officer told all officers and N.C.O.s to fall out. We were searched for maps, etc., but they did not find anything.

"The officers were taken away from the N.C.O.s and men. We then marched behind the line until we came to a dressing station, where we were halted and told to pick up wounded who were already on stretchers. Some were English and some German. There were four men to a stretcher. We marched along the road for miles, it seemed, halting for rest now and then, being of course under guard all the time. We wondered how much farther we had to go (there was no guide to meet us and say: 'Only one more kilometre!'), as everybody was dead beat and had had nothing to eat since the previous afternoon.

"Sergt. J. McFie, two others and myself, carried a stretcher together on which there was a man covered over with a khaki overcoat. Several times we asked him how he felt and if he was in pain, but no response came to our enquiries. At last whilst resting at a halt I lifted the overcoat and saw he was a dead German.

"After walking the greater part of the day with these stretchers on our shoulders, we were told to lay them down and to continue our march without them. We eventually got to a place where we stopped for the night in a building, and looked forward to having something to eat, the first that day, but did not get it, so we had to go to sleep with an empty stomach."

At 1.0 a.m. on the 26th orders were received to withdraw to Bucquoy, and the Battalion arrived two hours later, resting in a field south of the village until 8.0 o'clock, when it was ordered to take up a line about three miles further west, near Gommecourt. In that position the day was passed quietly, Bucquoy being on the line where the German advance in this area was held up. At 1.0 a.m. on the 27th the Battalion moved to Bienvillers, where another quiet day was passed resting in a field to the south of the village.

Moving on the 28th, the Battalion proceeded viâ Fonquevillers to a line south of Gommecourt, where Major C. T. Williams reported from the Detail Camp. There was considerable shelling of the back areas during the day. After a quiet day on the 29th another move was made through Gommecourt to relieve the 7th Manchesters in support to the 124th Brigade in front of Bucquoy, where the Details joined the rest of the Battalion.

Let us now take the adventures of the Details whom we had left at Savoy Camp. Soon after the Battalion moved off, they were ordered to proceed to Achiet-le-Petit, where they were billeted in tents, and were able to see many incidents of the retreat. Along the road from Achiet-le-Grand a vast stream of traffic of all kinds was making its way together with Labour Companies and other miscellaneous units who were trying to find fresh quarters. Staff cars were flying hither and thither. Alongside the roads were horse lines and reinforcement camps. Meanwhile German planes hovered overhead dodging the shells from the many anti-aircraft batteries which made a terrific din all day long. The evening arrived, and with it the German planes. Most of those in the camp where the Details were, turned out to watch the "Gothas" in the searchlights which were beginning to play on them. Suddenly a loud swishing through the air was heard, and the next second a bomb had fallen on the camp with a tremendous explosion. It fell on a tent, and there were loud groans. The other men in the camp fell flat on their faces while the plane above dropped some more bombs which burst in the horse lines across the road. The plane, having unloaded, then made for home. Cries were heard for stretcher-bearers, and those who were not fatally injured were conveyed to an ambulance which drew up on the road. By this time the men in the camp were in no humour to remain in the tents, for they knew that the planes would probably return. They were right in their assumption, and soon after another batch of the death-dealing craft arrived. Orders were then issued for the men to try to find cover. There were a few old dugouts in the vicinity, and in these shelter was taken for the night. The droning of the engines, intermingled with the explosions of bombs, continued throughout the night.

On the 23rd a move was made by way of Beaumont Hamel and Mailly-Maillet to Bertrancourt, where accommodation was provided in barns. The march was made difficult by the fact that the British guns were retiring. We asked the gunners where they were bound, but they had not the slightest idea. It looked as though the artillery was leaving the infantry to its fate, and some of the Details expressed this view to the gunners in no uncertain manner, but of course they were only carrying out their orders. It was rumoured that a certain general gave orders for batteries to retire, and that this was not a British general but a German spy dressed in a British general's uniform. According to the Corps and Divisional reports this rumour appears to have been an actual fact, for warnings were issued regarding German agents who were trying to spread panic among the troops.

Stragglers were also met, but these were rounded up, formed into composite companies and sent to the line again. Wild rumours from these and others made the situation a great deal worse than it was. In an action such as this there was bound to be much confusion and perhaps a lack of control. For instance, it was possible for unwounded men to mingle with the wounded who were forced to walk long distances if they wished to receive proper attention. The clearing station at Achiet-le-Grand had to be evacuated, and most of the wounded had to retire on foot, but some were able to get on trains and lorries which were making their way back. There was a story that a train arriving in Achiet-le-Grand was loaded with troops who reached the base. The guard is supposed to have shouted in jest: "Last train for Etaples!" and many boarded it and were conveyed there, only to be returned to their units under escort.

When it was known that the Germans were close at hand, the Expeditionary Force Canteens and other institutes were thrown open to the troops, who loaded themselves up with cigarettes, chocolate and other things to prevent them passing into the hands of the enemy.

From one particular canteen we entered all the stock was taken by our men, and barrels of beer were poured away. Some of the thirsty ones thought this a shame, but it was the most sensible thing to do, for some of the men in the March retreat consumed too much whisky and beer in these places and were consequently unable to get away from the enemy. Rudolf Binding, a prominent German writer, who participated in the battle, has asserted in one of his books that his own troops lost the great offensive through over-indulgence in the good things found in the British canteens, and this seems to be borne out to some degree by an incident related by C.Q.M.S. Tice, who writes:—

"The nearest I ever got to being captured was in March, 1918. I and the C.Q.M.S. of C Company were trying to find our companies, none too easy a job in those nearly fatal days of the war. We came across what I should think had been an E.F. Canteen: anyway, we went in and got a shock, for at the other end were a lot of Jerries having a pretty good time by the noise they were making. Strangely enough nobody saw us, and needless to say, we beat a hasty retreat. By luck we came across Capt. Whiteway, whom we knew; but he was wounded a few minutes later. We could not find the Battalion that night, but discovered parts of it next morning."

It was dark when the Details passed through Beaumont Hamel, but perhaps the quaintest thing noticed there was a white board over a sandbagged villa with the inscription "Town Major of Beaumont Hamel." As there was not the least semblance of a town there, just a mere heap of bricks and masonry, some amusement was caused by the inscription.

During the 24th and 25th the Details moved to other places where the order to stand to was frequently given. Extra ammunition had been given out, and it was thought that reinforcements had been called for by the Battalion.

Thièvres was reached on the 26th, and on the way a Composite Battalion consisting of instructors from the IV Corps School was passed. Refugees were streaming along the road with all their belongings packed in farm carts and other means of transport. It was a distressing sight to see old men and women with little children, tired and weary, clinging to them. The terror of war struck into our hearts. During the night of the 26th the German air raiders were active, and many bombs were dropped near the tents in which the men were sleeping.

On the 27th the Australians who were hastening from Belgium passed the Details camp. Apparently they had been experiencing plenty of artillery fire where they had come from, the enemy no doubt trying to make them believe that he was going to attack in the north. The Details did not move again until the 29th, when they proceeded to the Transport lines at Couin, where, after alarums and excursions and a short rest, they proceeded to rejoin the Battalion at Bucquoy.

An incident at Couin which shows the state of tension which existed at the time has been recorded by Cpl. Nugent:—

"A party of Signallers about 15 strong who had comprised part of the Brigade Forward Party (usually referred to by the Signallers as the Brigade Fatigue Party) had received orders to return to the Battalion, although owing to the *débacle* no one had any definite knowledge as to its whereabouts. There was considerable confusion on the roads, guns in retreat, troops moving forward, and G.S. waggons moving in all directions. Another N.C.O. and myself were in charge of the party and on reaching some fork roads, being uncertain as to the route, he decided to go one way with some of the party whilst I elected to go the other with the remainder. Strangely enough we converged at Couin and reached Details. We had not been there long when with others at the camp we were told to fall in, and every man was served out with one day's rations and 150 rounds of ammunition. I distinctly remember Cpl. Jack McFie walking along the ranks distributing letters which had accumulated since the day we had left Halloy en route for Achiet-le-Grand. There was no time for speculation as to our destination or for distributing between ourselves the bread, cheese, etc., and we were hurried off in the opposite direction from which we had arrived, some carrying 2lb. tins of jam, and others with loaves of bread. The ammunition was in bandoliers which we slung round our necks. We had not proceeded more than 400 yards when a G.S. waggon came tearing down the road, the driver whipping his horses to a furious rate and yelling as he tore past us, 'German cavalry in the next village!' On hearing this the officer in charge, Capt. Edgar, said in a matter of fact way, 'Come on lads, fix your toothpicks.' These were the exact words used, and there was no time lost in doing so. Tins of jam were dumped by the roadside and we were instructed to cover the fields on both sides of the road in extended order. This we did immediately and commenced to dig in with our entrenching tools. Directly in front of us was a small ridge, and it was our intention if the German cavalry came over, to pick them off as they topped the skyline. There was an ominous silence and we waited for the enemy to appear, occasionally sending one of the party to the top of the ridge to see if anything was approaching. By the late afternoon, as it seemed obvious that a false alarm had been given, we were allowed to wander about, and subsequently found a farmhouse where we obtained some hot water and made tea with our Iron rations.

"In company with a Signaller (Knox) I discovered a deserted army hut in which were dozens of packs and pieces of equipment lying about, together with a revolver and ammunition. It appeared to us that these had been dumped some time earlier owing to an emergency, and knowing that spare shirts and socks were useful, we helped ourselves and I took also the revolver and ammunition.

"We did not go short of food or cigarettes as we had on the first portion of our journey discovered an abandoned B.E.F. Canteen and many men carried a sandbag full of 'Caporal' cigarettes, besides chocolate and biscuits.

"Just before dark we were told to find what accommodation we could for the night and not move away until further orders were received. By a stroke of luck we found a large barn containing hay or straw and slept soundly until the next morning.

"No developments had taken place during the night, and we marched the next morning for some time until we reached what remained of the Battalion in a village some distance further back."

It may be that Cpl. Nugent's account has some bearing on the appearance of some of our cookers on the horizon, to which Cpl. Southall refers later on in this chapter.

The Battalion, now re-united with the Details, remained in support in the Bucquoy area. On the 30th the enemy showed very little activity, but on the 31st there was a bombardment of about three hours duration, during which 2nd Lieut. A. E. Bell was slightly wounded.

We had now come to the end of one of the most critical months of the whole war. The Germans, boastful of victory, as we shall see from 2nd Lieut. John's account at the end of this chapter, had failed in their endeavour to separate the Allies, mainly owing to the fighting retreat made by the Fifth Army and the dogged determination of the Third, in which the 12th, in common with the rest of the 41st Division, had nobly played its part.

The fatal casualties—a full list of which appears in the appendix—suffered by the 12th during March were: three officers (Capt. E. V. Whiteway, who died of wounds later, and Lieuts. F. R. Matthews and F. L. Warland) and 59 other ranks. Some were at first reported as missing, but their deaths were afterwards accepted as having occurred during the period.

In addition Capt. A. F. Copp; Lieuts. G. C. Davenport, L. L. Linford, J. F. Tamblyn and J. A. Golding; 2nd Lieut. A. E. Bell; and 91 other ranks were wounded.

Of the officers who passed from our midst, two, Capt. Whiteway and Lieut. Matthews, were well known to the majority of the Battalion but more particularly to the Brigade and Regimental Transport men. Capt. Whiteway, as already recorded by Q.M.S. Tice, was wounded and reached the base hospital at Etaples, where we thought there was a chance of his recovery. Unfortunately nephritis supervened and he passed away on the 28th of April. As one of our original officers and the Brigade Transport Officer, his services had recently been recognised by the award of the Military Cross. He was well liked and respected by all ranks. References have already been made to Lieut. Matthews in other chapters of this history, but it is not generally known that he was one of three officers of the Brigade who offered to swim the Piave in Italy to gain information as to the enemy's movements. He was not selected to do the job, but the fact that he volunteered for such a perilous mission is proof enough of the stuff of which he was made.

Among the wounded officers we are happy to number Capt. Copp and Lieut. Linford as members of our Association. Capt. Copp has suffered from his wounds ever since that day, and it is only with difficulty that he is able to attend any of our functions. Lieut. Linford is perhaps better known to us to-day than he was then. Although gazetted to the East Surrey Regt. early on in the war after active service as a Tommy with the L.R.B. in France, he was posted to the 11th Battalion and sent over to France where he was attached to the 11th "Queen's" at "Plug Street" and Flers. After many wanderings he eventually joined us before we went to Italy.

Another sad blow to both the Battalion and the Brigade was the loss of Lce.-Cpl. E. E. ("Scotty") Williams, who died of his wounds at Etaples on the 3rd of April.

The number of officers and men reported as "Missing" was considerable, but after a time it was verified that the following were made Prisoners of War:—

Lieut. L. Dawson; 2nd Lieut. R. C. Johns; Sergts. E. Clark, W. G. Cornish, A. Currie, J. McFie, J. Radcliffe and L. L. Withers; Lce.-Sergt. W. T. Ayling; Cpls. M. Coghlan, H. C. Goddard, T. Page, and T. H. Payne; Lce.-Cpls. G. Bullard, B. Lewis, C. Meek, G. Ponman, R. Rogers, W. A. Sherwood, and E. Tuck; Ptes. R. Anthony, E. Bailey, J. Baker, S. W. Bartram, H. Baughan, G. Beech, F. Bigg, W. Billingsley, A. Bird, S. C. Browne, J. Buckley, M. C. Burgess, W. Burkin, W. Carter, F. W. Chitty, E. Colstone, H. Connor, J. Cox, M. Cox, A. Creamer, A. J. Crittenden, H. Crump, J. D. Dalpiaz, R. Dixon, B. W. C. Douthwaite, S. Eales, J. N. Edgerley, F. Edgley, C. Elam, J. Elam, E. Erridge, A. Flack, H. Fordham, C. W. Freeman, J. H. Gilchrist, W. Gladwin, L. H. C. Glassett, J. H. Graham, J. Gregory, R. E. Grimbley, F. Grist, G. Hall, J. Hall, A. Halsey, G. Hankin, E. Harbridge, W. Harraden, J. Hayward, H. Hesketh, C. Hiams, A. Hoare, G. H. Hobday, E. J. C. Holderness, H. Honeycombe, W. Houghton, E. Hubbard, W. Janes, W. Jenkinson, J. Jinks, G. B. Kirby, E. Lack, H. Leach, B. Lewin, J. T. Lewis, G. S. Lumb, G. Mathias, E. W. Matthews, A. E. May, W. Messenger, K. Mileuski, F. Neale, F. J. Neller, E. Nelson, S. Newman, A. Nichols, T. O'Brien, J. O'Hara, W. Peace, W. F. Perrin, H. Petch, T. Probert, G. Rawlings, G. Reeves, C. J. Rickard, J. A. Robbins (36421), H. J. Rose, F. Rowe, J. Russell, A. Smart, R. Smithson, A. Smith-West, G. Stephens, R. Stewart, J. Stromberg, T. W. Styles, W. A. Tapsell, H. Taylor, A. Thurley, C. G. Treby, P. Uden, H. Wainwright, L. Wall, H. Ward, G. West, R. Westbrook, A. R. C. Wheatley, S. Willsmer, A. J. Wilmott, M. J. Woods and A. C. Wright.

Reports subsequently received showed that our men were incarcerated in the following Prisoners' Camps:—Gelf, Munster 2, Minden, Friedrichsfeld, Frankfurt, Dulmen, Cassel, Limburg and Parchim. 2nd Lieut. R. C. Johns eventually reached Pforzheim, a small town on the Rhine, while Lce.-Cpl. R. Rogers, a man of advanced years who joined A Company at Rotherhithe was repatriated and admitted to the 1st London General Hospital at Camberwell on the 19th of May, 1918. Pte. J. A. Robbins died at Alldam on the 20th of May and Cpl. T. Page at Minden on the 21st. Two officers, Capts. E. B. Gillett and H. S. Todd, had been sent sick to England earlier in the month.

The 1st of April was spent in support in Bucquoy without incident except that Padre Williams came along and broke the joyful news that we were about to be relieved and he was under the impression that we were going to have a long rest from the line. In pleasant anticipation we awaited evening, when parties of the 1st/5th Lancashire Fusiliers gradually took over. The Battalion then marched to a point on the Bienvillers-Souastre Road where field-kitchens were waiting to supply the troops with hot soup. The majority of the Battalion left that evening and boarded lorries which conveyed them to the Thièvres area. A march was then made to an aerodrome at Marieux, where billets were found in the hangars. Unfortunately for B Company, the guides who were supposed to have met them and led them out must have lost their way. They were just about giving up hope of being relieved that night, when some voices in Lancashire dialect enquired where the East Surreys were supposed to be. In no happy frame of mind did B Company hand over their positions, although they were not aware at the time that these Lancastrians had already had their full share of the battle. B Company got to the road only to find that no hot meal awaited them as promised, and later on they were crowded into lorries in such a way that it was impossible to sit down. Jolted along the road, tired as could be, hungry as hunters, poor old B Company cursed "Fritz" and the company cooks right along to Marieux. After de-bussing the worst was to come for them: they were expected to find accommodation in a hangar already crowded to suffocation with sleeping figures.

Luckily Ted Holland and his cooks provided the promised hot meal; it was explained that they in company with the other company cooks had kept their tryst, but, after waiting for a long time after the rest of the Battalion had gone off, they decided that B Company must have disappeared altogether and so determined to get back to the transport lines.

We stayed in the sheds at Marieux until the 2nd, when a further move was made viâ Sarton and Orville to Amplier, not far from Halloy, so that after all we had arrived back at approximately the same place as we were in before our move on the 21st of March.

On the 3rd we took the road to Thièvres again, but this time for the last march in the Department of the Somme. Buses were here provided to convey us to Frévent. A wait of six hours, and then the Battalion entrained for Poperinghe.

Thus ended the adventures of the Twelfth in a battle which had been most trying to men who had never before had to fall back towards their own lines. We took toll of the enemy however for what he had accomplished in the area held by the Battalion. C Company in particular made him pay a heavy price before he was able to surround them, and the Lewis-gunners worked like Trojans.

Looking back over the years many of us must have asked ourselves frequently: "How did we manage to survive the German onslaught?" Only those who were

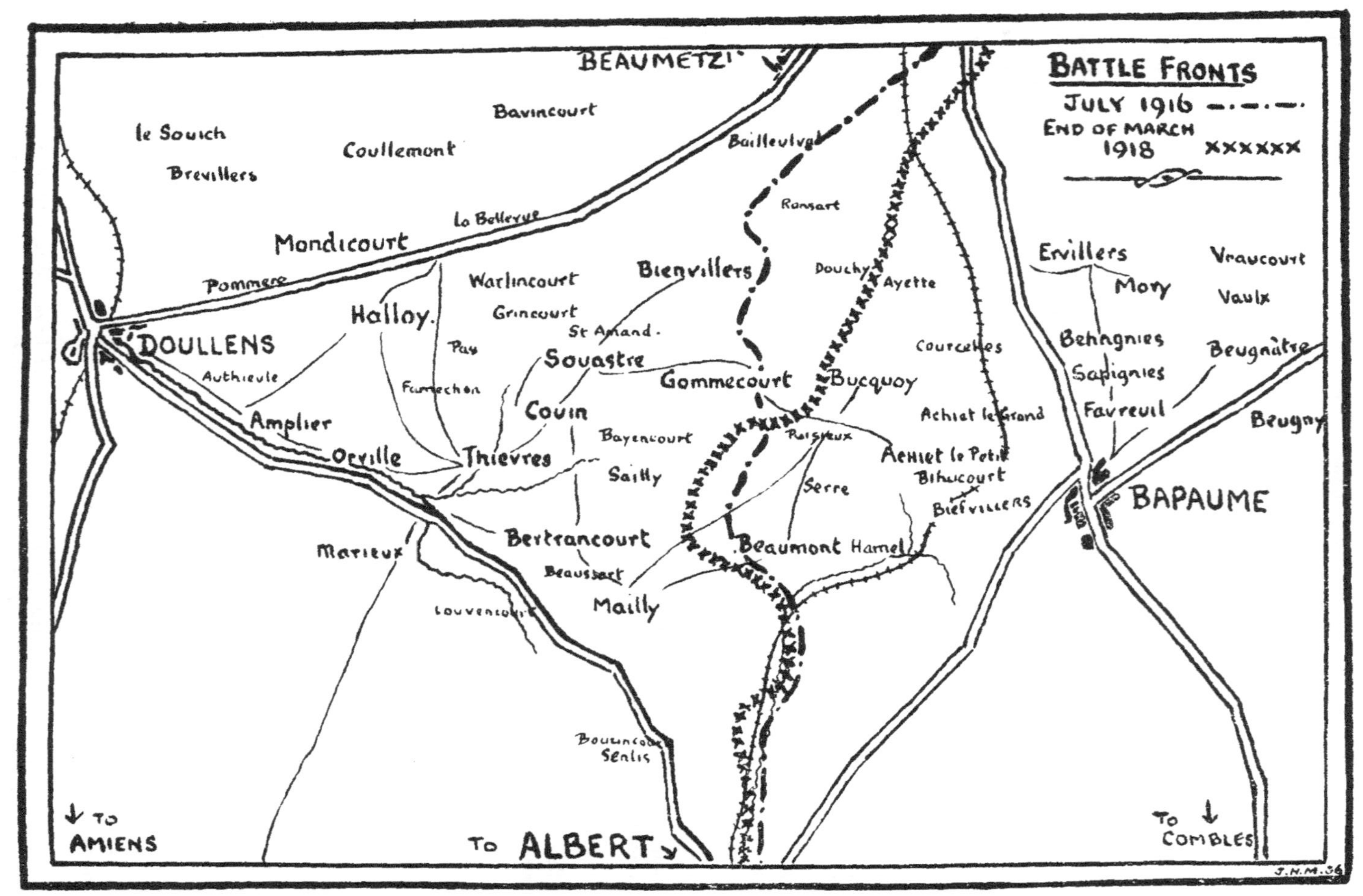
BATTLE FRONTS
JULY 1916
END OF MARCH 1918
XXXXXX
BEAUMETZ
Bavincourt
le Souich
Coullemont
Brevillers
Bailleulval
Ransart
La Bellevue
Mondicourt
Pommera
Warlincourt
Bienvillers
Douchy
Ayette
Halloy.
Grincourt
St Amand.
DOULLENS
Pas
Souastre
Gommecourt
Bucquoy
Courcelles
Authieule
Famechon
Couin
Achiet le Grand
Amplier
Bayencourt
Puisieux
Achiet le Petit
Orville
Thievres
Sailly
Serre
Bihucourt
Biefvillers
Bertrancourt
Beaumont Hamel
Marieux
Beaussart
Mailly
Louvencourt
Bouzincourt
Senlis
Ervillers
Mory
Vraucourt
Vaulx
Behagnies
Sapignies
Beugnâtre
Favreuil
Beugny
BAPAUME
TO AMIENS
TO ALBERT
TO COMBLES
J.H.M.36

present at the time can realise the utter feeling of despondency which seized us at times. We groused and grumbled and often felt the position was hopeless; but behind all this there was still a feeling that order would be restored from the chaotic conditions which followed the German advance. Panic, if it did exist, was more evident in the back areas than in the firing line. When our infantry did get a chance to face their enemy, they did so in a manner which reflected great credit on the Regimental officers and men who were called upon to bear the greatest burden.

For services rendered during the fighting the following awards were afterwards made:—

D.S.O.—Lieut.-Col. G. L. Brown.

Bar to Military Cross—Capts. H. S. Walker and J. A. Rogers.

Military Cross—A/Capts. F. B. B. Dowling and A. F. Copp; Lieut. G. C. Davenport; 2nd Lieut. R. McKechnie.

D.C.M.—Lce.-Cpl. N. A. Philpott and Pte. H. J. Sherborne.

Military Medal—Sergts. J. Lewis, A. V. N. Thompson, E. Davey, P. Newble; Cpl. W. H. Mann; Lce.-Cpl. W. E. Smith; Ptes. T. Chappell, T. Moore, J. Hester, A. Beck, A. F. Dennington and E. A. Smith.

The award of the D.S.O. to the Commanding Officer was richly merited, as we have already recorded.

Both Captains Walker and Rogers were two of the hardest working officers who ever served with the 12th. Both were regarded with the greatest esteem by the men who served under them. Capt. Rogers could be described as the quietest Company Commander we had. Many enquiries have been made by the members of the Association as to his whereabouts, but the only information we have comes from Cpl. J. Malone of A Company, who says he met him soon after the war and understood from the Captain that he was returning to America as soon as his repatriation papers were through.

Of the officers who received the M.C., 2nd Lieut. R. McKechnie of the Hants Carabineers who joined the Battalion from the 15th Hants as Transport Officer, was in some ways an object of curiosity to us all. He was a veteran of many wars and could probably show as many decorations as even Sergt. Jock Turner, the Master Cook, if not more. Mac, as he was known to us, could generally be depended upon to cause a laugh in many of the things he did, although he himself was a most serious looking individual. It was said that in the March retreat he brought the rations up to within a few hundred yards of the enemy and then created a fearful din in getting them unloaded. It was only when he was remonstrated with for giving our positions away that Mac decided that it was time he got his Transport safely off before the enemy took it. As it was, the Hants lost their cookers, while most of the packs and stores at Achiet-le-Grand had to be burned to save them falling into Fritz's hands.

The name of Capt. Dowling appears several times in the history of the Battalion, for as a young officer he had his share of the fighting and was entrusted with great responsibility for his years. He is still a serving officer in the East Surrey Regt.

The actions of Capt. Copp and Pte. Sherborne have already been referred to and perhaps it would be as well to quote the actual commendation which Lce.-Cpl. N. A. Philpott received from General Lawford in reference to the award of his D.C.M., as it throws some light on the movements of A Company, who have not received much mention in the narrative of operations.

16320, Lce.-Cpl. N. A. Philpott, 12th Btn. East Surrey Regiment (Bermondsey).

"For conspicuous gallantry and devotion to duty during an enemy attack. He protected his Company's flank with his Lewis-gun, and covered their withdrawal. He finally worked single handed, the rest of his team being casualties, and collected sufficient magazines to keep his gun in action, under heavy shell fire, until it was knocked out.

"He showed great courage and determination.

(Sgd.) Sydney Lawford,
Major-General, Comdg. 41st Divn.

Like another D.C.M. holder of the 12th (Giles), Philpott was one of those individuals whom we least expected to rise to the occasion. He was a frail slip of a boy, quiet and unassuming, but conscientious at his job. He had already been wounded while serving with the Battalion. After all, it was fellows such as Philpott who gave us the will to stick it out when things looked darkest.

The most noteworthy award amongst the Military Medalists was that of Pte. A. F. Dennington of B Company. Dennington had been sentenced a year before at Reninghelst to a heavy term for being asleep on his post whilst a gas sentry. His crime merited the extreme penalty, which no doubt because of his youth (he was a mere boy) had been commuted to ten years penal servitude. The sentence was as usual suspended to allow him the chance of making good. Right well he did this, and with a mention in despatches in Italy and the Military Medal his sentence was washed out.

How many of C Company earned decorations in that determined stand it would be hard to say. No honours were theirs, only the irony of being taken prisoner after they had saved others.

The story of the operations of March, 1918, would not be complete without some reference to the Transport and Medical Staff. First of all let R.Q.M.S. Speller tell us in brief his experiences.

"A peaceful stay in Halloy was succeeded by perhaps the worst period the 'Transport-wallahs' struck in a usually troubled existence.

"On March 20th part of the transport cleared off; I left late that evening and picked them up at Achiet-le-Grand just as the R.T.O. had been shelled off the premises. Working through a chaotic night, we managed to get forward with the officers' kits, packs, tools, band instruments, etc., which we dumped between Achiet-le-Grand and Achiet-le-Petit.

"That night the troops came through, getting to Savoy Camp early in the morning and after a meal deployed towards Sapignies where we delivered supplies for the next two days. Owing to the unfamiliar *terrain*, we did nearly lose a couple of cookers which ambled to within shouting distance of the enemy, but were warned in time by the front line troops of an adjoining division.

"On the night of the 23rd/24th I left Battalion H.Q. after delivering water and S.A.A. and found S. M. Horswell, whom I usually dug out if he was within reach. His greeting was, 'Hop it quick!' and I hopped accordingly. As I got back to Savoy Camp, inferno broke loose. Troops had already commenced retiring, and the E.F.C. had been abandoned and was being 'dismantled' by our troops. One gunner I saw with an arm hanging uselessly, his head swathed in a bloody bandage, clutching a half-empty bottle which he offered to all and sundry as he sang and picked an unsteady trail westward.

"The poor old Canteen man, who was later killed at Brandhock, implored me to save his stock which with the rest of the Regimental baggage was then the target of several low flying German planes. I ordered him back, and, as he refused to leave his charge, I encouraged him to safety by pouring a drum of spirit over the lot and sending it up in flames..

"Finally I reached the Transport lines where Nuttman had already hooked in, but all the roads were impassable with traffic. We then decided which vehicles to abandon and which to take across country with the spare pairs in lead should the necessity arise. I fancy we got them all away except one G.S. waggon, a damaged cooker, and the transport 'Coach,' a souvenir with farrier's kit and odds and ends.

"The next few days remain a haze of retirement, map references, Bucquoy, gas shells, wounded animals, and finally Gommecourt. When we were brought out of the line, I slept for 20 hours on top of a jolting G.S. waggon—my brain had gone completely numb after what seemed endless days and nights without a moment's rest."

Lastly the adventures of the small party which composed our Medical Staff gives a very good insight into the conditions which existed from the 21st of March until we arrived at Bucquoy. The writer is Cpl. Southall, who came very near to being captured.

"At last however the urgent summons came, and towards the evening of the 21st we were really on our way. We entrained in ordinary carriages, and I remember the journey in that train very vividly as we played cards by the light of candles stuck on the sides of the compartment. As we detrained in the middle of the night at a very much damaged railway station and lined up along the track preparatory to moving off somewhere in the blue, a shell landed in the street outside. The war had started for us again.

"We discovered as we moved off that the place was Achiet-le-Grand, and we didn't think a great deal of it. We marched for some time feeling dead tired and at last came to some wooden huts in a field to the left of the road. We packed down in these about 5 o'clock in the morning and received the joyful news that we should probably be going into action that day. The guns were going hard all night, and we knew that the Boche's new attack had started and that he had made alarming progress.

"The early morning was spent in getting together dressings likely to be needed for the show. The troops moved forward across the Arras-Bapaume Road, and during the day we lay out in the open near Mory. We went round exploring a bit and found an evacuated dressing station but no R.A.M.C. people with whom we could get in touch.

"At nightfall we moved forward and then over to our right. Where we got to that night I do not know, but I remember going down a sunken road and coming to one of our abandoned aerodromes, where we dug in. We then left this place and went somewhere else, where we dug in again. After moving for a third time, we finally arrived back where we started, having had a very exciting walk round without achieving much except keeping ourselves warm. I had no idea that I could dig so fast.

"Just after dawn the next morning we started off again, the Battalion taking over the front line. We found what I believe to be some sort of communication trench where we deposited ourselves not far from Battalion H.Q. We spent the night here, and, as it was bitterly cold, we went out in the middle of the night to find some sort of covering and were finally successful in finding a sheet of tarred felt which we spread over us. There was no great desire to tuck the sheet up round our necks, but it did keep some of the cold out.

"The next afternoon the doctor told us that we should be moving forward shortly to be nearer the line and he would let us know when we should be starting. Later in the afternoon he came to tell us to get ready to move. We said: 'What! Forward?' 'No. Back!' said he. I understood him to say that nobody knew where they were, and the Hants on our right had gone back without leaving word that they were going, leaving our right flank in the air and nobody knew which way little Fritz was coming next. We formed up with the rest of H.Q. at the top of the trench, and just so that we should be as conspicuous as possible we started to retire in fours. Suddenly out of the blue came two enemy planes which swooped down on us and from a very low altitude sprayed us with machine-gun bullets. By what seems a miracle none of us was hit, and the planes, instead of staying round and having a few more shots, flew off. We spread out a bit after this and continued our march down to the old position we had taken up to the south of Mory the morning after arriving at Achiet-le-Grand.

"Engineers had prepared two lines of trenches at right angles to each other, one facing eastward and the other practically south, with its right resting on the Bapaume-Arras Road. The doctor, Dick Henwood and I dug a small trench sufficient to hold the three of us at the rear of the trenches described above. As darkness fell, a magnificent firework display took place in Bapaume where apparently something set fire to a dump of Verey lights. Later there was a terrific burst of firing from the direction of the trench on our right and shouts and cries. Machine-gun bullets whizzed over the top of our trench, and men came running past us. We heard afterwards that there was tremendous confusion when the Boche attacked, and that the Battalion which should have linked up with our right across the Bapaume-Arras Road was finally posted somewhere in front of our southerly-facing trench unknown to us. The result was that these troops were forced back on us when the Boche attacked, and many were shot by our own men mistaking them in the darkness for the attacking enemy.

"Morning found the Battalion holding a line to the east of Achiet-le-Grand. We took up a position in a short bit of trench just behind the line and from here watched three tanks waiting just below the distant ridge. Suddenly over the ridge appeared hordes of the enemy, and the tanks cut loose. They went right through them and over the ridge, that being the last we saw of them. A battery of 18-pounders somewhere in and around the village was putting in some good work, and Fritz was dropping fairly heavy stuff in the place, one of the shells landing within a yard or two of where we were standing watching the tanks tearing about.

"The doctor decided to find a place which we could use as an Aid Post, so we walked across the railway crossing to the other side of the village, where we found a large farmhouse with all the upper part knocked away by shell fire. Opening a door, we entered a small room communicating with another with brick arched roofs or ceilings. This being a suitable spot we gave the stretcher-bearers notice as to our whereabouts and awaited events. The stretcher-bearers had no light job. We were not many yards from the line, but there were no R.A.M.C. bearers within miles, and our bearers after bringing the wounded to us for dressing had to wait till they were attended to and then go off into the blue to find the nearest advanced ambulance station which was some distance away. Luckily we had some wheeled stretchers which they were able to use.

"However, as they could not take a number of cases at once, we found ourselves with three cases—artillerymen—which we could not send down owing to lack of bearers. We were all weary from want of sleep, and about midnight the M.O. said he would have ten minutes' nap, that then I could do the same and then Dick Henwood. Dr. Christie lay down for his ten minutes, leaving strict orders not to let him sleep longer. I sat with my elbows on the table holding my eyelids open with my fingers for fear of dropping off to sleep where I sat. At the end of ten minutes I awoke the doctor and got down for my nap. The doctor said he would go into the village and see what was doing. He was back in two minutes saying: 'Pack up quickly, Corporal; we've got to move and do it in a hurry.' Dick looked with sadness at the 2,000 cigarettes he had scrounged from an abandoned B.E.F. Canteen and (let it be whispered) a bottle of whisky also, realising that he had to travel light and not be encumbered with luxuries. 'What has happened?' I asked the doctor. 'The Battalion must have moved out some time ago without notifying us, and there is not a soul between us and the German Army,' he said. It did not take us long to pack our stores of dressings, splints and the like on a wheeled stretcher and get off. It was quite impossible for us to take the wounded artillerymen with us, and it was a very sad thing to have to leave them behind. However, we found some R.A.M.C. bearers a little way down the road and gave them instructions where to find the wounded men, and we hope they were rescued, although we never heard. I wonder whether we could have taken any other course regarding them. If we had stayed with them, we couldn't have done anything more to make them comfortable than we had done. It would have been impossible to get them away, as nobody would have come back to the spot once the Battalion had evacuated the position, and, if we had stayed, it is quite possible that we as well as the wounded artillerymen would have been captured. As it turned out, there was just the chance that they were rescued.

"We carried on down the road and early in the morning reached a village which I believe was Achiet-le-Petit. We could not get on the cross-roads as it was occupied by streams of artillery going back to take up new positions. Making the best of things, we threw ourselves down in the road where we stood and went to sleep. I had my head on a large stone for a pillow and I believe might have slept the clock round, had the doctor not awakened me and told me that we could now continue our journey.

"We finally caught up with what was left of the Battalion, and the first one to greet me was Sam Lattimore (from Details). We got some hot tea and some food and then were off on the march again. We heard some good stories of what had been happening behind the lines. One fellow told us that a brass hat had got very alarmed when over the horizon he saw moving what he thought were enemy artillery on the march. He got together all the Details he could and lined them out in extended order for an expected attack. The enemy guns proved to be British Army Cookers! We also heard that our Battalion Transport had been spending its spare time travelling round France in circles.

"We then went back for a few miles to a small place, where we had a day or two's rest. The roll call was a pathetic affair. We then went into the line again at Bucquoy. The Boche attack seems to have slackened down at this point for a little, and this short period in the line was quiet and casualties few."

Note 1.

LIFE IN THE ENEMY COUNTRY AFTER MARCH 25th, 1918.

As in the case of Hollebeke, we are fortunate in being able to publish some experiences of two of our comrades who were captured on the 25th of March. Both belonged to C Company.

Sergt. Joe Radcliffe, M.M., has already recounted his experiences on the first day when he fell into the hands of the enemy, and now continues his narrative from the 26th:—

"When we awoke in the morning we were anxious to know two things: did we get any grub that day and where were we? Eventually we got a plate of gravy with a piece of meat and bread. The meat was horse, and, though we knew what we were eating, we enjoyed it.

"We then found that we were in a compound at Denain. During the day we were taken to 'Deutschland' by train and at the end of the journey found ourselves in the War Camp at Munster II. Here we met other prisoners, who told us that N.C.O.s would be separated from the men and sent to another camp, as N.C.O.s did not have to work. This caused us N.C.O.s to do a bit of 'fiddling.' The majority of N.C.O.s had four sets of stripes (one set on each arm of the tunic and overcoat). By taking three sets off we were able to make three privates into N.C.O.s.

"We stayed at Munster for about three weeks, and then some of us (about 300 in all) were moved to Minden. A few of C Company came with me. Those I remember for certain were Sergt. J. McFie, Sergt. F. Ayling and Cpl. T. Page. When we arrived at Minden on April 16th, we were put with other prisoners, mostly British, who had been captured about two or three years. In this camp the British prisoners were receiving parcels of food sent through the Red Cross by their Regimental Care Committee, which contained biscuits, bully, butter, dripping, cigarettes, etc., and weighed about 10lbs. These were sent to prisoners personally about every six days. In addition the British Red Cross Society in Rotterdam sent parcels now and again to the camp for new prisoners. These were distributed by the British Help Committee (a committee of about 10 British prisoners).

"On our arrival on April 16th we were given a parcel between two men, and how we enjoyed it. Bully and biscuits (how many times had we turned up our nose at them) and a drop of tea, the first we had had since we were captured. The weather at this time was very cold, and about a day after we arrived Cpl. T. Page (Gas Corporal of C Company) was not very well and went into hospital. We were not allowed to see him, and he died on May 2nd. Sergt. McFie, Ayling and myself and N.C.O.s from other regiments buried him on Sunday, May 5th, at 3 o'clock.

"On May 13th we were warned to move again to another camp, arriving at Sennelager on May 14th. Life at this camp was very much better for us three, and we met prisoners of the East Surreys who helped us along until our own parcels arrived. After staying here for about three months, we were again moved to Cottbus, where we stopped until January, 1919.

"The three of us came home together with a crowd of others from Cottbus, staying one night at Enschede (Holland), a couple of days at Rotterdam, and then went over to Hull. We had previously been fitted up with khaki, etc., at Rotterdam. We were then taken to Ripon in Yorkshire, given a jolly good feed, and then sent home on leave for two months. I reported back to the Depôt at Kingston and shortly afterwards was Depôt Orderly Sergt. One day I was detailed to go to Waterloo with such N.C.O.s and men of the 12th as were there. C.S.M. Wilkinson, Sergt. Ayling and myself duly reported at Waterloo and there met the Cadre of the 12th Battalion, this being the first time I had seen or heard of the Battalion since my capture. We marched with the Cadre behind the Colour which was duly handed over to the Bermondsey Borough Council, had a good feed at the Bridge House Hotel, London Bridge, and said good-bye to those present. So ended my happy (at most times) association with the 12th (Bermondsey) Battalion, East Surrey Regiment."

The other account comes from 2nd Lieut. Rex C. Johns, a young officer who was still in his teens:—

"The German 'Big Push' was at its height when, on the morning of March 25th, 1918, I was taken prisoner on the Somme near Bapaume. I had an immediate personal experience of the 'camaraderie' of the troops in the front line, of which so much has been heard. A young German subaltern engaged me in conversation and we discussed affairs in the friendliest manner, perhaps the predominant feature being the complete confidence of my new-found acquaintance that this 'Push' was to have its early culmination in Paris.

"Having proceeded further back from the trenches, I have a vivid recollection of a road which was absolutely straight and appeared to have no end, and along which thundered transports, conveying men and materials to hammer home the temporary advantage which the Boche was enjoying. On either side of the road were piled the dead harvest of the terrific action which had raged for the last five days, ally and foe being indiscriminately huddled together with horses and limber-mules, the whole creating a sickening stench.

"A German N.C.O., hearing me say that I was cold, offered me the khaki greatcoat from the corpse of a British private nearby. Continuing along the same straight road we were ordered to help carry German wounded on stretchers back to the dressing stations. Late that night we arrived at our first temporary camp for the night.

"In passing through the French villages on the following day, great precautions were taken to ensure that no demonstrations of sympathy should occur, the peasants being ordered to remain in their cottages until we had passed. At one such village however, occurred an incident which showed clearly that this sympathy, combined with a very real courage, existed in no mean measure.

"It was late evening, and we were standing outside the wire encampment in which we were to spend the night. Our principal sensation was that of acute hunger. The prevalent food shortage was keenly felt by all, and we naturally were not the first to receive consideration. Imagine our surprise, therefore, when, out of the semi-darkness, black bread was thrust into our hands by French peasant-women, who had in some manner evaded the guard. As there were very strict orders against any form of fraternising, and the people had endured such lengthy privation, we were profoundly moved by so kindly, not to say courageous, an action.

"For some days our march went steadily on, and I can well recall that my sympathy was aroused for the flying officers who still wore their tall flying boots; although most practicable when in the air, these were more than a slight hindrance when marching.

"Progress was not greatly speeded up when eventually we entrained, since almost all movements of trains were in the opposite direction. Troops were being rushed up to the front and here again evidence of the prevalent confidence asserted itself. 'Paris'—'Paris'—'Paris'—was chalked all over every train, the occupants being convinced that this was the ultimate, even early, destination. Trains bearing prisoners into Germany were naturally shunted on to sidings whenever the situation demanded. Thus on one occasion we were without food for 48 hours. When at length we drew into a wayside station, they gave us barley soup, which, although at the time truly welcome, taken in liquid bulk tended to chronic distention.

"Occasional hostile demonstrations were a feature of our journey, bitterness increasing as we progressed further into Germany. At length, after detraining, a further spell of marching found us at Rastatt in Baden. The camp here had been occupied by Russian prisoners, but, peace having been established with that country, its occupants were made to evacuate it in our favour, a few being retained in the capacity of cooks, orderlies and bath attendants.

"A series of army huts composed this camp, and rations took the form of 'vegetable' soup twice a day, a feeble imitation of coffee for breakfast and a small quantity of dark bread per day. After a few weeks on this diet our capacity for exercise was very limited. We very carefully saved all our potato peelings, which being roasted, were highly appreciated. The main conversation was centred on the subject of food, reminiscences being exchanged of the palatial meals which had been enjoyed in the past.

"Only two attempts at escape were made, both proving unsuccessful. The first was when a party managed to secrete itself under the flooring of a Russian Church, only to meet with early discovery. On the second occasion two officers endeavoured to get through the wire, but again the attempt was short-lived, one poor fellow being hit through the head, the other getting back in the nick of time. Shortly after this the camp was broken up, and we were sent to permanent camps in different parts of the country. I found myself at Pforzheim, a small town on the Rhine.

"I had then been a prisoner for some three months, and conditions here were vastly superior to any I had yet experienced. The commandant of the camp was a Count, really a good sort and complaints were seldom heard. One amusing event lingers in my memory. We were permitted to grow flowers in pots on our window sills, which were situated high up in the building, and one diminutive 'Jock' was arraigned before the authorities on a charge of pouring water on the heads of passing civilians. He was able to establish his innocence however, receiving nothing worse than a reprimand. When allowed out on parole, ample evidence was afforded us of the privation which the population had endured. The women and such old men as remained were pallid and emaciated; rickets was common amongst babies for want of milk after birth.

"Here again however my stay was short-lived, since I was transferred to hospital suffering from neurasthenia. A short spell in hospital was followed by the arrival of a repatriation order which enabled me to return home to England viâ Holland."

CHAPTER XIII.

4th April to 30th June, 1918.

Back in Flanders—Evacuation of Passchendaele—Trying period—Rest at Bayenghem—The Battalion takes over from the French.

JUST before dawn on April 4th the Battalion detrained at Poperinghe and marched to the Rue de Furnes, where billets were taken. The troops were housed in cellars, and it was soon apparent that they needed to be when heavy shells began to arrive from the enemy lines many miles away. At this time shops were still open in Poperinghe despite the bombs that were dropped and the shells that came over from the Boche daily.

Our stay at Poperinghe was short, for in the afternoon we moved on to School Camp, Watou, and the next day was spent in kit inspections, baths and delousing. In the absence of Colonel Brown, who was inspecting the part of the line which was going to be taken over by us, Major Williams commanded the Battalion when it was inspected by the G.O.C. VIII Corps on the 6th. Capt. R. O. Russell, M.C., left us that day to join the 10th R.W. Kents, who had suffered severely in the operations on the Somme.

The same day a draft of 102 other ranks from the 52nd (Graduating) Battalion, Royal Sussex Regt. joined us. These were mostly youths of about 18 years of age who had been hurriedly sent overseas to fill the gaps in the ranks created by the great German offensive. The older soldiers referred to them as the "War Babies," for some of them looked extremely youthful. However they soon showed that despite their youth they were not lacking in courage.

Another draft of over 100 other ranks came from the 1st Battn. Royal Fusiliers, amongst whom were some sturdy veterans besides a fair sprinkling of youth. A draft from the 22nd Battn. London Regt. also joined during the period together with drafts from the 8th, 9th and 13th battalions of the East Surreys. In all, the Battalion received about 400 reinforcements.

Although it was thought that after the fighting on the Somme the Battalion was bound to have a rest, this was not to be. The situation further south demanded that all available British troops should hold the line in the north to release those who could be sent to the south to help to stem the invasion there, which, although it had slackened off, was still serious. Accordingly on Sunday, April 7th, the Battalion set out to relieve the 1st Battn. Guernsey Light Infantry, which was holding the right front position of the right division of the VIII Corps on the Passchendaele Ridge. The Battalion marched to Quinton Station and entrained in the evening on the Light Railway for Borry Farm, to the left of the Zonnebeke Road. The Transport, Details, and some of the reinforcements moved to Toronto Camp, Reninghelst. The same day Major Stallard proceeded to take over the duties of Second-in-Command of the 10th R.W. Kents.

From the 8th to the 10th the situation was quiet on our front, which consisted of a series of outposts with supporting troops in rear. This was the method of defence adopted after the severe lesson learned from the fighting in this sector during the Third Battle of Ypres. There was heavy mist on the front during the period, making observation difficult.

On the 10th B Company took three prisoners and D Company one. Three of these Germans were apparently out on patrol and owing to the difficulty of finding one's way about in this region they had wandered into our lines; the other was a postman who was endeavouring to deliver mail to his comrades when he was snaffled by the imperturbable Battalion barber, Sam Webster of B Company. He was promptly despatched to Brigade H.Q. with his bundle of letters.

It was on the 9th of April that the Germans started their attack against the Portuguese near Neuve Chappelle. Before this it was obvious from the way the back areas, even on our front, were being shelled that the enemy was contemplating some sort of active operations. Intermittent shelling had taken place on the front we were holding on the 9th and 10th, and two other ranks were wounded.

At 5.30 a.m. on the 11th a creeping barrage of light calibre shells was put down on our outpost lines and was followed by a bombardment of 4.2's and 5.9's on the ridge, which lasted for one hour. As a result Pte. W. Weeks was killed and four other ranks wounded; Pte. T. Chidgey died of wounds the same day.

On the 12th the Battalion was relieved by the 2nd/6th North Staffs of the 59th Division and entrained at Iberian for St. Jean, whence it marched to Maiden Camp. 2nd Lieut. C. H. Ward, who was acting as entraining officer was badly burned and had to be admitted to hospital. Later the Battalion moved to a line through Square Farm and Low Farm, about 500 yards in rear of our original positions, in anticipation of the withdrawal from the existing front line. The companies then began to dig in. A and C Companies were in front: B was in reserve, whilst C was to be the counter-attack company in case of emergency. To augment the companies 150 men from the Details who had moved from Toronto Camp to Dirty Bucket Camp, Vlamertinghe, proceeded to join the Battalion in the new positions.

Before proceeding, let us turn to Cpl. Southall's account of the district we were about to evacuate. He says:—

"Any thought that we were going back to rest was soon dispelled when we found ourselves almost immediately back on our old front in Belgium and heading for the Passchendaele Ridge. The country we had been fighting over down South had been a Garden of Eden compared to this. As we marched along the duckboards raised high above the ground with on either side of us a dreary waste of huge shell-holes filled with water, mud and stench, it was impossible to feel other than depressed. We occupied a small German pill-box just below the summit of the ridge.

"One evening Giles went out to get rations; he was gone for some time when he was brought in by one of the boys. Giles was wet through; he had apparently slipped off the duckboards into a shell hole full of water and being in danger of drowning had raised a cry for help. 'When I got there,' said the rescuer, 'I found Giles almost up to his neck in water. His overcoat had floated up round him and there was Giles looking for all the world like a (something) water lily.'

"On another evening the doctor came to the dugout, called me outside, and, pointing to the Verey lights which were going up to our right and well behind us, asked me whose lights they were. 'Ours, I hope,' I replied. 'You are wrong; they are the Boche's lights,' he told me and then went on to explain that the enemy had pushed us back on our right around by our old front line before Ridgewood and that it was necessary for us to evacuate the Passchendaele Ridge for fear of being surrounded. A few hours after we were on our way back."

Cpl. T. Day relates the following story.—

"We were in the line near Passchendaele, and to get there we had to go along a duckboard track surrounded by water and mud.

"I was in charge of a Lewis-gun at B Company H.Q. and also a gas guard, nine men all told. One of them was a man named Chambers, a real Bermondsey boy. The night before we were relieved, an officer coming up to take over Company H.Q. fell off the duckboards and got a nasty soaking. The next morning the officer appeared in slacks and I was with Chambers, who was doing guard, when the officer related his experience of the night before. 'Blimey, mate, I bet yer got wet!' said Chambers. I reminded him he was talking to an officer. He replied: 'Sorry, mate, I didn't know yer in them clothes.' "

To appreciate the position which had arisen, we have to go back to the start of the Battle of the Lys on April 9th, when under cover of a mist an intense barrage fell on the British Front from Armentières to Lens which lasted for about six hours.

The first attack fell upon the Portuguese, who had not before been seriously engaged in a battle. One Portuguese battalion fought on stubbornly at La Couture, but the rest, overwhelmed by the enemy, had to retreat. Fortunately a gallant defence of the district around Givenchy by the 55th (Lancs) Division saved the day. Most of the English divisions had already been through the mill on the Somme, and it will be to their undying credit that they denied the enemy the Channel Ports at a time when he considered they were a spent force. To the men of the 55th Division we should raise our hats, for had we not handed over to these Lancastrians at Bucquoy only a few days before this new phase of the German operations after they had already seen severe fighting on the first days of the March offensive? Men of the 51st, 25th and 19th Divisions, all of whom were near us in the operations of a few weeks before, fought the enemy to a standstill where possible and only retreated in the face of overwhelming odds. On the 10th the enemy had taken Armentières, Ploegsteert and Messines, while further north the forward positions at Hollebeke were abandoned and the line fell back to the Wytschaete Ridge.

The Germans continued to advance on the 11th, when it is said that rumours of a complete defeat, the evacuation of G.H.Q. and a wild scramble to the coast were current in Britain. If there was panic at home, there certainly was not among the troops in the Ypres Salient. We knew that things were not going too well with us by the direction of the Verey lights, but our one desire was to be saved from that encirclement which threatened the Second Army.

The famous Order of the Day issued by Sir Douglas Haig was circulated and struck the right note. The otherwise silent Commander of the British Army poured out his soul to the men who he knew only too well were being called upon to bear more than their share of the fighting. "Many of us now are tired. To those I would say that victory will belong to the side which holds out the longest." . . . . "With our backs to the wall, and believing in the justice of our cause, each one of us must fight to the end." Such were some of the expressions of the Commander-in-Chief at a time when things looked desperate. The British line bent but did not break, and England without question has to be thankful for being spared, as the result of this battle, the sufferings endured by the Belgians and French.

In accordance with the situation further south it was decided to evacuate the ridge for which so many tens of thousands of lives had been sacrificed less than a year before. The Salient would thus be reduced, and man power could be economised in holding a shorter front. It must be remembered that there were little or no reserves behind us, only the promise that French and American reinforcements would reach us as soon as possible.

Although the Twelfth itself had thus far not come to grips with the enemy in this new offensive, some of its members who were on command or on courses of instruction had already been in action, as composite battalions were formed of all available troops in the back areas. One reads in the casualty lists of Sergt. E. R. Durrell dying of wounds on the 17th of April. As Durrell was attached to the Second Army Sniping School one can presume that he must have been called upon to help to stem the rush. Durrell was an immense figure of a man, who was noted for his enthusiasm in any job he undertook. From our Intelligence Section he had gone to Division and from there to Army. He was a brilliant linguist and in this direction was a very useful acquisition not only to A Company but the Battalion as a whole.

On the 14th the 26th Battn. Royal Fusiliers took over the front positions, and the Battalion moved back to Carte Keep and Mill Keep.

Another move was made on the 15th to a camp in the neighbourhood of Goldfish Château, but it was by no means a healthy one; the men were cantoned in huts which were not only a mark for the enemy airmen but also his artillery. Situated a little way outside of Ypres, the camp was surrounded by British batteries and was not a great distance from the enemy, who, following up the voluntary retirement in this sector, had reached a point near Hell Fire Corner, about two kilometres along the Menin Road by the railway crossing. Any place that was close to Ypres was bound to come in for some attention from the enemy, as he knew only too well that the way through this town was used daily by troops and transports going to and from the front positions. It was not surprising then that on the 16th the camp area was heavily shelled with H.E. and gas.

The Battalion worked from the 17th to the 24th on the Army Reserve Zone Trenches behind Ypres and between the Brielen and Poperinghe roads, the work being carried out by two companies from dawn to dusk.

On the 18th the enemy began to shell the huts in which Battalion H.Q. and B Company were accommodated, and a move had to be made. Arising out of the bombardment of B Company an incident happened which caused some amusement afterwards. C.S.M. F. Heydinger had recently rejoined the Battalion after having undergone some training in England for a Commission in the Artillery, and was in B Company H.Q. when the enemy opened up on a British battery which was situated almost opposite. This battery had been firing over our hut for some time, and we knew that sooner or later retaliation would follow. When the first shells from the Boche arrived, they cleared the hut all right and were certainly making for the battery. This went on for some time, and meanwhile C.S.M. Heydinger, utilising his knowledge of artillery shooting, was explaining to us how safe we were, when all of a sudden an enemy shell dropped behind the hut, and very soon Heydinger and all the other occupants scattered. He did not have time to explain the reason, but we presumed it must have been a "short" which he had not allowed for. This cleared half the camp, and on the following day another bombardment of H.E. and gas caused the whole camp to be temporarily evacuated, but not before one other rank had been killed and another wounded. About this time news was received of the death of Sergt. E. C. Selby on a ration dump near Poperinghe on the 17th. He had previously been employed in the Quartermaster's Stores and having been marked "permanent base" was attached to the A.S.C.

On the 21st the following officers joined:—2nd Lieuts. J. C. Carver, F. W. Crafter, F. C. Ells, G. H. Frischling, O. A. George, W. Greenhill, K. L. S. Lawton, R. M. Meadows, J. C. Waller and L. A. Ward, bringing the strength of the Battalion up to 43 officers and 1,087 other ranks.

Work was now intensified on the defended localities already referred to, three companies being employed there throughout the day, while another company was sent to work at St. Jean. We returned to camp after work was finished but very little real rest was our lot, as the enemy was consistently shelling the camp and neighbourhood, using a considerable amount of gas shells. The shelling was particularly severe between 3.0 a.m. and 8.0 a.m. on the 25th, when our casualty roll was two other ranks killed and 21 wounded. In addition 2nd Lieuts. F. C. Ells and O. A. George and 20 other ranks, mainly from C Company, who had suffered severely throughout the bombardment, were slightly gassed but remained with the Battalion. Working parties had been sent out at 6 o'clock as usual, but these were recalled at 10.0 a.m., as orders were received for the Battalion to stand by ready to move at short notice. In the evening a move was made to Dambre Camp; from here the Details moved again to B Camp, Brandhoek.

The enemy was expected to attack on the 26th; the Battalion had been allotted a counter-attack rôle against positions in front of Voormezeele and in the neighbourhood of Ridge Wood, which the C.O., the Second-in-command and the Company Commanders had reconnoitred on the 23rd and 24th. Accordingly the Battalion moved at noon to the Brigade rendezvous near Goldfish Château. Here we stayed resting in a field until the evening, waiting for the attack which did not materialise, when orders were received for us to return to Dambre Camp.

The 27th was a day of very great activity of the long-range guns of the enemy. From 9.30 a.m. until 3.45 p.m. a high velocity gun shelled the neighbourhood of Dambre Camp with shrapnel and H.E. and made a direct hit on an occupied stable. Down at B Camp, Brandhoek, much the same sort of conditions prevailed, but with more fatal results. At this time the enemy was in the region of Kemmel Hill, and in consequence every precaution had been taken along the road to Poperinghe in case he should break through. Trees were charged with explosives to be blown at a moment's notice in order to impede him should he come that way. Ammunition dumps (of which a good many existed in this area) were also mined ready to be destroyed should the worst happen. It was while the Details were listening to the high velocity shells falling around that a great calamity happened. One came over, and then a tremendous flash lit up the sky followed by a terrific explosion. The huts at B Camp collapsed like a pack of cards and the occupants were thrown to the floor. A hail of débris came like a whirlwind over the camp, and soon everyone was fleeing towards the Poperinghe Road. Shrapnel began to fall everywhere, and we wondered whether the enemy had let all his artillery loose. After a while, when things had subsided a bit, we discovered what had happened. A German shell had struck the mine in a large dump of our shells of different calibres. At the time the vicinity was crowded with men of the Labour Corps who were digging reserve trenches. An urgent call for stretcher-bearers was sent out, and soon the Details were doing what they could to pick up the wounded, mostly oldish men of the Labour Corps, under very trying conditions. It was expected that as a result of the first explosion other dumps would be involved, so that the men had to work like niggers before the next crash. Unfortunately the explosion had wrecked part of a C.C.S. near by, and it was a pitiable sight to see already wounded men trying to make their way to safety. Civilians also suffered, for the roofs were blown from their houses, which most of them quickly evacuated.

In all these things, tragic as they were, there always appeared the funny side. There were a few estaminets around, which the owners had left hurriedly, and some of the troops were soon in possession, helping themselves to wines and other things which were left behind. And this while the enemy continued to drop his heavies and the explosions from the dump made the place anything but a safe one to be in. Whether the proprietors of these estaminets ever returned we do not know, but at all events some

"Doc" Harrison and Corporal Southall at Tower Hamlets, September 1917.

of the troops were under the impression that their tenancy was over. However, there was one old lady with her daughter who still remained. On going to get some eggs and chips from her in the evening, we discovered that her estaminet had been partly demolished as a result of the explosion. "Where did you go, Madam" we enquired, "when the explosion took place?" "My daughter and I retired to our cellar," she replied. We then asked her why she did not move away now that things were getting so hot in the district. She politely informed us that she had lived there all her life, and, if she left, the possibilities of getting a livelihood elsewhere were very doubtful. The French Government might offer her refuge in some remote part of France, but there would be no compensation for the business she would have to give up. We came away admiring the old lady's courage, and her remark, "How would you liked to be turned out of the house where you were born?" gave us ample scope for debating what we should have done in her circumstances.

Near B Camp was another house which had been abandoned. We entered to find it full of British Army rations including "maconochies," bully, biscuits and potatoes. We left these, but a goat which was straying about in the garden was adopted and handed over to the Transport.

The Battalion stood by all day on the 28th and 29th, as things were rather uncertain in the neighbourhood of Kemmel, which, after a heroic defence by British and French troops, fell into the hands of the enemy on the 25th.

The loss of Kemmel, a hill 500 feet high, was a great blow to the defence in the Battle of the Lys. It was actually lost by our Allies who had sworn to hold it at all costs. Saturating the hill with gas, the Germans brought up some of their crack troops and managed to dislodge the French.

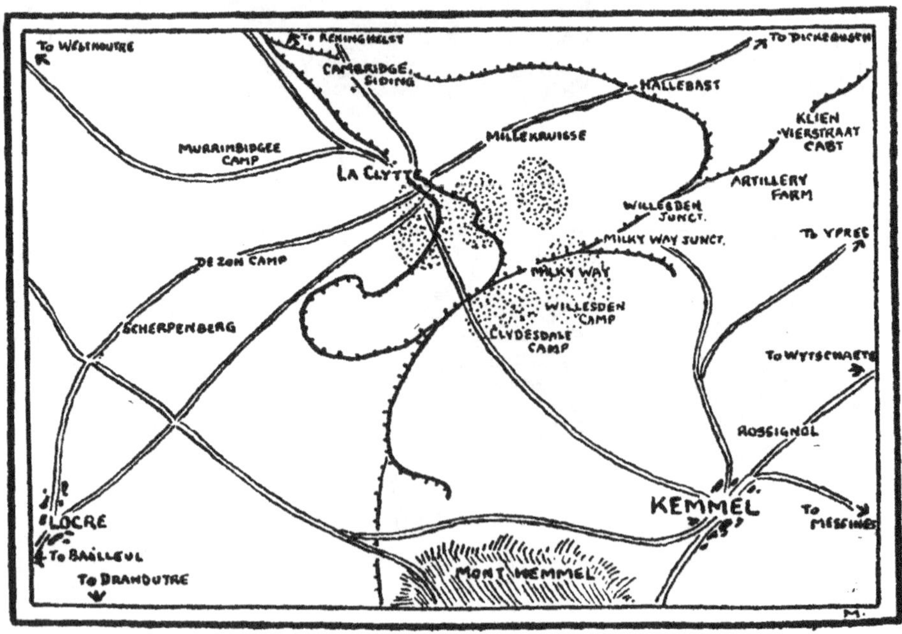

MONT KEMMEL *from* VIERSTRAAT—1917

drawn by John Aston, M.A.

It was not the privilege of many to enter the sacred precincts of the Observation Post which the British held on Mont Kemmel before the enemy captured it. In 1916 and 1917 we had seen the hill daily from our positions and must have passed it scores of times, but, as it was prohibited ground, we were unable to get any real idea of what an important position it was. Capt. H. S. Walker had the opportunity of visiting it while we were at Reninghelst. One day he went for a ride with Colonel Knapp and, reaching Kemmel, they dismounted. "Passing the sentry," he says, "we went up to the Observation Post, a wonderful place and an unforgettable experience. A large-scale map with all important points plotted and numbered; a powerful telescope on a tripod which could be swung to any number, and the place desired was easily picked up; it was extraordinary the number of places behind the enemy lines that one could see." Capt. Walker then relates how on his return to Reninghelst he was afterwards sent for by the C.O. and told to say nothing about the trip, as he had since discovered that Kemmel was out of bounds to everyone, except those with a special pass.

Tremendous inroads had also been made by the enemy on territory which we had known as rest billets; Steenwerck, Bailleul, Outtersteene were in his hands. The line now ran through Dickebusch, Locre and Strazeele to the outskirts of the Forest of Nieppe. Ploegsteert, Messines, St. Eloi, Voormezeele and Hollebeke no longer belonged to us, while the fighting had flowed to the foot of the Mont des Cats. Every inch of this ground was vital to our safety and, although greatly outnumbered and overwhelmed by shell fire, our troops made the Germans pay dearly for what they occupied. The Belgians too showed the do or die spirit, for on the 17th of April, after a terrific bombardment, which we heard in our sector, they were attacked by superior forces and, although losing ground at first, counter-attacked gallantly, recovered their line, and captured 600 prisoners. Those of us who were privileged to hear this bit of news had the greatest admiration for what the Belgians had done. Many had come to regard them as a spent force, but this latest exploit gave us the assurance that the spirit of King Albert was still behind the remnants of a very gallant nation. Had the Belgians given way, the Germans might have used this gap to surround the Second Army which was at the time retiring from Passchendaele.

On the 29th the last battle for the Channel Ports was fought. Attacking from Meteren to Zillebeke Lake against British and French troops and again trying the Belgian line further North, the enemy gained little success, as counter-attacks neutralised all his efforts.

It was the intention of the Germans to renew the attacks later, but, owing to the Allied offensive which Marshal Foch instituted when he found that the enemy had practically exhausted himself, these attacks never materialised. Instead the troops were sent south to try to hold up the advance which culminated in victory.

Capt. Hector Walker was wounded on April 30th together with Sergt. C. W. Field, the Provost Sergeant. He was sent to England on the 9th of May, and thus ended a very active and gallant career with the Battalion which had lasted for over 18 months. Arriving with the Surrey Yeomanry in October, 1916, on the Somme, Capt. Walker was soon given command of C Company. At varying times he had acted as C.O. and Second-in-Command. Then he took over as acting Adjutant and was finally appointed to the post in February, 1918, vice Capt. Clift. He was twice decorated and also mentioned in Despatches, and there were only two other officers, Capt. David Walker and Capt. J. A. Rogers, who saw more service, active or otherwise, during our whole existence. We were to lose one of the Walker Clan and regain another, for David, having rejoined on the 27th, was subsequently appointed Adjutant, a position which he occupied until the Battalion was disbanded.

During the month the following officers were sent to England sick:—Capt. G. P. G. Reah (Brigade Intelligence Officer) and Lieut. B. F. Dodd. In addition 2nd Lieut. C. H. Ward was sent home as the result of his injuries sustained at Iberian. The casualties suffered during April were 4 other ranks killed and 29 wounded. In addition to those already mentioned, Ptes. T. Sheldrick and J. Flannagan were killed outright on the 23rd and 25th respectively, while Pte. W. J. Hartley died of his wounds on the 25th and Pte. H. Gerrard on the 26th.

May opened with the Battalion finding the usual two officers and 100 other ranks per company for work on the new defences, known as the Green Line, behind Vlamertinghe. The enemy artillery was extremely active throughout the morning on the back areas, and as a result two other ranks were gassed.

This was the second anniversary of our arrival overseas, and the numbers of the old originals were beginning to dwindle. Of the officers who came over in May, 1916, there were none actually now serving with the Battalion. Some were on command and others rejoined later, but even they were few.

On the evening of May 2nd we relieved the 26th Battn. Royal Fusiliers in the Ypres sector near St. Jean, and sustained one casualty during the night. During the early hours of the morning of the 3rd our own artillery carried out a shoot between 3.0 a.m. and 4.0 a.m., which caused the enemy to retaliate and wound one of our men. Much shelling continued throughout the day, the front and reserve lines being well strafed as well as the back areas. B Company had a very bad time of it, for, besides Ptes. G. A. Howell and J. Pembroke being killed, ten other men were wounded. The airmen on both sides were also much in evidence.

The 4th was another day of considerable artillery activity on both our and the German front. It was also a tragic one for the Battalion. In the evening heavy shelling of our front and support lines together with Battalion H.Q. caused the following casualties:—Lce.-Cpl. E. Baker and Ptes. L. H. Acklin, P. E. Bartley and W. Cowell, killed, and eleven other ranks wounded. Ptes. T. Moore and G. Reynolds died of their wounds two days later. The death of Pte. Leo Acklin of A Company removed from our ranks one who, if he was not the first to enlist in the Battalion at Rotherhithe, held the first number allotted to the Battalion—12001.

The Details were now back at B Camp, Brandhoek, where daily we witnessed a terrific bombardment of Kemmel Hill by all types of guns from the French 75's upwards. The Boche was supposed to be holding the summit, but to those who watched it seemed incredible that any human beings could exist under such a tornado as swept the hill daily. Of course the enemy retaliated, and both the Transport and the Detail camps did not have too happy a time. Sunday, the 5th of May, was very rainy, and in consequence aerial and artillery activity was rather restricted. In the afternoon however the enemy put down a bombardment of gas shells on the Potijze and Menin Road, and one other rank was gassed.

Apart from planes flying low over our lines which were driven back by our anti-aircraft guns and Stokes mortars, there was little to record for the following morning. Later however a party of one officer and ten men from B Company raided James Farm for identification purposes, but found the farm empty. Pte. W. H. Russell was killed and four other ranks wounded during the day. The G.O.C. visited Battalion H.Q. on this day and presented the Colonel with a recommendation card for gallantry on the 25th of March.

Relief came from this sector on the 7th when the 15th Hants took over. The week had been a very trying one, as the casualties suffered show. It seemed as though the enemy, baulked of his efforts to reach the coast, was using up all his reserves of ammunition which had been accumulated for the great battle. But any thought that we were going to have an easier time was soon dispelled when we moved to the Ypres Defences and worked on them till the 9th. During the first day 2nd Lieut. W. Greenhill was gassed and seven other ranks were wounded.

Another move was made on the night of the 10th, when we took over on our right, half the front held by the 18th K.R.R.s and 50 yards of the front held by the 2nd York and Lancs Regt., after being relieved from our original front by the 9th Royal Inniskilling Fusiliers. We were now in the Ramparts and the Ypres Defences and as the enemy was only a short distance away at Hell Fire Corner, our positions were anything but healthy.

Rain occurred on the 12th and kept the planes quiet, but gas-shells fell in the vicinity of the front line and, although causing no casualties, kept the "Gas alert" order, which was prevalent on this front, very much in operation. Gas was the real danger in the Ramparts, for shells made very little impression on these strong fortifications.

During the 14th of May the enemy artillery was exceedingly active throughout the day and night, a large amount of gas-shells, both Mustard and Lachrymatory being used. The Dead End at Ypres was heavily shelled in the evening, and as a result three of the C.Q.M.S.s, A. Nash, W. H. Barnes and H. E. Tice, were wounded while bringing up rations.

R.Q.M.S. Speller says:—

"The nightly journeys viâ Dead End and Suicide Corner resulted in such casualties to the C.Q.M.S.s that no N.C.O. would take the job without suasion, although previously regarded as 'bombproof.' For some period the companies detailed N.C.O.s for the job in turn."

Enemy aircraft had also been active during the afternoon and brought down three of our observation balloons. One plane was brought down by our machines. Four other ranks were wounded in the course of the day.

Conditions were somewhat similar on the 15th, when 2nd Lieut. F. C. Ells was gassed and six other ranks wounded. Kemmel was again shelled heavily by our guns, when the French advanced their line to the north of it. Much shelling of Ypres and the back areas was experienced on the 16th, and enemy planes continued to bomb extensively.

The Battalion was relieved by the 23rd Middlesex on the 17th and then proceeded to Foster Camp near Brielen, three men being wounded before the relief was complete.

During the 18th the Battalion was employed on cleaning up and kit inspection. Gas-masks were worn as an exercise, for it was about this time that the enemy began to make great use of gas-bombs dropped from his planes. There was a battery situated near the camp, and in consequence several H.E. shells fell in its vicinity during the day, and at night time over came the enemy planes, dropping their bombs all over the place. Similar conditions prevailed on the following day, when Pte. E. T. Mardell was killed.

Musketry and gas-respirator drill was carried out on the 20th, gas-masks again being worn for half an hour. There was some shelling of H.Q. in the morning, and a hasty retreat had to be made to new quarters in a wood near by. Fortunately we had no casualties, although a battery 400 yards away had several.

During the 21st training was carried out as usual, the enemy remaining quiet. He made up for this in the evening though, as the opening up of his guns coincided with the arrival of his bombing planes. 2nd Lieut. A. J. Rodd was gassed and one man wounded during his moments of hate. Again on the following evening we were bombed from the air, the machines flying very low over the camp, but not being successful in causing any casualties. Nevertheless it was an experience which we did not relish, as this constant night bombing was beginning to tell on the nerves, besides robbing us of sleep which we sorely needed.

Despite the trying days and nights we had spent during the last few days we found time to get ourselves into a condition to earn the praise of General Towsey who, inspecting us in the morning of the 22nd, complimented us on our smart turn-out.

Training, including P.T., was carried out on the 24th, whilst the Boche continued to shell the batteries in our area. In the evening the "Crumps" gave a performance in the camp by way of a change. One cannot remember whether their performance was disturbed by the other "crumps," but one does remember the praiseworthy efforts of our own brass band, which during the period gave daily concerts to cheer us up. Occasionally a shell would land close to where they were playing, but never once was their programme curtailed because of the enemy "strafing."

Another period of so-called "rest" had now been completed, and in the evening of the 25th the Battalion marched to the Ypres sector to relieve the 26th Royal Fusiliers. The next day was spent in repairing trenches and completing the Ecole Switch Line which was situated midway between the Menin Gate and Hell Fire Corner, and was now under construction. The aircraft on both sides showed great activity during the day, which, although recorded in the Diary as being reasonably quiet, was not free from casualties; Pte. A. Golder was killed and seven other ranks wounded. On this day Pte. P. Hoffman died of wounds in England.

A patrol of one officer and two other ranks went out in the evening of the 27th to reconnoitre the ground leading to a supposed enemy post on the right of the Menin Road, but there were no signs of the enemy here.

Notification was received on the 28th of the Mention in Despatches of the following:—Acting Lieut.-Col C. F. Stallard; Major C. T. Williams; Capts. F. B. B. Dowling and G. P. G. Reah; 2nd Lieut. R. N. Haine (now attached to the 122nd T.M.B.); C.S.M. G. Hammond; Lce.-Sergt. W. Hall; and Ptes. A. Dennington and J. McSweeney.

Aircraft was again active on the 28th. Baulked in his effort to reach the coast, the Hun had now started a campaign of "Frightfulness" in the air. Men returning from the base at Etaples told how his planes had been over and bombed the hospitals and camps, killing nurses and wounded men. A wave of indignation began to spread amongst the troops and demands for retaliation. Soon we began to see hordes of our own planes making towards the German lines and we understood they were bound for the Rhine. In addition our airmen were now dropping leaflets behind the Boche lines giving a true insight into what had been actually happening along the front. With Lord Northcliffe in charge of British propaganda this phase of warfare very soon began to tell on the enemy, who for the first time during the war started to learn the true condition of things.

The work of completing the Ecole Switch was being pushed on with the utmost vigour and to the end of the month all available men were pressed into service. Things had not been going well down at the Transport lines, for the enemy, being in possession of Kemmel and the ridges which dominated the Salient, was alive to every movement of troops miles behind our own particular bit of front. On the 29th "A" Echelon was shelled out and suffered four casualties. The Details, having moved on the 26th to Tanner Camp, Peselhoek, were also shelled there on the 27th and 28th, and so a further move was made to Dublin Camp. Here they spent the last day of May in recreational training, which included a game of football. This was played in full view of a German observation balloon, and before the final whistle the enemy began to shell near by. This did not deter the footballers at first, but, when a large shell landed about 50 yards from the pitch, followed a minute or two later by another behind one of the goal-posts, the game was brought to a hasty conclusion just as the centre forward of one side was in the act of putting the deciding goal through. The men scattered to a hut close by, and then followed a long argument as to the result of the match. The centre forward claimed that he had scored before the goalkeeper had rushed to cover. The goalkeeper in turn claimed that, at the time the centre forward had shot, he was lying prone to save himself from the explosion of the shell behind his goal. After a long discussion it was agreed that "Jerry" had the honours for shooting so straight from such a long distance.

The London Gazette of May 31st made known the award of the Meritorious Service Medal to the following:—Acting R.S.M. D. Saunders, R.Q.M.S. N. Speller, and Sergts. G. Nuttman and W. Turner. "Polly" Saunders was the R.S.M. of the 41st I.B.D. at Etaples, which position he had occupied since leaving A Company before the Battalion came overseas. Saunders was an excellent instructor and also a good sportsman who had been wounded early in the war. Speller had at last got a well merited but belated decoration. Why he never got any other decoration many of us could never understand. He was not the man to shirk his duty wherever it took him. Night after night he had come up with the rations under conditions which were at most times particularly trying. George Nuttman, the Transport Sergt., and "Jock" Turner, the Master Cook, and acting Q.M.S. of H.Q. Company, were in the same boat as Speller. Their job was to see that the wants of the men in the line were not neglected, and they succeeded, despite all obstacles, in achieving this very essential service. But the driving force behind all was Speller.

The casualties during the month of May were: 8 other ranks killed, and 3 officers and 47 other ranks wounded or gassed. In addition to those already mentioned, Pte. W. Russell (attached 122nd T.M.B.) was killed on the 6th, and Pte. F. G. Skinner died of wounds on the 15th.

During the month Lieut. T. B. McWalter and 2nd Lieut. W. S. Hall rejoined, and Capt. G. O. Searle and 2nd Lieut. C. C. Simpson joined, but the latter soon left for England and was posted to the M.G. Training Centre at Grantham. In addition 2nd Lieuts. J. T. Thornton, A. Graves and C. W. Skellett joined the Divisional Wing; and Capt. A. R. K. Edsell was posted to the 1st Battn. Royal West Surrey Regt.

For the first three days of June the Battalion continued to occupy and consolidate the positions in the Ypres sector, during which the artillery and planes of the enemy continued to annoy us. On the 3rd two American officers were attached for instructional purposes.

Major G. O. Searle relates an amusing incident concerning two American soldiers who visited the front during this period.

"It was, I believe," he states, "whilst we were in the Ypres sector that the first two American N.C.O.s were sent up to see what it was like in the line. I remember taking them round the front line. They seemed very decent coves and pretty tough, but the equanimity of one gave way somewhat when a machine-gun opened up at a distance of at least half a mile. With a wild yell he leapt on the parapet and drew his revolver shouting, 'Where are the ——? Let me get at them.' "
72.—Regimental History.—C.D.

We were relieved by the 4th Battalion, The Manchester Regt., on the night of the 3rd, and marched to Mission Siding, where entrainment was made for Proven. The relief was not without incident, for, as Colonel Brown has recorded in his diary, we sustained ten casualties coming out of the line. Ptes. E. Ferry and A. E. Tickner were killed, whilst Pte. W. Stevens died of his wounds on the 5th.

Before we leave the sector around Ypres, a few points from Cpl. Southall's reminiscences are worth recording:—

"One night while we were sitting by candlelight playing cards, Fritz came over on an air raid. Sergt. Field, the Provost Sergt., came round shouting: 'Put all lights out there.' It seemed a shame to stop a good game of cards for an air raid, so we put the candle on the floor under the table, blocked up the window and sat on the floor carrying on with the game. The raid continued for some time, and at last we got down to sleep with the noise of dropping bombs and anti-aircraft fire still sounding in our ears. When we awoke, the crashing of falling missiles was still going on, and in my semi-wakened state I thought it was the air-raid still in progress. However the door opened, and in came some casualties; we realised that it was not a continuation of the previous night's raid, but that Fritz was shelling our huts. We had, if I remember rightly, about 14 casualties, and as a result we were moved back to some huts in a small copse near Vlamertinghe. It was quite comfortable here, except that a battery of naval 4.7's on the road to Dirty Bucket Camp used to blow our heads off, or so it felt, every time they fired.

"After a few days here the doctor announced that we were going forward again the next day. Before this there had been one day of alarums and excursions when the Battalion had lain out in the fields in extended order expecting to go into action in the direction of Ridge Wood, but nothing happened and we went back to our billets at the close of the day.

"The night before we were due to go up to Ypres I developed a temperature. The next day I had not improved, so the doctor suggested that I had better have a few days at the Transport lines. So I set off after mid-day to Dirty Bucket Camp and then turned to the left on the road towards Brandhoek past the shell dump which had gone up a few days before. The area looked as though a tornado had struck it.

"I finally reached the Transport lines and packed myself down in one of the huts. At night the Boche artillery spent a few hours searching for a newly arrived British battery of 8in. guns in a neighbouring field. Jerry didn't find the guns, but he certainly found the Transport lines. After a most uncomfortable night I got up in the morning to find that a shell had landed through the door of an unoccupied hut behind ours, blowing the roof up into the air. In a line with the front of our hut about 20 yards away was a series of four 5.9 shell holes, whilst another shell had gone through the Q.M. Stores and done a lot of damage. The Transport could not stand this sort of thing, so they packed up and moved up the road till they came to a cross-road on our right. Here they pulled up into a field and we were accommodated in a bivouac. Q.M.S. Speller found a small hut and set to work to put up his plates and cups on the shelf. He had just got them fixed when there was a tremendous crash, and all the crockery was shaken off the shelf. My head felt as if it was well on its way to Ypres. Well camouflaged down the side road was a battery of French long range guns and we were right in their line of fire. When they fired, the noise was deafening.

"I felt that, if I was supposed to be enjoying a rest, I would rather be up the line, for it couldn't be more noisy than this. The next day a message came from the doctor to say that the remainder of the Medical staff had developed temperatures, and would I go up? I found the boys in a dugout along the Canal bank at the Dead End, Ypres, where they seemed to be having a quiet time. Scott of the Signallers and one or two of his pals were amusing themselves paddling up and down the canal in a home-made boat with shovels as paddles.

"From here we moved over to the Ramparts, where we also had a quiet spell. One day we were watching a Stokes gun being used to fire at a German plane which was slowly flying up and down. It was amusing to see the Stokes shells going up into the air and speculating how near the plane they would be when they burst. I went in for something when suddenly the doctor came rushing in for dressings. I started to follow him, but he told me to stay where I was, as it wasn't a nice sight to see. Apparently a Stokes shell had burst in the gun practically blowing the crew to pieces. Strangely enough the plane was eventually brought down by a lucky hit from an 18-pounder shell.

"We had a few casualties whilst at the Ramparts, and these had to be brought down at night. Fritz occasionally dropped a shell on top of the bank which blew out our candles.

"We eventually left Ypres and then went back for a short rest to a spot near Dirty Bucket Camp where we were billeted in huts. One day, just as dinner was about to be served, Fritz started shelling round the huts, so we decided to go for a short walk to A Company's premises, where there was also a canteen. While there we were entertained by the spectacle of four Boche planes trying to get at a kite balloon around which a very effective barrage had been put by our artillery. While Fritz was hovering around, four of our planes appeared on the scene, took one opponent each and, so we were later informed, brought the four down. Deciding to go back, we crossed the light railway line, and there was a sudden screech as a high velocity shell made its way towards us. We dropped, and my tin hat fell off. The shell hit the ground about a yard from me and as I picked up my helmet and jammed it on my head bits of mud dropped on to it. It was only mud however, as luckily for us the shell was a dud. Expecting more we legged it to a neighbouring trench, where we sat down and howled with laughter at one another as we recalled our antics."

Cpl. Nugent in the following account, throws further light on the accident referred to by Cpl. Southall:—

"While we were at the Ramparts, many men at H.Q. witnessed one afternoon a very unfortunate accident. As it was a nice day, a number of Signallers and Runners, etc., not on duty were sitting down sunning themselves, while on the opposite side of the road which ran parallel with the Ramparts was a small sand-bag emplacement inside which was a Stokes trench mortar. This was being operated by a sergeant of the K.R.R.s, and with him stood a corporal of the Hampshires. Outside the enclosure was a lad, whose duty it was to pass the Stokes mortars, one at a time, to the corporal, who in turn dropped them into the muzzle of the gun. This was put there to fire at low flying enemy aircraft and was, I believe, in the nature of an experiment. Anyway, we were having a quiet time; one of H.Q. was feeling merry, as I well remember hearing him, whoever he was, whistling a tune from the 'Bohemian Girl' (when I hear it now, a picture of what subsequently happened always comes before me).

"An enemy aeroplane, flying low, came into view and bang went the Stokes gun, to be followed by a burst of the shell, a little to the rear, but nevertheless a good shot. Some yelled encouragement to the sergeant, and we were awaiting the result of the next shell, when there was a blinding flash and a terrific explosion. Someone dashed past me and rushed into the sap. When the smoke had cleared, what a sight met our eyes. Of the sergeant very little could be seen whilst the sandbags had been knocked flat. The metal at the muzzle of the gun was split into many strips and bent towards the base similar to the skin of a banana when partially peeled. The corporal lay on the ground with both legs and one arm off. Some of us rushed over with a coil of signal wire to tie up his limbs and stop the bleeding, but it was of little avail; he was carried into the sap, where he mercifully passed away soon after. The lad had rushed into the sap and was suffering from shell-shock. It was said at the time that the sergeant was due for leave next day. The accident was ascribed to the use of a defective mortar, the supply having been taken from a salvage dump, many of which existed around this part."

Another item of interest is contributed by Nugent in connection with the use of message-carrying dogs while we were in the Ecole-Switch Line. He says:—

"Dogs were tried during the Great War as a means of carrying messages, but, so far as the experience of the 12th Battalion is concerned, they were more of a nuisance than a help. The Germans were reputed to have kept dogs in their trenches owing to their keenness of hearing, in order to give the alarm in case of attack, but whether these were successful or not I cannot say. It is extremely doubtful in any case whether they would be of much use, as dogs are terrified of fireworks, to say nothing of H.E. shells.

"The one occasion when dogs were brought up to the 12th Battalion as a means of communication was in 1918, when the line was held in the vicinity of Ypres, H.Q. being in the Ramparts, near the Menin Gate.

"Along the Menin Road, just off 'Hell Fire Corner,' was a heap of ruins with capacious cellars known as 'The School.' On this occasion it was utilised to house one company and also formed a Battalion Forward Post with two signallers, a linesman and a runner, the writer being in charge. A telephone exchange was maintained which kept communication between Battalion H.Q. in the rear, the other three companies, a machine-gun post, and an artillery O.P.

"One day word came through that two dogs were being sent up by runner after dark and that these were to be released separately at given times and the usual form used by the signallers was to bear the name of the Battalion in code and the time of release only. In due course a scurry was heard, and into the signal office came a runner, out of breath and in a muddy state, hanging on to the collars of two dogs of a nondescript appearance. One was of the sheep-dog variety, rather on the shaggy side, and the other a mongrel type with the strain of Irish Terrier, both being of strong build. Each wore a heavy collar to which was attached a metal cylinder to contain the messages.

"To judge from the lurid remarks of the runner, one could only assume that he had had a rough time, and after a short spell he related his experiences. Apparently he should have arrived about an hour earlier, but it transpired that, after starting off all right along the Menin Road, trouble commenced as soon as he turned off the main road. One dog spotted a rat and immediately broke away after it, over the shell holes. The runner dragging the other went in pursuit and after a struggle managed to get a grip on its collar. Soon after a shell burst near by, and both dogs, now terrified, started to drag the runner along through the mud and filth until at last he managed to get them to their destination.

"While we were listening to this account, the dogs had been wandering round the cellars sniffing at everything, and one was observed going up some steps leading to one of the exits which at that time was not being used. Knowing that he might get free again we rushed up the steps in time to grab his collar and haul him back. There was a broken door at the top badly damaged by shell splinters and much holed by bullets, where on a clear morning a splendid view of Hill 60 could be obtained, as the School was situated on a slight rise. If the dog had escaped through this door there is little doubt he would have eventually found his way into the front line.

"When the time came, the arranged message was written and placed in the receptacle on the dog's collar, and the runner took the dog out the same way as it had come in. The runner was absent for about twenty minutes and then returned to inform us that the dog would not leave the place. Shortly afterwards we went out and found the animal wandering round the ruins searching for rats. All other means having failed, we threw some brickbats at him and then he bolted.

"By this time the other dog was ready, and being taken out in the same manner, curiously enough seemed to know what was required of him and trotted off in the right direction. The first dog was released at about 11.0 p.m. and the other half-an-hour later. Nothing further was heard until the next morning, when an enquiry was made whether the dogs had been released overnight. Neither of them had been seen, but from accounts received afterwards it transpired that the second dog had turned up at Brigade H.Q. two days later, but the first dog had not been seen or heard of after leaving the ruins. He may have been killed by a shell or more likely wandered along until he came to an inhabited village to become the property of a Belgian and used to draw a vehicle.

"This was the one and only experience we had of dogs as messengers, and many of us were not sorry."

On arrival at Proven, in the early hours of the morning of the 4th of June, the Battalion marched to Road Camp, where it joined the Details who had previously moved in. The men rested here until the evening, when they moved to Proven Siding and entrained at midnight. Watten was reached at 5.30 a.m. on the 5th, and then a march was made to rest billets at Bayenghem in the Eperlecques Training Area.

Once again we found ourselves away from the Salient with all its horrors and nightmares, and gladly we looked forward to the belated rest, which, but for the new developments which had arisen since our return to Flanders, should have been our lot after the worrying and exasperating times on the Somme in March. There was a feeling that things were going much better with us, although one could not fail to see that, with guns bristling in the vicinity of Cassel, the danger was not yet over. Still, if they could afford to dispense with our services in the line, even for a week or two, there were hopes, not without foundation, that the tide was turning in our favour. Rest we needed, and, if we were to enjoy that rest to the full, then the only thing was to try to banish from our minds, temporarily at any rate, what we had been through for the last three months. To this end we now found ourselves established in the pleasant little village of Bayenghem, a few miles away from another village of pleasant memories—Nordausques.

From now till the 24th of June we were to spend a fairly enjoyable time in a district which was well supplied with billets of the barn type and many of the amenities of life which to-day we might think trivial, but which were then very much looked forward to by the average Tommy in the Second Army Training area. A thorough programme of training was arranged, but, as it was being carried out in very congenial surroundings, we had little cause to grumble.

Nothing was more conducive to putting fresh life into the troops than a complete change of diet when facilities were available. The Second Army Staff not only encouraged this, but tried to ensure that cooks were well instructed in making the best use of the rations issued to them. But even then much depended upon the master-cooks of the battalions. The 12th was fortunate in having Sergt. "Jock" Turner as Sergeant Cook, for his previous active service in many campaigns had been of the utmost assistance to him and the Battalion in providing the troops with the best fare possible in every kind of circumstances. The time had now come when "Jock" found that with his activities in connection with the Canteen and the spare-time job of Q.M. Sergt. of H.Q., he would need an assistant. This assistant was found in the person of Cpl., later Sergt., Jack Greenslade, of B Company. Since joining us Jack had made himself well known throughout the Battalion as a first-class boxer and footballer and all-round sportsman. In addition he was a smart and cheery N.C.O., very well liked and respected in his company. The test of his ability as a cook came when we reached Bayenghem. Soon after our arrival our two expert cooks got busy. Field ovens were built under their direction, and instead of bully and other stews, roast joints made their appearance. Plum puddings also found a place on the diet sheets which were hung up in the cookhouse. Altogether the "inner man" was well provided for during the next three weeks.

Only one thing marred the respite from the line, and that was a severe outbreak of influenza. A wave of this mysterious malady was sweeping Europe at the time, and we were beginning to wonder whether the Germans had released these germs to make up for their failure to beat the Allies with their soldiery. At all events a large proportion of the Battalion was down at one time or another with this sickness. A special billet was used as an isolation ward, as it was impossible to evacuate all the cases to hospital. However, the duration of the illness was not more than three or four days. As smoking was supposed to stave it off, men began to invest their pay in buying cigarettes from the Canteen which Sergt. Turner had established as soon as we had settled down in the village. Unfortunately the Americans, who were also in the district, were purchasing their smokes from our canteen, and very soon our supplies began to fall short. As soon as this happened the "Yanks" had to be refused. They were attracted by such brands as "Lucky Strike" and "Richmond Gem," which with their arrival had gained a sale in France hitherto unknown.

Bayenghem not being far from our old billets at Nordausques, many journeys were made to that village to renew friendships forged with the civilians there before the Battle of Messines. Passes to St. Omer were also available, and great advantage was taken of the concession. Sports were held and football often played.

For the time war was forgotten, and the familiar sound of "Housey, Housey" (the cry of the "Lotto" merchants) was heard daily in the billets when parades were over. Colonel Brown, ever a good sort and sportsman, was inclined to turn a deaf ear to this gambling, but one could not expect him to tolerate this sort of thing outside his own H.Q. Some of the bravest "Lotto" and "Crown and Anchor" experts had the audacity to do this, but the arrival of "Wag" Love, the R.S.M., and Charlie Field, the Provost Sergeant, made them seek more obscurity in barns to carry on their nefarious trade of "fleecing" the troops.

On June 8th General Towsey, to the profound regret of all ranks who had served under him, handed over command of the 122nd Brigade to Brigadier-General S. V. P. Weston, D.S.O., M.C. The strain of two years and four months of arduous work on foreign service had told heavily on his health, so that he who had borne the burden and heat of the day was not privileged to lead his beloved brigade to final triumph. No commander was ever more sympathetic with the troops under him, so that he gained not mere respect, but from many a much rarer thing, affection.

The 12th was a pay day. The usual five francs was not doled out to the troops, as by this time credit sheets had arrived from the Pay Office at Hounslow, showing most of the men in very good standing. Some were allowed as much as 50 francs, as Company Commanders were beginning to realise that the men were desirous of spending while the opportunity was afforded.

On the 17th the Battalion took part in the Divisional Platoon Rifle Competition and lost by three points to the 15th Hants, the competition being finally won by the 18th K.R.R.s. A Battalion Concert Party, which had recently been formed, gave a performance on the 19th, and the "Crums" entertained us on the 21st.

Training had gone on steadily day after day, gas drill, musketry training and open order fighting being carried out constantly. The Brigade had a field day on the 20th, the object of the scheme being to practise units in keeping direction, and on the following day a practice attack and withdrawal was carried out in Eperlecques Wood. From this it was becoming clear that the idea of trench warfare was receding from the minds of our General Staff. A war of movement, such as many of us had visualised before we went overseas, was now accepted by both sides to be the only solution to ending the conflict, and, though the Germans had been the first since 1914 to make a real start in this direction, the Allies, under General Foch, were equally determined that, once the German progress had been stayed, no time should be lost in making counter offensives before the enemy had time to dig in and shelter behind the almost impregnable fortifications which had proved so costly to us between 1915 and 1917. These counter-offensives had already been launched on the French front with much success, and there were signs that the enemy was gradually losing the initiative.

The three weeks' training at Bayenghem came to an end on June 25th, when the Battalion paraded and marched to Rubrouck, a distance of 18 kilometres, where billets were occupied for the night. Here a draft of twenty-three other ranks joined from the Divisional Wing.

Next day we moved forward to occupy the East Poperinghe Line which was held by the 3rd Battalion, 52nd French Regt. The march was made viâ Cassel, where a rest was taken and dinner supplied. Further along the Steenvoorde-Abeele Road we reached the little hamlet of Beauvoorde, where we remained till the end of the month. Here and in the adjoining hamlet of La Cornette billets were taken over from the French, three of their officers remaining with us for 24 hours. The billets consisted of old barns and outhouses situated near a wood and amidst growing crops. The inhabitants were few but industrious, and besides tending the crops also did a fair trade in supplying the men with coffee, beer, and cigarettes of the "Flag" variety. There was one habitation near B Company's billets which drew attention. It consisted of an old shack made with the aid of biscuit tins and corrugated iron which sheltered three sisters who were found to be refugees. As far as we could make out, their parents had been killed in the old house from which they had been driven and they were trying to eke out an existence by supplying coffee to our fellows. One of the sisters was quite a child, whilst the other two were in their 'teens. All had a careworn expression, and it was apparent that they had been through much suffering during the last few months. The men in B Company took pity on them and whilst we were in occupation there saw to it that they were not wanting for food.

During June, Sergt. A. V. N. Thompson was sent to Hayling Island on a Lewis-gun course, and Lce.-Sergt. P. Coffin proceeded home as a candidate for a Commission. 2nd Lieuts. C. A. Watts and R. W. Davis were posted to the Battalion from the 1st Royal West Surreys. 2nd Lieut. Watts had already served in the Battalion as a private soldier and was eventually posted to his old company, "D," after joining on the 30th. Other officers joining were Lieut. H. Graves and 2nd Lieut. A. F. Topham. The following died in hospital during the month:—Lce.-Sergt. J. W. Hewitt, and Ptes. J. G. Clubb and J. A. Pout. The casualties during June had been 3 other ranks killed and 19 other ranks wounded.

CHAPTER XIV.

1st July to 27th September, 1918.

In the La Clytte-Westoutre Line—Fighting over the old rest area of 1916/17—Breaking in the Americans—Move to Esquerdes—Rest cut short again—Relief of 27th American Division—Hot action at Bois Quarante —Heavy Casualty List—Preparations for final advance.

THE 1st of July, 1918, found the Battalion parading at 10.0 p.m. and proceeding to take over reserve positions in the La Clytte-Westoutre Line. The march was made to Reninghelst, where relief of the 103rd French Regiment was carried out. Special precautions had to be taken to prevent the enemy discovering that the French were being relieved.

It was strange how the fortune of war had changed. Here we were in positions which had served us as rest billets less than a year before. The capture of Kemmel had somewhat altered the landscape, and Reninghelst was suffering severely from the enemy artillery. It was apparent that the inhabitants had beaten a hasty retreat, for in what remained of the houses were still to be seen articles of apparel as well as furniture.

The work of the Battalion was principally that of finding working parties. Although not officially recorded, the following incident will probably be recalled by some members of B Company. There were two sergeants in the Company who could always be depended upon to see the lighter side of things, and so it was that journeying through Reninghelst they came across a house which actually boasted a piano. Investigating further, they came across a top hat and also a straw hat. Arrayed in this head-gear they assembled a working party near the house, and, to the strains of "Colonel Bogey" played on the piano, the party proceeded to its duties. Such is war!

During the 3rd the enemy was active at night, when five other ranks were wounded on a working party on the La Clytte-Reninghelst Road.

The Transport was situated at Lappe (a mile north of Boeschepe), while the Details, under Capt. G. P. Cooper, were near Beauvoorde. But neither of these enjoyed much rest during the night, for enemy planes began to get troublesome, nightly paying visits and dropping bombs in the neighbourhood. The chief sufferers were the horses, as the Boche used a type of bomb which exploded without burying itself in the ground, scattering splinters over a very wide range. There were several stampedes, and drivers had a hard time in trying to keep their charges under control.

On the 5th the Battalion relieved the 15th Hants in the front line, and a continuous trench on the right, half a mile east of La Clytte, was also taken over from one company of the 2nd Yorks and Lancs Regt. The remainder of the front line companies were disposed in isolated posts.

The 7th of July will be remembered by the Details as the day when we got our first glimpse of the "Doughboys" going to war. It was a Sunday morning, and some of us were standing about in groups discussing an air raid of the night before, when in the distance we perceived a winding column as much unlike British troops on the march as we could wish to see. We had seen certain French and Italian troops at times marching all over the road, but somehow these were different. March discipline in the British Army was always very strict, no matter how tired the troops might be, so we were certain these were not British. However, we had not long to wait before discovering by their dress that the column was in reality an American one. As the "Yanks" approached us, we straightened ourselves up to give the salute to the officer in charge. As we saluted him, he stopped and enquired where the "shooting gallery" was. We were a little amused at this description of the line, but when we told him that it was still some miles away, he remarked that his men had been "hiking" all the morning and then passed on to a camp which was situated some little distance from Beauvoorde. As the "Sammies" passed, we realised that we had a new addition of the pack mule on the Western Front. The Labour Corps were renowned for carrying great packs on their backs, despite their supposed infirmities, but the American troops had them beat on that score. They seemed to be carrying, in addition to the ordinary impedimenta such as great-coat, blanket, etc., that we bore, pots and pans and an extra pair of boots. Our packs were usually neat, but the Americans appeared to be anything but that. Whoever devised their pack must have left out of consideration the fact that there is a limit to the endurance of the "footslogging" infantryman. Major Searle, in recalling this march past of the American battalion, says that the whole road was littered with their impedimenta. He believes that the above description of their kit leaves out quite a lot. "I seem to remember that they carried a pepper pot, mustard pot and salt cellar as well! And also half a tent? But perhaps this is an exaggeration," says the Major. We cannot vouch for what was actually contained in the large bundles on their backs, but at all events we sympathised with these new warriors, and, if their march discipline was not as good as ours, there was every reason to excuse them because of the heat and the burdens which they bore. It must be remembered that by now the British Army had learned a lesson, and packs were not only lightened but at times dispensed with, fighting order being considered a good substitute for the awkward bundle more familiarly known as "Charley."

Within a few days more Americans began to arrive, and it was clear that they were now to take a very active part in the war on the side of the Allies. They were concentrated in woods near Steenvoorde, where later they were inspected by General Pershing. The men of the 12th found them a very curious lot, similar in manner to the Australians, and spent many hours telling them about the line and listening to their stories of enlistment. Some had evidently come over for a tour of the Western Front and were quite unconcerned as to what was expected of them. It was said by some people that they boasted of what they were going to do to finish the war, but there was little of this spirit exhibited by the Americans at Steenvoorde. Most of them realised that the British and French had suffered terribly, and they intended to do what they could to help in bringing the war to an end. As yet they were in a raw state, and, although they were to make mistakes through inexperience, they were not lacking in courage nor the will to win through.

On July 7th Battalion H.Q. in the line received some attention from the enemy artillery, and at night our Transport was shelled while bringing up rations, with the result that two horses were wounded and later on destroyed. Two men were also wounded.

Many tales are told of our new Brigadier, General Weston. He was a man devoid of fear and was always turning up where one least expected him. It was on the 7th, Major Searle believes, that in the evening, while pretty heavy shelling was going on and he was walking between two of our isolated posts, that he saw the Brigadier walking in from No Man's Land, which, to say the least, was a surprising direction from which to see one's Brigade Commander approaching.

On the 9th an enemy patrol attempted to reach our lines, but Sergt. MacKenzie and the men of his platoon in B Company drove them off. Two other ranks were wounded during the day.

The Battalion was relieved on the night of the 10th/11th of July after having spent a miserable day, when the rain made things uncomfortable and the enemy trench-mortars and guns made great play on our front and support lines. The 18th K.R.R.s took over, and the Battalion went into support, relieving the 15th Hants. From now until the 15th the Battalion remained in support, supplying working parties for the R.E., being occasionally troubled by artillery fire and enemy bombers from the air.

Sergt. Jack Greenslade had now taken over the position of Sergeant Cook from that sturdy veteran, Sergt. Turner, who was at last on his way to England. Things were too unhealthy for cooks to do justice to the rations near the line, so Greenslade decided that at the Transport lines some of his cooks could turn their attention to producing some dainties which would find favour with the troops. Accordingly some of them remained behind and spent their time in making rissoles which could be sent up each night with the C.Q.M.S.s. Puddings made from ground biscuits were flavoured with raisins, and the hot food containers were brought into action for conveying real pea-soup, cocoa and tea to the men in the line, but judge the surprise of all when one night fishcakes arrived with the ration parties! Everyone wondered where the fish had been caught. Never before had such a delicious dish been offered to the troops. How did Jack do it then? First of all he "won" two hundredweight of potatoes from somewhere. Then he managed to procure some fish paste from surrounding canteens. Mixing these ingredients with bully beef, he produced the dish which everyone took for the genuine article. Greenslade's first consideration was for the men in the line, and he saw to it that his cooks showed no favours to Quartermaster-sergeants or others who might try to get more than their share of the rations. As a corporal of B Company, before taking over his new appointment, Greenslade had reason to know that occasionally there were some who did not always share the rations out as fairly as they should have done. As he was a huge fellow with a great sense of justice and a terrific punch, there were few who cared to get on the wrong side of him.

We were now to lose the services of our C.O. for a month as, after serving three years in France, he was granted a month's leave to England on the 15th. In his absence Major Williams assumed command, Capt. G. O. (later Major) Searle acting as Second-in-Command. The Battalion went into reserve at Reninghelst until the 20th, carrying out working parties, despite the continuous shelling, and indulging in baths.

The shelling of the reserve area nearly resulted in the loss of our two senior officers, as Major Searle relates in a humorous vein:—

"I remember rather an amusing incident with Major Williams. We were sitting outside a deep concrete dugout, somewhere between Reninghelst and La Clytte, when we were in reserve. Anyway, the time was about 10.0 a.m., the morning sunny and warm, the war apparently a long way off, and we had two perfectly good chairs. Major Williams suggested a drink which I virtuously refused as being too early. After a short argument, however, I surrendered, and we had only gone down a couple of steps when a terrific blast landed us on all fours at the bottom. After making sure of the drink, and perhaps another for luck, we put our heads out again to find our two perfectly good chairs had disappeared and a nice shell crater decorated the exact spot were we had been sitting. I therefore swore never to hesitate about accepting a drink in future."

On the 18th a raid was carried out by the Brigade on our right, which resulted in three prisoners and one machine-gun being captured. For this raid the Battalion stood to, all working parties being stopped.

Before we proceed further, a personal account of the period from Cpl. Southall will help us to visualise the change which had come over the district we knew so well in easier times, besides recalling to many certain incidents of the period under review.

"Our next move was to Kemmel, where we relieved the French. We occupied three Aid Posts on this sector—a house just round the corner from the Ouderdom-Reninghelst Road, a concrete dugout just off the road about a quarter of a mile up the road to Kemmel, and further up still another house alongside the road. These Aid Posts we occupied in succession for periods of a week, according to whether the Battalion was in reserve, support or the front line.

"Movement during the day was restricted, as the Boche held Kemmel Hill and had wonderful observation of our activities in spite of the camouflage with which the roadside was draped. To illustrate how well the Boche was able to observe our movements, it is only necessary to mention the fate that befell two of our Archie guns. We were occupying the Reserve Aid Post when one day two anti-aircraft guns on lorries pulled into the field next to our house and fixed themselves up behind the hedge. They had settled down and got the guns ready for action when required, when the Boche opened fire on them and put one, if not both, out of action.

"Dr. Christie hated us to be idle, and, believing doubtless in the old saying about Satan and idle hands, got us busy filling sandbags with Belgium and sandbagging the space under the roof of the reserve Aid Post. One of the stretcher-bearers who was with me at the time was a miner in civil life, and he gave us an illustration of packing the sandbags in the restricted space available and of how the miners worked on their backs in some of the low-roofed mine workings. He certainly put the rest of us to shame by the speed with which he worked. Unfortunately none of the medical staff of the battalions who relieved us at this post attempted to continue the work we started, and finally the passion for sandbagging petered out and we were left to spend our time in our usual lazy fashion.

"The only other time Dr. Christie had an urge to make us do something was when somebody—the 15th Hants M.O.'s staff I believe—stole a wheeled stretcher from outside the reserve Aid Post during the night. I was reproached for being so careless as to leave it outside, but how was I to guess that the mere sight of a couple of wheels standing outside the house would arouse the thieving instincts of some passer-by? I was told to go and find it. Apparently it was considered an easy matter to do. One could almost imagine the fellows who 'knocked it off' sticking a large label on it to the effect that this was the property of the 12th East Surreys! I set off on my forlorn hope about 11.0 o'clock one morning and walked past the front battalion H.Q. without any success. I was promptly 'told off' for walking up the road in daylight. I next went over in the Reninghelst direction, where the 15th Hants M.O.'s staff was quartered. I found a wheeled stretcher outside their premises and was told by the Hants Orderly that they had had it for months. I didn't believe him, but there was nothing on it to identify it as ours, so I couldn't claim it.

"Beck, one of our stretcher-bearers, made a shove-halfpenny board while we were at the support Aid Post, and this provided a bit of a change from Bridge.

"The Boche used to shell the road pretty badly when the Transport came up at night, and one night while we were up at the front Aid Post we had several casualties, including one of the water-cart men who had a shocking wound in his back. I was just going down to the C.C.S. to have a loose crown to my top jaw fixed in again, when the trouble occurred, and I stopped to give the doctor a hand before carrying on. It was heartbreaking to see the terrible wound which this poor old water-cart man (I forget his name) had sustained. He had been out with the Battalion since the start, and I believe was one of the original 12th, but I couldn't see how he could possibly recover from this awful crack.

"One day Fritz started to shell all around the front and support Aid Posts with apparently one gun firing pretty heavy stuff. There was not much protection, and we were just wondering whether we shouldn't be safer in the fields, when the shelling stopped as suddenly as it had started. The gun we heard had been almost immediately located by our Artillery observation officer and quickly effaced. It didn't do much damage, except for one shell which dropped alongside the support Aid Post and blew the whole of the front entrance sideways, thereby blocking the exit and imprisoning the inmates until some help was obtained and they were got out unhurt.

"We had quite a good collection of books to read while we were on this sector. The Y.M.C.A. at the corner of Reninghelst had been shelled at some time, and the occupants had apparently not stayed to remove all the contents. We went round with a few sandbags and filled them full of books from the Y.M.C.A. library.

"A large cat used to wander round our front Aid Post. We went out one day to find that it had collected a number of kittens in some straw in a shed at the back of the house, and we took one with us when we finally left the abode.

"Another incident which amused us was the sight of Scott, of the Signallers, and a friend in top hats pushing a couple of reels of signalling wire along the Kemmel Road in a perambulator one evening.

"On another occasion when Fritz was searching for some of our batteries on the other side of the Ouderdom-Reninghelst Road, part of the base of one of the shells flew back and dropped right into the middle of a copper in which A Company's cooks were just making the tea. The cooks and sundry other members of the company were sitting around the copper when the tragedy occurred. I say tragedy, for this enormous piece of shell made a large hole in the bottom of the copper and the tea just dropped out. Nobody was hurt."

The Battalion had now relieved the 15th Hants and taken over the front line in the neighbourhood of La Clytte. Patrols were sent out from time to time to try to get in touch with the enemy. On the 22nd one such patrol of officers left our line to the east of La Clytte, and after thoroughly scouring No Man's Land, failed to encounter any of the enemy. But there was a sequel to this patrol which Major Searle tells:—

"I believe this was the only time that I was deliberately fired at whilst with the 12th. It was starting to get light, and I went out to see why the patrol had not come in and met it round the corner of a hedge. I have forgotten who the platoon commander was, but he was sufficiently uncomplimentary to take me for a Boche. He first lobbed a Mills bomb at me and then fired his revolver at approximately 10 feet range, but, being a rotten bad shot, he missed me completely. I begged the empty cartridge case off him and have kept it ever since as a mascot."

Pte. E. Caryl was killed on the 22nd.

There were a few casualties on the 23rd, mainly as a result of counter-preparation shoots carried out by our artillery, to which the enemy retaliated on the support line. 2nd Lieut. R. W. Davis, a recently joined officer, was wounded, and Pte. G. E. Wright was killed.

In order to obtain identification, the 15th Hants carried out a raid on the 24th, but, although they inflicted casualties on the enemy, they did not secure a prisoner. Retaliation fell heavily on the 12th, and in particular on B Company, who suffered the loss of Lce.-Cpls. H. J. W. Haywood and J. Gray, and Ptes. F. Iorns, E. Arnold, W. E. Fox, K. G. Cumming and F. Pharro who were killed, and three other men who were wounded Most of these men had been with the Battalion for close on two years.

A company of Americans was attached to the Battalion from the 25th of July for the purpose of being "broken in." They were found to be very apt pupils, if a

CLOTH HALL : YPRES : 1917 :
JOHN ASTON :

little too care-free at times. They often exposed themselves unnecessarily, even to the extent of attempting to play cards on the parapet! However, as soon as the Boche guns began to play havoc with them they realised that it was safer to keep well under cover.

Cpl. Southall speaks of their arrival thus:—

"One day we were sitting on the little seat outside the reserve Aid Post when two strange beings hove in sight. They were soldiers in canvas gaiters and brown boots with packs and other impedimenta attached to them in such quantities that the top of it nearly pushed their hats off. They left no doubt as to their nationality when, having dumped their kit and seated themselves wearily on our little form, one of them remarked, 'Gee! I have a pair of feet, believe me!' They were the advance guard of a section of Americans who were to be attached to us for instruction and subsequently to relieve us in this part of the front.

"A few days later, when we were occupying the front Aid Post, Sam Lattimore turned in one morning and told us a rich story of the Americans attached to his Lewis-gun section. Sam's gunners were holding a strong point, and, after he had given the Americans instructions how to carry on, they were left to hold the post. The morning after, to Sam's amazement and horror, the American sergeant in charge of the party was observed making his way across country in broad daylight to the spot where Sam was located. Apart from the danger to himself he had apparently quite overlooked the fact that he was giving away to the Boche where our posts lay. Having told the gentleman just what he thought of him, Sam asked what the trouble was. The sergeant then calmly informed Sam that they had taken their Lewis-gun to pieces and couldn't get it together again; would Sam come and kindly fix it up? Sam went over to the post and found the Americans calmly sitting about without any attempt at manning the post with their rifles. Goodness knows what use they would have been if the Boche had made any attempt to rush the post.

"We had one or two casualties one evening, including an American who had a small piece of shell through the wrist. He yelled and shouted so much that Dr. Christie got annoyed with him at last, and, pointing to one of our own men who had received a much worse wound, told the American that he was a very unedifying spectacle to our much more seriously wounded man and that he ought to be ashamed of himself for making such a row."

It is not our purpose to disparage the part taken by our American comrades during the war, but it is certain that many of the things they said and did before they had gained experience were not only amusing but sometimes led us into trouble with the enemy. For instance, it is on record that one of the American units in our sector on being relieved from the line, left their machine-guns behind them. They either did not want the trouble of carting them out again, or considered that they were in the nature of trench stores.

The enemy line was bombarded on the 27th, when a patrol of the 18th K.R.R.s went out for identification purposes with no better result than that which had attended the Hants and ourselves a few days before.

Relief came again on the 30th, when the 18th K.R.R.s took over, and we moved into reserve, taking over from the 15th Hants.

The casualties suffered during July had been—Killed or died of wounds: 11 other ranks; Wounded, 2 officers and 31 other ranks. Those who had died of wounds in hospital were Ptes. A. J. Martin, J. T. Andrews and R. T. Fisher. The following had gone home for commissions:—Sergt. E. Davey, Cpls. L. Maguire and S. J. Saunders, and C.S.M. G. Prosser.

On August 1st the Twelfth moved into Divisional Reserve at Wippenhoek. It was generally felt that it was about time that we had a complete rest from the line, for though things had not been so bad as we had experienced in other sectors, there was still that uncertainty whether the enemy was going to renew his attacks. His artillery and aircraft had shown a considerable amount of activity, and men were for ever on the alert in case the grey hordes attempted to advance. However, any doubts we may have had were soon dispelled when, after spending the morrow in cleaning equipment, kit inspections, etc., and the morning of the 3rd in extended order drill under company arrangements, orders were received to relieve the 4th Battalion Canadian Mounted Rifles in the line at La Clytte on the night of the 3rd/4th.

On the morning after we relieved the Canadians, the whole sector occupied by the Battalion was heavily shelled. This performance was repeated in the evening, when a patrol consisting of Lieut. H. Graves, 2nd Lieut. K. L. S. Lawton and three other ranks went out to reconnoitre with the result that they were all wounded. Pte. W. Brown was killed during the day. On the 7th the Battalion was relieved by the 18th K.R.R.s and moved into support.

August 8th is known as the Black Day for the German Army on the Western Front because of the very successful Battle of Amiens begun by the British Fourth Army and the French First Army on that date—the turning point of the campaign. Activity on the 122nd Brigade front was greater than usual. With C Company and one platoon of D Company of the 12th East Surreys attached to them, the 15th Hants carried out an attack during the night in order to straighten out a salient on the Brigade front. C Company was used as a carrying party while No. 13 platoon of D dug two strong points on either side of a position known as the Milky Way. The attack took place at midnight after a short bombardment supported by the 41st M.G.C. with twenty-three guns, and was successful in every way. Two machine-guns were captured and also 37 prisoners. The enemy was completely surprised, but at some points held out stoutly till near dawn. Owing to local fighting the platoon which had completed its task and dug the two posts was not relieved and had to remain there till the next night.

The enemy was not content to let matters rest as they were after the operation, for it subsequently transpired from the statements of prisoners that a counter-attack was intended on the night of the 9th, when a furious bombardment, lasting for about half-an-hour, was opened on our positions. At the last minute the Germans postponed the attack until the early hours of the 11th.

At 3.30 a.m. that morning three companies of the Boche attacked with bombs on the right and centre of our new front line. Several of the enemy had megaphones and were continually shouting through them. Our right company, holding from the Kemmel—La Clytte Road to the Milky Way, maintained its line intact, while the company on the left of the Brigade front easily beat off the attackers with Lewis-guns.

Thirty Germans were taken prisoners, but, as a sufficiently large escort could not be spared, they were sent down with only a few men. These prisoners succeeded in escaping from their escort and established themselves in the derelict huts of Willesden Camp "B." Before they could be rounded up, they managed to get back to their own lines. It should be stated for those who were with the Battalion in 1916 and 1917 that the ground over which the fighting took place was less than two miles from De Zon and Murrumbidgee Camps which we had occupied after the Battle of Messines. In consequence the region was covered with abandoned hutments, some of them actually in front of our positions. This made it fairly easy in an action for men to hide themselves. Where the enemy penetrated to some of our posts they were afterwards driven out in a counter-attack by the K.R.R.s.

The operations during the last few days cost considerable losses to the men engaged. The casualties for the week ending August 10th were 11 other ranks killed or died of wounds, and 2 officers and 32 others ranks wounded. In addition to those already mentioned, the names of the dead with the date of decease were as follows:—Pte. L. Bagg (9th), Lce.-Cpl. A. J. Edwards (9th), Pte. J. Gallagher (9th), Pte. F. T. George (10th), Pte. J. James (2nd), Pte. W. Rayner (9th), Lce.-Cpl. W. Angell (died of wounds, 5th), Pte. J. H. Furmidge (died of wounds, 9th), and Pte. E. Smart (died of wounds, 9th).

A curious incident took place in this action. Situated in advance of our front line was a Lewis-gun team of B Company, composed of three of the young boys who had joined the Battalion in April. When the enemy attacked, the team was taken unawares and treated to a fusillade of bombs. Two of them managed to get back to our lines, but the third did not return, and reports from his comrades stated that he had been hit and taken prisoner. When things were quieter, successful efforts were made to locate the post; his gun was found, but there were no signs of the body, which seemed to confirm the report that he had been taken by the enemy. The sequel came some weeks later when we were advancing over this ground and came across his body.

On the 11th the Battalion took over from the 18th K.R.R.s in the front line. During the relief the K.R.R.s were again attacked by the enemy and lost two posts. In the evening of the 12th we dug a post in front of Clydesdale Camp to straighten up the existing line.

Our patrols were again active on the 14th, and 2nd Lieut. G. H. Frischling was killed. Throughout the night of the 15th the artillery on both sides carried out bombardments, but this did not deter us from sending out our patrols who gained useful information of the enemy positions, which, owing to the fact that no continuous lines on either side existed in this sector, were difficult to locate. The work of patrols where a known line existed was difficult enough, but here it was courting disaster even to venture a short distance from the isolated posts with which we held the line.

The Boche seemed still determined to regain his lost positions, for, after a quiet day on the 17th, his guns livened up at night and under cover of a heavy bombardment a raiding party attacked the posts of No. 7 Platoon of B Company. With Lewis-guns and bombs our men frustrated all the Hun efforts to get through, and the party had to retire in haste. After this attack the Battalion was relieved by the 15th Hants and moved back to reserve in the Zevecoten area by Reninghelst.

The casualties for the week ending August 17th had again been heavy, one officer and 11 other ranks being killed, 29 other ranks wounded, and 2 other ranks missing. One of the missing men, as has already been recorded, was afterwards found to be killed, and the other's death was afterwards accepted for official purposes.

The following are the names and dates of death of those who died:—Pte. C. W. Standing (16th), Pte. S. H. Dax (12th), Pte. T. Hancock (12th), Lce.-Cpl. D. D. Lewis (14th), Pte. J. H. Jones (14th), Lce.-Cpl. T. Brown (16th), Pte. E. Dunster (16th), Lce.-Cpl. A. Rhodes (16th), Pte. J. Rollinson (12th), Pte. F. E. Butler (12th), Pte. J. C. Hammond (died of wounds, 15th), and Pte. J. W. Brown (12th).

On the 19th and 20th hostile batteries were extremely active on our guns in the back areas and also on the roads. The enemy's position on Kemmel made things very uncomfortable for us all, as he was able to observe almost every movement we made for miles behind our front positions. On the following day Capt. Reiner was wounded, and the Battalion moved into Divisional Reserve at Wippenhoek.

Times were very trying, and our casualties were mounting daily. Compared with those we had suffered during our previous long stay at St. Eloi they were serious. Nevertheless the spirit shown by the majority of the Battalion was remarkable. The old hands might have been feeling the strain to a great extent, but the young soldiers were far from despondent.

A Squadron Sergeant-Major of the Cavalry named Jackson was attached to B Company from the 22nd of August. The reason for this was that he had applied for a commission and, before being accepted, had to spend some time with an infantry unit. His stay with the Battalion was not long, but, as we shall see afterwards, rather hectic. He was a cheery soul and often whiled away his time singing classical excerpts from musical shows or operas. As Sergt. Rogers of the band had temporarily taken over C.Q.M.S., and C.S.M. Bry Horswell could always be depended upon to give his famous "Thora," B Company H.Q. became one of the "star" turns of the Battalion. "Thora" gave way to the famous "Dolores" who was Queen of the Eastern Sea, from Leslie Stuart's "Floradora." This haunting refrain could be heard nightly while the guns pounded and planes hummed overhead. By way of a change, Jackson would now and again break into a ditty, "Down where the water melons grow," one of the verses of which went as follows:—

"A man was milking a cow one day,
Down where the water melons grow.
A fat old lady chanced that way,
Down where the water melons grow.
She said, 'I hope I don't offend,
But why aren't you at the front, my friend?'
He said, 'There ain't no milk that end,'
Down where the water melons grow."

The chorus "Down where the water melons grow" would be taken up by the remainder of the H.Q. staff, and then Jackson would continue to elaborate on this with certain phrases in Hindustani, in which Horswell would join.

These were the days of the Great War, when Fortune seemed to hang her balances even. We knew that the enemy was beginning to get nervous because of the attacks further south, but it would be too much to say that his morale was yet shaken. Had such been the case, then the German prisoners who had escaped at Kemmel would not have been anxious to get back to their own lines. The men of B Company, like their comrades in the other units, were tired, but it was such joyful spirits as Horswell and platoon sergeants like MacKenzie, Turner, and afterwards Mills, that kept their "tails up." Most of the young officers who were now joining the Battalion had served as N.C.O.s in other units, and in consequence there was a great deal of sympathy and understanding between all ranks.

The casualties between the 17th and the 24th of August had been:—Ptes. S. R. Palmer and A. E. Bull, killed on the 19th; Pte. W. T. Merrill, died of wounds on the 19th; Pte. E. J. May, missing and afterwards reported killed on the 19th; and 19 other ranks wounded.

The following decorations for gallantry on the 8th/9th of August were notified on the 25th:—

D.C.M. and Médaille Militaire: Sergt. F. T. James, M.M.
Military Medal: Sergt. W. Hall, Cpl. G. Hurran, Pte. A. Pocock, Pte. D. Coutts, Pte. A. E. Brand (attached 122nd T.M.B.), Sergt. C. W. Turner and Cpl. G. Church.

During the period an Order of the Day was issued from Brigade H.Q., in which the Army Commander paid a tribute to the work carried out by the 122nd Brigade during the week ending the 16th of August; he stated that the operations had been well planned and reflected the greatest credit on all the troops concerned.

On the 26th the Battalion moved from Wippenhoek and proceeded to take over the area vacated by the 10th "Queen's" in the Goed Moet Mill Line, between Ouderdom and Mille-Kapelleken Farm. This was part of the route we used to take when proceeding to the line at St. Eloi.

There was joy amongst the men, when on the 28th a billeting party under Capt. Dowling was despatched to take over billets in the G.H.Q. reserve area. It was felt that a little respite would be given from the anxious times which were being experienced in the Kemmel sector. However, as things turned out, it was to be the shortest and most disappointing holiday from the line since the Battalion went overseas.

It was a very still night on the 28th when the Battalion was relieved by the 2nd/4th "Queen's" (34 Division) and proceeded to Abeele, where entrainment was carried out at 4.0 a.m. There was something in the stillness we left behind that savoured of the uncanny. It was not usual for these conditions to prevail in this sector at this time, and some of us were suggesting that the enemy was either preparing for another attack or was beginning to evacuate his positions. Still, what did that matter to us? We were now on our way to rest, and there were plenty of American and other troops at hand to deal with any situation which might arise. How wrong we were in these assumptions will be seen as the story proceeds.

We reached Lumbres Station early in the morning and marched to the old fashioned village of Esquerdes. Billets were allotted in barns, and, as the weather was fine, everything pointed to a pleasant rest from fighting.

Friday, the 30th, was a pay day, and in the evening a concert was organised for the troops. There may have been a couple of estaminets in the village, but otherwise there was little opportunity for enjoyment. St. Omer was not far away, so that it was anticipated that passes would be issued to this town. Saturday came with a route march through the pleasant countryside, with recreation to follow in the afternoon and the evening.

On this day a flutter was caused in B Company H.Q. by the holding of a Court of Enquiry into the loss of Company acquittance rolls at Achiet-le-Grand in the March retreat. The facts were simple enough. When the Boche was threatening Achiet, certain stores, packs, etc., were ordered to be burned to save them falling into enemy hands. In the inferno up went the company box of B and with it the acquittance rolls of two platoons and the Battalion H.Q. staff. The Pay Office, probably not realising that there was a war on, kept on demanding that these documents should be forwarded despite the fact that an explanation had been sent with the acquittance rolls of two platoons and the signatures on a duplicate roll of some of the survivors of the March "push" who had been good enough to sign after particulars of the payment were extracted from their pay-books.

In accordance with regulations this Court of Enquiry had to sit presumably to satisfy certain auditors in "Blighty" who were safeguarding public funds, but it would be interesting to know whether other courts of this description were held to deal with the enormous losses in material in the canteens and other places which eventually fell into the hands of the enemy. The story of one such interminable case runs through Mottram's novel "The Spanish Farm." One could imagine the court disposing of the matter by quoting the familiar phrase "Owing to the exigencies of the service."

Strolling through the little village of Esquerdes (near Wizernes) on this warm Saturday night, one would have been struck by the sounds of revelry. In the one estaminet near B Company billets men foregathered to drive away dull care. Times had changed the tunes the men used to sing. "Tipperary," "A long, long trail," and other popular songs of the British Army had now given way to "In Arizona" and "Over There," possibly a result of contact with the Yankees. In the billets by the light of candles would be seen little groups of men from which such expressions as "Twist" and "Bust" could be heard. These were the Pontoon "schools." In the "Drums" billet would be heard the sound of a flute played by one who was trying to enliven the few occupants. Apart from billet guards, orderly sergeants, who in collaboration with company clerks were getting out parade states for the morning or preparing the many returns of men due for leave or to go on courses, etc., and other details who were always on duty, the whole Battalion seemed to be making the best of this lovely summer night.

"Lights Out" sounded, and soon all was peaceful again in the village. With no thoughts of operations for a week or two men contentedly laid their heads on their valises and slept soundly. Last to retire, perhaps an hour or two after the rest, the Company H.Q. staffs had visions of a long rest after Reveillé in the morning; no inkling that their rest would be disturbed had so far reached them. Orders were in the hands of the responsible officers and N.C.O.s for quite ordinary routine in the morning.

All went well until the early hours of the morning, when runners from Battalion H.Q. burst into each Company Office and waking the occupants handed over an urgent message from the Adjutant. The message was in turn conveyed by a company runner to the Company Commander, who handed it back with the order that the C.S.M. should act in accordance with the instructions. The company was to strike billets as soon as possible and be on the road ready to move off again at 7.30 a.m. in full marching order. The Orderly Sergeant was then given the task of going round to the various billets and rousing the men to give them the orders. His reception was not a good one, for it was not yet light, and only those who lived in barns during the war could know the difficulty of collecting one's belongings in daylight, let alone by the aid of a spluttering candle in the dark. Rations for the day had to be distributed by the Orderly Corporal, while section commanders had the difficult job of issuing them to the men as there were many tins among the issue.

Before 7.0 a.m. the companies were out on the road looking very much like the Americans with large bundles on the men's backs. The Transport had in the meantime taken the road through Wizernes for its next concentration point, Steenvoorde. At 7.30 a.m. the column formed up on the road near Battalion H.Q. and marched to Lumbres, where, after some delay, all entrained. Detraining at Abeele at 5.0 p.m. on the 1st of September, the Battalion marched to the Abeele-Wippenhoek area, where it stayed the night. Thus we had come to the end of August with a peremptory order to move from quiet and peaceful surroundings back into the loathed war area once more.

The casualties for the month had been one officer and 18 other ranks killed, and three officers and 64 other ranks wounded. Besides those already mentioned, the following also died during the month:—Pte. L. D. Adlington (killed 24th), Pte. H. Crump (died 27th) and Pte. J. E. Thunder (died of wounds, 27th).

During August our new Quartermaster, Lieut. G. Haydock joined; also Lieut. P. R. Johnston and 2nd Lieuts. W. E. Bundy, F. E. Lewis and R. F. Howship. A draft of 40 other ranks from the 52nd Battn. Royal West Surreys also joined. Lce-Sergts. H. G. Velden and P. Coffin and Cpl. R. Cox had gone home for commissions. 2nd Lieuts. A. K. Watts, R. W. Davis (who had recently rejoined after being wounded) and F. C. Ells went sick to England; the last two were later medically boarded and struck off the strength.

At this time the situation in Flanders was undergoing an important change. The development of the Allied offensives further south had compelled the Germans on the night of the 29th/30th of August to begin an extensive retirement between Ypres and Bethune, and early on the 30th British patrols discovered that Bailleul had been evacuated. In following up the retirement stiff opposition was being met from German rearguards.

The 106th American Infantry Regiment, now in action in the sector previously occupied by the 41st Division, reached a line of trenches immediately east of, and parallel to, the Vierstraat-Kemmel Road on the night of the 31st of August. The next morning an advance was begun at 7.0 a.m., the objective being a general line from Vierstraat to V.C. Road, half a mile east of Rossignol Wood. The advance was held up by hostile machine-gun fire, and the situation was obscure. Instructions were issued for the 12th Battalion to relieve the troops holding the left Sub-sector of the Brigade Front from the Vierstraat Cross-Roads south-westwards. Each man had to carry 50 extra rounds of S.A.A. and his day's rations, which were cooked in billets and carried to the line. In addition 12 tins of water per company and 12 for Battalion H.Q. had to be carried. These were the orders issued to Colonel Brown, but circumstances were such that it was impossible to carry them out.

We left the billets at Wippenhoek in the gathering dusk on the 2nd of September and soon were amazed to see American troops passing us in little bunches. "Go on, Tommy, we've got them on the run!" was how some of them greeted us as they passed. Pte. Snell of D Company tells of how one of the "Yanks" shouted that we should need running-shoes to catch up the Boche.

Guides from the 27th American Division were supposed to meet the Battalion, but these failed to turn up. Accordingly when the troops arrived on the Vierstraat Road at 10.30 p.m., it was decided that, as the position was obscure, the Battalion should take up a line with two companies in front, facing Bois Quarante, and two companies in the Vierstraat Switch Line, the C.O. being wrongly informed that all this ground was cleared of the enemy.

At 1.30 a.m. on the 3rd, Capt. Rogers reported that A and C Companies had proceeded along the Vierstraat-Wytschaete Road and had met strong parties of the enemy on either side of the road half a mile beyond the Vierstraat cross-roads and had suffered casualties from machine-gun fire. This altered the plans of the Battalion, and A and C Companies joined D in the Vierstraat Switch Line, while B Company was ordered to advance down the Wytschaete Road as far as possible and as near as they could to Chinese Trench and dig in. This manœuvre was not completed until dawn.

The Americans were in a most disorganised state, and many were found wandering in this area. Orders were given to despatch these to the rear with all speed. They were mostly under the impression that they had reached their objectives in Grand Bois, a mile further to the south-east. The guides for the 15th Hants completely lost their way. By dawn the 12th was established in the area round Berghe Farm, but there were pockets of the enemy everywhere. The Americans, who were supposed to have driven the enemy back beyond Grand Bois and to be handing over to us a line as far forward as that point, did no handing over at all, and our troops had to find out the situation as best they could. The result was that the ground supposed to have been cleared was found to be strongly held, and many brave men's lives were sacrificed. The fact was that most of the American troops at this time were quite unused to war, and their staff work was hopeless.

At 3.0 p.m. a conference of the C.O.s of the three battalions of the Brigade was held by General Weston at the East Surrey H.Q., a mile to the rear of Vierstraat. Two hours later an order was received from Division that an attack would be launched against the Wytschaete Ridge at 5.30 a.m. in conjunction with the 34th Division on the right and the 35th on the left. Another Brigade conference was held and detailed orders issued. The 15th Hants and 12th East Surreys were to attack with two companies in two waves from Byron Farm to Catteau, the 18th K.R.R.s being in support.

Unfortunately during the day our H.Q. was badly gassed, and Capt. D. Walker (Adjutant), Capt. G. W. Christie (M.O.), and Lieut. A. E. Bell (Signalling Officer) were put out of action. Colonel Brown was also affected, but he managed to stay with us until the action was over. Capt. J. Ferguson, R.A.M.C., took over the evacuation of casualties which also included Cpl. Southall of the M.O.'s staff. Meanwhile the Colonel sent down for Major Searle who was in charge of the Details. When Major Searle arrived in the early hours of the morning he found Battalion H.Q. in a dugout at the side of the road just short of the Vierstraat cross-roads, with only Colonel Brown and one or two runners left and everything staged for the attack.

During the night A and B Companies advanced to the railway line that ran across our front and also gallantly cleared out the enemy from Chinese Trench astride the Vierstraat-Wytschaete Road, meeting heavy resistance and suffering severe casualties. The other two companies then advanced through them and were in position for the assault by 4.0 a.m. The 15th Hants could not get to their positions and eventually assembled behind Chinese Trench. C and D Companies of the 12th were now in front on the line of the railway the other side of Bois Quarante.

The barrage came down at 5.30 a.m. on the 4th of September, continuing on the enemy front line for 15 minutes, then moving forward in lifts of 100 yards every four minutes. Within three minutes of the start the enemy opened up on our forward positions with guns of all calibre, but by this time our men were advancing through the early morning mist and smoke of the bursting shells, and a few prisoners were coming back. By 6.15 C and D Companies had reached their objective, the western edge of Bois Quarante, and began to consolidate. According to a message sent to H.Q. at 6.30 a.m. by Capt. Dowling, casualties in D Company had been considerable and he had very few men left. He called for reinforcements, without which he could not hold on. Half an hour later he sent another message in which he stated that he could find no other officers, that he had only two small posts of men, and as there appeared to be no troops on either flanks with which he could get in touch, he was digging in where he was. Ten minutes later still he informed H.Q. that he was still losing men from machine-gun fire and shelling and had now only one post of seven men. Although he had heard that Lieut. Reynolds was up on his objective he was unable to find him. In the meantime Lieut. Reynolds of C Company had notified H.Q. that he was held up by strong machine-gun fire just in front of the crater, and had no picks and shovels or S.O.S. rockets. He also called for reinforcements. The cause of the trouble so far had been that soon after our barrage had halted, the companies were subjected to heavy machine-gun fire from Oak Trench on their right and two large pill boxes in Grand Bois. In endeavouring to keep the men together all the officers of the two companies, who exposed themselves freely, became casualties, with the exception of Lieut. T. E. S. Reynolds, as Capt. Dowling must have been wounded soon after he sent the message at 6.55 a.m., for no further messages appear to have been received from him. A and B Companies under Capt. J. A. Rogers moved from the Railway and endeavoured to form a defensive flank and fill up the gap between C and D Companies and the 15th Hants, who had been held up by fierce machine-gun fire and heavy casualties. About 7.15 a.m. the enemy, who realised that there was a lack of cohesion in the attack, counter-attacked C and D Companies, at the same time filtering through small parties with light machine-guns. D Company, which had suffered severe casualties, was driven back to the Railway, and C Company to a line immediately to the east of the craters in "Nag's Nose" blown in the Messines Ridge battle of 1917.

At 8.10 a.m. a runner was despatched by Capt. Wright of B Company to H.Q. with a message which is worth recording, as, in the words of Major Searle, it gives "a clear appreciation of the position by a gallant officer in a very tight corner."

To the Adjutant,
Root.

The situation appears to be as follows, as far as I can judge. C. and D Coys. appear to have reached their objective, but the Hants failed to keep pace on the right. The enemy counter-attacked here and reached a point about 17.c. Central. Two platoons of A Coy. and two of B Company under Capt. Rogers formed a defensive flank and subsequently advanced. They now appear to be on a line about CHINESE TRENCH 17. b. and d.

Sergt. Hargreaves of C Coy. (wounded) reports that when he left C Coy. an hour ago they had gone about a mile and were advancing again. I doubt the accuracy of this. I have two platoons of B Coy. and two of A, about 50 men in all on the railway embankment in 12. c. and d.

(Sgd.) A. A. Wright,
O.C. B. Coy.,
8.10 a.m.

By runner.

This was the last message written by Capt Wright, whom Cpl. Rushton "vividly remembers as a very fine officer, and just as vividly recollects seeing him killed by a sniper's bullet through the head."

The news of Capt. Wright's death and the wounding of Capt. Dowling, was conveyed by Pte. Brooks, a runner, to H.Q. in the following message from Lieut. Bundy, who had now taken over the remnants of D.

From O.C. D. Coy. Root. Situation Report. 11.0 a.m.

B and D Coys. in position along Railway track west of the first objective. Enemy is holding Wytschaete Ridge. Please send instructions. Capt. Dowling and Capt. Wright are both casualties. Companies are very weak and must have assistance.

(Sgd.) W. E. Bundy, Lieut.

Nothing further was heard from Lieut. Bundy, as he also became a casualty later on.

The remaining Company Commander who had gone into action (Capt. F. R. Barry of C Company was killed early on) was Capt. Rogers who gave his views on the situation in a wire timed 11.15 a.m.

To the Adjutant, Lozu. (Our correct code name for the attack).

Mr. McWalter wounded and C.S.M. Bignell. On the Hants sector west of the jumping-off place seems to be infested with Huns. The remains of B and A Coy. are facing south to watch them. They seem to have penetrated some distance towards the west judging by their double green lights. As far as I know, A Coy. numbers about 25. Enfilade fire on right (H sector) caused most of the casualties. Am at present trying to put out a Hun light M.G.

(Sgd.) J. A. Rogers, Capt.
A. Coy.

4.9.18. 11.15 a.m.

Our positions were held until 1.0 p.m., when A and B Companies, having suffered very severely from machine-gun and shell fire, fell back to the Vierstraat Switch Line. D Company withdrew to a line of trenches astride the Vierstraat-Wytschaete Road, thus leaving Lieut. T. E. S. Reynolds with C Company holding a forward post east of the Craters. These positions were maintained until handed over to the K.R.R.s, who were ordered up to relieve all posts of the Hants and East Surreys that could be found.

During the night the enemy heavily shelled the area behind the Vierstraat Ridge with H.E. and gas. A personal reconnaissance by the Brigade Major, Capt. S. R. Hogg, M.C., with 2nd Lieut. T. H. Lloyd (12th East Surreys) Brigade I.O., elucidated the position. By dawn the Twelfth, or what was left of them, had been relieved, and the 18th K.R.R.s were holding a line very little advanced from what it had been twelve hours before.

On the night of the 5th the Brigade was relieved and moved into Divisional Reserve, the 12th being billeted near Hoograaf Farm, midway between Reninghelst and Lijssenthoek.

The casualties of the Brigade were heavy in the whole operation—98 killed, 533 wounded, 60 missing. Our battalion suffered terribly. The casualties during September 3rd and 4th were—Killed: 3 officers and 42 other ranks (see appendix for names). Wounded or gassed: 11 officers and 180 other ranks. Missing: 7 other ranks. The officers killed were: Capts. F. R. Barry and A. A. Wright, and Lieut. R. M. Meadows. Those wounded were: Capt. F. B. B. Dowling; Lieuts. T. B. McWalter and P. R. Johnston; 2nd Lieuts. F. E. Lewis, and W. E. Bundy. Colonel Brown, Major C. T. Williams, Capts. D. Walker and G. W. Christie (R.A.M.C.) and Lieut. A. E. Bell were amongst the considerable number gassed and taken to hospital. The whole area of the operations was heavily gassed, and a large number of casualties resulted in the 122nd Brigade.

The total casualties reported in the War Diary for the week ending September 7th were 11 officers and 220 other ranks. These figures were nearly as much as those of Flers and Tower Hamlets, where operations of a much greater magnitude were carried out. Worst of all, there was little to show for them. First of all, much blame must attach to the Americans for not handing over properly and not sending guides to lead the Battalion to their positions. In fact, as Colonel Brown has stated in reviewing the narrative of the operations, the whole Brigade was badly let down by lack of information, and became involved in the first two hours when they expected a normal relief. Then it is for consideration whether it would not have been of advantage to have had a more prolonged preliminary preparation in view of the fact that the ground over which the Battalion was called upon to advance lent itself admirably to defence. There was no question of bad leadership, for, although some of the officers exposed themselves perhaps too freely, they did so to give heart to the men, who were surprised at the opposition put up by the enemy.

One thing did emerge from the operations, and that was that the Boche was not so demoralised as some writers are inclined to make people believe nowadays. In the main his machine-gunners fought their guns well as usual, and it is to the great credit of the men of the 12th, particularly the younger soldiers who had only been with us a few months, that in the face of such opposition they accomplished what they did.

What of those sterling men who sacrificed their lives in this galling operation? First of all, the name of Capt. A. A. Wright springs to the mind. Capt. Wright was one of a band of officers who joined the Battalion after Tower Hamlets. He was a quiet, unassuming, but very efficient company commander who took over B Company after Capt. E. B. Gillett had been evacuated to England sick. When B Company advanced down the Wytschaete Road, they had to dig in hastily while in the midst of the enemy. During the night the Boche moved about in the area, and one actually came up to the position where B Company H.Q. was situated. He enquired for one named "Carl," but, realising his mistake, attempted to run back, but S. M. Jackson (attached for instruction in infantry operations before going home for a commission) fired his revolver at him and killed him. B Company men speak of how Capt. Wright (an expert Lewis-gunner) took over a gun from the Lewis-gun section and silenced a German team which was giving much trouble. His coolness was an inspiration to those around him. Pte. Snell of D Company says that he remembers an officer of B Company, who he is almost sure was Capt. Wright, rallying the men when they were inclined to fall back. Standing up boldly in full view of the enemy, he called upon those around for the honour of the Regiment to go forward with him and not to retire.

Capt. F. R. Barry and Lieut. R. M. Meadows were both fatally wounded going into the attack. Capt. Barry commanded C Company and was one of the 5th Battalion officers who joined us at the same time as Capt. Wright.

Two very fine soldiers, C.S.M. C. Bignell and C.S.M. G. Hammond, were lost to the Battalion. Bignell had joined from the 4th Battalion in the preceding November and, after performing the duties of C.Q.M.S. for a time, had been made acting C.S.M. George Hammond joined us from the 3rd Battalion at the end of May, 1916, and had the distinction of winning the Military Medal and a bar to the decoration for excellent services rendered in most of the engagements in which the Battalion figured. With the demise of Bignell and Hammond the long line of Regular N.C.O.s who had been promoted to warrant officers came to an end, for Sergts. George Simpson and Billy Hall took over C.S.M.'s of A and D Companies respectively. Of the remaining other ranks who were killed, many were recently joined drafts.

Among the officers wounded was Capt. Dowling, commanding D Company, so that besides Battalion H.Q., all the Company Commanders, except Capt. Rogers, whose luck still held out, had been put out of action. For a very young officer, Capt. Dowling had had his share of the fighting since we returned from Italy. He had no easy a task in commanding D Company in the German offensive in March, and as his messages to H.Q. during these later operations show, he was terribly handicapped before he had reached his objective.

Lieut. T. B. McWalter, who was also wounded, was very much liked by those who came in contact with him. He hailed from South Africa and had a brother serving in the South African Brigade of the famous 9th Division. His merits as a fine soldier were acknowledged by Colonel Lee who appointed him as Adjutant, which position he held for some time. It was at his own request that he resumed regimental duties with C Company. When McWalter reached the C.C.S., he had a fairly bad wound, but he refused to be dressed until the orderlies had seen to some of the men who, he said, were worse off than he was. He was as usual cheery despite the fact that his wound must have been giving him much pain. It was a matter of great joy to most of us to know that he afterwards received the Military Cross for his services in the action.

Before coming to the honours awarded for the "show," let us quote the Brigadier in his report, as it has a great bearing on one award that was made. The Brigadier says:—

"The difficulties of the attack were greatly increased by the obscure situation taken over from the American Division, who had themselves been heavily engaged.

"The 15th Hants, being unable to form up on the line of the railway, as it was found, contrary to information received, to be strongly held by the enemy, never caught up with the barrage.

"The enemy, contrary to expectations, put up a very strong resistance. In spite of those adverse factors, both battalions advanced with the utmost courage and determination, until they sustained such casualties as made further progress impossible. These, in the case of officers, were especially severe and amounted to 85 per cent., and in the case of the men to between 60 per cent. and 70 per cent., of the number engaged. Most of the casualties were sustained from the high ground to the South. From Petit Bois and Oak Trench the enemy directly enfiladed our advance.

"Lieut. T. E. S. Reynolds, 12th East Surrey Regt., in maintaining and handing over an advance post of the Hollandscheshuur Crater displayed fine courage and determination.

"Lieut. G. J. Potter, M.C., 15th Hants, organised the remnants of the Hampshire Regt., again advanced his line at dusk, and refused to be relieved until he had completed this operation.

"My Brigade Major, Capt. S. R. Hogg, M.C., by his valuable reconnaissance in broad daylight cleared up a very obscure situation and gave orders which enabled the line to be advanced about 300 yards, and complete touch to be established on Right and Left.

"That the operation, owing to insurmountable difficulties, was only a limited success, cannot obscure the fine courage, determination and self-sacrifice displayed by all ranks.

(Sgd.) S. V. P. Weston,
Brigadier-General,
10.9.18. Commanding 122nd Brigade."

Our share of the Honours for the Bois Quarante action was:—

Military Cross: Lieut. T. B. McWalter; 2nd Lieuts. C. H. Fisher, T. E. S. Reynolds and G. L. White.

Bar to Military Medal: Pte. G. L. Huxley.

Military Medal: Sergt. D. E. Staines; Lce.-Cpls. B. C. Butling, A. E. Collins, W. Creasy, W. Felstead, N. J. Ketley, J. Rogers, G. Smith and G. E. Stenton; Ptes. S. Court, F. Cousins, G. Donaldson, J. E. Savage and Z. Spriggs.

Lieut. Reynolds' gallant deeds are already recorded. One is inclined to think that, had he held the rank of Captain, he might have been given the D.S.O. Colonel Brown is of the opinion that this young officer's determination in holding on to his forward post was deserving of high praise. If he had not done so, the line might easily have been driven back further than it was when the enemy attacked. The Colonel hoped at the time that he would be given a D.S.O.

At all events he was virtually the Company Commander of C, who again distinguished themselves in a similar manner to the action at Sapignies in March. 2nd Lieut. Fisher of A Company was considered by the men to be not only a thorough gentleman, but a saint. Even to-day men speak of his kindness and concern for those he commanded. There was grief in A Company when later on he was killed in action. 2nd Lieut. G. L. White was known among his brother-officers and the men as "Jumbo." One of two brothers who served with the 12th, he was very well liked in A Company because of a sense of humour which was not evident on the surface; at times he appeared to be a very serious sort of individual.

Pte. G. L. Huxley, M.M. (whom we have already had occasion to refer to) is spoken of by Lce.-Cpl. Stroulger as being a man devoid of fear, but with a distinct dislike of killing a fellow-man. In the thick of the action at Bois Quarante Huxley doing his duty as runner, disdained the use of his rifle, and, besides carrying his messages, gave confidence to his companions when they were in a very awkward predicament.

Most faithful of batmen and afterwards the "father" of the runners, "Jim" Rogers emerged from the action with a recommendation. At a later stage Rogers was recommended for the D.C.M., but was only awarded a bar to his M.M.

Lce.-Cpl. Bertie Butling of B Company was a mere boy with the cause of soldiering at heart. He was one of our "War Babies" who had joined in the preceding March.

Of the others Court and Ketley were ex-Surrey Yeomen; Cousins, Donaldson and Felstead ex-Middlesex men; Staines, Creasy and Stenton ex-Royal Fusiliers, the remainder being drafts from other battalions of the East Surreys.

As this was the last action in which Cpl. Southall participated, his account from the time we left the sector for rest until he was evacuated gassed is worth recording. He states:—

"Our time at Kemmel came to an end at last and we went out to rest. I took our kitten with me in the pocket of my great-coat, but on the way to the railhead it crawled out, climbed round my back and settled itself on my shoulder. When we finally reached our billets, our first job was to give it a feed of milk, and we were pleased to find that it was able to lap.

"We had a look round the village (Esquerdes) and found in a field a matting wicket laid out. I promised myself the enjoyment of a game of cricket in the near future, but alas! it was not to be. It is my recollection that either next morning or the morning after that there was a knock on the door about 1.0 a.m., and the doctor's voice announced that we must be prepared to move the next morning, as we were returning to the line. It transpired that the Boche had begun to retire, and it was rumoured that the Americans were not thought to be the best people to follow them up, so of course the 41st Division were again in the soup as usual!

"We went back by easy stages and finally learnt we were to relieve the "Yanks" on our old Brasserie (Vierstraat) front. As I knew this part of the neighbourhood fairly well from the old Reninghelst days, the doctor suggested that he, Henwood and I should set out in the afternoon to take over from the Americans. We took the old route viâ Hallebast Corner and up the Vierstraat Road and on the way met sundry American infantrymen strolling back from the line, who greeted us nasally with the information that they had got the Boche on the run and, unless we hurried, we should not catch them until they reached Berlin. The doctor, severely practical and knowing a little more about Fritz than the gentlemen who 'won the war,' was rude enough to ask the Americans what they meant by leaving the line before being properly relieved. Not in any way abashed, they informed him that there was no need to hand over the positions, as the Hun was running so fast that we should never catch him unless we hurried.

"We finally arrived at our dugout on the right-hand side of the road, and a filthy hole it was. The fug was awful and the floor littered with filthy dusty blankets, put down about fifteen deep for the comfort of the American orderlies, the bare floor being apparently too cold or hard for them. That night the Boche plastered the area with gas shells. As he was running away so fast, he must have fired them out of the wrong end of the guns. The following morning we decided to clean out the dugout and got all the blankets outside to start with. My eyes felt a bit sore, but I didn't take a great deal of notice. In the afternoon I heard that Dr. Christie had gone down with a touch of gas and Dr. Ferguson came to take over. Just after darkness fell, a number of casualties came down, including Cox, the doctor's servant, who had been shot in the leg. By this time I could hardly see out of my eyes, and the pain was pretty bad, so Dr. Ferguson kicked me out, and I finished up at Boulogne."*

At Hoograaf billets were fairly comfortable, some of the troops being accommodated in sandbagged cellars. Reserve trenches were being completed in this area and were observed to be a vast improvement on those we had seen before. They were wider, deeper and more substantially riveted. This was to be expected, as the place had been infested with men from the Labour Corps, whose main task was that of building defences behind the old front now that it was realised that front positions could be over-run far more easily than was thought at the time.

The companies practised attacks on the 12th, with special reference to strong points and machine-gun nests. On this day 2nd Lieut. Rodd rejoined the Battalion from duty at the Divisional Reception Camp, and the following new officers joined for duty:—2nd Lieuts. C. K. Adams, G. W. Sleath, R. Northwood, A. C. Cowlin, W. G. T. Summers, D.C.M., M.M., G. E. Smith and G. C. Saville.

On the 14th orders were sent out by Lieut. A. C. Edgar, who had recently returned from Brigade, where he had carried out staff duties for a time, and was now acting Adjutant in place of Capt. D. Walker, for relief of the 23rd Middlesex Regt. in the Vierstraat sector.

The Battalion, with Major G. O. Searle in command, marched to Ellarsyde Siding where it entrained for Cambridge Siding, north of La Clytte and less than a mile from Hallebast Corner. Detraining there, the companies proceeded to a point behind Vierstraat, where guides from the 23rd Middlesex met them, and then took over the line from a position west of Bois Quarante to Bois Confluent, less than 500 yards to the right of our old Headquarters at Dead Dog Farm. Only four officers per company proceeded to the line, the rest staying with the Details under Capt. Rogers.

Relief was not reported complete until the early morning of the 15th, and the course was not a smooth one, for heavy rain had rendered movement difficult and the enemy shelling was active, especially in the neighbourhood of Ridge Wood. As a result two officers and thirteen other ranks were wounded.

Enemy planes flying at a high altitude on the 17th dropped bombs near the front line and also brought down one of our observation balloons in flames at the back of Kemmel Hill.

A prisoner of the 134th Infantry Regiment was captured by one of our new posts on this day. It appears that the prisoner lost his way, a thing not to be wondered at in this region of desolation which had been fought over and over for more than three years, ploughed and seared by shell-fire and drenched with poison-gas.

* Pte. Griffiths, who took over from Cpl. Southall, says that Southall was so badly gassed that those present at the Aid Post did not expect him to recover. However, Southall was in hospital till January, 1919, when he was demobilised.

Relief came on the night of the 17th when the 15th Hants took over and we moved into Right Support. Next day Pte. S. Lodge died from wounds.

The 19th was a day of working parties and more enemy artillery activity, which was responsible for the killing of Pte. H. J. Barnett and the wounding of 2nd Lieut. G. K. Adams and one other rank. During the day 2nd Lieut. C. F. W. Faith, of B Company, proceeded down the line for England to join the R.A.F., and the following officers joined for duty:—2nd Lieuts. F. Combe-Seaton, L. H. Aldridge, P. V. James and L. W. Paviour.

Battalion H.Q., which was in Artillery Farm, Kleine Vierstraat, was heavily shelled throughout the day of the 20th and also received a direct hit, but no casualties are reported in the Diary, although, from the following story submitted by Major Searle, it appears there was a casualty which brought swift and furious retribution to the enemy.

"The Boche was putting one over about every ten minutes for twenty-four hours," writes Major Searle, "before they got a direct hit. It is wrong to say that there was no casualty; there was a very serious casualty! The direct hit smashed the very last bottle of whisky in B.H.Q.! This was reported to Brigade, who very decently sent up a replacement at once. They also arranged for the biggest retaliatory shoot I ever heard! I calculated that that bottle of whisky cost about £10,000 in shells."

This was to be our last day in the sector which held many memories for the old hands of the Battalion, as on the night of the 21st we were relieved by the 8th Battalion Scottish Rifles of the 34th Division and marched by platoons at 200 yards interval viâ Hallebast Corner to Ouderdom, where buses were taken to the new billeting area around Abeele. Capt. D. Walker and Lieut. A. E. Bell had now rejoined us from hospital, and the former arranged for billeting parties to proceed to the new location to take over Lynn House, Naval Farm, and the huts beside the road and railway. On the 24th Colonel Brown also returned from hospital and resumed command, so that, with the exception of Major Williams who had been sent to England on the 19th, our H.Q. officers who had been gassed in the Bois Quarante operations were now at duty again. As Major H. de C. Blakeney was no longer with the Battalion, having, after other jobs on command, being appointed to command the 10th Prisoners of War Company on August 23rd, 1917, Major G. O. Searle now assumed the duties of Second-in-Command. Although he says that his services with the Battalion were quite undistinguished, he nevertheless had to fill the breach at a very critical time when the C.O. was away in hospital.

A scheme of attack having reference to strong points and protection of the flanks was carried out on the 25th, and on the 26th the Battalion took part in a Brigade operation in the country between Godewaersvelde and the Mont des Cats. The main object of the latter was to practise keeping touch and dealing with strong points. From these operations it was apparent that ere long we would be called upon to chase the enemy. Everything suggested that a big action was pending, for there was feverish activity—the sign of offensives—everywhere. However, this did not deter the Boche artillery or his planes, for during our stay in the Abeele area we were bombed and shelled and spent a few uncomfortable hours in cellars and dugouts.

About this time notification was received that Lieut. J. F. Tamblyn, M.C., had been appointed Acting Captain on the 12th of July, while carrying out the duties of Brigade Major of the 71st Infantry Brigade. Lieut. Tamblyn, who was one of the officers who survived Flers, had seen good service with the 122nd T.M.B. and for varying periods had acted as Staff Captain of the 122nd Brigade and also as Brigade Major of the 120th Brigade. 2nd Lieut. T. H. Lloyd, M.C., was also posted to the General List as Brigade Intelligence Officer of the 122nd Brigade.

On September 24th Sergt. Charlie Turner, of B Company, proceeded home to England as a candidate for a commission. One of the original members of the 12th, Turner had shown himself a very capable and cheerful N.C.O. and had recently been awarded the M.M. Perhaps it was the loss of his old friend and joyful companion, Sergt. MacKenzie, who had now gone to England wounded, that decided Turner on the step he had taken to sever his connection with us. At all events it looked as though the old firm was breaking up.

VORMEZEELE VILLAGE—1917

drawn by John Aston, M.A.

CHAPTER XV.

28th September to 11th November, 1918.

The Final Advance to Victory—In the fighting at Gheluwe and on the Menin Road—The envelopment of Menin and the crossing of the Lys—Courtrai occupied—The Scheldt reached—The last casualties caused by air raid—Crossing of the Scheldt near Audenarde—News of the Armistice at Etichove.

WE reach the beginning of the end, the advance of the combined force commanded by H.M. The King of the Belgians, consisting of the Belgian Army, part of the Second British Army and certain French divisions.

On the 28th of September the Battalion moved to Ravine Wood, east of Hill 60, where we spent the night. To appreciate the position which had arisen it is necessary to relate what was taking place while the Battalion was making its way eastwards.

It is fairly clear that a drive of the enemy from Belgium was anticipated. Instructions on open warfare had been issued in which the importance of pushing on to final objectives, whether flanks were operating or not, was stressed. We had learnt something from the Germans about "Infiltration," which had proved so successful against the Italians a year before and also against the British in the following March. We were also instructed to report when there appeared to be an opportunity for horsemen to pass through, as French cavalry might be operating. The use of planes for delivering S.A.A. was also brought to notice. The 10th Squadron R.A.F. was to operate with the infantry, and boxes of ammunition would be dropped when a large V was placed on the ground at least 200 yards behind the line.

At 5.30 a.m. on the 28th of September, the XIX and II Corps of the Second British Army attacked on a front of four and a half miles south of the Ypres—Zonnebeke Road, the rôle of the 41st Division being to support the later stages of the operations. Further north the Belgian Army also attacked, with the result that in one day the enemy was driven from the high ground about Ypres: truly a remarkable performance when one realises the immense man-power and losses of the British Army which had been used a year before to gain in five months of warfare less *terrain* than was occupied on this one day. The conditions were not much better either, for heavy rains had made the going very hard, and the bringing up of guns and stores was a very difficult problem.

The Belgians entered Houthulst Forest, approached Staden and stormed Broodseinde in an advance of four miles, in which they took 5,000 prisoners and 300 guns; it was plain that the enemy began to see the writing on the wall.

General Plumer with battalions from the 9th, 29th, 35th and 14th Divisions had bitten into the Salient to such an extent that, on either side of the Menin Road, Bercelaere had been taken in an advance of five miles, Gheluvelt had fallen, and the 29th

Division careered over Kruiseecke, whilst the 35th Division taking Zandvoorde in their stride had progressed to a depth of nine miles. The Messines Ridge, stoutly defended as it was, was turned and taken by the troops of the 34th Division who had taken over before our move to Abeele.

Back on the ground close to Menin, where the 1st and 7th Divisions had been at the opening of the First Battle of Ypres in 1914, the young successors to the old "Contemptibles" had a bag of 3,600 prisoners and 100 guns to their credit at the end of the day of September 28th. This success has been described, and rightly so, as one of the most immediately decisive of all the Allied successes on the Western Front, as it liberated the Flemish coast, caused the enemy to evacuate his ground quickly, put a breaking strain on his last reserves and generally added to his confusion.

The foe was to be given no time to recuperate, and thus it was that the 12th Battalion, in common with the rest of the 41st Division now in the XIX Corps under General Watts, made its way to take a not inglorious part in the advance to Victory.

Leaving Ravine Wood on the 29th we moved forward as in open warfare past the terrible scenes of July and August, 1917, crossing the Ypres-Comines Canal to the concentration area south-east of Kortewilde. D Company furnished the advance-guard, encountering just beyond that village a strong point, which was soon dealt with. The concentration area was reached at 4.0 p.m. The advance so far was not made without casualties: Ptes. C. A. Field, A. F. Oakes, W. A. Wager and R. J. Watkins were killed, and 2nd Lieut. G. S. Savill and ten other ranks were wounded. Ptes. J. H. Austin and J. E. C. Falkner also died of wounds during the day.

A Company moved forward early on the 30th in an endeavour to make a good line towards Tenbrielen, two miles east of Kortewilde, and to get in touch with the 35th Division on the left. A Company having successfully carried out the task allotted to them, the Battalion moved to a new concentration area nearer Tenbrielen. During this advance 2nd Lieut. P. V. James was wounded.

September, always a fatal month for the Battalion during its career overseas, had come to an end with its usual heavy crop of casualties, for during the month, 3 officers and 62 other ranks had been killed or died of wounds; 14 officers and 199 other ranks had been wounded; while seven men were reported missing.

On the 1st of October the Battalion moved as the advance-guard of the Division in the direction of Menin, viâ Gheluwe (two miles north-west of that town). The starting point for the advance-guard and the main body was fixed at Tenbrielen cross-roads, but much delay was occasioned, as the spot could not be discovered, the whole place had been so completely obliterated by shell fire. This illustrates the immense difficulties encountered in the advance over this Inferno.

It was a misty morning, and in the early hours the advance of the whole column continued without opposition; at 7.40 a.m. Colonel Brown, in command of the advance-guard, reported having reached America, a mile north-east of Tenbrielen, without opposition. But at 8 o'clock the fog began to clear, and the column was seen by the enemy crossing the ridge east of the hamlet, and they at once opened a heavy and accurate artillery and machine-gun fire from the south. Our field guns came into action, and, shooting with open sights, succeeded in keeping down the fire from the machine-guns, but the hostile artillery brought down a heavy barrage on the America cross-roads. Our men however pushed on eastwards, encountering the Boche in various farms, copses and strong points. The 12th, still the foremost troops of the Division, was held up by a strong line of machine-gun posts south-west of Gheluwe, but succeeded in occupying a position a few hundreds yards west of the village. Our casualties were heavy. Lieut. A. C. Edgar and 2nd Lieuts. P. W. Targett, A. E. Bell, A. T. Topham and L. W. Paviour were wounded, and in addition to many wounded amongst the other ranks the following were killed:—Cpl. S. S. Hutchens; Lce.-Cpls. W. H. Collins and W. J. Smith; and Ptes. H. Alexander, E. Flowers, T. Goddard, J. Hennessey, B. Hiney, T. Ovall, W. H. Price, W. J. Rowsell and H. G. Terry. Altogether 84 officers and men had been put out of action during the day. This was part of the price we were to pay for victory.

Major Searle has already referred to the courage and utter disregard of danger of our Brigadier; here is another incident which occurred during this advance, showing the quality of General Weston. Sergt. L. C. Lunn who relates the incident writes:—

"The Battalion, which had been resting for a few days, was marching with transport along the Tenbrielen-America Road, preparatory to taking over the Front Line, which was being pushed forward between Menin and Wervicq (Menin had been reported clear of the enemy), when, about a mile from Menin, machine-guns and field guns opened out along the whole column. There was a hurried scamper of men and horses, and only one or two minor casualties were reported. General Weston arrived just at this moment, and quickly dismounting took cover with some men of our Battalion.

"(Afterwards we heard that the report that the enemy was clear of Menin was incorrect. How well we knew that phrase! He had seen us marching along the road from his Observation Post in the spire of Menin Church.)

"Owing to the nearness of the enemy and small cover afforded, it was impossible for some hours to get the Battalion together and also to get news of where the Front Line was supposed to be, and dispositions of any troops in front of us. Orders were later received to stay where we were and await further instructions. We remained there in shell-holes until evening.

"In the meantime there was great consternation at Brigade Headquarters: the Brigadier was missing! During the afternoon a report was received stating that the General had been seen advancing towards the enemy with a party of 12th East Surreys.

"When darkness came, the General did not return, neither was any message received from him nor from any Dressing Station he might have passed through, if wounded. The Brigade Major (Capt. S. R. Hogg) reluctantly reported to Divisional Headquarters that the General was 'Missing, believed killed.'

"The Divisional Commander (General Lawford) gave instructions that Lieut.-Col. Brown of the 12th East Surreys was temporarily to take command of the Brigade, and he assumed command of it that night.

"About noon on the following day, General Weston walked into Brigade Headquarters. The astonishment on everybody's face showed pretty plainly, and on learning the events that had taken place and that actually somebody else had been appointed to take over, he was, to put it mildly, very annoyed.

"The explanation:—He had got tired of waiting in a shell-hole and was chafing under enforced idleness, so decided to take a party and reconnoitre for himself. He and his party of the 12th East Surreys advanced until they came in touch with the enemy. They then drove them out of their positions from which they were machine-gunning the road, and forced them right back into Menin. The General then got his party to make their position tenable, which they did, and were comfortably holding on to it until the rest of the Battalion came up on the following morning to take over."

On the 2nd at dawn the 15th Hants and the 18th K.R.R.s advanced under a barrage through our lines to continue the attack and drove the enemy out of Gheluwe Switch, but did not entirely clear the village; at 10.0 a.m. Capt. J. A. Rogers was detailed to mop up part of Gheluwe with A Company. A counter-attack which took place at 6.30 p.m. on the Brigade front was repulsed.

It was impossible to clear these desperate Boche machine-gunners out of their lairs without paying the usual price in casualties, and the following were killed during the day:—Lce.-Cpls E. H. Heard and H. Langley; Ptes. W. H. Hatcher. W. S. Key and A. C. Pelling. The following died of wounds the same day:—Ptes. G. Donaldson, M.M., and J. W. French. Pte. J. T. Keeble, who was wounded in an earlier action, died of wounds in England on the 2nd of September.

The Battalion was relieved during the early morning of the 3rd by the 1st/1st Hereford Regt. and the 1st/7th Cheshire Regt. of the 34th Division and moved back to the neighbourhood of Zandvoorde, where it was attached to the 124th Brigade as support battalion. Pte. H. A. Gosling died of wounds during the day. We did not move again until the afternoon of the 4th, when we proceeded again in support of the 124th Brigade to a position near Terhand, several miles to the north-east.

During the day Pte. M. D. O'Malley died of his wounds. In connection with his death, Cpl. Jim Malone and Sergt. Sam Lattimore relate some interesting facts. Paddy, as he was known amongst his colleagues, was a stretcher-bearer in A Company. During the advance some cries came from a wounded German in front of our positions. These were heard by Paddy and others several times; he took compassion on the Boche and without further ado left our trenches and proceeded over the open to the wounded man. Picking him up, he made for our trenches again with his burden, but on the way was hit by a enemy bullet. Taken to the Aid Post (now in charge of Dr. Christie, who had rejoined after being gassed at Vierstraat), Paddy expired some little time later, while the German—an officer cadet—survived. Lattimore saw O'Malley in the Aid Post, where Paddy asked him for a drink of tea. Paddy's reward was a posthumous Military Medal; his example was typical of the men who wore the badge of the Red Cross. In common with others of the same section, O'Malley's first thoughts were for the wounded of whatever nationality. Whether the enemy realised what was happening will of course never be known, but if the shot that laid O'Malley low was intentional, then it reflects very badly on the humanity of the Germans.

It would not be out of place to mention here some of the practices to which the enemy resorted in his retirement. In dugouts, in the trenches and also on dumps he laid what we called "Boobytraps." This might consist of a German bayonet sticking out of the wall of the dugout or trench to which was attached a bomb. Knowing that our men were fond of collecting souvenirs, he intended that the bayonet should be removed with time-delayed fuses sometimes attached to the bells in the churches were also used by the enemy, with the result that often men, women and children who were taking refuge were killed.

Many casualties having been caused in this way, the troops were instructed to be very careful in entering dugouts and collecting souvenirs. The enemy was resorting to "frightfulness" again, now that there was not much question who was going to win. The Germans had tried these cowardly devices at the end of 1916, when their morale was so shaken and they evacuated the Somme area. Such foul methods only exasperated their foes and proved that their power of resistance was now cracking. Throughout history the German race, though endowed with many fine qualities, has done things which are inexplicable to the average Englishman. For instance Lieut. Mutch has produced a pamphlet which he picked up during the final advance, which was printed in block capitals and ran as follows:—

DEAR TOMMY,

YOU ARE QUITE WELCOME TO WHAT WE ARE LEAVING. WHEN WE STOP WE SHALL STOP, AND STOP YOU IN A MANNER YOU WON'T APPRECIATE.

FRITZ.

We mention these things not with the idea of condemning the German nation for the action of some individuals, but to record historical facts which even Ernst Jünger in "The Storm of Steel" does not deny. The only real effect it had upon us was to make us ultra-careful in touching things or occupying places, until our engineers had come along and made them safe for us.

During the night of the 4th/5th of October our area was heavily shelled. The Battalion remained in its positions on the 5th, on which day orders were received that we were again under the command of the 122nd Brigade. Four other ranks were wounded during the day, bringing our casualties for the past week up to 17 other ranks killed, 7 officers and 81 other ranks wounded, and 9 other ranks missing. The following officers joined on the 5th:—2nd Lieuts. J. H. Savage, M.M., and J. R. A. Cockayne from the 1st Battalion, and 2nd Lieut. B. E. C. Walker from the 9th.

For gallantry in the field in these operations known as the Battle of Ypres, 1918, the following honours were later awarded:—

Military Cross: Capt. G. W. Christie, R.A.M.C., Lieut. (A/Capt.) A. C. Edgar and 2nd Lieut. G. C. W. Sleath.

Military Medal: Sergt. S. Lattimore; Lce.-Sergt. H. Mills; Cpl. J. Drinkwater; Lce.-Cpl. R. Sadler; Ptes. D. J. Challis, T. Clarke, A. Head, M. D. O'Malley and S. Waddingham.

Of the recipients the bulk came from B Company. Sergt. Sam Lattimore and Pte. Tommy Clarke were two of the original 12th, who, as Lewis-gun Sergeant and runner respectively, had given good service. Both remained with the Battalion throughout its existence, and it is a great tribute to the popularity of Lattimore that since our Association was formed scores of men have written from different parts of the country enquiring after his welfare. His secret lay in the fact that not only was he an efficient instructor but was able to suit himself to the various types of individuals who made up his gun teams. Men obeyed Lattimore out of respect and not through fear of the rank he held.

Lce.-Sergt. Harry Mills of B Company was a quaint character. He hardly ever spoke above an undertone, but his manner was such that very little cajoling was necessary to get his men to do what he wanted. Contact with the Americans had led Harry occasionally to issue the order, "Twos into fours; Git!" His age we could never fathom. He used to say that he had borrowed his brother's birth certificate to enlist after having served many years in the Royal Navy. His method of issuing commands did not always appeal to peace time soldiers, but that he was not lacking in courage was shown when he afterwards received the Croix de Guerre and the D.C.M. Before we left him in Germany, where he was acting C.Q.M.S. of B Company, Harry told us that with all these honours thrust upon him at once there was the possibility of his being made Mayor of Isleworth, when he would have to wear a high hat and gown with sleeves! "It's a fine Army. You can't whack it. Four meals a day, three blankets, and everything found. What else could one wish for?" was one of his famous expressions.

Capt. Christie was a fearless and efficient Medical man who had probably had a longer life with the Battalion than any other M.O. Lieut. Edgar took over B Company and was made acting Captain after Capt. Wright. Like many more good officers we had, he came from the 5th Battalion and, besides being attached to Brigade for a time, had also acted as Adjutant.

On the 6th a warning order was received for the Battalion to move back to Abeele and in the afternoon we marched back to Ypres. The march was not an easy one, as it must be remembered that the line had now been advanced about ten miles down the Menin Road and in other parts a greater distance still. From Ypres buses conveyed the men to their billets in Abeele, which was reached in the evening.

From the Transport and Details point of view the latest advance was something very much out of the ordinary. For one thing most of us had not anticipated ever having the use of Ypres as a place where Q.M. Stores could be established. However, such was the case, for the stores were for a short time situated near the Cloth Hall. Ypres was full of dugouts among the ruins, and, although the enemy was being driven from all the ridges surrounding the ruined town, he still kept up his daily strafe, causing the usual casualties. Some of the Details were billeted in what looked like an old fortification near the Ramparts and were little troubled, except by aeroplanes at night. The Transport moved for a time to Hell Fire Corner, which before the "Push" was the British Front Line. As the Battalion advanced, the C.Q.M.S.s had a difficult task of finding their companies to deliver their rations. Of our old "Quarters" of the companies only Dick Calver of A Company was now with us; the others were Billy Steer, Haynes, Marshall and Blatch. The Menin Road, owing to the terrible fighting which had taken place between 1914 and 1918, was in an appalling condition, and, until the Labour Corps had begun to make it passable for all kinds of traffic, limbers had a hard job in negotiating the shell-holes, not to mention the mud. On either side of the road the débris of war was to be seen. German guns broken and abandoned, smashed wagons, dumps of stick-bombs, destroyed pill-boxes, besides dead Germans and horses, littered the ground over which we had to pass. Progress across these tracts towards Passchendaele was very slow at first, but, as the enemy was thrown further back, corduroy tracks were made which greatly accelerated the pace.

Passchendaele we found to be nothing more than a heap of bricks with a sign board to denote that a village had once existed there. Thereafter we began to strike a little bit of civilisation in villages where British troops had not trod since 1914. Thus far we had not come across the civilians in the occupied area, but that experience was not to be denied us much longer. The passage along the road to Menin was not a comfortable one, nor were the sights inspiring, but after passing that zone things were more congenial.

The Battalion stayed in the Abeele area between the 7th and the 11th of October reorganising and carrying out training for future operations.

Further reinforcements of officers joined during the period, Lieuts. J. H. H. Sands, F. C. Reed, W. D. Bayliss and K. G. Bancroft, and 2nd Lieuts. E. L. Morley, A. Stevens, R. C. Latham and C. L. Smith, making good any deficiencies of officers in the Companies. In addition we welcomed back Lieut. W. G. Robinson, who had been twice wounded while serving with us. At this period there was not one of our original officers with us, and of those who had joined us in France during 1916 only Capts. Rogers and Walker remained. So far Capt. Rogers had come through unscathed, but his luck was not to hold out much longer. Company and platoon commanders were, through casualties, being constantly changed, and it is extremely difficult for most of the survivors of the Battalion to recall now who their officers were. In some cases they were either killed or wounded before the men had time even to know their names.

On the 12th the Battalion entrained at Rémy Siding, Wippenhoek, and proceeded along to "Clapham Junction" on the Menin Road, where we detrained. We rested and had dinner close by "Stirling Castle" in the neighbourhood of Sanctuary Wood, before resuming the pursuit of the enemy. Meanwhile the Details moved to the Divisional Rest Camp at Brandhoek, "B" Echelon Transport to Hell Fire Corner and "A" Echelon Transport east of Gheluvelt.

It will be readily realised that in order to avoid confusion and congestion on the roads it had become necessary to divide the transports into two sections, known as "A" and "B" Echelons. For the purpose of administration "A" Echelon came under the orders of Brigade, and "B" Echelon under Division. "A" Echelon was composed of the following:—1 S.A.A. limber, 1 Grenade limber, 1 Maltese cart, 7 pack ponies and 4 officers' chargers for each battalion and 4 chargers and spares (8 in all), 1 limber for the Signallers section, 1 G.S. wagon for tools, and a D.R. Signal for each Brigade. "B" Echelon was made up of 2 S.A.A. limbers, 2 tool limbers, 4 L.G. limbers, 4 cookers, 2 water carts, 1 mess cart, 6 charges and 4 spare animals for each battalion, and a G.S. wagon for tools, a limber for cooks, a Maltese cart for the Signallers and a Veterinary Sergt. Rider for each Brigade. In addition the Quartermaster's staff for each battalion was attached to "B" Echelon. From now until the end this arrangement was carried out, each echelon moving up as the troops advanced.

The Battalion having reached Stirling Castle, orders were now issued explaining that the attack in the north was to be continued by the French, the Belgians, and the Second British Army, and that the 122nd Brigade was to attack with the three battalions in line, the 12th East Surreys being in the centre with the 18th K.R.R.s on the right and the 15th Hants on the left. In addition to the usual "doings" taken into action each man had to carry two egg-bombs and two sandbags. Various red, blue and green rockets, flares and smoke-bombs, large and small wire-cutters and 1,000 yards of white tape had also to be carried between them.

Resuming the march, we took over the positions of the 11th "Queen's" (123rd Brigade) about one mile north-east of Gheluwe. With the exception of occasional shelling the 13th passed off fairly quietly. One officer and three other ranks became casualties on this day.

The combined forces under the command of Albert, King of the Belgians, after the first successful attack which started on the 28th of September, were now to attack again on the whole front between Comines on the River Lys, and Dixmude. The 41st Division was to make a large advance in bold style, planned on unusual lines and intended to protect the right flank of the general operations, the whole movement of the Second Army being aimed at enveloping Menin and obtaining observation of the valley of the Lys with a view to the later crossing of the river. The depth of attack by the 41st Division was 2,000 yards for the first objective, decreasing to 1,750 yards at the second objective and increasing to 3,500 yards at the final objective, entailing a total advance of over four miles. The capture of the second objective was entrusted to the 122nd Brigade with the 12th Battalion as the pivot of the attack. Zero hour was fixed for 5.35 a.m. and three minutes before this the battalions, each on a two-company front, were formed in lines of sections close up to the artillery start line. To cover the advance smoke was to be used, and for the purpose of keeping direction special compass parties were posted on the flanks of the units. The ground was now open, practically undamaged by shell-fire and with few defences or wire entanglements.

The following report in the War Diary sums up the operations carried out:—

"On October 14th, the enemy carried out a counter-preparation shoot at 1.15 a.m. which lasted for 45 minutes. At 2.30 a.m. the Battalion, in conjunction with the 15th Hants on the left and the 18th K.R.R.s on the right formed up a mile north of Gheluwe on a two-company front. At 5.32 a.m. a short barrage opened out, and the Battalion pushed forward under it towards the Blue Line, which was reached at 7.45 a.m. The advance was then continued to the Red Line. The two front companies reached this point at 8.30 a.m. followed closely by the two support companies. The Battalion reached its objective at the time laid down, although extremely foggy conditions prevailed throughout the advance, and smoke was used, so that great difficulties were experienced in keeping touch with the flanks. Our casualties were light, although the line of advance was held by numerous concrete pill-boxes and machine-guns. The approximate casualties were three officers and 50 other ranks. Over 250 prisoners were taken and in addition a large number of machine-guns and trench mortars. At 10.0 a.m. the 124th Brigade passed through our lines and pushed forward to a distance of 1,500 yards. All men of the Battalion fought splendidly, and great credit was due to the leadership of the officers and N.C.O.s who kept direction in spite of the thick fog which prevailed. All objectives of the Division were gained by 4.0 p.m."

There is very little to add to the account entered in the Diary except that the Battalion accomplished a very successful advance in face of difficulties and had more to show for it than in any action in which we had taken part while on active service.

The Battalion was now near the Menin-Roulers Road about two miles north of Menin, and on the 15th remained in support, together with the rest of the Brigade, on the ground it had won.

That the operations met with the approval of the Higher Command was shown when the following decorations were afterwards awarded for the action:—

2nd Bar to Military Cross: Capt. J. A. Rogers.
Bar to Military Cross: Lieut. W. D. Mutch.
Military Cross: Capt. E. St. J. N. Ryan.
Bar to Military Medal: C.S.M. W. Hall and Lce.-Cpl. W. Haxton.
Military Medal: Sergt. F. James; Cpl. J. H. W. Draper; Lce.-Cpls. S. G. Brewster, O. J. George and W. H. James; Ptes. F. H. Fanner, P. Record, T. Rochford, S. J. Sadler and R. Seaman.
Croix de Guerre: Lce.-Cpl. S. G. Brewster.

Capt Rogers had again emerged from the operations with an addition to the honours already awarded him, thus making him the most decorated officer of the Battalion in its career. Lieut. Mutch too had added to his quota for his valuable work as I.O. during the advance. Capt. E. St. J. Ryan, given a company at last, had proved his worth, but he was not to live long to enjoy his honour. It was C.S.M. Billy Hall's turn now to collect some "gongs" for sterling services rendered not only in this action but throughout a career with the Battalion which was equalled by few. Sergt. F. James was an old "Contemptible" with a D.C.M. already to his credit for a previous action in which the Battalion had taken part. He too was to go the way of many others who distinguished themselves, for within a few days of the Armistice he was fatally wounded by an aerial bomb. Cpl. Draper, of B Company, was, we believe, one of the men who retrieved a football in the action in which the 8th Battalion took part at Montauban on July 1st, 1916. It will be remember that in this action of the 8th Battalion the Company Commander of one of the companies provided each of his platoons with a football to kick over the top with the idea of keeping their spirits up during the initial stages of the attack. Two footballs were picked up after the action. Brewster helped to put our own Battalion team on the map in the football matches which were played later on. Of Percy Record, one of our stretcher-bearers, we shall have something to say later on in our story.

Although the casualties, consisting of two officers and 14 other ranks killed and 2nd Lieut. R. C. Latham and 61 other ranks wounded, were light considering what had been accomplished, there was great regret amongst us for those fine fellows who had been left behind on the field of battle. Amongst these were 2nd Lieut. C. M. Fisher, of A Company, who was a great favourite with his men, and 2nd Lieut. F. Combe-Seaton, who had only recently joined the Battalion and, with his batman, Pte. W. J. Phillips, was killed and buried in the region of Dadizeele. Ptes. W. Asbury, R. Buick, G. Folly,

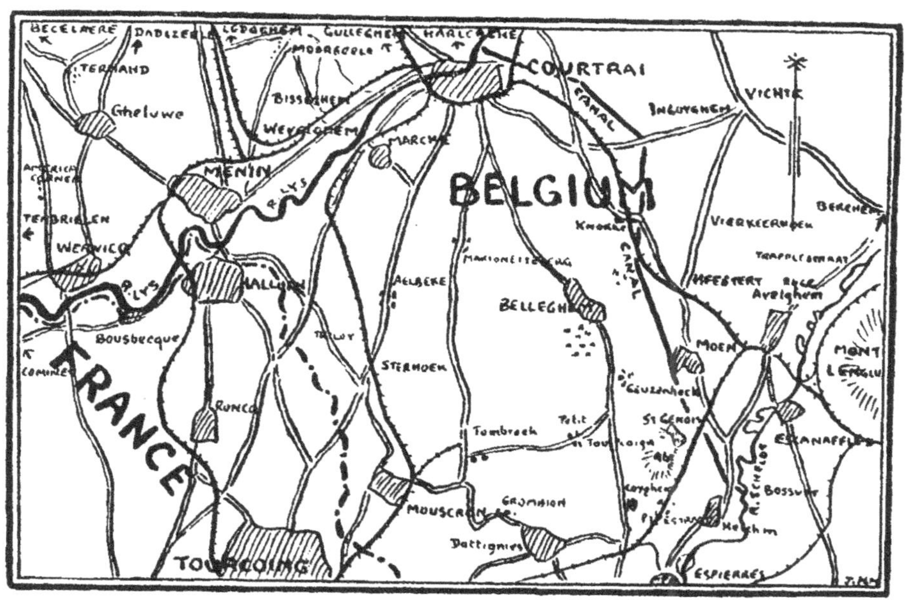
COURTRAI
BELGIUM
FRANCE
MENIN
LYS
CANAL
Gheluwe
WERVICQ
HALLUIN
Bousbecque
RONCQ
TOURCOING
MOUSCRON
Dottignies
BELLEGHEM
STERHOEK
Tombroek
AELBEKE
MARCKE
WEVELGHEM
BISSEGHEM
GULLEGHEM
DADIZEELE
BECELAERE
INGOYGHEM
VICHTE
VIERKEERHOEK
HEESTERT
Avelghem
MOEN
ESCANAFFLES
Bossuyt
ESPIERRES
COMINES

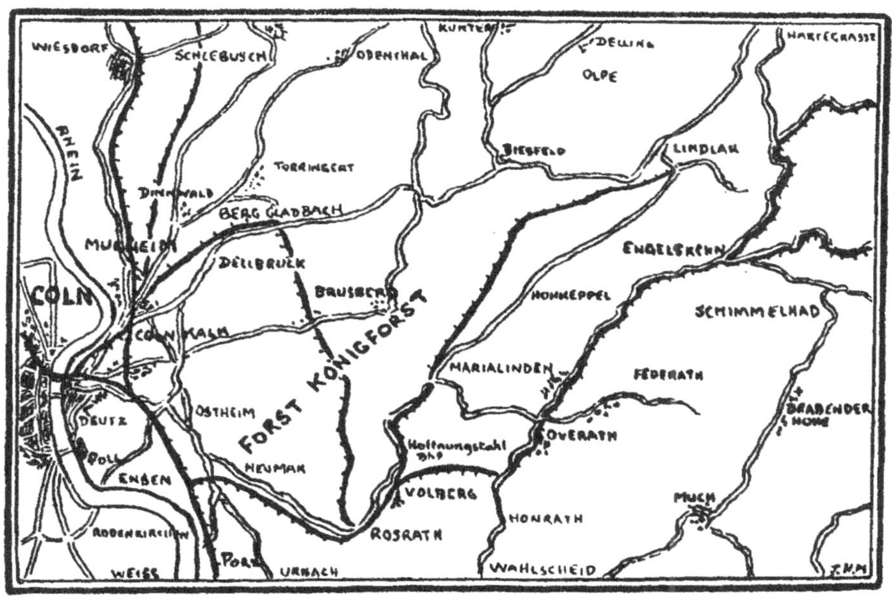
WIESDORF
SCHLEBUSCH
ODENTHAL
OLPE
RHEIN
BIESFELD
LINDLAR
BERG GLADBACH
MULHEIM
DELLBRUCK
BRUSBERG
COLN
COLN KALK
FORST KONIGFORST
HOHKEPPEL
MARIALINDEN
FEDERATH
OSTHEIM
DEUTZ
POLL
HEUMAR
VOLBERG
OVERATH
HONRATH
MUCH
ROSRATH
URBACH
WAHLSCHEID

C. Fountain, A. E. Healy, C. W. Latter, E. C. Laws, J. R. Morris, W. J. Sales, A. F. Seed, J. M. Stubbs and W. J. Wilson were also killed on the 14th of October, while Pte. W. G. Parr died of wounds on the following day, as also did Pte. H. S. Newton, who had been gassed.

As a direct result of this action the daily bombardment of Ypres was at an end. On the 13th, while some of the Details were in the town, the enemy shelled it and caused some casualties, but from all accounts these were parting shots.

As the advance proceeded, so the Railway Operating Department (known to us as R.O.D. or "Roll on Death") began to construct the broad-gauge railway running from Poperinghe eastwards. Stations were established at different points, and a system of signalling was instituted.

At Poperinghe the news of the advance had the effect of bringing many of the civilian population back again. Shops and estaminets began to open, and many of the men in the reinforcement camps round Brandhoek were permitted to visit the town on the night of the 14th to join with a few of the French troops in celebrating unofficially the deliverance of such a big slice of Belgium within a few days.

The Transport moved on down the Menin Road, and the Q.M.S.s were finding that open warfare was not going to be all honey for them. The length of the road was about ten miles, and it was no easy matter to walk even a mile over its surface. Cutting across country to find the Battalion was more difficult still, and the "Quarter Blokes" were usually dead beat after they had completed the double journey.

The Battalion remained in its positions north of Menin on the 15th. Shelling had practically ceased, and it was evident from the fires that were observed in Menin that the enemy was about to evacuate that town.

On the 16th we moved up to Moorseele several miles more to the east, and thence to Gulleghem, two miles beyond Moorseele, where support positions to the 123rd Brigade, holding the front line around Courtrai, were taken up. The Transport had in the meantime moved up to Dadizeele and were finding things not quite so difficult as hitherto.

We had now reached a part of the front which had served as rest-billets for the German Army, and most of us were surprised to see the amount of comfort Fritz must have enjoyed compared with us. We saw houses with notice boards exhibited outside showing the number of "truppen" to be accommodated; wire beds had been rigged up in sheds and other places to save the men sleeping on the floor. Dead horses with chunks carved out of their sides were often seen, and we learned afterwards that "dead horse" had become a staple article of diet among the Germans and civilians in the occupied area. In many parts the fields were under cultivation, and turnips and potatoes were pulled up by the troops as they pursued the enemy. Refugees from part of the country through which the enemy was retiring began to arrive in our area. Some made their temporary homes in the churches, where they were often seen huddled together. Tales were brought to us of how little children had been killed through tampering with the "boobytraps" left by the beaten Hun.

Yes, the game was up, and the Germans knew it. "Kaput" was their equivalent for "Napoo." Nothing could save them now, not all their terrible sacrifice of lives and treasure, not all the science and generalship of the War Lords. The most efficient military machine the world ever knew was tumbling into ruin. Yet they played the ghastly game to the end with a valour, doggedness and skill that will always astound the world. It was a fighting retreat, in the main orderly and disciplined, never a "Sauve qui peut!" What a pity it should have been disgraced by such wanton and impish tricks that could do no serious harm to the pursuer but only inflame his resentment.

Though, as always, the enemy had done his utmost to impede our advance by destroying railways and other points of military importance, he had not reckoned on the amazing efficiency of the different corps operating with the infantry. As we advanced, so the men of the Labour Corps and the Royal Engineers followed behind, toiling to make up roads and railways. Never before had the British Army, and particularly the Second, been so well organised. Where a railway track had been so completely destroyed as to render it incapable for use for some time, a new track was made alongside it by Canadians and others who had spent a life-time at this sort of work. Meanwhile lorries were used for transport as much as possible. To show how well organised was the advance, we read in the War Diary of the 17th of October that, although the Battalion was in support, the men received a bath and a clean change of clothing.

On the 17th we remained in Gulleghem, which was intermittently shelled throughout the day and bombed by several enemy planes which flew over during the night. Lieuts. R. F. Browne and T. C. Hill joined the Battalion during the day, together with Lieut. A. R. Puttock, who was again posted to us after recuperating in England. Here was another link with our St. Eloi days, but no doubt Lieut. Puttock, like Lieut. Robinson, found very many changes had taken place in the Battalion during the months which had intervened. Several gas shells fell in the village on the 18th, causing some casualties.

Before we proceed, a review of what had taken place on other parts of the front, would be useful in helping us to follow the course of events.

It had been the intention of the British Admiralty (possibly about September, 1917) to make a landing on the Belgian Coast with the aid of flat-bottomed boats carrying tanks, but the idea was eventually abandoned. In consequence of what they heard, the Germans began to fortify the Belgian Coast with shell-proof machine-gun positions and the sand dunes with steel traps and obstacles for dealing with tanks. The fortifications were made stronger than the cliffs of Gallipoli. The great coastal batteries were increased, and everything was set for any invasion from the sea that the British might try.

Information was received by the enemy that a great landing battle would be opened on October 14th, 1918, and the Admiral in charge of the German defences, who ever since the 28th of September had been busy trying to get away his big guns, stores and ships, was beginning to find the task a very difficult one. General Sixte von Arnim with 20 divisions of the Fourth German Army and other divisions borrowed from the Sixth Army at Lille under General von Quast, was making a dogged stand by Dixmude, Roulers and Menin, principally with the idea of helping the transport of guns and material from the coast to be carried out before the blow fell. In addition defences around Ghent and Antwerp were being strengthened.

The news of an intended landing caused panic among German officials and civilians as far back as Bruges. Realising that the German reserves were not sufficient for a stand in strength along the coast, these individuals fled. On the 14th of October, we did bombard the coast and carry out a demonstration. but only to mislead the enemy. Once again the British Intelligence had triumphed.

While this demonstration was taking place, the armies under the King of the Belgians resumed their advance between the River Lys at Comines and the Yser at Dixmude. The task allotted to the British under Sir Herbert Plumer was the most important one of all. They had to prolong their defensive flank down the River Lys so as to guard all the attacking troops of the French and Belgians from a thrust from the Sixth German Army around Lille. Then they had to inflict a great strategic defeat upon this Germany Army on their right flank by driving them with their left through the German Fourth Army to the middle reach of the Lys above the town of Courtrai. There on a position behind Lille, Roubaix, and Tourcoing they could cut the northern railway communications of the German Sixth Army running through Courtrai and outflank them.

Conducted by the II Corps (9th, 29th and 36th Divisions), the X Corps (30th and 34th Divisions) and the XIX Corps (41st and 35th Divisions under the command of General Sir H. E. Watts), the British advance was irresistible despite the fact that General von Arnim had decided to make a desperate struggle, in the hopes that a defensive victory for his arms might make up for the defeats the Germans were suffering on other parts of the Western Front.

The Germans were driven from Moorseele and Heule towards Harlebeke, on the Lys, north of Courtrai, a town some sixteen miles north-east of Lille. Whilst the II Corps had been doing this, the other two Corps had fought their way towards the rising ground by Comines, Wervicq and Menin west of Courtrai. The German Sixth Army sought protection by making walls of flame out of the outer buildings of the threatened towns. Frontal attacks on towns were avoided by us to prevent the enemy from firing on buildings where civilian populations were sheltered. By the use of smoke from 60-pounders and flanking thrusts by the infantry, who connected in rear of the German pill-boxes and other defences, the most heroic of the Germans were eventually overcome. Stout Bavarians, to whom we have already had occasion to refer a few times throughout this history, again fought like tigers, but were no match for the English, Irish and Scottish troops in the II Corps under Sir Claud Jacob. Our tutors, the 9th Division, drove the enemy towards Gulleghem, the Irish captured Moorseele, whilst the English stormed the fortifications and scattered the enemy above Menin, bringing some of his own guns into action against him to drive him out of Heule into Courtrai. In the early hours of the 15th of October, Irish troops closed with the German rear-guards in the northern part of Courtrai and carried the buildings as far as the Lys.

The enemy lined the farther bank with covered machine-guns, while most of the population, numbering 30,000, had to take refuge in their cellars; it looked as though Courtrai was going to share the fate of other towns. This, however, was not to be, as it was decreed by General Plumer that the enemy should be contained along the waterway, since, by the turning movement some miles northward at Harlebeke, it was only a question of time before Courtrai must be evacuated.

This was briefly the position when on the 19th of October the Battalion marched from Gulleghem and, crossing the River Lys near Bisseghem, south-west of Courtrai, spent the remainder of the day on the outskirts of the town. At the same time the Transport moved up to Heule. The 122nd Brigade were now temporarily attached to the 35th Division as reserve.

On the 20th the Battalion moved into Courtrai at a time when some of the German troops had not yet cleared out, and here billets were taken for the day.

This was a great day for our men. After being used to taking tiny villages and hamlets, they suddenly found themselves in a fairly large industrial town. Strict instructions were issued as to how the troops should conduct themselves. As the town was still subject to bombardment from land and air, refuge was found in many cellars where the inhabitants were living.

Activity on every side was the order of the day. R.E.s were busy throwing pontoon bridges across the Lys, and in some cases barrels with rafts on them were used for the infantry to cross. The order to break step was given in marching over these improvised bridges, and some of us did not feel too happy in risking the crossing.

British flags were very soon displayed in some parts of the town, and we wondered where they had come from. It was suggested by some that the Germans, with a true business instinct, had sold them to the inhabitants to welcome us. At all events our welcome was not confined to the hanging out of bunting, for the people seemed overjoyed and did what they could to make our stay, short as it was, very enjoyable.

Here is an incident related by one of our Company Clerks concerning the British entry into Courtrai.

"I was in a café in Courtrai a day or two after the Battalion and had a very interesting conversation with the proprietress. There were two or three others with me, and we were enjoying a feed of eggs and chips. The lady, who could speak English, informed us that she used to own a restaurant in Ostend, but had moved away from there when the British started to bombard the coast in 1914. She had then gone to Courtrai, where, from time to time, she had German troops billeted on her. On the whole she had little good to say for them, as they stole her chickens and often helped themselves to other things. She told us how our planes had caused much damage not only in Courtrai but in other towns behind the German lines. The Germans had kept the populace in ignorance, as far as possible, of what was taking place, but the people themselves could see that things were not going too well with them. Just before they evacuated the town, they spread false rumours of what the British troops were like and at the same time showed a changed attitude in their own conduct. However, this lady had gained the confidence of a German soldier whom she described as a good one. Before the British entry he had informed her that the British would be in occupation in a few days and told her to assure the people she knew that they would be well treated by them."

After a day's rest in Courtrai we went into action near Sweveghem, three miles east of the town, on October 21st. Our objective entailed a 9,000 yards advance to the River Scheldt, and for this purpose C Company on the left and D Company on the right formed the attacking waves, while A on the left and B on the right were in support.

The attack commenced at 7.0 a.m. The 18th K.R.R.s and the 15th Hants succeeded during the day in forcing the line of the canal with great gallantry and crossing by 2.0 p.m. At first there was little opposition on our front, but soon sharp fighting ensued and we were held up by very heavy machine-gun fire and a belt of wire. Altogether we advanced about two miles to the Courtrai—Bossuyt Canal, south of Knokke. During the advance 2nd Lieut. G. H. Savage, M.M., was killed, and 2nd Lieut. R. Northwood was wounded. The following were also killed: Lce.-Cpl. J. Taylor and Ptes. A. B. Carr, E. Chapman, G. Loveland and W. Welsh, while Ptes. W. F. Mulville and G. Songhurst died of wounds the same day. Notification was also received of the death from wounds of Pte. W. Hasler on the 20th.

The Battalion was again in action on the 22nd, when three companies crossed the Canal near Knokke. Much opposition was met with, particularly by C Company, as the enemy strongly held a tunnel with machine-guns, along the front over which our advance was made. C Company was held up at first and lost many men, but later in the afternoon succeeded in forcing the position. Capt. E. St. J. N. Ryan, recently decorated for his services in the field, was killed in making the attempt, and Capt. J. A. Rogers and Lieut. T. C. Hill were wounded. Eventually the Battalion got through every opposition and gained touch with the units on either flank. It had been a trying time for the attackers, for the enemy machine-gunners made good use of their positions and mowed our men down as they attempted to advance.

In addition to many wounded, the following other ranks were killed during the operations:—Cpl. H. Old; Ptes. J. Bacon, J. W. Balls, G. E. Barker, W. Chittock, C. H. Clark, N. Collins, G. Cressey, J. R. Dallinger, A. G. Day, F. Parker, P. S. Record, M.M., P. Revels, T. J. M. Reynolds, E. S. Tanner, A. J. Trim and C. Wright. Ptes. A. Linge and G. B. Tawn died of wounds on the same day; Ptes A. Howard and S. R. Convine on the 23rd and Pte. F. Clements on the 24th.

The wounding of Capt. Rogers brought to an end a career with the 12th Battalion which began soon after we went overseas. He was never spectacular, but invariably managed to get the best out of his men in his own quiet way. There were few operations he missed and in which his conduct was not the subject for recommendation for award. Considering that Capt. Rogers was awarded the Military Cross with two bars for operations in which he commanded companies and one where he commanded half the Battalion, it is surprising that the powers who dealt with the award of decorations did not see fit to award him the D.S.O. Not that one supposes that Capt. Rogers would have wished this, for his modesty was such that he would have considered that he had only done his duty in the circumstances as one who had been placed in charge. There could have been few officers in the whole Division who had been through so much fighting as he, for he was essentially a company officer, and, if his luck in not becoming a casualty had held out so long, it must have been a terrific strain on him to shoulder the responsibility of taking companies into action.

Many readers who were with the Battalion up to the last year of the war will look in vain for familiar names among the lists of the dead for this period. The fact is that many of them were hardly known to us, some only joining just before the final advance to victory was commenced. Some of the old hands still clung on, surviving miraculously, it seemed, until the end—but they were very, very few. Amongst the latest list of the fallen appeared the name of Pte. Percy Record, well-known at the time in B Company as a fearless stretcher-bearer, about whom Capt. David Walker has written another story.

"When we had advanced along the Menin Road, we were in a position west of the town, and from Battalion H.Q. to the front line communication was along a sunken road into which the enemy could fire. He certainly was not a good shot, but on one occasion, passing down the road, I got frightened and leapt headlong into a ditch and down on my stomach; I may add too there were six inches of water in the ditch. There I remained with no thought of moving for about five minutes, when I heard a voice. There standing upright and in full view of the enemy and taking no consequence of the risk, was our stretcher-bearer, Pte. Record. He called to me: 'Are you hurt, Sir?' I felt wet, but my discomfort came more from the thought of how brave a fellow that must be. I got up and marched back to Battalion H.Q., which I reached safely. Some time later I learnt of the death by a sniper of our brave stretcher-bearer."

For services rendered in connection with the operations, 2nd Lieut. R. F. Howship, a young officer of B Company, was subsequently awarded the Military Cross.

About midnight on the 22nd/23rd of October the Battalion was relieved by the 23rd Middlesex and moved back into the Divisional Rest Area, north of Knokke. One casualty occurred during the day, 2nd Lieut. J. R. A. Cockayne being gassed and subsequently transferred to England.

In these days of harrying the Boche there was little respite from the fighting, as there was no intention of letting him settle down again. In fact from the time we had started on the 28th of September it seemed to us as though we were on the move all the time, and it is difficult after so many years to recall many of the incidents which, although not officially recorded, would be of interest to the men who took part in the operations. We were never out of the line for more than a few days at a stretch, hardly long enough to know much about the places where we rested. Our latest rest lasted for two days, just enough time to re-organise again for another push forward.

The 26th was to see us again in action, this time for the assault on Avelghem on the Scheldt, 9 miles W.S.W. of Courtrai. The Battalion was to attack in co-operation with the 18th K.R.R.s.

The jumping-off point was reached at 8.30 a.m., but by 9 o'clock civilians had reported to Brigade H.Q. that the enemy had left Avelghem. Patrols who were sent into the village reported that there were no signs of the enemy, and the orders for the attack were therefore cancelled. A patrol was then sent to secure the damaged bridgehead across the River Scheldt, or, to give it its French name shown in the operation orders, Escaut. This was done, and posts were established there and in the hamlets of Rugge and Wafflestraat, after enemy groups had been dispersed, in spite of heavy fire from the right bank. The village was heavily shelled during the night.

This day Lieut. Robinson was wounded again while serving with us. As he had only rejoined us a fortnight before, his stay was shorter than hitherto. Ptes. V. J. Clark, I. L. Digby, F. Histed, A. L. Pattman, H. E. Samson and M. Angood were the fatal casualties suffered during the day, the last-named dying from his wounds.

2nd Lieut. W. G. T. Summers, D.C.M., M.M., an ex-N.C.O. of the 9th Battalion, was in charge of the three patrols which entered Avelghem and then secured the damaged bridgehead over the Scheldt and succeeded in establishing posts on the right bank. For his services he was afterwards awarded the Military Cross. On the following day he also was wounded.

Our casualties from the 14th to the 26th of October had been heavy, especially on the 21st and 22nd. Three officers and 33 other ranks were killed; seven officers and 167 other ranks wounded; and 30 other ranks missing. Ptes. E. B. Chambers and O. Ellis died from their wounds on the 27th, and the number of missing was gradually reduced towards the end of the month by reports from burial parties.

Another rest came on the 27th, when we moved back two miles west of Knokke, where we remained till the end of the month in reserve, training for the next offensive. As a welcome change from chasing the enemy, sports were held on the 29th.

While the Battalion was resting near Knokke, the enemy was very active in the air. His main objective was, of course, Courtrai, where endeavours were being made to rebuild the bridges and repair the roads. B Company was billeted in barns near Belleghem, and on two occasions bombs were dropped very close to them. On the night of the 29th of October the enemy came over in relays, and the raids lasted throughout the night. Coming right over B Company's billets, one Boche airman unloaded his bombs a couple of hundred yards away from the officers' mess which was situated in a farmhouse. As they dropped, it seemed as if they were falling on the farm itself, and the civilians inside quickly took to the cellars. Everybody inside thought that their last day had come, so near were the explosions. Lights were extinguished both in the mess and the barns around, and the ground shook like an earthquake. The "terror that flieth by night" was perhaps the most frightful of the miseries that marked the latter stages of the war. Men expected constant danger and hardships in the firing line, but to know no peace or rest when they were withdrawn, never to lie down to sleep without the expectation of being awakened by the sound of deafening explosions, the sight of mangled bodies and fear of imminent death set the nerves on edge and made everyone haggard and strained.

On the following morning we heard that a little party from Battalion H.Q. which had gone into Courtrai on pass had not returned. Enquiries were set on foot, and two of the Company Clerks visited the Casualty Clearing Stations in the area. It was eventually discovered that the Provost-Sergt. Charlie Field and Lce.-Cpl. Percy Sloots, of the Battalion Orderly Room staff had been killed by a bomb, and that the Sniping-Sergt., F. T. James, had been seriously wounded. These were the last fatal casualties suffered by the Battalion, apart from those who subsequently died from wounds received in previous actions. Sergt. Field was one of the original members of the 12th and had occupied the not altogether pleasant job of Provost-Sergeant since Messines. He had never shirked his duty and was awarded the M.S.M. for good work in the line. Percy Sloots was an ex-Surrey Yeoman who had entered the Orderly Room as a clerk at St. Eloi. He was a cheery companion and well liked by all. Sergt. F. T. James, who had been awarded the D.C.M., M.M., and Médaille Militaire while serving with the 12th, died of his wounds on the 8th of December. After being wounded a few times, he joined the Battalion after Flers, and his good work is shown by the awards he received. For a man with such a remarkable record of war service to be killed towards the end was one of our great tragedies of the war. He took over the snipers while Sergt. Jack Hill was on command.

Another death on the 30th was that of Pte. W. G. Kemp, who died aboard the Hospital-Ship, St. David, off Boulogne. In connection with the death of this man it was recently discovered that his name was not recorded by the Imperial War Graves Commission, and after the necessary enquiries had been made it was decided to add it to the Tyne Cot Memorial at Passchendaele.

The total casualties for October were four officers and 58 other ranks killed; 12 officers and 257 other ranks wounded, and 19 other ranks missing. The following subsequently died from their wounds:—Ptes. T. W. Saville (2.11.18), E. W. Stokes (3.11.18), T. Pack (7.11.18), R. G. Gunn and W. A. King (in hospital in England, 24.11.18), S. G. Samuels (24.11.18), P. J. Offord (28.11.18), P. W. Baxter and C. Simmonds (in hospital in England, 4.2.19). Gunn and Offord were with the Battalion when it was at St Eloi in 1916.

On the 31st of October the Battalion, now 38 officers and 677 other ranks strong, marched to Vierkeerhoek in Brigade support, the 122nd Brigade having relieved the 106th Brigade of the 35th Division.

From the 1st to the 3rd of November, the Battalion remained in support near Vierkeerhoek carrying out training in musketry and Lewis-gun.

Some of the Details had now moved up towards Courtrai, and, together with the Q.M. Stores, they moved to Sweveghem on the 2nd of November; here they were billeted in a factory where some of the smashed machinery bore the inscription "Babcock and

Wilcox"—an English firm in London. To the troops this was a reminder of home, until the enemy planes started bombarding in the evening.

On the 4th the Battalion moved back near Knokke. Here the C.O. and the Company Commanders reconnoitred the line of the River Escaut in preparation for a crossing which was to take place on the 10th and 11th of November.

Leaving billets on the 5th, we moved to Harlebeke, where the Details rejoined us together with "A" Echelon of the Transport.

As the time had now arrived for the Transport to move with the rest of the Battalion instead of having to make those nightly journeys over the shell-swept roads, it is right and proper to pay some little tribute to the work they accomplished. Although there were perhaps more of the old faces in this section than any other in the Battalion, their numbers had dwindled from time to time as the result of casualties. No one is better fitted to pay a compliment to them than Q.M.S. Speller, who says:—

"No record of the 12th Battalion could be regarded as complete without a generous reference to that cheery crowd, the Transport Section. I came in contact with them and depended upon them more perhaps than anybody, and my regret is that no words of mine will reflect them as they deserve to be reflected.

"There were Victor Whiteway, Matthews, and Libby, all of whom met death gallantly; Lieut. Ted Edwards, who brought from Africa rows of medal ribbons, polo sticks and enough sporting gear to fit out a modest 'safari'—alas, the majority of this found an early home at the base—whose years and near-blindness finally resulted in his going down the line; McKechnie who exuded 'horsiness'—all of these served their brief space as O. i/c Transport, and passed on.

"Nuttman, who had an uncanny 'knack' with both horses and dogs, I was fortunate in getting in 1915, and he served with the Battalion throughout. Joe Mills, our 'scrapper,' Brown, Tims, little Ruskin, Thornton, Horner, these I remember well after leaving them 17 years ago. Bill Maleed, whose ferocious eyebrows belied his gentleness, farrier and giant though he was. Henley, who earned a sack of medals for gallantry, and didn't anyway get one. When the roads around Ypres were at their 'unhealthiest,' Henley exuded a complete and cheerful disregard of sudden death. His calm 'Get up, you ——s!' was like a tonic, and amongst other things I imagine he held the record for France in the number of draught-poles he smashed! Reid, and his heavy draught, 'Lousy,' whose profiles were oddly similar as to Grecian curve.

"Others there were whose names ascape me now, but whether it was a quick 'hook in and get,' a visit from the Veterinary Nabobs, a 'finding' expedition, improvising an Xmas turkey (with four legs) in Italy, or cleaning a billet of squatter 'Austrylians,' I never found them lacking.

"The Battalion never missed getting rations on any day during the whole of their campaigning, and whatever kudos came my way on that account belonged almost entirely to the Transport."

At Harlebeke we were billeted in an old camp which had apparently been occupied by the Germans. Besides the hutments there was a large concrete dugout near by with straw on the floor. We had seen many of these bomb-proof shelters on our way up and presumed they were used for air raids. This one in Harlebeke could have housed a platoon comfortably, but the interior was in such a filthy state that the men fought shy of it. Harlebeke must also have been used as a rail-head, for there was a fair-sized station there which the enemy had wrecked before he retired. The rails had been blown up in the station itself, and along the track was evidence that stick-bombs had been inserted under the metals at intervals and gaps blown in the line. A few shops existed and were patronised for what little they could sell to us.

Apart from his planes, which nightly dropped bombs around, little was heard of the enemy. This led to the usual crop of rumours, but this time one proved to be correct. A temporary respite from fighting was spoken about, as it was understood plenipotentiaries were crossing the line to treat for an armistice. However, we took very little notice of this, as we had come to regard the Hun as a wily bird who would resort to anything to give him a chance of recovery. Whatever the rumours were, it did not make any difference to our mode of procedure. We had become so used to regarding the war as one without end that any one who seriously tried to suggest that an end was in sight would be laughed at and called a fool.

On the 8th after Divine Service the Battalion rehearsed the operations for the next action—that of crossing the river. The crossing by foot-bridge was followed by a practice attack at 11.0 a.m. In the evening we again assembled for another practice—this one on the lines for the actual attack. A and B Companies sent 40 men across the river in boats, while the remainder of the Battalion crossed by means of two foot-bridges, the whole operation being carried out in the dark. Despite the high morale of our men at the time this latest dangerous operation was not looked upon with great favour by those who would be called upon to do the actual stunt. Silence was an essential part of the programme, but it also required a sleeping or unwatchful enemy to make it a real success. Fortunately the actual attack was never delivered, otherwise the already heavy casualty-rolls of the 12th East Surreys would have been greatly swollen. Q.M.S. Speller has thrown a little more light on the impending advance when he writes:—

"Happily for the Battalion the attack ordered for the 10th-11th of November did not take place. Horswell had orders to regulate the direction of the companies' attack across a kilometre or two of open country until they should reach and endeavour to cross the Scheldt. A very small frontage was allotted to the Battalion and we all knew what that signified, especially as our immediate objective on the other side was a stone-built village protected by a 30 yards barbed-wire belt!

"Horswell was 'Harbour Master,' or so he said, and this title he retained throughout the 'Exercises of the Fleet,' which a few kindred souls in the Sergeants' Mess developed as a 'Tableau,' later.

"Apropos of the Scheldt crossing—for several nights previously we had dumped barrels, timber, and life-belts on the river bank for use during the attack. When we arrived in Germany about six weeks later, very urgent enquiries were made as to the whereabouts of sundry life-belts, the property of H.M. Navy! Verily we had come back to peace-time equipment accounting with a jolt."

On the 9th we marched to Ingoyghem, a distance of about 10 kilometres to the south-east, where billets were found in farmhouses in the surrounding district. Here two things were discovered which interested us. First of all the civilians informed us that the main German Army had passed through there several days before and only a few rear-guards had remained. Secondly we learned that our artillery was out of range of the Boche. This was news indeed, but still many of us thought that the enemy was leading us into a trap. At all events if his infantry had gone back, his planes had by no means finished with us yet, for in the evening a little bit of excitement was caused when a German plane was brought down near B Company's billets. There was a scamper over to the blazing wreckage, but the airman was burnt to a cinder.

We continued the march on the 10th, and after experiencing some difficulty in crossing swampy ground reached the banks of the Scheldt, which we crossed on pontoon bridges already prepared by the R.E. The river was crossed at Berchem, five miles S.W. of Audenarde, the scene of Marlborough's great victory, and silently through the night we made our way to Etichove. Nothing was seen or heard of the enemy; even his usual night-birds of the air seemed to have deserted us. There was something uncanny about it all. We had not been used to this stillness. Tired and footsore, the men were distributed about fairly comfortable barns, the luckier ones, like Battalion and Company H.Q., finding rest in some of the houses. The inhabitants greeted us warmly, freely distributing coffee and eggs as far as they went.

The rest, as far as the writer is concerned, must be the experiences of B Company, who were detached from the remainder of the Battalion. No doubt others were similar.

C.S.M. Bry Horswell and C.Q.M.S. Billy Steer, of B Company, were an ideal combination. They not only performed their respective jobs efficiently, but brought a fund of humour into the drabness of things. On the night before the Armistice, Horswell was the pessimist and Steer the optimist in a discussion on the duration of the war. Steer was fully convinced that there was a possibility of it ending soon and suggested that we should hear some news in the morning, while Horswell was certain that the quietness of things could be accounted for by the Hun preparing a new line farther back. However, the argument ended by both, in common with the rest of the H.Q. staff, falling fast off to sleep.

Early on the morning of the 11th of November Ted Holland, most famous of B Company cooks, came into the house and waking Steer told him that there was a "Froggy" soldier round his cooker, who kept on repeating "La Guerre finie." Steer dressed and went out to see the Frenchman, who jubilantly repeated what he had told Holland. Back again went Steer into the billet and woke Horswell and the others to break the news. Horswell was not having any, for at the time the sound of explosions could be heard in the distance. By this time more of the troops were awake and crowded round the Frenchman, who further explained that an Armistice would come into operation at 11.0 a.m. Some were inclined to believe the news, but others thought the Frenchman must be mad. It must be remembered that, although it was now known by us that the German delegates had come to sue for an Armistice, we had not the least inkling of what progress had been made. In point of fact the actual Armistice Terms were signed by the Germans some hours before 11.0 a.m., and no doubt the French troops were better informed than we were.

The Diary reports that the news of the Armistice was announced at 10.30 a.m. As far as B Company was concerned, the news was not received until some time later. Some of us were punting a football about, when we were surprised to see Colonel Brown come on the field. Without any fuss he conveyed to us the joyful tidings. One cannot remember any cheering breaking out; rather were we too dazed to give any expression to our feelings. However, after an hour or two had passed, we were given the freedom of the village. In two or three little estaminets that existed there we mingled with the French soldiers who had found their way into the place, sang their songs, helped them to sing ours, and generally cemented the Entente Cordiale. Later our brass and drum and fife bands got going, and soon the village was crowded by soldiers and civilians who were only too glad to give way to the pent-up feelings of four years of war.

At six o'clock in the evening Divine Service was held, which gave the men an opportunity not only of being thankful for being spared, but also of thinking of those fine fellows they had known and loved who had already finished their course.

This was how we received the news of the Armistice. Let us now turn to Capt. E. W. J. Neave's account of how the 11th "Queen's" received it. They were with the 123rd Brigade, and on the morning of the 10th went forward in support of the 23rd Middlesex, who advanced through Nukerke and Schoorisse and were assisted by machine-guns mounted in the side-cars of motor-cycles. The inhabitants gave them a rousing reception as they arrived on the heels of the retreating Germans. About mid-day a line of enemy machine-guns held up the "Diehards," and they had to dig in. The "Queen's" following them halted, and billeted 1½ miles south-east of Schoorisse.

At dawn on the 11th a party from the "Queen's" was sent to arrange billets at Hauwstraat, between Schoorisse and Nederbrakel, but on reaching the outposts the officer in charge was informed that the outposts were waiting the order to advance. Without further ado the advance party then crossed into the enemy's country and, pushing on cautiously, reached their destination at 10.30 a.m. and found out that the enemy had left half an hour ago. At 10.45 a mounted officer galloped into the village and ordered them to proceed no further, as an armistice had been arranged, which would commence at 11.0 a.m.

The men regarded this news as not meaning much to them at the time; with their limited knowledge of armistices, they only thought it might bring them a few days' rest. Capt. Neave continues:—

"The billeting party sent back to the Adjutant for instructions and retired to the one estaminet to await the runner's return. The proprietor produced a bottle of cognac and a bottle of white wine—all the Germans had left him—with which a dozen men proceeded to 'celebrate' the occasion. At 11.0 a.m. the Germans to our front emptied their machine-gun belts, and the French, on our left, fired several salvos of their '75's.' Then there was a silence."

In England and especially in London, as we know, the people in their delirium of relief and joy "mafficked" and danced. There was none of that among the troops. Dulled by constant peril, discomfort, toil and misery, they received the seemingly incredible news almost in a stupor. It couldn't be true that the War was over—poor old Tommy would, of course, go on "getting it in the neck." The older men were mostly silent and thoughtful; it was the youngsters who were noisy. The chief thought was—"Well, I'm lucky to be alive. Now let's get home out of this filthy hell. Then shan't I have a good time!" It was the great reprieve. We were like prisoners suddenly released from years in a dark and stinking dungeon, who stand blinking in the sunlight with no words to say.

A few points in connection with the operations preceding the Armistice would not be out of place here, especially as we were quite out of touch at the time.

While the Battalion was at Harlebeke, mutiny had broken out amongst the German forces; the outbreak among sailors and marines at Kiel spread to the soldiers in Brussels and elsewhere. The German officers, stern as ever, managed to restrain their men and to get together rear-guard forces from tired and dejected troops. But despite gallant stands here and there the Allied Offensive could not be stopped, though by flooding the region of the Scheldt the enemy hoped to arrest our progress.

On November 8th, the day of our practice attack, the Germans began a movement of withdrawal by Renaix and abandoned Tournai. In the meantime the Belgians and French, having won bridgeheads along the Scheldt between Ghent and Audenarde, began to move forward towards Brussels. In accordance with this movement the British Army took a leading part by advancing through Renaix on the 9th and reaching the outskirts of Grammont on the 10th. Ath also fell on this day. On Monday, November 11th, the foremost troops of the Second Army were in the region of Grammont, a place whence we were to go on leave later.

Much discussion takes place nowadays as to why we did not continue the advance once we had gained such a complete ascendancy over the enemy. Some would have liked us to continue to the Rhine, but, as we were afterwards to find out, the Germans had seen to it that as we advanced most means of communication were either destroyed or put temporarily out of use. Railways were put out of action and cross-roads mined. Our chief means for transport of supplies was the lorry. Apart from this consideration, there was no object in prolonging the slaughter for the sake of satisfying those who clamoured for giving the Germans a dose of their own medicine.

The forward sweep of the British Armies in the last three months was an amazing achievement, which should never sink into oblivion. They had few reinforcements; they had gone beyond range of the heavy artillery, which for long could not be brought across the wide area of grisly bogs left behind by the infantry in their rapid advance; even the transport could barely keep up, and often the troops had to be munitioned and fed by supplies dropped from aeroplanes. Casualties were heavy, and few battalions up to half strength. Yet our men, exhausted by the strain of constant fighting, racked by deadly H.E. and machine-gun fire and the equally maddening horror of night-bombing behind the front, tense, lousy and mudstained, yet still cheerful through all their trials, buoyed up in this last hour by the exaltation of final success, staggered on like the "weary Titan" of Matthew Arnold's poem:—

> "Bearing on shoulders immense,
> Atlantean, the load,
> Well-nigh not to be borne,
> Of the too vast orb of her fate."

It was not the French, exhausted by the interminable struggle of over four years, gallant and almost incredible as their last efforts were, that dealt the Hun his death-blow. It was not the Americans, although the knowledge that their fresh millions were coming fast into the field caused the German High Command to realise with despair that victory had for ever eluded their grasp. It was the British Army that dealt the hammer strokes which broke in pieces the armed might of Germany. Marshal Foch has generously acknowledged this, and Ludendorff has stated it without reserve. It is in no boastful spirit we record this plain fact of history, which many forget, but only that honour may be given where honour is rightly due.

CHAPTER XV.

28th September to 11th November, 1918.

The Final Advance to Victory—In the fighting at Gheluwe and on the Menin Road—The envelopment of Menin and the crossing of the Lys—Courtrai occupied—The Scheldt reached—The last casualties caused by air raid—Crossing of the Scheldt near Audenarde—News of the Armistice at Etichove.

WE reach the beginning of the end, the advance of the combined force commanded by H.M. The King of the Belgians, consisting of the Belgian Army, part of the Second British Army and certain French divisions.

On the 28th of September the Battalion moved to Ravine Wood, east of Hill 60, where we spent the night. To appreciate the position which had arisen it is necessary to relate what was taking place while the Battalion was making its way eastwards.

It is fairly clear that a drive of the enemy from Belgium was anticipated. Instructions on open warfare had been issued in which the importance of pushing on to final objectives, whether flanks were operating or not, was stressed. We had learnt something from the Germans about "Infiltration," which had proved so successful against the Italians a year before and also against the British in the following March. We were also instructed to report when there appeared to be an opportunity for horsemen to pass through, as French cavalry might be operating. The use of planes for delivering S.A.A. was also brought to notice. The 10th Squadron R.A.F. was to operate with the infantry, and boxes of ammunition would be dropped when a large V was placed on the ground at least 200 yards behind the line.

At 5.30 a.m. on the 28th of September, the XIX and II Corps of the Second British Army attacked on a front of four and a half miles south of the Ypres—Zonnebeke Road, the rôle of the 41st Division being to support the later stages of the operations. Further north the Belgian Army also attacked, with the result that in one day the enemy was driven from the high ground about Ypres: truly a remarkable performance when one realises the immense man-power and losses of the British Army which had been used a year before to gain in five months of warfare less *terrain* than was occupied on this one day. The conditions were not much better either, for heavy rains had made the going very hard, and the bringing up of guns and stores was a very difficult problem.

The Belgians entered Houthulst Forest, approached Staden and stormed Broodseinde in an advance of four miles, in which they took 5,000 prisoners and 300 guns; it was plain that the enemy began to see the writing on the wall.

General Plumer with battalions from the 9th, 29th, 35th and 14th Divisions had bitten into the Salient to such an extent that, on either side of the Menin Road, Bercelaere had been taken in an advance of five miles, Gheluvelt had fallen, and the 29th

On our arrival at Everbecq comfortable billets were allotted in houses and other places which the enemy had made fit for his troops to occupy. As soon as we arrived we found the civilians getting busy to supply us with coffee. As usual we found that the Germans had spread the rumour that we should commandeer whatever we wanted, and, when we offered to pay for what we had, they were agreeably surprised. We knew they could ill afford to give us anything and saw to it that they were recompensed for their trouble.

An inter-company football tournament was started on the 15th, when H.Q. drew with C Company 4—4. On the 16th B Company beat D Company 4—1. The replay between H.Q. and C Company took place on the 17th, resulting in a win for the former by 5—2.

During the stay photographs of the companies were taken by a local photographer, B Company's being taken outside a lovely château where the officers were billeted. On the 17th 2nd Lieuts. J. Walker and A. R. Wilkins joined the Battalion, and a few days later Lieuts. H. D. Gold and A. W. England rejoined. Lieut. England was another of our officers who had been with us at St. Eloi and was wounded in the Battle of Messines.

The Battalion was on the road again on the 18th, when it moved to Bievene. It was an inspiring march, for lining the roads were civilians who cheered us as we passed, and in the villages and hamlets flags and bunting began to appear from the windows. Again we were fairly comfortably billeted, for in an effort to make our stay enjoyable these simple country folk, glad no doubt to have us with them, did everything to make us happy.

This was the extent of our advance towards Germany for the time being, for owing to the difficulty of supplying the troops it was decided that some should stay where they were until the lines of communication were better organised. It was therefore decreed that our old friends, the 9th Division, should take our place in the vanguard, and the Battalion marched back to Everbecq on the 20th. Although there may have been some regrets at our not having the honour of being some of the first troops to enter the Rhineland, there was no begrudging the honour to one of the finest divisions in the British Army. Since our early associations with them at "Plug Street," where they initiated us into trench warfare, we had come in contact with them many times and sometimes relieved them, and it was strange that at the end we should again be in the same area as they were. However, they had to march the distance which we afterwards accomplished partly by rail. From now until the end of November we were pleasantly settled in Everbecq, carrying out training and route marches, but also enjoying ourselves when the opportuntities were given.

On the 22nd a party of officers from the Division, in which several of ours were included, proceeded to Brussels to take part in the official entry of the King of the Belgians into his beloved capital. These officers spoke in glowing terms of the great reception they received on this occasion.

The final of the Football Competition between A Company, who had drawn a bye, and H.Q. resulted in H.Q. winning, 3—1, on the 23rd.

On the 26th Colonel Brown took over the command of the Brigade in the absence of General Weston, who proceeded to England, and in his absence Major Searle commanded the Battalion. On this day a sports committee was appointed, composed of Lieuts. Gold and Browne, and 2nd Lieuts. Sleath and Aldridge.

So great was the football fever at this time that cooks and other people who had never turned out before were enticed to try their skill. Six-a-side matches were arranged which caused a great deal of fun. This was all for the good of the football prestige of the Battalion, and later on we were champions of the 41st Division and took part in the final of the Corps Cup. To select a representative team a Probables v. Possibles Match was played on the 30th, when the former won by the big score of 11—0. Concerts were also given by the various companies. On the 30th we also underwent another change in command, as Major C. T. Williams returned, having recovered from the effects of his gassing at Vierstraat.

There had only been one casualty during November, one other rank wounded. At the date of the Armistice the strength of the Battalion was 36 officers and 650 other ranks, but these numbers had been slightly increased by the end of the month.

Leave to England was continued while we were at Everbecq. Parties had to parade at Brigade H.Q. and proceed from Grammont by motor bus through Renaix to Courtrai. The party which left on the 1st of December experienced what was probably the lot of others. The bus used was one of the oldest type seen on the London roads before the war. Crowded with troops in the highest of glee, the bus slowly made its way along the road to the entraining point. Everything went well until a hill was reached, and then the vehicle point blank refused to take it, so the men were instructed to get off and help to push it up the hill. A few stops more for breakdowns occurred before Courtrai was reached. The rail journey from Courtrai to Calais took about 10 hours, and some precarious parts of the road had to be negotiated. One can remember crossing an archway—evidently a broken railway bridge—which had been temporarily strutted up by the Royal Engineers. In normal times one would not dream of taking the risk, but times were different now; we had taken risks far worse than this, and the thoughts of getting home again, even for a few days, were enough to make us dismiss the incident as trifling.

Some of those who went on leave did not return, as they discovered that by getting an offer of work from a late employer a man could be demobilised in England without delay. This had a marked effect on those still serving with the Battalion, who considered for various reasons their claims were better. Those who returned were usually sent to the Cavalry Barracks at Namur, as by this time we were on the move again. Later they proceeded by rail to Huy to rejoin the Battalion when it reached that area.

To revert to those at Everbecq, the 1st of December will be remembered as the day on which a special Memorial Service was held for those who had fallen in the war.

Playing in the final of the Brigade Football Tournament on the 7th, our team beat the 18th K.R.R.s by 3—2.

Our stay at Everbecq should not be passed over without some account of the fancy dress parade and sports meeting which was held on the 9th of December. Through the kindness of Sergt. B. G. Burgess, we are able to reproduce the actual programme, whish will help to revive memories besides causing some amusement to those who were not privileged to participate.

Commence
9.30 a.m.
Sharp.

On the
Football
Ground.

EVERBECQ.

Mon. DEC. 9th.

GRAND — UNIQUE — IMPROMPTU — SPORTS MEETING.

MONEY FOR NOTHING!!! PRIZES FOR ALL!!! ROLL UP!!! ROLL UP!!!
— ALL —
PROBABLES — POSSIBLES — IMPOSSIBLES — & N.B.G.s.

SPECIAL FEATURES:—

1. OPEN AIR BOXING. IS THERE ANYONE YOU WANT TO HAVE A SCRAP WITH!!! PERSUADE HIM TO COME ALONG AND WE WILL PROVIDE THE RING AND FRANCS, 5 FOR THE WINNER.
   N.B.—IF ANYONE CHOOSES A SERGEANT-MAJOR HE MUST DEPOSIT FRANCS, 20, TO BE RETURNED IF HE IS RETURNED IN GOOD CONDITION.

2. BLINDFOLD BOXING.

3. SPECIAL FOR COMPANY COOKS!!!
   FRANCS, 40, FOR BEST TURNED OUT COOKER.
   FRANCS, 20, FOR BEST DINNER.
   TO BE JUDGED BY COMMANDING OFFICER AT DINNERS ON MONDAY.

4. BLINDFOLD SQUAD DRILL. TEAMS OF 9.
   BRING YOUR OWN TEAM AND HANDKERCHIEF.
   WE PROVIDE THE PRIZE.

5. CARNIVAL RACE. FANCY DRESS. THE FANCIER THE BETTER!!
   100 YARDS. PRIZE FOR BEST DRESS PLUS POSITION IN RACE.

6. COCK FIGHT. ONE TEAM OF 12 FROM EACH COMPANY.
   PRIZE: FRANCS 5 PER PAIR OF WINNING TEAM WHO REMAIN MOUNTED.

7. THREE-LEGGED CIVILIAN RACE. BRING YOUR OWN CIVILIAN!!!!
   AGE, SEX AND SIZE AT YOUR DISCRETION.
   FRANCS 10 FOR 1st. FRANCS 5 FOR 2nd.

8. WHEELBARROW RACE. BRING YOUR OWN WHEELBARROW AND LIVING CONTENTS. PRIZE: 5 FRANCS.

9. BOOT AND TUNIC RACE. THE MORE COMPETITORS THE MERRIER.
   PRIZE: FRANCS 10 FOR 1st. FRANCS 5 FOR 2nd.

10. OFFICERS & W.O.'s MULE RACE. PRIZE SPECIALLY PRESENTED BY M.O. (ONE BRAND NEW UNUSED No. 9.).

11. BAND AND DRUM RACE (WALKING HANDICAP).

12. BACK TO BACK S.D.R. RACE. 100 YARDS.

13. SPECIAL FOR SANITARY MEN. TEAMS OF TWO. THE BEST CONSTRUCTED LATRINE. 15 MINUTES ALLOWED.
    OWN MATERIAL TO BE SCROUNGED, FOOTBALL POSTS AND PRESENT LATRINES NOT TO BE USED!!! SPECIAL PRIZE: FRANCS 10.

14. LADIES' RACE. (CIVILIANS ONLY MAY COMPETE.)
    SPECIAL PRIZE: ONE LOAF, ONE TIN BULLY, AND A BAR OF SOAP.

15. PLATOON RACE. PLATOONS LIMITED TO 15. ALL COMPETITORS ROPED TOGETHER. PRIZE: 30 FRANCS FOR WINNING TEAM, 15 FRANCS FOR 2nd.

2.30 p.m.

16. GRAND OPEN AIR CONCERT ON THE FOOTBALL GROUND, AND DISTRIBUTION OF PRIZES.
    FOLLOWED BY KISS-IN-THE-RING, IF SUFFICIENT COMPETITORS(?) ARE PROCURED.

ALL ENTRIES TAKEN ON THE FIELD.

THE BAND AND DRUMS WILL GIVE SELECTIONS.

Of the results of the different events no evidence exists to-day. No doubt there are some members in our Association who enriched themselves to the extent of from 10 to 5 francs, but there is ample evidence of the Carnival and Fancy Dress in photographs possessed by several. Perhaps the star turn was Lieut. "Jumbo" White, who, with a tattered and torn civilian suit, complete with tweed cap and choker, and with a bundle of papers tucked under his arm, represented a paper boy. Lieut. Haine, arrayed in shorts and with a child's straw hat perched perilously on his head, was seated on a child's tricycle: C.S.M. Simpson and Lce.-Cpl. Giles were attired as old dames: Lieut. Puttock sported a shiny topper with a dilapidated morning dress coat and trousers, while two murderous looking individuals with a bag of "swag" and an entrenching tool handle to complete their guise no doubt were meant to represent the "Black Hand Gang." We have an idea that Major Searle is represented in one of the groups, but he is so completely disguised as to make him unrecognisable. The really respectable looking people in the groups are the Pierrots, among whom one recognises Cpl. MacKriell, of C Company and the "Dickybirds." The story is also told of one member of the Battalion who managed to unearth a German uniform and masqueraded as a Fritz. By all accounts he did not get a great reception, for, being taken for the genuine article, he was unceremoniously dumped into a pond. We were often accused by our late enemies of being mad, but it was such foolish antics that enabled us to forget the greater things which, had we dwelt upon them too much, would surely have driven us crazy. It was the Englishman's sense of humour among other qualities which helped us to win through.

On the 11th the medal ribbons of the Croix de Guerre were presented by the Divisional Commander to the following:—C.Q.M.S. W. J. Steer; Sergt. H. Mills, D.C.M., M.M.; Cpl. E. J. Bailey; Lce.-Cpls. S. Brewster, M.M., and O. J. George; Pte. W. Felstead, M.M.

The time had now come to say goodbye to Everbecq and the good folk there, who made our stay most enjoyable. Who can forget the old man in the house where B Company H.Q. were? During the German occupation he had hidden many things from them, including some excellent cigars. On our arrival he got these out of their hiding place and presented them to us. On the inside of the front door of every house in the village was inscribed the names of all the occupants with certain particulars. This was done by the Germans to keep a check on the movements of the civilians, who also had to have passes containing photographs. These passes were often sought by us as souvenirs, but the holders were rightly reluctant to part with them in view of the tragic and historic part they had played in their lives.

During the occupation of the district electric lighting had been installed by the enemy in this and other villages. Some crude looking coins made from very common metal were in circulation, and fuel consisted of briquettes which were obtained from a kind of army dump in the village.

While the majority of the inhabitants of the village were glad to be rid of the Boche, there was one exception brought to our notice, a young lady near B Company's billets, who every day could be seen looking towards the east. She never spoke to a British Tommy, and we wondered what the reason was, till we found out that she had a lover, a German officer, who had promised to return as soon as he could.

On the 12th the march to the frontier was continued as far as Herinnes, where billets were taken for the night. The following day we reached Bierges. Taking the Enghien—Hal road on the 14th, we proceeded to Wanthier-Braine, close to the historic field of Waterloo. Here we remained until the 16th, when the march was resumed to Vieux-Genappe. On the way the British Monument at Waterloo was seen, and not far away the King of the Belgians watched us pass.

Here we were truly in the "Cockpit of Europe." Within a few miles were Ligny and Quatre Bras, scenes of the two furious fights of the French against the Prussians and the British on June 16th, 1815, two days before Napoleon's final overthrow, and close by were Fleurus (1690 and 1794) and Namur, the capture of which was one of the fine exploits of our King William of Orange in 1695.

The 17th found the Battalion wending its way through Quatre Bras and Petit Marbais to the Glassworks at Tilly. En route the G.O.C. took the salute and afterwards sent his congratulations on the turnout of the Battalion. Ligny was reached on the 18th; Belgrade on the 19th and Pontillas on the 20th, after passing through the famous town of Namur.

Continuing on the 21st, the Battalion marched to Warnant-Dreye, 25 miles west of Liége, and close to Ramillies, scene of Marlborough's great victory over the French in 1706. Here we were to settle down in comfortable billets until orders were issued to proceed to Germany.

Situated not many miles from the town of Huy on the River Meuse, Warnant was an ideal spot for the troops to be cantoned. Billets were as good as could be expected, the farmhouses and barns being utilised for this purpose. There were a few shops and estaminets, besides a concert and dance hall in the village, and some fields near by which were used for football and other sports.

The 23rd was spent in cleaning up. Now that hostilities had ceased things were beginning to savour of peace-time soldiering. R.S.M. C. J. Love, who had been wounded during the final advance, had now returned to us, and in due course made himself busy seeing that the turnout of the Battalion was as good as possible. Hitherto most of the warrant officers had been regular soldiers, but through casualties a great change had taken place. Speller was the sole remaining W.O. who had gone out to France with us in 1916. C.S.M. B. Horswell, of B Company, who was C.Q.M.S. of A Company in 1916, had been promoted to C.S.M. at "Plug Street" and had, at various times, acted as R.S.M. Of the other C.S.M.s, Mayston of C Company was an ex-Surrey Yeoman, G. Simpson of A Company was one of the original members of the Battalion who had joined at Rotherhithe, and W. Hall of D Company was one of the draft from the 11th Battalion which had joined at Aldershot. From this it will be seen that both Simpson and Hall had risen to the rank of C.S.M. from privates whilst serving with the Battalion. And well they deserved it, for they were real fighting soldiers, both having been through most of the engagements in which the Battalion participated, and both being decorated for their services.

We have already had occasion to refer to the different changes in the command of the companies, but now the time had come when all the Company Commanders were officers who had only been with us for a short while. Most of them were experienced officers, well fitted for the posts they occupied. In a short while they got to know their men, and very keen competition in turnout, drill and sport was the order of the day once we had settled down to soldiering as the regulars knew it in peace time.

On Christmas Day Divine Service was held in the morning, after which the men had a feast which was probably the best they had ever had on active service. No pains were spared by the officers and the good folk in England to see that unstinted Christmas cheer should be available for the men. Major Searle has something to say about our Christmas dinner.

"The Battalion little knew how close they were to missing a large part of the Christmas dinner. I was given 3,000 francs and sent to Amiens to buy the necessaries for the Brigade. There was nothing in Amiens, so I went to Paris. Even there it was difficult to get what one wanted, as everything was so dear. Anyhow I accumulated dozens of cases of oranges and apples, nuts and what-nots and hundreds of ducks and turkeys, and then had the frightful job of scrounging three lorries and drivers as I was in Paris without leave. We had only three days for the long trek from Paris to Warnant and it was slow going across the Somme battlefield. It was mild weather, and what with the lorry drivers sleeping on top of the ducks, I know I was glad to get them back before they got too high!"

From the 26th of December until the end of the year we remained at Warnant-Dreye carrying out parades under company arrangements, interspersed with football and cross-country running. Tours to the Battlefield of Waterloo were provided, Division making arrangements to convey the parties in lorries or buses. A recreation room was started, which was much appreciated by all. A dance was organised by the sergeants, and to it were invited the local village belles.

We had left behind the dangers of the battlefields, but the malady known as influenza still pursued us and men were being sent to hospital with it. Notification was received during the period that Pte. E. Paine had died from it on the 29th of November. Here was a man who had been with us at Rotherhithe, and it was just the luck of the war that, after going through so much, he should be laid low by a germ which, although we considered it a nuisance, was not thought to be fatal. Lieut. G. E. Head joined during December.

The dawn of the year 1919 found the Battalion still at Warnant-Dreye carrying on very much as usual, but within a few days we were to enter upon another journey, which marked a milestone in the history of the 12th.

On the 5th of January warning orders were received for the relief of the 5th Canadian Battalion, 1st Canadian Division, in the outpost area of the Rhineland, and the 6th was spent in making preparations for the move. On the 7th we marched out of Warnant-Dreye and proceeded to Huy, where entrainment was carried out.

Here a little digression is necessary, to follow the events connected with the occupation of the Rhineland.

After the Battalion had discontinued the march to the frontier, the British troops who were to occupy the bridgeheads of Cologne made their way forward day by day in accordance with the terms of the Armistice. Although the German troops were supposed to be clear by a certain time, this did not always turn out according to plan. In fact in Brussels itself the Allied troops are said to have entered before many of the Germans had left.

A certain amount of disorganisation had taken place in the ranks of the Boche through many of the soldiers casting off their officers and making their way back independently. Looting was naturally rife amongst these men, but on the whole German commanders managed to enforce some sort of discipline with the majority, and we read of how some of the enemy returned to the Fatherland like conquering heroes.

The first British troops crossed the German frontier on Sunday, December 1st, and, even if they were not received with great joy, there were no incidents which augured badly for the occupation. On December 6th the British entered Cologne, and six days later crossed the Rhine and occupied the Cologne Bridgehead. It will thus be seen that our troops had been in occupation for close on a month before the 12th Battalion proceeded to take its part in the occupation.

Entraining at Huy, the Battalion proceeded down the lovely valley of the Meuse into the hilly and beautiful country of the Ardennes. A short halt was made in Liége station, where a train-load of troops, who were returning from the Rhine, gave us a vivid account of their experiences in the short time at their disposal. As we left these lucky fellows who were going home to Blighty for demobilisation and leave, we broke into the chorus which was our new war cry, "When we've wound up the Watch on the Rhine."

We journeyed throughout the 8th, passing towns famous in history. When the German frontier was reached, two officers—one of whom was Lieut. "Jumbo" White—were detailed to look after the driver in case anything happened to the train. Apart from a sudden jerk which we experienced when the officers produced their revolvers to demonstrate what would happen if the driver tried any monkey tricks, the journey passed uneventfully. In passing we should mention that on the back of a postcard which has come into our possession, appears the cryptic messages:—

"What is our destination? D'you know? We've just been stopping the ——— trying to win a truck full of English cooks. Our blinking Hun Engine hasn't rolled up yet!"

(Sgd.) Jumbo.

"Jumbo, for the sake of all that is good and hopeful—GET A MOVE ON AND STOP THE BUMPS!"

(Itd.) D. W. Capt.

Aix-la-Chapelle, or Aachen, to give it the name we saw, looked very pretty in the distance, while Spa suggested to us a place at which we should have liked to stop and investigate.

In the early hours of the 9th the 12th Battalion crossed the famous Rhine by the Hohenzollern Bridge. Slowly the train made its way over, while tired eyes peeped out of the truck doors to get a glimpse of this wonderful river which the German Army had immortalised in song. The legend "Koln" which had just been passed in the station left no doubt in our minds as to where we were, but in the darkness it appeared no different to crossing Hungerford Bridge in London with "Old Father Thames" slowly coursing along below.

The train then wended its way along until it reached Overath, where detrainment took place. Billeting parties had already been in search of quarters, and these met us at the station and guided us to Marialinden, 15 miles east of Cologne, where the 5th Canadian Battalion was relieved, one company and two platoons proceeding to take over the outpost lines. On arrival in Marialinden the troops were accommodated in houses where possible, although concert halls and other places were pressed into service.

Tired and hungry, some of us went into a house near the village church and found the proprietor and his wife busy making coffee and cutting up black bread. This was given to us, and most of us proffered payment for it. Our arrival must have created a good impression in this respect, for within a few days the inhabitants accepted us, not as foreign invaders, but as friends.

Cpl. Nugent contributes an article on the move into Germany:—

"Christmas was over, having been spent in the small Belgian village of Warnant-Dreye, and orders were received for the Battalion to proceed to Germany and form part of the Army of Occupation.

"One sunny morning the whole battalion paraded and, with the band playing, marched towards Huy, the point where we had to entrain. On arrival at this point some delay was occasioned, and in consequence the loading of the stores, etc., was not completed until fairly late in the afternoon. At last the train moved out of the station and the troops settled down to play cards or look through the doorway of the trucks at the surrounding countryside. As usual these were of the type generally used, suitable for horses and men, bearing the inscription: 'Hommes 40, Chevaux 8' in spite of the fact that two men required more space than one horse, taking into account the equipment carried.

"The train rattled along merrily until we reached the frontier, when a stop was made for a change of engine. At this point a German engine backed on to the train and was the cause of an incident which accounted for one or two broken limbs and damaged heads amongst the troops. We had not been standing long, when, with a terrible jerk the train jumped forward, throwing men off their feet and causing the sliding doors to jump back on the steel runners. In a few moments many men had cracked their heads against ends of the trucks, one at least had a broken arm, and in several cases the steel edges of the truck doors had cut cheeks to the bone. It was not possible to do anything until the next stop, when the medical staff quickly got to work and patched up the wounded. The reason for this unfortunate occurrence was not apparent at the time, but it subsequently transpired that two officers had been detailed to ride for a time on the footplate in order to ensure that no action would be taken by the German driver to imperil the safety of the train. Owing to the fact that the officers knew no German and the driver no English signs were of no avail, and in order to impress upon the latter the necessity of being careful in his driving, one officer drew his revolver merely as a gesture. This was presumably interpreted by the German wrongly and he immediately opened the throttle with the result mentioned.

"No further untoward incident occurred, and we proceeded through the German countryside at a good rate. Many comments were made on the depths of the pine forests which abounded on either side and the peaceful aspect of everything, to which we had not yet become accustomed.

"The outskirts of Cologne were reached about midnight, and, as the train stopped just on the Hohenzollern Bridge, a good view of the city was obtained, as the whole place appeared to be illuminated for a considerable distance on either side. Passing over the Rhine many commenced singing 'Die Wacht am Rhein' or, as we knew it, the parody on this, 'The Watch on the Rhine.'

"At last we stopped in a wayside station and were ordered to detrain. It was very dark, the time being about 1.0 a.m. and no lights were on the platform. We discovered the name of the place to be Overath, although this conveyed nothing to us, being more interested in our ultimate destination and somewhere to sleep. The companies formed up, H.Q. leading, followed by the band, and at the word of command marched off through the main street of the village. In spite of the time and circumstances the band struck up the old favourite 'Colonel Bogey,' which of course sounded very loud owing to the quietness which prevailed all round and the narrowness of the street. We had not been marching very long before a number of upstairs windows were flung open, but closed again quickly, when the occupants had seen what was happening. However, the band soon petered out as we encountered a long winding road which ran steadily uphill for what seemed to us hours on end. The actual distance was not more than three miles, as we afterwards discovered, and in due course we came to the straggling village of Marialinden, which was perched on top of a hill, with a church which could be seen in daylight for miles around owing to its twin spires towering above everything else on the skyline. This was our destination. Here we halted and fell out to make our way individually round the small square in an endeavour to find a place where a few hours sleep could be obtained while billets were being arranged. Many found a resting-place against the church walls between the buttresses, which afforded some measure of protection. Equipment was laid down, and some men managed to sleep, others dozed, and some sat smoking until sleep overcame them. By dawn everybody had been accommodated in barns and houses. Part of H.Q. Company was billeted in the post office, which comprised one half of a house, the other half being a 'Wirtschaft' or beer house. Many souvenirs were purchased from the small shops and sent home, there being such a run on the German porcelain tobacco pipes that supplies were quickly exhausted."

We must remember that everything had to be arranged by our G.H.Q. in case the enemy should rearm and attack us. Pill-boxes were constructed, trenches dug and fortifications erected, guns placed in position, M.G. posts sited, and a whole scheme arranged for defence or attack east of Cologne.

The section of the outpost line occupied by the Battalion detachment at Drabenderhohe, 22 miles from the Rhine at Cologne, was the most easterly post of the British zone. Platoons and sections were somewhat scattered, but they passed their time away by catching rabbits and occasionally shooting game.

Those not on the actual outposts did the usual parades and company training, which had by now become part of our daily life. An Inter-Company Drill Competition which was to be judged by the C.O. and afterwards by the G.O.C. was held at a later stage. This necessitated much intensive training by companies, and the entries in the Battalion diary for this period are full of it. It does not state which company won it or whether the best company judged by the G.O.C. on January 27th was the ultimate winner in the Brigade.

The men were now beginning to get a bit restless. They had heard of demobilisation, and that was enough to set most of the older hands thinking of home. They were fed up with the war and no doubt thought they would soon be enjoying the good things of which a grateful nation had practically assured them through statesmen and others in authority. Means were therefore devised to keep them from taking their thoughts too seriously. Football and boxing came to the aid of these who were responsible for the welfare of the troops.

On the 17th of January educational classes were held for the first time in Bookkeeping, Shorthand, French and German. 2nd Lieut. J. C. Waller of B Company bravely took a language class, but, like other officers and men who volunteered for the task of educating Tommy, he no doubt found his pupils keen for a few days, but, finding the experience of going back to school again too irksome, they soon lost interest and like naughty boys started to play truant. Sport was enjoyed far more than education, and there was no lack of support for it, despite the fact that snow often made the ground unfit for play.

We have already made some reference to the "Fleet" over which C.S.M. Bry Horswell presided as "Harbour Master." Composed of W.O.s and sergeants, it was a sort of "crazy gang" which gave performances of their drama, "The Fleet at anchor," in the Sergeants' Mess, which had now been established, with an occasional visit to B Company Office. From evidence received it would appear that one of the acts in the drama consisted of throwing a bucket of water over one of the actors who had asked for a water wave. B Company Office was also used by the gang for glee parties, etc. With such joyful souls as Horswell and Noad the sergeants had plenty of scope for driving away dull care.

Meanwhile the Sports Committee was working well, and with the aid of that great sportsman, Sergt. Jack Greenslade, and Major C. T. Williams, the Battalion eventually won great prestige in the boxing and football world.

The Demobilisation Office was now set up, and was placed in charge of Lieut. Mutch with Sergt. S. Lattimore as his able assistant.

The correct and most efficient method of demobilisation had been exercising the minds of the authorities for some time. A group system had been planned, and each man had recorded in his pay book the category into which his occupation in civilian life fell. One began to hear of "Pivotal" and "Starred" men, whose rapid demobilisation was essential for the country's well-being. A miner became a most important person, so too an agricultural worker. Even the sleeping partner in a firm was looked upon as one deserving of special consideration, while a man with a guaranteed letter from his late employer could produce arguments as to his usefulness to the community that would make his early release imperative. The result of all this was that some of the "Cease fire" drafts, even the youths of 18, were being demobilised in preference to men who had had three years and even more overseas. This could not last long without a great outcry, and consequently priority of release eventually came to those with the longest service, and quite rightly too.

The first batch of men from the Battalion is recorded as having proceeded home on the 26th of January. There were eight of them, and these were followed on the 28th by another seven and on the 29th by twelve more.

In connection with demobilisation the following incident happened in B Company:—

There was a certain genial acting corporal, who at the time of the Armistice was waiting to go home for a commission. He was a Company Director, and, as soon as Demobilisation started, pressed his claims as a pivotal man. His representations were not received favourably, and, when a request for the company to submit the names of two men as clerks in the Demobilisation Office was received from Orderly Room, this man's name was submitted with one other. It was thought that by sending him into the Office his demobilisation would be delayed, but strangely enough he accepted without much demur.

At this time passes to Cologne were being freely issued to officers and men alike. The trains were for the free use of the troops, and in Cologne itself accommodation was first of all found in the hotels and later in a kind of boarding house, with permission to remain all night if desired. Men had to report to the British Town Major at the Dom Hotel, who issued them with a billeting ticket written in English and German, upon which was a tariff of charges for meals for which the men had to pay. Accommodation was free, but meals consumed in the hotel had to be paid for.

Sergt. Lattimore had decided to have a night in Cologne, and so he left the Office in charge of the acting corporal of B Company. The next morning, judge the surprise of B Company's C.S.M. to find the corporal who he thought would be retained for some months making his way past B Company Office with full marching order on. The C.S.M. hailed him and enquired where he was going. "Home," promptly came the reply. There was no doubt about it; he was actually in possession of his movement orders. On enquiry later it transpired that Orderly Room had in the usual manner called for the names of so many men per company for demobilisation, and that the corporal had submitted his and probably made out his own papers. With the exception of the Orderly Room staff with the Cadre at the end, this is the only incident we had of a man demobilising himself.

From now onwards daily batches left the Battalion, and by the end of February four officers and 146 other ranks had severed connection with us. Those who remained tried to make the best of things until their turn came.

Platoons and even sections often led a separate existence, as billets were spread over a fairly wide area. The country was hilly, and when the snow came it was difficult to get about. Toboggans, both the genuine article and improvised ones, began to make their appearance. Besides forming a useful mode of transport they were also a source of enjoyment. Men frolicked about in the keen exhilarating atmosphere, much to the amusement of the local "kinder," who had come to regard Tommy as something different from what they had been told.

Fraternising was strictly forbidden—officially, Unofficially it was rampant. You could trust the English troops to make themselves friendly wherever they went. In the billets there were no military police to enforce regulations, and, whilst the officers and N.C.O.s had a duty to perform in this direction, they were blind to many things they witnessed. One could go round to many of the billets and find the troops sitting at table with the civilians. Romance was not to be denied, and if you saw a *fraulein* in the street followed by a British Tommy, you could be almost sure that they were friends.

In a few of the billets the womenfolk cooked for Tommy, and, while the Germans were suffering severely as the result of the blockade which was only lifted at the express wish of our G.O.C., Sir H. Plumer, Tommy saw to it that they were not wanting for food, if he could possibly manage to help them from his own rations. "Sauerkraut" was all they were able to offer in return, for black bread was not relished by the troops. Soap and chocolate, practically unprocurable by the Germans, were obtained in the B.E.F. canteens which were now established in Cologne. Tommy supplied these commodities when the opportunity came.

Respect for the female sex was another trait in the English soldier which surprised the women of the Rhineland. Trains to Cologne were usually crowded, and it was not an uncommon sight to see the women standing and the men sitting. Tommies would offer their seats to the women, while the Germans would glare at them for doing so. One incident happened in a crowded train when one of our W.O.s yanked a German out of his seat and promptly pushed a *fraulein* into it. Other Germans looked on, but there were too many Englishmen present for them to make a scene.

If we can take the example of a typical woman of the Rhine, living in a village where the Battalion stayed, we shall not be far wrong in summing up what the German women thought of our men. Lena's father had been killed at the front, her mother in an air-raid on Cologne. She had several brothers and sisters whom she was "mothering" at the time when our men occupied billets in her house. She told us that, with her experience of German troops, she would much prefer the English because of their kindness and courtesy. Their behaviour, she said, was exemplary, and, far from the fear she had had when she knew that the English would occupy the village, she was glad they had come. She could speak our language a little, and she told us of cases where local German girls were going to classes with the express purpose of learning the English language.

As far as the men were concerned, we remained affable towards them, although at first they treated us coldly and with a certain amount of reserve. This wore off in time, and German ex-soldiers with their badges torn from their tunics would often want to join our company, and were welcomed.

There was one particular individual, who, so rumour ran, was once a Zeppelin commander. We called him Franz, and, visiting him frequently in his flat, we would call upon him for a rendering of his favourite march "Alten Kameraden" (Old Comrades) on his grand piano. In B Company H.Q. at Marialinden the lady of the house would often get two of her young boys who were excellent pianists to play for our amusement. We occupied her drawing-room, probably the finest billet we ever had.

All this only goes to prove the almost universal truth that individuals of different race nearly always form friendships and get on most happily together. It is nations in the aggregate that quarrel with each other, or their governments that find causes of offence, and one of the most fruitful sources of trouble is the newspaper. Prejudice against foreigners is usually the result of ignorance. Englishmen can be excessively "insular," but this tendency rapidly diminishes with modern travel and knowledge. Such bodies as the League of Nations, Boy Scouts and Girl Guides, and Travel Associations are potent workers for peace because they bring individuals of different nationalities into close touch and consequent amity, which is the chief reason why Dictators hate them.

On February 5th a rehearsal for the Ceremonial of the handing over of the King's Colour was held. The Divisional Commander inspected the parade on this occasion. Other rehearsals were held on the 8th and 10th, and in order to give the men an opportunity of getting things in order for the occasion there were no parades on the 11th.

The 12th of February, 1919, marked the ceremony of the handing over of the King's Colour. The Battalion marched to Overath, and there General Sir Herbert Plumer, after a suitable speech and a recital of the deeds of the Battalion, handed over the Colour with due ceremony.

Notification was received on the 10th of the award of the Belgian Croix de Guerre to the following:—2nd Lieut. A. J. Rodd, Sergt. B. G. Burgess (Orderly Room), Cpl. J. McFie (Post-Corporal) and Cpl. F. Goble (H.Q. Officers' Mess and Canteen).

Relief in the outposts came on the 14th of February, when the 18th K.R.R.s took over, and the Battalion went into reserve in the Volberg-Hoffnungstahl area. The bulk of those billeted in Volberg experienced similar conditions to those in the area they had just left. Perhaps there was a little more leisure, for cinemas were being established and men found time to seek out photographers to have their photos taken to give their pals as a token of remembrance. B Company H.Q. was established in the country residence of a gentleman who paid us a visit during our occupation. The Company Office was the drawing-room, partly furnished, and two or three bedrooms with real beds and coverlets were used as sleeping quarters. Never before had we experienced such luxuries on active service.

The first visitor here was a German who wanted to sell us some good razors made in Solingen. He informed us that he had spent 20 years in America and was visiting his home town in Germany when war broke out. The Authorities stopped him from returning to the U.S.A., but he was going back again at the first opportunity.

The owner turned up one day and with a polite, "Good morning, gentlemen," ushered himself into the Company Office. He told us that he was the owner and in his best English asked us if we would be good enough to look after his property while we occupied it. We told him we would. Then taking us out into the garden, he showed us the remains of a mahogany table which he informed us the last troops billeted there had chopped up for firewood.

The Germans indeed, after having trampled their foes and the occupied territories under the heel of the Prussian jackboot so long, had now, like all bullies when knocked out, begun to cringe and fawn. They knew well enough that this was useless with the French and Belgians, whose sufferings had been too poignant and wrongs too foul to be easily forgiven. To hear the intensity of hatred with which they almost spat out the words "Sales Boches" was enough. But the Englishman, as the Hun knew well enough, is a very poor hater, tolerant, fair-minded and easily pacified. To our troops they had as a rule been the fierce but fair fighter; the atrocities committed at times upon our wounded and prisoners were forgotten by us or slurred over. "The war is over; let us be friends again," was their attitude.

They were also desperately anxious to win our friendship as a safeguard against the implacable hate and vengeance of the Belgians and French. After all, they had devised refinements of cruelty and had indulged in utterly wanton destruction when they had most of Belgium and large areas of France in their power. They had gone out of their way to make the very name of Germany a stench and abomination in the nostrils of their ancient foes, and could not have rightly complained if they had suffered at their hands double for all their sins. Besides, they believed—as they do to-day—that they only fought the war as a defensive one against a deliberate policy of "encirclement" cunningly engineered by France, and had only lost it in the end because they were overcome, not in fair fight, but by lying propaganda, the hunger blockade and "Marxist" treachery at home. Their rulers to-day go even further and teach the youth of Germany that their country really won the war!

In England of course a very different sentiment towards the enemy was the rule. "Hang the Kaiser, and make Germany pay to the last farthing!" was the cry, especially of those journals who to-day applaud dictators for Prussianism of the deepest dye! They were indeed horrified and outraged by the fraternisation of our troops with the enemy and his kith and kin: but, as they were "our heroes," they turned a blind eye to it all.

Divine Service, which was held weekly since we arrived in Germany, was held in the village church on the 23rd, and a lecture on Imperialism was given to the men on the 26th.

March, 1919, was ushered in with the usual parades but ended with the Battalion practically defunct as a unit.

On the 3rd the Battalion team in the Divisional Cross-Country run came in second to the 1st Field Ambulance, with the 20th D.L.I. third. As a final winding up, a Concert was held in the Battalion Concert Hall on the 4th.

The 41st Division was now in the course of re-organisation. It had been decided to transfer certain units to it and rename it the London Division. Accordingly on the 8th of March the 9th Battalion East Surreys from the 24th Division took the place of the 12th Battalion in the 1st London Brigade of the London Division. Nine officers and 300 other ranks of the 12th Battalion who were to be retained with the army of Occupation were accordingly transferred. A great many of these were young soldiers who had joined us in 1918, but there was also a good sprinkling of old "veterans," who, being offered the enticement of a bounty for continuing to serve for one, two, three or four years, had accepted. Most of the time-serving soldiers were returned to join the regular battalions of the regiment and to assist at the demobilisation centres in England. The remainder awaiting demobilisation went into billets in the Kaiserin Krankenhaus near by to await the instructions which would carry them home to Blighty.

The award of a bar to the Military Medal to Cpl. Jim Rogers, who had all through done such fine service in charge of the Runners, was notified on the 5th.

The remainder of the story so far as the remnants of the Battalion are concerned can be summed up in the words of the Diary: "Men employed in cleaning up stores, etc."

The story of the gradual demobilisation would not be complete without reference to the Corps Football Championship, in which the Battalion team participated at Koln-Kalk, a suburb of Cologne. After winning the Divisional Championship, we thought we were going to pull off the other. Accordingly the men of the 12th turned up in force to cheer the team on to victory. Our opponents were a Scottish unit, and after play had been in progress for some time it looked as though we were their masters. However luck was against us. A swerving ball carried by the wind completely fogged our goalkeeper, Sadler, while later a bouncing ball which could have been cleared by Lieut. J. Walker playing at back, was left to Sadler to deal with. He had the ball well covered, but again he was deceived by the bounce and it went just over his head into the goal which he had left. A goal scored for us made it look as though we still had a sporting change, when the change of ends took place. In the second half, under instructions from Major Williams, the team went all out, and our opponents' goal was ever in jeopardy. Towards the end we were awarded a penalty for some infringement. One can picture C.S.M. Billy Hall of D Company taking the spot kick with the Scottish goalkeeper taking up a stance near a goalpost. There appeared to be nothing to stop such a sure shot as Hall from scoring, and it was his intention to see that we were not disappointed. He aimed at the left hand corner of the goal, and a gasp went up from us all as we saw the ball strike the post and with one bound the goalkeeper scramble the ball away. Try as we might, the equaliser would not come, and it was with a heavy heart that Hall and the rest of the team left the field at the final whistle. The joke of the whole affair was that the team was accused by some of playing for demobilisation. The team, as far as can be remembered, was:—Sadler, Lieut. J. Walker, Boxall, Day, Hall, Spencer, Chamberlain, Lieut. W. S. Hall, Greenslade, Brewster and Exall.

Nor should we forget the Second Army Boxing Championships, for which Sergt. Jack Greenslade took a team down to Cologne that won many prizes. Greenslade, after reaching the final in the Heavies, had to retire, beaten by a black man. In delivering a blow Jack dislocated a bone through hitting what one could describe as a cast-iron man. However, Jack had his revenge later on when he won the championship while serving with the 9th Battalion, and, incidentally trained and assisted a tug-of-war team which was practically unbeatable.

At the hospital in which we were billeted we got a glimpse into the life of the youth of Germany. Periodically we saw parties of youths and their blue-eyed Mädchen friends, knapsacks on back, strolling along to the accompaniment of mandolines and guitars. These were the "Wandervögel," or hikers, of whom we were to hear much in our own country later on. They would stop in the woods around, picnic and then dance on the green, living in an enchanted dream-world of revolt against convention and the old philosophy that had brought their Fatherland to ruin.

Passes into Cologne were plentiful, "French leave" abundant. It was only a question of going down to Overath, hopping on the train and then trusting to luck that the military police would not examine passes.

There was plenty of life in Cologne. Cafés did a roaring trade and, with German business acumen, most of the shops had something to sell us, such as a replica of the

Iron Cross for about sixpence, bottles of Eau de Cologne from the original makers, and other objects which would serve us as souvenirs.

The Café Germania (previously known as the Piccadilly) a highly respectable place frequented by the bourgeois of Cologne, boasted a very fine orchestra which played special request pieces for the benefit of their English visitors. Tips to the waiters consisted in the main of English cigarettes, their own being a very poor substitute.

The "Princess" Café and Cabaret shows drew many of the troops. One could hear the "Merry Widow Waltz," "Love me and the World is mine," and "Yip-i-addy-i-ay," tunes heard in England before the war, constantly played in the cafés. Did the Germans want us to forget the war and bring us back to the time when their German bands paraded our country? In no small measure did they succeed. The lights, the music and the whole atmosphere of Cologne suggested the palmy days of peace with one great exception—food. Horse-meat might have been relished by the Germans and others not so fussy as we were. There was no option if you entered a restaurant; horse-meat was the fare. The result was that in Cologne most of us became vegetarians.

A few British concert parties, including the "Crumps," had use of the majority of the theatres in the town, the price of admission being a few marks. Quite an enjoyable evening could be spent listening to these men, who for many years had catered for the amusement of the troops behind the lines. Some were "stars" already, others have since won fame on the music-halls and the radio. The Y.M.C.A. soon established itself, and there was one particular place known as "The Crystal Palace," where meals could be procured at any time of the day.

The great Dom, or Cathedral, of Cologne was an object of interest to many of us, particularly as we were told that at least one of the bells in the belfry had been removed and melted down to make munitions. Other places of interest were plentiful. One striking notice was that placed round the statue of a famous German soldier, "To the British Officers' Club."

The statue of the Kaiser at the entrance to the Hohenzollern Bridge served to remind us how the mighty had fallen, while the sight of a *schutzmann* (policeman) saluting our colours and our officers brought home to us the fact that a proud and haughty foe was getting a dose of the bitter medicine given to the people of France and Belgium when the tide of war had flowed the other way.

Steamers full of British troops, including batches from the 12th, made the trip daily from Cologne to Coblenz to see the wonderful scenery spoken and sung about by the Rhinelanders, and we were not disappointed. Many of us vowed we would return again in the piping times of peace. Trams were free to us, and in this way we reached many of the suburbs of Cologne. The trams with trailers attached were so well patronised that crowds used to hang on to them in the rear. There seemed to be no limit to the accommodation as long as you were able to hang on somewhere. Trips were also made to the Opera House, where the highbrows could spend an interesting evening.

Very little difficulty was experienced in the matter of the language, as it was found that the shopkeepers of Cologne were fairly well versed in our own. Money speaks all languages, and, if a shopkeeper found any difficulty in understanding us, he usually had an interpreter (probably an ex-waiter in England) ready at hand to help him out with the transaction. The news of the Army of the Rhine was printed by Germans in a paper called the "Cologne Post." This was a welcome addition to the English papers which were reaching us from Blighty.

The whole atmosphere, particularly in the Hohe Strasse, suggested that of the West End of London round Regent Street and Piccadilly. Perhaps this was the real attraction to the British troops after the dullness of French towns and even London. At all events while the Cadre was waiting for its demise daily trips were made to the town.

The names of two men who died after the cessation of hostilities appear in Part 2 Orders: Pte. W. J. Baker died on the 15th of January and Sergt. J. Sparks on the 3rd of February.

The passing of Sergt. Sparks, who was the Battalion Master Tailor, was sad news. He was well advanced in years and had been with the Battalion since its early days. He succumbed to influenza and was buried by the sergeants in Cologne.

On the 17th of March the following officers proceeded to the concentration camp for demobilisation and dispersal:—Lieuts. G. E. Head and R. N. Haine and 2nd Lieuts. C. W. Skellet and J. Walker. Major Williams went to England on the following day for transfer to Russia, followed on the 19th by Capt. A. C. Edgar and Lieuts. W. S. Hall, A. R. Puttock and A. J. Rodd for demobilisation. 2nd Lieuts. R. Northwood and A. C. Cowlin left on the 26th.

Signs that the Shiny Twelfth was on its last legs came when on the 26th those that remained turned up in force to pay their tribute to their Commanding Officer, Lieut.-Col. G. L. Brown, D.S.O., who was relinquishing command and returning to England. In addition many members who had transferred to the 9th Battalion were also there. One cannot remember what the Colonel said on parting, but one distinctly remembers the loud cheers given as he waved us goodbye. We had lost a C.O. who, joining in the dark days of March, 1918, had led us to final victory. His kindly consideration and deep understanding of the type of soldiers he was dealing with earned him the affection and esteem of officers and men alike. Returning to his regiment, the Middlesex, he was eventually appointed to command their 1st Battalion. It is only recently that he finished his command. After Colonel Brown left, the command of the Cadre devolved upon Capt. David Walker.

While all this was going on, we read in Part 2 Orders of some of our comrades, whom we lost at Hollebeke, Sapignies, and other places as prisoners of war, arriving at Leith, Hull and Dover from the end of November onwards, glad to get a glimpse of Blighty again, perhaps after months of torment. Lieut. L. Dawson is shown as arriving at Hull on the 29th of November, and 2nd Lieut. L. Jennings and Lieut. F. A. Samuels at Leith on the 25th and 26th of December respectively. Some of the ex-prisoners on arrival are shown as admitted to hospital, a fact which speaks for itself.

For operations which preceded the Armistice the following awards were notified in due course:—

Distinguished Conduct Medal: Sergts. H. Mills, M.M., and R. J. Mutimer; Lce.-Cpl. W. Rainbow.

Bar to Military Medal: Sergt. D. Staines and Pte. A. Pocock.

Military Medal: Lce.-Cpls. G. Bunnet, J. Malone, J. Ralph and E. C. West; Ptes. G. Church, A. E. Collings, W. C. Humphreys, H. C. Keith, E. Lugo, G. Roud, J. Rutty, W. H. Tilley, J. W. Trout and R. Watts.

Meritorious Service Medal. Sergts. L. C. Lunn (122nd Brigade Office) and C. W. Field; Cpl. G. A. Elliott.

French Croix de Guerre: Lieut.-Col. G. L. Brown, D.S.O.; C.Q.M.S. W. J. Steer; Sergt. H. Mills; Cpl. E. J. Bailey; Lce.-Cpl. O. J. George; Pte. W. Felstead.

Médaille Militaire: C.S.M. W. Hall.

As in so many other cases in the records of the Battalion, full details of what the above awards were made for are lacking, but, as we have already stated in other cases, this in no way detracts from the merit. Some were given for consistently good work and for no particular action in which the men participated. In come cases decorations were bestowed on men who were on the administrative side of the Division, Brigade and Battalion. Instances of this occur in the cases of Sergt. L. C. Lunn, who was in the 122nd Brigade Office during the time the Brigade was overseas; Sergt. C. W. Field, who was on the Battalion police staff from 1916 until he was killed just before the Armistice; Cpl. G. A. Elliott, who was on Division and the G.H.Q. staff in Italy. Pte. G. Church, a Transport man, was one of the original members of the 12th Battalion.

One fact the above list does bring out, and that is that in the operations before the Armistice the Battalion well performed the work allotted to it, for decorations usually depended upon the measure of success attained.

With these awards the decorations won by members of the Battalion during the time we were overseas were as follows:—

Distinguished Service Order: 3.
Second Bar to Military Cross: 1.
Bar to Military Cross: 3.
Military Cross: 33.
Distinguished Conduct Medal: 15.
Bar to Military Medal: 10.
Military Medal: 130.
Meritorious Service Medal: 7.
French Croix de Guerre: 7.
Belgian Croix de Guerre. 8.
Médaille Militaire (*avec palme*) Belgian: 2.
Mentions in Despatches: 24.
Total: 243.

In addition there were cases where men had received cards from the Divisional Commander testifying to their good work or bravery, but for which no medal was forthcoming. Cpl. Chamberlain has referred to these as "soup tickets," in relating a brave action of Signaller Taylor at Tower Hamlets, so the reader can gauge from Taylor's experience how unfortunate these men were in not securing a medal.

At Koln Kalk the remnants were billeted in a part of Humboldt's factory. This firm had apparently been supplying the Germans with much of their supplies of munitions, and a tour round the works to look at the most up to date machinery installed there was very instructive. In the grounds were some concrete emplacements which had no doubt been used as refuges from our planes.

The Battalion Orderly Room Staff and the four Company clerks were busily engaged in preparing the papers for the men who were going home daily, while the remainder were cleaning up stores and making the necessary arrangements for the return of the Cadre to England. Plenty of leisure was also enjoyed, and Koln Kalk was thoroughly explored.

By the 22nd of May, 1919, the numbers had been reduced to four officers and 36 other ranks, when a move was made to Antwerp, where a most amusing incident occurred, which we give in Capt. David Walker's own words.

"Actually the Battalion demobilisation was complete, but there still remained some duties towards final disbandment to be done, and in accordance with demobilisation plans about forty personnel, including officers and N.C.O.s, formed the Cadre unit. This comprised transport, headquarter staff and a few others drawn from the companies. Our Colonel having gone to England and to an Army Course, I was left in command in the early spring of 1919. The responsibility was not great, and to all of us soldiering was of the past. We had a few parades, and most of us enjoyed a bath daily, for the weather was very warm.

"We first had a daily existence for two months in Koln Kalk, a suburb of Cologne; then the expected orders to move to embarkation port arrived, and we entrained for Antwerp. There we were among our own kind; we were a small section in a large encampment on the docks some six miles from the town of Antwerp itself. The only thing that mattered was that, during the hours of daylight, we were under one hour's notice to get on board a ship for old England.

"During the period there was nothing of the serious Orderly Room, and everyone was well behaved, even though it was the case of 'Do as you please' when the day was over. As officer commanding the Cadre unit, I was however brought back into the serious business of duty by an incident while at Antwerp, which luckily had a happy ending.

"Our Transport Sergeant* had, I believe, a reputation as a Bermondsey 'bruiser,' and, fine soldier though he was, when on a drinking bout he was a fighter. At least once he had been reduced in rank, and disciplinary action against him was usually due to his only weakness.

"I was in Antwerp one evening, and entering a restaurant I saw at the bar our Transport Sergeant and a corporal. Both were doing much the same as myself, and out for any enjoyment offering. I felt some responsibility and called over the corporal, who assured me that the sergeant was always all right when with him, and that he would see him home to camp safely. I thought no more about it until next morning, when, during a shave outside my tent, the R.S.M. approached to report to me that Sergeant —— had not returned to camp the previous night. I questioned him, but he knew nothing, so I sent for our sergeant's friend the corporal. I am afraid that the corporal did not mean to be helpful either, and all I got from him was: 'Sergeant —— was with me and coming back to camp quite all right, when something happened and I lost him!'

"I had not long to wait, as I thought, and within the hour I received a message from the powers at the camp to send to the Civil Prison an escort to collect our sergeant, who the previous night had been arrested, and it was added there was a charge against him.

"This struck me immediately as being very serious, and the idea of the Civil Authorities made it rather worse.

"The R.S.M. was ordered to detail an escort to proceed to the prison, and meanwhile I myself went to the A.P.M. Antwerp, to see what it was all about and to do anything I could to get our sergeant on board ship and away. Any civil charge was going to make a difference to him on demobilisation. I went to the Provost Marshal with some misgivings as to how I should be received, but my mind was full of all the good deeds that our valiant sergeant had done when the real business of the war was the common purpose of us all. This purpose was over, and I was prepared to plead strongly if it was going to do any good.

"It was a small room, and I was put into a chair opposite an office desk where the A.P.M. sat. He had an encouraging grin on his face as I proceeded to unfold my tale, and I spared our sergeant nothing in making him a real hero. The other listened, and his expression did not alter from the wily grin. I finished all I could say before he spoke a word, and then he said to me:—

*Not Sergt. Nuttman.

" 'Do you know what happened last night?'

"I had to reply 'No, Sir,' and added that the reason of my being there was to find that out. The A.P.M. proceeded: 'Then I will tell you,' and he gave me the following account in these words:—

" 'I was in bed, when about 1.30 a.m. I received a message from the Gendarmerie to send an escort to arrest a drunken English sergeant. This was nothing so very unusual, and a N.C.O. and two men were despatched. They were gone twenty minutes when I got another message to send the squad—a M.P. sergeant and eight men. In turn the squad was gone twenty minutes when I received a further message from the N.C.O. to send reinforcements. This was altogether unusual, and to grasp the situation I got out of bed and took twenty men with me to the seat of operations. There I was faced with an amazing spectacle. A crowd of civilians all driven into a frenzy, numbering about 150, round your sergeant, and no one able to approach within half a dozen yards of him in the centre.'

"At this point the Provost Marshal stopped, and I felt that this was going to be even more serious than I had bargained for. He pushed across the desk a formidable document of five sheets with the remark:—

" 'This is the translation of the civil charge.'

"I read this through. The first three pages were the names and addresses of civilians numbering some fifty odd who had claims against our sergeant for theft. The articles stolen were, I should say, almost every conceivable article of wearing apparel: hats, coats, raincoats, umbrellas, shoes, walking-sticks—I believe umbrellas and walking-sticks were the most numerous.

"Following this detail there was an account given by two Belgian policemen, who really were, in part, the cause of our sergeant's war on so many unoffending Antwerpians. This statement finished up with a paragraph which in all sincerity showed how nearly our sergeant never reached the shores of England. It was:—

" 'Of course we were only armed with swords, but, had we had revolvers, we would never have been beaten.'

"The Provost Marshal and myself had a good laugh, and he said there was nothing he could do, but he would advise me to get the sergeant on board ship for England as soon as possible.

"To cut the story short, I was thankful that the authorities were in the same mood as myself. In 36 hours the 12th East Surreys got orders to embark. I had to report to the G.O.C. at the camp on the sergeant under close arrest. He was to have the last say, and when I faced him I was up against it properly. He stared at me fiercely. On his breast he wore D.S.O. (two bars), D.C.M.. (bar), M.M., and many decorations. He commanded the utmost respect and only asked one question:—

" 'Are you telling me the truth?'

"Trembling I said, 'Yes, Sir,' and the reply came:—

" 'Then deal with the case yourself.'

"An Orderly Room was extemporised, and our sergeant, terribly sorry for himself, was before me, not knowing what was going to happen.

"The usual formalities, then 'Severely reprimanded.'

"All the 12th East Surrey Cadre Unit reported present and correct on board the good steamship within the next hour."

Thus the Cadre sailed away from Antwerp and reached Aldershot on the 28th of May.

The men of the Battalion on command or in hospital at the time the Cadre returned to England were posted to a Details Battalion of the East Surreys, from which they were eventually demobilised.

After two days at Aldershot the Cadre, at very short notice, proceeded to Bermondsey, where it was entertained to luncheon at the Bridge House Hotel, London Bridge, by the Mayor of Bermondsey on May 31st.

The following extracts taken from a report in the "South London Press" of the period gives a true account of the last days of the 12th Battalion.

" 'Bermondsey's Own,' or at least what was left to represent them, has returned from Germany. The borough did not have much opportunity to show its gratitude to the men who have fought so nobly, not because of any default of the inhabitants, but information that the Cadre of the 12th Battalion East Surrey Regt. was to return to Waterloo on Saturday was not received until 24 hours beforehand. With such notice, what could be done? At any rate no stone was left unturned by the Mayor (Councillor Arthur J. Fells, J.P.), Councillor J. H. Hart, who raised the Battalion during his mayoralty, Mr. James Buckman (Borough Treasurer), whose work in the formation of the Battalion can never be estimated, and the Town Clerk (Mr. Fredk. Ryall), to see that the men had a welcome fitting to the occasion.

"Marching from Waterloo, headed by the band of the 1st East Surrey Regt., and followed by the Mayoress and Civic representatives, they came to the boundary at Tower Bridge Road. Here the Mayor headed the procession and, figuratively speaking, opened the gates of the Borough to the four officers and 38 men. They proceeded to the Town Hall, and at the entrance Capt. D. Walker, M.C., who was in command, presented to his Worship the colours of the Regiment to be hung in the Council Chamber as a permanent record of Bermondsey's contribution to the war. Capt. Walker said the colours had been presented by General Plumer with the hope that the battalion would uphold the great tradition of the East Surrey Regt. The men of the 12th had always striven to carry out that hope."

The report goes on to describe how the Cadre, among whom were Capt. D. Walker; Lieuts. H. D. Gold and W. D. Mutch; Hon. Lieut. and Quartermaster G. Haydock C.S.M. J. Wilkinson and Sergt. J. Radcliffe (from the Depôt), was entertained to luncheon at the Bridge House Hotel, when the Mayor (accompanied by the Mayoress) presided. Councillor J. H. Hart and Messrs. J. Buckman and F. Ryall were also present, and during the proceedings paid eloquent tribute to the work accomplished by the Battalion, after the Mayor had, in his speech, referred to the death at Flers of Capt. J. T. Buckman (son of the Borough Treasurer) who had refused a staff appointment in order to go to France with his men.

When Councillor Hart rose to speak, he received an ovation from the men. In conveying his gratitude he mentioned the pride he felt in raising the Battalion, but regretted that, since Colonel Lee had left it, not a word had been received of the deeds of the men except from those he had met who came home on leave.

Replying on behalf of the Battalion, Capt. David Walker stated:—

"The Prince of Wales had said that the war had made a man of him. The speaker, and he believed those with him, could say the same of themselves. They had a lot for which to thank Bermondsey. The fine spirit with which the Battalion had started had been with the men all through."

Capt. Walker then paid a tribute to the different colonels who had been in command, and also to the men, and after wishing them every success, asked them to drink the toast of "Absent Friends."

Other speeches were delivered by Lieuts. Mutch and Haydock.

The report of the proceedings is ended with the following:—

"The 12th East Surreys have become known as the 'Silent Battalion,' and it is characteristic of them. These lads, for most of them are still young, sat with bronzed, grim, set faces, practically silent during the meal."

On the 3rd of June, 1919, a historic interlude in the meeting of the Bermondsey Borough Council took place in the evening, when Capt. David Walker accompanied by Lieuts. Mutch and Gold and Capt. Wray of the 1st/22nd "Queen's" formally handed to the Mayor the Battalion Colour with the request that, if possible, it should be placed in the Council Chamber.

After expressing his thanks for the reception given to the Cadre on the preceding Saturday, Capt. Walker outlined the part taken by the 12th since it was formed. Among other things he said the Battalion was sometimes known as the "Black Hand Gang," because on the occasion of their first raid the men left a board with a black hand painted on it in the German trenches. Referring to the capture of Flers, he mentioned that the Battalion was not given full credit for taking the place, but it was the first unit there.

Accepting the flag, the Mayor said:—

"I accept these Colours in the name of the Council and the Borough of Bermondsey. I am sure they will be valued through time immemorial."

Councillor Hart agreed with the suggestion of Councillor Hansom that the names of the battles in which the 12th took part should be placed upon the flag.

"Bermondsey had never received the houours due to her," said Councillor Hart. "It seems to me that the Battalion was called upon at all sorts of times to fill up gaps, and yet those at home had not received any information of what had been done except through the officers and men who had come home on leave." He continued (amid applause), "I am sure I am expressing the sentiments of all in the Borough when I say we are grateful for what they have done to honour Bermondsey."

Councillor D. Richmond said Bermondsey owed a great deal to Councillor Hart for raising the Battalion. He wanted to say on behalf of the Council that the Borough owed the men more than it could express for volunteering and performing the work they did so nobly. Councillors Vezey and Bustin also added their tribute to "Bermondsey's Own."

In the same edition of the "South London Press" appeared extracts from letters received by Councillor Hart deprecating the manner in which the "Silent Battalion" had passed away. Old comrades, parents of the fallen, and other people were greatly annoyed to learn that such short notice was given of the Cadre's return. One ex-signaller of the Battalion mentioned how the men of the 12th after being directly responsible for the taking of Flers were surprised to find that an English newspaper had given the credit to the Guards.

The above shortened account from the "South London Press" brings out two important points in connection with the war service of the 12th. First of all it is plain that the borough which had raised the Battalion knew little or nothing of what it had done, and secondly the action of the War Office in not giving more notice to the local Mayor was resented strongly by the man through whose efforts the Battalion came into existence. Once again officialdom had triumphed over common sense. There were many of the members of the Battalion recently demobilised in London at the time who would have been only too glad of the opportunity of being present on the occasion of the handing over of the Colour, but the first they heard of it was in the press after the ceremony had taken place. Looking back over that time, one wonders whether the action of a seemingly ungrateful department of state was responsible for the apparent lack of interest afterwards taken by the Bermondsey Borough Council in matters concerning our Association as well as those connected with the World War. However, if the War Office failed to thank the Mayor and members of the Battalion, the Divisional Commander, Sir Sydney Lawford, made some amends by having the following letter despatched to all the men who had been recently demobilised:—

"Now that the time has come for you to leave the Army and go back to civil life, I wish, both personally and officially, to thank you for the service you have given.

"You take away with you the priceless knowledge that you have played a man's part in this great war for freedom and fair play. You will take away with you also your remembrances of your comrades, your pride in your Regiment and your love for your country.

"You have played the game; go on playing it, and all will be well with the great Empire which you have helped to save."

"I wish you every prosperity and happiness.

(Sgd.) Sydney Lawford,
Major-General,
Commanding London Division.

The handing in of stores and equipment went on until June 10th, 1919, when, the last members of the Cadre being demobilised and Sergt. B. G. Burgess having made out his own papers, the 12th Battalion officially ceased to exist.

To quote the Official History of the East Surrey Regt:—

"During its two and a half years of active service in France, Flanders and Italy, the Battalion saw much hard fighting, and by its gallantry and endurance added much to the great reputation of the Regiment to which it belonged."

The actual casualties, exclusive of sickness, suffered by the Battalion during its existence, were as follows:—

	Officers.	Other Ranks.
Killed in action (including those previously reported "Missing") and died of wounds	38	683
Wounded	86	1,826
Prisoners of War	4	166
Total ...	128	2,675

The following are the numbers of officers and other ranks who served with the Battalion during the war:—

Officers	217
Other Ranks	4,487
Total ...	4,704

The "Silent" Battalion thus passed away in a similar manner to many other units of Kitchener's Army, unsung and unheard of except for an occasional reference by one of the Generals under whose command they came. Scattered all over the world, its members wanted to forget the horrors of the War, but to retain the memory of a comradeship which had never before been experienced in their lives. In their hearts they had a contempt for those who did not serve, and, if they are honest with themselves, they still have, even to-day. Some have allowed themselves to be submerged by unpatriotic propaganda emanating mostly from those who during the war found refuge at home or are of foreign origin, while the wrangles of soldiers and statesmen since the war have served only to show in brighter colours what Tommy Atkins achieved.

And so it was all over.

Over? Yes, the 12th Battalion East Surrey Regt. had ceased to be. What of its members? Hundreds of them sleep in the soil of France and Flanders, some perhaps forgotten but almost all remembered with tender affection by relatives and friends. This book, we trust, may recall to these something of what their loved ones achieved in "the War to end War."

What of those who survived? Many cannot now be traced. Some have passed over to the Great Beyond. But some hundreds now are linked in an Association to preserve while they live something of that ardent comradeship that once inspired them as a unit. To them this book, we hope, will recall something of what must be the biggest thing in their lives, and will help to pledge themselves anew to the service of their country and of their fellow-men.

For we who went through the actual fighting should know what War is in a sense totally different from those who took no combatant part. It was, we all realise in our hearts, a monstrous horror, a crime against humanity that never need have happened. The comman man in every Army knew it. The English Tommy and the French Poilu, the German and Austrian, the Russian, the Italian, the Turk, they felt themselves to be victims of a common madness that had stricken all alike, caught in the toils of a devilish net, loathed but inextricable. And to-day, nearly 20 years later, we all know in our hearts that War as a means of solving the world's hard problems and removing international discord is a delusion and a lie.

Yet to-day, in this mad Europe of ours, far larger standing armies than in 1914, equipped with weapons infinitely more deadly, wait ready for the signal to begin the hateful and futile game. The nations are spending on armaments more than £2,500,000 a day! There are far more causes of quarrel than 20 years ago, deeper hatreds, intenser ambitions, more bitter feelings of revenge. And all this in a world where plenty beyond the dreams of former ages is ready to our hands, if it were not for man's insensate and perverse folly. Another European War, everyone realises, must mean the end of our civilisation. And yet those who urge that reason should prevail over sentiment and law over force by co-operation in a Council of the Nations are jeered at as "pacifist cranks" and vilified by an obscurantist gutter press. It is a situation to make angels weep.

Let us end with some wise words of Sir Philip Gibbs:—

"There is no one cure for all these troubles, but they may be lessened and their greatest evils averted surely by a spirit of reason against unreason, by tolerance against intolerance, by ideals of peace against ideals of force, by conciliation against conflict, by a change of heart in the Individual as well as in the Nation."

We say with all our heart—Amen.

CHAPTER XVII.

THE ASSOCIATION OF 12th (BERMONDSEY) BATTALION, THE EAST SURREY REGIMENT.

By C. A. JAMES.

IN days of post-war demobilisation, there appeared in some newspapers a brief paragraph announcing that a cadre of the 12th Battn. East Surrey Regt. was embarking for home at a Belgian port: this cadre the press paragraphs intimated as consisting of a mere handful of men. It was this "handful," bearing back with the Colours won upon the field the live embers of a former patriotic offering, this meagre residuum which held the spark to be fanned later into the glow of comradeship's re-union.

To the world at large perhaps the old 12th was snuffed out. Anyhow, the war was over, and the Battalion's service no longer required; its record might have added further pages to the volume of forgotten history, had not chance, here and there, thrown into contact a few who had shared the never-to-be-forgotten days.

A friendly invitation extended by the East Surrey Regt. had drawn to an annual dinner at Harrods a good number of the old 12th, thus linking the Bermondsey boys with the fame attaching to the entire body of the East Surreys. It must not pass unnoticed that these early gatherings included among the numbers attending that prominent citizen Mr. John Hart, who, as former Mayor of Bermondsey had sponsored and initiated the raising of the 12th Battalion in his Borough. Thus from 1919, the torch kindled in 1915 was preserved from extinction.

The Chamber of the Bermondsey Borough Council no longer echoed its glory in the achievements of its own citizen soldiers, and cynical disregard of the solemn sacrifices offered up by their own flesh and blood was manifested in the fact that, although considerable sums of money had been contributed towards the local memorial at Mill Pond Bridge, Rotherhithe, there is no record of a wreath ever being placed there in commemoration of those who fell—men of the 12th (Bermondsey) Battn., The East Surrey Regt.

Far away from the capricious disdains of post-war borough councils however, accident disclosed that, in a probably less reprehensible measure of neglect, the 41st Divisional Memorial, erected at Flers in 1923, had never been officially unveiled. A party of the 11th "Queen's," during a pilgrimage to the battlefields, chanced to include L. M. Duggan of "Ours," and, observing that the 12th Battalion was wrongly inscribed on the memorial as the "10th," Duggan found occasion to draw attention through the press to the error. It was happily rectified when at Whitsun, 1932, again a party of the 11th "Queen's" with L. M. Duggan among them, together with official representatives and a large crowd of old comrades from every unit of the 41st Division (except sad to relate the 12th East Surreys) took part in the solemn unveiling of this memorial to the fallen by Sir Sydney Lawford. Thus late, was remedied a seeming negligence, thanks to a committee set up and presided over by Brig.-General S. Lushington, late C.R.A. of the division.

Whatever the causes, it became noticeable that at the East Surrey annual gatherings at Harrods ever depleted numbers of the old 12th Battalion were in evidence. In November, 1932 a muster of six embraced Capt. E. C. Solomon; Lieut. N. Speller; Lieut. and Quartermaster H. Amoore; Messrs. R. J. Calver, W. J. Steer and L. M. Duggan. Perhaps the desperate plight acted as a stimulus; at any rate it fired this half-dozen into getting a move on, and, before the annual dinner was well digested, discussion had advanced to the installing of Duggan as Chief Scout with the remainder standing to in support trenches.

The 11th "Queen's" and 11th Royal West Kents had by this time organised their associations, and Duggan was fortunate in having the helpful advice and experience of Messrs. H. C. Burberry and L. W. Dawson of these societies. The poor response to announcements in newspapers, many and varied, was enough to freeze the warmest enthusiasm, but a quick tot of moral rum, and Duggan was out again scanning the black horizon eager to gather in scattered individuals of the living remnant. Either the scent of the moral rum or Duggan's mode of search eventually succeeded in attracting some forty old lads of the 12th and rousing their interest in the scheme of founding the Association by means of which old comradeships might be renewed in general meetings from time to time. A meeting held at the Raglan, St. Martin's-le-Grand, on February 23rd, 1933, brought together sixty-five old members of the Battalion who then and there decided on the Association becoming a reality. Colonel H. H. Lee, D.S.O., owing to the uncertainty of his movements, was unable to accept an invitation to become President. Major H. de C. Blakeney with Capts. R. A. V. Brearey and E. C. Solomon became Vice-Presidents and Lieut. Norman Speller Chairman, but these represented the entire strength of officers who had rallied to the call for re-union; however better luck was ahead. L. M. Duggan was chosen Hon. Secretary and Treasurer; S. Lattimore Vice-Chairman; E. C. Howell Hon Asst. Secretary, and a committee consisting of J. T. Hawkins, H. G. Levett and C. B. Smith with Hon. Auditors B. G. Burgess and J. Kirk completed the establishment.

Following another meeting on March 24th in the Tower Bridge Hotel, at which our membership was considerably swollen with some of our local lads, the first Dinner of the Association took place at the Tower Bridge Hotel on Saturday, April 8th, where a glad assembly learned that the Battalion's original constructor, Colonel L. F. Beatson, O.B.E., had been traced, made President and was there present in the chair, supported by several officers of the old Battalion. On this occasion also many of us saw for the first time the Battalion Colour which decorated the walls for the evening.

The fare provided was most enjoyable, while the items on the menu, given below, helped to recall many memories.

MENU.

Potage Voormezeele.

Soles Dickebusche Lake
Sauce "Wipers"

Rosbif Jack Greenslade
Yorkshire Pudding
Crême Jock Turner

Legumes de Menin

Tartes d'Armentières
Trifles—"Minnies" and "Coalboxes"

Biscuits — Fromage

Café

Some activities of the Committee were disclosed at the Annual General Meeting which was held in the London Commercial Restaurant, Mincing Lane, the ensuing September. It seems that somebody nosing about the Bermondsey Town Hall had become cognisant of the fact that the Battalion Colours were reposing, not in the Mayor's Parlour, not fluttering in the breeze from the Town Hall flag-mast, but being probably deemed by the borough's elected incompatible with materialist conceptions, this emblem of former bellicosity had in the Council's judgment a more suitable home available in the department reserved for discarded lumber—the Town Hall basement.

An impulse of generosity, however, was not lacking, and the Council, responding to representations, very kindly consented to a transfer of the Colours to the Association for the purpose of "Laying up" in the Parish Church of Rotherhithe, the authority of the War Office being sought and obtained for the projected ceremony.

There is a sensation of thrill about the mystical rites of re-union celebrated in a spot hallowed by events such as birth and growth; Southwark Park was the old Twelfth's nursery; the hectic days within its cage-like sports oval left ineffaceable recollections of buoyant infancy, and when on Sunday, October 29th, 1933, there assembled plain-clothed veterans at the place where, as khaki-clad soldiers, they had once paraded for regular duty, something of a sacramental atmosphere prevailed.

Cheery greetings exchanged denoted personal acquaintanceships, as these bemedalled clusters lined the park's pathways prior to the supreme moment, when, after a lapse of eighteen years, they again were called to "Fall in" upon their cradle parade-ground. The ranks number and prove: perhaps while they stand at ease some flittings of bygone scenes come to mind, and once familiar voices and forms revivify in fancy's world: the old parade-ground has not changed; many will never again tread its turf, but their shades live on.

The local branch of the British Legion kindly lent its band for the occasion. Over the old foot-ways we tramp again; the strains of martial music reanimate the pace of matured ex-service men into the debonair tread of earlier devil-may-caredom; into Southwark Park Road we march, where people flock to their windows and doors or stand on sidewalks, all wonderbound at the unusual spectacle. As most befitting, Colonel Beatson heads the column. With him are Major G. R. P. Roupell, V.C., from the Depôt and a number of visiting officers, as well as about twenty former officers of the old 12th. Then follows Lieut. W. S. Hall with the Colour, escorted by two of our old Quartermaster-Sergeants, Calver and Tice, and behind them 150 of the old Battalion's other ranks. The occasion is honoured by the attendance of members of the 11th "Queen's" Royal Regt. O.C.A.; the Association of 11th (Lewisham) Battn. The Queen's Own R.W. Kent Regt.; the Bermondsey and Rotherhithe Branch of the British Legion and the 21st and 22nd London Regts.—more popularly known as the First Surrey Rifles and the "Queen's"—have also sent detachments to grace the event.

Mill Pond Bridge is an unpretentious district, but it accommodates, with simple dignity, the local war memorial. Here the parade halts and the assembled townsfolk stand in reverent respect whilst Colonel Beatson places a wreath at the foot of the memorial. Then there resounds that heart-tearing bugle call, "Last Post"; and then—a minute of dead silence, until "Reveillé" breaks the solemn hush. It is a brief ceremony but packed full of deep significance. The band gets us again on the stride and we march on to church.

As if from retiring modesty, the Church of St. Mary, Rotherhithe, conceals itself from main thoroughfares: an antique, bent and narrow street is the approach, lending picturesque colour to its old English centre of religious life, for the church interior is a striking relic of long-gone generations and their sober worship: we are back again in old England.

Rapidly filled pews testified widespread interest: from near and far—as distant as Lancashire—members had strained to be present, while more deeply affecting was the company of bereaved relatives there present in memory of some once near and dear. Though the Bermondsey Council could not find it convenient to be represented at the service, Mrs. N. C. Runge, the people's parliamentary representative, was kind enough to mark the occasion by active participation.

The clergy and choir filed in, and beside Padre Daniels, M.C., Rector of Rotherhithe, was noted the vested figure of one known among the 12th as Capt. G. P. Cooper; now in Holy Orders, he was assisting the Rector at this impressive rite.

We sang, "All people that on earth do dwell" to the well-known "Old Hundredth" tune, while the Colour Party advanced towards the chancel and handed over the flag to Colonel Beatson.

"This consecrated Colour, formerly carried in the service of The King and Empire, I now deliver into your hands for safe custody within these walls."

So the Colonel spoke as he handed the Colour to the Rector of Rotherhithe, who replied:

"We receive this Colour for safe custody within this Church. It shall remind us of the courage and self-sacrifice of those who have gone before, and inspire all who see it to love the brotherhood, fear God, and honour the King."

Then the dense congregation who had stood in fervent witness united in singing the nation's hymn, "God Save the King."

Brigadier-General F. W. Towsey, C.M.G., C.B.E., D.S.O., J.P., had travelled from his home in Colchester, Essex. Hardly any of us had met him since the time we all wore the King's uniform and marched to war, yet his genial command was quickened in memory and warm feelings went out as, facing us at the lectern, no longer "Brass hatted," he appeared just a plain English gentleman reading to us from the Prophet Isaiah.

The sermon preached by the Rev. F. E. A. Williams, M.C., Rector of Temple Ewell and River with Guston, Dover, became an intimate discourse to old comrades in arms, for Padre Williams was no stranger, and indulgence in a reminiscent perspective became the happy medium for clinching edifying precept.

Another hymn, and then a deep silence of two minutes brought us to the central act of all services of this kind—remembrance of our fallen comrades.

The silence was broken by the Priest's voice: "Their bodies are buried in peace," to which we responded: "But their name liveth for evermore." Thanking Almighty God for the renewal of old friendships and associations we stood while the Blessing was then imparted, and the service was over.

We left the hard-won Colours in Sanctuary; the band playing the East Surrey's regimental march "The Lass O' Gowry" led us past Rotherhithe Town Hall, once the Battalion H.Q., where Capt. Hector S. Walker in command gives "Eyes left": our Brigadier-General took the Salute in company with our Colonel and Mrs. N. C. Runge, M.P.

At the rear of the Town Hall the column halted, and General Towsey delivered some homely words in the manner expressive of genuine old friendship.

"Parade—dismiss." The day has become one catalogued in red letter.

After the enthusiasm evidenced in such stirring response to the honouring of the colours an annual Association pilgrimage to Rotherhithe has been made, assembling in Southwark Park and marching to St. Mary's for a service specially arranged for the Battalion. For four years in succession these commemoration services—usually on the Sunday preceding Armistice Day—have afforded an agreeable change from those other occasions during the year when old comrades are drawn together.

Since the solemn laying-up in the church, the colours have received additional honour. Through the generosity of an anonymous donor, the old spear-head was replaced by one of the official lion and crown type and the chief battle honours, "Ypres 1917-18," "Somme 1916-18," "Flers-Courcelette," "Arras 1918," "Messines 1917," "Menin Road," "St. Quentin," "Bapaume," "Courtrai," and "Italy 1917-18," were embroidered upon the flag in February, 1935. A suitable tablet with the inscription, "King's Colour of the 12th (Bermondsey) Battn. The East Surrey Regt., 1915-1918," fixed below the colours was a further benefaction of the same generous donor. The whole arrangements were carried through by Lieut. N. Speller, Mr. W. G. Robinson and the Rev. A. P. Daniels. The care expended in thus erecting an abiding shrine to the memory of deeds accomplished at the price of noble sacrifice should spur the old comrades and their families into a perpetuation of this rally at Armisticetide.

September, being a month in which many events of importance in the life of the old 12th Battalion are commemorated, has been set aside for holding annual general meetings. The official ways and means of running the Association are dealt with at these meetings, each member present constituting a useful unit in the moulding of the Association and its affairs. The time devoted to reviewing business matters finds ample reward in the thoughtful provision of a canteen, a song or two, together with that never-failing delight, a vigorous gossip with former company mates over episodes that happened in the old days.

Conviviality perhaps reaches its summit at the Annual Dinner which occurs at the end of February each year. Beaming smiles scintillate around the festive board; genial repartee darts hither and thither, and the amiable grace of a family muster diffuses itself.

Each year has recorded a steady increase at table, the gathering of something over 100 at the first dinner, gaining a score each year, expanded the muster to 140 in 1936. Defying the obstacle of distance, members from far remote parts, whether by road, rail or air, have been brought to these annual dinners. Pte. Cottam has twice journeyed from Chorley, Lancs.: C.S.M. Horswell came from Gloucester in 1934, as well as Cpl. Rushton from Southport, Lancs.: Capt. David Walker has repeatedly left Edinburgh to be present: Major G. O. Searle has come from King's Lynn: Dr. Christie (late Capt. and Battalion M.O.) from Ulverston, Lancs.: Lieut W. D. Mutch (late I.O.) from Yorkshire, and Cpl. W. Fuller from Ramsgate. Two other medical officers, Drs. Binney and Harrison, have also attended, and soon after his return from British West Africa Capt. Dowling put in an appearance.

To the 1936 dinner held in the London Commercial Restaurant, Mincing Lane, came Colonel Pennell of the 18th K.R.R.s who was the Twelfth's C.O. at Hollebeke in July and August, 1917, when he was awarded the D.S.O., Major S. R. Hogg (late Brigade Major), and Capt. Kerr (late Staff Capt.). Colonel Corfe of the 11th West Kents, as at a previous dinner, enlivened the proceedings with some anecdotes which provoked hilarious laughter. To the toast of "Our General," proposed by Colonel Beatson, we responded with the lusty chorus of "For he's a jolly good fellow," to our old Brigadier, General Towsey. Greatly touched with emotion at the wonderful reception accorded him, the General, in a speech teeming with sound thoughts, reviewed the past, present and future, carrying his attentive listeners in sympathetic accord punctuated by wholehearted applause. The General stayed right to the end of the dinner conversing with the guests of all ranks.

Another most pleasing feature of the 1936 dinner was practical recognition of the unremitting work performed by L. M. Duggan, the Association's Hon. Secretary, in the presentation of a canteen of cutlery.

From Mincing Lane to Flanders is a bit of a stretch; yet a few members have contrived to bridge the span. As far back as 1933 there began pilgrimages to places on the Western Front where the Battalion was in action. At Whitsun that year Mr. Aston with Duggan and Rogers toured the Salient and in particular the old sector of St. Eloi. Still visible was the old crater as well as the one blown under the German lines on June 7th, 1917

In 1934 Crosby, Duggan, Herbert and Snell made the journey and delved round the neighbourhood of the Brasserie at Elzenwalle, Ridgewood, Vierstraat, Dickebusch and other places of interest. They also visited Flers on the Somme where they placed a wreath on the 41st Divisional Memorial. This was the first act of homage paid to our fallen comrades in the village where so many of them fell in 1916.

Six members of the Association, Duggan, Farrell, Herbert, Percival, Snell and G. W. Wells, with three friends and relations, went over at Whitsun, 1935, and spent three most enjoyable and interesting days in which they must have covered hundreds of miles. A special trip was made to Passchendaele, Hollebeke and Reninghelst, in addition to most of the other places covered on previous tours. Again a wreath was placed on the Memorial in Flers.

At Whitsun, 1936, Mr. and Mrs. G. Percival, Mr. and Mrs. R. R. Rampling, Mr. and Mrs. C. E. MacKriell, Mr. H. G. Herring and three friends, and the Hon Secretary, making their Headquarters at La Panne, toured the Salient and Somme (including Flers, where a wreath was deposited) and enjoyed a most interesting trip.

The Association purposes to continue its organisation of a pilgrimage each year: many who have enjoyed the facilities afforded have expressed the desire to go again. By a wonderful recovery a land known to us only as a battle-ground now presents the charm of a peaceful countryside risen upon territory that, when we quitted it, was a howling wilderness.

The days of peace, once yearned for, inspire fellowship among former belligerents, and these excursions, contributing streams of pilgrims, French, Belgian and British, establish contacts ripening into friendly relations, while now the Germans are also arriving to view scenes of past horrors. These people, determined on peace, surveying memorials to their honoured dead together with those visible relics of their old slaughter-yard, are moved to united resolve that neither the rash gambles of unscrupulous statesmen nor fanatical bellowings of ignorant tub-thumpers shall again recklessly plunge civilization into destruction.

In an age confronted with new problems, the Association endeavours to preserve the spirit of patriotic fervour and the *esprit de corps* engendered during days of national trial. The ill-requited lot of many enduring undeserved affliction is a rankling sore in several breasts, and a value of Association gatherings is that these hard facts, as well as the glad knowledge of others' well being, are unveiled. At the various meetings we can dilate on stirring incidents of an eventful past, dwell on the state of the living present and with trustful effort fall in on parade for a future route march throughout which the links of old war comradeships shall not be broken.

IN A WAR CEMETERY.

The misty eve was dying in
A sullen smear of rain,
And in the West the sun had dipped,
Flushed with a sanguine stain.

To right and left, to front and rear,
There stretched in endless file
The myriad headstones of the dead,
As I stood there awhile.

But I went on in awful thought
Oppressed, and compassed twice
With halting step the Altar Stone
And Cross of Sacrifice.

As there I stood, Another came
And entered by the gate,
Pausing, like me, to read the names
And deeply meditate.

Nearer He paced, and as He came,
He spoke no word aloud,
But His form faltered, and His head
Was low and lower bowed.

At length He stayed and raised His arms
Aloft as if in prayer:
And in a flash I saw the hands—
The print of nails was there.

JOHN ASTON, 1927.

Roll of Honour

Members of the 12th (Service) Battalion, The East Surrey Regiment, who were killed in action, or died of wounds or disease, during the Great War, 1914-1918 (number in parentheses denotes Cemetery):—

Rank and Name.

Acklin, L. H., Pte. (46)
Adcock, A. H., Pte. (14)
Adlington, F. C., Pte. (81)
Adlington, L. D., Pte. (62)
Alexander, H., Pte. (51)
Allchin, W. T., Pte. (56)
Andrews, A. C., Pte. (70)
Andrews, J. F., Pte. (28)
Angell, W., L./Cpl. (90)
Angood, M., Pte. (35)
Armstrong, R., Pte. (18)
Arney, J., Pte. (13)
Arnold, E. A., L./Cpl. (14)
Arnold, H. E., Pte. (73)
Asbury, W. J., Pte. (17)
Askew, J., Pte. (14)
Aston, H. F., Pte. (13)
Aucourt, C. O., Sgt. (36)
Austin, G. E., Pte. (41)
Austin, J. H., Pte. (14)
Backhouse, W., Pte. (18)
Bacon, A. J., Pte. (13)
Bacon, J., Pte. (21)
Bagg, L., Pte. (14)
Bailey, E., Pte. (55)
Bailey, H. P., M.C., 2nd Lieut. (13)
Bailey, T. B., Cpl. (14)
Baines, W., Pte. (13)
Baisden, A., Pte. (55)
Baker, E., L./Cpl. (46)
Baker, J. A., M.M., L./Cpl. (44)
Baker, W. J., Pte. (71)
Ball, J., Pte. (14)
Balls, F. J., Pte. (18)
Balls, J. W., Pte. (21)
Barker, G. E., Pte. (21)
Barker, H. W., Pte. (14)
Barnard, H., Pte. (18)
Barry, F. R., Capt. (41)
Barnett, H. J., Pte. (31)
Bartlett, W. H., Pte. (14)
Bartley, P. E., Pte. (46)
Baskeyfield, S., L./Cpl. (41)
Bateman, G. H., Pte. (41)
Bates, A., Pte. (73)
Baxter, P. W., Pte. (8)
Beadon, W., Pte. (72)
Beard, N. S., L./Cpl. (72)
Beckett, W. J., L./Cpl. (28)
Bednall, E., Pte. (45)
Beehag, J., Pte. (56)
Belsham, J., Pte. (55)
Belcher, E. F., L./Sgt. (71)
Bennett, A. E., L./Cpl. (13)
Bennett, A. W., Pte. (72)
Bennie, J. C., Pte. (55)
Benson, A., Pte. (14)
Benson, W. A., Pte. (50)
Benzie, W., Pte. (56)
Betteley, R., Pte. (14)
Bickerdyke, W., Pte. (55)
Bickerton, W., Pte. (55)
Biggs, J. W., Pte. (13)
Bignell, C., C.S.M. (70)
Birch, A. T., Pte. (71)
Bird, W. C., Pte. (26)
Bishop, J. W., Pte. (28)
Bishop, L. T., Cpl. (13)
Bisson, C. C., Pte. (77)
Blowers, B., Pte. (14)
Blythe, C., Pte. (55)

Rank and Name.

Bolton, E. E., M.M., L./Cpl. (42)
Botting, G., Pte. (56)
Bowles, C. F., Pte. (81)
Bowry, A., L./Cpl. (39)
Brand, W. G., Pte. (41)
Breakspear, F., Pte. (55)
Brenton, W. J., Pte. (13)
Bridger, F., Pte. (43)
Broomfield, J., Pte. (79)
Brown, A. S., Pte. (13)
Brown, G. R., L./Cpl. (88)
Brown, P. C., Pte. (18)
Brown, T., L./Cpl. (14)
Brown, W., Pte. (28)
Brunt, F. W., Pte. (41)
Buck, J. H., L./Cpl. (29)
Buckman, J. L., Capt. (56)
Budd, P. J., M.M., Pte. (13)
Buick, R., Pte. (17)
Bull, A. E., Pte. (14)
Buller, E. F., Pte. (41)
Bundle, W. J., Pte. (14)
Burbridge, B., Pte. (18)
Burgess, A. E. B., Pte. (49)
Burkin, W. H., Pte. (55)
Butler, F. E., Pte. (28)
Button, L. J., Pte. (41)
Bye, E., Pte. (15)
Cahill, F. W., Pte. (56)
Campbell, F., Pte. (84)
Campbell, G., Pte. (13)
Cansdale, J. P., Pte. (13)
Carey, B., Pte. (72)
Carpenter, A. V., Pte. (50)
Carr, A. B., Pte. (53)
Carter, H. J., Pte. (14)
Carter, W., D.C.M., Sgt. (83)
Caryl, E. T., Pte. (28)
Caton, J., Pte. (72)
Chamberlain, W. R., Pte. (71)
Chambers, E. B., Pte. (24)
Chaplin, J. W., Pte. (97)
Chapman, A. E., Pte. (41)
Chapman, E. A., Pte. (21)
Chappel, W., Pte. (13)
Charge, W. V., Pte. (56)
Charles, H., Pte. (33)
Charman, W. H., Pte. (28)
Charman, W. J., Pte. (56)
Chase, A., Pte. (56)
Chasteauneuf, E. H. B., Pte. (29)
Chatfield, C. J., Pte. (23)
Cheshire, R., Pte. (55)
Chesters, J. R., Lieut. (56)
Chidgey, T., Pte. (45)
Child, R. V., Pte. (72)
Chipping, P. L., Pte. (30)
Chittock, W., Pte. (21)
Churcher, H. G., Pte. (56)
Clark, A., Pte. (61)
Clark, F., Pte. (56)
Clark, T., Pte. (26)
Clarke, C. H., Pte. (21)
Clarke, G., Pte. (14)
Clarke, V. J., Pte. (21)
Clary, E. A., Pte. (41)
Claydon, A. C., Pte. (14)
Clements, F., Pte. (24)
Clifford, A., Pte. (41)
Clipsham, W. H., Cpl. (55)
Cloak, H. T., Pte. (13)

Rank and Name.

Clubb, J. G., Pte. (70)
Cockshutt, W., Pte. (55)
Coeshall, P., L./Cpl. (85)
Cogger, C. F., Pte. (73)
Cogger, G., Pte. (30)
Coleby, E., Pte. (15)
Collcutt, G. E., Pte. (41)
Collett, P. F., Pte. (26)
Collier, J. T., Pte. (72)
Collins, F., Pte. (28)
Collins, F. L., Pte. (14)
Collins, H. J., L./Cpl. (72)
Collins, N., Pte. (22)
Collins, W. H., Pte. (71)
Collins, W. H., L./Cpl. (51)
Collis, R. E., Pte. (76)
Combe-Ceaton, H. N., 2nd Lieut. (17)
Condon, V. B., Sgt. (94)
Convine, S. R., Pte. (16)
Cook, E. J., L./Sgt. (56)
Cook, H. P., Pte. (64)
Cooper, C. V., Cpl. (14)
Cooper, F., Pte. (30)
Cooper, G. F., Pte. (59)
Cooper, N., Pte. (56)
Cooper, W. H., Pte. (44)
Cornell, J. A., Pte. (41)
Cowell, W., Pte. (46)
Cox, W., Pte. (13)
Cox, W. T., Pte. (56)
Cressey, G. E., Pte. (16)
Croft, G. J. V., Pte. (14)
Cross, H., Pte. (41)
Crump, H., Pte. (93)
Cullinane, J., Pte. (41)
Cullip, J. W., Pte. (39)
Cumming, K. G., Pte. (28)
Cuthbert, W. H., Pte. (14)
Dallinger, J. R., Pte. (21)
Daston, W., Pte. (40)
Davies, F. L., Pte. (56)
Davis, C. York, Capt. (56)
Dawes, A. J., Pte. (72)
Dax, S. H., Pte. (32)
Day, A. G., Pte. (21)
Day, G. W., Pte. (55)
Day, W., Cpl. (57)
Dean, F. C., Pte. (55)
Dennett, A. R., Pte. (32)
De Rider, H. T., Pte. (13)
Devey, A., Pte. (55)
Digby, I. L., Pte. (22)
Diplock, T. H., Pte. (13)
Dolwin, R., Pte. (56)
Donaldson, G., M.M., Pte. (20)
Donnelly, T., Pte. (28)
Donnely, J., D.C.M., Sgt. (72)
Dormer, C. E., Pte. (56)
Doulton, A. E. J., Pte. (14)
Dove, P. W., Cpl. (86)
Drake, H., Pte. (41)
Drinkwater, J., Pte. (13)
Duncan, A. T., 2nd Lieut. (18)
Dunford, A. C., Pte. (81)
Dunkley, H. N., 2nd Lieut. (14)
Dunn, A. E., L./Cpl. (96)
Dunn, J., Pte. (56)
Dunster, E. W., Pte. (14)
Durrell, E. R., Sgt. (30)
Dyson, F. T., Pte. (55)

Rank and Name.

Eagle, J., Pte. (72)
Eason, V. W., Pte. (78)
Easter, T., Pte. (13)
Ede, E. G., Pte. (23)
Edlin, W., Sgt. (81)
Edmonds, J., Pte. (41)
Edmunds, E., Pte. (55)
Edwards, A. J., L./Cpl. (14)
Edwards, E., Cpl. (41)
Ellis, C., Pte. (24)
Ellis, W. G. T., Pte. (18)
Essom, H. W., Pte. (14)
Eves, G., Pte. (56)
Eveling, A. G., Pte. (56)
Eyles, B., Pte. (55)
Falkner, J. F. C., Pte. (47)
Farmborough, A., Pte. (14)
Ferry, E., Pte. (46)
Fewtrell, A., Pte. (18)
Fibbens, G., Pte. (14)
Field, C. A., Pte. (47)
Field, C. W., M.S.M., Sgt. (16)
Finch, L. J. G., Pte. (77)
Findlay, J., Pte. (56)
Finnigan, W. G., Pte. (55)
Fishburn, E., Pte. (14)
Fisher, C. H., M.C., 2nd Lieut. (17)
Fisher, H. F., Pte. (56)
Fisher, R. T., Pte. (70)
Flannagan, J., Pte. (38)
Flowerday, P., Pte. (56)
Flynn, D. J., Pte. (13)
Folly, G., Pte. (17)
Fookes, E. B., Pte. (41)
Fountain, C., Pte. (17)
Fowler, S., L./Cpl. (60)
Fowler, W. F., Pte. (56)
Fox, A. R., L./Cpl. (41)
Fox, C. C., Lieut. (56)
Fox, W. E., Pte. (14)
Franks, S., Pte. (56)
French, J. W., Pte. (28)
Frischling, G. H., Lieut. (28)
Furmidge, J. H., Pte. (28)
Fryer, W., Pte. (29)
Gale, S., Pte. (14)
Gallagher, J., Pte. (14)
Garrard, A., Cpl. (26)
Gatford, T. W., Pte. (67)
Gay, T. H., Pte. (18)
George, F. T., Pte. (14)
George, J. A., Pte. (14)
George, J. T., M.M., Pte. (55)
Gerrard, H. J., Pte. (20)
Gibbons, P. J., 2nd Lieut. (56)
Gibson, M., Pte. (13)
Gibson, T. G., Pte. (72)
Giles, H., Pte. (41)
Giles, J., L./Cpl. (47)
Goddard, T., Pte. (51)
Godfrey, A., Pte. (32)
Godfrey, T., Pte. (56)
Golder, H. A., Pte. (37)
Golding, G., Pte. (63)
Goodman, A., Pte. (72)
Goodwin, S. G., Pte. (28)
Gordon, R., Pte. (56)
Gosby, A., Pte. (56)
Gosling, H. A., Pte. (20)
Gould, G. H., Pte. (97)
Graham, A., Pte. (70)
Grainge, H. L., Pte. (83)
Gray, J., L./Cpl. (28)
Green, H., Pte. (97)
Grenway, L. H., Pte. (15)
Grove, E., Sgt. (41)
Groves, W. R. T., Pte. (14)
Guest, A., Pte. (56)
Gunn, R. G., Pte. (3)
Currin, R. W., 2nd Lieut. (48)
Guy, J. S., Pte. (18)
Gwynn, R. A, Pte. (86)
Hailer, E., Pte. (10)
Hall, A. C., Pte. (73)
Hall, G. H., Pte. (87)
Hambleton, E., Sgt. (13)
Hammond, G., M.M., C.S.M. (41)

Rank and Name.

Hammond, J. C., Pte. (28)
Hammond, J. R., Pte. (18)
Hammond, J. W., Pte. (13)
Hancock, T. C., Pte. (12)
Harber, S. G., Pte. (28)
Harding, F. J., 2nd Lieut. (47)
Harper, T., Pte. (65)
Hart, S. L., Pte. (9)
Hartley, W. J., Pte. (38)
Hasler, L., Pte. (90)
Hatchard, A. E., Pte. (55)
Hatcher, W. H., Pte. (50)
Haywood, J., L./Cpl. (14)
Healey, A. E., Pte. (17)
Heard, E. H., L./Cpl. (50)
Hemmings, W. J., L./Sgt. (18)
Hennessey, J., Pte. (14)
Hesmer, T. W., Pte. (14)
Hewitt, A. T., Pte. (28)
Hewitt, J. W., L./Sgt. (90)
Hewitt, P., Pte. (20)
Hickey, D., Pte. (86)
Hicks, W., Pte. (55)
Hider, H., Pte. (14)
Hilborn, E. A., Cpl. (41)
Histed, F., Pte. (89)
Hoadley, W., Pte. (71)
Hoare, A. H., M.M., L./Cpl. (14)
Hobbs, H. F. S., Sgt. (72)
Hoffman, P., Pte. (6)
Holmes, C., Pte. (14)
Honey, B., Pte. (14)
Hooker, A. C., Pte. (56)
Hooker, S., Pte. (18)
Hotston, S., Pte. (14)
Howard, A., Pte. (28)
Howat, A. F., Pte. (41)
Howell, G. A., Pte. (46)
Howlett, F. J., L./Sgt. (18)
Howitt, A. G., M.C., Capt. (13)
Hoyland, W. P., Pte. (55)
Hughes, W., Pte. (13)
Humby, F. W., Pte. (13)
Humphrey, Albert, Pte. (26)
Humphrey, Alex., Pte. (14)
Hutchen, S. S., Cpl. (14)
Hutcheson, J. McL., 2nd Lieut. (14)
Hyam, T. J., Pte. (32)
Hyam, W. C., Pte. (13)
Iles, H., Pte. (13)
Iorns, F. A., L./Cpl. (14)
Irish, F. J., Pte. (55)
Jackson, D. H., Pte. (14)
Jackson, G., Pte. (14)
Jackson, H., C.S.M. (72)
James, A., Pte. (41)
James, F. T., D.C.M., M.M., Sgt. (90)
James, J., Pte. (28)
James, W., Pte. (26)
Jarrett, T. E., Pte. (41)
Jessop, J. D., M.C., Capt. (72)
Johnson, E. V., Pte. (41)
Johnson, F. N., Pte. (55)
Johnson, G., Pte. (43)
Johnson, M. T., 2nd Lieut. (98)
Johnson, S., Pte. (56)
Jolly, T. B., 2nd Lieut. (14)
Jones, J. H., Pte. (14)
Jones, J. J., Pte. (55)
Jordan, A. C., Pte. (71)
Jotcham, W., L./Cpl. (55)
Joyce, A. A., Pte. (56)
Joyce, T., Pte. (56)
Keeble, J. T., Pte. (4)
Keefe, H. J., Pte. (56)
Kellow, E. H., L./Cpl. (26)
Kelly, H. J., L./Cpl. (14)
Kelly, J., L./Cpl. (13)
Kemp, W. G., Pte. (14)
Kendall, E., Pte. (28)
Key, W. S., Pte. (51)
Killick, H. F., Pte. (56)
Kinanan, T., Pte. (14)
King, Albert, E., Pte. (61)
King, Alfred, Pte. (65)

Rank and Name.

King, Arthur Edwin, Pte. (72)
King, Arthur John, L./Cpl. (5)
King, W. A., Pte. (2)
King, Wm. F., Pte. (13)
Kirby, H. W., Pte. (41)
Kirby, W. G., Pte. (13)
Klippel, S., Pte. (41)
Knight, Frank H., Pte. (13)
Knight, Fredk., Pte. (14)
Knowles, F., Pte. (41)
Ladbury, G. S., Pte. (1)
Laidler, E. A., Pte. (41)
Lambert, E. C., Lieut., R.A.M.C. (61)
Lane, W. J., Pte. (41)
Lang, F. C. E., Pte. (56)
Langley, A. E., Pte. (14)
Langley, H., L./Cpl. (14)
Lasenby, S., 2nd Lieut. (14)
Latter, A., Pte. (18)
Latter, C. W., Pte. (17)
Lavender, G. H., L./Cpl. (14)
Laws, E. C., Pte. (17)
Laws, J., Pte. (14)
Lay, F., Pte. (14)
Leakey, S., Pte. (56)
Lewington, A. E., Pte. (18)
Lewis, D. D., L./Cpl. (32)
Lewis, I. A., Pte. (13)
Lewis, R. A., Pte. (39)
Libby, A. T., Lieut. (14)
Lincoln, A. C., Pte. (49)
Linford, A. J., L./Cpl. (14)
Linge, A., Pte. (28)
Littlejohn, E. C., Pte. (56)
Lock, F. C., Pte. (28)
Locke, F. J., Pte. (14)
Lodge, G., Pte. (90)
Longbottom, C. D., Pte. (14)
Looker, J. R., L./Cpl. (40)
Loveland, G., Pte. (21)
Luckie, F. J., Pte. (55)
Ludlow, S., Pte. (55)
McCallum, D., Capt. (14)
McDonald, A. E., Pte. (41)
Maddison, D. S., M.M., A.C.S.M. (14)
Maguire, C., M.M., Sgt. (80)
Mallett, W. R. G., M.M., L./Cpl. (55)
Manby, J. C., Pte. (14)
Mardell, E. T., Pte. (14)
Maris, E. A., Pte. (55)
Mark, A. J., Pte. (18)
Martin, A. J., Pte. (66)
Martin, G. F., Pte. (56)
Martin, H. R., Pte. (72)
Maskell, A. H., Pte. (14)
Mason, J. W., Pte. (14)
Mathias, C., L./Cpl. (59)
Matthews, F. R., Lieut. (55)
Maud, A. J., Pte. (14)
May, H. J., Pte. (14)
Maybin, A. E., Pte. (55)
Meadows, R. M., Lieut. (41)
Mellor, J., Pte. (70)
Menzie (Manszi), L., Pte. (99)
Mercer, T., Pte. (55)
Merrill, W. T., Pte. (28)
Merritt, C. E., Pte. (56)
Miles, A., Cpl. (14)
Miller, C., Pte. (14)
Miller, T., Pte. (13)
Mitchell, H. F., Cpl. (61)
Moffatt, D. W., Pte. (14)
Moffatt, S. F., L./Cpl. (14)
Monk, J. C., Pte. (68)
Morgan, A., Cpl. (72)
Morgan, S. H., 2nd Lieut. (18)
Moore, T., M.M., Pte. (70)
Morris, G., L./Sgt. (56)
Morris, J. R., Pte. (17)
Morris, W. R., Pte. (71)
Mortimer, C. T. J., Pte. (13)
Moss, E. W., Pte. (55)
Mullins, H. W., Pte. (14)
Mulville, W. F., Pte. (21)

Rank and Name.

Myers, A. J., L./Cpl. (14)
Neville, S., Pte. (26)
Newman, S., Pte. (46)
Newton, H. S., Pte. (28)
Nightingale, W., Pte. (14)
Noonan, E., Pte. (72)
Norman, G. A., Pte. (14)
Norman, W. H., Pte. (18)
Norwood, E., Pte. (14)
Nutley, F. V., Cpl. (55)
Oakes, A. E., Pte. (47)
Offord, P. J., Pte. (90)
Old, H., Cpl. (21)
O'Malley, M. D., M.M., Pte. (20)
Osborne, S., Pte. (72)
O'Sullivan, T., Pte. (26)
Oswell, L. C., Pte. (14)
Ovall, T., Pte. (50)
Pack, T., Pte. (90)
Page, T., Cpl. (93)
Page, W., Pte. (26)
Paine, E. H., Pte. (90)
Paisley, E. G., C.Q.M.S. (33)
Palmer, F. W., Pte. (72)
Palmer, S. R., Pte. (14)
Parker, F., Pte. (22)
Parr, W. G., Pte. (28)
Parsons, D. G., Pte. (40)
Parsons, W. G., Pte. (73)
Parsons, W. H., Pte. (18)
Pattman, A. L., Pte. (14)
Pavey, W. H., Pte. (56)
Peachey, R. A. V., Pte. (18)
Peacock, P., L./Cpl. (79)
Pearce, F. H., Pte. (56)
Peirce, H., Pte. (58)
Pelling, A. C., Pte. (51)
Pembroke, J., Pte. (46)
Perrin, E., Pte. (14)
Peterson, A. E., C.S.M., (56)
Pettitt, W., Pte. (15)
Pharro, F., Pte. (14)
Phillips, D. J., Pte. (56)
Phillips, W. J., Pte. (17)
Phipps, J. W. J., Pte. (55)
Pickard, J. I. Pte. (56)
Piggott, E. H., Pte. (28)
Piggott, F. F., Pte. (52)
Pink, T. J., L./Cpl. (72)
Pocknell, F. A., L./Cpl. (72)
Pope, J., L./Cpl. (26)
Porter, W., Pte. (56)
Pout, J. A., Pte. (69)
Price, W. H., Pte. (50)
Prior, G., Pte. (56)
Pullum, W. H., Pte. (28)
Purkiss, E. W., Pte. (21)
Quinnell, H. J., Pte. (73)
Randall, H., Pte. (13)
Rands, T., Pte. (41)
Rawlings, W., L./Cpl. (86)
Rayner, W., Pte. (14)
Read, G. A., Pte. (18)
Record, P. S., M.M., Pte. (21)
Reeve, J. W., Pte. (71)
Reeves, S. E., Pte. (14)
Reid, G., Pte. (73)
Rendell, J. W. H., Pte. (55)
Revels, P., Pte. (21)
Reynolds, G., Pte. (70)
Reynolds, T. J. M., Pte. (22)
Reynolds, W. G., Pte. (13)
Rhodes, A., L./Cpl. (14)
Rice, H. V., M.M., Pte. (12)
Richards, K. A., Pte. (71)
Richards, W. L., Sgt. (72)
Richardson, Harold, Pte. (72)
Richardson, Henry, Pte. (13)
Richardson, Henry Chas., M.M., L./Cpl. (13)
Richardson, Herbert, F., Cpl. (56)
Richens, W. A., L./Cpl. (13)
Ridley, A. E., Pte. (43)
Robbins, J. A., Pte. (91)
Robbins, W., Pte. (55)
Roberts, A. G., Pte. (55)
Roberts, J. F., Pte. (55)

Rank and Name.

Roberts, L., M.C., 2nd Lieut. (82) (Attd. R.W. Surrey Regt.)
Robins, A. C., Pte. (13)
Robinson, W. A., L./Cpl. (14)
Rollinson, J., Pte. (28)
Rook, L. G., Pte. (14)
Rose, H. G., Pte. (13)
Rosier, C. W., Pte. (26)
Rothery, A. C., Pte. (14)
Rowell, H. E., L./Cpl. (72)
Rowsell, W. J., Pte. (50)
Rummery, A. C., Pte. (52)
Russell, E., Pte. (26)
Russell, L. W. B., 2nd Lieut. (14)
Russell, W. H., Pte. (46)
Ryan, E. St. J., M.C., Capt. (21)
Sadleir, G. H., Pte. (56)
Sadler, H., Pte. (13)
Sales, W. J., Pte. (17)
Samson, H. E., Pte. (22)
Samuels, S. G., Pte. (90)
Sandford, J. H., L./Cpl. (26)
Saunders, C. E., Sgt. (13)
Savage, G. H., M.M., 2nd Lieut. (34)
Saville, R. W., Pte. (14)
Saville, T. J., Pte. (7)
Sawyer, T. E., Pte. (56)
Scobell, T. H., Pte. (56)
Scott, G. A. T., Pte. (55)
Scott, H., Pte. (74)
Seabrook, G., Pte. (81)
Seager, W. T., Pte. (72)
Seaman, R. J., Pte. (13)
Seagrief, J. W., Pte. (18)
Seed, A. F., Pte. (17)
Selby, E. C., Sgt. (27)
Seward, A., Pte. (73)
Shanks, W. P., Pte. (72)
Sharp, C., Pte. (56)
Sharp, G. R., Pte. (14)
Sharp, W., Pte. (56)
Shaw, F., Pte. (13)
Sheasby, A. R., Pte. (13)
Sheldrick, T. E., Pte. (38)
Shepherd, A. H., Pte. (56)
Sherborn, G. R., Pte. (30)
Shilling, W. E., Pte. (55)
Simmons, C., Pte. (11)
Skeels, R., Pte. (18)
Skelton, E., Pte. (87)
Skinner, F. G., Pte. (61)
Slacke, C. O., Capt. (13)
Sloots, P. H., L./Cpl. (25)
Smart, E., Pte. (70)
Smith, A. J., Pte. (72)
Smith, C. J., L./Cpl. (72)
Smith, F. C., L./Cpl. (56)
Smith, G. A., Pte. (56)
Smith, L. G., L./Cpl. (49)
Smith, W. J., L./Cpl. (50)
Songhurst, G., Pte. (24)
Sparkes, J. W., Pte. (56)
Sparkes, W., Pte. (55)
Sparks, J., Sgt. (92)
Spicer, A. L., Pte. (21)
Spink, J. H., Pte. (18)
Springett, T. C., Pte. (56)
Standing, C. W., Pte. (14)
Starling, A., Pte. (13)
Stern, E. W., Pte. (13)
Stenning, B. C., 2nd Lieut. (73)
Stevens, C. R., Pte. (55)
Stevens, E. C. J., Pte. (55)
Stevens, J., Pte. (13)
Stevens, W. (alias Smith, H.), Pte. (70)
Steward, R., Pte. (13)
Stocker, S. E., Pte. (56)
Stocks, A., Pte'. (14)
Stokes, E. W., Pte. (90)
Stray, G., Pte. (56)
Stubbs, J. M., Pte. (17)
Stutter, J., Pte. (56)
Sumner, S. D. S., Pte. (75)
Sutton, W. W., Pte. (15)
Swannell, J. R., Pte. (13)

Rank and Name.

Tanner, E. S., Pte. (21)
Tawn, G. B., Pte. (16)
Taylor, A. S., Sgt. (77)
Taylor, Henry, Pte. (56)
Taylor, Horace, Pte. (14)
Taylor, J., L./Cpl. (22)
Teniers, R., Pte. (56)
Terrell, F. J., Pte. (26)
Terry, H. G., Pte. (50)
Thacker, C. P., Pte. (55)
Thornton, T. C., Pte. (56)
Thorogood, G. O., Pte. (71)
Thorogood, T., Pte. (28)
Thrussell, C., Pte. (13)
Thunder, J. E., Pte. (70)
Thurlow, R. J., Pte. (56)
Tickner, A. E., Pte. (19)
Tindell, A., L./Cpl. (56)
Tinsley, R., Pte. (18)
Tomlinson, C., Pte. (55)
Toms, C. A. G., Sgt. (72)
Toms, J. E., Pte. (13)
Tondeur, A. F., Pte. (13)
Treby, C. G., Pte. (92)
Trim, A. J., Pte. (21)
True, W. G., Pte. (13)
Tucker, C. S., Pte. (13)
Turnill, N., Pte. (14)
Tutty, J. C., Pte. (14)
Tweedale, A., Pte. (41)
Underhill, F. W., Pte. (95)
Underwood, C., Cpl. (14)
Valentine, W., Cpl. (55)
Veal, W. W., Pte. (14)
Wager, W. S., Pte. (47)
Walker, F. J., L./Cpl. (14)
Walker, W. H., Pte. (14)
Wallis, F., Pte. (26)
Walmisley-Dresser, H. J., Lieut.-Col. (81)
Walton, E. W., Pte. (71)
Walton, J. E., Lieut. (13)
Ward, U. W., Pte. (55)
Warland, F. L., Lieut. (55)
Warr, E. M., C.S.M. (74)
Warrington, H., Pte. (74)
Wassell, G. J., Pte. (56)
Watkins, R. J., Pte. (47)
Weatherley, S., Pte. (72)
Webb, F. W., Cpl. (56)
Weeks, W., Pte. (14)
Weller, W., Pte. (13)
Wells, T., L./Cpl. (49)
Wells, T., Pte. (13)
Welsh, W., Pte. (22)
Wenham, A., Pte. (56)
Westbrook, R., Pte. (14)
White, C. H., Pte. (56)
White, D. A., Pte. (13)
White, R. E., 2nd Lieut. (28)
Whitehead, H. W. W., Pte. (13)
Whitfield, S., Pte. (55)
Whiteway, E. V., M.C., Capt. (71)
Wicker, A. J., Pte. (55)
Wilkins, H. W., Pte. (72)
Wilkinson, B., Sgt. (56)
Williams, A. M., Pte. (33)
Williams, C., Pte. (26)
Williams, E. E., M.M., L./Cpl. (71)
Williams, S., Pte. (41)
Williams, W. C., L./Sgt. (72)
Willows, G. F., Pte. (32)
Wilson, J., Pte. (17)
Wolstenholme, J., Pte. (15)
Wood, A., Pte. (14)
Wood, Ernest, A., L./Cpl. (13)
Wood, Evelyn, Pte. (54)
Wood, H. E., Pte. (13)
Woodhams, J. H., Pte. (41)
Worrell, H., Pte. (14)
Wright, A. A., Capt. (14)
Wright, G. E., Pte. (28)
Wright, P. C., Pte. (21)
Wright, W. J., Pte. (26)
Wyatt, F., Pte. (13)
Yates, C. E., Pte. (14)

Index to location of Cemeteries and Memorials where the Fallen of the 12th Battalion East Surrey Regt. are buried or, having no known grave, are commemorated.

ENGLAND AND WALES:—

1. Brighton Borough Cemetery, Sussex (1)
2. Brighton and Preston Cemetery, Heathfield, Sussex (1)
3. Colchester Cemetery, Essex (1)
4. Croydon (Queens Road) Cemetery, Surrey (1)

London:

5. Battersea Cemetery, Morden, Surrey (1)
6. City of London and Tower Hamlets Cemetery, Stepney (1)
7. East London Cemetery, Plaistow (1)
8. Putney Vale Cemetery (1)
9. Long Ditton (St. Mary) Churchyard, Surrey (1)
10. Netley Military Cemetery, Hound., Hants. (1)
11. Burlingham St. Andrew Churchyard, Norfolk (1)
12. Cardiff Cemetery, Wales (1)

BELGIUM:—

13. Menin Gate Memorial, Ypres (69)
14. Tyne Cot Memorial, Passchendaele (108)
15. Ploegsteert (Hyde Park Corner) Memorial (6)
16. Courtrai (St. Jean) Communal Cemetery (4)
17. Dadizeele New British Cemetery (15)
18. Dickebusch New Military Cemetery (27)
19. Elverdinghe: Hagle Dump Cemetery (1)
20. Haringhe (Bandanghem) Military Cemetery, Haringhe-Rousbrugge (5)
21. Harlebeke New British Cemetery (19)
22. Heestert Military Cemetery (8)
23. Kemmel: Klein Vierstraat British Cemetery (2)
24. Moorseele Military Cemetery (4)
25. Moorseele: Kezelburg Military Cemetery (1)
26. Ploegsteert: London Rifle Brigade Cemetery (18)
27. Poperinghe: Gwalia Cemetery (1)
28. Poperinghe: Lijssenthoek Military Cemetery (32)
29. Poperinghe New Military Cemetery (3)
30. Proven: Mendinghem British Cemetery (5)
31. Reninghelst: Grootebeek British Cemetery (1)
32. Reninghelst: La Clytte Military Cemetery (7)
33. Reninghelst New Military Cemetery (3)
34. St. Genois Churchyard (1)
35. Sweveghem Churchyard (1)
36. Vlamertinghe: Brandhoek Military Cemetery (1)
37. Vlamertinghe: Brandhoek New Military Cemetery No. 3 (1)
38. Vlamertinghe New Military Cemetery (3)
39. Voormezeele: Bus House Cemetery (3)
40. Voormezeele Enclosures 1 and 2 (3)
41. Voormezeele Enclosures No. 3 (3)
42. Voormezeele: Oak Dump Cemetery (1)
43. Voormezeele: Ridge Wood Military Cemetery (3)
54. Wytschaete Military Cemetery (1)

FRANCE:—

44. Ypres: Duhallow A.D.S. Cemetery (2)
45. Ypres: Reservoir Cemetery (2)
46. Ypres: Town Cemetery Extension (Menin Gate) (9)
47. Zantvoorde British Cemetery (7)
48. Zillebeke: Bedford House Enclosure No. 3 (1)
49. Zillebeke: Bedford House Enclosure No. 4 (4)
50. Zillebeke: Hooge Crater Cemetery (9)
51. Zillebeke: Perth Cemetery (China Wall) (5)
52. Zillebeke: Larch Wood (Railway Cutting) Cemetery (2)
53. Zillebeke: Sanctuary Wood Cemetery (1)

FRANCE:—

55. Arras Memorial (53)
56. Thiepval Memorial (78)
57. Abbeville Communal Cemetery Extension (1)
58. Achiet Le Grand Communal Cemetery Extension (1)
59. Bailleul Communal Cemetery Extension (2)
60. Beaumont Hamel: Serre Road Cemetery No. 2 (1)
61. Boulogne Eastern Cemetery (5)
62. Bray-Sur-Somme: Bray Hill British Cemetery (1)
63. Bully-Grenay Communal Cemetery British Extension (1)
65. Cerisy Gailly French National Cemetery (1)
66. Chauny Communal Cemetery British Extension (1)
67. Douchy-les-Ayette British Cemetery (1)
64. Calais Southern Cemetery (1)
68. Doullens Communal Cemetery Extension No. 1 (1)
69. Eperlecques: Bleue Maison Military Cemetery (1)
70. Esquelbecq Military Cemetery (11)
71. Etaples Military Cemetery (14)
72. Flers: Bulls Road Cemetery (35)
73. Godewaersvelde British Cemetery (9)
74. Hazebrouck Communal Cemetery (3)
75. Hem Monacu: Hem Farm Military Cemetery (1)
76. Le Treport: Mont Huon Military Cemetery (1)
77. Les Boeufs: Guards Cemetery (3)
78. Longuenesse (St. Omer) Souvenir Cemetery (1)
79. Longueval: Caterpillar Valley Cemetery (2)
80. Mametz: Flatiron Copse Cemetery (1)
81. Maricourt L'Abbe: Heilly Station Cemetery (6)
82. Meaulte Military Cemetery (1)
83. Mory Abbey Military Cemetery (2)
84. Puchvillers British Cemetery (1)
85. Rouen: St. Sever Cemetery Extension (Grand Quevilly) (4)
86. Rouen: St. Sever Cemetery Extension (Petit Quevilly) (1)
87. Sans Les Marquion: Ontario Cemetery (1)
88. Tamines Communal Cemetery (1)
89. Vichte Military Cemetery (1)
90. Wimille: Terlincthum British Cemetery (7)

GERMANY:—

91. Berlin South Western Cemetery, Stahnsdorf (1)
92. Cologne Southern Cemetery (2)
93. Hamburg Cemetery, Ohlsdorf (2)

ITALY:—

94. Arquata Scrivia Communal Cemetery Extension (1)
95. Bordighera British Cemetery (1)
96. Genoa: Staglieno Cemetery (1)
97. Giavera British Cemetery (3)
98. Oneglia Town Cemetery (1)
99. Tezze British Cemetery (1)

NOTE.—**The figures in brackets at the end of the name of the cemetery or memorial represent the number of old comrades buried in the cemetery or commemorated on the memorial.**

HONOURS, DECORATIONS AND AWARDS GRANTED TO MEMBERS OF THE 12TH BATTALION.

DISTINGUISHED SERVICE ORDER:—

Brown, G. L., Lieut.-Col.
Knapp, C., Lieut.-Col.
Pennell, R., Major (A./Lieut.-Col.)

MILITARY CROSS AND TWO BARS:—

Rogers, J. A., Capt.

MILITARY CROSS AND ONE BAR:—

Mutch, W. D. D., Lieut.
Walker, H. S., Capt.

MILITARY CROSS:—

Bailey, H. P., 2nd Lieut.
Beechman, H. A., 2nd Lieut.
Christie, G. W., R.A.M.C., Capt.
Copp, A. V., Capt.
Davenport, G. C., Lieut.
Dowling, F. B. B., Capt.
Edgar, A. C., Capt.
Fisher, C. H., 2nd Lieut.
Harrison, W. L. A., R.A.M.C., Capt.
Horswell, B. P., C.S.M.
Howitt, A. G., Capt.
Howship, R. F., 2nd Lieut.
Jessop, F. D., Capt.
Lloyd, T. H., Lieut.
Mackintosh, A. M., 2nd Lieut.
McKechnie, R., Lieut.
McWalter, T. B., Lieut.
Openshaw, H. S., Capt.
Palk, W. J., Lieut.
Reynolds, T. E. S., Lieut.
Ryan, E. St. J., Capt.
Samuels, F. A., Lieut.
Sleath, G. G. W., 2nd Lieut.
Summers, W. G., D.C.M., M.M., 2nd Lieut.
Tamblyn, J. F., Lieut.
Todd, H. S., Capt.
Walker, D., Capt.
Ward, C. H., Lieut.
White, G. L., Lieut.
Whiteway, E. V.. Capt.

DISTINGUISHED CONDUCT MEDAL:—

Carter, W., Sgt.
Donnely, J., Sgt.
Giles, A. B., Pte.
Hill, W. C., C.S.M.
Huggett, P., Pte.
James, F. T., Sgt.
Love, C. J., R.S.M.
Mayston, R. W., C.S.M.
Mills, H., Sgt.
Mutimer, R. J., Sgt.
Philpott, N. A., Cpl.
Prosser, G. D., C.S.M.
Sherborne, H. J., Pte.
Trussler, A. W., Cpl.

MILITARY MEDAL AND ONE BAR:—

Greaves, J. G., Sgt.
Hall, W. G., C.S.M.
Hammond, G., C.S.M.
Haxton, W., L./Cpl.
Huxley, G. L., L./Cpl.
Kenyon, H., Cpl.
Pocock, A., Pte.
Rogers, J. R., Cpl.
Southall, L. C., Cpl.
Staines, D., Sgt.

MILITARY MEDAL:—

Aitken, W. A., L./Cpl.
Baker, J. A., L./Cpl.
Barnes, W., C.Q.M.S.
Beck, A., Pte.
Bolton, E. E., L./Cpl.
Brand, A. E., Pte.
Brewster, S. G., L./Cpl.
Broderick, A., Pte.
Budd, P. J., Pte.
Bunnet, G., L./Cpl.
Butler, F. A., Pte.
Butlin, B. C., L./Cpl.
Calver, R. J., C.Q.M.S.
Camp, W. C., Pte.
Challis, D. J. S., Pte.
Chappell, T., Pte.
Church, G., Cpl.
Clarke, T., Pte.
Coghlan, M., Cpl.
Cole, W., Pte.
Collins, A. E., Pte.
Collins, R., L./Cpl.
Conner, E., Pte.
Coomes, F. C., Pte.
Court, S. J., Pte.
Cousins, F., Pte.
Coutts, D., Pte.
Creasey, W., L./Cpl.
Cunningham, T., Pte.
Davey, E., Sgt.
Davey, F., Pte.
Daw, C., Pte.
Dawe, J., L./Sgt.
Dennington, A. F., Pte.
Dickson, M., Sgt.
Donaldson, C., Pte.
Dove, J., L./Cpl.
Draper, J. H. W., Cpl.
Drinkwater, J., Sgt.
Durrant, A., Cpl.
Fanner, F. H., Pte.
Felstead, W., L./Cpl.
Floyd, A., Pte.
George, J. T., Pte.
George, O. J., L./Cpl.
Hammond, W., Pte.
Harbridge, E., Pte.
Head, A. F., Pte.
Hester, J., Pte.
Hill, W. G., C.S.M.
Hoare, A., L./Cpl.

MILITARY MEDAL:—

Humphreys, W. C., Pte.
Hurran, G. P., Sgt.
Jones, G., L./Cpl.
Keith, H. C., Pte.
James, F. T., Sgt.
James, W., L./Cpl.
Ketley, N. J., L./Cpl.
Kitchen, A. R., L./Cpl.
Langley, R., Sgt.
Lattimore, S., Sgt.
Long, T. W., Cpl.
Lewis, J., Sgt.
Lugo, E., Pte.
Lynch, D., Pte.
McKenzie, T. G., Sgt.
Maddison, D., C.S.M.
Mallett, W. R. G., Cpl.
Maguire, C., Sgt.
Malone, J., L./Cpl.
Manley, H., Pte.
Mann, W. H., Sgt.
Mayston, R. W., C.S.M.
Mills, H., Sgt.
Moore, T., Pte.
Morris, E., L./Cpl.
Newble, P. E., Sgt.
Newton, J., Cpl.
O'Malley, M. D., Pte.
Pegg, A., Pte.
Ponman, G., L./Cpl.
Radcliffe, J. F., Sgt.
Ralphs, J., L./Cpl.
Richardson, H. C., L./Cpl.
Rice, H. C., Pte.

Record, P., Pte.
Rochford, T., Pte.
Roud, G., Pte.
Rutty, J., Pte.
Sadler, R., L./Cpl.
Sadler, S. J., Pte.
Sarvant, S. F., Cpl.
Savage, E. J., Pte.
Scott, H. W., Pte.
Seaman, R., Pte.
Simpson, G. W., C.S.M.
Smith, E. A., Sgt.
Smith, G., L./Cpl.
Smith, W. A., Pte.
Smith, W. E., Cpl.
Southwood, W. A., Pte.
Spriggs, Z., Pte.
Stenton, G. E., Pte.
Thompson, A. V. N., Sgt.
Thompson, W. J., L./Cpl.
Tilley, W. H., Pte.
Trout, J. W., Pte.
Trussler, A. W., Cpl.
Turner, C., Pte.
Turner, C. W., Sgt.
Tustin, C., Pte.
Varrow, W. J., L./Cpl.
Waddingham, S. J., L./Cpl.
Watts, R., L./Cpl.
Wells, H., Pte.
West, E. C., L./Cpl.
Wilkins, G., L./Cpl.
Williams, E. E., L./Cpl.
Woodcock, S., Cpl.
Young, T. J., Sgt.

MERITORIOUS SERVICE MEDAL:—

Elliott, G., Sgt.
Field, C. W., Sgt.
Lunn, L. C., Sgt.
Nuttman, G., Sgt.
Saunders, D., R.S.M.
Speller, N., R.Q.M.S.
Turner, W., Sgt.

CROIX DE GUERRE—FRENCH:—

Bailey, E. J., Cpl.
Brown, G. L., Lieut.-Col.
Brewster, S. G., L./Cpl.
Felstead, W., L./Cpl.
George. O. J., L./Cpl.
Mills, H., Sgt.
Steer, W. J., C.Q.M.S.

CROIX DE GUERRE—BELGIAN:—

Burgess, B. G., Sgt.
Goble, F., Cpl.
Hall. W., C.S.M.
McFie, J., Cpl.
Mayston, R. W., C.S.M.
Reeves, G., Pte.
Rodd, A. J., 2nd Lieut.
Todd, H. S., Capt.

MEDAILLE MILITAIRE (*avec palme*)—BELGIAN:—

Hall, W., C.S.M.
James, F. T., Sgt.

MENTIONED IN DESPATCHES:—

Acklin, L. H., Pte.
Burgess, B. G., Sgt.
Cleave, J. H., A./R.S.M.
Dennington, A. F., Pte.
Dowling, F. B. B., Capt.
Durrant, A., Cpl.
Hagen, W., Capt.
Haine, R. N., Lieut.
Hall, W., C.S.M.
Hall, W. S., Lieut.
Hammond, G., C.S.M.
Lattimore, S., Sgt.
Lee, H. H., D.S.O., Lieut.-Col.
Love, C. J., R.S.M.
Lunn, L. C., Sgt.
McSweeney, J., Pte.
Matthews, F. R., Lieut.
Osborn, E. I., Sgt.
Reah, G. P. G., Capt.
Speller, N., R.Q.M.S.
Stallard, C. F., Major
Tice, H. E., C.Q.M.S.
Webster, S. T., Pte.
Williams, C. T., Major

ROLL OF OFFICERS WHO SERVED WITH THE BATTALION.

Lieut.-Col. L. F. Beatson, O.B.E.
" G. L. Brown, D.S.O.
" E. Knapp, D.S.O.
" H. H. Lee, D.S.O.
" H. J. Walmisley-Dresser.

Major (A./Lieut.-Col.) C. H. Kitching
" R. Pennell, D.S.O., M.C.
" A. W. Puttick, M.C.
" C. F. Stallard, M.C.

MAJORS

H. de C. Blakeney
C. C. Clifton
R. E. C. Edye
L. H. Hickson
G. O. Searle
L. Tenbosch
C. T. Williams

CAPTAINS

F. R. Barry
H. Benbow
R. A. V. Brearey
Z. N. Brooke
J. L. Buckman
G. P. Cooper
A. V. Copp, M.C.
A. D. Crow
F. B. B. Dowling, M.C.
R. A. Down
A. C. Edgar, M.C.
A. R. K. Edsell
A. Fewings
E. B. Gillett
W. Hagen
A. G. Howitt, M.C.
F. D. Jessop, M.C.
D. McCallum
J. A. C. McCalman
R. A. McCulloch
E. Newington
H. S. Openshaw, M.C.
C. N. Pridham
G. P. G. Reah
A. V. Reiner
H. C. Reynard
J. A. Rogers, M.C.
R. O. Russell, M.C.
E. St. J. Ryan, M.C.
C. O. Slacke
—. Spencer
H. S. Todd, M.C.
J. W. Tunwell
D. Walker, M.C.
H. S. Walker, M.C.
E. V. Whiteway, M.C.
A. A. Wright
C. York-Davis

LIEUTS and 2nd LIEUTS.

C. K. Adams.
L. H. Aldridge
J. Aston
E. Aucutt
H. P. Bailey, M.C.
A. V. Baker
J. Baker
R. C. Baker
K. G. Bancroft
J. W. Barrow
E. H. Barry
W. D. Bayliss
F. Beard
C. J. F. Beauchamp
L. S. Beaufoy
H. A. Beechman, M.C.
A. E. Bell
S. E. Bennett
W. H. C. Binns
G. G. Briggs
R. D. Brown
R. F. Browne
W. E. Bundy
J. C. Carver
J. R. Chesters
L. V. W. Clark
V. L. Clift
J. R. A. Cockayne
F. Combe-Ceaton
W. B. Cooke
A. C. Cowlin
F. W. Crafter
J. E. M. Crowther
G. C. Davenport, M.C.
R. W. Davis
L. Dawson
B. F. Dodd
E. M. Dove
A. T. Duncan
H. N. Dunkley
R. E. Edwards
W. M. Edwards
F. C. Ells
T. H. Elphicke
A. W. England
C. F. W. Faith
C. H. Fisher, M.C.
C. C. Fox
G. H. Frischling
O. A. George
P. J. Gibbons
H. D. Gold
J. A. Golding
H. G. Graves
W. Greenhill
R. W. Gurran
R. N. Haine
W. S. Hall
N. G. W. Hancock
F. J. Harding
C. R. Haynes
G. E. Head
A. Hemsley
T. C. Hill
R. F. Howship, M.C.
L. C. A. Hudson
W. V. B. Hughes
L. McL. Hutcheson
P. V. James
A. G. Jennings
L. H. Jennings
R. C. Johns
M. T. Johnson
P. R. Johnston
T. B. Jolly
B. E. Langford
S. Lasenby
R. C. Latham
K. L. S. Lawton
C. C. A. Lee
F. E. Lewis
A. T. Libby
L. L. Linford
T. H. Lloyd, M.C.
A. M. Mackintosh, M.C.
R. McKechnie, M.C.
T. B. McWalter, M.C.
F. R. Matthews
R. M. Meadows
W. L. Miller
S. H. Morgan
E. L. Morley
M. C. Morris
W. D. Mutch, M.C.
R. Northwood
R. L. Oates
W. J. Palk, M.C.
L. W. Paviour
H. T. Pike
J. H. H. Pritchard
A. R. Puttock
F. C. Reed
T. E. S. Reynolds, M.C.
L. Roberts, M.C.
(Attd. 6th R.W.S.)
W. G. Robinson
A. J. Rodd
L. A. Rossiter
L. W. B. Russell
F. A. Samuels, M.C.
J. H. H. Sands
J. H. Savage, M.M.
G. S. Saville
W. P. Selbie
C. C. Simpson
C. W. Skellett
G. C. W. Sleath, M.C.
C. L. Smith
G. E. Smith
J. W. Staddon
B. C. Stenning
A. Stephens
S. Stimson
A. Straker
W. G. T. Summers, M.C., D.C.M., M.M.
E. W. Symons
J. F. Tamblyn, M.C.
P. W. Targett
J. T. Thornton
A. F. Topham
W. A. Vanner
B. E. C. Walker
J. Walker
J. C. Waller
J. F. Walton
C. H. Ward, M.C.
L. A. Ward
F. L. Warland
A. K. Watts
C. A. V. Watts*
S. A. Wheeler
G. L. White, M.C.
R. E. White
A. R. Wilkins
H. E. Winder
O. E. Woollard

HON. LIEUTS. and QMRS.

H. Amoore
W. W. Easter
G. Haydock
G. W. Lander
W. McEnuff

R.A.M.C. MEDICAL OFFICERS

Capt. C. N. Binney
Lieut. C. Cameron
Capt. G. W. Christie, M.C.
Capt. J. J. H. Ferguson, M.C.
Lieut. F. Gamm
Capt. W. L. A. Harrison, M.C.
Capt. R. T. Herdman
Lieut. E. C. Lambert
Capt. C. Newton-Bennett
Lieut. L. W. Oliver
Capt. H. H. Prentiss
Lieut. F. W. Wilson
Lieut. G. W. Young

*Also served as a private in the Battalion.

NOMINAL ROLL OF OTHER RANKS WHO SERVED WITH THE BATTALION, OTHER THAN THOSE ALREADY MENTIONED IN THE APPENDICES.

Abbott, H.
Abbott, H. L.
Abbott, W. J.
Abrehart, G. T.
Ackland, G.
Acraman, E. G.
Adams, E. E.
Adams, F. J.
Adams, H. (11091)
Adams, H. (14233)
Adams, W. (17051)
Adams, W. (25995)
Adams, W. H.
Adcock, E. S.
Adlington, G.
Agar, F. W.
Ainge, C. A.
Akers, A. W.
Alberici, L.
Albrice, J.
Alden, A. W.
Alderman, R.
Alderson, E.
Aldridge, T.
Alexander, E.
Alexander, W.
Allam, C. G.
Allard, R. B.
Alldis, A. (12547)
Alldis, A. (37155)
Alldis, H.
Alldridge, H. G.
Allen, A.
Allen, A. E.
Allen, A. T.
Allen, E. J.
Allen, F.
Allen, F. R.
Allen, G. H.
Allen, G. W.
Allen, H.
Allen, J. (14300)
Allen, J. (202265)
Allen, M. K.
Allery, H.
Allmand, E. H.
Allsup, H.
Ambrose, C.
Ambrose, W.
Anderson, A.
Anderson, D.
Anderson, J.
Anderson, R.
Anderson, T. E.
Anderson, W. J.
Andrews, A. W.
Andrews, F. C. G.
Andrews, H.
Andrews, J.
Andrews, S. J.
Angell, A. E.
Angus, J.
Annetts, W. T.
Ansell, F. G.
Anthony, R.
Appleby, E.
Apps, R. J.
Argent, H. J.
Aris, A. S.
Aris, C. C. (12711)
Aris, C. C. (204024)
Armes, G.
Armitage, W. H.
Arnold, F.
Arnold, F. B.
Arnold, G. E.
Arnold, W.
Arnold, W. G.
Arnott, J.
Arnott, J. W.
Arthur, W. H.
Ash, E.
Ash, W.
Ash, J. W.
Ashby, C.
Ashby, E. G.
Ashby, H. L.
Ashelford, A. W.
Ashelford, G.
Ashley, H. J. A.
Ashley, J. W.
Ashpole, C. W.
Aslin, W.
Aspin, J.
Aston, G.
Atkin, R.
Atkins, E. (7694)
Atkins, E. (26992)
Atkins, H.
Atkinson, G. P.
Attoe, T. W.
Attridge, A.
Aubrey, E.
Austin, F.
Avery, A.
Aves, E.
Aviston, R.
Axford, A. T.
Ayers, S.
Aylen, L.
Ayling, W. T.
Aylott, F.
Aylward, S.
Aylward, W.
Ayres, A.
Back, R.
Bacon, B.
Bacon, G.
Badham, F. A.
Bagnall, S.
Bailey, A.
Bailey, C. J.
Bailey, F. J.
Bailey, G.
Bailey, H. (12661)
Bailey, H. (32251)
Bailey, R. C.
Bailey, S.
Bailey, T. G.
Bailey, W. H.
Baird, A.
Baker, A.
Baker (4141)
Baker, D.
Baker, E. (17501)
Baker, F.
Baker, G. E.
Baker, J. (12996)
Baker, J. (20829)
Baker, J. E.
Baker, W. H.
Baker, W. J.
Balch, T. E.
Balcombe, C. S.
Balcombe, W. H.
Baldock, T. H.
Baldwin, F. G.
Baldwin, T.
Ball, W.
Ball, W. H.
Ballard, A. H.
Balman, W. J.
Bamber, H.
Bament, J. W.
Banfield, G.
Banger, E. F. J.
Banks, F. G.
Banks, J.
Barden, W. F.
Barfield, V.
Bargen, J.
Barham, A.
Barham, P. E.
Barham, W.
Barker, G. (25255)
Barker, G. (34342)
Barker, H.
Barker, R.
Barker, S.
Barker, S. W.
Barker, W. F.
Barlthrop, F. J.
Barnard, E. A.
Barnard, F. A.
Barnes, A.
Barnes, G.
Barnes, P.
Barnett, A. E.
Barnett, B.
Barnett, F.
Barnett, H.
Baron, E. C.
Barr, P.
Barrans, E.
Barrett, F. (204555)
Barringer, H. J.
Barron, H. (20911)
Barron, H. (37567)
Barrow, A. E.
Barry, F.
Barry, M.
Barry, T.
Barson, E. C.
Bartlett, E. G.
Bartlett, H.
Bartlett, W. R.
Barton, A.
Barton, H.
Bartram, S. W.
Bashford, A.
Bashford, J.
Bass, A. W.
Bassett, W.
Basted, A.
Batchelor, A.
Batchelor, C.
Batchelor, G.
Batchelor, H. M.
Bateman, H.
Bateman, H. J.
Bates, A. C. S.
Bates, F.
Batey, H.
Bath, C.
Battersby, F. W.
Battes, P.
Baughan, H.
Baxter, P. (9064)
Baylis, D.
Baylis, F. H.
Bayliss, J.
Baysting, A. W.
Bayton, W. C.
Beach, B.
Beach, E. C.
Beacham, C. H.
Beadle, G. J.
Beadle, W.
Beasley, R.
Beard, F.
Beard, J. (12343)
Beard, J. (204086)
Beardwell, F.
Beaumont, C. A.
Beaumont, G.
Beckett, F. J.
Beckingham, J.
Bedingfield, C. R.
Bednell, W. G.
Bedwell, A. W.
Beech, G.
Beechey, S.
Behannon, G. W.
Belchamber, L.
Bell, S.
Bendall, H. C.
Bending, W.
Benham, S. A.
Bennett, C. W. O.
Bennett, J. F.
Bennett, J. R.
Bennett, J. W. (14310)
Bennett, J. W. (14321)
Bennett, S.
Bennett, F. C.
Bennett, G. H.
Bennett, R.
Bennett, S.
Bennett, W.
Bennett, W. F.
Bennett, W. S.
Benniman, F.
Benson, W. A.
Bentley, H.
Bentley, J.
Bentley, L.
Bentley, T. E.
Bernas, A.
Berwick, C.
Berry, A. C.
Berry, H.
Best, J. C.
Best, W. L.
Betts, G.
Betts, H.
Bevan, P.
Beveridge, J.
Beveridge, S.
Bewley, J. W.
Bexley, A.
Bezant, J.
Bibby, H. (16114)
Bibby, H. (204019)
Bicknell, S.
Bicknell, S. J.
Biggerstaffe, A. E.
Biggin, F. J.
Biggs, A. A.
Billam, C.
Billingsley, W.
Binns, S.
Birch, H. (547)
Birch, H. (242207)
Birch, L.
Bird, A. (25147)
Bird, A. (25301)
Bird, T. F.
Bird, T. F. J.
Birmingham, W. A.
Birtchenell, P. J.
Bishop, C. J.
Bishop, F.
Bishop, H. J.
Bishop, W. (12156)
Bishop, W. (17915)
Bisson, W. J.
Blackford, F.
Blackford, O. G.
Blacklin, R. D.
Blackman, C.
Blackman, F.
Blackman, J. A.
Blackmore, A.
Blackmore, S. R.
Blackwell, F. T. G.
Blagden, A. J.
Blagdon, A. J.
Blain, F. H. G.
Blake, A.
Blake, W. A.
Blaker, E.
Blake, F. C.
Blake, G.
Blake, H. G.
Blaker, W. J.
Blanchard, J. E.
Bland, B.
Blandford, S.
Blaney, A. E.

Blatch, T.
Blatch, W.
Blencowe, R.
Bliss, F. W.
Bliss, H.
Bloomfield, R.
Blowers, S. G.
Blows, E. J.
Blundell, A.
Blundell, L. E.
Blunt, G.
Blyth, G. A.
Blyth, T. B.
Boatfield, J. H.
Boddington, T. H.
Bodley, J. J.
Body, H. G.
Boeg, J.
Bolton, F.
Bolton, W.
Bolton, W. G.
Bolton, W. H.
Bond, A. W.
Bond, L. C. H.
Bonfield, P. V.
Booth, J. C.
Booth, W.
Bostridge, W.
Botting, A.
Boulter, H.
Bourne, G. P.
Bourne, R.
Bournes, E.
Bowden, C. H.
Bowdery, W.
Bowen, A.
Bowen, N.
Bowen, W.
Bowerman, L.
Bowers, T. W.
Bowler, F.
Bowler, J. G.
Bowler, W.
Bowles, A.
Bowles, C.
Box, G. C.
Boxall, F. L.
Boyer, G. W.
Bozzett, W. T.
Bracken, E.
Brackett, J.
Bradbury, H. E.
Bradford, W. J.
Bradshaw, A. E.
Bradshaw, J.
Bradshaw, V. H.
Bradshaw, W.
Brady, A.
Brady, T.
Bragg, R.
Braim, J.
Bramley, P.
Brawn, E.
Brazier, J.
Brenchley, R. P.
Brenchley, W. E.
Brest, A. G.
Brett, H.
Brewer, F. W.
Brewer, H. J.
Brewin, J. T.
Brewster, W.
Brewster, W. J.
Brice, E. L.
Bridge, C. W.
Bridger, A. A.
Briggs, G. J.
Briggs, J. W.
Bright, A. E.
Bright, M.
Brinson, F. P.
Briscey, C. H.
Brisenden, D.
Brister, T. A. C.
Broadley, W. H.
Bromley, A.
Brondon, G.
Brook, A. B.
Brooker, R.
Brooker, T. F.
Brookes, F. L.
Brookling, A. T.
Brookman, W.
Brookman, W. T.
Brooks, A.
Brooks, F. W.
Brook, K.
Browett, A.
Brown, C. (2274).
Brown, E. (3097).
Brown, E. (12757).
Brown, E. (17640).
Brown, E. J.
Brown, F.
Brown, G.
Brown, H. (1126).
Brown, H. (12815).
Brown, H. C.
Brown, J. D.
Brown, J. W.
Brown, N.
Brown, P. (12314).
Brown, P. (26782).
Brown, R.
Brown, S. F.
Brown, T. (12418).
Brown, T. (23497).
Brown, T. J.
Brown, V. (38080).
Brown, V. (204557).
Brown, V. J.
Brown, W. (12071).
Brown, W. (12112).
Brown, W. (25300).
Brown, W. (241577).
Browne, P. J.
Browne, S. C.
Bryan, C. G.
Bryant, C.
Buckland, A. B.
Buckland, L.
Buckle, F. A.
Buckley, J.
Buckley, L.
Bucknell, A. E.
Budd, H.
Bugden, S.
Buggy, J. W.
Bulbrook, R. W.
Bull, A. R. H.
Bull, J.
Bullard, F.
Bullard, G. W.
Bulley, A. E.
Bullock, F. C.
Bunn, F.
Bunting, H. C.
Burbridge, A.
Burden, D.
Burden, H.
Burden, W.
Burford, C. A.
Burgess, A.
Burgess, C.
Burgess, J.
Burgess, J. H.
Burgess, M. C.
Burgess, R. E.
Burgoyne, A.
Burke, T.
Burkin, G. W.
Burles, G.
Burnand, H.
Burnett, F. O.
Burnham, J.
Burns, F. J.
Burr, C.
Burrill, R.
Burrows, A.
Burrows, G.
Burry, R.
Burton, A.
Busby, H.
Busby, W. H.
Busher, C. C.
Buswell, J.
Butcher, C.
Butcher, C. W.
Butcher, E.
Bute, A.
Butler, A. H.
Butler, E.
Butler, E. J.
Butler, G.
Butt, J.
Butterworth, R.
Buttery, A. E.
Button, J. H.
Button, J. P.
Button, O. W.
Byford, W.
Byles, A.
Cairns, G.
Cake, C. H.
Callaghan, J.
Calnon, J.
Cambridge, F.
Cantallow, P.
Capleton, W. C.
Capp, J. W.
Carey, A. (24822)
Carlton, G. W.
Carmichael, G.
Carney, H. W.
Carpenter, A.
Carpenter, E.
Carpenter, J.
Carr, A. A.
Carr, E. E.
Carr, P. L.
Carrell, A. T.
Carroll, J.
Carrod, P.
Carrodus, H. W.
Carter, C. E.
Carter, C. T.
Carter, F. W.
Carter, H. A.
Carter, J. T.
Carter, J. W.
Carter, S.
Carter, W. (26758).
Carter, W. (32756).
Cartmell, G.
Cartwright, J.
Cartwright, J. S.
Casbolt, H. J.
Case, G. A.
Case, H. C.
Cassidy, R.
Cathie, E. C.
Catt, W. J.
Causebrook, J. E.
Chalk, G.
Challis, F.
Chamberlain, J.
Chambers, H. R.
Chambers, P. H.
Champion, M.
Chandler, W. H.
Chapman, E.
Chapman, H.
Chapman, J. W.
Chapman, M. E.
Chapman, R.
Chapman, R. J.
Chapman, W. C.
Charles, G. E.
Charlwood, W. A.
Chase, A.
Chase, E. R.
Chatfield, R.
Chatters, C. A.
Chattle, V. K.
Cheeseman, H.
Cheeseman, J.
Chennell, F. G.
Chifney, J. E.
Child, A.
Childs, A.
Childs, A. W.
Childs, J.
Chillingworth, C. H.
Chismon, G. A.
Chitty, F. W. C.
Choat, R.
Chubb, T. A.
Chudley, H. E.
Church, F. G.
Church, F. W.
Church, H. J.
Clack, A. W.
Clacy, C.
Claridge, H. A.
Claridge, G. J.
Clark, A. F.
Clark, A. G.
Clark, E. (12226).
Clark, E. (29427).
Clark, G.
Clark, H.
Clark, H. J.
Clark, T. A.
Clark, W.
Clark, W. J.
Clarke, A. N.
Clarke, C.
Clarke, E.
Clarke, E. A.
Clarke, E. F.
Clarke, E. R.
Clarke, H. A.
Clarke, H. W.
Clarke, J.
Clarke, L. R.
Clarke, S.
Clarke, W.
Clatworthy, E.
Claxton, G.
Claxton, R.
Claxton, W.
Clayton, W. G.
Clements, E.
Clements, W. A.
Clews, W. A.
Clifford, R. F.
Clifford, H.
Clifton, F.
Clifton, F. J.
Clinche, W. A.
Clist, H. G.
Clover, F.
Coates, A.
Coates, J. R.
Cobb, C.
Cobb, W.
Cobbard, D.
Cobham, J. E.
Cockerton, J. G.
Cocks, G. C.
Cocks, R. F.
Coe, A. E.
Coffin, P.
Coggins, W. G.
Cole, A. C.
Cole, A. T.
Cole, C. (12955)
Cole, C. (14231).
Cole, F.
Cole, J. (17338).
Cole, J. (30628).
Cole, J. H.
Cole, P. J.
Cole, W. G.
Coleman, J. A.
Coleman, L.
Coleman, P.
Coleman, R.
Coleman, S. F.
Coleman, W. W.
Coles, S. C.
Coles, F.
Coles, G.
Collett, W. J. L.
Collier, E. J.
Collier, H. A.
Collier, R.
Collier, R. W.
Collins, A. W.
Collins, E. J.
Collins, E. W.
Collins, H.
Collins, M. F.
Collins, R.
Collins, S.
Collins, W. R.

Collinson, J.
Collis, H.
Colls, C. C.
Colstone, E.
Colton, D.
Colwell, H. R.
Comber, R.
Conche, A.
Condon, W.
Congrave, J.
Connell, A.
Connor, H.
Conoway, T. C.
Constable, E. E. F.
Conybeare, J. W.
Cook, A. E.
Cook, A. W.
Cook, E. T.
Cook, J.
Cook, J. G.
Cook, N. G.
Cook, P. W.
Cook, T.
Cooke, F. C.
Cooksey, E.
Cooley, J. E.
Coombes, A. L.
Cooper, A.
Cooper, A. B.
Cooper, A. W.
Cooper, C. D.
Cooper, F. (2947)
Cooper, F. (17267).
Cooper, F. R.
Cooper, H.
Cooper, J.
Cooper, L.
Cooper, P. H.
Cooper, R. (16159).
Cooper, R. (25202).
Cooper, W.
Cooper, W. H.
Coote, G.
Cope, E.
Cope, J.
Cope, S.
Coram, E.
Cornelius, P.
Cornish, A. H. G.
Cornish, E. J.
Cornish, F.
Cornish, P.
Cornish, W. G.
Cossburn, J. W.
Coster, A.
Coston, J. W.
Cottam, T.
Cotter, H.
Coughlan, W.
Couldridge, T. F.
Coulson, R.
Coulton, A.
Courteney, E. F.
Cousen, P. B.
Cousins, C. J. F.
Cousins, E. G.
Coutts, W.
Couzens, F.
Covill, T.
Cowan, P.
Cowdroy, G.
Cowey, T.
Cowhig, C.
Cowlin, F. K.
Cox, A.
Cox, A. W.
Cox, G. E.
Cox, H. E.
Cox, J. (19139).
Cox, J. (32313).
Cox, M.
Cox, R.
Cox, W.
Coyne, M.
Crabtree, J. W.
Craddock, H. A.
Craig, T.
Cramp, W. R.
Cranstone, E.
Crawford, J. (12992).
Crawford, J. (26099)
Crawley, E.
Crawley, G.
Crawley, W.
Craydon, H. M.
Cream, W.
Creamer, A.
Creamer, J.
Creed, C. A.
Creed, E. T.
Creek, H.
Cressey, J.
Crighton, F.
Cripps, A. E.
Cripps, J.
Critcher, E.
Crittenden, A. J.
Crockett, G.
Croft, H.
Croker, W. R.
Crompton, J.
Cronin, J.
Crook, F.
Croome, R. W.
Crosby, H. E.
Cross, W.
Cross, W. A.
Crouch, W.
Croucher, H. J.
Crowther, R.
Croxford, W.
Croxford, W. G.
Cullabine, N. C.
Culley, H.
Culling, E.
Cunningham, E.
Currie, E.
Curtis, C. (337).
Curtis, C. (17084).
Curtis, E.
Curtis, H. G.
Curzon, C. W.
Curzon, R.
Custance, A.
Cutler, J. W.
Cutmore, E. H.
Dalby, C. J.
Dale, H. (25494).
Dale, H. (38793).
Dalligan, A.
Dalligan, J.
Dalpiaz, J.
Dalton, R. G. F.
Dalveen, W. R.
Daly, J.
Dance, E. G.
Daniell, N.
Daniells, H. J.
Daniells, J.
Daniells, W. C.
Daniels, G. (25223).
Daniels, G. (203303).
Daniels, H.
Darby, H.
Dark, J.
Dark, T.
Darkin, J. F.
Darling, A.
Daughterly, A. L.
Davey, A. (12349).
Davey, A. (49094).
Davidson, H.
Davies, A. H. E.
Davies, E.
Davies, F. (23472).
Davies, F. (25351).
Davies, G.
Davies, J. (25282).
Davies, J. (609).
Davies, J. (29361).
Davies, J. (32302).
Davies, T.
Davis, A.
Davis, C. F.
Davis, C. R.
Davis, D. W. (12612).
Davis, D. W. (34518).
Davis, G.
Davis, J.
Davis, T. J. (15851).
Davis, T. J. (242739).
Davis, W.
Davis, W. D.
Davy, R.
Daw, W.
Dawkes, J.
Dawson, A.
Day, A.
Day, C.
Day, C. H.
Day, H.
Day, J.
Day, R. A.
Day, T.
Day, W. T.
Deacon, A.
Deacon, F. G.
Deadman, G. A.
Deadman, R.
Deadman, W. J.
Deakins, P. J.
Deamer, G.
Deamer, W.
Dean, A. (6830).
Dean, A. (26804).
Dean, F.
Dean, H.
Dean, P.
Dean, W. A.
Dear, T.
Dearman, W. (12128).
Dearman, W. (14273).
Debenham, E. W.
Dedman, J.
Deeprose, H. F.
Degray, D.
Delaney, A.
Denby, F.
Denese, J. G.
Denham, H. J.
Denton, A.
Denyer, A.
Denyer, F.
Denzey, H.
Depledge, J.
DePothonier, F. G.
Dew, A. W.
Dewbury, A.
Dewdney, F.
Dewe, E. H.
Dexter, G. S.
Diales, R.
Dibdin, C. T.
Dickens, A. H.
Dickeson, M.
Dickinson, P.
Dilley, E.
Dilley, H.
Dimmock, S.
Dimmock, W. A.
Dineen, J.
Dinkele, C. W.
Dix, H. G.
Dixon, A.
Dixon, F. W.
Dixon, G. E.
Dixon, R.
Dixon, T.
Docura, J.
Dodd, G. H.
Dodman, C.
Dodshon, F. G.
Doherty, S.
Dolton, W. L.
Donaldson, E.
Donn, E.
Donovan, J. A.
Dooley, T.
Dore, R. H.
Dorney, J.
Dorrell, A.
Doubtfire, H.
Doughty, J. G. C.
Douthwaite, B. W.
Down, A.
Down, A. W.
Downard, A.
Downie, W.
Downing, P.
Downs, A.
Downs, G. C.
Downs, H. J.
Drake, S. E.
Draper, W.
Drawbridge, J.
Drenon, C.
Drew, A. J.
Drew, C. R.
Driscoll, H.
Driscoll, M. P.
Driver, C.
Dumbrell, W.
Drury, R.
Ducker, A.
Dudley, J.
Dudley, R. G.
Dudman, S. F.
Duffield, J.
Duggan, L. M.
Dunbar, C. F.
Duncan, G. P. W.
Duncan, J. S.
Duncan, R.
Dunham, G.
Dunkley, H. J.
Dunkley, W.
Dunn, W.
Dunstan, T. P.
Durbridge, E.
Durrant, L.
Duthie, C. A.
Dwan, T.
Dyer, G.
Dyson, F.
Eagle, R.
Eaglen, W. J.
Eagles, A. C.
Eagling, A.
Eales, S.
Earley, A.
East, C.
East, G.
East, W. H.
Easter, A. E.
Easter, E. E.
Eastlake, C.
Eastland, W. A.
Easton, L. E.
Easton, S. H.
Eaton, G.
Eaton, H. W.
Eaton, T.
Eatwell, F. T.
Ebsworth, A.
Edgerley, J. N.
Edginton, R.
Edgley, F.
Edleston, E.
Edmonds, G.
Edmonds, W.
Edney, E.
Edwards, A.
Edwards, A. J.
Edwards, B. W.
Edwards, F. C. E.
Edwards, F. J.
Edwards, F. S.
Edwards, G.
Edwards, G. A. P.
Edwards, J. (12212).
Edwards, J. (12769).
Edwards, J. (14261).
Edwards, J. (17524).
Edwards, W. (11982).
Edwards, W. (36411)
Edwards, W. A.
Egan, J. E.
Eggett, F. W.
Eggleton, P. J.
Elam, C.
Elam, J.
Elbourne, G.
Elcombe, G. E.
Eldridge, A. C.
Eldridge, F. E.
Ellard, E.

Ellery, W. S.
Elliott, A. C.
Elliott, A. W.
Elliott, D. A.
Elliott, H. (25353).
Elliott, H. (48271).
Elliott, H. W. M.
Elliott, J. W.
Ellis, A. G. T.
Ellis, G.
Ellis, J.
Ellis, J. R.
Ellis, L.
Ellison, W. J.
Ellner, L.
Ellwood, W. C.
Elmer, E. J.
Elsmore, J.
Elson, C.
Elves, A.
Elves, R.
Emery, G. W.
Emms, F.
Engall, W. H.
Englefield, S. S.
Erridge, E.
Ervine, F. H.
Etches, A. H.
Eunson, W. H.
Evans, A. B.
Evans, C.
Evans, C. T.
Evans, E.
Evans, J.
Evans, R.
Eve, D.
Eveling, E. A.
Evenden, E. F.
Evenden, P.
Everett, E. T.
Everett, S.
Everitt, J.
Exall, A. E.
Eydman, H.
Eydman, R.
Eyles, W.
Faint, L. H.
Fairhurst, W.
Farley, A. R.
Farley, E. V.
Farley, G.
Farmer, R. J.
Farmer, W.
Farnes, C.
Farrah, H.
Farrant, W. G.
Farrar, J. A.
Farrell, H. G.
Farrell, W.
Farin, A.
Farrow, A.
Farrow, J.
Farrow, W.
Favell, E. E.
Feakins, C. J.
Featherstone, G.
Feddon, H.
Feeley, A. G.
Feist, S. W.
Fellingham, T. M.
Fennell, W. C.
Fenner, E.
Ferminger, G.
Ferney, J. G.
Ferris, F. C.
Feston, W. H.
Fewings, G. H.
Fewkes, G. H. D.
Field, J. (12393).
Field, J. (26159).
Field, J. T.
Filce, A.
Finch, J.
Finch, O. J. W.
Finch, W. H.
Fincham, H.
Fish, R.
Fisher, A. N.
Fisher, C. G.
Fisher, E. A.
Fisher, H.
Fisher, J.
Fisher, V. R.
Fitzgerald, E.
Fitzgerald, J.
Fitzgerald, J. G.
Fitzjohn, E.
Fitzjohn, W.
Flack, A.
Flack, E. D.
Flack, W.
Flanagan, F. W.
Flemming, A. J.
Fletcher, F.
Flowers, L. J.
Floyd, A. W.
Fluskey, T.
Flynn, J.
Foley, J.
Follen, J. W.
Foord, E.
Foot, J. A.
Foot, P.
Ford, F.
Ford, G. W.
Ford, H. (7210).
Ford, H. (14308).
Ford, J.
Ford, R.
Ford, W. J.
Fordham, G. R.
Fordham, H.
Foreman, W.
Forman, G.
Forster, W. A.
Forward, H.
Fosbrook, F.
Foster, E. J.
Foster, F.
Foster, G.
Foster, J.
Foster, W. J.
Fountain, F.
Fountain, H.
Fountain, J.
Fox, B.
Fox, F.
Fox, P.
Fox, P. J.
Fox, W. D.
France, C. A.
Francis, F.
Francis, E. L.
Francis, G.
Francis, H. (17277).
Francis, H. (28436).
Francke, R. G.
Franklin, C. (4458)
Franklin, C. (17243)
Freak, C.
Frearson, C. H.
Fredericks, J.
Free, C. W.
Free, W. J.
Freeman, C. W.
Freeman, F.
Freeman, G. A.
Freeman, W.
Freestone, F. W.
French, A.
French, C.
French, R.
French, W.
Frewin, A. E.
Frewin, W. H.
Fridd, H.
Friend, R. E.
Frisby, J.
Frith, H.
Frost, G. J.
Frost, J. (23949).
Frost, J. (48275)
Frost, S.
Frost, T. A.
Frostwick, H. V.
Fruitrell, G.
Fry, A.
Fryer, S. W.
Fuller, W. F.
Furse, J. H.
Fury, J.
Fynn, H. E.
Gadbury, G. W.
Gadd, B. J.
Gage, —.
Gaines, W. G.
Gale, J. C.
Galloway, C. C.
Galloway, F. F.
Galesworthy, H. H.
Galter, A. H.
Galvin, F.
Gant, J.
Gardham, G.
Gardner, E.
Gardner, H. J.
Gardner, W.
Garman, H. W.
Garner, C.
Garnham, G.
Garrett, A. L.
Garrett, R.
Gardiner, G. H.
Gascoyne, J. E.
Gasser, H.
Gaston, J.
Gates, C. H.
Gatty, G.
Gearing, S. W.
George, A. (28406).
George, S. C.
George, —. (203977).
Gent, F.
Gentry, W. A.
Gerhardt, C.
Germain, T. A.
Gibbons, O.
Gibbons, F. M.
Gibbs, A.
Gibbs, H. (21283).
Gibbs, H. (12882).
Gibson, A. E.
Gibson, V.
Gilbert, G.
Gilbert, H. W.
Gilchrist, J. H.
Gilder, P. C.
Giles, —. (12269).
Giles, W. R.
Gillespie, J.
Gillett, C. T.
Gilliard, A.
Gillingham, H. G.
Gillingham, J.
Gillingwater, C.
Gillison, H.
Gillson, C. J.
Gilmour, J.
Gilpin, A.
Ginn, A.
Gipson, W.
Girling, W.
Gissing, E.
Gladman, J. T.
Gladwin, W. C.
Glassett, L. H. C.
Glasspoole, S. T.
Glazier, G. W.
Glazier, W.
Gliddon, M.
Glue, J.
Goacher, H. G.
Gobbett, H. E.
Goddard, A.
Goddard, E.
Goddard, H. C.
Goddard, S.
Goddard, T. W.
Goddard, W.
Godfrey, J.
Golden, C.
Golder, A.
Goldsmith, A. V.
Goldsmith, T. T.
Gondrill, C.
Good, R.
Goodchild, J. G.
Goodenough, H.
Goodenough, W. H.
Goodfellow, H.
Goodsell, J. T.
Goodspeed, B. T.
Goodwin, A. E. D.
Goodwin, C.
Goodwin, D. W.
Goody, W.
Goold, N.
Gordon, A. H.
Goshawk, C. J.
Gosling, A.
Gosling, G. C.
Gosnald, O. G.
Goss, H. T.
Goss, T. E.
Gossington, J.
Gossington, S. V. J.
Gough, A. E. W. D.
Gough, C. H.
Gough, E. R.
Gough, W. J.
Gould, E. J.
Goulds, L.
Gourlay, R. W.
Gower, C. F.
Grady, G. A.
Graham, J. A.
Graham, J. H.
Graham, R.
Graham, W.
Grant, E. O.
Grant, G.
Gray, A.
Gray, E. W.
Gray, F. G.
Gray, G.
Gray, G. H.
Gray, P.
Gray, W. G. (12915).
Gray, W. G. (15816).
Gray, W. H.
Green, A. (49107).
Green, A. (5652).
Green A. W.
Green, C. R.
Green, J.
Green, J. B.
Green, V. J.
Greenaway, A. E.
Greenfield, B.
Greenfield, C. F.
Greenhall, W.
Greenslade, J.
Greenslade, W. J.
Greenland, W. J.
Greenwood, J.
Greenwood, W. S.
Gregg, A.
Gregory, F. C.
Gregory, H.
Gregory, H. H.
Gregory, J.
Gregson, J. H.
Greves, T. S.
Grey, W. C.
Greygoose, L. E.
Grief, R. J.
Griffiths, H. A.
Griffiths, C. J. F.
Griffiths, J.
Griffiths, L. R.
Grimes, F. W.
Grimbley, R. E.
Grimwood, F.
Grist, A. E.
Grist, F. (204029).
Grist, F. (9490).
Gristwood, W. G. J.
Grogan, F. F.
Grogan, T.
Grove, J.
Grover, J.
Grover, T. G.

Gubbens, C.
Guiler, W.
Gull, G. A.
Gurman, G.
Gumbrill, G.
Gunner, L.
Gunton, F.
Gurney, F. C.
Gurney, P.
Gurry, H. S.
Guy, H.
Guyatt, P. A.
Habgood, P. E.
Hacker, H. T.
Hackett, A. H.
Hackett, R.
Hacquoil, H. C.
Hadakin, J. F.
Hadingham, G. A.
Hadley, T.
Haggerty, M.
Haigh, T. T.
Haines, T.
Hale, J. W.
Hall, D.
Hall, J.
Hall, J. P.
Hall, L. G.
Hall, R. P. L.
Hall, W. (205970)
Hall, W. (38134)
Hall, W. (12652)
Hallett, A.
Halliday, A.
Halliwell, D.
Halls, A.
Halsey, A.
Hammond, A.
Hammond, E.
Hammond, G. (12012)
Hammond, T. E.
Hammond, W. (14237)
Hammond, W. (10714)
Hammerton, F.
Hampton, B.
Hamshire, J. E.
Hancock, H. R.
Hancock, J.
Hand, F. C.
Hands, F.
Hankin, W.
Hankin, W. J.
Hann, A. E.
Hannah, —
Harding, A.
Harding, C.
Harding, F.
Harding, H. J.
Harding, W. (48156)
Harding, W. (34919)
Hardy, W.
Hargreaves, E.
Harkness, A.
Harley, E. J.
Harmer, W.
Harper, P.
Harper, W. J.
Harraden, W. A.
Harries, E.
Harrington, E.
Harrington, T. N.
Harris, A.
Harris, A. J.
Harris, C. D.
Harris, C. E. L.
Harris, G. H.
Harris, H. R.
Harris, J. (28257)
Harris, J. (12926)
Harris, J. E.
Harris, R. McD.
Harrison, A. E.
Harrison, F.
Harrison, G.
Harrison, H.
Harrop, W. F.
Hart, A.
Hart, C.
Hart, R.
Hart, S.
Hartfield, A. J.
Hartley, J. G.
Hartley, T.
Hartley, W.
Hartnell, C. S.
Harvey, A. E.
Harvey, B. H. E.
Harvey, G.
Harvey, G. W.
Harvey, W. D.
Hartwell, E. M.
Harwood, A.
Hastler, H.
Hastings, T.
Hathaway, H. W.
Hathaway, W.
Hatt, R.
Hattley, J. G.
Hatton, A. H.
Hattley, W.
Hatton, G.
Hatton, H. C.
Hawes, S. E.
Hawes, W. E.
Hawes, W. F.
Hawkes, H.
Hawkins, A.
Hawkins, H. J.
Hawkins, J.
Hawkins, J. T.
Hawkins, W. (14211)
Hawkins, W. (21230)
Hawkins, W. G.
Hawley, J.
Hawthorn, F. E.
Hawthorn, J.
Hawtin, H. R.
Hawtrey, J.
Haxton, J. C.
Hayes, M.
Haynes, A. J.
Haynes, C. E.
Haynes, N.
Haynes, W.
Hayward, W.
Hayward, H. W. J.
Hayward, J. H. H.
Hazard, J.
Hazel, H.
Hazelgrove, T.
Hazelgrove, W.
Hazell, A. G.
Head, F.
Head, F. C.
Head, H. R. V.
Heale, B.
Heasman, C.
Heard, J.
Hearn, H. J.
Hearson, G.
Heath, J.
Heath, R.
Heath, R. J. F.
Hedge, E.
Hedges, H.
Hedges, J. J.
Hedges, S. A.
Hedley, A.
Heffer, T.
Heighney, T. W.
Helliar, A. A.
Helliar, C. F.
Helliar, H.
Hemmings, H. A.
Henley, H.
Henley, J.
Henstridge, A. F.
Henwood, R. J.
Hepher, C. R.
Herbert, E.
Hergert, F.
Herring, H. G.
Hersey, W.
Hesketh, H.
Hesketh, R.
Hester, H. W.
Hewett, A.
Hewitt, A. (26980)
Hewitson, A.
Hewson, G.
Hexter, W. C.
Heydinger, F. C. H.
Heywood, E. H.
Heyworth, W.
Hiams, C.
Hickey, A. (14179)
Hickey, A. (12332)
Hickey, H.
Hicks, F. A. D.
Hicks, H. J.
Hicks, J. W.
Higgins, D.
Higgins, W.
Highley, R.
Hill, A. (35581)
Hill, C.
Hill, F.
Hill, H. A.
Hill, J. F.
Hill, J. W.
Hill, R.
Hill, S. H.
Hill, W. (12160)
Hill, W. G.
Hilleard, J.
Hillerby, G. W.
Hilliard, F.
Hillier, F.
Hillier, L. C.
Hills, A. J.
Hills, E.
Hills, J.
Hilsdon, G.
Hilson, C. T.
Hilton, J. H.
Hilton, W.
Hind, H.
Hinds, J. R.
Hines, F.
Hinge, F.
Hiscocks, H. A.
Hitch, E. A.
Hitchman, J.
Hoadley, J.
Hobbs, G.
Hobbs, W. F.
Hobday, G. H.
Hodges, E.
Hodgson, G. A.
Hoile, W. J.
Holderness, E. J.
Holding, A. G.
Holland, E.
Holland, G.
Holland, W. (26836)
Holland, W. (16323).
Holloway, R.
Holman, J. (22412).
Holman, J. (13466).
Holmes, C. H.
Holmes, H. J.
Holmes, R.
Holmes, T.
Holt, R.
Holt, W.
Holter, F.
Holvey, A. E.
Homerton, W.
Homewood, C.
Homewood, E.
Homewood, F.
Honeycombe, H. C.
Hook, N.
Hookham, F. G.
Hooton, S.
Hope, M.
Hopkins, J.
Hopkins, R.
Hopkins, W.
Horn, H. L.
Horne, F.
Horne, J.
Horne, P. E.
Horner, F.
Horrex, H.
Horsepool, T. W.
Hough, P. A.
Houghton, A.
Houghton, H. B.
Houghton, T. A.
Houghton, W.
Hounson, R.
Hovey, J.
Howard, E.
Howard, F. A.
Howard, H.
Howard, H. A.
Howard, S.
Howard, V.
Howard, W.
Howarth, J. A.
Howden, A. C.
Howe, E. A.
Howe, D. W.
Howell, E.
Howell, H.
Howes, A. C.
Howes, C.
Howes, H. B.
Howson, H. H.
Hubbard, E.
Hubbard, F.
Hubbard, H. A. F.
Hubbard, W.
Huggett, C. E.
Huggins, A. G.
Huggins, W. H.
Hughes, C. (2795).
Hughes, C. (16074).
Hughes, J.
Hughes, S.
Hughes, W. (4885).
Hughes, W. (26841).
Hughes, W. (12125).
Hull, C.
Hull, W.
Hume, J.
Humphreys, A. E.
Humphreys, E.
Humphreys, E. G.
Humphreys, G. W. C.
Humphreys, H. (8654).
Humphreys, H. (19123)
Humphreys, W.
Humphreys, W. S.
Humphries, A.
Hummerston, G.
Hunt, J.
Hunt, J. T.
Hunter, H. G.
Hunter, J. W.
Hunter, J. (14290).
Hunter, J. (12280).
Hunter, H. C. M.
Hunter, W. F.
Huntingford, J. E.
Huntley, S. W.
Hurd, G.
Hurdle, A. G.
Hurley, A.
Hussey, A.
Hussey, E.
Hutchings, F. W.
Hutchins, F. G.
Hutchinson, C.
Hutchinson, E. E.
Hutchinson, G. F.
Hutchinson, H.
Hutchinson, J.
Hutchinson, J. W.
Hutchinson, R.
Hutchinson, S. J.
Hyett, H.
Hyde, A.
Hyde, C.
Hyde, J.
Hyde, S. A.
Hyde, W.
Illsley, T.
Ince, G.
Ingham, S.
Ingleton, C.
Ingleton, F.

LAYING UP OF THE COLOUR, OCTOBER 1933.

Copyright Daily Sketch

Ingram, W.
Ireland, W. H.
Ison, E. J.
Israel, —.
Isted, H. J. S.
Ives, H. P.
Ives, W. J.
Ivey, A.
Ivey, D.
Ivey, F. J.
Ivory, J. J.
Jackett, E.
Jackman, G.
Jackson, A. (16180).
Jackson, C. (Wise).
Jackson, C. (12039).
Jackson, H.
Jackson, J. E.
Jackson, W.
Jackson, W. J.
Jago, W.
Jakens, T. C.
Jakes, C.
James, C.
James, C. A.
James, E.
James, G. P.
James, H.
James, J. (12119)
James, J. (14280)
James, W. (26461)
James, W. (12144)
James, W. F.
James, W. H.
Janes, W.
Jarrett, C. F.
Jarvis, A.
Jeal, H.
Jeal, L. F.
Jeeves, J.
Jeff, E. J.
Jefferies, H. W.
Jefferies, P. W.
Jelley, H.
Jelly, A. T. W.
Jenkerson, C.
Jenkins, G.
Jenkins, H.
Jenkins, J.
Jenkinson, W.
Jenks, J.
Jenner, A. E.
Jenner, G. H.
Jennings, A. C.
Jennings, G.
Jennings, S. H.
Jerrom, E.
Jerrom, J.
Jesse, F. W.
Jesty, G. E.
Jewell, W.
Joel, A. J.
Johnson, A. (12015)
Johnson, A. (27417)
Johnson, C.
Johnson, E.
Johnson, F.
Johnson, G. A.
Johnson, J. (48453)
Johnson, J. (12803)
Johnson, J. (12876)
Johnson, S. W. J.
Johnson, W.
Johnson, W. H.
Johnson, W. R.
Johnston, R.
Johnstone, H. T.
Jolliffe, H.
Jolly, J. W.
Jolly, T.
Jonas, R. H.
Jones, A. (11112)
Jones, A. A. (12309)
Jones, A. E.
Jones, C. S.
Jones, F.
Jones, G. (12498)
Jones, G. E.
Jones, G. H.
Jones, J. (14930)
Jones, J. (19330)
Jones, J. H. (25532)
Jones, J. P.
Jones, S.
Jones, T.
Jones, W.
Jones, W. T.
Jons, A.
Jordan, R. (16291)
Jordan, R. (6363)
Jordon, E.
Jordon, J.
Jordon, T.
Joyce, C.
Joyce, R.
Justice, P.
Kasey, A. J.
Kearns, G.
Keating, W.
Kebby, E. C.
Keegan, T. W.
Keeley, P. E.
Keen, A.
Keene, F.
Keiller, W.
Kelleher, W.
Kelleher, J.
Kelley, W.
Kember, A.
Kelly, W.
Kemp, C.
Kemp, F.
Kemp, W.
Kennett, W. R.
Kennedy, F.
Kent, C.
Kent, F. A.
Kenward, J. G.
Kerr, W. (25079)
Kerr, W. (26845)
Kersey, E. C.
Kettle, G. W.
Keylock, W. J.
Keywood, W.
Kidman, F.
Kidman, L.
Kilborn, J.
Killick, C. A.
Killick, W. A.
Kimber, H.
Kinane, T.
Kinchin, E.
King, C. (48255)
King, C. (8594)
King, C. E.
King, C. F. G.
King, C. J.
King, E.
King, E. J.
King, E. V.
King, F.
King, F. W.
King, G. V.
King, J.
Kingdon, A.
Kingsnorth, A.
Kinsman, W.
Kipps, D. W.
Kirby, E. H.
Kirby, G.
Kirby, G. B.
Kirby, H. G.
Kirby, J.
Kirk, J.
Kirkum, A. G.
Kirsch, H.
Kitchener, W.
Kitterman, T. H.
Kitto, J. P.
Knibbs, A.
Knight, C. E.
Knight, C. H.
Knight, C. W.
Knight, F. W. J.
Knight, G.
Knight, W.
Knight (30883)
Knighton, R. E.
Knights, D. R.
Knights, J. A.
Knock, J. W.
Knott, A. G.
Knox, J. A.
Kraushaar, H. F.
Kuspert, C. C.
Kynaston, R. H.
Lacey, E.
Lack, E.
Laker, E.
Lallow, W. R.
Lambert, A.
Lambert, G.
Lambert, H.
Lambert, W. G. F.
Lamerton, C.
Lampard, S. F.
Lampett, A.
Lancaster, F. W.
Lancaster, J.
Landamore, W. A.
Lander, A.
Lander, A. E. (10654)
Lander, A. (34453)
Lane, E.
Lang, C.
Langley, C.
Langridge, H.
Laporte, C.
Larkin, A. E.
Larkin, E.
Larkin, J.
Larrett, S. R.
Laurie, W.
Laurie, W. C.
Laver, J.
Laverick, W. E.
Law, H.
Lawrence, A.
Lawrence, E.
Lawrence, E. E.
Lawrence, G.
Lawrence, J.
Lawrence, W. A.
Lawis, F.
Laws, F. G.
Laws, W. H.
Laye, G.
Layzell, G.
Lazarus, L.
Lea, A.
Leach, H.
Leaman, G. H.
Lear, A. E. W.
Leavers, F.
Ledger, G.
Lee, A.
Lee, G. (12582)
Lee, G. (48376)
Lee, H. A.
Lee, H. J.
Lee, J.
Lee, M. N.
Lee, N. H.
Lee, P.
Lee, S. G.
Lee, T. J.
Leeming, E.
Leggett, G.
Leggett, W.
Lemmon, W. R.
Lemon, H.
Lemon, W.
Leonard, A.
Leonard, H. E.
Letford, E.
Letts, H.
Levett, J.
Levett, H. G.
Levi, A.
Levitt, A.
Levy, J.
Lewin, A.
Lewin, B.
Lewis, B.
Lewis, G.
Lewis, H. A.
Lewis, J. (12291)
Lewis, J. T.
Lidbury, W.
Liddell, F. B.
Lightfoot, G. J.
Lincoln, E.
Lincoln, E. G.
Lindsay, C.
Linford, S.
Ling, S.
Lingwood, J. W.
Linstead, T. E.
Lipscombe, W. H.
Lloyd, A.
Lloyd, J. C.
Lloyd, P. N.
Lloyd, W. (32935)
Lock, A.
Lock, J.
Longcluse, E. C.
Longden, J.
Longland, F.
Loosley, C. H.
Love, C.
Loveday, E. W.
Loveday, J.
Lovell, J.
Lowdell, H. J.
Lowe, H.
Lowe, R.
Lowers, S. F.
Lucas, N.
Lucas, J.
Lucas, R. J.
Lucas, T. F.
Lucas, W. F.
Luck, C. B.
Luck, W. P.
Luetchford, C.
Lulham, C.
Lumb, G. S.
Lumbis, G.
Lumby, H.
Lumley, E.
Lunn, C. T.
Lunn, P.
Lunn, W.
Lunnon, W.
Lust, W. A.
Lutz, T. H.
Luxford, A.
Lynch, J.
Lynes, B.
Lynn, H. E.
Lyons, J.
Macfarlane, D. W.
Macher, H. C.
Mackie, T.
Maddocks, A.
Maddox, T. H.
Maddy, J.
Maguire, T. J. M.
Maguire, T. H.
Maguire, W. R.
Maher, W.
Maiden, W. C. J.
Major, R. K.
Makin, A.
Malcher, F. G.
Maleed, W. J.
Males, M. G.
Malham, A.
Mallett, W.
Malley, E.
Mallyon, W.
Malone, J. (5053)
Maloney, W.
Maloy, G.
Mangham, C. J.
Manktelow, W.
Manley, A. A.
Mann, H.
Mannell, D.
Manners, F. W.
Manning, H.
Manning, P. R.
Mansfield, G. E. W.
Mansfield, S.
Mansfield, W.
Mant, L.
Manuel, A. H. J.
Manville, A.
Marcham, A.

Marchant, F. J.
Marfleet, H. C.
Margetts, G.
Markes, P.
Markley, H. S.
Marks, A. (204624)
Marks, A. (204019)
Marney, A.
Marriott, L.
Marsh, H. H. M.
Marsh, L. B.
Marshall, C.
Marshall, R. J.
Marshall, S. (34345)
Marshall, S.
Marshall, S. H.
Marshall, T.
Mart, H.
Martin, A.
Martin, D.
Martin, J.
Martin, R.
Martin, T.
Martin, W.
Martin, W. E.
Martin, W. H.
Martin, W. J.
Masco, L.
Maskell, A.
Maskell, G. W.
Maskell, T.
Mason, G. (14)
Mason, G. (14203)
Mason, G. (12839)
Mason, H. W.
Mason, J. (12159)
Mason, J. (21241)
Mason, W.
Massey, J.
Massey, J. E.
Masters, A. C.
Masters, F.
Masters, P.
Mathews, A.
Mathias, G. (30154)
Mathis, A.
Matthews, B.
Matthews, E. W.
Matthews, H.
Matthews, P. F.
Matthewson, J.
May, A. C.
May, F.
May, G. W.
May, R.
Mayfield, A.
Mayhew, T. A.
Mayhill, J.
Maynard, G. E.
Maynard, W.
Mayne, W. G.
McAleavy, J.
McAllister, J.
McBride, W.
McCann, G. A.
McCarthy, E.
McCarthy, H.
McCarthy, T. (14263)
McCarthy, T. (12257)
McCaskill, R.
McCollock, A. C.
McCormack, E.
McDermott, T. E.
McDonald, A. E.
McDonald, J.
McDougall, D.
McEwan, D.
McFadyean, G.
McFie, W.
McFie, James
McGill, A. G.
McGuire, H.
McGuire, L.
McIntosh, A. J.
McKay, A.
MacKriell, C.
McLaren, R.
McLean, T.
McLeod, R.
McLoughlin, H.
McManus, G.
McMarniss, H. J.
McPherson, W. B.
McQuillan, C.
McShee, H.
McShee, J.
Mead, W.
Mead, J.
Meader, T. M.
Medhurst, R. D.
Medlock, E.
Meek, C.
Meekins, L.
Melling, J.
Melluish, F. W.
Menlove, W. H.
Mepham, H.
Mepham, J.
Mercer, F. J.
Mercer, G.
Mercer, R.
Mercer, S. F.
Meredith, H.
Merritt, A. W.
Messenger, F.
Messenger, W.
Myers, F. G.
Myers, W. E.
Mynott, A.
Middleton, H.
Middleton, W. H.
Midson, C. D.
Miles, E. A.
Miles, F. (124251)
Miles, F. (31802)
Miles, T.
Mileuski, K.
Millard, E.
Miller, G. T.
Miller, H.
Miller, J.
Miller, J. H.
Miller, S.
Miller, W. A. T.
Millett, C.
Millgate, W.
Millichamp, J.
Millington, J.
Mills, E.
Mills, E. F.
Mills, G.
Mills, H.
Mills, H. G.
Mills, J. J.
Millward, A.
Milsom, F.
Minehan, J.
Mingay, H.
Minns, A.
Mitchell, A.
Mitchell, T.
Mitchell, S. T.
Moir, G. A.
Mollett, J.
Monckton, M.
Monk, J.
Montague, P.
Montague, L.
Moon, J.
Moore, C. A.
Moore, G.
Moore, F. S.
Moore, J.
Moore, T.
Moore, W. A.
Morath, A. J.
Moran, A.
Morling, F.
Morey, A.
Morley, P. W.
Morgan, A.
Morgan, A. E.
Morrill, P.
Morris, A. J.
Morris, G. H.
Morris, J. M.
Morris, N.
Morrisey, J.
Mortimer, C. F.
Mortimer, W.
Morton, F.
Morton, G.
Moseley, F.
Moseley, H. C.
Motts, W.
Moule, F.
Mower, L.
Mudge, W. H.
Mulville, C.
Munday, A.
Munday, H. N.
Munday, H. S.
Munden, S. S.
Munns, J. A.
Munns, T. E.
Munro, D.
Munson, A.
Murchison, R. G.
Murphy, D.
Murphy, H. H.
Murphy, J. (17301)
Murphy, J. (12950)
Murray, G.
Murray, H. C.
Murray, P. W.
Murrell, S.
Musgrave, R.
Musgrove, A. P.
Muspratt, H. M.
Mussard, B. C.
Mussard, F.
Mustard, D.
Myers
Mynott, A.
Nagel, M.
Nainby, S. R.
Nash, A.
Nash, G.
Nash, S.
Nash, W. H.
Nastri, F.
Nation, C. E.
Neal, H. E.
Neal, P.
Neal, W.
Neale, C.
Neale, F.
Neale, S. A.
Needham, E.
Neller, F. J.
Nelson, C.
Nelson, E.
Nelson, S. H.
Netherton, E. J.
Neville, W.
New, H.
New, J.
Newbon, W.
Newing, G.
Newman, A.
Newman, A. E.
Newman, C.
Newman, W. F.
Newnham, H.
Newson, G. A.
Newton, A.
Nicholls, T. G.
Nichols, A.
Nichols, F. H.
Nicholson, J.
Nickels, J. W.
Nicol, A.
Nieland, J. H.
Nightingale, C.
Nixon, H.
Nixon, W.
Noad, E. C.
Noad, W.
Noakes, E.
Noble, A. G.
Nolan, R.
Nolan, J.
Noonan, W. H.
Nordeman, F. W.
Norris, A.
Norris, C.
Norris, E.
Norris, W. A.
Norton, H. G.
Norwood, B. C.
Nye, C.
Nugent, S. J.
Nunn, G.
Nutley, A. E.
O'Brien, D.
O'Brien, J. (12533)
O'Brien, J. (14127)
O'Brien, R.
O'Brien, T. (12077)
O'Brien, T. (38656)
O'Connor, F.
Ogier, L. M.
O'Hara, J.
O'Hara, W.
O'Leary, A. D.
O'Leary, J. (12450)
O'Leary, J. (2842)
O'Leary, J. (12106)
Oliver, S. W.
O'Neill, F.
O'Reilly, B.
Orpin, J.
Orton, H.
Orvis, F.
Osborn, A.
Osborn, H. W.
Osborn, W. A.
Osborne, F.
Osborne, E. H.
Osborne, R.
Osborne, T.
Osmond, A. H.
Ovenden, V. R.
Overy, H. R.
Owen, D. A.
Packham, L. A.
Packwood, L.
Page, C.
Page, C. E.
Page, C. T.
Page, E.
Page, P.
Page, W. H.
Page, W. T.
Paine, E. (16119)
Paine, S. C.
Palfrey, H. J.
Palmer, A.
Palmer, A. T.
Palmer, F. (33233)
Palmer, F. (48290)
Palmer, T.
Palmer, W. C.
Pankhurst, C.
Pannell, J.
Pantlin, A.
Pantry, F. C.
Paollillo, A.
Papps, C.
Parfitt, C.
Parfrey, J. C.
Parkes, G. E. (46021)
Parker, E. A.
Parker, H.
Parker, J.
Parker, W. (12909)
Parker, W. (30945)
Parkin, M. E.
Parkins, T. W.
Parkinson, E. M.
Parkinson, P.
Parks, J. A.
Parr, F. C.
Parr, J. H.
Parramore, J.
Parrett, A.
Parsons, F.
Parsons, J.
Parsons, W. (25562)
Parsons, W. (25571)
Parsons, W. (204580)
Parsons, W. H. (12954)
Partridge, R.
Pascoe, J.
Pasfield, G.
Paskitt, W.

Patch, W. J.
Patey, C. E.
Patrick, F.
Patrick, H. W.
Patterson, R.
Patterson, T.
Pattinson, C. H.
Paul, A. F. J.
Paul, F. J. H.
Payne, A. H.
Payne, A. J.
Payne, C. E. (26759)
Payne, C. E. (35233)
Payne, G.
Payne, H.
Payne, H. A.
Payne, J.
Payne, T. H.
Peace, W. C.
Peachey, H.
Peacock, W. T.
Pearce, A.
Pearce, J.
Pearce, R. W.
Pearce, W. R. A.
Pearcey, J. H.
Pearl, C. E.
Pearl, G.
Pearl, W.
Pearman, R. S.
Pearman, T. W.
Pearson, A.
Pearson, A. C.
Pearson, H.
Pearson, W. H.
Peasley, A.
Peck, A.
Peck, J.
Peddle, H.
Pedler, J. R.
Pegler, F.
Peile, H.
Pemberton, A.
Pembroke, W.
Pendred, E.
Pendry, R.
Penfold, G.
Penfold, W.
Pennell, J.
Penney, W. (2492)
Penney, W. (14632)
Pennifold, L.
Pennington, J.
Pentecost, A.
Pepper, R. W.
Pepperell, S. C.
Percival, G.
Perkins, T.
Perkins, W. G.
Perrin, A. R.
Perrin, W. E.
Perry, H.
Perry, S.
Perry, T. W.
Perry, W.
Perryman, G. W.
Petch, H.
Peters, A.
Peters, F.
Peters, J.
Peters, T.
Peto, T.
Petry, E. W.
Pettitt, J.
Pettyfor, G.
Pharoah, G. R.
Phelps, P.
Phelps, W. T.
Phillips, C. (12190)
Phillips, C. (29481)
Phillips, H.
Phillips, H. C.
Phillips, H. H.
Phillips, H. J.
Phillips, I. P.
Phillips, J.
Phillips, P.
Phillips, T. W.
Philp, A. W.
Pickett, L. J.
Pickford, A.
Picking, A. I.
Pike, J. A.
Pike, J. S.
Pillcher, W. J.
Pinder, H.
Pinder, W. A. G.
Pines, W.
Piper, W.
Piper, W. H.
Pitney, W. E.
Pitts, S.
Pitts, S. L. B.
Plant, S. J.
Platt, S.
Plowright, R.
Plum, A. J.
Plumbridge, H.
Plumley, C.
Plumley, P.
Plumpton, C. S.
Poat, E.
Pocklington, R. S.
Pocock, A. J.
Pocock, F. M.
Pocock, L. A.
Pollard, A. (5282)
Pollard, A. (28227)
Ponton, E. W.
Poole, E. A.
Poole, F. D.
Pooley, C. E.
Pope, A. J.
Popple, R. W.
Potier, A. E.
Potkins, V.
Potter, A. A.
Potter, C. E.
Potter, H.
Potter, J.
Potter, L. S.
Potter, W. F.
Poulter, G.
Poulter, S.
Poulter, W. E.
Povey, F. J.
Powell, E.
Powell, E. F. J.
Powell, G. A.
Powell, J.
Powell, W.
Powell, W. A.
Poyner, W. T.
Pratt, F. W.
Preedy, H. P.
Preedy, W. S.
Prentice, A.
Preslent, W.
Press, R.
Preston, H. W.
Price, C.
Price, C. J.
Price, F. A.
Price, H. (26495)
Price, H. W.
Price, J.
Price, P.
Price, P. H.
Priest, W. T.
Prigmore, H.
Prior, P.
Probert, T.
Proctor, C.
Prosser, G.
Prout, M.
Pryce, J. P.
Pryer, T.
Pryor, P.
Pudney, A.
Pugh, A.
Pull, E.
Pullen, P.
Punston, A. A.
Punter, H.
Purcells, L.
Purkiss, A. H.
Purkiss, C. R.
Pursey, A. H.
Pursey, G.
Pursey, L. H.
Purssey, W.
Puta, C. P.
Putman, G. E.
Puttock, D. W.
Puttock, G.
Quesnell, W.
Quinton, A. E.
Quirk, —. (19814)
Race, H.
Radcliffe, T.
Radford, G.
Radnor, A. C.
Raggett, W. P.
Rainbow, W.
Rainforth, G. H.
Ralph, W. H.
Rampling, R. R.
Ramsbottom, J.
Ramsey, J. J.
Rand, H.
Randall, A.
Randall, G.
Ransom, J. F.
Rapley, T. W.
Rasey, W. C.
Ratcliffe, L.
Ratcliffe, N.
Rawlings, A.
Rawlings, C.
Ray, J.
Rayner, T.
Read, G. J.
Read, M. T.
Read, L.
Read, W. B.
Reader, G. A.
Reardon, J.
Reckie, H.
Reddick, H.
Redding, C. F.
Reddington, J. R.
Redwin, T.
Reed, A. E.
Reed, G. V.
Reed, J. A.
Reed, J. W.
Reed, R.
Reeder, S.
Reeve, H. A.
Reeve, A. H.
Reeve, F. G.
Reeve, J. C.
Reeve, H. W.
Reffell, H.
Reid, C.
Read, R.
Reid, W.
Reigate, W. J.
Reinbach, L.
Remnant, W. G.
Render, A.
Renton, R.
Repsch, T.
Retford, T. F.
Revell, F.
Rex, W. W.
Reynolds, E. G.
Reynolds, G. (12679)
Reynolds, G. (26847)
Reynolds, W. C.
Rham, B. E.
Rhodes, A.
Rhodes, F. W.
Rice, H.
Rice, M.
Richards, A. F.
Richards, C. H.
Richards, D. J.
Richards, E. F.
Richards, G.
Richards, J.
Richards, T. F.
Richards, V.
Richardson, F.
Richardson, F. J.
Richardson, H. (1332)
Rickarby, W. A.
Rickard, C. J. H.
Ridge, A.
Ridley, C. H.
Ridley, T.
Rigden, A. R.
Rigler, F. S.
Riley, G.
Riley, J. P.
Rippington, R.
Rivett, E.
Roach, M.
Robbins, A.
Roberts, A. (19998)
Roberts, C. (204403)
Roberts, C. (204543)
Roberts, F. G.
Roberts, H.
Roberts, J.
Roberts, J. W.
Roberts, W. F.
Robertson, J. W.
Robertson, W. W.
Robinson, E. J.
Robinson, E. J. V.
Robinson, J. C.
Robinson, T.
Robinson, T. H.
Roffe, W.
Roffey, E. R.
Roffey, G.
Roffey, W. G.
Roffey, W. J.
Rogers, A. T.
Rogers, C. R.
Rogers, J. (12466)
Rogers, J. (241756)
Rogers, R.
Rogers, T.
Rogers, W. (9379)
Rogers, W. T.
Rolf, J. G.
Rolfe, G.
Rose, A. G.
Rose, H. J.
Rose, W. R.
Rosindell, W.
Ross, J. H.
Ross, R.
Rotherham, H. J.
Routledge, F. S.
Rowcroft, G.
Rowcroft, H. G. C.
Rowe, A.
Rowe, C.
Rowe, F. (24736)
Rowe, F. (26967)
Rowe, F. H.
Rowe, G. R.
Rowe, J. (12038)
Rowe, J. (25399)
Rowe, J. J.
Rowe, K.
Rowe, W.
Rowland, A.
Rowland, N.
Rowlett, E.
Rowling, J. W.
Roxburgh, G.
Rubery, C. Y.
Rudrum, R.
Rule, J.
Rumble, F. B.
Rumbold, C. W.
Rumbold, W. T.
Rumsby, J. E.
Rush, A.
Rush, T. R.
Rushton, G. I.
Ruskin, W. G. A.
Russell, F. J.
Russell, J.
Russell, J. G.
Russell, W.
Ryan, G.
Ryan, P. S.
Ryan, W.

Saberton, H.
Sabin, T.
Sabine, T. W.
Sadler, J. S.
St. Julien, C. W.
Sale, G.
Sale, S.
Salisbury, F.
Salmons, L. S.
Salzmann, T.
Sandell, G. F.
Sanders, A. J.
Sanders, B. (11511)
Sanders, J. F.
Sands, V.
Sargeant, W.
Sargent, A.
Sargent, A. E.
Sargent, A. L.
Saul, S. E.
Saunders, A.
Saunders, B.
Saunders, E. (25247)
Saunders, F. J. (21250)
Saunders, F. J. (34995)
Saunders, R.
Saunders, S. J.
Saunders, T. A.
Saunders, W. G.
Saville, A. E.
Sawyer, H.
Sawyer, W. D. G.
Saych, F.
Sayer, G.
Sayers, G.
Sayers, G. H.
Scales, J. A.
Scammell, F.
Scanlon, C.
Scarborough, S. C.
Scarlett, F. S.
Schen, J. B.
Schofield, C.
Schofield, J.
Schooling, J.
Scotcher, W. J.
Scott, C.
Scott, G. (25217)
Scott, J. A.
Scott, H. T.
Scott, M.
Scott, O. P.
Scott, R. H.
Scott, W.
Scrace, A.
Scroggins, J.
Scroggins, W. H.
Scudder, J. C.
Seabrook, F. J.
Seabrook, G. (12199)
Seager, G.
Seaman, B.
Seaman, H. C.
Seaman, R. (2875)
Searchfield, J.
Searle, J.
Sears, J.
Seaward, H. P.
Sedgwick, G.
Seels, G.
Selfe, A. G.
Sell, J. J. T.
Sellens, W. J.
Sellers, P.
Senior, F. H.
Setchell, C.
Seward, C. C.
Sewell, F.
Sewell, J. H.
Sexton, J.
Sharp, J.
Sharp, W. M.
Sharp, W. R. T.
Shaw, A.
Shaw, B.
Shaw, F. (26989)
Shaw, S.
Shawl, R.
Shea, E.
Sheedy, J.
Sheen, E. G.
Sheldrick, G.
Shepherd, A.
Shepherd, J.
Sheppard, A.
Sheppard, G. H.
Sheppard, W. H.
Sherwin, C.
Sherwood, W. A.
Shields, C.
Shields, W. J.
Shilcock, A. N.
Shine, J.
Shinn, C.
Shinn, J.
Shipp, B.
Shirley, F.
Shoobridge, J.
Shore, F. E.
Short, F. C.
Short, W. F.
Shulman, A.
Siese, V.
Siggers, T. R.
Siley, C.
Silverside, W.
Simkin, F.
Simmonds, C.
Simmonds, R. G.
Simmons, A. C.
Simmons, A. J.
Simmons, E.
Simmons, G.
Simmons, H.
Simms, H. E.
Simner, J. A.
Simon, F. W.
Simpson, C.
Simpson, F.
Simpson, H. L.
Simpson, T. A.
Sims, M. L.
Sinclair, R.
Sinden, A.
Sinden, C. E.
Singer, S.
Singleton, F.
Singleton, J.
Sippetts, C. A.
Sissons, E. L.
Skews, H.
Skiggs, A. E.
Skinner, A.
Skinner, C.
Skinner, E.
Skivens, A.
Slade, W.
Slater, B.
Slater, J.
Slaughter, F.
Sly, C. A.
Smale, W.
Smallbone, J.
Smallpiece, A. J.
Smart, A.
Smart, W. J.
Smith, A.
Smith, A. A.
Smith, A. G. (12524)
Smith, A. G. (46032)
Smith, A. J. E.
Smith, A. S.
Smith, C. B.
Smith, C. H.
Smith, C. L.
Smith, E. (12047)
Smith, E. (12346)
Smith, E. (12470)
Smith, E. (18991)
Smith, F. (25395)
Smith, F. (37685)
Smith, F. G. (16332)
Smith, F. G. (31315)
Smith, F. J.
Smith, F. S.
Smith, F. W.
Smith, G. (11924)
Smith, G. (14152)
Smith, G. (28086)
Smith, G. (28330)
Smith, G. E.
Smith, H.
Smith, H. A.
Smith, H. B. R.
Smith, H. C.
Smith, J. (7670)
Smith, J. (11308)
Smith, J. (48269)
Smith, J. A.
Smith, J. E. (12241)
Smith, J. E. (12488)
Smith, J. M.
Smith, J. N.
Smith, J. W. (37630)
Smith, L.
Smith, R. (21192)
Smith, R. (26277)
Smith, R. (30389)
Smith, S.
Smith, S. W. (12253)
Smith, S. W. (12420)
Smith, S. W. (25588)
Smith, T. (12853)
Smith, T. (32699)
Smith, T. A.
Smith, T. H.
Smith, W. (5781)
Smith, W. (26500)
Smith, W. C.
Smith, W. F.
Smith, W. H. (10213)
Smith, W. H. (32693)
Smith, W. T.
Smith-West, A.
Smithson, R.
Smye, W. J.
Snell, A. E.
Snelling, F. R.
Snook, S.
Snow, B.
Snow, G.
Snow, H.
Soer, W. H.
Solley, A. T.
Solomon, E. C.
Somers, M.
Songhurst, D.
Souster, W.
South, B. H.
South, P. H.
Southern, A. H.
Spain, J. T.
Sparrow, A. G.
Sparrow, E. J.
Spearing, F. G.
Spearpoint, S.
Spelzini, W. J.
Spencer, A.
Spencer, A. H.
Spencer, C. H.
Spencer, W.
Spencer, W. E.
Sponton, J. H.
Spooner, W. G.
Spring, J.
Sprooles, W. J.
Stacey, P. H.
Stacey, R. C.
Stacey, W. H.
Staines, H.
Staines, S.
Stanbridge, A. W.
Standen, E. E.
Standing, J.
Stanley, A.
Stanley, G.
Stanley, J.
Stanley, J. L.
Stanley, W.
Stanton, W. F.
Stapleton, E. A.
Stapleton, J. B.
Stapley, H.
Starck, G.
Starling, A. (39210)
Staunton, H.
Stead, W.
Stearn, C.
Stebbings, J. W.
Stedman, T. (26464)
Stedman, T. (12046)
Steel, A.
Steel, A. W.
Steel, W.
Steen, E.
Steen, H.
Steer, F.
Steer, J. F.
Stein, H. J.
Stelling, E.
Stephens, J. G.
Stephens, W.
Stephenson, J.
Sterry, J. A.
Sterry, W. H.
Stevens, A.
Stevens, C.
Stevens, F.
Stevens, H. (26965)
Stevens, H. (12255)
Stevens, J.
Stevens, T. F.
Stevenson, E. W.
Stevenson, J. (32230)
Stevenson, J. (37681)
Stevenson, R.
Stevenson, W. H.
Steward, G.
Stewart, D. C.
Stewart, F.
Stewart, J.
Stewart, R.
Stiles, G.
Still, W. T.
Stimson, T.
Stock, F.
Stock, H. J. W.
Stockbridge, W. J.
Stocker, G. F.
Stocker, T. B.
Stocking, H. G. D.
Stockman, C. J.
Stokes, R. W. S.
Stone, C. W.
Stoner, C. A.
Stoneham, C. F.
Storer, W. H.
Storey, F.
Storey, J.
Stoton, W.
Strange, H.
Stratton, A.
Stray, W. F.
Stredwick, H. J.
Stringer, R.
Stromberg, J.
Strong, E.
Strong, J.
Stroulger, W.
Stuart, D.
Stump, R. J.
Styles, C.
Styles, E. J.
Styles, T. W.
Sucklings, A.
Suffolk, H. R.
Sulch, A.
Sullivan, P. (12441)
Sullivan, C.
Sullivan, D. G.
Sullivan, E. W.
Sullivan, J.
Sumpter, G.
Sutcliffe, J.
Sutton, J. S.
Sutton, W.
Swain, A. R.
Swain, J. W.
Swan, G.
Swane, H. E.
Swann, D.
Swaysland, H. C.
Sweatman, J. A.
Sweet, W. G.
Sweetman, E. H.
Symonds, G. H.

Symonds, T.
Tagg, T.
Tanner, C. E.
Tapper, E. H.
Tapsell, W. A.
Tarling, W.
Tarr, F. W.
Tarry, H.
Taverner, R.
Taylor, A. (12622)
Taylor, A. (12799)
Taylor, B.
Taylor, C.
Taylor, C. R. M.
Taylor, E.
Taylor, E. J.
Taylor, F. A. H.
Taylor, F. G. (12510)
Taylor, F. G. (32729)
Taylor, G.
Taylor, G. R.
Taylor, H. (203451)
Taylor, J. (27021)
Taylor, J. R.
Taylor, J. W.
Taylor, W. (25249)
Taylor, W. (25595)
Taylor, W. (37250)
Taylor, W. J.
Taylor, W. W.
Telford, R. H. H.
Templeman, F.
Terry, A. W.
Thackeray, W. J. J.
Thatcher, W. (11212)
Thatcher, W. (25558)
Theobald, G.
Thomas, A. J.
Thomas, E.
Thomas, H. P.
Thomas, S.
Thompsett, A.
Thompson, A. (25600)
Thompson, A. (33802)
Thompson, A. E.
Thompson, A. R.
Thompson, C. (6447)
Thompson, (11765)
Thompson, C. (25220)
Thompson, G.
Thompson, H.
Thompson, J. W.
Thompson, R.
Thompson, T.
Thompson, T. C. E.
Thompson, W.
Thompson, W. R.
Thomson, A. (33926)
Thomson, A. (205003)
Thomson, H.
Thorne, A.
Thorne, H.
Thorne, W.
Thornton, G.
Thornton, H.
Thornton, T.
Thorogood, F.
Thorogood, H.
Thorpe, G.
Thorpe, W. A.
Thorrington, A. C.
Thurley, A.
Thurston, S.
Tibbitts, W. A.
Tickel, A. H.
Tidy, A.
Tidy, W. C.
Tierney, J.
Till, J. G.
Tilley, A. A.
Tilley, A. W.
Tilley, S.
Tilston, W.
Timms, A. B.
Tinworth, J. H.
Tipping, J. W.
Tipple, A.
Tite, A.
Tizzard, —.
Todd, J.
Tomlinson, R.
Tomsett, J. G. A.
Tooke, E. A.
Tooms, G. H.
Tooms, W. J.
Tovey, T.
Towlson, G. S.
Townsend, E.
Townsend, E. W.
Townsend, H. (32728)
Townsend, H. (242346)
Townsend, W.
Travers, H.
Treagus, H.
Tregear, C.
Tremain, G. A.
Trigg, J.
Trowbridge, F. J.
Trumble, J.
Trundle, G. R.
Trussler, G.
Tuck, E.
Tucker, A. E.
Tucker, H. E.
Tucker, W.
Tugwell, E. A.
Tulley, T. M.
Tuppen, H.
Turland, A. E.
Turnbull, J. B.
Turner, E. A.
Turner, E. C.
Turner, E. J.
Turner, H. B.
Turner, J.
Turner, W. (11625)
Tween, C.
Twiner, F. S.
Tye, F.
Tyler, H. J.
Tyler, J.
Tyrer, S.
Tyrrell, R. F. L.
Tyson, W.
Uden, P.
Vaine, W.
Varley, E. G.
Varrow, T.
Varrow, T. J.
Vass, R. C.
Velden, H. G.
Vernon, J. H.
Vickers, A. J.
Vidler, R. G.
Vince, C.
Vince, T. W.
Vince, W.
Viner, M. C. E.
Viney, A.
Vivian, A.
Voak, A.
Wackett, W.
Wade, J.
Wade, W.
Wadman, H.
Waghorn, W. T.
Wain, A.
Wainwright, H.
Waite, A.
Wakefield, W.
Wakelin, B.
Wale, G. C. E.
Walker, A.
Walker, A. A.
Walker, A. V.
Walker, H.
Walker, J. J.
Walker, R. E.
Walker, T.
Walker, W. (25297)
Walker, W. A.
Wall, H.
Wall, L.
Wallace, C. F.
Waller, F.
Waller, T.
Waller, J.
Walmsley, H.
Walsh, F.
Walters, S.
Walters, W. P.
Walton, G. A.
Walton, H. F.
Walton, J. A.
Wanstall, R. L. A.
Want, T.
Ward, A.
Ward, E. T.
Ward, G. W.
Ward, J. (14148)
Ward, J. (17143)
Ward, L. D.
Ward, P.
Ward, P. E.
Ware, A.
Warne, E.
Warner, J.
Warren, F.
Warren, G. E.
Warren, R. T.
Warrier, A.
Warwick, S.
Wass, J. W.
Watcham, W.
Waterman, E. G.
Waters, A.
Watford, S. G.
Watkins, E.
Watkinson, W.
Watson, G.
Watson, G. W.
Watson, H.
Watson, H. J.
Watson, J. (17519)
Watson, J. (26995)
Watson, W. A.
Watts, C. A. V.
Watts, F.
Watts, G.
Watts, H. (12980)
Watts, H. (26055)
Watts, L. A.
Watts, W.
Weaver, H. T.
Weaver, W. A.
Webb, G. H.
Webb, G. W.
Webb, H. H. J.
Webb, S. E.
Webb, W.
Webster, J. C. N.
Wedgbury, E. A.
Wedge, W. G.
Weeding, W. G.
Weedon, J. F. L.
Weldon, S.
Weller, A.
Weller, B.
Weller, C. P.
Weller, J.
Weller, P. B.
Welling, P. R.
Wellings, T.
Wellock, C.
Wells, A.
Wells, A. R.
Wells, C. F.
Wells, D.
Wells, D. G.
Wells, G. W.
Wells, J.
Wells, O. H.
Wells, W.
Wellstead, A.
Wemyss, K.
Wendon, L. A.
West, A.
West, A. S.
West, C.
West, G. A.
West, H.
West, R. A.
West, W. (12135)
West, W. (25298)
West, W. E.
Westaway, S.
Westgarth, A.
Westlake, —.
Weston, A.
Westwood, W.
Whale, A. W.
Whale, J.
Whalley, J. T.
Wharfe, H. A.
Wheatley, A. R. C.
Wheeler, C.
Wheeler, H.
Wheeler, J. A.
Wheeler, J. W.
Wheeler, J. W. E.
Wheeler, R. F.
Wheeler, W. E.
Wheeler, W. G.
Whelan, W. (49176)
Whelan, W. (49195)
Wheller, H.
Wheelhouse, H.
Whenham, J.
Whenham, R.
Whiffen, H.
Whitaker, B.
Whitburn, J. W.
Whitby, H.
Whitcher, W. F.
Whitcomb, A.
White, A. E.
White, A. J.
White, A. V.
White, A. W.
White, B. C.
White, F.
White, F. J.
White, G. P.
White, H. G.
White, J.
White, J. A. C.
White, J. J.
White, P.
White, P. J.
White, R.
White, W.
White, W. J.
White, W. T.
Whitehorn, R.
Whitehouse, W.
Whiteman, J. G.
Whiterod, C.
Whiting, A. G.
Whiting, E. F.
Whiting, F.
Whiting, J. (6945)
Whiting, J. (9493)
Whiting, W.
Whiting, W. S.
Whitlock, W.
Whitnell, G.
Whittaker, (17878)
Whittaker, R.
Whittle, H. F.
Whitton, H. P.
Wicken, J.
Wickens, C. R. W.
Wickens, C. W. R.
Wickham, J. C.
Wiffen, A.
Wigg, C. W. C.
Wightman, V.
Wilden, L. F. W.
Wildish, H.
Wilkins, E.
Wilkins, W.
Wilkinson, C.
Wilkinson, J.
Willcox, H.
Willey, A.
Willey, C.
Williams, A.
Williams, C. (6849)
Williams, E.
Williams, H. (242761)
Williams, H. C.
Williams, H. G.
Williams, I.
Williams, J.
Williams, J. H.
Williams, J. J.
Williams, L.
Williams, P. A.
Williams, R. G.
Williams, T.
Williams, W. (12825)
Williams, W. (14059)
Willis, H.
Willis, W. H.

Willmott, A. J.
Willmott, J. J.
Wills, W.
Willsher, W. G.
Willsmer, S.
Wilson, —. (34256)
Wilson, A. (12604)
Wilson, A. (23800)
Wilson, F.
Wilson, G. W.
Wilson, H.
Wilson, H. L.
Wilson, J. C.
Wilson, T. C.
Wilson, W. (12246)
Wilson, W. (242045)
Wilson, W. F.
Wilson, W. H.
Wilson, W. J.
Wiltshire, J. R.
Wimble, A. H.
Winch, A. E.
Winder, J.
Windmill, A. R.
Windmill, S. J.
Winfield, C.
Wing, J. B.
Winsall, T.
Winsbury, E. W.
Winter, A.
Winter, H.
Winyard, C.
Witherden, J.
Withers, L. L.
Withey, A.
Witts, W. F.
Witty, G.
Wolstenholme, T.
Wooberry, J. T.
Wood, A. (25616)
Wood, A. H.
Wood, G.
Wood, J. H.
Wood, W. A.
Wood, W. E.
Wood, W. H.
Woodbine, E. M.
Wooder, W. G. A.
Woodgate, F.
Woodhams, J.
Woodhead, J. R.
Woodhouse, R. E.
Woodhouse, W.
Woodley, G. S.
Woodley, J. H.
Woodley, W. C.
Woodman, F. W.
Woods, A.
Woods, F. C.
Woods, H.
Woods, M. J.
Woods, S. W.
Woods, T.
Woods, W. J.
Woodward, A. A.
Woodward, C. A.
Woodward, J.
Woodward, N.
Wooldridge, G. J.
Woolgar, F.
Woolgar, W.
Woolnough, H. J.
Woolnough, J.
Wootten, J.
Wootton, G. F.
Worcester, W.
Workman, C.
Worsfold, W.
Wortley, S.
Worton, H.
Wratten, H. W.
Wrenn, C. H.
Wright, A. C.
Wright, C.
Wright, C. S.
Wright, F. W.
Wright, J. E.
Wright, J. R. J.
Wright, L. M.
Wright, M. C.
Wright, S. C.
Wright, T. (12033)
Wright, (33268)
Wright, W.
Wright, W. A.
Wright, W. S. (33084)
Wright, W. S. (37228)
Wyard, O.
Wyatt, A.
Wyatt, C.
Wyatt, R. C.
Wyeth, H.
Wyllie, G. A.
Wyman, S.
Yallop, B. A.
Yallop, W.
Yambo, A. H.
Yardley, S.
Yarnton, C.
Yates, —. (6167)
Yates, A. E.
Yates, D.
Yates, G. W.
Yates, W.
Yeardil, J.
Yeulett, S. E.
Young, A.
Young, A. B. C.
Young, C.
Young, F. J.
Young, G. (14900)
Young, G. (25725)
Young, J. (3251)
Young, J. (11630)
Young, J. (14145)
Young, J. T.
Young, L.
Young, R. H.
Young, W.
Young, W. D.
Young, W. P.
Younger, R. W.
Youthed, C.
Yuill, C.

NOTE.—This list does not include absconded recruits and certain men posted to the Battalion and transferred to Labour units, etc.

OFFICERS WHO APPEAR IN PHOTOGRAPH TAKEN AT ALDERSHOT IN MARCH, 1916.

Back Row: 2nd Lieut. C. N. Pridham, Lieut. C. C. A. Lee, 2nd Lieut. R. Lambert-Oates, Lieut. H. Templeham Pike, Lieut. H. S. Openshaw, Lieut. E. V. Whiteway, Lieut. R. A. Victor-Breary, 2nd Lieut. F. H. Elphicke, Lieut. J. W. Tunwell, 2nd Lieut. A. T. Libby, Lieut and Qmr. W. McEnuff, 2nd Lieut. D. McCallum.

Middle Row: Lieut. E. C. Lambert, R.A.M.C., Lieut. G. G. Briggs, 2nd Lieut. J. E. M. Crowther, 2nd Lieut. A. V. Reiner, Lieut. J. R. Chesters, Lieut. C. O. Slacke, 2nd Lieut. E. M. Dove, Lieut. C. C. Fox, Lieut. F. D. Jessop, 2nd Lieut. F. Beard, Lieut. J. Wilfred Staddon, Capt. W. Hagen, 2nd Lieut. S. Stimson.

Front Row: Capt. A. D. Crow, Capt. York Davis, Major L. Tenbosch, Major Gwyn Thomas (Brigade Major), Lieut.-Col. L. F. Beatson, Brig.-Gen. F. W. Towsey, Lieut.-Col. H. H. Lee, D.S.O., Major H. J. Walmisley-Dresser, Capt. H. de C. Blakeney, Capt. and Adjt. R. A. McCulloch, Capt. J. L. Buckman.

NAMES OF OFFICERS IN GROUP TAKEN AT NORDAUSQUES, APRIL, 1917.

Back Row: 2nd Lieut. S. E. Bennett, 2nd Lieut. F. B. B. Dowling, 2nd Lieut. L. W. B. Russell, 2nd Lieut. A. Hemsley, 2nd Lieut. L. A. Rossiter, 2nd Lieut. L. H. Jennings, 2nd Lieut. A. W. England, 2nd Lieut. H. S. Todd, 2nd Lieut. R. N. Haine, 2nd Lieut. W. G. Robinson.

Middle Row: 2nd Lieut. F. A. Samuels, 2nd Lieut. R. W. Curran, 2nd Lieut. A. G. Howitt, 2nd Lieut. R. D. Brown, 2nd Lieut. F. J. Harding, Lieut. D. Walker, 2nd Lieut. W. J. Palk, M.C., Lieut. V. L. Clift, 2nd Lieut. A. R. Puttock, 2nd Lieut. B. F. Dodd, 2nd Lieut. W. A. Vanner.

Front Row: 2nd Lieut. F. R. Matthews, Lieut. R. A. Victor-Breary, Capt. C. N. Binney, R.A.M.C., Capt. H. S. Walker, Capt. C. T. Williams, Lieut.-Col. H. H. Lee, D.S.O., Lieut and Adjt. T. B. McWalter, Capt. W. Hagen, Capt. H. S. Openshaw, M.C., Capt. J. A. C. McCalman, Lieut. J. A. Rogers.

THE LATE JOHN ASTON, M.A. (Oxon.)

It is with deepest regret that we have to record the death of our very dear friend, John Aston, shortly before the publication of this book. After a short illness he passed from our midst on January 12th at the age of 56.

A godly man, he was greatly admired and respected by his brother officers and the men he commanded.

Of him, Colonel H. H. LEE, D.S.O., his Commanding Officer has written :

"One of the officers who joined us in October, 1916, he always took the greatest interest in the Battalion and whilst serving with it was severely wounded. His keenness and zeal were apparent in every undertaking and his loss will be much felt by all those who are left. It is due to his efforts that this volume is published."

Truly we mourn the loss of a great and gallant gentleman.

ERRATA.

Acknowledgments. Paragraph 6. After "Roland Dorgeles" insert "Ernst Junger."
Page 5. Paragraph 3. Line 4. "2nd" should read "1st."
Page 15. Last paragraph. Line 2. "a former" should read "at present a."
Page 22. Last line. "Outtersteen" should read "Outtersteene."
Page 23. Line 19. "keen in" should read "keen on."
Page 26. Line 30. "out" should read "our."
Page 34. Line 11. "of" should read "or."
Page 34. Last line. "Delenelle" should read "Delennelle."
Page 38. Line 3. "Fixecourt" should read "Flixecourt."
Page 44. "*Appendix to Operation Orders" should precede the penultimate paragraph.
Page 45. Lines 8 and 9. "respondered" should read "responded."
Page 45. Line 10. "Mantauban" should read "Montauban."
Page 46. Line 5. "followed" should read "following."
Page 46. Paragraph 5. Line 1. "objectives were in" should read "objectives were reached in."
Page 52. Paragraph 2. Lines 1 and 2. "Steenwreck" should read "Steenwerck."
Page 52. Line 23. Omit "T.M.B.)"
Page 71. Line 1. Omit "of."
Page 75. Line 12. "growd" should read "crowd."
Page 84. Penultimate paragraph. Last line. After "photograph" insert "facing page 69."
Page 112. Paragraph 2. Line 5. "through out lines" should read "through our lines."
Page 133. Paragraph 5. Line 2. "remember " should read remembered."
Page 134. Quotation marks should be inserted at the commencement of paragraphs 5 and 6.
Page 135. Quotation marks should be inserted before and after the paragraph commencing "It was" and ending "East Surreys."
Page 137. "* The capture of these prisoners" etc. refers to the account by Cpl. Day on page 136.
Page 140. Footnote refers to account of Major Pennell on page 139.
Page 142. Note 1. Lines 2 and 3. "therefor" should read "therefore."
Page 148. Paragraph 2. Line 3. * should be after "village" in line 2.
Page 148. Paragraph 2. Last line. "inhabitant " should read "inhabitants."
Page 162. Paragraph 4. Line 5. Omit "Billy Warr."
Page 165. Fifth line from end and last line. Substitute † for *.
Page 166. Line 13. After "knew" omit *.
Page 183. Paragraph 6. Line 1. and second footnote, line 1. Substitute † for *
Page 185. Cpl. Southall's account. Paragraph 2. End of line 3. and second footnote. Substitute † for *
Page 189. Line 16. "on" should read "own."
Page 189. Lines 48 * and 51 †. The first two footnotes on page 190 refer.
Page 206. Line 22. "post" should read "posts."
Page 216. Last paragraph. Line 1 "Brandhock" should read "Brandhoek."
Page 223. Paragraph 3. Line 2. "Chappelle" should read "Chapelle"
Page 234. Line 9. Delete line.
Page 238. Paragraph 5. Last line. "Crums" should read "Crumps."
Page 258. Line 10. "Cox" should read "Cocks."
Page 258. Paragraph 2. Line 4. "riveted" should read "revetted."
Page 264. Line 18. "a enemy" should read "an enemy."
Page 264. Paragraph 3. After 5th line insert, "fatal results.
A German helmet on a dump would likewise be arranged. Bombs with "and then continue "time-delayed," etc.
Page 268. Line 37. "remember" should read "remembered."
Page 277. Paragraph 7. Line 1. "ascape" should read "escape."
Page 277. Paragraph 7. Line 3. "cleaning" should read "clearing."
Page 296. Paragraph 3. Line 12. Third word. "change" should read "chance."
Page 298. Paragraph 4. Line 3. "Skellet" should read "Skellett."
Page 298. Bottom of page. Distinguished Conduct Medal. Omit "Lce.-Cpl. W. Rainbow."
Page 302. Paragraph 4. Line 8. "J.T. Buckman" should read "J. L. Buckman."
Page 303. Paragraph 4. Line 1. "houours" should read "honours."
Page 303. Line 21. "D. Richmond" should read "Dr. Richmond."
Appendix. Page 313. Column 3. "Combe-Ceaton, H.N." should read "Combe-Ceaton, F."
Appendix. Page 316. Column 1. After 54 delete "France."
Appendix. Page 317. D.S.O. "C. Knapp" should read "E. Knapp."
Appendix. Page 331. Lines 5 and 24. "Breary" should read "Brearey."

Lightning Source UK Ltd.
Milton Keynes UK
UKOW06f0153010214

225661UK00001B/17/P